SUBSCRIPTION NOTICE

Y0-DBU-098

This Wiley product is updated on a periodic basis with supplements to reflect important changes in the subject matter. If you purchased this product directly from John Wiley & Sons, we have already recorded your subscription for this update service.

If, however, you purchased this product from a bookstore and wish to receive (1) the current update at no additional charge, and (2) future updates and revised or related volumes separately with a 30-day examination review, please send your name, company name (if applicable), address, and the title of the product to:

Supplement Department
John Wiley & Sons, Inc.
One Wiley Drive
Somerset, NJ 08875
1-800-225-5945

THE CONSTRUCTION LAW LIBRARY FROM WILEY LAW PUBLICATIONS

ALTERNATIVE CLAUSES TO STANDARD CONSTRUCTION CONTRACTS
James E. Stephenson, Editor

ALTERNATIVE DISPUTE RESOLUTION IN THE CONSTRUCTION INDUSTRY
Robert F. Cushman, G. Christian Hedemann, and Avram S. Tucker, Editors

ARBITRATION OF CONSTRUCTION DISPUTES
Michael T. Callahan, Barry B. Bramble, and Paul M. Lurie

ARCHITECT AND ENGINEER LIABILITY: CLAIMS AGAINST DESIGN PROFESSIONALS
Robert F. Cushman and Thomas G. Bottum, Editors

CONDOMINIUM AND HOMEOWNER ASSOCIATION LITIGATION
Wayne S. Hyatt and Philip S. Downer, Editors

CONSTRUCTION ACCIDENT PLEADING AND PRACTICE
Turner W. Branch, Editor

CONSTRUCTION BIDDING LAW
Robert F. Cushman and William J. Doyle, Editors

CONSTRUCTION CLAIMS AND LIABILITY
Michael S. Simon

CONSTRUCTION DEFAULTS: RIGHTS, DUTIES, AND LIABILITIES
Robert F. Cushman and Charles A. Meeker, Editors

CONSTRUCTION DELAY CLAIMS
Barry B. Bramble and Michael T. Callahan

CONSTRUCTION ENGINEERING EVIDENCE
Loren W. Peters

CONSTRUCTION FAILURES
Robert F. Cushman, Irvin E. Richter, and Lester E. Rivelis, Editors

CONSTRUCTION INDUSTRY CONTRACTS: LEGAL CITATOR AND CASE DIGEST
Wiley Law Publications Editorial Staff

CONSTRUCTION INDUSTRY FORMS (TWO VOLUMES)
Robert F. Cushman and George L. Blick, Editors

CONSTRUCTION LITIGATION FORMBOOK
  David M. Buoncristiani, John D. Carter, and Robert F. Cushman

CONSTRUCTION LITIGATION: REPRESENTING THE CONTRACTOR
  Robert F. Cushman, John D. Carter, and Alan Silverman, Editors

CONSTRUCTION LITIGATION: REPRESENTING THE OWNER (SECOND EDITION)
  Robert F. Cushman, Kenneth M. Cushman, and Stephen B. Cook, Editors

CONSTRUCTION LITIGATION: STRATEGIES AND TECHNIQUES
  Barry B. Bramble and Albert E. Phillips, Editors

CONSTRUCTION SUBCONTRACTING: A LEGAL GUIDE FOR INDUSTRY PROFESSIONALS
  Overton A. Currie, Neal J. Sweeney, and Randall F. Hafer, Editors

DRAFTING CONSTRUCTION CONTRACTS: STRATEGY AND FORMS FOR CONTRACTORS
  Samuel F. Schoninger

HANDLING FIDELITY, SURETY, AND FINANCIAL RISK CLAIMS (SECOND EDITION)
  Robert F. Cushman, George L. Blick, and Charles A. Meeker, Editors

HAZARDOUS WASTE DISPOSAL AND UNDERGROUND CONSTRUCTION LAW
  Robert F. Cushman and Bruce W. Ficken, Editors

1990–1991 DIRECTORY OF CONSTRUCTION INDUSTRY CONSULTANTS
  Wiley Law Publications, Editors

1991 WILEY CONSTRUCTION LAW UPDATE
  Steven M. Goldblatt, Editor

PROVING AND PRICING CONSTRUCTION CLAIMS
  Robert F. Cushman and David A. Carpenter, Editors

SWEET ON CONSTRUCTION INDUSTRY CONTRACTS
  Justin Sweet

1991 WILEY CONSTRUCTION LAW UPDATE

STEVEN M. GOLDBLATT

Editor
Associate Professor
University of Washington

Wiley Law Publications
JOHN WILEY & SONS
New York · Chichester · Brisbane · Toronto · Singapore

Library of Congress Cataloging-in-Publication Data

ISBN 0-471-52126-4

Printed in the United States of America

10 9 8 7 6 5 4 3 2 1

To Joan and Sarah

"Law never *is*, but is always about to be."
Justice Benjamin Cardozo
of the Court of Appeals of New York
in a 1921 lecture to Yale Law School,
The Nature of the Judicial Process.

PREFACE

Wiley's Construction Law Library offers a rich collection of volumes, each one created with an eye toward a primary audience such as owners, design professionals, or constructors—as well as their attorneys. The book's purpose is not to comprehensively treat a discrete body of law, but instead to highlight contemporary issues from the viewpoints of expert industry attorneys. This is envisioned as the first in a series of annual Wiley construction law anthologies.

The book's essays are brought together under four themes. The first, contract formation and standard form documents, presents essays on contract format, AIA Document A201 modifications for owners, incorporation by reference in subcontracts, a system of construction management, and the ASCE and NAAG documents.

The second, management of claims, features essays on claims strategies, progress payments as claim waivers, quantum meruit, jointly caused delay, and landmark CPM decisions of the past decade.

The third, design professionals' liability, presents essays on the effect of administrative proceedings on civil liability, construction administration services, the impact of construction safety, the defense of qualified privilege in defamation claims, software and computer liability, and a review of recent significant case decisions.

The fourth, strategies, techniques, and observations, offers essays on organized labor's agenda, the right to stop work, asbestos liability strategies, and construction litigation discovery.

We look forward to readers' reactions to this update and encourage their suggestions for future topics.

My thanks to Tom Conter, Mary Hope, Beverly Payne, and Sharon Kincaide at Wiley Law Publications for their professionalism and patience; to the chapters' contributors for sharing their expertise; to Tom Porterfield of Schinnerer Management Services, Joan Barnett of CMC on behalf of Andrews Conferences, Karl Borgstrom of CMAA, and Bill Heavey of AGC of America for their cooperation; and to Gale Shinozaki of Scan Text and Mary Ellen Mill Rolson and Sue Poffenroth of MDCS/datatran for their services. My special thanks to Justin Sweet and Milton Lunch for their time, interest, and counsel, and to Gordon Varey, Jana Keil, and Vi Throckmorton at the University of Washington for their support.

Seattle, Washington
December 1990

STEVEN M. GOLDBLATT

ABOUT THE EDITOR

Steven M. Goldblatt is chairman and associate professor of the Department of Building Construction in the College of Architecture and Urban Planning at the University of Washington, Seattle. His teaching and research focus on design and construction law, and he holds adjunct appointments in the Departments of Architecture and Civil Engineering. Previously, he was a faculty member at Purdue University following nine years' experience in California as an engineer, attorney, and consultant. Recently, he has mediated many Puget Sound construction disputes. A member of the board of trustees of the American Council for Construction Education, he served as 1989-90 president of the Associated Schools of Construction after six years as founding editor of ASC's *Construction Education Chronicle*. The author of many articles and book chapters, Professor Goldblatt has been responsible for four Wiley Construction Law Library supplements: the 1989 and 1990 supplements to both *Construction Industry Contracts: Legal Citator and Case Digest* and *Construction Industry Forms*. He is a member of the American Arbitration Association and its panel of construction arbitrators, the American Bar Association and its Forum on the Construction Industry, the American Institute of Constructors, the California State Bar Association, and the National Association of College and University Attorneys. As the Washington State Public Policy Fellow in Summer 1990, Professor Goldblatt reported to the state legislature on how various state agencies procure design and construction services.

He holds a B.S.E.E. degree from the University of California, Berkeley, and a J.D. degree from Golden Gate University, San Francisco.

ABOUT THE CONTRIBUTORS

Frederic I. Albert is an associate with the law firm of Thelen, Marrin, Johnson & Bridges in Irvine, California, and a 1987 graduate of the University of Toledo College of Law.

Bradley H. Bagshaw is a partner in the Seattle, Washington, law firm of Helsell, Fetterman, Martin, Todd & Hokanson. He practices commercial litigation, concentrating in the areas of construction and appellate practice.

Louise A. Behrendt is a clerk to United States Magistrate Franklin L. Noel in Minneapolis, Minnesota, and a 1989 graduate of William Mitchell College of Law in St. Paul.

Mark R. Berry is an associate with the law firm of Wickwire Gavin in Vienna, Virginia, and a graduate of George Washington University's National Law Center.

Richard D. Conner is a partner in the law firm of Patton, Boggs & Blow in Greensboro, North Carolina. His practice is devoted to the construction industry and concentrates in the area of resolving construction disputes. He is general counsel to CMAA and is an arbitrator, lecturer, and author.

Philip R. Croessmann practices law with the Seattle, Washington, firm of Bassett & Morrison, primarily representing design professionals and environmental consultants. He is former deputy general counsel for the AIA and now serves as general counsel for the Seattle chapter of the AIA and the Alaska/Washington chapter of the National Asbestos Council.

Overton A. Currie, senior partner of the Atlanta, Georgia, law firm of Smith, Currie & Hancock, founded and heads the firm's construction department. He is a founding fellow and 1989-91 president of the American College of Construction Lawyers, a national director of AAA, and past chairman of the ABA Section of Public Contract Law.

Randall L. Erickson is a partner in the law firm of Thelen, Marrin, Johnson & Bridges in Irvine, California. His primary area of practice is civil litigation, specializing in construction, project finance, and real estate development. He is a lecturer for California Continuing Education of the Bar.

B. Clarence Hart is chairman of the board of the law firm of Hart, Bruner & O'Brien in Minneapolis, Minnesota. He is past chairman of the ABA Tort and

Insurance Practice Section, a fellow of the American College of Trial Lawyers, a fellow of the American College of Construction Lawyers, an ABA fellow, and an advocate of the American Board of Trial Advocates.

David J. Hatem, a partner in the Boston, Massachusetts, law firm of Posternak, Blankstein & Lund, teaches legal aspects of architecture and engineering at Boston Architectural Center, and serves as legal advisor to the American Consulting Engineers of New England. He is a lecturer and author.

Thomas W. Hayton is a partner in the law firm of Ferguson & Burdell in Seattle, Washington. A former Washington state assistant attorney general in special litigation and transportation, he practices in the areas of general litigation, construction litigation, and government contracts.

Jeff A. Hellinger is a clerk with the law firm of Lawrence & Syria in Bellevue, Washington, and a third-year student at the University of Puget Sound School of Law in Tacoma.

Julian F. Hoffar is a senior partner in the law firm of Watt, Tieder, Killian & Hoffar in McLean, Virginia. He specializes in the representation of contractors, subcontractors, engineers, sureties, and developers involved in construction disputes in the United States and internationally. He has also written and lectured extensively.

Ralph L. Kaskell, Jr., of counsel to the New Orleans law firm of Deutsch, Kerrigan & Stiles, is a charter member and past chairman of the ABA Forum on the Construction Industry.

John A. Knutson is a partner in the law firm of Kenney, Burd, Knutson & Markowitz in San Francisco, California. He practices in the areas of products liability, commercial and business tort litigation, and construction matters, as well as design professional liability defense.

Michael E. Kreger practices construction law in the Anchorage, Alaska, office of the Seattle-based law firm of Perkins Coie. He is Alaska state chairman of the ABA Section of Public Contract Law.

Michael J. Ladino is a partner in the Washington, D.C., law firm of Gadsby & Hannah. He is past chairman of the international division of the ABA Forum on the Construction Industry, the A/E and professional services committee, and state and local procurement division of the ABA Section of Public Contract Law. He has taught at four area universities.

Kerry C. Lawrence is a partner in the law firm of Lawrence & Syria in Bellevue, Washington. He limits his practice to construction-related matters. He is an arbitrator, mediator, lecturer, and author and serves as deputy chairman of the Washington State Bar Association's Section of Public Procurement and Private Construction Law.

Judd H. Lees is a partner in the law firm of Williams, Kastner & Gibbs in Bellevue, Washington. His practice concentrates on construction labor law, including practice before the NLRB, contract negotiations, and prevailing wage cases. He is past president of the Western Washington chapter of ABC and is a lecturer and author.

Lance J. Lerman is an associate with the law firm of Wickwire, Gavin in Vienna, Virginia, and is a graduate of George Washington University's National Law Center. He is vice chairman of the federal contract claims and remedies committee of the ABA Section of Public Contract Law.

Milton F. Lunch, former long-time general counsel of NSPE, is an A/E liability consultant in Chevy Chase, Maryland, and a frequent commentator on design professional liability issues.

John J. Lynch is a partner in the Chicago, Illinois, law firm of Haskell & Perrin. His civil litigation practice emphasizes professional liability, environmental, and excess insurance coverage. He is past chairman of the professional, officers and directors liability law committee of the ABA Tort and Insurance Practice Section.

Robert C. Nauheim is an associate in the Anchorage, Alaska, office of the Seattle-based law firm of Perkins Coie and is a 1989 graduate of the University of Oregon School of Law.

Christopher L. Noble is a partner in the Boston law firm of Hill & Barlow, specializing in architectural and construction law. He is a fellow of the American College of Construction Lawyers and has taught design and construction law at the Harvard Graduate School of Design and the Boston Architectural Center.

David C. Romm is a senior litigation partner in the law firm of Watt, Tieder, Killian & Hoffar in McLean, Virginia. He specializes in construction claims evaluation, preparation, negotiation, and litigation on behalf of contractors, subcontractors, owners, and bonding companies, with a particular expertise in jury trials of complex construction disputes.

Laurence Schor, a partner in the Washington, D.C., office of Schnader, Harrison, Segal & Lewis, concentrates his practice on all phases of construction and government contract law. He was formerly with the offices of general counsel for the Army Corps of Engineers and NASA. A founding member and director of the American College of Construction Lawyers, he is past chairman of the construction committee of the ABA Section of Public Contract Law.

Neal J. Sweeney is a partner in the Atlanta, Georgia, law firm of Smith, Currie & Hancock. He practices exclusively in the area of construction law and litigation, concentrating on public contracting and bid protests. He is a lecturer and author.

John B. Tieder, Jr., is a partner and founder of the law firm of Watt, Tieder, Killian & Hoffar in McLean, Virginia. He specializes in government contracts and construction litigation in the United States and internationally and has written and lectured extensively.

Richard C. Walters, a senior attorney in the Washington, D.C., office of Schnader, Harrison, Segal & Lewis, specializes in government contracting and construction law. He is former assistant counsel to the Naval Facilities Engineering Command in Philadelphia and is a lecturer and author.

Jon M. Wickwire, a partner in the law firm of Wickwire Gavin in Vienna, Virginia, practices in the area of construction claims and litigation. He is vice chairman of the construction law committee and the state and local contract claims and remedies committee of the ABA Section of Public Contract Law. He is also a lecturer and author.

SUMMARY CONTENTS

PART I   CONTRACT FORMATION AND STANDARD
FORM DOCUMENTS

Chapter 1   **Choosing a Contracting Format**   3

Chapter 2   **Modifications to AIA A201 1987 Edition from
Owner's Viewpoint**   17

Chapter 3   **Incorporation by Reference in Subcontracts**   39

Chapter 4   **A System of Construction Management for the
1990s**   61

Chapter 5   **What Went Wrong with the ASCE and NAAG
Documents?**   121

PART II   MANAGEMENT OF CLAIMS

Chapter 6   **Keys to Success in Avoiding and Managing Claims**   139

Chapter 7   **Progress Payments as Claim Waivers, Trust Funds,
and Partial Lien Releases**   171

Chapter 8   **Quantum Meruit**   187

Chapter 9   **Recovery for Jointly-Caused Delay**   201

Chapter 10   **Landmark CPM Decisions from 1980 to 1990**   219

PART III   DESIGN PROFESSIONALS' LIABILITY

Chapter 11   **Administrative, Regulatory, and Registration
Proceedings Involving Design Professionals**   243

Chapter 12   **Construction Administration Services and the
Architect's Liability Dilemma**   265

Chapter 13   **Impact of Construction Safety on Design
Professionals**   281

Chapter 14   **The Defense of Qualified Privilege in Defamation
and Commercial Tort Claims Against Architects**   297

Chapter 15   **Liability of Architect/Engineers for Erroneous
Software and Computer Data**   315

Chapter 16   **Review of Recent Significant Cases Involving
Design Professionals**   335

PART IV   STRATEGIES, TECHNIQUES, AND
OBSERVATIONS

Chapter 17   **The Work Force Shortage and Organized Labor's
Agenda for the 1990s**   367

Chapter 18   The Right to Stop Work   379

Chapter 19   Asbestos Liability Strategies   387

Chapter 20   Discovery in Construction Litigation   409

Index   443

DETAILED CONTENTS

PART I   **CONTRACT FORMATION AND STANDARD FORM**
                  DOCUMENTS

Chapter 1   **Choosing a Contracting Format**

                  Randall L. Erickson
                  Frederic I. Albert

§ 1.1   Introduction

PRICE CONSIDERATIONS IN PRIVATE CONTRACTS

§ 1.2   In General

§ 1.3   Fixed Price Contracts: Owner Advantages, Contractor Risk

§ 1.4   —Contractor Advantages, Owner Risk

§ 1.5   Cost Contracts: Contractor Advantages, Owner Risk

§ 1.6   Guaranteed Maximum Contracts

§ 1.7   Abandonment

COMPETITIVE BIDDING AND COMPETITIVE NEGOTIATION

§ 1.8   Competitive Bidding: Policy and Frustration

§ 1.9   —Owner Risk: Performance Risk and Bonds

§ 1.10   —Competence Risk Avoidance in Public Sector

§ 1.11   —Private Owners

§ 1.12   —Cost Estimating Risks and Excessive Change Orders

§ 1.13   —Contractor Risk: Cost Estimating Risk and Subcontractor Quotes

§ 1.14   —Computation Errors

§ 1.15   —Private Contracts

§ 1.16   —Public Contracts

§ 1.17   —Extra Work Compensation in Public Contracts

§ 1.18   —Private Contracts

§ 1.19   Competitive Negotiation in General

§ 1.20   —Owner Risk

§ 1.21   —Contractor Cost Estimating Risks

STANDARD TRADE ASSOCIATION CONTRACTS

§ 1.22   Standard Contracts in General

§ 1.23   —AIA Documents

§ 1.24   Standard Contract Cautions

DESIGN-BUILD CONTRACTS

§ 1.25   In General

§ 1.26   Joint Venture Design-Build Team

§ 1.27   Sole Contractor

Chapter 2   **Modifications to AIA A201 1987 Edition from Owner's Viewpoint**

B. Clarence Hart
Louise A. Behrendt

§ 2.1   Introduction

OWNER'S OBLIGATIONS

§ 2.2   Define Scope of Work
§ 2.3   Provide Information
§ 2.4   Provide Assurance of Ability to Pay
§ 2.5   Provide Insurance

OWNER'S RIGHTS

§ 2.6   Make Changes
§ 2.7   Be Protected from Risks Which A/E and Contractor Should Bear and Insure
§ 2.8   Suspend or Terminate the Contract
§ 2.9   Have Work Completed on Schedule

OWNER'S EXPOSURE TO CLAIMS AND HOW TO PROTECT AGAINST THEM

§ 2.10   Delay Damages
§ 2.11   Differing Site Conditions
§ 2.12   Defective Plans
§ 2.13   Lack of Coordination of Separate Prime Contractors

OWNER'S RELATIONSHIPS WITH OTHER PARTIES

§ 2.14   Contractor
§ 2.15   Architect
§ 2.16   Effect of Dispute Resolution Provisions on Owner
§ 2.17   Conclusion

Chapter 3   **Incorporation by Reference in Subcontracts**

Michael E. Kreger
Robert C. Nauheim

§ 3.1   Introduction

TYPES OF INCORPORATING CLAUSES

§ 3.2   Conduit Clauses
§ 3.3   Incorporation by Reference Clauses

GENERAL RULES GOVERNING ENFORCEABILITY

§ 3.4   Basic Rules of Interpretation
§ 3.5   —Scope of Incorporation Must Be Clear
§ 3.6   —Implied Incorporation

§ 3.7   —Subcontract Consistency
§ 3.8   —Surrounding Circumstances
§ 3.9   Third-Party Beneficiary Status: Who Can Enforce Incorporated Provisions?

INCORPORATION OF SUBSTANTIVE TERMS
§ 3.10   Indemnification Clauses
§ 3.11   —Scope
§ 3.12   —Indemnification for Negligence
§ 3.13   —Workers' Compensation and Indemnity
§ 3.14   Arbitration Clauses: Public Policy Supports Arbitration
§ 3.15   —Incorporated Arbitration Clauses and the Miller Act
§ 3.16   No Damages for Delay and Other Remedy Clauses
§ 3.17   Incorporation of the Implied Warranty of the Adequacy and Suitability of Plans and Specifications

Chapter 4   A System of Construction Management for the 1990s
          Richard D. Conner

§ 4.1   Construction Management: A Concept with a Definition
§ 4.2   CMAA Documents: Construction Manager as Agent

SUMMARY OF THE CMAA SYSTEM
§ 4.3   Project Planning and Selection of a Design Professional
§ 4.4   Construction Management Plan
§ 4.5   CM as Owner's Agent
§ 4.6   CM and Design Professional Cooperation
§ 4.7   Reliance on CM Cost Estimates
§ 4.8   Design Criteria
§ 4.9   Compliance with the Project Budget
§ 4.10   Design Documentation
§ 4.11   Design Professional's Basic Construction Phase Services
§ 4.12   CM Determinations During the Construction Phase

CM'S LEADERSHIP ROLE
§ 4.13   During the Design Phase
§ 4.14   During the Construction Phase
§ 4.15   CM's Exposure to Liability
§ 4.16   Performance Standards of Care
§ 4.17   Professional Liability Insurance Coverage
§ 4.18   CMAA A-1 Standard Form of Agreement Between Owner and Construction Manager
§ 4.19   CMAA A-4 Standard Form of Agreement Between Owner and Design Professional

Chapter 5   **What Went Wrong with the ASCE and NAAG Documents?**

Ralph L. Kaskell, Jr.

§ 5.1   The Kansas City Hyatt Regency Skywalk Collapse

ASCE MANUAL

§ 5.2   Overreaction of ASCE

§ 5.3   ASCE Manual of Professional Practice for Virtually Everybody

NAAG DOCUMENTS

§ 5.4   Overreaction of NAAG

§ 5.5   Agreement Between Owner and Design Professional

§ 5.6   Construction Contract

§ 5.7   Confusion Reigns

PART II   **MANAGEMENT OF CLAIMS**

Chapter 6   **Keys to Success in Avoiding and Managing Claims**

Overton A. Currie
Neal J. Sweeney

§ 6.1   Life in the Construction Industry: Avoiding Risks and Preserving Awards

§ 6.2   Involving Reputable and Reliable Participants in the Project

§ 6.3   Defining Rights, Responsibilities, and Risks

§ 6.4   Contract Framework

§ 6.5   Standard Contract Forms and Key Contract Provisions

§ 6.6   Interpreting and Applying Express and Implied Terms

§ 6.7   Contract Modification

§ 6.8   The Arbitration Alternative

§ 6.9   —Time and Costs of Arbitration

§ 6.10   —Selection of Arbitrators

§ 6.11   —Informality and Limited Appeals in Arbitration

§ 6.12   —Enforceability of Agreements to Arbitrate

§ 6.13   —Special Problems Involving Multiple Parties

§ 6.14   Avoiding and Preparing for Claims Through Proper Management and Documentation

§ 6.15   Prudent and Responsible Estimating

§ 6.16   Establishing Standard Operating Procedures

§ 6.17   Establishing Lines of Communication

§ 6.18   Project Documentation

§ 6.19   —Correspondence

§ 6.20   —Meeting Notes

§ 6.21   —Jobsite Logs or Daily Reports

§ **6.22**   —Standard Forms and Status Logs

§ **6.23**   —Photographs and Video Tapes

§ **6.24**   Cost Accounting Records

§ **6.25**   Monitoring the Work Through Scheduling

§ **6.26**   Effective Claim Development

§ **6.27**   Early Claim Recognition and Preparation

§ **6.28**   Early Involvement of Experts and Attorneys

§ **6.29**   Use of Demonstrative Evidence

§ **6.30**   Components of a Well-Prepared Claim Document

§ **6.31**   Importance of Calculating and Proving Damages

§ **6.32**   —Basic Damage Principles

§ **6.33**   Methods of Pricing Claims

§ **6.34**   —Total Cost Method

§ **6.35**   —Segregated Cost Method

§ **6.36**   Project Cost Reviews and Audits

§ **6.37**   Pursuing Negotiation and Settlement

Chapter 7   **Progress Payments as Claim Waivers, Trust Funds, and Partial Lien Releases**

Kerry C. Lawrence
Jeff A. Hellinger

§ **7.1**   Introduction

§ **7.2**   Establishing the Ground Rules

§ **7.3**   Prompt Identification of Claims

§ **7.4**   Waiver of Claims for Extra Cost or Time Extension

§ **7.5**   Release of Lien Rights

§ **7.6**   Trust Funds

§ **7.7**   Restrictive Indorsements

§ **7.8**   Form—Contractor's Application for Payment

§ **7.9**   Form—Conditional Release/Unconditional Release of Lien

Chapter 8   **Quantum Meruit**

Bradley H. Bagshaw

§ **8.1**   Introduction

§ **8.2**   A Source of Payment When There Is No Contract

§ **8.3**   A Source of Payment When the Contract Is Silent about a Particular Aspect of the Work—Extra Work

§ **8.4**   —Work Done under Unanticipated Conditions

§ **8.5**   —Owner Interference

§ **8.6**   —Owner Control of Methods and Materials

§ **8.7**   Payment for Work Despite the Contract

§ 8.8   Recovery Despite a Clause Limiting or Controlling Recovery
§ 8.9   —The No Damages for Delay Cases
§ 8.10   —The Cardinal Change Cases
§ 8.11   Recovery Despite Inequitable Contract Provisions That Purport to
             Cover the Changed Work

Chapter 9   Recovery for Jointly-Caused Delay
             Thomas W. Hayton

§ 9.1   Introduction
§ 9.2   Both Parties Must Prove Causation and Delay to Whole Job
§ 9.3   Concurrent Cause Rule
§ 9.4   —Apportionment Still Possible under Liberal Rule
§ 9.5   —Other Criteria Not Useful in Concurrent Cause Rule Analysis
§ 9.6   —Breach versus Price Adjustment
§ 9.7   —Suspension of Work and Government Delay of Work Clauses
§ 9.8   —Hopelessly Intertwined Causes
§ 9.9   —Concurrent Cause Rule Used to Analyze Government Claims of
             Delay
§ 9.10   —No Apportionment Possible under Conservative Version of Concur-
             rent Cause Rule
§ 9.11   Presumed Sharing Rule
§ 9.12   —Application of Presumed Sharing Rule to Costs Not Time-Related
§ 9.13   —Application of Presumed Sharing Rule to Delay
§ 9.14   —Criteria Used in Apportioning under Presumed Sharing Rule
§ 9.15   Consequence of Choosing Particular Rule

Chapter 10   Landmark CPM Decisions from 1980 to 1990
             Jon M. Wickwire
             Lance J. Lerman
             Mark R. Berry

§ 10.1   Introduction
§ 10.2   What Is CPM?
§ 10.3   Use of CPM for Delay Analysis and Contract Claims
§ 10.4   Delay Claim Analysis
§ 10.5   —The Parameters
§ 10.6   Acceleration Claim Analysis
§ 10.7   Loss of Productivity Analysis
§ 10.8   The Decisions
§ 10.9   —*Fortec Constructors versus United States*
§ 10.10   —*Gulf Contracting, Inc.*
§ 10.11   —*Weaver-Bailey Contractors, Inc. versus United States*
§ 10.12   —*Williams Enterprises versus Strait Manufacturing & Welding, Inc.*

§ 10.13   The Major Cases and Issues
§ 10.14   —*Utley-James Inc.*
§ 10.15   —*Haney versus United States*
§ 10.16   —The *Santa Fe* Decisions
§ 10.17   —*Ealahan Electric Co.*
§ 10.18   —*Titan Pacific Construction Corp. versus United States*
§ 10.19   State Recognition of CPM Principles

PART III   DESIGN PROFESSIONALS' LIABILITY

Chapter 11   **Administrative, Regulatory, and Registration Proceedings Involving Design Professionals**
              David J. Hatem

§ 11.1   Introduction
§ 11.2   Case Study

GENERAL DISCUSSION AND BACKGROUND
§ 11.3   OSHA Proceedings
§ 11.4   Board of Registration Proceedings
§ 11.5   —Kansas City Hyatt Case
§ 11.6   Civil Actions Arising Out of Construction Accidents

IMPACT OF DETERMINATIONS IN ADMINISTRATIVE AND REGISTRATION PROCEEDINGS ON SUBSEQUENT CIVIL LIABILITY
§ 11.7   Issue Preclusion Generally
§ 11.8   Issue Preclusion in Case Study
§ 11.9   Admission of Findings into Evidence
§ 11.10   Effect of Professional Practice Standards
§ 11.11   Guidelines

Chapter 12   **Construction Administration Services and the Architect's Liability Dilemma**
              John A. Knutson

§ 12.1   Introduction
§ 12.2   Background
§ 12.3   Supervision
§ 12.4   —Early Case Law
§ 12.5   —AIA Standard Form Contract
§ 12.6   —*Mounds View*
§ 12.7   —Modern Statutes
§ 12.8   —Recent Cases
§ 12.9   Limiting Liability by Contract
§ 12.10   Recommendations

Chapter 13   **Impact of Construction Safety on Design Professionals**

Milton F. Lunch

§ **13.1**   Introduction
§ **13.2**   The Master Builder Concept
§ **13.3**   Early Supervision Cases
§ **13.4**   Stop the Work Cases
§ **13.5**   Current Document Language
§ **13.6**   Relationship of Workers' Compensation Laws
§ **13.7**   Labor Laws
§ **13.8**   Impact of OSHA
§ **13.9**   Pending Safety Legislation
§ **13.10**   Defense by Indemnification
§ **13.11**   Construction Safety Guidelines

Chapter 14   **The Defense of Qualified Privilege in Defamation and Commercial Tort Claims Against Architects**

Christopher L. Noble

§ **14.1**   Introduction
§ **14.2**   Defamation
§ **14.3**   Tortious Interference
§ **14.4**   Privilege Defenses
§ **14.5**   Communications
§ **14.6**   —Communications with Owner
§ **14.7**   —Communications with Persons Other than Owner
§ **14.8**   Case Summaries
§ **14.9**   —*Riblet Tramway Co. versus Ericksen Associates, Inc.*
§ **14.10**   —*Somers Construction Co. versus Board of Education*
§ **14.11**   —*Joba Construction Co. versus Burns & Roe, Inc.*
§ **14.12**   —*Conway Corp. versus Construction Engineers, Inc.*
§ **14.13**   —*Kecko Piping Co. versus Town of Monroe*
§ **14.14**   —*Vojak versus Jensen*
§ **14.15**   —*Certified Mechanical Contractors, Inc. versus Wight & Co.*
§ **14.16**   —*Dehnert versus Arrow Sprinklers, Inc.*
§ **14.17**   —*George A. Fuller Co. verus Chicago College of Osteopathic Medicine*
§ **14.18**   —*V.M. Solis Underground Utility & Paving Co. versus City of Laredo*
§ **14.19**   —*Alfred A. Altimont, Inc. versus Chatelain, Samperton & Nolan*
§ **14.20**   —*Santucci Construction Co. versus Baxter & Woodman, Inc.*
§ **14.21**   —*Ballou versus Basic Construction Co.*
§ **14.22**   —*Waldinger Corp. versus CRS Group Engineers, Inc.*
§ **14.23**   Guidelines to Protect Architects

Chapter 15   Liability of Architect/Engineers for Erroneous Software and Computer Data

Michael J. Ladino

§ 15.1   Introduction

TRADITIONAL AREAS OF A/E LIABILITY

§ 15.2   Legal Background and Development of the Concept of Malpractice
§ 15.3   Liability to Persons with Whom the A/E Is in Privity of Contract
§ 15.4   Negligence
§ 15.5   Third-Party Beneficiary
§ 15.6   Indemnification
§ 15.7   Tortious Interference with Contractual Relations
§ 15.8   Implied Warranty

LIABILITY OF SOFTWARE DESIGNER FOR DEFECTIVE SOFTWARE

§ 15.9   Scope of Problem
§ 15.10   Sale of Goods versus Sale of Services: Rights and Responsibilities of Software Designer to Software User and Third Parties
§ 15.11   UCC Problems Facing Software Dealers
§ 15.12   —Express Warranties
§ 15.13   —Implied Warranties
§ 15.14   —Limitation on Remedy Provisions
§ 15.15   Software Manufacturer's Exposure to Professional Malpractice Liability
§ 15.16   Substantive or Mechanical Errors
§ 15.17   CADD Use Guidelines

Chapter 16   Review of Recent Significant Cases Involving Design Professionals

John J. Lynch

CONTRACTUAL LIABILITY

§ 16.1   Architect's Contract and Poor Work
§ 16.2   Exculpatory Clause Does Not Absolve Architect
§ 16.3   Contract Disclaimer
§ 16.4   Engineering Firm Liable for Failure to Detect Fraud
§ 16.5   Excess Cost of Construction Does Not Defeat Architect's Fee Claim

CONTRIBUTION AND INDEMNITY

§ 16.6   Contribution or Indemnity from Designer
§ 16.7   Architect Not Entitled to Contribution or Indemnity
§ 16.8   Equitable Indemnity Not Available from Engineer
§ 16.9   Architect Allowed Indemnity for Attorneys' Fees
§ 16.10   Indemnification of Joint Tortfeasor
§ 16.11   Defendant Can Maintain Contribution Action

§ 16.12   Engineer Not Entitled to Contribution or Implied Indemnity

§ 16.13   Design Engineer Could Not Obtain Contribution from EPA

§ 16.14   Indemnity or Contribution from Design Drawing Company

§ 16.15   Apportioned Fault Verdict Upheld

ECONOMIC LOSS

§ 16.16   Negligent Misrepresentation Case Requires Functional Equivalent of Privity

§ 16.17   Tort Recovery for Economic Loss Not Allowed Regardless of Relationship Between Parties

§ 16.18   Tort Recovery for Economic Loss Not Allowed Even to Supplier of Services

§ 16.19   Claim for Negligent Review of Shop Drawing

ENVIRONMENTAL LAW

§ 16.20   Waste Disposal Problems

EXPERT WITNESS LITIGATION

§ 16.21   Expert Witness Immune from Suit

§ 16.22   Expert Opinion Necessary to Prove Negligence

§ 16.23   Non-Architect as Expert Witness Against Architect

§ 16.24   Statute Requires Filing of Expert's Affidavit with Complaint Against Architects

§ 16.25   Surveyor Liable as a Matter of Law

§ 16.26   Architect's Own Expert Establishes Architect's Negligence

MEASURE OF DAMAGES

§ 16.27   Cost to Repair

§ 16.28   Consequential Damages from Engineer

PATENT AND LATENT DEFECTS

§ 16.29   Question of Fact

§ 16.30   Owner's Allegation of Latent Defect

§ 16.31   Subsequent Owner Could Not Recover

PRIVITY

§ 16.32   Condominium Owner Third-Party Beneficiary

PUBLIC OFFICIAL IMMUNITY

§ 16.33   Suit Against State Employee Engineer Barred

RACKETEERING

§ 16.34   Engineering Firm Supplying Reports and Studies

SAFETY ON THE JOBSITE

§ 16.35   No Duty to Notify Workers

§ 16.36   Architect Not Liable to Injured Worker

§ 16.37   No Duty to Supervise

STATUTES OF REPOSE

§ 16.38   Wisconsin's Statute of Repose Held Unconstitutional

§ 16.39   Utah's Statute of Repose Held Unconstitutional
§ 16.40   Ohio's Statute of Repose Held Constitutional
§ 16.41   Oklahoma's Statute of Repose Held Constitutional

STATUTES OF LIMITATIONS
§ 16.42   A/E Firm Estopped from Asserting Statute of Limitations
§ 16.43   Damage Claim Did Not Change Contract Action Into Tort Action
§ 16.44   Economic Loss Action Governed by Tort Statute of Limitations
§ 16.45   Suit by Governmental Agencies Not Barred by Statute of Limitations

PART IV   STRATEGIES, TECHNIQUES, AND OBSERVATIONS
Chapter 17   The Work Force Shortage and Organized Labor's Agenda for the
              1990s
              Judd H. Lees

§ 17.1   Introduction
§ 17.2   Agenda Item 1: Continue the Apprenticeship Battle
§ 17.3   Agenda Item 2: Employ More Sophisticated Top-Down Organizing
           Techniques
§ 17.4   Agenda Item 3: Engage in More Aggressive Bottom-Up Organizing
§ 17.5   Agenda Item 4: If All Else Fails, File an Unfair Labor Practice Charge

Chapter 18   The Right to Stop Work
              Laurence Schor
              Richard C. Walters

§ 18.1   Introduction
§ 18.2   Impossibility and Commercial Impracticability
§ 18.3   The McCarthy Case
§ 18.4   The New AIA Clause
§ 18.5   Observations

Chapter 19   Asbestos Liability Strategies
              Philip R. Croessmann

§ 19.1   Introduction

REGULATORY HISTORY OF ASBESTOS IN BUILDINGS
§ 19.2   Federal Regulatory History
§ 19.3   State Regulation
§ 19.4   Criminal Enforcement

COST RECOVERY
§ 19.5   Strict Liability
§ 19.6   Product Liability
§ 19.7   Negligence

§ **19.8**   Warranty

§ **19.9**   Miscellaneous Theories

COST RECOVERY DEFENSES

§ **19.10**   Economic Loss versus Property Damage

§ **19.11**   Statute of Limitations

§ **19.12**   Safe Product Defense

§ **19.13**   Product Identification

LIABILITY AND ASBESTOS ABATEMENT

§ **19.14**   Owner

§ **19.15**   Architects and Engineers

§ **19.16**   Asbestos Consultants

§ **19.17**   Asbestos Contractors

§ **19.18**   Other Groups

PROTECTION AND ALLOCATIONS OF LIABILITY

§ **19.19**   Contracts

§ **19.20**   Supervision

§ **19.21**   Recordkeeping

§ **19.22**   Workers' Training

§ **19.23**   Worker Release

§ **19.24**   Liability Insurance

§ **19.25**   Incorporation

§ **19.26**   Legislation

Chapter 20   **Discovery in Construction Litigation**

John B. Tieder, Jr.
Julian F. Hoffar
David C. Romm

INTRODUCTION

§ **20.1**   Purposes of Discovery

§ **20.2**   Defending Against Discovery

OTHER SOURCES OF INFORMATION

§ **20.3**   Client Sources

§ **20.4**   Third Parties

§ **20.5**   Former Employees or Representatives of Opponent

§ **20.6**   Experts

§ **20.7**   Published Materials

ORGANIZING CLIENT INFORMATION

§ **20.8**   Basic Case Established from Client Data

§ **20.9**   Gathering Documents

§ **20.10**   —Indexing

§ 20.11 — Indentification and Removal of Privileged or Exempt Documents
§ 20.12 Witness Interviews

AVAILABLE METHODS OF AFFIRMATIVE DISCOVERY

§ 20.13 Document Requests: Identifying the Records
§ 20.14 — Organizing the Documents
§ 20.15 — Analyzing the Documents
§ 20.16 Interrogatories
§ 20.17 Depositions
§ 20.18 Requests for Admissions
§ 20.19 Discovery Through Negotiations

NONCOMPLIANCE OR OBJECTIONS TO DISCOVERY

§ 20.20 Motion Practice
§ 20.21 Sanctions
§ 20.22 Duty to Preserve Documents
§ 20.23 Attorney Liability

DEFENSIVE DISCOVERY

§ 20.24 General Considerations
§ 20.25 Interrogatories: When and How to Object
§ 20.26 — Preparation of Responses
§ 20.27 Requests for Production of Documents
§ 20.28 — Responding to a Request
§ 20.29 Depositions: Preparing the Witness
§ 20.30 — Objections
§ 20.31 — Memory of Witnesses
§ 20.32 — Designating Witnesses
§ 20.33 — Requests for Admissions
§ 20.34 — Duty to Supplement

EXPERT DISCOVERY

§ 20.35 Who Is an Expert?
§ 20.36 Discovery of Nontestifying Experts
§ 20.37 Discovery of Testifying Experts
§ 20.38 Impeachment of the Trial Expert

Index

PART I

CONTRACT FORMATION AND STANDARD FORM DOCUMENTS

CHAPTER 1

CHOOSING A CONTRACTING FORMAT

Randall L. Erickson
Frederic I. Albert

§ 1.1   Introduction

PRICE CONSIDERATIONS IN PRIVATE CONTRACTS

§ 1.2   In General

§ 1.3   Fixed Price Contracts: Owner Advantages, Contractor Risk

§ 1.4   —Contractor Advantages, Owner Risk

§ 1.5   Cost Contracts: Contractor Advantages, Owner Risk

§ 1.6   Guaranteed Maximum Contracts

§ 1.7   Abandonment

COMPETITIVE BIDDING AND COMPETITIVE NEGOTIATION

§ 1.8   Competitive Bidding: Policy and Frustration

§ 1.9   —Owner Risk: Performance Risk and Bonds

§ 1.10   —Competence Risk Avoidance in Public Sector

§ 1.11   —Private Owners

§ 1.12   —Cost Estimating Risks and Excessive Change Orders

§ 1.13   —Contractor Risk: Cost Estimating Risk and Subcontractor Quotes

§ 1.14   —Computation Errors

§ 1.15   —Private Contracts

§ 1.16   —Public Contracts

§ 1.17   —Extra Work Compensation in Public Contracts

§ 1.18   —Private Contracts

§ 1.19   Competitive Negotiation in General

§ 1.20   —Owner Risk

§ 1.21   —Contractor Cost Estimating Risks

STANDARD TRADE ASSOCIATION CONTRACTS

§ 1.22　Standard Contracts in General

§ 1.23　—AIA Documents

§ 1.24　Standard Contract Cautions

DESIGN-BUILD CONTRACTS

§ 1.25　In General

§ 1.26　Joint Venture Design-Build Team

§ 1.27　Sole Contractor

§ 1.1　Introduction

Contractors, owners, and architects have many options when deciding what type of construction contract to utilize and how best to implement a contract given the nature of a project. Price considerations, competitive bidding and negotiation, standard trade association contracts, and the design-build arrangement are just a few of those options on private contracts.

PRICE CONSIDERATIONS IN PRIVATE CONTRACTS

§ 1.2　In General

A major factor in the determination of the appropriate contract format is the contract price and the risk allocation involved in choosing the means of compensating the contractor.

In this process a conflict often arises between allocating the risk of cost escalation and cost cutting incentives. In general, there are two approaches. First, there is the fixed price contract in which the contractor agrees to complete the project for a specific amount. Second, there are cost base contracts wherein the contractor will be paid separately for costs plus an additional amount representing profit. This amount can be a percentage of the costs or it can be a fixed amount.

§ 1.3　Fixed Price Contracts: Owner Advantages, Contractor Risk

Pure fixed price contracts benefit owners since they are only liable to pay the fixed ceiling price for the total contract. Conversely, this places the risk of cost overruns on the contractor. Contractors would be wise to avoid this risk where project plans are not well defined or involve experimental designs. Furthermore, the contractor must take into account the risk of long term cost escalation when preparing its bid.

§ 1.4 — Contractor Advantages, Owner Risk

One advantage that the contractor has in a fixed price contract is that a reduction of cost increases profits. Since the owner is obligated to pay the fixed price regardless of cost, a penny saved is a penny earned for the contractor.

Thus, the owner runs the risk that the contractor will sacrifice quality in order to enlarge its profit. Although there is a set of specifications which must be met, the contractor under this format may use whatever shortcuts it can to meet those minimum requirements. This risk is also accentuated by the fact that owners are less concerned with the contractor's record keeping in the fixed price format. This again highlights the importance of selecting a contractor with integrity and concern for its reputation.

§ 1.5 Cost Contracts: Contractor Advantages, Owner Risk

Cost base contracts ostensibly guarantee contractors that they will make some profit. The owner agrees to pay all construction costs and to compensate the contractor pursuant to an agreed formula based on a percentage of cost or a fixed fee. The cost base contract completely shifts the risk of cost overruns to the owner. However, the extent of this risk varies greatly depending on the specific type of formula used for fixing the contractor's fee.

Owners usually should avoid the cost plus percentage of cost formulas. Obviously, where the contractor's fee is based on a percentage of total cost, there is no incentive to cut costs. In fact, the contractor's interests are best served if they are increased. In cost plus a fixed fee contracts, the contractor's fee is fixed up front and the contractor is reimbursed for all costs. Here, there is no longer an incentive to increase costs, but neither is there an incentive to reduce them.

§ 1.6 Guaranteed Maximum Contracts

Guaranteed maximum contracts essentially seek a middle ground on allocating the risk of cost escalation between the owner and the contractor. Like the cost plus a fixed fee format, the owner pays all costs and the contractor is paid a fixed fee. But like the fixed price format, there is a contract ceiling provision requiring that the total cost and fee not exceed a specific dollar figure.

Consequently, the owner bears the risk of costs up to the specific ceiling. Unlike the fixed price contract, however, the contractor has no inherent incentive to sacrifice quality in order to enlarge its profit. Regardless of the final cost to the contractor, it must meet the contractual specifications and the owner's liability cannot exceed the ceiling price. By penalizing the contractor for cost overruns above the target ceiling and by rewarding it for cost savings, this type of contract provides financial motivation to the contractor to perform at the lowest reasonable cost.

Once cost plus the fee reaches the ceiling level, the risk has shifted to the contractor. However, such contracts will often contain price escalation clauses to protect the contractor against general price increases caused by inflation. Other clauses should be added to protect the contractor against radical changes in the scope of the work.

§ 1.7   Abandonment

A major risk to owners in most contract and pricing formats is the contract theory of abandonment. *Abandonment* occurs when an owner imposes excessive performance changes and is said to have abandoned the original contract. The contractor is then entitled to receive the fair market value of its services rather than the contract price.

This can occur in all contract and pricing formats except the percentage of costs formula. In fact, in a 1985 case, it occurred in the guaranteed maximum context.[1] In that case, the owner and contractor had entered into a guaranteed maximum contract with a guaranteed fee of $300,000 provided that the total price did not exceed $4.7 million. Due to owner initiated changes, inadequate drawings, and delays which caused expenditures and services to escalate to over $8 million, the court held that the owner abandoned the contract and rendered the guaranteed maximum provisions inapplicable. Instead, the contractor recovered the actual value of its work.

Again, even the most well drafted contract and compensation provision will not guard against lack of detailed planning and adequate contract administration.

COMPETITIVE BIDDING AND COMPETITIVE NEGOTIATION

§ 1.8   Competitive Bidding: Policy and Frustration

In both the public and private sectors, the policy behind the competitive bidding process is to review bids impartially and obtain the lowest available price from a

---

[1] C. Norman Peterson Co. v. Container Corp. of Am., 172 Cal. App. 3d 628, 218 Cal. Rptr. 592 (1985).

responsible bidder. However, competitive bidding can be frustrated by contractor collusion. Where contractors agree to take turns or submit fictitious bids, there is obviously no true competition and the lowest bid will not be obtained. Furthermore, contractors who participate in collusive practices may be violating the antitrust laws.

Also, private owners often frustrate the competitive bidding process by entering into post-bidding negotiations. They reserve the right not to accept the lowest bid, and they subsequently negotiate with their favorite contractor to see if they can match the lowest price. Unfortunately for contractors, any concerted effort to prevent this practice again would probably be violative of the state and federal antitrust laws.[2]

§ 1.9   — Owner Risk: Performance Risk and Bonds

The competitive bidding process presents common performance risks to both public and private owners. First, there is the risk that the particular bidder is either not willing or not able to perform the work promised. Also, there are risks that the contractor might become bankrupt. These are some of the main reasons that owners require various bonds for their protection.

There are basically four types of bonds used in construction contracts. First, *bid bonds* insure owners that a surety will pay for damages caused by a bidder's later refusal to enter into an awarded contract. Second, *performance bonds* are used to protect owners against prime contractors who render improper performance. Third, *payment bonds* are used to pay off unpaid subcontractors and suppliers in order to avoid the effects of mechanics' liens. And, finally, *subcontractor bonds* are used by prime contractors to protect against unreliable subcontractors. Most often, the law requires that bid, performance, and payment bonds be furnished in public construction contracts.

In private contracts, owners should be sure to state in the bid invitation the type of bonds required, the desired amount, the surety to be used by the bidders, and the right to refuse any substitution of surety without express written approval.

§ 1.10   — Competence Risk Avoidance in
Public Sector

Competitive bidding statutes, being price oriented, present inherent competence risks that the lowest bidder will not be the most reliable bidder. Thus, to avoid an award to an unproven or questionable bidder, public authorities are generally

---

[2] Oakland-Alameda County Builders' Exchange v. F.P. Lathrop Constr. Co., 4 Cal. 3d 354, 482 P.2d 226, 93 Cal. Rptr. 602 (1971).

given the right either to award the contract to the lowest responsible bidder or to simply reject all bids and readvertise.

If the public authority does not give the contract to the lowest bidder, it must determine, in good faith, that the low bidder is not responsible.[3] However, this discretion does not necessarily allow the public authority to give the award to the "most responsible bidder."[4]

Alternatively, some courts have given public authorities nearly complete discretion when the right to reject all bids and readvertise is reserved and exercised in the public interest.[5] The courts have held that a public authority's discretion to do so is only subject to only proof that: (1) its actions were in the public interest, and (2) it had not solicited bids without any intention of considering them.

§ 1.11 —Private Owners

In private contracts, owners may protect themselves from competence risks by reserving the right to accept or reject any and all bids, including the lowest bid. However, rejection of the lowest bid is subject to liability for damages if bad faith rejection is proven. If an owner uses the bidding process in order to check the price offered by a favored, preselected contractor with no intention of awarding the job to the low bidder, the owner may risk liability to the other bidders to whom the contract was not awarded. Here, the owner might be liable in damages to each of the other bidders measured by the cost to them of preparing and submitting bids. Thus, a contract clause, such as the reservation to reject the low bidder, cannot be used in bad faith.[6]

Also, assuming that the owner has reserved the right not to accept the lowest bid, it is free to enter into post-bidding negotiations as discussed earlier. Here, a favored high bidder may approach the owner and offer to do the work for less than the low bid. Alternatively, the owner may take the low bid to all bidders and ask if any of them wish to bid even lower, or the owner may negotiate with the low bidder alone in an attempt to further reduce the contract price.

---

[3] *See* Raymond v. Fresno City Unified School Dist., 123 Cal. 2d 626, 267 P.2d 69 (1954) (court upheld rejection of a low bid on grounds of poor construction of another building by the low bidder).

[4] Swinerton & Walberg Co. v. City of Inglewood-Los Angeles County Civic Center Auth., 40 Cal. App. 3d 98, 103 Cal. Rptr. 689 (1974).

[5] Universal By-Products, Inc. v. City of Modesto, 43 Cal. App. 3d 145, 117 Cal. Rptr. 525 (1974).

[6] Milton v. Hudson Sales Corp., 152 Cal. App. 2d 418, 313 P.2d 936 (1957).

§ 1.12   —Cost Estimating Risks and Excessive Change Orders

In competitive bidding, the contractor will often bid the project at or even below actual cost. Furthermore, the bid will price only items shown by the plans even though the plan may only be 75 to 90 percent complete. Contractors may be forced by incomplete plans to bid below cost and make up the loss through change orders.

Generally, construction contracts contain change clauses which compensate the contractor at a percentage of cost. Although expensive to the owner, design flexibility cannot be accomplished without such a mechanism. Frequently, however, disputes arise as to whether particular extra work requested is required by the contract. Where plans are relatively incomplete, the contractor is in a better position to argue that they do not call out certain work and that it should be compensated pursuant to the changes clause in the contract. In other words, one of the easiest ways for an owner to minimize cost increases due to change orders is to start with a complete set of drawings.

§ 1.13   —Contractor Risk: Cost Estimating Risk and Subcontractor Quotes

In competitive bidding, the contractor will generally have only a few weeks to analyze plans and prepare its bids. To make matters worse, subcontractors often are forced to wait until the final minutes before the bid deadline to call in their quotes. Because of the last minute nature of preparing the bid, contractors run the risk that the subcontractors' quotes do not represent the full scope of the work requested by the contractor.

To minimize this risk, contractors should make it clear to the subcontractors from the outset exactly what their quotes should represent. Otherwise, the contractor's bid will not reflect all the work to be done and the contractor will have to do the work itself or hire a subcontractor at its own expense.

§ 1.14   —Computation Errors

Before a bid is accepted, the general rule is that it is only an offer and can be withdrawn at any time. This technically would allow the contractor to withdraw an erroneous bid at any time before the owner accepts it. However, both public and private owners now often require bid bonds which guarantee contractor performance if awarded the project. Furthermore, some bid invitations require that the bid will be made irrevocable for a stated time.

The contractor should be very careful when submitting its bids that computation errors are not made. As mentioned, subcontractors often wait until the last minute before submitting their quotes. Thus, such errors are easily understandable. However, judicial relief from such mistakes is often difficult to obtain.

§ 1.15   —Private Contracts

Relief for computation errors in private contracts is governed by the legal theory of unilateral mistake. Here, the contractor will only be able to rescind its bid in situations in which the owner knows, or should know, that a bid was unreasonably low.

Although there is a limited right of rescission, the contractor will not be able to have the contract reformed to correct the error. In other words, the contractor cannot enter into the contract and then try to increase the price due to its bidding error. An action for reformation is available only when, through mistake, the contract as finally written does not express the mutual intention of the parties. The contract entered into after a bid mistake may not reflect the contractor's intention. But it does reflect the owner's intention. Therefore, reformation is not available to the contractor.[7]

§ 1.16   —Public Contracts

In California, the public contract bidder who submits a mistaken bid may be relieved from the bid by consent of the awarding authority, or may bring an action in the Superior Court to recover the amount forfeited, without interest or cost. The complaint must be filed and served within ninety days after the bid opening. The bidder must establish to the satisfaction of the court that a mistake was made, that the bidder gave written notice to the public entity within five days after the bid opening, and specify in detail how the mistake occurred, and that the mistake was material and not due to an error in judgment or to carelessness.[8]

§ 1.17   —Extra Work Compensation in Public Contracts

Contractors should never rely on representations of field personnel as to payments for extra work in public contracts. Often state, county, and city engineers have no power to obligate their respective entities to pay for extra work claims. Even if the contract authorizes the engineer to order the extra work, the courts may find the authorization beyond the scope of legal authority. Essentially,

---

[7] Lemoge Elec. v. County of San Mateo, 46 Cal. 2d 659, 297 P.2d 638 (1956).

[8] Cal. Pub. Cont. Code §§ 5100, et seq. (West).

public contractors are charged with knowledge of the public entity's agent's limitations and no relief will be rendered.

§ 1.18   —Private Contracts

Private contracts generally contain clauses which require written change orders before the contractor is paid for extra work. Unlike public contracts, the courts will be quick to invoke the doctrine of waiver to prevent unjust enrichment to the owner. Thus, if the work is requested by the owner or is done with its knowledge, the owner will have waived the extra work clause of the contract.

§ 1.19   Competitive Negotiation in General

In private contracts, owners will often bypass the competitive bidding process and enter into a procedure known as competitive negotiation. In competitive negotiation, the contractor enters into the construction project at a much earlier stage. Here, the owner will choose a contractor at a time when the owner's drawings are only conceptual or schematic rather than near completion as in competitive bidding.

This allows the contractor to participate in the design process and advise the owner about the costs of architectural design proposals. Contractors are selected on the basis of their presentation to the owner in which they submit their ideas on the project, a guaranteed maximum price, their fee, the conditions of employment, and previous work history.

§ 1.20   —Owner Risk

In competitive negotiations, the owner's selection of a contractor becomes even more important. Because the contractor has greater control over the project, it also has more opportunity to increase its fee with hidden costs. Also, since the owner now relies on the contractor to quantify and approve architectural proposals, the owner runs the risk that the architect and the contractor may not get along, thus presenting great obstacles to the project's completion.

§ 1.21   —Contractor Cost Estimating Risks

In competitive negotiation, the estimating techniques used by the contractor depend on the type of specifications available, unlike in competitive bidding where the contractor should bid at the lowest available price to get the award. This is because the cost estimations occur after the contractor is selected.

Instead, the contractor will estimate as high as possible to protect itself from cost overruns.

If the designs happen to give detailed specifications, the contractor will estimate costs by the unit pricing method. Using the design specifications which enumerate how many units of a given building material are needed, the contractor can get more precise price quotes from suppliers who can gear their estimates by the predicted number of units required under the plans. Unit pricing enables a contractor to give a reasonably accurate bid because the detailed specifications provide an excellent guideline for compiling the bid, a unit of material at a time. Unit pricing has the advantage of allowing the contractor to check out prevailing prices for the owner-estimated quantities of material and labor.

As the owner's plans become less detailed and more conceptual, the contractor must rely more on historical cost estimations. Here, the owner's plans are more result oriented and it expects the contractor to help select the means to accomplish the desired end. The contractor must then give the owner a budget figure that is based in most part on similar projects built in the past.

In competitive negotiation, the contractor's estimating risks are enhanced because it is pinned down to a figure early without the benefit of detailed planning. It can minimize these risks by (1) avoiding giving a budget estimate as long as possible to allow some detailed planning to develop, (2) qualifying the budget as an estimate and subject to change, and (3) building an added margin of safety into the price. On the other hand, by being more involved in the design process, the contractor enters into the domain of the architect. This could expand its scope of responsibility and increase its exposure.

STANDARD TRADE ASSOCIATION CONTRACTS

§ 1.22   Standard Contracts in General

One option which the contractor, as well as the owner and architect, should seriously consider at the contract formation stage is the use of a standard trade association contract. These contracts include documents of the American Institute of Architects (AIA), Associated General Contractors (AGC), and the National Society of Professional Engineers (NSPE).

§ 1.23   —AIA Documents

The AIA documents are widely used and generally accepted as stating the best and most standard practices in the construction industry. The AIA meets and confers with the AGC and generally receives approval and/or endorsement for its two most commonly used documents, A101 (basic agreement) and A201 (general conditions).

The AIA maintains that fairness is more than a passing consideration in the drafting of these documents. It is apparent, however, that the architect's perspective is embodied in a number of ways. For example, as a rule, the AIA prefers to separate the design and construction aspects of construction in its documents. This structure, of course, serves to protect the architect's traditional role on any given building endeavor. Although the AIA documents do maintain a slant toward an architectural perspective, they are generally considered fair to all parties.

One excellent feature of the AIA documents is that they reflect an ongoing real world approach. For example, an AIA document will never call for the issuing of an insurance policy or bond which is obsolete, unavailable, or unrealistically expensive at the time of document publication. Because AIA documents are frequently updated, they continue to reflect this real world approach throughout the different revisions.

AIA documents A101 and A201 combine to form the standard construction agreement. AIA documents—A101 and A201 are perfect examples—are interrelated with many provisions referencing other sections within the text. Therefore, standardized documents should be used together. Because the modification or deletion of a certain provision can change other provisions of the agreement, extreme caution should be used in making any changes. AIA construction documents are excellent forms if the project being contracted for is one which fits into the profile of the type of project the AIA considered when drafting the provisions. Generally, any mid-priced project where design and construction are separated and in which the architect has a central administrative role is an excellent choice for an AIA document.

The combination of the A101 and A201 works best if:

1. A single contract is used
2. A fixed price is determined by competitive bidding
3. The design is prepared by an independent architect engaged by the owner and it is completed before the award
4. No construction manager is used and
5. The architect, in addition to designing, plays a significant role during construction.[9]

Most courts treat these standardized documents as though they were negotiated and drafted by both parties. Therefore, the standard documents are interpreted neutrally, rather than against the one who "prepared" them.

---

[9] J. Sweet, Sweet on Construction Industry Contracts 178 (John Wiley & Sons 1987).

§ 1.24   Standard Contract Cautions

Some courts, however, are critical of standardized construction documents, but this criticism often seems to reflect situations where the documents were used improperly, i.e., for the wrong type of project. One court called AIA A201 "a voluminous printed form contract mass produced."[10]

Normally, in a commercial context such as the construction agreements, standardized contracts are not considered contracts of adhesion. A contract of adhesion is one in which a person (generally a consumer) has no realistic opportunity to bargain and cannot obtain the desired product or services except by acquiescing in a form contract. However, some courts have recently held that even in a commercial setting, if there is an uneven bargaining position, a standard form contract such as an AIA document could be found unconscionable and unenforceable.[11]

The bottom line on standard association contracts is that if they fit the project to be contracted they can be a great advantage in continuity and reduction of legal costs. It is generally held that AIA documents, along with other standardized association contracts, can be used with confidence if no changes are made in the terms. However, even if changes become necessary, attorneys' costs should be limited. The number of hours it would take an attorney to review the changes to an already legally sound standardized contract should be far fewer than it would take to fully and satisfactorily review a construction contract entirely prepared by the contractor, architect, or owner.

DESIGN-BUILD CONTRACTS

§ 1.25   In General

A design-build arrangement is one in which a party or a group of parties contract with the owner to produce the completed construction product from beginning to end. At first blush, there is an obvious advantage in the centralization of responsibility and expertise. The potential advantage of this arrangement is, however, tempered with disadvantages that should be carefully considered before adopting this approach. Chiefly, the range of critical and analytic dialogue which normally occurs between architect and general contractor on a project may be severely diminished or lost altogether. Two conceivable ways of implementing the design-build approach are utilizing a joint venture format or a sole contractor.

---

[10] Fletcher v. Laguna Vista Corp., 275 So. 2d 579 (Fla. Dist. Ct. App.), *cert. denied,* 281 So. 2d 213 (Fla. 1973).

[11] Bos Material Handling, Inc. v. Crown Controls Corp., 137 Cal. App. 3d 99, 186 Cal. Rptr. 740 (1982).

§ 1.26   Joint Venture Design-Build Team

One way of implementing a design-build format is for an architect or engineering firm to form a joint venture with a general contractor, thus becoming a design-build team. The advantage of this approach is that the general contractor is involved very early on in coordinating the cost of the various architectural and structural features with the architect. The team can lay out specifically and practically the concepts to be followed in construction and the prices contemplated. Under this approach, there is more motivation for the architect and general contractor to work together in cooperation since they are, in effect, one entity as joint venturers.

The subtle, though obvious, disadvantage to the owner is that the architect under a design-build format is not the owner's agent the way the architect under traditional construction formats would be. This is so because the architect is now a partner with the general contractor. Another potential result of this relationship is a limitation on the creative design talent available on the project and the absence of an independent expert engaged by the owner to monitor performance.

Any confusion this may cause in terms of liability for project delays, errors, etc., at least from the owner's standpoint, can be minimized if the joint venture and the individual joint venturers are made jointly responsible for the entire design-build product. In this way, the owner can then look to the design-build team for a finished product and leave the venturers to sort out their individual responsibilities to each other.

§ 1.27   Sole Contractor

Architects and experienced, full-service engineering companies may undertake to be responsible for the design, procurement of materials and equipment, and management of construction. The result under this approach may be that the project can be sped from conception to completion. This approach can also clarify legal responsibility and relationships which might be less clear under a joint venture approach. Unfortunately, however, the critical analysis of suggestions and approaches that inevitably results from having independent architects and contractors is more likely lost in this approach.

CHAPTER 2

MODIFICATIONS TO AIA A201 1987 EDITION FROM OWNER'S VIEWPOINT

B. Clarence Hart
Louise A. Behrendt*

§ 2.1   Introduction

OWNER'S OBLIGATIONS

§ 2.2   Define Scope of Work

§ 2.3   Provide Information

§ 2.4   Provide Assurance of Ability to Pay

§ 2.5   Provide Insurance

OWNER'S RIGHTS

§ 2.6   Make Changes

§ 2.7   Be Protected from Risks Which A/E and Contractor Should Bear and Insure

§ 2.8   Suspend or Terminate the Contract

§ 2.9   Have Work Completed on Schedule

OWNER'S EXPOSURE TO CLAIMS AND HOW TO PROTECT AGAINST THEM

§ 2.10   Delay Damages

§ 2.11   Differing Site Conditions

§ 2.12   Defective Plans

§ 2.13   Lack of Coordination of Separate Prime Contractors

---

* This chapter is adapted from a paper presented in December 1989 to the Fourth Annual Construction Litigation Superconference sponsored by Andrews Conferences.

OWNER'S RELATIONSHIPS WITH OTHER PARTIES

§ 2.14   **Contractor**

§ 2.15   **Architect**

§ 2.16   **Effect of Dispute Resolution Provisions on Owner**

§ 2.17   **Conclusion**

§ 2.1   Introduction

According to the *Encyclopedia Brittanica,* elephants have a gestation period of 20 to 22 months. By comparison, it is evidently easier to give birth to elephants than it is for the American Institute of Architects to give birth to a new edition of the AIA General Conditions of the Contract for Construction, AIA Document A201. The 14th edition of that document, published in April 1987, consumed the efforts of 16 volunteer architects, with the support of AIA staff and attorneys over a period of seven years.

The changes made in the 1987 edition are so extensive, both in form and substance, that literally no complete article, paragraph, or subparagraph remains unmodified; only twelve sentences in the entire document were unchanged. Titles are changed. Organizational content and sequences are changed. The index is changed. Definitions are added and altered. Legal rights, obligations, and relationships are modified and in some instances even the format of presentation has been altered.

Such extensive and far reaching changes have predictably resulted not only in the usual expository comment but an unusual barrage of criticism from representatives of owners, design professionals, and contractors. This chapter will provide information concerning the nature and effect of the changes as well as suggestions from several commentators for counteracting or nullifying the changes. It will also provide insights of our own concerning changes that may be desirable to protect the interests of the owner.

When reviewing and negotiating any contract, owners should keep in mind that no form document, such as A201, can be suitable for all owners and all types of projects. There is no such thing as a standard construction document or set of documents which will be suitable for the wide variety of different construction projects which occur in the construction industry. No standard construction document can be used properly as a "cookie cutter" to serve construction projects in an infinite variety of sizes, characteristics, and complexity.

Each set of contract documents must be tailored to fit each individual project. Factors to be considered include the following:

1.   Whether the project is public or private
2.   Whether the project is in an urban, suburban, rural, or wilderness area

3.   The type of project, e.g., highway and heavy projects, hospitals and clinics, educational facilities, high-rise buildings, solid waste incinerators, garden variety housing projects, petroleum pipelines, sewer and water projects, and so forth

4.   The relative sophistication of the parties involved. Sophisticated owners and design firms have standard contract supplements, computer-generated, to serve each particular type of project

5.   Whether the project involves a single prime or multiple prime contractors

6.   Whether there is a construction manager or not.

Criticism concerning the 1987 changes to A201 represents a complete spectrum of positive and negative commentary. For example, veteran architect-attorney Carl Sapers believes that the 1987 edition of A201 essentially "fails" to serve not only the owner but the contractor and architect as well, and this failure is "of grave concern to all of us connected with the design and construction of buildings in America."[1] On the other hand, Justin Sweet, in his comprehensive treatise on construction industry contracts, describes all AIA documents as good ones; they "clearly inform" each party of their responsibilities and entitlements, and anticipate likely problems.[2]

It is not our intention in this chapter to provide all-encompassing owner-oriented commentary, criticism and suggested changes to A201. Several able commentators have already performed that task. Due to partisan partiality and strength of position, some suggested changes are more aggressive than others and thus may not be appropriate for all owners in all circumstances. Relative bargaining power is always a factor and harsh, overreaching contracts often produce their own retribution in the form of desperation reactions and ultimate litigation. Generally, we hope that you will be able to use some of the suggestions which follow to negotiate a contract which is fair, reasonable and workable for all parties concerned.

OWNER'S OBLIGATIONS

§ 2.2   Define Scope of Work

A201-1987 substantially expands the definition of "work." Paragraph 1.1.3 states that "work" includes "construction and services required by the Contract Documents, whether completed or partially completed," and covers all work in

---

[1] Sapers, *The New AIA General Conditions: A Flawed Document that Architects Will Use at Their Peril,* Architectural Record 37 (Feb. 1988) [hereinafter Sapers].

[2] J. Sweet, Sweet on Construction Industry Contracts 14 (1987) [hereinafter Sweet].

progress whether on or off the construction site. This broad definition appears to include all temporary facilities, safety programs, testing, and other services provided by the contractor in addition to permanent construction.

Paragraph 1.1.4 defines "project" as "construction by the owner or by a separate contractor." Both 1.1.3 and 1.1.4 contemplate that the contract itself will outline and define the "work" required for the "project."

According to Article 4 of AIA B141-1987, Standard Form of Agreement between Owner and Architect, the owner is to provide "full information regarding requirements for the project, including a program which shall set forth the owners objectives, schedule, constraints and criteria . . . ." It has been suggested that this section is so all-encompassing, and imposes such far-reaching obligations on the owner to define scope of work that, if it were to be followed literally, architect services for design development would not be necessary. Therefore, to define the work and the scope of the project as referenced in ¶¶ 1.1.3 and 1.1.4 of A201, a prudent owner needs to negotiate the terms of the standard owner-architect agreement so that the owner is not obligated literally to conceptualize the entire project before the architect becomes involved.[3]

§ 2.3   Provide Information

Article 2 of A201-1987 significantly added to the owner's responsibilities to provide information to the contractor. For example, ¶ 2.1.2 now requires that the owner provide the contractor with information "which is necessary and relevant for the contractor to evaluate, give notice of or enforce mechanic's lien rights," including "a correct statement of the record legal title to the property on which the project is located. . . ." These new requirements were obviously added to make it easier for the contractor to obtain legal description information, which is often difficult for a contractor to obtain without owner cooperation.

This subparagraph has come under strong attack by owner advocates. Gregory Hummel suggests that the language in ¶ 2.1.2 is ambiguous concerning how much information the owner must provide, and how often the contractor can request this information of the owner. He suggests that such potential ambiguities be resolved before the contract is executed.[4]

---

[3] G. Hummel, *Negotiating the Owner-Architect Agreement (Owner's Viewpoint): Supplemental Conditions to AIA Document B141 Standard Form of Agreement Between Owner and Architect, 1987 Edition,* Design and Construction Contracts 1, 22-23 (ABA 1989).

[4] G. Hummel, *Negotiating the Owner-Architect Agreement (Owner's Viewpoint): The General Conditions of the Contract for Construction 1987 Edition of AIA Document A201,* Design and Construction Contracts 127, 131 (ABA 1989) [hereinafter Hummel].

A more extreme position is taken by Hugh King and Marc Epstein. They recommend the deletion of ¶ 2.1.2 in its entirety because it "requires the owner to furnish to the contractor certain information that the owner may not desire to disclose."[5]

Paragraph 2.2.2 requires the owner to "furnish surveys describing physical characteristics, legal limitations and utility locations." Hummel suggests that this language be changed to require the contractor to review any materials (such as surveys, soil tests, etc.) submitted by the owner and corroborate their accuracy or notify the owner within 20 days of the discovery of any inaccuracy. It is suggested that the contractor not be allowed to recover damages from any such inaccuracy if it fails to notify the owner as required.[6]

For an inexperienced owner, Sweet suggests the deletion of this subparagraph entirely. He believes that, if the owner is inexperienced, it makes more sense to place responsibility for site survey and investigation on the architect, and make the expense reimbursable.[7]

King and Epstein again suggest substantial and radical changes and additions to ¶ 2.2.2. They suggest adding language to the effect that furnishing of surveys by the owner shall not relieve the contractor of its duties under the contract documents. They also suggest inclusion of language stating that neither the owner nor the architect shall be required to furnish the contractor with information concerning subsurface characteristics or conditions of the areas where the work is to be performed. King and Epstein admit that the suggested additions to ¶ 2.2.2 effectively make the contractor assume the risk of unknown site conditions.[8] This type of disclaimer, if expressed in explicit terms, may be effective but may also generate higher bids to cover unknown conditions.

Paragraph 2.2.3 contemplates that, "[e]xcept for permits and fees which are the responsibility of the Contractor under the Contract Documents, the Owner will secure and pay for necessary approvals, easements, assessments and charges required for construction . . . ." Hummel suggests that the permits and approvals to be obtained by the owner be specifically identified in this subparagraph. Specific identification of the owner's responsibilities would imply that the contractor is responsible to obtain all other approvals and permits. This is a proper inference since the contractor is usually in a better position to know which permits and approvals will be necessary to perform the work.[9]

---

[5] King & Epstein, *Owner's Counsel Reviews (and Suggests Changes to) the New (1987) AIA General Conditions of the Contract for Construction (Part 1),* The Practical Real Estate Lawyer 9, 21 (Mar. 1989) [hereinafter King I].

[6] Hummel at 131-32.

[7] Sweet at 138.

[8] King I at 21-23.

[9] Hummel at 132.

§ 2.4   Provide Assurance of Ability to Pay

Paragraph 2.2.1 mandates that the owner disclose to the contractor information regarding financial arrangements to fulfill its contract obligations prior to the execution of the agreement and "promptly from time to time thereafter." This is a significant change from the 1976 edition, where ¶ 3.2.1 only required the owner to furnish to the contractor reasonable evidence that financial arrangements had been made to fulfill the owner's obligations prior to the execution of the contract. The 1987 edition contemplates that the failure of the owner to provide financial information may permit the contractor to avoid commencing work, and presumably may allow the contractor to stop work if the owner does not provide reasonable evidence of ability to pay.

Sweet believes that this subparagraph was created to put contractors on notice of so-called "spec" owners who put little of their own money into speculative projects.[10] Despite this apparent good intention on the part of the AIA to "protect" the contractor from speculative projects, the term "reasonable evidence of ability to pay" in ¶ 2.2.1 is undefined and will undoubtedly generate much controversy.[11] The most foreseeable ambiguity will arise in situations where the owner can provide reasonable evidence of ability to pay the original contract price but refuses or is unable to show ability to pay for changes and/or disputed claims for extras.

Many commentators suggest limiting the language in 2.2.1 to require the owner to provide financial information to the contractor only prior to the commencement of the work.[12] King and Epstein, of course, recommend the deletion of ¶ 2.2.1 in its entirety. They believe that "the owner should not be required to furnish contractor with evidence of its financial arrangements."[13]

§ 2.5   Provide Insurance

Paragraph 11.2.1 provides that "the owner shall be responsible for purchasing and maintaining the owner's usual liability insurance." The owner has the option to "purchase and maintain other insurance for self-protection against claims which may arise from operations under the contract." Sweet has suggested that the 1987 version of ¶ 11.2.1 is the unfortunate compromise product of "committee drafting." For example, the clause requiring the owner to maintain the owner's "usual" liability insurance will provide confusion for the first-time

---

[10] Sweet at 486.

[11] J. Watson, *Using the New AIA Form A201: An AGC of California White Paper,* Associated General Contractors of California Legal Briefs 4 (1988).

[12] *See* F. Schnall, *An Owner's Commentary on the Revised AIA General Conditions of the Contract for Construction,* Design and Construction Contracts 161, 174 (ABA 1989) [hereinafter Schnall]; Sweet at 189; Hummel at 131.

[13] King I at 21.

construction owner. For this owner, "usual" may mean a "usual" business public liability policy.

Sweet explains that the contractor would obviously like to have the owner carry its own liability insurance to reduce the contractor's liability exposure and liability premiums. To clarify ambiguities, Sweet prefers returning to the 1976 language of ¶ 11.2, which stated in substance that the owner would buy and maintain its own liability insurance.[14]

King and Epstein recommend deleting 1987 Article 11 in its entirety, and replacing it with their own recommended sections. Regarding owner's liability insurance, King and Epstein recommend stating that the owner shall be responsible for purchasing and maintaining its own liability insurance and may, at its option, purchase and maintain insurance to protect the owner against claims which may arise from operations under the contract.[15]

The subject of property insurance is covered by ¶ 11.3 in the 1987 edition. Property insurance plays a much more important role than liability insurance in the construction contract. This is evidenced by the fact that liability insurance is covered by just four paragraphs, and property insurance is covered by 15 paragraphs.

Paragraph 11.3.1 requires that property insurance be purchased and maintained by the owner, even though it has been generally assumed that both the owner and the contractor have an insurable interest in the project. King and Epstein recommend replacing the entire section on property insurance with a section entitled "Builder's Risk Insurance"; they advocate limiting the owner's obligation to procure builder's risk insurance, and give the owner an alternative to require the contractor to obtain the policy.[16]

OWNER'S RIGHTS

§ 2.6   Make Changes

Article 7 of A201 discusses changes in the work. The 1987 edition distinguishes between changes which the owner, architect, and contractor have all fully accepted and signed ("change orders") and those which only the architect and owner have signed ("construction change directives").

Robert Flinn and Jonathan Gerlach have compared the 1976 edition change clauses with those in the 1987 edition. They indicate that under the 1976 edition, the owner—without invalidating the contract—was entitled to order changes in

---

[14] Sweet at 463-64.

[15] King & Epstein, *Owner's Counsel Reviews (and Suggests Changes to) the New (1987) AIA General Conditions of the Contract for Construction (Part 3)*, The Practical Real Estate Lawyer 45, 66-75 (July 1989) [hereinafter King II].

[16] *Id.* at 69-71.

the work within the general scope of the contract, with contract amount and time being adjusted accordingly. Only the owner could order changes. This procedure attracted complaints in situations where the contractor disagreed with some or all of the changes. These complaints were addressed in the 1987 edition by the creation of the construction change directive concept embodied within ¶ 7.3.1.[17]

Hummel believes that the owner should be concerned with the amount of authority and discretion the new construction change directive vests in the architect.[18] To address this concern King and Epstein recommend deleting language in ¶ 7.3.1 which requires all construction change directives to be prepared by the architect.[19]

Justin Sweet has stated that the power to direct changes is essential to the owner because design needs to be changed as the owner changes its mind.[20] Therefore, King and Epstein have suggested substantial changes to those Article 7 provisions which would require owner approval for all changes. For example, suggested changes to 7.3.4 would require the contractor to tell the owner of any disagreements with an architects directive regarding changes in time or money. Suggested modifications to 7.3.6 would provide a formula to determine the compensation payable to a contractor for changes in the work. It is suggested that 7.4.1 be changed to require owner approval for even minor changes.[21]

§ 2.7   Be Protected from Risks Which A/E and Contractor Should Bear and Insure

Critics and commentators have made extensive suggestions to many sections of A201-1987 which would reduce the owner's liability in a wide variety of circumstances. Areas for suggested changes include increasing the contractor's standard of care, making the contractor more responsible for errors and inconsistencies in the contract documents, eliminating qualifying language which would reduce the contractor's warranty obligations, and adding to the architect's contract administration responsibilities as they pertain to shop drawing review and detection and reporting of contractor work defects.

Hummel suggests adding a higher standard of care in ¶ 1.2.3 if a contractor has held itself out to possess a particular expertise or skill. If the owner is induced to retain the contractor because of this special skill, Hummel contends

---

[17] Flinn & Gerlach, *The 1987 AIA Document A201: Basic Principles and Guidelines,* Construction Briefings, Federal Publications (Aug. 1988) [hereinafter Flinn].

[18] Hummel at 146.

[19] King & Epstein, *Owner's Counsel Reviews (and Suggests Changes to) the New (1987) AIA General Conditions of the Contract for Construction (Part 2),* The Practical Real Estate Lawyer 51, 81-82 (May 1989) [hereinafter King III].

[20] Sweet at 217.

[21] King III at 79-86.

that the owner should be entitled to hold the contractor to a higher standard of care.[22]

Article 3 of A201-1987 outlines the contractor's responsibilities. Several changes have been recommended to this section which would give the contractor even greater responsibility and limit owner liability. For example, ¶ 3.2.1 requires the contractor to "study and compare" "information furnished by the owner pursuant to ¶ 2.2.2." An owner must therefore be careful of what items are included in this paragraph. Hummel suggests that 3.2.1 be revised to make the contractor responsible for errors or inconsistencies in the contract documents that it "should have recognized."[23]

Former contractor warranty language embodied in the 1976 edition of A201 required that the work would be of "good quality, free from faults and defects." In 1987, the warranty found at ¶ 3.5.1 has been replaced with a qualifying provision stating that the work will be "free from faults and defects not inherent in the quality required or permitted."

Flora Schnall believes that the contractor's warranty has been reduced in scope to the detriment of the owner. From the owner's perspective, only the contractor is capable of making certain that the products used are permitted by the contract documents and not inherently defective or unsuited for the work.[24] King and Epstein would revise 3.5.1 to require the contractor to warrant that the materials and equipment furnished under the contract would be of "the best quality" and would completely eliminate the qualifying language.[25]

Paragraph 3.7 outlines the contractor's responsibilities regarding permits, fees, and notices. Hummel suggests revising ¶ 3.7.1 to coordinate with the requirements of ¶ 2.2.3, which outlines the owner's responsibilities to secure and pay for approvals, easements, assessments, and permits. The suggested revision would change 3.7.1 so that the contractor is responsible for all approvals and permits not specifically enumerated as the owner's responsibility in ¶ 2.2.3.

Hummel also suggests adding language which would require the contractor to keep the owner informed of any changes in laws or ordinances or in approvals or permits required for the project. He also suggests striking ¶ 3.7.3 regarding the limitation of the contractor's responsibility to ascertain that contract documents are in accordance with applicable law. Hummel believes that this clause is inconsistent with the other requirements of the entire A201 document.[26]

Paragraph 3.12 sets forth the contractor's obligations regarding shop drawings, product data, and samples. This section emphasizes that the contractor alone must review and approve shop drawings, product data, and samples for conformity with the contract documents, making the contractor solely responsible for errors or omissions in shop drawings. Schnall suggests that this section

---

[22] Hummel at 130.

[23] *Id.* at 133.

[24] Schnall at 175-76.

[25] King I at 33.

[26] Hummel at 134.

may place the owner in the middle of a dispute between the architect and the contractor in the event of a dispute about the accuracy and correctness of shop drawings. She suggests that changes be made to ¶ 3.12 to make the architect solely responsible for shop drawings.[27]

The architect's role as outlined by A201-1987 has also been reviewed and criticized. The 1987 edition no longer dedicates an exclusive article outlining the role of the architect. Rather the architect's role is included as part of Article 4, Administration of Contracts. Hummel states that this change was ostensibly made to reflect more accurately the fact that the general conditions are part of the owner-contractor agreement and are not binding upon the architect.[28] Both owners and contractors may disagree with that conclusion.

Paragraph 4.2 outlines the architect's contract administration responsibilities. Hummel has stated that the architect's contract administration duties were ambiguous as provided in the 1976 edition, but the 1987 edition made those duties even more ambiguous. He suggests rewriting ¶ 4.2 in its entirety to make the architect clearly responsible for detailed contract administration; i.e., he suggests that ¶ 4.2.2 be changed to clarify that the architect will exercise "care and diligence" in discovering and reporting contractor work defects and deficiencies.

Additionally, Hummel believes that the architect should be held to the highest professional standards in performing architectural services. Any defective design or specification should be promptly corrected by the architect at no cost to the owner. Also, the architect should promptly reimburse the owner for all damages resulting from the use of defective design or specification.[29] There is, of course, ample case law to support this latter obligation with or without change in contract language.[30] However, prompt reimbursement is not so easily achieved.

§ 2.8   Suspend or Terminate the Contract

Paragraph 2.3.1 gives the owner the right to stop the work if the contractor fails to provide work which is in accordance with the requirements of the contract, or if the contractor "persistently fails" to carry out work in accordance with the contract. This paragraph may be read in conjunction with ¶ 14.2, which outlines requirements for termination by the owner for cause.

Hummel suggests that ¶ 2.3.1 be changed to clarify that the right to stop the work, as provided by this section, is in addition to—and not in restriction or

---

[27] Schnall at 170.

[28] Hummel at 137.

[29] *Id*. at 138-40.

[30] Zontelli & Sons v. City of Nashwauk, 373 N.W.2d 744 (Minn. 1985); Annotation, *Responsibility of One Acting as Architect for Defects or Insufficiency of Work Attributable to Plans*, 25 A.L.R.2d 1085, 1087 § 3 (1952).

derogation of—the owner's right to terminate under Article 14. He explains that this change is necessary because ¶ 2.3.1, as written, does not provide for a situation where an owner fails to stop the contractor's performance of non-conforming or defective work and later wishes to exercise its termination rights. The pitfall here is the possibility that in a comparative negligence jurisdiction, it might be implied that the owner has forfeited its right to terminate under Article 14 by "negligently failing" to exercise its rights to stop the work under ¶ 2.3.1.[31]

King and Epstein suggest changes to ¶ 2.3.1 which would expand the owner's right to stop the work. For example, they suggest the elimination of the adjective "persistently" in the third line of ¶ 2.3.1, to enable the owner to suspend work if the contractor just simply fails to carry out the work. They also suggest that changes be made which would allow the owner to stop the work if the contractor fails or refuses to provide a sufficient amount of labor, materials or equipment or fails to supervise and coordinate the work.[32]

Werner Sabo cautions, however, that any expansion of the owner's rights to stop the work pursuant to ¶ 2.3.1 carries with it the implied obligation of the owner to assume responsibility for job site safety.[33] The AIA deleted the architect's right to stop the work in the 1976 edition of A210, the first revision of A201 after an architect was held liable for job site safety, in the now famous decision in *Miller v. Dewitt*.[34]

As previously mentioned, Article 14 contains requirements for termination or suspension of the contract. Paragraph 14.1 outlines requirements for termination by the contractor. Paragraph 14.1.1.5 gives the contractor the right to terminate if the owner has failed to furnish the contractor with financial information as required by ¶ 2.2.1. Schnall suggests that this provision be deleted in its entirety as it may provide the contractor with an "easy out" on a losing job.[35]

Paragraph 14.1.2 gives the contractor the right to terminate the contract for any of the reasons enumerated in ¶ 14.1.1 upon seven days' written notice to the owner and architect. King and Epstein sensibly suggest that ¶ 14.1.2 be revised to give the owner a reasonable time to cure the condition which caused the contractor to seek termination, and would put a "reasonable limitation" on costs recoverable by the contractor.[36] The latter suggestion is more difficult to specify and to enforce.

Paragraph 14.2 provides the conditions permitting the owner to terminate for cause. King and Epstein suggest changes to this paragraph which would eliminate the requirement that the architect certify that sufficient cause exists to justify termination by the owner. In addition, King and Epstein propose a new

---

[31] Hummel at 132.

[32] King I at 24-25.

[33] W. Sabo, *A Legal Guide to AIA Documents* 97, AIA (1987-88) [hereinafter Sabo].

[34] 37 Ill. 2d 273, 226 N.E.2d 630 (1967).

[35] Schnall at 178-79.

[36] King II at 91.

¶ 14.2.5 which would essentially allow the owner to terminate for "convenience" reasons. This additional language would allow the owner to terminate any or all remaining work for "any reason whatsoever" by giving seven days' prior written notice to the contractor.[37] Early drafts of the 1987 edition contained such a provision but it was negotiated out of the final edition due to AGC complaints.

Sweet explains that ¶ 14.2.4 was changed in the 1987 edition to reflect the fact that the Bankruptcy Reform Act bars contractual termination based solely upon the contractor's bankruptcy. He suggests that ¶ 14.2.1 may be changed to include broad performance-oriented grounds for termination to get around the prohibition against terminating due to bankruptcy. Some writers seem to be unaware of the potential advantage of being able to terminate an insolvent contractor before it files for bankruptcy or is declared bankrupt.[38]

Sweet has also criticized Article 14 in its entirety as being "badly drafted." This suggests the desirability of wholesale revisions and perhaps redrafting the entire section. King and Epstein have suggested wholesale revisions.[39]

Sweet generally cautions that regardless of whether or not changes are made to Article 14 which expand termination rights, owners should be aware of the consequences of wrongful termination. The principal risk in contract termination is that a court may determine that an owner was not justified in terminating the work. Such a wrongful termination may give the contractor a right to recover the reasonable value of the services it has provided, even if the contractor has entered into a losing contract.[40]

§ 2.9   Have Work Completed on Schedule

Paragraph 3.10 of the 1987 edition outlines the contractor's construction schedule responsibilities. Paragraph 3.10.1 requires the contractor to prepare a construction schedule which does "not exceed time limits current under the Contract Documents," and to submit same to the owner and the architect for review. It requires the contractor to keep the schedule current, and also to provide a schedule of submittals, allowing for architectural review.

Sweet states that historically the AIA has paid little attention to schedules, appearing to assume a "leisurely construction process with emphasis on quality." He does not believe that ¶ 3.10.1 imposes any rigorous schedule commitments, and essentially leaves construction pace and scheduling in the hands of the contractor.[41]

For these reasons, commentators have suggested additions to ¶ 3.10 which would expand upon scheduling requirements. For example, Sabo suggests that if

---

[37] *Id.* at 91-95.

[38] Sweet at 409-10.

[39] King II at 89-95.

[40] Sweet at 400.

[41] *Id.* at 332.

an owner wants a more detailed schedule, or a specific type of schedule, that requirement should be spelled out in 3.10.1, or in supplementary conditions.[42] King and Epstein suggest a major addition to 3.10.1 which does spell out detailed scheduling requirements of the kind suggested by Sabo. They also recommend that 3.10.1 be changed to reflect the fact that the contractor is responsible to ensure timely completion without any adjustments to the contract sum.[43]

Scheduling requirements may differ depending upon the type of facility involved. For example, the owner of a power generation facility may wish to secure and exercise the right to review and comment upon the reasonableness or accuracy of a critical path method (CPM) schedule. Failure to do so could result in a determination that the owner acknowledged the adequacy and reasonableness of the schedules by remaining silent.[44]

Paragraph 8.2.1 provides for a "time is of the essence" clause. Hummel suggests that this subparagraph be augmented by a statement to the effect that the contractor, by executing the agreement, confirms that it is capable of properly completing the work within the contract time.[45] It should be noted, however, that 8.2.1 already provides that, "by executing the agreement the contractor confirms that the contract time is a reasonable period for performing the work."

OWNER'S EXPOSURE TO CLAIMS AND HOW TO PROTECT AGAINST THEM

§ 2.10 Delay Damages

Paragraph 8.3 of the 1987 edition deals with delays and extensions of time. Paragraph 8.3.1 allows the contractor additional time for justifiable delay. Paragraph 8.3.3 states that the entirety of ¶ 8.3 "does not preclude recovery of damages for delay."

Hummel suggests revising ¶ 8.3.1 to include a "no damage for delay" clause, making an extension of time the contractor's sole remedy for delay.[46] King and Epstein provide substantial changes to ¶ 8.3.1 which would also include a "no damage for delay" clause, and narrowly restrict circumstances under which contract time could be extended, restrict the circumstances justifying time extensions, and require "float" time to be credited to the owner by deducting it from any alleged time extension claim for delay.[47]

---

[42] Sabo at 106-07.

[43] King I at 39.

[44] *Guidelines,* Construction Briefings 23-24 (Apr. 1989).

[45] Hummel at 146.

[46] *Id.* at 147.

[47] King III at 87-88.

Paragraph 4.3 outlines the requirements for bringing claims and resolving disputes. Claims for additional time are dealt with in ¶ 4.3.8. King and Epstein outline changes to ¶ 4.3.8.2 regarding adverse weather conditions. They expand upon this section to require that requests for extensions of time due to adverse weather conditions include U.S. Weather bureau climatological reports for the months involved plus a report indicating the average precipitation, temperature, etc. for the past ten years from the nearest reporting station. They suggest this addition to clarify what data is necessary to substantiate a delay because of adverse weather conditions.[48]

§ 2.11   Differing Site Conditions

Paragraph 4.3.6 of the 1987 edition deals with claims for concealed or unknown conditions. It provides for a possible increase or decrease in the contractor's cost of or time required for performance if physical conditions are encountered which are either subsurface or "otherwise concealed" and which "differ materially" from the contract documents. The section also provides for cost or time adjustments for encountering unknown physical conditions of an "unusual nature," which differ from those ordinarily found to exist or those generally recognized as inherent in construction activities.

Hummel believes that the term "physical condition" referred to frequently in ¶ 4.3.6 is ambiguous. For example, there is ambiguity concerning whether this term means only natural conditions, such as those beneath the surface of the ground, or existing conditions in a building scheduled for renovation. He would also add a condition to 4.3.6 making the contractor responsible for those conditions which "reasonably should have been discerned by the contractor's prior work, inspection, tests and reviews."[49]

King and Epstein suggest an entirely new approach to differing site conditions, which would eliminate ¶ 4.3.6 in its entirety. Generally, they advocate creating an entirely new ¶ 1.2.2, enlarging the contractor's obligations as a result of site visits. This new and detailed clause would specify broadly and explicitly what a contractor becomes responsible for as a result of the execution of the construction contract. They also suggest substantial additions to ¶ 2.2.2 (the section requiring the owner to furnish surveys describing physical characteristics) which would effectively shift the entire risk of unknown site conditions to the contractor.[50] On any job having a significant component of underground work, these changes would be likely to carry a substantial contingency price.

---

[48] King III at 65-66.

[49] Hummel at 141-42.

[50] King I at 15, 22-23.

§ 2.12   Defective Plans

Under ¶ 1.1.1, the AIA defines the "Contract Documents" to include "the Agreement between Owner and Contractor . . . Conditions of the Contract, . . . Drawings, Specifications, addenda issued prior to execution of the Contract, other documents listed in the Agreement as well as Modifications issued after execution of the Contract." Paragraph 3.2.1 requires the contractor to "carefully study and compare the Contract Documents" and requires the contractor to "report to the architect any errors, inconsistencies, or omissions." The contractor will be liable for any construction activity it performs if it knows "it involves a recognized error, inconsistency, or omission." This subparagraph specifically refers to information required to be furnished by the owner pursuant to ¶ 2.2.2. For this reason, Hummel suggests that the owner be particularly careful of what items are included in ¶ 2.2.2 (recall that 2.2.2 requires the owner to furnish surveys describing physical characteristics, legal limitations, and utility locations for the site of the project).[51]

Because the standard AIA language in ¶ 3.2.1 makes the contractor responsible only for errors and omissions actually discovered, King and Epstein suggest making additions to 3.2.1 which make the contractor responsible for errors and omissions which it "reasonably should have recognized." In addition, they recommend the addition of new language, numbered 3.2.1.1. This additional language requires the contractor to notify the owner and the architect in writing of any errors, inconsistencies, or omissions before proceeding with the work. The architect's decision under this new subparagraph would be subject to the owner's approval. If the contractor goes forward with the work in spite of the knowledge of the error or inconsistency, the contractor is responsible to correct the error or inconsistency at no additional cost to the owner.[52]

§ 2.13   Lack of Coordination of Separate Prime Contractors

The owner's right to contract with separate prime contractors is provided in Article 6 of the 1987 edition. As a cautionary note, Sweet recommends that the separate prime contractor system be used only by sophisticated owners. The key concern in the separate prime contract situation is lack of coordination. Failure to provide for coordination of the work of separate prime contractors is usually disastrous.[53]

For example, James Hawkins, Michael Wilson, and Timothy Thornton believe that Article 6 presents significant conflicts if the owner uses nonunion labor

---

[51] Hummel at 133.

[52] *Id.* at 27-28.

[53] Sweet at 175, 372-74.

while the contractor uses union labor. They also note significant confusion regarding the owner's obligations when the owner awards separate prime contracts.[54]

Here again, King and Epstein recommend extensive changes to Article 6. At the outset, they recommend deleting ¶ 6.1.4, which subjects the owner's forces to the same obligations as the contractor under the general conditions of the contract. Since the owner's duties are extremely limited, they consider it inappropriate to subject the owner to the general conditions. They also recommend deleting ¶ 6.2.5 regarding claims between separate prime contractors.

They recommend that these subparagraphs be replaced with language requiring separate prime contractors to promptly attempt settlement of any dispute they may have with any other separate prime contractor. The proposed new paragraph would also require the contractors to indemnify, defend, and hold harmless the owner, the owner's partners, and any agents of the above-mentioned parties, to the "full extent as agreed to under ¶ 11.8 of the supplementary general conditions."[55]

Sweet believes that the legal problems which may be generated by the separate prime contract system reveal the "lack of care" the AIA has paid to these issues. He recommends that a tailor-made contract should be prepared if a project is of a size sufficient to warrant the use of separate prime contractors. Such a contract could be one to which all major contractors would be a party. Alternatively, separate contracts could be created which would clearly indicate that each contractor would deal with and be responsible only to the owner.[56]

OWNER'S RELATIONSHIPS
WITH OTHER PARTIES

§ 2.14   Contractor

Sweet has characterized the relationship between and among the owner, the contractor and the architect as a kind of "partnership" in which the owner, through the architect, plays a part in performance of the contract while the contractor uses its skill to detect design errors. However, he cautions that the owner must be careful not to overstep its intervention powers. Contractors are wary of aggressive owners who simply cannot keep their hands off their own projects. Sweet warns that an owner who acts in this manner may open up itself to risks and responsibilities which are properly borne by the contractor. For example, Sweet states that excessive intervention can make an owner responsible

---

[54] Hawkins, Wilson, & Thornton, *Changes in the New 1987 Edition of AIA 201 General Conditions of the Contract for Construction,* Associated General Contractors of St. Louis (Dec. 3, 1987).

[55] King III at 75-79.

[56] Sweet at 382.

to public authorities for unsafe methods as well as increased liability risk exposure.[57]

Generally, commentators agree that some method must be used to clarify each party's rights and responsibilities, and to set forth a "chain of command." Sabo suggests that a "separate memorandum" be prepared which would outline the functions and responsibilities of all parties. Such a document should make it clear that the contractor is not an agent of the owner, but rather an independent contractor.[58]

King and Epstein suggest that such a clarification be added in ¶ 3.3.2. They suggest that at the end of this paragraph, the following language be added: "It is understood and agreed that the relationship of contractor to owner shall be that of an independent contractor. Nothing contained herein or inferable herefrom shall be deemed or construed to 1) make the contractor the agent, servant or employee of the owner, or 2) create any partnership, joint venture, or other association between owner and contractor."[59]

As already noted, Sapers has provided significant criticisms of A201-1987. Among his criticisms, Sapers notes that several sections of the 1987 edition lead to the conclusion that the owner has somehow given up its possessory right to the premises when it enters into a construction contract. For example, ¶ 3.16.1 sets forth the owner's right of access to the work. Sapers states that this permission should not be necessary. Also, ¶ 9.9.1 bars the owner from occupying any portion of the work without agreement from the contractor, public authorities and the builder's risk insurer. Sapers finds it "particularly galling" to read that public authorities must approve the owner's move-in.[60] Nevertheless, many states and municipalities require owners to obtain certificates of occupancy before occupying new or remodeled structures.

Cautious contractors prefer that owners accept the contractor's work as complete or at least substantially complete before taking occupancy because the troublesome dividing line between punch list work and owner maintenance responsibilities becomes blurred after occupancy. Also, taking occupancy is or should be the dividing line between builder's risk insurance coverage and the owner's responsibility for permanent fire and extended coverage insurance after occupancy.

§ 2.15   Architect

The architect is obviously not a party to the contract for construction. However, A201 obviously refers to the architect's rights, duties, and responsibilities in

---

[57] *Id.* at 257, 281-82.

[58] Sabo at 98.

[59] King I at 29-30.

[60] Sapers at 37.

several sections. An owner should remember that if any changes are made in the owner-architect relationship as reflected in the standard owner-architect agreement, the A201 general conditions should be amended to alert the contractor to the architect's modified duties.

A201-1987 does not contain an article which specificially outlines the architect's responsibilities. Rather, the responsibilities of the architect are included in Article 4, Administration of the Contract. The critical items concerning the architect's responsibilities for administration of the contract appear in ¶ 4.2.

As previously suggested, ¶ 4.2 takes items that were ambiguous in the 1976 edition and makes them even more ambiguous. For example, ¶ 4.2.2 only requires that the architect "become generally familiar with the progress and quality of the completed work." Hummel would change this subparagraph to require the architect to become familiar in detail with the progress and quality of the work. This change would be in accordance with the architect's duty of detailed administration of the construction contract. Hummel also suggests changing the last sentence in ¶ 4.2.2 which, as it stands, only requires the architect to "endeavor to guard the owner against defects and deficiencies in the Work." Proposed changes would add language to the effect that the architect will exercise "care and diligence in discovering and promptly reporting to the owner any defects or deficiencies in the work of the contractor."[61]

Additionally, it is suggested that language be added to 4.2.2 which would require the architect to follow the highest professional work standards in performing all architectural services under the agreement. Under such a standard, any defective design or specifications furnished by the architect must be promptly corrected by the architect at no cost to the owner. Likewise, the architect would be required to reimburse the owner for all damages resulting from the use of such defective designs. Hummel also suggests that ¶ 4.2.2 be rewritten entirely so that it clearly states the architect's responsibilities. For example, it could specify the minimum number of weekly on-site visits the architect must make, and could require the architect to submit a written report to the owner subsequent to each on-site visit.[62]

King and Epstein also advocate far-reaching changes to ¶ 4.2. For example, they recommend that almost all of the language in 4.2.1 be deleted. The corrected section would merely state that "the Architect will provide administration of the Contract as described in the Contract Documents. . . ." They suggest this change, because the existing language of the 1987 edition provides an "overly broad delegation of authority" to the architect. As revised, this subparagraph would provide the architect with the authority to act on behalf of the owner only to the extent provided in the contract documents.[63]

---

[61] Hummel at 138-39.

[62] *Id.*

[63] King III at 54-61.

King and Epstein also recommend additions to ¶ 4.2.3 which would obligate the architect to notify the owner of any contractor failure to use proper construction means, methods, techniques and sequences. Additionally, the architect would be responsible for any such problem it should have been aware of in the exercise of due professional diligence. They also suggest adding, to ¶ 4.2.4, language which allows the owner to correspond or negotiate directly with the contractor as long as the owner forwards a copy of any writing to the architect.

Other changes and additions would expressly require the architect to reject defective work unless the owner instructs otherwise (¶ 4.2.6), limit the effect of the architect's interpretations and decisions regarding matters concerning performance under requirements of the contract documents (¶ 4.2.11), and eliminate the architect's power with respect to aesthetic matters (¶ 4.2.13).[64] This suggested deletion of the architect's control over aesthetic matters seems inexplicable considering the architect's classic traditional and legal responsibility for a pleasing aesthetic design.

§ 2.16 Effect of Dispute Resolution Provisions on Owner

If a complex claim procedure helps the owner then the claims procedures in the 1987 edition should be a boon to the owner. Paragraph 4.3 Claims and Disputes, ¶ 4.4 "Resolution of Claims and Disputes," and ¶ 4.5, Arbitration contain all of the 1987 edition provisions regarding dispute resolution.

Commentators have been highly critical of the 1987 edition dispute resolution provisions. For example, Sapers has stated that the arbitration process provided by ¶ 4.5 is "convoluted," and has made the arbitration process "virtually impossible to understand." He states that a contractor can avoid the whole arbitration process by filing a mechanic's lien at the same time it commences arbitration. This, however, is only partially true because contractors on government-owned projects, those who waive or forfeit their lien rights, and owners have no such escape hatch.[65]

Paragraph 4.4.1 allows the architect to review all claims and take any one of five preliminary actions within ten days of receipt. Sweet has indicated that these terms in the 1987 edition show that the AIA "went overboard in making the architect a claims officer." Sweet believes that owners who review this paragraph are not likely to let it remain intact. However, he cautions that any deletion of the architect's role here must be done carefully, because the role of the architect is carefully built into the general conditions.[66]

---

[64] *Id.*

[65] Sapers at 40.

[66] Sweet at 206.

Flinn and Gerlach have calculated that the entire claims process contemplated by the 1987 edition should not take any longer than 45 days. However, they believe that the complexity of these new claim procedures will generate controversies regarding whether the very specific time frames have been violated. These controversies may detract from the substantive issues that gave rise to the dispute in the first place.[67]

Several commentators have suggested the deletion of ¶ 4.5 in its entirety. For example, King and Epstein believe that it is "seldom in the owner's best interest to be forced to arbitrate claims with the contractor."[68] Less drastic changes would allow for the paragraphs on nonjoinder of architects in arbitration to be replaced with paragraphs stating that joinder and consolidation may be achieved. Bernard Goldstein has stated that "if the need arises for conflict resolution let it be done once and for all with everyone involved."[69]

Sweet indicates that arbitration clauses are among those most frequently changed or deleted in the AIA documents. He adds that in deciding to delete or change arbitration provisions, the owner must consider the alternatives, i.e., availability of private dispute resolution forums and strengths or weaknesses of local courts. He also suggests that the arbitration paragraph may be tailored to make the process more attractive to the parties by eliminating or modifying certain feature of a general arbitration clause.

"Tailoring" an arbitration clause, drafters could, for example, specify the place of arbitration, limit arbitration to claims which do not exceed a specified dollar amount, limit disputes to those which occur while the work is proceeding, allow consolidation of separate arbitrations, provide a right to full or limited discovery, eliminate the use of attorneys, make the award nonbinding, and make the award of attorneys' fees and costs to the prevailing party mandatory.[70]

§ 2.17   Conclusion

As indicated at the outset, since the 1987 edition of A201 has come into being, vast amounts of commentary have been published concerning its merits and its shortcomings. No single chapter should pretend to provide the definitive critique of this document.

Detractors believe that the owner is significantly under-represented in the 1987 edition. This fact is represented by the aggressive changes advocated by

---

[67] Flinn at 4-5.

[68] King III at 68-70.

[69] Goldstein, *General Conditions of AIA Contract for Construction,* 1 N.Y.L.J. 25, 28 (Sept. 23, 1987).

[70] Sweet at 422-25.

commentators like Hummel and King and Epstein. On the other hand, representatives of the AIA believe that they have done everything possible to insure owner input into the 1987 edition.[71]

The subjective fairness of the entire document depends upon who is doing the evaluation. Thus, careful and diligent owners may change A201 to suit their own needs, but they should remain aware that contractors will not be eager to commit to a project in which they have no rights at all.

---

[71] Ellickson, *The AIA Defends A201/1987,* Architectural Record 40, 42 (Mar. 1988).

CHAPTER 3

INCORPORATION BY REFERENCE IN SUBCONTRACTS

Michael E. Kreger
Robert C. Nauheim

§ 3.1   Introduction

TYPES OF INCORPORATING CLAUSES

§ 3.2   Conduit Clauses

§ 3.3   Incorporation by Reference Clauses

GENERAL RULES GOVERNING ENFORCEABILITY

§ 3.4   Basic Rules of Interpretation

§ 3.5   —Scope of Incorporation Must Be Clear

§ 3.6   —Implied Incorporation

§ 3.7   —Subcontract Consistency

§ 3.8   —Surrounding Circumstances

§ 3.9   Third-Party Beneficiary Status: Who Can Enforce Incorporated Provisions?

INCORPORATION OF SUBSTANTIVE TERMS

§ 3.10   Indemnification Clauses

§ 3.11   —Scope

§ 3.12   —Indemnification for Negligence

§ 3.13   —Workers' Compensation and Indemnity

§ 3.14   Arbitration Clauses: Public Policy Supports Arbitration

§ 3.15   —Incorporated Arbitration Clauses and the Miller Act

§ 3.16   No Damages for Delay and Other Remedy Clauses

§ 3.17   Incorporation of the Implied Warranty of the Adequacy and Suitability of Plans and Specifications

§ 3.1   Introduction

Faced with a dispute, the parties to a construction subcontract turn quickly to the swords and shields available to them in the subcontract. Frequently, however, the important legal weapons are not set out in the contract at all. Instead, they are incorporated by reference by innocuous boilerplate clauses that purport to incorporate the entire general contract or mysteriously transpose all of the contractor's obligations in the general contract onto the subcontractor.

To the extent incorporation by reference clauses are even considered during negotiations, they are generally favored by the contractor who desires to pass to the subcontractor those obligations imposed upon the contractor by the owner. More commonly, however, incorporation by reference and "flow down" or "conduit" clauses receive scant attention as harried project managers interlineate the standard form subcontracts. Prime contractors and subcontractors alike often fail to recognize, much less reconcile, the provisions of the prime contract purported to be incorporated by the subcontract. As a result, terms which neither party considered, much less negotiated, are raised in disputes in which they may be dispositive on important issues such as dispute resolution, substantive remedies and indemnity obligations.

Courts often disagree over the level of specificity or magic language needed to incorporate terms from the prime contract. Certain principles, however, are recognized by the courts. This chapter discusses some of the principal factors courts consider in deciding whether to enforce subcontract language claimed to incorporate such upstream contract provisions. Identifying these principles will enable the practitioner to draft contract documents more effectively and predict the enforceability of incorporated terms. Even after identifying these principles, however, the first practical advice must remain: general incorporation language is not an effective substitute for specific clauses in the subcontract which address the issue.

TYPES OF INCORPORATING CLAUSES

§ 3.2   Conduit Clauses

Two kinds of clauses are typically employed in construction subcontracts to incorporate obligations from an upstream contract. The first attempts to bind a subcontractor to a contractor in the same fashion and to the same extent as the contractor is bound to the owner by the prime contract documents. These so-called "conduit" or "flow down" clauses purport to provide a general contractor and subcontractor the same rights and duties specifically afforded to the owner and the general contractor in the prime contract.

A typical conduit clause frequently employed in construction subcontracts is the clause provided in the standard form subcontract prepared by the American Institute of Architects (AIA).[1]

A more abbreviated conduit clause is used in the standard form contract prepared by the Associated General Contractors of America (AGC): "The Subcontractor binds itself to the Contractor under this agreement in the same manner as the Contractor is bound to the Owner under the Contract Documents."[2]

There are important differences between the AIA and AGC conduit clauses. First, unlike AIA, the AGC conduit clause does not specifically limit the scope of its effect to the extent the contract documents "apply to the work of the subcontract and insofar as applicable to the subcontract." As a result, the AGC conduit clause may be viewed with skepticism because of the overly broad sweep of incorporation. In contrast, the AIA pass-through clause is more specific: At once, it is arguably more narrow—incorporating terms only to the extent they apply to subcontract "work"—and more broad, incorporating all contractor obligations and all contractor remedies.

Second, the AGC clause fails to delineate any correlative rights to the subcontractor; the clause states only that the subcontractor "binds itself" to the contractor without any reference to parallel subcontractor rights. Accordingly, the AGC conduit clause may not always cause all prime or other upstream contract rights to "flow down" to the subcontractor.

§ 3.3   Incorporation by Reference Clauses

A second source of incorporation comes from clauses which refer to and specifically incorporate into the subcontract the general contract or specific provisions from that contract. Typical of such "incorporation by reference" clauses in construction subcontracts is the general incorporation clause contained in the AIA standard form subcontract, which incorporates the general contract and the plans and specifications into the subcontract.[3]

In contrast to the AIA standard form subcontract, the AGC document provides only a space in which "applicable contract documents" may be listed and, presumably, incorporated as a part of the subcontract.[4]

In their efforts to glean the intent of the parties to the subcontract, courts do not usually distinguish the "conduit" and "incorporation by reference" clauses

---

[1] AIA Document A401-1987, Standard Form of Agreement Between Contractor and Subcontractor, art. 2.1 [hereinafter AIA A401].

[2] AGC Document No. 600-1984, Subcontract for Building Construction, art. 8.1 [hereinafter AGC 600].

[3] AIA A401 art. 1.

[4] *See* AGC 600, art. 16.5.

noted above. Courts are apparently satisfied that both clauses are generally intended to have a comparable effect. While there are theoretical and potentially practical differences between the two clauses, unless a court draws a distinction relevant to the discussion below, we will refer to both clauses generally as incorporation by reference clauses.

GENERAL RULES GOVERNING ENFORCEABILITY

§ 3.4   Basic Rules of Interpretation

With some exceptions, courts interpret incorporation by reference and conduit clauses in construction contracts using well-established principles of contract interpretation. The most fundamental is that a court must attempt to give effect to the expressed intent of the parties at the time they contracted.[5] Unfortunately, determining what terms the contracting parties actually agreed to incorporate from a prime contract is usually not apparent from the subcontract, particularly from the standard form subcontracts. The following rules of contract interpretation most frequently guide courts attempting to divine the intent of the parties when terms or obligations in the general contract are argued to have been incorporated by the subcontract.

§ 3.5   —Scope of Incorporation Must Be Clear

Courts often state that the terms of an extrinsic document will be incorporated into a contract only to the extent of the purpose specified by the incorporating contract.[6] Other cases state that, in order to be enforceable, incorporated terms must have a reasonably clear and ascertainable meaning with respect to the incorporating contract.[7] The thrust of the foregoing requirements in the context of incorporation by reference clauses in construction contracts is that the scope of intended incorporation must be relatively clear.

This rule avoids ambiguities created when terms in general contracts are applied to subcontracts in which the performance may be significantly different. It is not common for a subcontractor to assume all of the general contractor's obligations to the owner. Accordingly, the precise scope of incorporation must

---

[5] *See* Jensen v. Ramas, 792 P.2d 668 (Alaska 1990).

[6] Guerini Stone Co. v. P.J. Carlin Constr. Co., 240 U.S. 264, 36 S. Ct. 300 (1916); Omega Constr. Co. v. Altman, 147 Mich. App. 649, 382 N.W.2d 839 (1985); Lincoln Welding Works, Inc. v. Ramirez, 647 P.2d 381 (Nev. 1982); 17 Am. Jur. 2d, *Contracts* § 263 at 667 (1964).

[7] *See* Hartline-Thomas v. Arthur Pew Constr. Co., 151 Ga. App. 598, 260 S.E.2d 744 (1979); Binswanger Glass Co. v. Beers Constr. Co., 141 Ga. App. 715, 234 S.E.2d 363 (1977).

usually be clear in order to determine which provisions of an upstream contract were intended to be incorporated.

This concern was recognized in the seminal case of *Guerini Stone Co. v. P.J. Carlin Construction Co.*,[8] which is cited often for the proposition that the incorporation by reference clause only incorporates the plans and specifications for the project, and not the remedial, or procedural aspects of the prime contract.[9] In *Guerini Stone,* however, the subcontract provided only that the subcontract was to be performed in a fashion "agreeable to the drawings and specifications" provided in the prime contract.[10] The subcontract contained no other incorporation by reference clause.

In *Guerini Stone*, contractor was faced with a delay claim by the subcontractor caused by an owner's change order. The contractor argued, despite the absence of a no damages for delay provision in the subcontract, that the subcontract had incorporated the prime contract change order provision via the subcontract language. Rejecting this argument, the court concluded that the parties incorporated the plans and specifications into a subcontract only for the purpose of "indicating the work to be done and in what manner done by the subcontractor" and that no other purpose had been specified.[11]

Unfortunately, some courts have relied on *Guerini Stone* to support broader principles. For example, relying largely on *Guerini Stone,* one line of cases adopts an inflexible rule of construction which holds that a subcontract can incorporate upstream contract provisions only to the extent such provisions "relate to the scope, quality, character and manner of the work performed by the subcontractor."[12] Under this approach, upstream indemnification, arbitration and other remedial, general conditions cannot be made a part of the downstream contract absent an express indication of intent in the subcontract to specifically incorporate such terms.[13]

In contrast, some courts do not require that the particular purpose of incorporation be specified in the subcontract so long as the contract language and surrounding circumstances indicate that the particular provision was intended to become a part of the subcontract. In fact, at least one court turned the *Guerini Stone* "specified purpose" rule on its head by announcing that subcontract incorporation of a prime contract is effective to the extent such incorporation is not limited to any specified purpose.[14] Furthermore, where a clause incorporating a general contract is "general and unlimited," it has been held sufficient to

---

[8] 240 U.S. 264 (1916).

[9] *E.g.,* S. Leo Harmonay, Inc. v. Binks Mfg. Co., 597 F. Supp. 1014 (S.D.N.Y. 1984); United States Steel Corp. v. Turner Constr. Co., 560 F. Supp. 871 (S.D.N.Y. 1983); McKinney Drilling Co. v. Collins Co., 517 F. Supp. 320 (N.D. Ala. 1981).

[10] 240 U.S. 264, 265 (1916).

[11] *Id.* at 277.

[12] S. Leo Harmonay, Inc. v. Binks, 597 F. Supp. at 1014.

[13] *Id.* at 1019.

[14] Lincoln Welding Works, Inc. v. Ramirez, 647 P.2d 381 (Nev. 1982).

impose on the subcontractor the provisions in the prime contract concerning the notice requirements in damages for delay.[15] It should be noted however that, unlike *Guerini Stone,* these cases involved subcontracts containing conduit clauses and clauses incorporating the entire general contract, not only the plans and specifications.

Recognizing the issue of scope in incorporation by reference clauses, the AIA Document A401 conduit clause is limited "to the extent that the provisions of the [c]ontract [d]ocuments between the [o]wner and the [c]ontractor apply to the work of the subcontractor." Several courts have impliedly rejected arguments that such language limits incorporation to the plans and specifications contained in the general contract and instead extend incorporation to include applicable general condition as well.[16] Moreover, even where limiting language similar to that used in the AIA clause is absent, a conduit clause in a subcontract is usually effective in creating rights and duties analogous to those possessed by the upstream contractor only "insofar as applicable."[17]

Other courts have noted that conduit clauses "are designed to incorporate into the subcontract those provisions of the general contract relevant to the sub-contractor's performance" thereby causing the parties to the subcontract to "assume the correlative position of the parties to the prime contract."[18] Since a subcontractor agrees to perform only a portion of the work originally contracted by the general contractor, the obligations and rights which "flow down" to the subcontractor by a conduit clause will, with some exception, extend only to "correlative" obligations and rights incidental to the specific work being performed by the subcontractor.[19]

In contrast, courts have not always construed general incorporation by reference clauses to contain the limitation of conduit clauses to applicable or "correlative" obligations. A result of this lack of an implied limitation is often a patent ambiguity between general contract clauses or subcontract clauses. For example, a general contract may contain an arbitration clause while the sub-contract does not. The general contractor will defend the claims by a sub by arguing the intent to arbitrate. Various clauses in the subcontract will then be asserted for the consistency or inconsistency of arbitration with a subcontract which is altogether silent on the matter. In short, to be effective in incorporating the administrative and remedial provisions of a prime contract, a general

---

[15] Sime Constr. Co. v. Washington Pub. Power Supply Sys., 621 P.2d 1299 (Wash. Ct. App. 1980).

[16] *Id.* at 1303.

[17] Frommeyer v. L.&R. Constr. Co., 261 F.2d 879 (3d Cir. 1958).

[18] Industrial Indem. Co. v. Wick Constr. Co., 680 P.2d 1100, 1104 (Alaska 1984).

[19] Unfortunately, the courts are not uniform in the treatment of general conduit clauses. On several occasions, courts have reasoned that such clauses are ambiguous because they could be reasonably understood to transfer all of the rights and obligations of the contractor to the subcontractor, something clearly not contemplated in normal contractor-subcontractor relations. *See, e.g.,* Mountain States Constr. Co. v. Tyee Elec., Inc., 43 Wash. App. 542, 718 P.2d 823 (1986).

incorporation by reference clause should specifically refer to such provisions or, at least, to the "general and supplemental conditions" of the prime contract.[20]

§ 3.6   —Implied Incorporation

Some courts have acknowledged that a subcontract's express incorporation of the obligations of a contractor in an upstream contract through a conduit clause necessarily implies the incorporation of the contractor's rights even if the conduit clause does not generally or specifically incorporate such rights. For example, in *Industrial Indemnity Co. v. Wick Construction Co.,* the court noted, "[I]t is patently unreasonable for a general contractor to attempt to bind the subcontractor to the provisions of the general contract while the general contractor does not give the corresponding rights, remedies and redress to the subcontractor."[21]

According to *Industrial Indemnity,* the subcontract's incorporation of duties analogous to those owed by the contractor to an owner will necessarily imply the incorporation of corresponding rights and remedies held by the contractor. Similarly, in *Turner Construction Co. v. Midwest Curtainwalls, Inc.,*[22] the court rejected a prime contractor's argument that a subcontract conduit clause expressly providing the prime contractor with all of the "rights and remedies" it had against the owner as against the subcontractor did not pass through the same rights and remedies to the subcontractor. Thus, in some jurisdictions, a conduit clause has the effect of incorporating correlative rights and remedies even if the clause addresses only the obligations of the subcontractor and the rights of the contractor.

§ 3.7   —Subcontract Consistency

A second rule of construction frequently applied by the courts requires that express terms in the subcontract control over terms which are inconsistent or conflict with terms incorporated from the prime contract.[23] Unfortunately, the courts are not consistent in judging just what constitutes a "conflict" or

---

[20] *See, e.g.,* McGrath v. Elec. Constr. Co., 230 Or. 295, 364 P.2d 604 (1961); John W. Johnson, Inc. v. Basic Constr. Co., Inc., 429 F.2d 764 (D.C. Cir. 1970); United States Steel Corp. v. Turner Constr. Co., 560 F. Supp. 871 (S.D.N.Y. 1983); McKinney Drilling Co. v. Collins Co., 517 F. Supp. 320 (N.D. Ala. 1981); Batter Bldg. Materials Co. v. Kirschner, 142 Conn. 1, 110 A.2d 464 (1954). *But see* Westinghouse Elec. Supply Co. v. Fidelity & Deposit Co., 560 F.2d 1109 (3d Cir. 1977).

[21] 680 P.2d at 1106 (citing R. Cushman, The Construction Industry Form Book, § 5.04 (John Wiley & Sons 1979)).

[22] 187 Ill. App. 3d 417, 543 N.E.2d 249 (1989).

[23] *See, e.g.,* APAC-Tennessee, Inc. v. J.M. Humphries Constr. Co., 732 S.W.2d 601 (Tenn. Ct. App. 1986); John W. Johnson, Inc. v. Basic Constr. Co., 429 F.2d 764 (D.C. Cir. 1970); McKinney Drilling Co. v. Collins Co., 517 F. Supp. 320 (N.D. Ala. 1981).

"inconsistency" with respect to express provisions in the subcontract. Some courts, for example, hold that incorporated terms conflict with the subcontract even though the extrinsic term reasonably can be viewed to supplement, not contradict, the specific terms of the subcontract.

For example, one court ruled that an indemnity clause in a prime contract which is broader than the indemnity clause contained in a subcontract conflicts with the subcontract and should be disregarded.[24] Similarly, where a subcontract was "quite explicit" in addressing the amount to be paid to a subcontractor but lacked any price adjustment provision, a price adjustment clause in a general contract was held to be "inconsistent" with the express terms of the subcontract and therefore was not incorporated into the subcontract.[25] By contrast, other courts have held that, where an incorporated term is more specific than a term in a subcontract, the general contract language modifies, rather than conflicts with, the more general subcontract provisions and should be enforced.[26]

§ 3.8   —Surrounding Circumstances

The third principle in determining the intent of the parties is to look to the four corners of the subcontract and the circumstances surrounding the formation of the subcontract in order to determine if incorporation is consistent with the reasonable expectations of the parties at the time they entered the agreement. In other words, incorporation by reference clauses are to be construed "consistent with the most reasonable interpretation under the totality of circumstances."[27] Courts are reluctant to enforce an incorporated term if the presence or absence of other terms in either the subcontract or the general contract cast doubt on the

---

[24] Brown v. Prime Constr. Co., 684 P.2d 73 (Wash. 1984); Jones v. Strom Constr. Co., 527 P.2d 1115 (Wash. 1974).

[25] APAC-Tennessee Inc. v. J.M. Humphries Constr. Co., 732 S.W.2d 601 (Tenn. Ct. App. 1986). *See also* Industrial Indem. Co. v. Wick Constr. Co., 680 P.2d 1100 (Alaska 1984) (liquidated damages clause in prime contract limiting delay damages was not inconsistent with specific subcontract provisions granting contractor the right to terminate a subcontractor's work on a project).

[26] *See* Sears, Roebuck & Co. v. Shamrock Constr. Co., 441 So. 2d 379 (La. Ct. App. 1983); Ajax Magnolia Ore Corp. v. Southern Cal. Edison Co., 167 Cal. App. 2d 743, 748, 334 P.2d 1053, 1056 (1959). In Gibbons-Grable Co. v. Gilbane Building Co., 34 Ohio App. 3d 170, 517 N.E.2d 559 (1986), the court reasoned that specific language of a prime contract's arbitration clause controlled over the more general reservation of remedies clause in the subcontract because if the reservation of remedies clause in the subcontract were enforced the arbitration clause in the prime contract would be rendered meaningless. On this basis the court concluded that the prime contract arbitration clause was not inconsistent with the subcontract reservation of remedies provision and therefore intended to be incorporated.

[27] *See, e.g.,* North W. Pac. Indem. Co. v. Junction City Central Water Dist., 658 P.2d 1209 (Or. 1983); Jensen v. Ramas, 792 P.2d 668 (Alaska 1990) (goal of interpreting contracts is to give effect to the reasonable expectation of parties as manifest by the language of the contract provisions, relevant extrinsic evidence, and case law interpreting similar provisions).

reasonableness of incorporation. Thus, the absence of a clause in a subcontract requiring a subcontractor to carry insurance covering its potential liability resulting from an obligation to indemnify the general contractor may cast doubt on the subcontractor's intent to incorporate indemnification language from the prime contract.[28]

§ 3.9   Third-Party Beneficiary Status: Who Can Enforce Incorporated Provisions?

Unlike the assignment or delegation of contract rights and duties, construction subcontracts ordinarily do not purport to directly assign rights or delegate duties created between the upstream parties. Instead, construction subcontracts attempt to embody the independent legal relations as established between the subcontractor and the immediate upstream contractor. For this reason, subcontract incorporation by reference clauses do not usually establish legal relations between the subcontractor and remote upstream parties.[29]

Thus, ordinarily, there is no privity of contract between an owner and a subcontractor.[30] Consequently, while general incorporation by reference to a second contract may be sufficient to bind the immediate parties to each other according to the incorporated provisions, the incorporation may, nevertheless, be ineffective in binding the subcontractor to the owner or to another remote upstream contractor.

The extent of the subcontractor's obligations to and rights against such remote parties must be examined in terms of the remote party's status as third-party beneficiary under the subcontract or the subcontractor's status as a third-party beneficiary under the upstream contract.[31] A third party will be able to enforce terms of an incorporating contract only if such third party is an intended, rather than incidental, beneficiary of the incorporating contract.[32] It follows that an upstream party, such as an owner, gains no rights as against a subcontractor

---

[28] *See* Loughman Cabinet Co. v. C. Iber & Sons, Inc., 361 N.E.2d 379 (Ill. App. Ct. 1977) (a subcontractor's cause of action based on incorporated terms in prime contract made effective by general incorporation by reference clause in subcontract; court ruled subcontractor cannot reasonably assert that other provisions of general contract were not incorporated).

[29] Coleman v. Pearman, 159 Va. 72, 165 S.E. 371 (1932). *See generally* Note, *Contracts for the Benefit of Third Parties in the Construction Industry,* 40 Fordham L. Rev. 315 (1971).

[30] Warren Bros. Roads Co. v. United States, 105 F. Supp. 826 (Ct. Cl. 1152). *Accord* Matirano Constr. Corp. v. Briar Contracting Corp., 104 A.D.2d 1028, 481 N.Y.S.2d 105 (App. Div. 1984).

[31] *See generally* Majestic Mfg. Corp. v. L. Riso, 27 N.Y.S.2d 845 (1940), *aff'd,* 261 A.D. 1099, 27 N.Y.S.2d 846 (1941); Corbin on Contracts, Ch. 41, *Third Party Beneficiaries* §§ 779D, 787 (2d ed. 1976).

[32] *See* Restatement (Second) of Contracts §§ 302, 304 (1981); Corbin, Ch. 41, §§ 779D, 787.

under the downstream subcontract absent a provision in the subcontract indicating an intent by the subcontract parties to benefit the upstream party.[33]

In a recent Georgia case, an owner sued a subcontractor on account of a flow down indemnity obligation. A clause in the subcontract stating that the general contract became "a part" of the subcontract was deemed sufficient to incorporate into the subcontract a prime contract provision requiring the general contractor to include in any subcontract on the project a provision calling for the indemnification of the owner by the subcontractor.[34] The prime contract required the general contractor to include in the subcontract a provision binding the subcontractor to indemnify the owner. While the prime contractor failed to include such an express obligation in the subcontract, the court reasoned that the general incorporation language of the subcontract was effective in incorporating this prime contract clause into the subcontract.

In effect, the subcontract was held to incorporate language in the prime contract requiring that the subcontract incorporate the prime contract obligation to indemnify the owner.[35] Despite the incorporation of the indemnification clause, however, the court found that the subcontract precluded the owner as an intended beneficiary of the subcontract.[36] Accordingly, the owner could not enforce the incorporated indemnity clause against the subcontractor.[37]

Similarly, other cases have held that, absent an indication that the subcontractor is an intended beneficiary of an upstream contract or an assignee of contract rights of the contractor, the subcontractor cannot assert rights against an owner which have been incorporated by the subcontract.[38]

INCORPORATION OF SUBSTANTIVE TERMS

§ 3.10   Indemnification Clauses

The risks of personal injury, property damage, or economic loss as a result of design errors, changes, and delay are well known in the industry. One of the functions of a contract is to identify which party bears these risks. Indemnity and

---

[33] Kaiser Aluminum & Chem. Corp. v. Ingersoll-Rand Co., 519 F. Supp. 60 (D. Ga. 1981); Pierce Assocs., Inc. v. Nemours Found., 865 F.2d 530 (3d Cir. 1988). *But see* Sears, Roebuck & Co. v. Jardel Co., 421 F.2d 1048 (3d Cir. 1970) (terms incorporated by subcontract from general contract gave owner rights as against subcontractor).

[34] Walls, Inc. v. Atlantic Realty Co., 186 Ga. App. 389, 367 S.E.2d 278 (1988).

[35] *Id.*

[36] *Id.* at 281.

[37] *Id.*

[38] Port Chester Elec. Constr. Corp. v. Atlas, 357 N.E.2d 983 (N.Y. 1976); E.C. Ernst Inc. v. Manhattan Constr. Co., 551 F.2d 1026 (5th Cir. 1977), *cert. denied,* 434 U.S. 1067, 98 S. Ct. 1246 (1978).

insurance clauses are the means to do that. In public contracts and most private contracts, the contractor generally assumes certain risks via an indemnity clause and by agreeing to insure itself (and the owner as a named insured) on account of these risks.

Contractors prudently pass down these risks to their subcontractors, certainly to the extent the subcontractors' acts or omissions create the risk. The careful contractor will spell out the duty to indemnify and to insure in the subcontract. But such express risk-shifting often does not occur. Instead, whether by intent or blind luck, a contractor may be forced to rely on a modest incorporation by reference clause to assert that a subcontractor has a duty to indemnify a contractor on account of a risk the contractor agreed to assume.

Early cases addressing the incorporation by reference of prime contract indemnity provisions generally did not enforce indemnity obligations against the subcontractor.[39] However, many of these cases involved incorporation by reference clauses but not conduit clauses and relied on the overbroad understanding of *Guerini Stone,* discussed in § 3.6. More recent cases involving contracts with conduit clauses as well have concluded that indemnity provisions may be incorporated by reference.[40] Still, special problems attend the enforcement of subcontract clauses purporting to incorporate indemnity provisions. These problems arise largely from the scope of incorporating language in the subcontracts and from principles governing the enforceability of indemnification provisions in general.

§ 3.11   —Scope

Where a subcontract incorporates broad indemnity provisions from the general contract, the general contractor facing liability to the owner will argue that the subcontractor "stands in the shoes" of the prime contractor for such claims, even though unrelated to the subcontracting work. While such a contractual relationship is possible, it is usually not contemplated by parties to a subcontract. As noted earlier, conduit clauses are effective at incorporating obligations delineated in general contracts only to the extent that such obligations relate to or arise out of the subcontractor's performance of work on the project. Consequently, unless a contrary intent is expressed in the subcontract, the subcontractor's obligation to indemnify the prime contractor will extend only to those claims relating to or arising out of the subcontractor's performance of its work on the project.[41]

---

[39] *See, e.g.,* Schull Constr. Co. v. Koenig, 121 N.W.2d 559 (S.D. 1963).

[40] *E.g.,* Walls, Inc. v. Atlantic Realty Co., 186 Ga. App. 389, 367 S.E.2d 278 (1988); Arthur Pew Constr. Co. v. Bryan Constr. Co., 148 Ga. App. 114, 251 S.E.2d 105 (1978); Donald S. Whittle v. Pagani Bros. Constr. Co., 383 Mass. 796, 422 N.E.2d 779 (1981); Binswanger Glass Co. v. Beers Constr. Co., 141 Ga. App. 715, 234 S.E.2d 363 (1977).

[41] *See* Industrial Indem. Co. v. Wick Constr. Co., 680 P.2d 1100, 1104 (Alaska 1984); Donald S. Whittle v. Pagani Bros. Constr. Co., 383 Mass. 796, 422 N.E.2d 779 (1981).

§ 3.12 —Indemnification for Negligence

At one time, indemnification clauses were strictly construed against the party seeking indemnification.[42] Courts in most jurisdictions will now enforce the provisions of indemnity contracts consistent with the most reasonable interpretation of the contract terms. Many jurisdictions, however, strictly construe provisions purporting to obligate the indemnitor for the indemnitee's own negligence.[43] In such jurisdictions, a subcontract clause requiring the subcontractor to indemnify the contractor against losses or liability resulting from the contractor's own negligence may be enforceable only if such coverage is specifically expressed in the subcontract in clear and unequivocal terms.[44]

The rationale for strict construction is that the potential liability of an indemnitor is so extensive and the character of the indemnity so unusual that "there can be no presumption that the indemnitor intended to assume the liability unless the contract puts it beyond doubt by express stipulation."[45] Courts also recognize that a subcontractor performing a portion of the work on a construction contract does not ordinarily expect to be liable for damages resulting from the negligence of the general contractor.[46] For this reason, it has been said that the test for the enforcement of a subcontract indemnification clause purportedly covering the contractor-indemnitee's own negligence is whether the subcontract language specifically focuses attention on the fact that, by the agreement, the indemnitor was assuming liability for the indemnitee's own negligence.[47]

In addition to the rule favoring a strict construction against indemnification for negligence, some states by statute have prohibited indemnification by a construction subcontractor for damages resulting from the sole negligence or willful misconduct of the contractor.[48]

Consistent with strict construction, many courts are reluctant to enforce subcontract clauses purporting to incorporate language which would impose on

---

[42] *See, e.g.,* Hooey v. Airport Constr. Co., 171 N.E. 752, *reh'g denied,* 175 N.E. 331 (N.Y. 1931).

[43] *See generally* 41 Am. Jur. 2d, *Indemnity* § 13, 699-702 (1968); Wajtasiak v. Morgan County, 633 S.W.2d 488 (Tenn. Ct. App. 1982); Mostyn v. Delaware L.&R. Co., 160 F.2d 15 (2d Cir. 1947); Kansas City Power & Light Co. v. United Tel. Co. of Kansas, 458 F.2d 177 (10th Cir. 1972); First Am. Nat'l Bank v. Tennessee Gas Transmission Co., 58 Tenn. App. 189, 428 S.W.2d 35 (1967); Ethyl Corp. v. Daniel Constr. Co., 725 S.W.2d 705 (Tex. 1987).

[44] *E.g.,* Allison Steel Mfg. Co. v. Superior Court, 22 Ariz. App. 76, 523 P.2d 803 (1974); Paul Hardeman Inc. v. J.I. Hass Co., 246 Ark. 559, 439 S.W. 2d 281 (1969); Wajtasiak v. Morgan County, 633 S.W.2d 488 (Tenn. Ct. App. 1982); Kansas City Power & Light Co. v. United Tel. Co. of Kan., 458 F.2d 177 (10th Cir. 1972).

[45] George J. Dingledy Lumber Co. v. Erie R. Co., 102 Ohio St. 236, 131 N.E. 723 (1921).

[46] *See* MacDonald Kruse, Inc. v. San Jose Steel Co., 29 Cal. App. 3d 413, 105 Cal. Rptr. 725 (1973); Brown v. Prime Constr. Co., 684 P.2d 73 (Wash. 1984); Gonzales v. R.J. Novick Constr. Co., 20 Cal. 3d 798, 575 P.2d 1190 (1978); Calkins v. Lorain Div. of Koehring Co., 613 P.2d 143 (Wash. Ct. App. 1980).

[47] Sweetman v. Strescon Indus., Inc., 389 A.2d 1319 (Del. 1978).

[48] *See, e.g.,* Alaska Stat. § 45.45.900; Ga. Code Ann. § 20-504; Minn. Stat. §§ 337.01 et seq.

the subcontractor the duty to indemnify the contractor for the contractor's negligence. A conduit clause in the subcontract, for example, is often not "a clear and unequivocal agreement" to indemnify the general contractor for its own negligence, even where the general contractor's obligation to indemnify the owner for negligence is unequivocal in the prime contract.[49]

For example, in *Goldman v. Ecco-Phoenix Electric Corp.,*[50] a subcontract conduit clause was found to be insufficient to incorporate in the subcontract a specific provision in the prime contract requiring the contractor to indemnify the owner for the owner's negligence. Referring to the boilerplate conduit clause in the subcontract, the court reasoned that "an indemnification agreement calling for financial protection against one's own negligence cannot rest upon language so loose and obscure."[51]

Courts in more recent cases have also concluded that a conduit clause in the subcontract is not sufficient to bind a subcontractor to indemnify a contractor for the owner's negligence, even where the incorporated provision is clear with respect to negligence coverage as between the upstream parties.[52] Similarly, language in the subcontract purporting to make all the prime contract documents a part of the subcontract is not usually sufficient to bind the subcontractor to indemnify the contractor for the owner's negligence.[53]

The strict construction of indemnity provisions alleged to cover the indemnitee's negligence has eroded in some states. For example, clauses failing to explicitly provide for indemnification for a contractor's negligence may nevertheless be enforceable if such negligence was "passive" rather than "active"[54] or if the indemnitor's breach of contractual obligations or its own negligence contributed to the loss incurred by the indemnitee.[55] In such jurisdictions, incorporation by reference clauses may be sufficient to incorporate the duty to indemnify.[56]

Only a few courts, however, have addressed whether an incorporation by reference clause is enough to require a subcontractor to indemnify an upstream contractor for liability resulting from the contractor's contractual obligation to indemnify an owner or other third party for such party's negligence. At least one court has found a broad subcontract indemnification clause sufficient to cover a contractor's liability resulting from its contractual obligation to indemnify the owner.[57]

---

[49] Allison-Steel Mfg. Co. v. Superior Court, 22 Ariz. App. 76, 523 P.2d 803 (1974).

[50] 62 Cal. 2d 40, 396 P.2d 377, 41 Cal. Rptr. 73 (1964).

[51] 396 P.2d at 382.

[52] Wyoming Johnson Inc. v. Stag Indus., 662 P.2d 96 (Wyo. 1983).

[53] *See* Wajtasiak v. Morgan County, 633 S.W.2d 488 (Tenn. Ct. App. 1982).

[54] C.J. Abbott, Inc. v. Gilpatrick Constr. Co., 731 P.2d 1188 (Wyo. 1987).

[55] Whittle v. Pagani Bros. Constr. Co., 383 Mass. 796, 422 N.E.2d 779 (1976); Burns v. Ford Motor Co., 331 N.E.2d 325 (Ill. 1975); Arthur Pew Constr. Co. v. Bryan Constr. Co., 188 Ga. App. 114, 251 S.E.2d 105 (1978).

[56] *See* MacDonald Kruse, Inc. v. San Jose Steel Co., 29 Cal. App. 3d 413, 105 Cal. Rptr. 725 (1973).

[57] Brown v. Prime Constr. Co., 684 P. 2d 73 (Wash. 1984).

§ 3.13   —Workers' Compensation and Indemnity

Where a subcontractor's employee brings suit against the general contractor for a work-related injury, workers' compensation statutes may affect the enforceability of an indemnity clause incorporating from the general contract the obligation to indemnify the contractor. Workers' compensation statutes exclude other remedies against employers; specifically, lawsuits by their employees for work-related injuries. While an employer may waive immunity to such suits, courts hold that such waiver must generally be clear to be effective.[58]

Accordingly, some states require that the subcontract show clearly that the subcontractor intended to waive workers' compensation immunity prior to finding that the subcontractor agreed to assume the contractor's liability.[59] In Washington, for example, subcontract indemnification provisions are enforceable for the injuries sustained by the subcontractor's employees only if such clauses "clearly and specifically contain a waiver of the immunity of the workers' compensation act, either by so stating or by specifically stating that the indemnitor assumes potential liability for actions brought by its own employees."[60] Thus, a conduit clause purporting to incorporate an indemnification provision in the prime contract which specifically waived the contractor's workers' compensation immunity may not be sufficient to indicate the subcontracting waiver of statutory immunity.

In contrast, other courts hold that workers' compensation immunity does not apply to subcontractors who have contractually undertaken the obligation to indemnify an upstream contractor.[61] In such jurisdictions, workers' compensation statutes are irrelevant to the enforcement of incorporation by reference clauses.

Contracting parties desiring indemnification of the contractor by the subcontractor for claims grounded in negligence, whether on the part of the contractor or another party, should insure that the subcontract contains language sufficiently explicit to indicate that the parties intended such coverage. Undoubtedly, the safest route is to avoid a dispute regarding the enforceability of incorporation by reference or conduit clauses by including an adequate indemnification provision in the subcontract. Furthermore, where a clear waiver of workers' compensation statute immunity is necessary, subcontracts should include a separate provision containing an explicit waiver of such immunity. Finally, contractors should examine local statutes to see if there is a statutory prohibition of indemnification under a construction contract for damages caused by the contractor's sole negligence.

---

[58] Gonzales v. R.J. Novick Constr. Co., 20 Cal. 3d 798, 575 P.2d 1190 (1978).

[59] Calkins v. Lorain Div. of Koehring Co., 613 P.2d 143 (Wash. Ct. App. 1980).

[60] Brown v. Prime, 684 P.2d at 75.

[61] Arthur Pew Constr. Co. v. Bryan Constr. Co., 148 Ga. App. 114, 115 (1978) (workers' compensation statute does not bar prime contractor's contractual right to indemnify from subcontractor for work-related injuries to subcontracting employers).

§ 3.14   Arbitration Clauses:
Public Policy Supports Arbitration

The obligation to submit to arbitration is consensual; it depends on an agreement between the parties to do so.[62] Since the obligation to arbitrate will usually preclude a party from the opportunity to litigate in a court of law, some courts state the general rule that it must be clear and unmistakable that the parties to a contract agreed to arbitration.[63]

With the passage of the Federal Arbitration Act (FAA)[64] and the adoption by many states of the Uniform Arbitration Act or similar arbitration statutes, arbitration has become a favored method of resolving construction contract disputes.[65] Courts refer to the policy embodied in the FAA to buttress orders requiring arbitration where the intent of the parties to arbitrate is not clear in the subcontract documents.[66] For example, courts routinely enforce arbitration provisions contained in AIA Document A201 against downstream subcontractors, where such downstream contracts contain only a general conduit clause.[67]

The courts continue to apply the factors noted above in determining whether upstream arbitration clauses may be effectively incorporated into a subcontract. However, the state and federal policy favoring arbitration appears to predispose courts toward finding incorporation. In one case, a subcontract provided that the subcontractor was entitled to "the benefit of all rights, remedies and redress against the Contractor that the Contractor . . . has against the Owner."[68] The prime contract contained the general conditions of AIA A201 which provide that the contractor had the right of arbitration against the owner for "[a]ll claims, disputes and other matters" arising out of the contract.[69] In summary language, the court concluded that the general incorporation language was sufficient to

---

[62] *See generally* 5 Am. Jur. 2d, *Arbitration and Award* § 11; R.W. Roberts Constr. Co. v. St. John's Management Dist., 423 So. 2d 630 (Fla. Dist. Ct. App. 1982).

[63] *See, e.g.,* Titan Group v. Sonoma Valley County Sanitation Dist., 164 Cal. App. 3d 1122, 211 Cal. Rptr. 62 (1985).

[64] 9 U.S.C. § 1 (1988).

[65] Volt Information Sciences, Inc. v. Board of Trustees, 109 S. Ct. 1248 (1989) (FAA only requires courts to enforce privately negotiated agreements to arbitrate, like other contracts, according to their terms).

[66] *E.g.,* E&F Constr. Co. v. Rissil Constr. Assocs., Inc., 181 Conn. 317, 435 A.2d 343 (1980); Jim Carlson Constr., Inc. v. Bailey, 769 S.W.2d 480 (Mo. Ct. App. 1989).

[67] Gibbons-Grable Co. v. Gilbane Bldg. Co., 517 N.E.2d 557, 582 (Ohio Ct. App. 1986); Godwin v. Stanley Smith & Sons, 386 S.E.2d 464, (S.C. Ct. App. 1989); Turner Constr. Co. v. Midwest Curtainwalls, Inc., 187 Ill. App. 3d 417, 543 N.E.2d 249 (1989); J.S.&H. Constr. Co. v. Richmond County Hosp. Auth., 473 F.2d 212 (5th Cir. 1973). *See also* Home Lumber Co. v. Appalachian Regional Hosp., Inc., 722 S.W.2d 912 (Ky. Ct. App. 1987). *But see* Omega Constr. Co. v. Altman, 147 Mich. App. 649, 382 N.W.2d 839 (1985).

[68] ADC Constr. Co. v. McDaniel Grading, 177 Ga. App. 223, 338 S.E.2d 733 (1985).

[69] 338 S.E.2d at 736.

incorporate into the subcontract the right to arbitration even though the sub-contract made no explicit reference to arbitration.[70]

Even with the willingness of courts to enforce arbitration clauses incorporated by reference, specific subcontract language will still control over inconsistent language incorporated by reference. For example, one court rejected an incorporated prime contract clause limiting arbitration to claims of less than $50,000, where a specific clause in the subcontract provided for the arbitration of all claims.[71] The court reasoned that a general conduit clause could not be construed to impose obligations set forth in an upstream contract since such a construction would entail the "wholesale incorporation of the entire prime contract."[72] More importantly, the court noted that the placement of the conduit clause in the "scope of work" section of the subcontract could be reasonably read only to require the subcontractor to follow the requirements of the "specifications, drawings and other prime contract documents."[73] In addition, the court noted that specific provisions in the subcontract were to control in the face of "inconsistent" terms purported to have been incorporated from the prime contract.[74]

In a more recent case, the court rejected a subcontractor's argument that an additional subcontract clause relieved the subcontractor from the duty to arbitrate claims otherwise covered by incorporated prime contract provisions.[75] The prime contract bound the contractor and owner to arbitration. The subcontractor asserted that the conduit clause of the subcontract was not sufficiently clear to impose on the subcontractor the obligation to arbitrate. It argued further that specific language in the subcontract stating that "in the matter of arbitration . . . rights and all procedures shall be analogous to those set forth in the contract documents" applied to the rights and duties of the parties in the event of arbitration, but did not impose arbitration.[76] Rejecting this argument, the court found that the conduit clause had incorporated the obligation to arbitrate and that the specific clause in the subcontract was not inconsistent with the incorporated obligations.[77]

Finally, it has also been held that under the FAA, an incorporation by reference clause in a contractor's payment bond incorporated an obligation to arbitrate set forth in the prime contract.[78]

---

[70] *Id.*

[71] Falcon Steel Co. v. Weber Eng'g Co., 517 A.2d 281 (Del. Ct. App. 1986).

[72] *Id.* at 289.

[73] *Id.* at 286.

[74] *Id.*

[75] First Fin. Sav. v. H.L.B. Corp., 1988 W.L. 10964 (Ohio Ct. App. 1988) (not reported in N.E.2d).

[76] *Id.* at 3.

[77] *Id.*

[78] Exchange Mut. Ins. Co. v. Haskell Co., 742 F.2d 274 (6th Cir. 1984).

Most federal courts have found incorporation by reference and conduit clauses sufficient to bind a prime and subcontractor to arbitration provisions in the prime contract.[79] Since state law regarding the enforceability of arbitration provisions may be preempted by the FAA, a subcontract conduit clause incorporates a prime contract arbitration provision even though the provision is unenforceable under state law.[80]

§ 3.15 —Incorporated Arbitration Clauses and the Miller Act

Incorporation by reference clauses in subcontracts do not incorporate upstream arbitration clauses where the federal Miller Act[81] remedies are available to the subcontractor.[82]

Some of the early decisions seem to rest on a broad construction of *Guerini Stone,* noted in § **3.5,** especially where no conduit clause was present in the subcontract.[83] The rationale for more recent cases is twofold. First, since the purpose of the Miller Act is to provide security for subcontractors who cannot obtain a lien on government property, "the courts do not favor finding that a subcontractor has abandoned his rights under the Act."[84] Second, the right to sue may be waived only by "clear and express provisions."[85] The same rationale has been used to bar the enforcement of general incorporation by reference clauses where a subcontractor's right to sue was not based on a statutory bond.[86]

In sum, incorporation by reference clauses are effective in passing through to the subcontracting parties arbitration obligations set forth in the prime contract. Subcontractors desiring to avoid arbitration incorporated by such clauses should include the desired venue selection clauses in their subcontracts, arbitration clauses in prime contracts notwithstanding.

---

[79] Moses H. Cone Memorial Hosp. v. Mercury Constr. Corp., 460 U.S. 1, 103 S. Ct. 927 (1983).

[80] *See* Godwin v. Stanley Smith & Sons, 386 S.E.2d 464 (S.C. Ct. App. 1989).

[81] 40 U.S.C. § 270(a) (1988).

[82] Fanderlik-Locke Co. v. United States, 285 F.2d 939 (10th Cir. 1960); United States *ex rel.* B's Co. v. Cleveland Elec. Co., 373 F.2d 585 (4th Cir. 1967); H.W. Caldwell & Son, Inc. v. United States, 407 F.2d 21 (5th Cir. 1969); Industrial Contractors Corp. v. William Clairmont, Inc., 341 F. Supp. 940 (D. Neb 1972); United States v. Gulf Ins. Co., 650 F. Supp. 557 (S.D. Fla. 1986).

[83] *See, e.g.,* J.W. Johnson, Inc. v. Basic Constr. Co. 429 F.2d 764 (D.C. Cir. 1970) (incorporation by reference is not effective in incorporating procedural or remedial provisions).

[84] H.W. Caldwell & Son, Inc. v. United States, 407 F.2d 21 (5th Cir. 1969).

[85] Cleveland Elec. Co., 373 F.2d at 586.

[86] Washington Metro. Area Transit Auth. *ex rel* Noralco v. Norair Eng'g Corp., 553 F.2d 233 (D.C. Cir. 1977).

§ 3.16　No Damages for Delay and
Other Remedy Clauses

Where a prime contract includes a no damages for delay clause, it is in the contractor's interest to insure that a similar provision is contained in the subcontract. Without a no damages for delay clause in the subcontract, a contractor may be faced with the situation in which it is liable to the subcontractor for delays caused by the owner but cannot, in turn, recover from the owner.[87]

Most of the jurisdictions which have addressed the question hold that subcontract conduit clauses are sufficient to incorporate no damages for delay provisions of the prime contract. In an early case, a court held that under a conduit clause in the subcontract "the main contract became part and parcel of the subcontract so far as that provisions are consistent."[88] Therefore, the subcontractor could not obtain delay damages by virtue of the incorporated "no damages for delay" clause in the prime contract.[89]

Other more recent decisions have reached similar results.[90] In one case, the Alaska Supreme Court held that a liquidated damages clause in the prime contract limiting delay damages to $400/day was incorporated by a general conduit clause in the subcontract.[91]

Courts have not been reluctant to hold subcontract incorporation by reference clauses effective at incorporating prime contract no damages for delay clauses. In one typical case, the court presumed, absent contrary evidence, that the subcontract was drafted in accordance with a prime contract provision requiring the subcontract to bind the subcontractors to the contractor by the terms of the prime contract.[92] Thus, inasmuch as the no damages for delay clause barred the contractor from obtaining damages from the engineer, the subcontractor could not obtain delay damages.[93]

At least one court has specifically refused to acknowledge the effective incorporation of no damages for delay provisions into subcontracts. Relying on

---

[87] Of course, if the subcontractor's action against a contractor is based on specific remedies of the subcontract, incorporation of the no damages for delay provisions would probably be inconsistent with the specific provisions of the contract, and therefore not incorporated. Moreover, some courts hold that, absent a contractual commitment to the contrary, a general contractor is not liable to its subcontractor for damages flowing from delays incurred by a subcontractor unless the delays were caused by the general contractor or some agency or circumstance under its direction or control. W. Wright, Inc. v. Korshoj Corp., 250 N.W.2d 894, 899 (Neb. 1977).

[88] Walter R. Cliffe Co. v. DuPont Eng'g Co., 298 F. 649, 652 (D. Del. 1924).

[89] *Id.*

[90] *See* Sime Constr. Co. v. Washington Pub. Power Supply Sys., 621 P.2d 1299 (Wash. 1980) (notice requirements of damages for delay provisions in prime contract incorporated by conduit clause); McDaniel v. Ashton-Mardian Co., 357 F.2d 511 (9th Cir. 1966); Coast Sash & Door Co. v. Strom Constr. Co., 65 Wash. 2d 279, 396 P.2d 803 (1964).

[91] Industrial Indem. Co. v. Wick Constr. Co., 680 P.2d 1100, 1104-05 (Alaska 1984).

[92] Bates & Rogers Constr. Corp. v. Greeley & Hansen, 109 Ill. 2d 225, 486 N.E.2d 902 (1985).

[93] 486 N.E.2d at 905.

the strict approach embodied in the misbegotten offspring of *Guerini Stone,* the court in *S. Leo Harmonay, Inc. v. Binks Manufacturing Co.*[94] held that, because general incorporation language is effective at incorporating only those prime contract provisions relating to the scope, quality, character, and manner of the subcontractor's work, a no damages for delay provision in the prime contract could not be incorporated in the subcontract.[95] As noted earlier, however, *Guerini Stone* properly stands for the narrower proposition that, when a subcontract expressly incorporates only the plans and specifications set forth in the general contract, a greater scope of incorporation should not be implied.

§ 3.17   Incorporation of the Implied Warranty of the Adequacy and Suitability of Plans and Specifications

An interesting and unresolved question involves the effect of incorporation provisions in subcontracts on terms implied at law in the general contract. Terms implied in law are not created by the assent, whether by word or conduct, of the parties to the contract. They are imposed without any words or conduct that might be interpreted as promissory in nature.[96] Implied at law terms are imposed by courts in order to avoid an injustice and are based on matters of policy fairness.[97]

One of the most important terms implied at law in construction contracts is the implied warranty of the adequacy and suitability of plans. While there are numerous exceptions to the rule, the owner of a construction project who furnishes detailed plans or specifications to be followed by its contractor in carrying out the work of the project is deemed by law to impliedly warrant that the plans and specifications are accurate and suitable for their intended use.[98]

Under the general rule, a contractor will not be responsible for defects in the work resulting from inadequate or defective plans or specifications furnished by the owner.[99] Similarly, a contractor, who incurs expenses in excess of the contract price as a result of the inadequacy or unsuitability of the places provided by the owner, may be entitled to recover the extra expenses incurred in correcting the differences from the owner.[100]

---

[94] 597 F. Supp. 1014 (S.D.N.Y. 1984).

[95] *Id.* at 1028.

[96] *See* 3 Corbin § 561 (1976).

[97] *See* Restatement of Contracts 2d, § 4(b) (1974); Holmes, The Path of the Law, 10 Harv. L. Rev. 457, 466 (1897).

[98] The seminal case for this principle is United States v. Spearin, 248 U.S. 132 (1918). *See also* J. L. Simmons Co. v. United States, 412 F.2d 1360 (Ct. Cl. 1969).

[99] *See generally* J. Harrington, R. Thum, & J. Clark, *The Owner's Warranty of Plans and Specifications for a Construction Contract,* 14 Pub. Cont. L. J. 24 (1984).

[100] *See, e.g.,* Souza & McCue Constr. Co. v. Superior Court, 370 P.2d 338 (Cal. 1962). This rule has apparently been rejected in several jurisdictions, most notably Pennsylvania and Texas.

This same rule has been applied to subcontractors. The Alaska Supreme Court in *Lewis v. Anchorage Asphalt Paving Co.*[101] stated:

> [If] the contractor is bound to build according to detailed plans and specifications prepared by the owner or prime contractor, he will not be held liable for defects in the end product which are caused by deficiencies in the specifications as long as he performs the work according to the plans and in a workmanlike manner.[102]

The court then concluded that a subcontractor, who has followed the plans and specifications provided to it by the prime contractor, cannot be held to guarantee to the prime contractor that the work will be free of defects or accomplish the intended purpose. Several other courts have agreed with the Alaska court.[103] The question thus becomes: Are conduit or incorporation by reference clauses needed to impose the implied warranty as between the contractor and the subcontractor?

If the implied warranty of the adequacy and suitability of plans and specification is "deemed" to be given by prime contractors as well as owners, there may not be any need to incorporate such an obligation by provisions in the subcontract. In holding that the implied warranty was made by a contractor who passed plans and specifications on to a subcontractor, an Oklahoma court explained the relative positions of the parties in "pass-through" terms:

> We construe the underlying rationale of [the implied warranty] to shift the risk of loss from the least culpable party back up the contract chain to either the party who created the defective plans or the first party in the chain who contractually agreed to assume the risk.[104]

The court concluded that the subcontractor was entitled to recover costs from the contractor due to the inadequacy of the owner's plans and specifications merely provided by the contractor.[105] The court, however, did not address whether the implied warranty flowed to the subcontractor by virtue of incorporation by reference.[106]

See, e.g., Central Penn. Indus. Inc. v. Commonwealth, 358 A.2d 445 (Pa. 1976); Lonergan v. San Antonio Loan & Trust Co., 104 S.W. 1061 (Tex. 1907).

[101] 535 P.2d 1188 (Alaska 1975).

[102] *Id.* at 1196. Note that the court here qualified the protection afforded by the implied warranty: The subcontractor has the duty to warn the contractor of defects in the plans and specifications of which it has knowledge.

[103] Puget Sound Nat'l Bank v. C.B. Lauch Constr. Co., 73 Idaho 68, 245 P.2d 800 (1952); Bradford Builders, Inc. v. Sears, Roebuck & Co., 270 F.2d 649 (5th Cir. 1959); Wood-Hopkins Contracting Co. v. Masonry Contractors, Inc., 235 So. 2d 548 (Fla. 1970).

[104] Miller v. Guy James Constr. Co., 653 P.2d 221, 224 (Okla. 1982).

[105] *Id.* at 225.

[106] *Id.*

If it can be said that incorporation by reference or conduit clauses effectively incorporate prime contract provisions implied in law, we have come full circle. Subcontracts which incorporate by reference the conditions, plans, and specifications of the prime contract and require the subcontractor to assume the contractor-owner obligations also make the contractor an implied warrantor of plans over which the contractor had no control. The flow-down obligations can flow up, as well.

CHAPTER 4

A SYSTEM OF CONSTRUCTION MANAGEMENT FOR THE 1990S

Richard D. Conner*

§ 4.1   Construction Management: A Concept with a Definition

§ 4.2   CMAA Documents: Construction Manager as Agent

SUMMARY OF THE CMAA SYSTEM

§ 4.3   Project Planning and Selection of a Design Professional

§ 4.4   Construction Management Plan

§ 4.5   CM as Owner's Agent

§ 4.6   CM and Design Professional Cooperation

§ 4.7   Reliance on CM Cost Estimates

§ 4.8   Design Criteria

§ 4.9   Compliance with the Project Budget

§ 4.10   Design Documentation

§ 4.11   Design Professional's Basic Construction Phase Services

§ 4.12   CM Determinations During the Construction Phase

CM'S LEADERSHIP ROLE

§ 4.13   During the Design Phase

§ 4.14   During the Construction Phase

§ 4.15   CM's Exposure to Liability

§ 4.16   Performance Standards of Care

§ 4.17   Professional Liability Insurance Coverage

§ 4.18   CMAA A-1 Standard Form of Agreement Between Owner and Construction Manager

§ 4.19   CMAA A-4 Standard Form of Agreement Between Owner and Design Professional

* This chapter is adapted from a paper presented in May 1990 to the 29th Annual Meeting of Invited Attorneys sponsored by AIA, NSPE, and Victor O. Schinnerer & Company. CMAA Form No. A-1 and Form No. A-4 are © by Construction Management Association of America and are reprinted with permission of CMAA.

§ 4.1   Construction Management:
A Concept with a Definition

"Construction management is the process of professional management applied to a construction program from conception to completion."[1]

"Construction management consists of that group of management activities that is distinct from normal architectural and engineering services and is related to a construction program."[2]

§ 4.2   CMAA Documents:
Construction Manager as Agent

During 1990 the Board of Directors of the Construction Management Association of America (CMAA) authorized the distribution of "standard" forms of agreement for a one year period of trial use and comment.[3] The forms consist of the following documents:

CMAA Document No. A-1 (1990 edition) Standard Form of Agreement Between Owner and Construction Manager (CM as Owner's Agent)

CMAA Document No. A-2 (1990 edition) Standard Form of Contract Between Owner and Contractor

CMAA Document No. A-3 (1990 edition) General Conditions of the Construction Contract; Owner-Contractor Contract

CMAA Document No. A-4 (1990 edition) Standard Form of Agreement Between Owner and Design Professional.

The process of developing these documents began in 1983, and the documents came together with the completion of the A-4 during 1990. Persons too numerous to name here have volunteered their time at considerable expense in making contributions to the content of the documents. One individual should, however, be recognized: Albert W. Heyer, Chairman of the Contracts Committee, who has held the drafting effort on course.

The strategy in drafting the CMAA documents was to provide contractually specified duties and avoid concurrent responsibility. Documents drafted in such a manner should minimize conflicts between the CM and design professional and

---

[1] CMAA official statement on construction management.

[2] *Construction Management Responsibilities During Design*, 113 ASCE J. of Constr. Eng'g & Mgmt. (Mar. 1987, Paper No. 21341, George Stukhart, ed.).

[3] The CMAA was founded in 1981. The CMAA, through its Contracts Committee has, in addition to the documents detailed in this chapter, developed drafts of contracts for use when the CM provides a Guaranteed Maximum Price.

promote cooperation.[4] The contractual relationships established under CMAA documents A-1 through A-4 (CMAA documents) are the same as when using American Institute of Architects (AIA) documents B141/CM-1980 and B801-1980.

There are one or more contracts for construction between owner and contractors and separate agreements between owner, designer, and CM. The CM "system" implemented by the CMAA documents is, however, significantly different from that of the AIA. Under the CMAA the CM is the owner's principal agent and responsible for contract administration. The architect's role is limited to design. Copies of CMAA A-1 and A-4 appear in §§ **4.18** and **4.19**, and copies of A-2 and A-3 are available through the CMAA office.[5]

This chapter deals with responsibilities as allocated between the CM and the design professional in the CMAA documents, as compared to the AIA documents.

SUMMARY OF THE CMAA SYSTEM

§ 4.3   Project Planning and Selection
of a Design Professional

The CM is employed prior to the design professional. The CM prepares a management plan which includes a project budget, master schedule and other components for acceptance by the owner. Following acceptance of the management plan by the owner, the CM prepares a milestone schedule for the design and assists the owner in selecting a design professional and preparing the contract between owner and design professional.

§ 4.4   Construction Management Plan[6]

The CMAA system emphasizes predesign and construction planning through use of the construction management plan (CM plan). The CM plan defines the

---

[4] *See generally* R. Kaskell, *How Architects and Engineers in the Contractual Arrangements can Anticipate and Avoid Exposure to Liability,* 48 Ins. Counsel 650 (1984).

[5] The initial editions of the A-1, A-2, and A-3 documents were circulated in 1988, and the 1990 edition contains modifications to each of those documents. Copies of all documents specified in this chapter and other CMAA publications are available from Karl F. Borgstrom, CMAA, 12355 Sunrise Valley Drive Suite 640, Reston VA 22091, (703) 391-1200.

[6] CMAA Document A-1 [hereinafter CMAA A-1] ¶¶ 3.2.1.1 and 3.3.1.1. The basic components of a CM plan are listed in the CMAA Manual of Standard CM Services and Practice as follows: project description; milestone schedule; master schedule; reference to project documents; project organization chart and staffing plan; explanation of roles, responsibilities, and authority of team members; project budget; reference to project procedures manual; management

project requirements in narrative form and outlines the strategy for fulfilling those requirements. As the project progresses and its documentation becomes more definitive, various aspects of the CM plan may be revised and refined.[7]

The design professional makes recommendations for revisions to the CM plan including the project requirements, master schedule, project budget, and the information system.[8]

§ 4.5   CM as Owner's Agent

The CM is the owner's principal agent in connection with the project. The design professional renders, and has sole responsibility for, all professional design services in connection with the project.[9] The CM and design professional each recognize the other's authority and role. The documents detail the CM's services as principal agent.[10]

§ 4.6   CM and Design Professional Cooperation[11]

CM and design professional services are not intended to be duplicative but rather complementary.[12] The CM and design professional are each entitled to rely on the other for proper performance of services.[13]

§ 4.7   Reliance on CM Cost Estimates[14]

The project costs as estimated by the CM are incorporated into the CM plan and the design professional is entitled to rely on such data while preparing its

---

information system; bid packaging and contracting strategy; and site mobilization and utilization.

[7] The AIA documents place no emphasis on predesign project planning and are not specific on how a plan, if developed, would be followed or updated.

[8] CMAA Document No. A-4 [hereinafter CMAA A-4] ¶ 1.2. Under the AIA documents, the procedure for preparation of design documents according to a schedule is less clear. *See* B801 ¶ 1.1.3.

[9] CMAA A-1 art. 3; CMAA A-4 ¶ 2.3.

[10] Under the AIA documents the architect is the owner's principal agent during contract administration.

[11] CMAA A-1 ¶ 1.4; CMAA A-4 ¶¶ 2.4 and 2.5.

[12] Under the AIA documents the obligations and responsibility of the architect and CM appear duplicative in the areas of project budgeting and contract administration. *See* B141/CM ¶¶ 1.1, 1.2, 1.3, and 1.5; B801 ¶¶ 1.1 and 1.2.

[13] B801 states that the CM is entitled to rely on the architect's services. B141/CM does not emphasize reliance on the CM's services.

[14] CMAA A-1 ¶ 3.3.3.2; CMAA A-4 ¶ 3.5.1.

drawings and specifications.[15] The design professional has sole responsibility for design and makes final determination as to the specification of materials and equipment for the project (subject to any directives issued by the owner).

§ 4.8   Design Criteria[16]

The design professional develops design criteria based on the information set forth in the CM plan. The design criteria will evolve from preliminary to detailed in the manner established in the CM plan.

§ 4.9   Compliance with the Project Budget[17]

During design the CM and design professional are required to maintain close liaison and have constant interchange of information and documentation. The design professional provides to the CM submittals of drawings and specifications as required in the CM plan. During design, the design professional receives from the CM advice, cost analyses, value analyses and information as to constructability, clarity, consistency and coordination in the documentation.

§ 4.10   Design Documentation[18]

Design documentation is prepared in the form for contracting (single or multiprime) as indicated in the CM plan. Design documentation is prepared and coordinated so as to permit such scheduling and sequencing of construction as required by the CM plan. During the bid and award phases, the design professional prepares addenda, attends conferences and determines the acceptability of substitutions.

§ 4.11   Design Professional's Basic Construction Phase Services[19]

The design professional is not obligated to visit the site to become generally familiar with the work.[20] During the construction phase, the design professional

---

[15] Under the AIA documents the CM provides estimates after the architect prepares design documents. The CM has less authority in controlling cost.

[16] CMAA A-4 ¶ 3.1.

[17] CMAA A-1 ¶¶ 3.3.1.5 and 3.3.1.6; CMAA A-4 ¶ 3.5.1.

[18] CMAA A-4 ¶ 3.8 and art. 4.

[19] CMAA A-4 art. 5.

[20] Under the AIA documents there is a duplication of authority and responsibility for inspecting the construction work. B141/CM requires the architect to visit the site periodically (¶ 1.5.4) to

visits the site as necessary in order to: render interpretations, determine the acceptability of substitutions, prepare design documents arising from change orders, review shop drawings and submittals, and prepare design documents arising from subsurface conditions.

§ 4.12　CM Determinations During the Construction Phase[21]

The CM determines contractor compliance with the contract documents and reviews and approves contractors' applications for payment.[22] Any coordination, scheduling, or sequencing of contractors' work that is required by the owner is the CM's responsibility to administer. The CM issues certificates of substantial and final completion.[23] The design professional provides as additional services those services resulting from significant changes in the general scope, extent or character of the project or its design as fixed in the CM plan, and in connection with certain visits to the site requested by the owner or CM.

CM'S LEADERSHIP ROLE

§ 4.13　During the Design Phase

The CMAA documents are innovative by defining the responsibilities between the CM and design professional in a system where the CM is entrusted by the owner to lead the process of design and construction. During the design phase, the CM's services relate principally to the following:

Matters of scheduling and coordination of the activities of all parties involved

Coordinating and expediting communications

Evaluation of constructability

Estimating and cost

Maintaining the project budget

Time and sequencing considerations related to designs developed by the design professional

---

determine generally that the work is proceeding according to the contract documents. B801 (¶ 1.2.7) requires the CM to determine in general that the work is performed according to the contract documents.

[21] CMAA A-1 ¶ 3.5; CMAA A-4 Art. 5 and Art. 6.

[22] Under the AIA documents the architect approves applications for payments while the CM is limited to making recommendations. B141/CM ¶ 1.5.7 and B801 ¶ 1.2.3.4.

[23] Under the AIA documents, the architect issues certificates of completion and the CM assists. *See* B141/CM ¶ 1.5.16 and B801 ¶ 1.2.14.

Recommendations as to the separation of the construction contracts into various categories of work

Commenting on clarity and consistency of the design documentations.

§ 4.14   During the Construction Phase

During the construction phase, the CM's services involve:

Serving as the owner's principal agent at the site

Project scheduling

Administering on the owner's behalf all of the prime contracts for construction

Monitoring the quality and quantity of the work

Monitoring cost and time considerations during construction

Coordinating and expediting of communications

Functioning as the initial arbiter of disputes between the owner and contractors concerning the work.

The CM has the obligation to determine during construction that the work is being completed in accordance with the contract documents. The CM will also determine the amounts owing to the contractors and issue a certificate for payment.

The design professional's services during the construction phase are limited. It is not intended by the CMAA documents that the design professional will, as a part of basic services, visit the site to become generally familiar with or check the quality or quantity of work, or to determine that the work is proceeding in accordance with the contract documents.[24]

As a part of its basic services provided in CMAA A-4, the design professional will during the construction phase perform certain services in connection with interpretations and clarifications, substitutions, change orders, submittals and subsurface and physical conditions. For example, ¶ 5.3 of the A-4 agreement provides:

> Upon receipt from the CM . . . of written requests for interpretation and clarifications of the Drawings, Specifications and other technical design related information, the Design Professional will review the same and issue (through the CM) in writing appropriate clarifications and interpretations.

Visits by the design professional to the site in addition to those necessary to enable the design professional to perform basic services in connection with the items specified above are treated as additional services. Other items of additional services, such as the design professional's participation in review or

---

[24] As is provided in AIA B141/CM ¶ 1.5.4.

approval of applications for payment, are described in Article 6 of the A-4 agreement.

§ 4.15   CM's Exposure to Liability

Along with the CM's leadership role and responsibility goes exposure for the CM to liability if the services are not performed properly.[25] Basic to the CMAA system is the belief that providing services and assuming authority while having clearly defined responsibilities allows the CM to more effectively gain control over the risks which create exposure to liability. For example, the management services provided by the CM in connection with the design schedule increase the likelihood that design documents will be developed and delivered without delaying construction.[26] The CM's obligation to certify amounts owing to contractors,[27] rather than "making recommendations to the architect for certification,"[28] enhances the CM's ability to require a contractor's compliance with the project schedule.

The scope of the design professional's construction phase administration services under the CMAA A-4 agreement are reduced compared to the scope provided in AIA B141/CM-1980. Consequently, the exposure to liability of the design professional during construction phase administration is reduced.

§ 4.16   Performance Standards of Care

The CMAA documents maintain the legal principle that the duty owed by the CM and design professional in their performance is measured by a "standard of care." The CM agrees to perform the services specified in the A-1 agreement with that degree of skill and judgment which can be reasonably expected from a similarly situated CM.[29] The design professional agrees as follows in the A-4 agreement: "The Design Professional will perform its services hereunder properly and in accordance with the standards of its profession."[30]

---

[25] Areas of liability exposure for the CM are not the subject of this chapter. Various publications and articles have thoroughly discussed the liability subject. *See, e.g.,* P. Partridge & V. Noletto, Jr., Construction Management Revisited: Evolving Roles and Exposures of Construction Managers and A/E's (V.O. Schinnerer & Co.'s 27th Annual Meeting of Invited Attorneys, 1988). For a collection of articles concerning CM liability, *see also Construction Management and Design-Build/Fast Track Construction,* 46 Law & Contemp. Probs. 1 (1983), Duke University School of Law.

[26] CMAA A-1 ¶¶ 3.2.2.2 and 3.3.2.2.

[27] CMAA A-1 ¶ 3.5.3.6.

[28] As is provided in AIA B801 ¶ 1.2.3.4.

[29] CMAA A-1 ¶ 1.1.1.

[30] CMAA A-4 ¶ 2.5.

Neither the CM nor the design professional warrant or guarantee perfect results. Whether the CM or design professional has performed according to the required standard of care will be determined by a variety of factors such as the manner in which professionals generally perform, experience, and the requirements of the contract and the project.

§ 4.17   Professional Liability Insurance Coverage

Professional liability insurance policies appear to cover the services of architects or engineers performing as construction managers.[31] However, the policies exclude coverage for construction activities.[32]

How the policies would apply if an architect/engineer (A/E) contracted to provide CM services under the CMAA documents would depend on the scope and extent of the agreement between the owner and the CM. Under the CMAA A-1 agreement where the CM acts as the agent of the owner, an architect or engineer performing CM services does not assume responsibility for construction activity. The A-1 agreement specifies that:

> [N]othing in this Agreement shall be construed to mean that the CM assumes any of the responsibilities or duties of the Contractors. . . . The Contractors are solely responsible for the construction means, methods, techniques, sequence and procedures used in the construction of the Project.[33]

Thus, it appears that the A/E providing services under the CMAA A-1 agreement would have coverage. It must be noted, however, that current professional liability policies are not generally available to those performing CM services who are not licensed as architects or engineers. The CMAA has identified a demand for errors and omissions type coverage for CMs who are not licensed as architects or engineers. Efforts are under way through CMAA to investigate the availability of coverage in such situations if the insured utilizes the CMAA documents.

---

[31] For example, CNA Policy 1-87503-A (Ed. 8/83). The policy states coverage for negligent acts arising out of the performance of or failure to perform professional services." Professional services" include those services which one is legally qualified to perform for others in the capacity as a construction manager. IV. Definitions. The term "professional services" as stated in a policy written by Continental Casualty Company has been interpreted to include the services of an architect who was alleged to be "in charge of" construction at the jobsite, and whose jobsite activities were argued to be more in the nature of a "design/build architect" rather than a traditional architect." United States Fidelity & Guar. Co. v. Continental Casualty Co., 505 N.E.2d 1072 (Ill. App. Ct. 1987).

[32] Exclusions, A.9.

[33] CMAA A-1 ¶ 1.4.

§ 4.18   CMAA A-1 Standard Form of Agreement Between Owner and Construction Manager

THE CONSTRUCTION MANAGEMENT ASSOCIATION OF AMERICA, INC.

CMAA Document No. A-1 (1990 edition)

Standard Form of Agreement Between
<u>OWNER and CONSTRUCTION MANAGER</u>

(Construction Manager as Owner's Agent)

This document is to be used in connection with the Standard Form of Contract Between OWNER and CONTRACTOR (CMAA Document No. A-2), the General Conditions of the Construction Contract (CMAA Document No. A-3), and the Standard Form of Agreement Between OWNER and DESIGN PROFESSIONAL (CMAA Document No. A-4), (all being 1990 editions).

<u>CONSULTATION WITH AN ATTORNEY IS RECOMMENDED WHENEVER THIS DOCUMENT IS USED.</u>

AGREEMENT
made this   day of   the year Nineteen
Hundred and

BETWEEN the Owner:

and the Construction Manager:

For services in connection with the Project known as:

as further described in Article 2.

The Owner and Construction Manager, (hereinafter referred to as the "CM"), in consideration of their mutual covenants herein agree as set forth below:

1

(Page intentionally left blank.)

SAMPLE AGREEMENT

72

TABLE OF CONTENTS
CMAA Document No. A-1 (1990 edition)

Article:

1. Relationship of the Parties 5
2. Project Definition 5
3. Construction Manager's Basic Services 6
4. Duration of the Construction Manager's Services ....:................................... 15
5. Changes in the Construction Manager's Basic Services and Compensation 15
6. Owner's Responsibilities 16
7. Compensation for CM Services and Payment 17
8. Insurance and Mutual Indemnity 20
9. Termination and Suspension 21
10. Dispute Resolution 22
11. Additional Provisions 23

(Page intentionally left blank.)

SAMPLE AGREEMENT

CMAA Document No. A-1 (1990 edition)

ARTICLE 1
RELATIONSHIP OF THE PARTIES

1.1 Owner and Construction Manager

The CM shall be the Owner's agent in providing the Construction Manager's Services described in Article 3 of this Agreement. The CM and the Owner shall perform as stated in this Agreement and each CM and Owner accepts the relationship of trust and confidence between them, which is established herein.

1.1.1 Standard of Care

The CM covenants with the Owner to furnish its services hereunder properly, in accordance with the standards of its profession, and in accordance with applicable federal, state and local laws and regulations which are in effect on the date of this Agreement first written above.

1.2 Owner and Design Professional

The Owner shall enter into a separate agreement, the "Owner-Design Professional Agreement", with one or more Design Professionals to provide for the design of the Project and certain design-related services during the Construction Phase of the Project. The Project is defined in Article 2 of this Agreement. The Owner shall not change the Owner-Design Professional Agreement in any way that is prejudicial to the CM. If the Owner terminates the Design Professional's services, a substitute acceptable to the CM shall be appointed.

1.3 Owner and Contractors

The Owner shall enter into a separate contract with one or more Contractors for the construction of the Project.

1.4 Relationship of the CM to Other Project Participants

In providing the Construction Manager's Services described in this Agreement, the CM shall endeavor to maintain a working relationship with the Contractors and Design Professional on behalf of the Owner. However, nothing in this Agreement shall be construed to mean that the CM assumes any of the responsibilities or duties of the Contractors or the Design Professional. The Contractors will be solely responsible for construction means, methods, techniques, sequence and procedures used in the construction of the Project and for the safety of its personnel, property, and its operations and for performing in accordance with the Contractor's contract with the Owner. The Design Professional is solely responsible for the design requirements and design criteria of the Project and shall perform in accordance with the agreement between the Design Professional and the Owner. The CM's services shall be rendered compatibly and in cooperation with the Design Professional's services under the Owner-Design Professional Agreement. It is not intended that the services of the Design Professional and the CM be competitive or duplicative, but rather be complementary. The CM will be entitled to rely upon the Design Professional for the proper performance of services undertaken by the Design Professional pursuant to the Owner-Design Professional Agreement.

ARTICLE 2
PROJECT DEFINITION

2.1 The term "Project", when used in this Agreement, shall mean the total construction to be performed under this Agreement.

2.2 The Project name and locations are as follows:

_____
_____
_____
_____
_____ .

2.3 The Project is intended for use as: _____
_____
_____
_____
_____
_____ .

5

CMAA Document No. A-1 (1990 edition)

ARTICLE 3
CONSTRUCTION MANAGER'S
BASIC SERVICES

3.1 CM Basic Services

The CM shall perform the Basic Services described in this Article. It is not required that the Basic Services be performed in the sequence in which they are described.

3.2 Pre-Design Phase

3.2.1 Project Management

3.2.1.1 Construction Management Plan: The CM shall prepare a Construction Management Plan for the Project. In preparing the Construction Management Plan, the CM shall consider the Owner's schedule, cost and general design requirements for the Project. The CM shall then develop various alternatives for the sequencing and management of the Project and shall make recommendations to the Owner. The Construction Management Plan shall also include a description of the various Bid Packages recommended for the Project. The Construction Management Plan shall be presented to the Owner for acceptance.

3.2.1.2 Design Professional Selection: The CM shall assist the Owner in the selection of a Design Professional by developing lists of potential firms, developing criteria for selection, preparing and transmitting the requests for proposal, assisting in reviewing written proposals, assisting in conducting interviews, evaluating candidates and making recommendations.

3.2.1.3 Design Professional Contract Preparation: The CM shall assist the Owner in review and preparation of the Agreement between the Owner and Design Professional.

3.2.1.4 Design Professional Orientation: The CM shall conduct, or assist the Owner in conducting, a Design Professional orientation session during which the Design Professional shall receive information regarding Project, schedules, costs and administrative requirements.

3.2.2 Time Management

3.2.2.1 Master Schedule: In accordance with the Construction Management Plan, the CM shall prepare a Master Schedule for each component of the Project. The Master Schedule shall specify the proposed starting and finishing dates for each contract and the dates by which certain construction activities must be complete. The CM shall submit the Master Schedule to the Owner for acceptance.

3.2.2.2 Design Phase Milestone Schedule: After the Owner accepts the Master Schedule the CM shall prepare the Milestone Schedule for the Design Phase, which shall be a method for judging progress during the Design Phase.

3.2.3 Cost Management

3.2.3.1 Construction Market Survey: The CM shall conduct a Construction Market Survey to provide current information regarding the general availability of local construction services, labor, material and equipment cost and the economic factors related to the construction of the Project. A report of the Construction Market Survey shall be provided to the Owner and the Design Professional.

3.2.3.2 Project and Construction Budget: Based on the Construction Management Plan and the Construction Market Survey, the CM shall prepare a Project and Construction Budget based on separate division of the Work required for the Project. The CM shall review the budget with the Owner and Design Professional and the CM shall submit the Project and Construction Budget to the Owner for acceptance. The Project and Construction Budget shall be revised as directed by the Owner.

3.2.3.3 Cost Analysis: The CM shall analyze and report to the Owner and the Design Professional the cost of various design and construction alternatives. As a part of the cost analysis, the CM shall consider costs related to efficiency, usable life, maintenance, energy and operation.

6

CMAA Document No. A-1 (1990 edition)

3.2.4 Management Information System (MIS)

3.2.4.1 Establishing the Project MIS: The CM shall develop a MIS in order to establish communication between the Owner, CM, Design Professional, Contractor and other parties on the Project. In developing the MIS, the CM shall interview the Owner's key personnel, the Design Professional and others in order to determine the type of information for reporting, the reporting format and the desired frequency for distribution of the various reports.

3.2.4.2 Design Phase Procedures: As a part of the MIS the CM shall establish procedures for reporting, communications and administration during the Design Phase.

3.3 Design Phase

3.3.1 Project Management

3.3.1.1 Revisions to the Construction Management Plan: During the Design Phase the CM shall make recommendations to the Owner regarding revisions to the Construction Management Plan. Revisions approved by the Owner shall be incorporated into the Construction Management Plan and accepted by the Owner.

3.3.1.2 Project Conference: At the start of the Design Phase, the CM shall conduct a Project Conference attended by the Design Professional, the Owner and others. During the Project Conference the CM shall review the Construction Management Plan, the Master Schedule, Design Phase Milestone Schedule, the Project and Construction Budget and the MIS.

3.3.1.3 Design Phase Information: The CM shall monitor the Design Professional's compliance with the Construction Management Plan and the MIS and the CM shall coordinate and expedite the flow of information between the Owner, Design Professional and others.

3.3.1.4 Project Meetings: The CM shall conduct periodic Project meetings attended by the Owner, Design Professional and others. Such meetings shall serve as a forum for the exchange of information concerning the Project and the review of design progress. The CM shall prepare and distribute minutes of these meetings to the Owner, Design Professional and others.

3.3.1.5 Review of Design Documents: The CM shall review the design documents and make recommendations to the Owner and Design Professional as to constructibility, as to cost, sequencing, scheduling and time of construction, as to clarity, consistency and coordination of documentation among Contractors, and as to the separation of the Project into construction contracts for various categories of the Work. The recommendations resulting from such review will be provided to the Owner and Design Professional in writing and as notations on the design documents.

3.3.1.6 Limitations on the CM's Review and Recommendations: In making reviews and recommendations as to design documentation or design matters the CM shall not be responsible for providing nor will the CM have control over the Project design, design requirements, design criteria or the substance or contents of the design documents. By performing the reviews and making recommendations described herein, the CM shall not be acting in a manner so as to assume responsibility or liability, in whole or in part, for any aspect of the project design, design requirements, design criteria or the substance or contents of the design documents. The CM's actions in making such reviews and recommendations as provided herein are to be advisory only to the Owner and to the Design Professional.

3.3.1.7 Owner's Design Reviews: The CM shall expedite the Owner's design reviews by compiling and conveying the Owner's comments to the Design Professional.

3.3.1.8 Approvals by Regulatory Agencies: The CM shall coordinate transmittal of documents to regulatory agencies for review and shall advise the Owner of potential problems in completion of such reviews.

3.3.1.9 General Conditions: The General Conditions to the Contract Documents for the Project shall be CMAA Document No. A-3. Separate General Conditions for materials and for equipment procurement shall be

7

CMAA Document No. A-1 (1990 edition)

prepared by the CM to meet the specific requirements of the Project.

3.3.1.10 Project Funding: The CM shall assist the Owner in preparing documents concerning the Project and Construction Budget for use in obtaining or reporting on Project funding. The documents shall be prepared in a form approved by the Owner.

3.3.2 Time Management

3.3.2.1 Revisions to the Master Schedule: While performing the services provided in Paragraphs 3.3.1.1, 3.3.1.2 and as necessary throughout the Design Phase, the CM shall recommend revisions to the Master Schedule. The Owner shall issue, as needed, change orders to the appropriate parties to implement the Master Schedule revisions.

3.3.2.2 Monitoring the Design Phase Milestone Schedule: While performing the services provided in Paragraphs 3.3.1.3 and 3.3.1.4, the CM shall monitor compliance with the Design Phase Milestone Schedule.

3.3.2.3 Pre-Bid Construction Schedules: Prior to transmitting Contract Documents to bidders, the CM shall prepare a Pre-Bid Construction Schedule for each part of the Project and make the schedule available to the bidders during the Bid and Award Phase.

3.3.3 Cost Management Task

3.3.3.1 Project and Construction Budget Revision: The CM shall make recommendations to the Owner concerning design changes that may result in revisions to the Project and Construction Budget and divisions of the Work required for the Project.

3.3.3.2 Cost Control: The CM shall prepare an estimate of the construction cost for each submittal of design drawings and specifications from the Design Professional. This estimate shall include a contingency acceptable to the Owner, CM and the Design Professional for construction costs appropriate for the type and location of the Project and the extent to which the design has progressed. The Owner recognizes that the CM will perform in

accordance with the standard of care established in this Agreement and that the CM has no control over the costs of labor, materials, equipment or services furnished by others, or over the Contractors' methods of determining prices, or over competitive bidding or market prices. Accordingly, the CM does not guarantee that proposals, bids or actual construction costs will not vary from budget figures included in the Construction Management Plan as amended from time to time. If the budget figure is exceeded the Owner will give written consent to increasing the budget, or authorize negotiations or rebidding of the Project within a reasonable time, or cooperate with the CM and Design Professional in revising the Project's general scope, extent or character in keeping with the Project's requirements and sound design practices, or modify the requirements appropriately. Instead of the foregoing, the Owner may abandon the Project and terminate this Agreement in accordance with Article 9. The estimate for each submittal shall be accompanied by a report to the Owner and Design Professional identifying variances from the Project and Construction Budget. The CM shall coordinate and expedite the activities of the Owner and Design Professional when changes to the design are required to remain within the Project and Construction Budget.

3.3.3.3 Value Analysis Studies: The CM shall provide value analysis studies on major construction components. The results of these studies shall be in report form and shall be distributed to the Owner and Design Professional.

3.3.4 Management Information Systems (MIS)

3.3.4.1 Schedule Reports: In conjunction with the services provided by Paragraph 3.3.2.1, the CM shall prepare and distribute Schedule Maintenance Reports that shall compare actual progress with scheduled progress for the Design Phase and the overall Project.

3.3.4.2 Project Cost Reports: The CM shall prepare and distribute Project Cost Reports that shall indicate estimated costs compared to the Project and Construction Budget.

SAMPLE AGREEMENT

3.3.4.3 Cash Flow Report: The CM shall periodically prepare and distribute a Cash Flow Report.

3.3.4.4 Design Phase Change Order Report: The CM shall prepare and distribute Design Phase Change Order Reports that shall list all Owner-approved change orders as of the date of the report and shall state the effect of the change orders on the Project and Construction Budget and the Master Schedule.

3.4 Bid and Award Phase

3.4.1 Project Management

3.4.1.1 Prequalifying Bidders: The CM shall assist the Owner in developing lists of possible bidders and in prequalifying bidders. This service shall include the following: preparation and distribution of questionnaires; receiving and analyzing completed questionnaires; interviewing possible bidders, bonding agents and financial institutions; and preparing recommendations for the Owner. The CM shall prepare a bidders list for each bid package.

3.4.1.2 Bidder's Interest Campaign: The CM shall conduct a telephonic and correspondence campaign to attempt to increase interest among qualified bidders.

3.4.1.3 Notices and Advertisements: The CM shall assist the Owner in preparing and placing notices and advertisements to solicit bids for the Project.

3.4.1.4 Delivery of Bid Documents: The CM shall expedite the delivery of Bid Documents to the bidders. The CM shall obtain the documents from the Design Professional and arrange for printing, binding, wrapping and delivery to the bidders. The CM shall maintain a list of bidders receiving Bid Documents.

3.4.1.5 Pre-bid Conference: In conjunction with the Owner and Design Professional, the CM shall conduct Pre-bid Conferences. These conferences shall be forums for the Owner, CM and Design Professional to explain the Project requirements to the bidders, including information concerning schedule requirements, time and cost control requirements, access requirements, the Owner's administrative requirements and technical information.

3.4.1.6 Information to Bidders: The CM shall develop and coordinate procedures to provide answers to bidders' questions. All answers shall be in the form of Addenda.

3.4.1.7 Addenda: The CM shall receive from the Design Professional a copy of all Addenda. The CM shall review Addenda for constructibility, for effect on the Project and Construction Budget, sequencing and time of construction, and for clarity and coordination in documentation. The CM shall distribute a copy of all Addenda to each bidder receiving documents.

3.4.1.8 Bid Opening and Recommendations: The CM shall assist the Owner in the bid opening and shall evaluate the bids for responsiveness and price. The CM shall make recommendations to the Owner concerning the acceptance or rejection of bids.

3.4.1.9 Post-bid Conference: The CM shall conduct a Post-bid Conference to review contract award procedures, schedules, Project staffing and other pertinent issues.

3.4.1.10 Construction Contracts: The CM shall assist the Owner in the assembly, delivery and execution of the Contract Documents. The CM shall issue to the Contractors the Notice of Award and the Notice to Proceed on behalf of the Owner.

3.4.2 Time Management

3.4.2.1 Pre-bid Construction Schedule: The CM shall emphasize to the bidders their responsibilities regarding the Pre-bid Construction Schedule specified in the Instructions to Bidders or the Contract Documents.

3.4.2.2 Contractor's Construction Schedule: The CM shall provide a copy of the Master Schedule to the bidders.

3.4.3 Cost Management

3.4.3.1 Estimates for Addenda: The CM shall prepare an estimate of costs for all Addenda and shall submit a copy of the estimate to the Design Professional and to the Owner for approval.

CMAA Document No. A-1 (1990 edition)

3.4.3.2 Analyzing Bids: Upon receipt of the bids, the CM shall evaluate the bids, including alternate prices and unit prices, and shall make a recommendation to the Owner in regard to the award of each construction contract.

3.4.4 Management Information System (MIS)

3.4.4.1 Schedule Maintenance Reports: The CM shall prepare and distribute Schedule Maintenance Reports during the Bid and Award Phase. The Reports shall compare the actual bid and award dates to scheduled bid and award dates and shall summarize the progress of the Project.

3.4.4.2 Project Cost Reports: The CM shall prepare and distribute Project Cost Reports during the Bid and Award Phase. The Reports shall specify actual award prices and construction costs for the Project compared to the Project and Construction Budget.

3.4.4.3 Cash Flow Reports: The CM shall prepare and distribute Cash Flow Reports during the Bid and Award Phase. The Reports shall be based on actual award prices and construction costs for the Project and the Reports shall specify actual cash flow compared to projected cash flow.

3.5 Construction Phase

3.5.1 Project Management

3.5.1.1 Pre-Construction Conference: In consultation with the Owner and Design Professional, the CM shall conduct a Pre-Construction Conference during which the CM shall review the Project reporting procedures and other rules.

3.5.1.2 Permits, Bonds and Insurance: The CM shall verify that the required permits, bonds, and insurance, have been obtained. Such action by the CM shall not relieve the Contractor of its responsibility to comply with the provisions of the Contract Documents.

3.5.1.3 On-Site Management and Construction Phase Communication Procedures: The CM shall provide and maintain a management team on the Project site to provide contract administration as an agent of the Owner and the CM shall establish and implement coordination and communication procedures among the CM, Owner, Design Professional and Contractors.

3.5.1.4 Construction Administration Procedures: The CM shall establish and implement procedures for reviewing and processing requests for clarifications and interpretations of the Contract Documents; shop drawings, samples and other submittals; contract schedule adjustments; change order proposals; written proposals for substitutions; payment applications; and the maintenance of logs. As the Owner's representative at the construction site, the CM shall be the party to whom all such information shall be submitted.

3.5.1.5 Review of Requests for Information, Shop Drawings, Samples, and Other Submittals: The CM shall review the Contractors' requests for information, shop drawings, samples, and other submittals to determine the anticipated effect on compliance with the Project requirements, the Project and Construction Budget, and the Master Schedule. The CM shall forward to the Design Professional for review the request for clarification or interpretation, shop drawing, sample, or other submittal, along with the CM's comments. The CM's comments shall not relate to design considerations, but rather to matters of constructibility, cost, sequencing, scheduling and time of construction, and clarity, consistency, and coordination in documentation. The CM shall receive from the Design Professional, and transmit to the Contractor, all information so received from the Design Professional.

3.5.1.6 Project Site Meetings: Periodically the CM shall conduct meetings at the Project site with each Contractor and the CM shall conduct coordination meetings with all Contractors, the Owner and the Design Professional. The CM shall record, transcribe and distribute minutes to all attendees, the Owner and Design Professional.

3.5.1.7 Coordination of Other Independent Consultants: Technical inspection and testing provided by others shall be coordinated by the CM. The CM shall receive a copy of all inspection and

10

CMAA Document No. A-1 (1990 edition)

testing reports on the day of the inspection or test. The CM will not be responsible for providing, nor will the CM control, the actual performance of technical inspection and testing. The CM is performing a coordination function only and the CM is not acting in a manner so as to assume responsibility or liability, in whole or in part, for all or any part of such inspection and testing.

3.5.1.8 <u>Minor Variations in the Work</u>: The CM may authorize minor variations in the Work from the requirements of the Contract Documents that do not involve an adjustment in the contract price or the contract time and which are consistent with the overall intent of the Contract Documents. The CM shall provide to the Design Professional copies of such authorizations.

3.5.1.9 <u>Change Orders</u>: The CM shall establish and implement a change order control system. All changes to the Contract between the Owner and Contractor shall be only by change orders executed by the Owner.

3.5.1.9.1 All proposed Owner-initiated changes shall first be described in detail by the CM in a request for a proposal issued to the Contractor. The request shall be accompanied by drawings and specifications prepared by the Design Professional. In response to the request for a proposal, the Contractor shall submit to the CM for evaluation detailed information concerning the price and time adjustments, if any, as may be necessary to perform the proposed change order Work. The CM shall review the Contractor's proposal, shall discuss the proposed change order with the Contractor, and endeavor to determine the Contractor's basis for the price and time proposed to perform the Work.

3.5.1.9.2 The CM shall review the contents of all Contractor-requested changes to the contract time or price, endeavor to determine the cause of the requests, and assemble and evaluate information concerning the request. The CM shall provide to the Design Professional a copy of the change requests, and the CM shall consider the Design Professional's comments regarding the proposed changes in the CM's evaluations of the Contractors' requests.

3.5.1.9.3 The CM shall make recommendations to the Owner regarding all proposed change orders. At the Owner's direction, the CM shall prepare and issue to the Contractor appropriate change order documents. The CM shall provide to the Design Professional copies of all approved change orders.

3.5.1.10 <u>Subsurface and Physical Conditions</u>: Whenever the Contractor notifies the CM that a surface or subsurface condition at or contiguous to the site is encountered that differs from what the Contractor is entitled to rely upon or from what is indicated or referred to in the Contract Documents, or that may require a change in the Contract Documents, the CM shall notify the Design Professional. The CM shall receive from the Design Professional and transmit to the Contractor all information necessary to reflect any design changes required to be responsive to the differing or changed condition and, if necessary, shall prepare a change order as indicated in Paragraph 3.5.1.9.

3.5.1.11 <u>Quality Review</u>: The CM shall establish and implement a program to monitor the quality of the construction. The purpose of the program shall be to assist in guarding the Owner against defects and deficiency in the Work of the Contractors. The CM shall reject Work and transmit to the Owner and Contractor a notice of nonconforming Work when it is the opinion of the CM, Owner or Design Professional that the Work does not conform to the requirements of the Contract Documents. Except for minor variations as described in Paragraph 3.5.1.8, the CM is not authorized to change, revoke, alter, enlarge, relax or release any requirements of the Contract Documents or to approve or accept any portion of the Work not performed in accordance with the Contract Documents. Communication between the CM and Contractor with regard to Quality Review shall not in any way be construed as binding the CM or Owner as releasing the Contractor from the fulfillment of any of the terms of his Contract Documents. The CM will not be responsible for, nor does the CM control, the means, methods, techniques, sequences and procedures of construction for the Project. It is understood that the CM's action in providing Quality Review as stated herein is a service to the Owner and by performing as

11

CMAA Document No. A-1 (1990 edition)

provided herein, the CM is not acting in a manner so as to assume responsibility or liability, in whole or in part, for all or any part of the construction Work for the Project. No action taken by the CM shall relieve any or all of the Contractors from their obligation to perform their work in strict conformity with the Contract Documents and in strict conformity with all other applicable laws, rules and regulations.

3.5.1.12 Contractor's Safety Program: The CM shall require each Contractor that will perform Work at the site to prepare and submit to the CM for general review a safety program, as required by the Contract Documents. The CM shall review each safety program to determine that the programs of the various prime Contractors performing Work at the site, as submitted, provide for coordination among the Contractors of their respective programs. The CM shall not be responsible for any Contractor's implementation of or compliance with its safety programs or for initiating, maintaining, monitoring or supervising the implementation of such programs or the procedures and precautions associated therewith, or for the coordination of any of the above with the other prime Contractors performing the Work at the site. The CM shall not be responsible for the adequacy or completeness of any Contractor's safety programs, procedures or precautions.

3.5.1.13 Disputes Between Contractor and Owner: The CM shall render within a reasonable time decisions in writing concerning disputes between the Contractor and the Owner relating to the acceptability of the Work, or the interpretation of the requirements of the Contract Documents pertaining to the performance and furnishing of the Work.

3.5.1.14 Operation and Maintenance Materials: The CM shall receive from the Contractor operation and maintenance manuals, warranties and guarantees for materials and equipment installed in the Project. The CM shall deliver this information to the Owner and provide a copy of the information to the Design Professional.

3.5.1.15 Substantial Completion: The CM shall determine when the Project and a Contractor's Work is substantially complete. In consultation with the Design Professional, the CM shall, prior to issuing a Certificate of Substantial Completion, prepare a list of incomplete Work or Work which does not conform to the Contract Documents. This list shall be attached to the Certificate of Substantial Completion.

3.5.1.16 Final Completion: In consultation with the Design Professional, the CM shall determine when the Project and the Contractor's Work is finally completed, shall issue a Certificate of Final Completion and shall provide to the Owner a written recommendation regarding payment to the Contractor.

3.5.2 Time Management

3.5.2.1 Master Schedule: The CM shall adjust and update the Master Schedule and distribute copies to the Owner and Design Professional. Adjustments to the Master Schedule shall be made for the benefit of the Project.

3.5.2.2 Contractor's Construction Schedule: The CM shall review each Contractor's Construction Schedule and shall verify that the schedule is prepared in accordance with the requirements of the Contract Documents and that it establishes completion dates that comply with the requirements of the Master Schedule.

3.5.2.3 Construction Schedule Report: The CM shall, on a monthly basis, review the progress of construction of each Contractor, shall evaluate the percentage complete of each construction activity as indicated in each Contractors' Construction Schedule and shall review such percentages with each Contractor. This evaluation shall serve as data for input to the periodic Construction Schedule Report that shall be prepared and distributed to the Contractor, Owner and Design Professional by the CM. The Report shall indicate the actual progress compared to scheduled progress and shall serve as the basis for the progress payments to the Contractors. The CM shall advise and make recommendations to the Owner concerning the alternative courses of action that the Owner may take in its efforts to achieve contract compliance by the Contractor.

12

CMAA Document No. A-1 (1990 edition)

3.5.2.4 Effect of Change Orders on the Schedule: Prior to the issuance of a change order, the CM shall determine and advise the Owner as to the effect on the Master Schedule of the change. The CM shall verify that Work activities and adjustments of time, if any, required by approved change orders have been incorporated into the Contractors' Construction Schedule.

3.5.2.5 Recovery Schedules: The CM may require the Contractor to prepare and submit a Recovery Schedule, as specified in the Contract Documents.

3.5.3 Cost Management

3.5.3.1 Schedule of Values (Each Contract): The CM shall, in participation with the Contractors, determine a Schedule of Values for each of the construction contracts. The Schedule of Values shall be the basis for the allocation of the contract price to the activities shown on the Contractor's Construction Schedule.

3.5.3.2 Allocation of Cost to the Contractor's Construction Schedule: The Contractor's Construction Schedule shall have the total contract price allocated among the Contractor's scheduled activities so that each of the Contractor's activities shall be allocated a price and the sum of the prices of the activities shall equal the total contract price. The CM shall review the contract price allocations and verify that such allocations are made in accordance with the requirements of the Contract Documents. Progress payments to the Contractor shall be based on the Contractor's percentage of completion of the scheduled activities as set out in the Construction Schedule Reports and the Contractor's compliance with the requirements of the Contract Documents.

3.5.3.3 Effect of Change Orders on Cost: The CM shall advise the Owner as to the effect on the Project and Construction Budget of all proposed and approved change orders.

3.5.3.4 Cost Records: In instances when a lump sum or unit price is not determined prior to the Owner's authorization to the Contractors to perform change order Work, the CM shall request from the Contractors records of the cost of payroll, materials and equipment and the amount of payments to subcontractor's incurred by the Contractor in performing the Work.

3.5.3.5 Trade-off Studies: The CM shall provide Trade-off Studies for various minor construction components. The results of the Trade-off Studies shall be in report form and distributed to the Owner and Design Professional.

3.5.3.6 Progress Payments: The CM shall review the payment applications submitted by each Contractor and determine whether the amount requested reflects the progress of the Contractor's work. The CM shall make appropriate adjustments to each payment application and shall prepare and forward to the Owner a Progress Payment Report. The Report shall state the total contract price, payments to date, current payment requested, retainage and actual amounts owed for the current period. Included in this report shall be a Certificate of Payment that shall be signed by the CM and delivered to the Owner.

3.5.4 Management Information System (MIS)

3.5.4.1 Schedule Maintenance Reports: The CM shall prepare and distribute Schedule Maintenance Reports during the Construction Phase. The Reports shall compare the actual construction dates to scheduled construction dates of each separate contract and to the Master Schedule for the Project.

3.5.4.2 Project Cost Reports: The CM shall prepare and distribute Project Cost Reports during the Construction Phase. The Reports shall specify actual Project and construction costs compared to the Project and Construction Budget.

3.5.4.3 Project and Construction Budget Revisions: The CM shall make recommendations to the Owner concerning changes that may result in revisions to the Project and Construction Budget. Copies of the recommendations shall be sent to the Design Professional.

3.5.4.4 Cash Flow Reports: The CM shall periodically prepare and distribute Cash Flow Reports

13

CMAA Document No. A-1 (1990 edition)

during the Construction Phase. The Reports shall specify actual cash flow as compared to projected cash flow.

3.5.4.5 Progress Payment Reports (Each Contract): The CM shall prepare and distribute the Progress Payment Reports. The Reports shall state the total construction contract price, payment to date, current payment requested, retainage and actual amounts owed this period. A portion of this Report shall be a Certificate of Payment that shall be signed by the CM and delivered to the Owner for use by the Owner in making payments to the Contractor.

3.5.4.6 Change Order Reports: The CM shall periodically prepare and distribute Change Order Reports during the Construction Phase. The Report shall list all Owner-approved change orders by number, a brief description of the change order work, the cost established in the change order and percent of completion of the change order work.

3.6 Post-Construction Phase

3.6.1 Project Management

3.6.1.1 Record Documents: The CM shall coordinate and expedite submittals of information from the Contractors for record drawings and specification preparation and shall coordinate and expedite the transmittal of Record Documents to the Owner.

3.6.1.2 Organize and Index Operation and Maintenance Materials: Prior to the Final Completion of the Project, the CM shall compile manufacturers' operations and maintenance manuals, warranties and guarantees and bind such documents in an organized manner.

3.6.1.3 Occupancy Permit: The CM shall assist the Owner in obtaining an Occupancy Permit by accompanying governmental officials during inspections of the Project, preparing and submitting documentation to governmental agencies and coordinating final testing and other activities.

3.6.2 Time Management

3.6.2.1 Occupancy Plan: The CM shall prepare an Occupancy Plan that shall include a schedule for relocation for furniture, equipment and the Owner's personnel. This schedule shall be provided to the Owner.

3.6.3 Cost Management

3.6.3.1 Change Orders: The CM shall continue to provide services related to change orders as specified in Paragraph 3.5.3.3 during the Post-Construction Phase.

3.6.4 Management Information Systems (MIS)

3.6.4.1 Close-out Reports: At the conclusion of the Project, the CM shall prepare final Project accounting and close-out reports.

3.6.4.2 MIS Reports for Move-in and Occupancy: The CM shall prepare and distribute reports associated with the Occupancy Plan.

3.7 Additional Services

3.7.1 At the request of the Owner, the CM shall perform Additional Services and the CM shall be compensated for same as provided in Article 7 of this Agreement. The CM shall perform Additional Services only after the Owner and CM have executed a written Amendment to this Agreement providing such services. Additional Services may include:

3.7.1.1 Services during the Design or Construction Phases related to investigation, appraisal or evaluation of surface or subsurface conditions at or contiguous to the site, or other existing conditions, facilities, or equipment that differs from what is indicated in the Contract Documents, or determination of the accuracy of existing drawings or other information furnished by the Owner;

14

CMAA Document No. A-1 (1990 edition)

3.7.1.2 Services related to the procurement, storage, maintenance and installation of the Owner-furnished equipment, materials, supplies and furnishings;

3.7.1.3 Services related to determination of space needs;

3.7.1.4 Preparation of space programs;

3.7.1.5 Services related to building site investigations and analysis;

3.7.1.6 Services related to tenant or rental spaces;

3.7.1.7 Preparation of a Project financial feasibility study;

3.7.1.8 Preparation of financial, accounting or MIS reports not provided under Basic Services;

3.7.1.9 Performance of technical inspection and testing;

3.7.1.10 Preparation of an Operations and Maintenance Manual;

3.7.1.11 Services related to recruiting and training of maintenance personnel;

3.7.1.12 Services provided in respect of a dispute between the Owner and the Contractor after the CM has rendered its decision thereon in accordance with Paragraph 3.5.1.13;

3.7.1.13 Performing warranty inspections during the warranty period of the Project;

3.7.1.14 Consultation regarding replacement of Work damaged by fire or other cause during construction and furnishing services in connection with the replacement of such work;

3.7.1.15 Services made necessary by the default of the Contractor;

3.7.1.16 Preparation for and serving as a witness in connection with any public or private hearing or arbitration, mediation or legal proceeding;

3.7.1.17 Assisting the Owner in public relations activities, including preparing information for and attending public meetings; and

3.7.1.18 Services related to move-in including preparing and soliciting responses to requests for proposals, preparing and coordinating the execution of contracts, conducting pre-moving conferences, administering the contract for moving activities in conjunction with move-in for the Project and providing on-site personnel to oversee the relocation of furniture and equipment by the movers while actual move-in is in progress.

ARTICLE 4
DURATION OF THE CONSTRUCTION MANAGER'S SERVICES

4.1 The commencement date for the CM's Basic Services shall be the date of the execution of this Agreement.

4.2 The duration of the CM's Basic Services under this Agreement shall be _____ consecutive calendar days from the commencement date.

ARTICLE 5
CHANGES IN THE CONSTRUCTION MANAGER'S BASIC SERVICES AND COMPENSATION

5.1 <u>Owner Changes</u>

5.1.1 The Owner, without invalidating this Agreement, may make changes in the CM's Basic Services specified in Article 3 of this Agreement. The CM shall promptly notify the Owner of changes that increase or decrease the CM's compensation or the duration of the CM's Basic Services or both.

15

CMAA Document No. A-1 (1990 edition)

5.1.2 If the scope or the duration of the CM's Basic Services is changed, the CM's compensation shall be adjusted equitably. A written proposal indicating the change in compensation for a change in the scope or duration of Basic Services shall be given by the CM to the Owner within thirty (30) days of the occurrence of the event giving rise to such request. The amount of the change in compensation to be paid shall be determined on the basis of the CM's cost and a customary and reasonable adjustment in the CM's fixed, lump sum, or factor fee consistent with the provisions of Article 7.

5.2 Authorization

Changes in CM's Basic Services and entitlement to additional compensation or a change in duration of this Agreement shall be made by a written amendment to this Agreement executed by the Owner and the CM. The amendment shall be executed by the Owner and CM prior to the CM performing the services required by the amendment. The CM shall proceed to perform the services required by the amendment only after receiving written notice directing the CM to proceed.

5.3 Invoices for Additional Compensation: The CM shall submit invoices for additional compensation with its invoice for Basic Services and payment shall be made pursuant to the provisions of Article 7 of this Agreement.

ARTICLE 6
OWNER'S RESPONSIBILITIES

6.1 The Owner shall provide to the CM complete information regarding the Owner's knowledge of and requirements for the Project. The Owner shall be responsible for the accuracy and completeness of all reports, data, and other information furnished pursuant to Paragraph 6.1. The CM may use and rely on the information furnished by the Owner in performing services under this Agreement, and on the reports, data, and other information furnished by the Owner to the Design Professional.

6.2 The Owner shall be responsible for the presence at the site of any asbestos, PCB's, petroleum, hazardous materials and radioactive materials, and the consequences of such presence.

6.3 The Owner shall examine information submitted by the CM and shall render decisions pertaining thereto promptly.

6.4 The Owner shall furnish legal, accounting and insurance counseling services as may be necessary for the Project.

6.5 The Owner shall furnish insurance for the Project as specified in Article 8.

6.6 If the Owner observes or otherwise becomes aware of any fault or defect in the Project or any nonconformity with the Contract Documents, the Owner shall give prompt written notice thereof to the CM.

6.7 The Owner shall furnish required information and approvals and perform its responsibilities and activities in a timely manner to facilitate orderly progress of the work in cooperation with the CM consistent with this Agreement and in accordance with the planning and scheduling requirements and budgetary restraints of the Project as determined by the CM.

6.8 The Owner shall retain a Design Professional whose services, duties and responsibilities shall be described in a written agreement between the Owner and Design Professional. The services, duties and responsibilities set out in the agreement between the Owner and the Design Professional shall be compatible and consistent with this Agreement and the Contract Documents. The Owner shall, in its agreement with the Design Professional, require that the Design Professional perform its services in cooperation with the CM, consistent with this Agreement and in accordance with the planning and scheduling requirements and budgetary restraints of the Project as determined by the Owner and documented by the CM. The Owner shall provide to the CM a copy of the Owner-Design Professional Agreement, and the Owner represents to the CM that all the terms of that agreement have been acknowledged by and are acceptable to the Design Professional. The CM agrees to perform for the benefit of the Design Professional

CMAA Document No. A-1 (1990 edition)

all duties and responsibilities that the Owner has agreed the CM will perform for the benefit of the Design Professional in the Owner-Design Professional Agreement. The terms and conditions of the agreement between the Owner and the Design Professional shall not be changed without written consent of the CM and the consent shall not be unreasonably withheld.

6.9 The Owner shall accept the Project and Construction Budget and any subsequent revisions as provided in Paragraph 3.2.3.2 of this Agreement.

6.10 The Owner shall cause any and all agreements between the Owner and the Contractor to be compatible and consistent with this Agreement. Each of the agreements shall include waiver of subrogation and shall expressly recognize the CM as the Owner's agent in providing the Construction Manager's Basic and Additional Services specified in this Agreement.

6.11 At the request of the CM, sufficient copies of the Contract Documents shall be furnished by the Owner at the Owner's expense.

6.12 The Owner shall in a timely manner secure, submit and pay for necessary approvals, easements, assessments, building permits and charges required for the construction, use or occupancy of permanent structures or for permanent changes in existing facilities.

6.13 The Owner shall furnish evidence satisfactory to the CM that sufficient funds are available and committed for the entire cost of the Project. Unless such reasonable evidence is furnished, the CM is not required to commence the Construction Manager's Services and may, if such evidence is not presented within a reasonable time, suspend the Services specified in this Agreement upon fifteen (15) days written notice to the Owner. In such event, the CM shall be compensated in the manner provided in Paragraph 9.2.

6.14 The Owner, its representatives and consultants shall communicate with the Contractors only through the CM.

6.15 The Owner shall send to the CM and shall require the Design Professional to send to the CM copies of all notices and communications sent to or received by the Owner or the Design Professional relating to the Project. During the Construction Phase of the Project, the Owner shall require that the Contractors submit all notices and communications relating to the Project directly to the CM.

6.16 The Owner shall designate in writing an officer, employee or other authorized representatives to act in the Owner's behalf with respect to the Project. This representative shall have the authority to approve changes in the scope of the Project and shall be available during working hours and as often as may be required to render decisions and to furnish information in a timely manner.

6.17 The Owner shall make payments to the Contractors on the basis of the Contractor's applications for payment as recommended by the CM.

ARTICLE 7
COMPENSATION FOR CM SERVICES AND PAYMENT

7.1 The CM shall receive compensation for its services in accordance with Paragraph 7.2 (Cost Plus Fixed Fee) or Paragraph 7.3 (Lump Sum Fee).

7.2 Cost Plus Fixed Fee

The Owner shall compensate the CM on the basis of the CM's cost plus a fixed fee in accordance with the terms and conditions of this Agreement and specifically as follows:

7.2.1 Compensation for Basic Services

The CM shall be compensated for performing the Basic Services described in Article 3 as follows:

7.2.1.1 A Fixed Fee of _____ _____ Dollars ($_____);

17

CMAA Document No. A-1 (1990 edition)

7.2.1.2 The cost of employees working on the Project, other than principals, in an amount which equals the multiples established in subparagraphs 7.2.1.2.1 and 7.2.1.2.2, multiplied by the personnel expense for each such employee. Personnel expense for an employee shall be _____ times the base hourly wage. Personnel expense includes the base hourly wage, payroll taxes, employee benefits and Workers' Compensation Insurance. The cost of the CM's principals shall be paid at the rate specified in subparagraph 7.2.1.3. The specified multiples and rates shall remain constant for a twelve month period following the date of this Agreement. Thereafter, the multiples established in the referenced subparagraphs shall be adjusted by the CM if the CM's personnel expense changes;

7.2.1.2.1 Employees assigned to the Project and working at the construction site or employees for which the Owner provides all office facilities and services, excluding the project manager and assistant project managers, a multiple of _____ (_____);

7.2.1.2.2 Employees assigned to the Project and working in the CM's administrative office, including the project manager and assistant project managers, a multiple of _____ (_____);

7.2.1.3 Principals of the CM who participate in the Project, a fixed rate of _____ _____ (_____) per hour. The principals to be compensated according to these terms are:

_____
_____
_____
_____
_____
_____;
and;

7.2.1.4 Engineers, architects and consultants employed by the CM and performing services related to the Project, a multiple of _____ _____ (_____) times the amount of the invoice for such services.

7.2.2 Direct Expenses

7.2.2.1. In addition to the compensation for services stated herein, the CM shall be reimbursed for its direct expenses for Basic and Additional Services. Direct expenses are those actual expenditures made by the CM, its principals, employees, engineers, architects and consultants in the interest of the Project, including, without limitation:

7.2.2.1.1 Long distance telephone calls, telegrams and fees paid for securing approval of authorities having jurisdiction over the Project;

7.2.2.1.2 Handling, shipping, mailing and reproduction of materials and documents;

7.2.2.1.3 Transportation and living expenses when traveling in connection with the Project;

7.2.2.1.4 Computer equipment rental;

7.2.2.1.5 Computer software purchased;

7.2.2.1.6 Electronic data processing service and rental of electronic data processing equipment;

7.2.2.1.7 Word processing equipment rental;

7.2.2.1.8 Premiums for professional liability insurance and other insurance beyond the limits normally carried by the CM that are required by the terms of this Agreement;

7.2.2.1.9 Relocation of employees and families;

7.2.2.1.10 Temporary living expenses of employees who are not relocated, but assigned to the Project;

7.2.2.1.11 Gross receipts taxes, sales or use taxes, service taxes and other similar taxes required to be paid as a result of this Agreement;

7.2.2.1.12 Field office expenses including the cost of office rentals, field telephones, utilities, field furniture, equipment and supplies; and

18

CMAA Document No. A-1 (1990 edition)

7.2.2.1.13 Premium time work.

7.2.3 Construction Manager's Accounting Records

7.2.3.1 Record of the CM's personnel expense, engineers, architects and consultant fees and direct expenses pertaining to the Project shall be maintained on the basis of generally-accepted accounting practices and shall be available for inspection by the Owner or the Owner's representative at mutually convenient times for a period of two years after completion of the Construction Phase Basic Services.

7.2.4 Payments

Payments to the CM shall be made monthly, not later than fifteen (15) days after presentation of the CM's invoice to the Owner, as follows:

7.2.4.1 Payment of the Fixed Fee as indicated in Paragraph 7.2.1.1 shall be in amounts prorated equally over the duration of the CM's Basic Services. The duration shall be as set out in Article 4;

7.2.4.2 Payment of personnel expense and the fixed hourly rate for principals shall be in amounts equal to the actual hours spent during the billing period on the Project multiplied by the rates and multiples stated in Paragraphs 7.2.1.2, 7.2.1.3, and 7.2.1.4.

7.2.4.3 Payment of engineer, architect and consultant services shall be in amounts equal to the invoice in receipt by the CM for the billing period times the multiplier stated in Paragraph 7.2.1.4;

7.2.4.4 Reimbursement for direct expenses shall be in amounts equal to expenditures made during the billing period and during previous billing periods not yet invoiced;

7.2.4.5 No deductions shall be made from the CM's compensation due to any claim by the Owner, Contractors or others not a party to this Agreement or due to any liquidated damages, retainage or other sums withheld from payments to the Contractors or others not a party to this Agreement; and

7.2.4.6 Payments due the CM that are unpaid for more than thirty (30) days from the date of the CM's invoice shall bear interest at the legal rate from the due date, compounded annually. In addition, the CM may, after giving seven (7) days' written notice to the Owner, suspend services under this Agreement until the CM has been paid in full all amounts due for services, expenses and charges.

7.2.5 Compensation for Additional Services: The CM shall be compensated and payments shall be made for performing Additional Services in the same amount and manner as provided in Article 7 for Basic Services. There shall be an increase in the fixed fee set out in Paragraph 7.2.1.1 in an amount which is mutually agreeable between the Owner and CM.

7.3 Lump Sum Fee

The Owner shall compensate the CM on the basis of a lump sum fee in accordance with the terms and conditions of this Agreement as follows:

7.3.1 Compensation for Basic Services

The CM shall be compensated for performing Basic Services described in Article 3, a total Lump Sum in the amount of _____

($_____), which amount shall be paid in _____ monthly installments as follows:

Installment No.	Installment Due Date	Installment Amount
_____	_____	_____
_____	_____	_____
_____	_____	_____
_____	_____	_____
_____	_____	_____
_____	_____	_____
_____	_____	_____
_____	_____	_____
_____	_____	_____
_____	_____	_____
_____	_____	_____
_____	_____	_____
_____	_____	_____

19

CMAA Document No. A-1 (1990 edition)

7.3.2 Direct Expenses

The cost of direct expenses incurred shall be included in the lump sum fee.

7.3.3 Payments

Payments shall be made monthly, not later than fifteen (15) days after receipt of the CM's invoice by the Owner.

7.3.3.1 No deductions shall be made from the CM's compensation due to any claim of the Owner, Contractors or others not a party to this Agreement or due to any liquidated damages, retainage or other sums withheld from payments to Contractors or others not a party to this Agreement.

7.3.3.2 Payments due the CM that are unpaid for more than thirty (30) days from date of the CM's invoice shall bear interest at the legal rate from the due date, compounded annually. In addition, the CM may, after giving seven (7) days' written notice to the Owner, suspend services under this Agreement until the CM has been paid in full all amounts due for services, expenses and charges.

7.3.4 Compensation for Additional Services

The CM shall be compensated and payments shall be made for performing Additional Services in an amount and on terms mutually agreeable between the Owner and CM.

ARTICLE 8
INSURANCE AND MUTUAL INDEMNITY

8.1 CM's Liability Insurance

8.1.1 The CM shall purchase and maintain insurance as shall protect the CM from the claims set forth below that may arise out of or result from the CM's performance of services pursuant to this Agreement:

8.1.1.1 Claims under Workers' Compensation, disability benefits and other similar employee benefits acts that are applicable to the work performed;

8.1.1.2 Claims for damages because of bodily injury, occupational sickness or disease or death of CM's employees under any applicable employer's liability law;

8.1.1.3 Claims for damages because of bodily injury or death of any person other than CM's employees;

8.1.1.4 Claims for damages insured by usual personal injury liability coverage that are sustained (1) by any person as a result of an offense directly related to the employment of such person by the CM or (2) by any other person;

8.1.1.5 Claims for damages, other than to the work itself, because of injury to or destruction of tangible property, including loss or use therefrom; or

8.1.1.6 Claims for damages because of bodily injury or death of any person or property damage arising out of the ownership, maintenance or use of any motor vehicle.

8.1.2 The CM's comprehensive General and Automobile Liability Insurance, as required by Paragraph 8.1.1, shall be written for not less than the following limits of liability:

a. Comprehensive General Liability

1. Personal Injury:
   _____ Each Occurrence
   _____ Aggregate

2. Property Damage:
   _____ Each Occurrence
   _____ Aggregate

b. Comprehensive Automobile Liability

1. Bodily Injury:
   _____ Each Person
   _____ Each Occurrence

2. Property Damage:
   _____ Each Occurrence

20

CMAA Document No. A-1 (1990 edition)

8.1.3 Comprehensive General Liability Insurance may be obtained under a single policy for the full limits required or by a combination of underlying policies with the balance provided by an excess or umbrella liability policy.

8.1.4 The foregoing policies shall contain a provision that coverages afforded under the policies shall not be cancelled or expire until at least thirty (30) days written notice has been given to the Owner and shall include either a liability endorsement covering this Agreement or an endorsement making the Owner an additional insured under the policies. Certificates of insurance showing such coverages to be in force shall be filed with the Owner prior to commencement of the CM's services.

8.2 Owner's Insurance

8.2.1 The CM, as agent of the Owner, shall be named as an additional insured in any insurance policy obtained by the Owner for the Project.

8.3 Notices and Recovery

8.3.1 The Owner and CM each shall provide the other with copies of all policies thus obtaining for the Project. Each party shall provide the other thirty (30) days notice of cancellation, non-renewal or endorsement reducing or restricting coverage.

8.4 Waiver of Subrogation

8.4.1 The Owner and the CM waive all rights against each other and against the Contractor, Design Professional, consultants, agents and employees of the other for damages during construction covered by any property insurance as set forth in the Contract Documents. The Owner and the CM shall each require similar waivers from their contractors, consultants and agents.

8.5 Indemnity

8.5.1 The CM hereby indemnifies and holds harmless the Owner, the Design Professional and their employees, agents and representatives from and against any and all claims, demands, suits and damages for bodily injury and property damage for which the CM is liable that arise out of the negligent acts or omissions of the CM in performing the Construction Manager's Services under this Agreement provided, however, that the CM does not assume any risk of damages to property that is incorporated in or shall be incorporated in or is located at the Project site which is not within the possession of the CM or under the CM's direction or control. The total liability of the CM arising by reason of this indemnity for losses that are not insured shall not exceed the amount of the total compensation actually paid to the CM by the Owner pursuant to this Agreement.

8.5.2 The Owner shall cause the Design Professional to indemnify and hold harmless the CM, its employees, agents and representatives to the same extent and in the same manner that CM has provided indemnification for the Design Professional under Paragraph 8.5.1.

8.5.3 The Owner hereby indemnifies and holds harmless the CM and its employees, agents and representatives from and against any and all claims, demands, suits and damages for bodily injury and property damage that arise out of or result from, in whole or in part, wrongful acts or omissions of the Owner, its employees, agents, representatives, independent contractors, material suppliers, the Contractors and Design Professional.

8.5.4 The Owner shall cause the Contractors to indemnify and hold harmless the CM from and against any and all claims, demands, suits, damages, including consequential damages and damages resulting from personal injury or property damage, costs, expenses and fees that are asserted against the CM and that arise out of or result from wrongful acts or omissions by the Contractor in performing the Work.

ARTICLE 9
TERMINATION AND SUSPENSION

9.1 Termination

9.1.1 This Agreement may be terminated by the Owner for convenience after seven (7) days' written notice to the CM.

21

CMAA Document No. A-1 (1990 edition)

9.1.2 This Agreement may be terminated by either party hereto upon seven (7) days' written notice should the other party fail substantially to perform in accordance with the terms hereof through no fault of the other or if the Project in whole or substantial part is stopped for a period of sixty (60) days under an order of any court or other public authority having jurisdiction or as a result of an act of government.

9.1.3 In the event of termination under Paragraph 9.1.1, the CM shall be paid its compensation for services performed to the date of termination, services of engineers, architects and consultants then due and all termination expenses. Termination expenses are defined as those expenses arising prior, during and subsequent to termination that are directly attributable to the termination, plus an amount computed as a percentage of the total compensation earned at the time of termination computed as follows:

9.1.3.1 Twenty (20) percent if the termination occurs during the Pre-design Phase, Design Phase or Bidding Phase; or

9.1.3.2 Ten (10) percent if the termination occurs during the Construction Phase or Post-Construction Phase.

9.1.4 In the event of termination under Paragraph 9.1.2, the CM shall be paid its compensation for services performed to the date of termination, services of professional consultants then due and all termination expenses. No amount computed as provided in Paragraphs 9.1.3.1 and 9.1.3.2 shall be paid in addition.

9.2 Suspension

9.2.1 The Owner may in writing order the CM to suspend all or any part of the Construction Manager's Services for the Project for the convenience of the Owner or for Work stoppage beyond the control of the Owner or the CM. If the performance of all or any part of the Services for the Project is so suspended, an adjustment in the CM's compensation shall be made for the increase, if any, in the cost of the CM's performance of this Agreement caused by such suspension and this Agreement shall be modified in writing accordingly.

9.2.2 In the event the Construction Manager's Services for the Project are suspended, the Owner shall reimburse the CM for all of the costs of its construction site staff, assigned Project home office staff and other costs as provided for by this Agreement for the first thirty (30) days of such suspension. The CM shall reduce the size of its staff for the remainder of the suspension period as directed by the Owner and, during such period, the Owner shall reimburse the CM for all of the costs of its reduced staff. Upon cessation of the suspension, the CM shall restore the construction site staff and home office staff to its former size.

9.2.3 Persons assigned to another project during such suspension periods and not available to return to the Project upon cessation of the suspension shall be replaced. The Owner shall reimburse the CM for costs incurred in relocating previous staff persons returning to the Project or new persons assigned to the Project.

9.2.4 If the Project is suspended by the Owner for more than three (3) months, the CM shall be paid compensation for Services performed prior to receipt of written notice from the Owner of the suspension, together with direct expenses then due and all expenses and costs directly resulting from the suspension. If the Project is resumed after being suspended for more than six (6) months, the CM shall have the option of requiring that its compensation, including rates and fees, be renegotiated. Subject to the provisions of this Agreement relating to termination, a suspension of the Project does not void this Agreement.

ARTICLE 10
DISPUTE RESOLUTION

10.1 The Owner and the Construction Manager shall submit all unresolved claims, counterclaims, disputes, controversies, and other matters in question between them arising out of or relating to this Agreement or the breach thereof ("disputes"), to mediation prior to either party initiating against

22

SAMPLE AGREEMENT

CMAA Document No. A-1 (1990 edition)

the other a demand for arbitration pursuant to Paragraph 10.2 below, unless delay in initiating or prosecuting a proceeding in an arbitration or judicial forum would irrevocably prejudice the Owner or the CM. The Owner and the CM shall agree in writing as to the identity of the mediator and the rules and procedures of the mediation. If the Owner and the CM submit the dispute to mediation it shall be under the then current Construction Industry Mediation Rules of the American Arbitration Association.

10.2 All disputes that the Owner and the CM are unable to resolve by mediation as aforesaid shall be decided by arbitration, subject to the limitations stated in Paragraph 10.4 below. The agreement to arbitrate, and any other agreement or consent to arbitrate entered into in accordance herewith shall be specifically enforceable under the prevailing law of any court having jurisdiction. The Owner and the CM shall agree in writing as to the identity of the arbitrator(s) and the rules and procedures of the arbitration. If the Owner and the CM do not so agree, then the Owner and the CM shall submit the dispute to arbitration under the then current Construction Industry Rules of the American Arbitration Association.

10.3 Notice of demand for arbitration must be filed in writing with the other party to this Agreement and with the arbitrator(s). The demand must be made within a reasonable time after the dispute has arisen, but not prior to or during the pendency of the mediation as agreed in Paragraph 10.1. In no event may the demand for arbitration be made after the date when institution of legal or equitable proceedings based on such dispute in question would be barred by the applicable statute of limitations.

10.4 No arbitration arising out of, or relating to, this Agreement may include, by consolidation, joinder or in any other manner, any person or entity who is not a party to this Agreement unless both parties agree otherwise in writing. No consent to arbitration in respect of a specifically-described dispute will constitute consent to arbitrate any other dispute which is not specifically described in such consent or which is with any party not specifically described therein.

10.5 The award rendered by the arbitrator(s) will be final, judgment may be entered upon it in any court having jurisdiction thereof, and the award will not be subject to modification or appeal. In any judicial proceeding to enforce this Agreement to arbitrate, the only issues to be determined shall be those set forth in 9 U.S.C. Section 4 Federal Arbitration Act, and such issues shall be determined by the Court without a jury. All other issues, such as but not limited to, arbitrability, prerequisites to arbitration, compliance with contractual time limits, applicability of indemnity clauses, clauses limiting damages and statutes of limitations shall be for the arbitrator(s), whose decision thereon shall be final and binding. There shall be no interlocutory appeal of an order compelling arbitration.

ARTICLE 11
ADDITIONAL PROVISIONS

11.1 Confidentiality

11.1.1 The CM will keep all information concerning the Project confidential, except for communications between the CM, Design Professional, Contractor and their independent professional engineers, architects and other consultants and subcontractors incident to completion of the Project, and except for publicity approved by the Owner and in connection with filings and communications with governmental bodies having jurisdiction over the design of the Project.

11.2 Limitation and Assignment

11.2.1 The Owner and the CM each binds itself, its successors, assigns and legal representatives to the terms of this Agreement.

11.2.2 Neither the Owner nor the CM shall assign or transfer its interest in this Agreement without the written consent of the other, except that the CM may

23

CMAA Document No. A-1 (1990 edition)

assign accounts receivable to a commercial bank for securing loans without approval of the Owner.

11.3 Governing Law

11.3.1 This Agreement shall, unless otherwise provided, be governed by the law of the state where the Project is located.

11.4 Extent of Agreement

11.4.1 This Agreement constitutes the entire agreement between the parties and incorporates all prior agreements and understandings in connection with the subject matter hereof. This Agreement may be amended only in writing signed by the party against whom enforcement is sought. Nothing contained in this Agreement is intended to benefit any third party other than the Design Professional as specifically indicated herein. The Contractors, subcontractors, or suppliers are not intended third party beneficiaries of this Agreement.

11.5 Severability

11.5.1 If any portion of this Agreement is held as a matter of law to be unenforceable, the remainder of this Agreement shall be enforceable without such provisions.

11.6 Meaning of Terms

11.6.1 References made in the singular shall include the plural and the masculine shall include the feminine or the neuter.

11.6.2 The meaning of terms used herein shall be consistent with the definitions expressed in the CMAA Standard Form Agreements, Contracts and General Conditions.

11.7 Notices

11.7.1 All notices required by this Agreement or other communications to either party by the other shall be deemed given when made in writing and deposited in the United States Mail, first class, postage prepaid, addressed as follows:

To the Owner:

_____

_____

_____

_____

To the CM:

_____

_____

_____

_____

(Remainder of the page is intentionally left blank.)

24

SAMPLE AGREEMENT

CMAA Document No. A-1 (1990 edition)

This Agreement is executed as of the day and year first written above.

OWNER: CONSTRUCTION MANAGER:

_____   _____

Title: _____   Title: _____

Attest: _____   Attest: _____

§ 4.19   CMAA A-4 Standard Form of Agreement Between Owner and Design Professional

THE CONSTRUCTION MANAGEMENT ASSOCIATION OF AMERICA, INC.

CMAA Document No. A-4 (1990 edition)

Standard Form of Agreement Between
OWNER and DESIGN PROFESSIONAL

This document is to be used in connection with the Standard Form of Agreement Between OWNER and CONSTRUCTION MANAGER (CMAA Document No. A-1), the Standard Form of Contract Between OWNER and CONTRACTOR (CMAA Document No. A-2), and the General Conditions of the Construction Contract (CMAA Document No. A-3), (all being 1990 editions).

CONSULTATION WITH AN ATTORNEY IS RECOMMENDED WHENEVER THIS DOCUMENT IS USED

AGREEMENT
made this   day of   the year Nineteen Hundred and

BETWEEN the Owner:

and the Design Professional:

For Services in connection with the Project known as:

(hereinafter called the Project) as further described in "Exhibit A" attached hereto and made a part hereof.

Owner has employed   (the "CM") to provide professional construction management services as Owner's agent in connection with the Project in accordance with an agreement dated   , 19   (the Owner-CM Agreement). A copy of all portions of the Owner-CM Agreement pertinent to the Design Professional's services under this Agreement including the terms and conditions in connection with interrelationships and the complementary nature of services of the CM and the Design Professional for the Project is attached hereto, made a part of this Agreement and marked "Exhibit B".

1

SAMPLE AGREEMENT

(Page intentionally left blank.)

SAMPLE AGREEMENT

TABLE OF CONTENTS
CMAA Document No. A-4 (1990 edition)

Article:

1. The Construction Management Plan 5
2. Relationship of the Parties 5
3. Basic Services: Design Phase Services 6
4. Basic Services: Bid and Award Phase 8
5. Basic Services: Construction Phase Services 9
6. Additional Services 12
7. Owner's Responsibilities 13
8. Duration of Design Professional Services 15
9. Compensation for Design Professional's Services and Payment 15
10. Changes in Design Professional's Basic Services and Compensation 20
11. Insurance and Mutual Indemnification 20
12. Termination and Suspension 21
13. Dispute Resolution 22
14. Owner's Rights in Documents and Reuse 23
15. Additional Provisions 24

Exhibit A - Project Description
Exhibit B - Pertinent Parts of Owner-CM Agreement
Exhibit C - Construction Management Plan

3

(Page intentionally left blank.)

4

CMAA Document No. A-4 (1990 edition)

Owner and Design Professional in consideration of their mutual covenants herein agree as set forth below:

ARTICLE 1
THE CONSTRUCTION MANAGEMENT PLAN

1.1 The Owner's description and statement of requirements for the Project are set forth in the Construction Management Plan, which is acceptable to the Owner and the CM, and to the extent that it relates to the Design Professional's services hereunder is also acceptable to the Design Professional. The Construction Management Plan dated _____, 19___ is attached hereto, made a part hereof and marked "Exhibit C". A preliminary Master Schedule specifying the starting and finishing dates for construction and a Milestone Schedule for the Design Professional's Design Phase services (including interim and final submittals) is included in the Construction Management Plan. A preliminary Project and Construction Budget and a preliminary Management Information System covering and regulating communication between the key participants in the Project are included in the Construction Management Plan. The Design Professional shall perform the services specified by this Agreement in a manner consistent with the Construction Management Plan.

1.2 It is recognized that as the Project progresses and its documentation becomes more definitive, various aspects of the Construction Management Plan (including the Owner's requirements, Master Schedule, Project and Construction Budget and Management Information System) may be revised and refined after consultation between the Owner, CM and Design Professional, and those revisions will be incorporated into the Construction Management Plan by formal amendments as appropriate.

ARTICLE 2
RELATIONSHIP OF THE PARTIES

2.1 The Design Professional is to render to the Owner and have sole responsibility for all professional design services in connection with the Project (except as specifically provided otherwise in this Agreement). In the Owner-CM Agreement the

CM has agreed to cooperate with the Design Professional in this regard and to recognize the Design Professional's authority, responsibility and separate professional role for the Project. The CM has received all portions (other than terms of compensation) of this Agreement that relate to the CM's services under the Owner-CM Agreement, including terms and conditions relative to the interrelationships and cooperative nature of services to be rendered by the Design Professional and CM, and the Owner represents to the Design Professional that the CM has acknowledged that they are acceptable to the CM.

2.2 The Design Professional shall provide to the Owner professional architectural and engineering services for all design phases of the Project and professional design services during construction as provided in this Agreement. The services shall include customary architectural and civil, structural, mechanical and electrical engineering services.

2.3 The CM will serve as the Owner's principal agent in connection with the Project. The CM's services during the design phase will relate principally to matters of scheduling and coordination of the activities of all parties involved, coordinating and expediting communications, evaluation of constructibility, cost, sequencing, scheduling and time considerations related to designs developed by the Design Professional, recommendations as to the separation of the construction contracts into various categories of the Work of Contractors and commenting on clarity, consistency and coordination of the design documentation. The CM's services during the construction phase will involve administering on the Owner's behalf all of the prime contracts for construction, monitoring the quality and quantity of the Work of the Contractors, monitoring cost and time considerations during construction, coordination and expediting of communications and functioning as the initial arbiter of disputes between the Owner and Contractors pertaining to the Work.

5

CMAA Document No. A-4 (1990 edition)

2.4 The Design Professional is an independent contractor responsible for its own means and methods of providing services and is not a joint venturer with the Owner or CM, or a subcontractor or agent of the CM. The Design Professional recognizes the authority, responsibility and role assigned to and undertaken by the CM under the Owner-CM Agreement. The Design Professional's services shall be rendered compatibly and in cooperation with the CM's services under the Owner-CM Agreement. It is not intended that the services of the CM and Design Professional be competitive or duplicative but rather complementary. The Design Professional shall communicate with the Owner, Contractors and others involved in the Project only in accordance with the Management Information System included in the Construction Management Plan.

2.5 The Design Professional shall perform its services hereunder properly and in accordance with the standards of its profession. The Design Professional acknowledges its sole responsibility as a professional for the design of the Project and for performing certain design related services during its construction. The Design Professional also acknowledges that in the performance of services under the Owner-CM Agreement, the CM will be relying upon the performance by the Design Professional of services under this Agreement. Except as set forth herein, the Design Professional shall not have any other duties and responsibilities in respect of the Project. The Design Professional shall be entitled to rely upon the CM for the proper performance of services undertaken by CM pursuant to the Owner-CM Agreement.

2.6 The Design Professional shall participate in the orientation sessions provided by the CM in accordance with the Owner-CM Agreement Paragraph 3.2.1.4, and, as the design of the Project progresses, shall provide advice as requested and suggestions in respect of revisions to the various aspects of the Construction Management Plan.

ARTICLE 3
BASIC SERVICES: DESIGN PHASE SERVICES

The Design Professional shall perform Basic Services as described in Articles 3, 4 and 5 and any

Additional Services that are authorized, all in accordance with the provisions of Article 2.

3.1 Design Criteria

Based on the preliminary description and statement of the Project requirements as set forth in the Construction Management Plan, the Design Professional, in consultation with the Owner and the CM, shall develop design criteria and design requirements for the Project. During this process the Design Professional shall receive from the CM advice in respect of constructibility, cost, scheduling, sequencing and time of construction and clarity, consistency and coordination of the documentation, but shall not have responsibility in respect of any thereof. As the Design Professional develops the design criteria and design requirements, and they evolve from preliminary to detailed and definitive, they shall be submitted to and reviewed by the Owner and CM, and ultimately accepted by the Owner. As the design criteria and design requirements are so accepted they shall be furnished to the CM in written form. In performing services under the Owner-CM Agreement the CM will be entitled to rely on all design considerations and determinations provided by the Design Professional.

3.2 Owner-Supplied Information

Design Professional shall advise the CM of the necessity of the Owner or CM obtaining from others and providing to the Design Professional subsurface and other data of the types described in Paragraph 7.12, on all of which the Design Professional may rely in rendering services hereunder and in preparing the design documentation.

3.3 Governmental Approvals

The Design Professional shall be responsible for identifying governmental bodies having jurisdiction to approve the design of the Project. As part of such responsibilities as a licensed professional, the Design Professional shall be responsible to see that the documents and services furnished by the Design Professional conform to the laws, regulations and other legal requirements applicable at the time they are furnished, and that the final design documentation complies with the requirements of

6

CMAA Document No. A-4 (1990 edition)

Paragraph 3.8 below. The Design Professional shall not have responsibility as part of Basic Services to obtain any governmental approvals or permits but may rely on the Owner doing so on his own or through the CM. Information in respect of such approvals shall be furnished to the Design Professional in a timely manner, and the Design Professional shall be entitled to rely upon the accuracy and completeness of what has been so furnished.

3.4 Construction Management Plan

The Design Professional shall make recommendations for revisions to the Construction Management Plan as the design progresses and shall evaluate and comment on revisions proposed by the CM. These may include revisions to the Project requirements, Master Schedule, Project and Construction Budget, and Management Information System. Revisions of the Construction Management Plan made by the CM will be issued to the Design Professional only with the written approval of the Owner and CM. The Design Professional may rely upon all information and data included in the Construction Management Plan in rendering services hereunder and in preparing the design documentation.

3.5 Cost Control

3.5.1 During design of the Project, the CM and Design Professional shall maintain close liaison and have constant interchange of information and documentation. Both will cooperate to achieve compliance with the Project and Construction Budget, which will include a contingency acceptable to the Owner, CM, and Design Professional for construction costs appropriate for the type and location of the Project and the extent to which the design has progressed and been finalized. The Design Professional shall provide to the CM submittals of design drawings and specifications as required in the Construction Management Plan. The Design Professional shall receive, comment on and give due consideration to advice, cost analyses, Value Analyses, information as to constructibility, as to costs, sequencing, scheduling and time of construction, and as to clarity, consistency and coordination in documentation as submitted by the CM. While the Design Professional may rely upon

such data submitted by the CM, the Design Professional as the party having sole responsibility for design of the Project shall, after taking into consideration any budgetary restraints imposed by the Construction Management Plan, make the final determination as to the acceptability, selection and specification of materials and equipment for the Project (subject to any directives issued by the Owner). Final determinations with respect to construction sequencing, the separation of construction into separate contracts for various categories of work, and the estimated Project and construction costs will be made by the CM and will be incorporated in the Construction Management Plan as amended from time to time; and the Design Professional shall be entitled to rely upon such data provided by the CM.

3.5.2 The Owner recognizes that while the Design Professional is to cooperate with the CM to the end that actual construction costs will not exceed budget figures included in the Construction Management Plan as amended from time to time, the Design Professional has no control over the costs of labor, materials, equipment or services furnished by others, or over the Contractors' methods of determining prices, or over competitive bidding or market prices, or over construction costs projections prepared by the CM. Accordingly, the Design Professional does not give any assurance or guarantee that proposals, bids or actual construction costs will not vary from budget figures included in the Construction Management Plan as amended from time to time. If the budget figure is exceeded the Owner shall give written consent to increasing the budget, or authorize negotiations or rebidding of the Project within a reasonable time, or cooperate with the Design Professional and CM in revising the Project's general scope, extent or character in keeping with the requirements and sound design practices, or modify the requirements appropriately. The preparation by the Design Professional of additional or amended Drawings, Specifications and other design documents in order to reflect design changes made necessary to respond to such changes in the Project's general scope, extent, character or requirements shall be provided by the Design Professional as an Additional Service under Article 6. Instead of the foregoing the Owner

7

CMAA Document No. A-4 (1990 edition)

may abandon the Project and terminate this Agreement in accordance with Article 12.

3.6 Times of Performance

In preparing the design documentation the Design Professional shall comply with the Master Schedule and Milestone Schedule for Design Phase Services as included in the Construction Management Plan.

3.7 Conferences and Meetings

The Design Professional shall attend Project conferences and meetings called by the Owner or CM.

3.8 Design Documents

Before conclusion of the Design Phase, and after receipt of comments, recommendations and advice from the CM, who will also convey the Owner's comments, the Design Professional shall prepare the final design documentation for construction consisting of:

3.8.1 Final Drawings to show the general scope, extent and character of the Contractor's Work;

3.8.2 Specifications prepared in accordance with the Construction Specification Institute sixteen division format;

3.8.3 Technical criteria, written descriptions and design data information for use by the Owner in filing applications for governmental approvals and permits;

3.8.4 General Conditions using CMAA Document No. A-3 (1990 edition) and Supplementary Conditions; General Conditions for separate material and equipment procurement shall be prepared by the CM;

3.8.5 Bid Documents which may include requests for alternate bids as required by the CM (subject to the provisions of Paragraph 6.1.8); and

3.8.6 Addenda or other customary design documents.

3.8.7 The final documentation shall be in form for contracting (single or multi-prime) as indicated in the Construction Management Plan. The final design documentation furnished hereunder shall be prepared in accordance with professional standards, shall be in such detail as is appropriate for the nature and character of the Work to be performed by the Contractors, and shall be prepared and coordinated so as to permit such scheduling and sequencing of construction as may be required by the Construction Management Plan. The CM will assemble bid packages and handle all administrative aspects of bidding. The Owner shall be responsible for obtaining appropriate legal reviews of all documents.

ARTICLE 4
BASIC SERVICES: BID AND AWARD PHASE

4.1 The Design Professional shall participate in pre-bid conferences.

4.2 The Design Professional shall receive from the CM requests from Contractors for clarification of the Contract Documents and shall prepare the design documentation for Addenda, which will be reviewed by the CM for constructibility, cost, scheduling, time, coordination, clarity and consistency, and will be issued by the CM after being processed by the CM and approved by the Owner.

4.3 The Design Professional shall, on request of the CM, provide advice on the prequalification of bidders and the evaluation of bids.

4.4 The Design Professional shall attend post-bid conference and pre-construction conference.

4.5 The Design Professional shall not be involved in accepting or rejecting subcontractors or suppliers.

4.6 If substitutions are to be permitted during the bidding period, the Design Professional shall determine their acceptability and prepare the necessary design documentation for inclusion in Addenda.

8

CMAA Document No. A-4 (1990 edition)

ARTICLE 5
BASIC SERVICES: CONSTRUCTION PHASE SERVICES

5.1 Visits and Access to Site

The Design Professional shall make visits to the site as necessary to enable the Design Professional to carry out its Basic Service responsibilities under Paragraphs 5.3 through 5.7, inclusive, and Paragraphs 5.16 and 5.17. However, it is not intended that during such visits the Design Professional shall be obligated as part of Basic Services to become generally familiar with or check the quality or quantity of the Work or to determine that the Work is being completed in accordance with the Contract Documents. The Owner shall be responsible to see that the Design Professional is given access to the site as necessary to carry out its services under this Agreement.

5.2 Communications

The Design Professional shall only communicate with Contractors, subcontractors and suppliers through the CM or in the presence of the CM.

5.3 Interpretations and Clarifications

Upon receipt from the CM (with the CM's comments as appropriate) of written requests for clarifications and interpretations of the Drawings, Specifications and other design related information, the Design Professional shall review the same and issue (through the CM) in writing appropriate clarifications and interpretations.

5.4 Substitutions

Upon receipt from the CM of written proposals for substitutions of materials and equipment (with the CM's comments, including Trade-off studies, as appropriate), the Design Professional shall evaluate the same and shall have final authority to accept or reject such proposals as being appropriate for the Project.

5.5 Changes

Upon receipt from the CM of written requests for changes in the Contract Documents (with comments, including Trade-off studies, as appropriate) the Design Professional shall prepare the necessary Drawings and Specifications (subject to the provisions of Paragraphs 6.1.5 and 6.1.7). Whenever a directive for a work change is issued by the Owner, a copy will be sent to the Design Professional. Whenever the CM authorizes minor changes in the Work pursuant to authority under the Owner-CM Agreement, written confirmation will be given to the Design Professional, who shall review the information submitted and advise the Owner and CM whether or not the change is compatible with, or will prejudice the integrity of the design concept of the completed Project as a functioning whole as indicated in the Contract Documents. The Design Professional shall be the sole judge of whether or not a minor change involves design or aesthetic considerations and no such change shall be made without the Design Professional's concurrence.

5.6 Submittals

The Design Professional shall cooperate and participate in meetings conducted by the CM to establish procedures for submission and review of shop drawings, samples and other submittals. Upon receipt from the CM of the Contractors' shop drawings, samples and other submittals with the CM's comments (including Trade-off studies, as appropriate), the Design Professional shall review, approve or reject and return the same to the CM for transmission to the Contractors. The review and approval shall be for the limited purpose of checking conformance with the information given in the Contract Documents and compatibility with the design concept of the completed Project as a functioning whole as indicated in the Contract Documents. The Owner shall require the CM to transmit to the Design Professional all data on variations and deviations from the requirements of the Contract Documents received from Contractors and to insist on Contractors' compliance with the procedures established. All reviews of shop drawings, samples and other submittals shall be in accordance with the Contractors' Construction Schedule, which will have been established by the CM with the Contractors' and the Design Professional's participation.

9

CMAA Document No. A-4 (1990 edition)

5.7 Surface and Subsurface Conditions

The information with respect to surface and subsurface conditions at or contiguous to the site on which Contractors will be entitled to rely shall be identified by the Design Professional in the Contract Documents. Contractors' responsibility for other surface and subsurface conditions will be as provided in the General Conditions [CMAA Document No. A-3 (1990 edition)]. The Owner shall require the CM to consult with the Design Professional whenever a surface or subsurface condition is uncovered that differs from what a Contractor is entitled to rely on, or from what is indicated in the Contract Documents, or that may require a change in the Contract Documents. In that event the Design Professional shall visit the site to examine the condition and determine if the Owner should obtain further examination or testing. The preparation by the Design Professional of additional or amended Drawings and Specifications for incorporation into a Change Order to reflect any design changes required to be responsive to the changed conditions shall be provided by the Design Professional as an Additional Service under Article 6.

5.8 CM's Comments and Advice

The Owner shall require that all transmittals to the Design Professional requesting interpretations or clarifications, or proposals for substitutions, or change orders, or reviewing and approval of submittals, or evaluations of changed subsurface conditions shall include the CM's comments regarding the request or proposal and its anticipated effect on compliance with the Project requirements, the Project and Construction Budget, and the Master Schedule. The CM's comments will not relate to design considerations but rather to matters of constructibility, cost, sequencing, scheduling and time of construction, clarity, consistency and coordination of the design documentation. The Owner shall require the CM to give the Design Professional prompt notice (confirmed in writing) of apparent defects in the design documents (Drawings, Specifications, approved submittals, samples, changes, change orders and other design documents referred to in Paragraphs 3.8 and 5.3 through 5.6, inclusive) of which the CM obtains actual knowledge,

but the CM shall not have responsibility for detecting the existence of any such defects.

5.9 Tests and Inspections

The Design Professional may request the CM to call for special inspections and tests of the Work to enable the Design Professional to carry out its services under Paragraphs 5.3 through 5.7, inclusive, and shall be entitled to rely upon the accuracy and completeness of the results provided.

5.10 Quality Control of the Contractor's Work

The Owner shall not cause or permit the CM to allow or accept, and the Owner shall not allow or accept, any Work by the Contractors involving a deviation from the requirements of the Contract Documents unless the Design Professional shall have given written approval, which approval shall not be unreasonably withheld; however, the foregoing restriction shall not apply to variations from the design documentation which do not affect the design concept or the integrity of the completed Project as a functioning whole (aesthetically, structurally, or otherwise). Any participation by the Design Professional in programs or procedures to observe, review or monitor the quality of the Contractors' Work, or any participation in the review and acceptance or rejection of the Contractors' Work that the Owner or CM may require (except as provided in Paragraphs 5.16 and 5.17) shall be provided by the Design Professional as an Additional Service under Article 6. If during the course of any such visits to the site, or other site visits furnished as Additional Services in accordance with Paragraphs 5.10 and 5.11 and Article 6, the Design Professional obtains actual knowledge of Contractors' Work that does not conform to the requirements of the Contract Documents, or will not be compatible with or will prejudice the integrity of the design concept of the completed Project as a functioning whole as indicated in the Contract Documents, the Design Professional shall give prompt written notice thereof to the CM, but the Design Professional shall not have responsibility to detect the existence of any such condition.

CMAA Document No. A-4 (1990 edition)

5.11 Progress Payments

As requested by the CM, the Design Professional shall comment in writing on specific aspects of any Schedule of Values developed by the CM for the Work. Any participation by the Design Professional in the review and approval of applications for payment, and the review and acceptance of the quality and quantity of the Contractors' Work that the Owner or CM may require in connection with applications for payment, shall be provided by the Design Professional as an Additional Service under Article 6.

5.12 Not Responsible for Contractor's Work

The Design Professional shall not have responsibility for or guarantee the Contractors' performance of the Work or the construction contracts, or the acts of subcontractors or suppliers, but shall be beneficiary of the customary guarantees by the Contractors that the Work furnished is in accordance with the requirements of the Contract Documents.

5.13 Copies of Notices

The Design Professional shall furnish the CM copies of all written notices and communications sent to or received by the Design Professional which relate to the aspects of the Project for which the CM has responsibility under the Owner-CM Agreement.

5.14 Coordination and Scheduling of Contractors' Work

Any coordination, scheduling or sequencing of the Work of the Contractors that is required by the Owner will be the responsibility of the CM. The Design Professional's documentation shall be prepared as required by the Construction Management Plan to permit such coordination, scheduling and sequencing.

5.15 Time and Cost Control

The CM will have authority as the Owner's agent to develop and monitor Contractors' cost control procedures and time schedules with respect to the Work and will receive, as requested, comments and suggestions from the Design Professional, who shall have no other authority or responsibility in connection with Contractors' timely performance, scheduling, sequencing or costs incurred during construction.

5.16 Substantial Completion

The Design Professional shall visit the site and consult with the CM as requested in respect of the readiness of certain specific items of the Work for substantial completion. While such visits and consultation shall involve assistance in the preparation of lists of incomplete Work or Work which does not conform to the requirements of the Contract Documents for each prime construction contract, a detailed examination or inspection of all of the Work shall not be required. Final decisions on substantial completion will rest with the CM, who will issue a Certificate of Substantial Completion. A copy of the Certificate of Substantial Completion will be given to the Design Professional.

5.17 Final Completion

The Design Professional shall visit the site and consult with the CM as requested in respect of completion of items on the list prepared in connection with substantial completion, but the Design Professional's Basic Services shall not include making a final examination or inspection of the Work under each prime construction contract or the Project, or determining if it is finally complete, or monitoring the assembly and submission of data by the Contractors as required by the Contract Documents.

5.18 Confidentiality

The Design Professional shall keep all information concerning the Project confidential, except for communications between the Design Professional, CM, Contractors and their independent professional engineers, architects and other consultants, subcontractors, and suppliers incident to completion of the Project, and except for publicity approved by the Owner and in connection with filings and

11

CMAA Document No. A-4 (1990 edition)

communications with governmental bodies having jurisdiction over the design of the Project.

5.19 Means and Methods

The Design Professional shall not have responsibility for means, methods, techniques, sequences or procedures of construction, or for safety precautions and programs incident thereto.

5.20 Overtime Work

The Owner shall require the CM to give the Design Professional immediate written notice whenever Work at the site is to be carried on other than during regular working hours.

5.21 Stopping the Work

The Design Professional shall have no authority or responsibility to recommend to the Owner or CM that the Work be suspended, stopped or taken over by the Owner, or that any of the construction contracts be terminated.

ARTICLE 6
ADDITIONAL SERVICES

6.1 As requested by the Owner or CM, the Design Professional shall perform Additional Services and the Design Professional shall be compensated therefor as provided in Articles 9 and 10. Additional Services shall be performed only after execution of a written amendment or supplement to this Agreement authorizing such services. Additional services may include:

6.1.1 Services rendered to investigate, appraise or evaluate existing conditions, facilities or equipment, or to verify the accuracy of existing drawings or other information furnished by the Owner, including information of the types described in Paragraph 7.12.

6.1.2 Services of independent professional associates or consultants for other than Basic Services; services to provide data of the types described in Paragraph 7.12 where the Owner employs the Design Professional to provide such services in lieu of furnishing the same in accordance with Paragraph 7.12; services relating to determination of space needs for the preparation of space programs; and services related to tenant and rental operations.

6.1.3 Services related to building sites investigations and analyses.

6.1.4 Services of the types described in Paragraph 4.5.

6.1.5 Services resulting from significant changes in the general scope, extent or character of the Project or its design, including but not limited to, changes in size, complexity of the Project or in the Construction Management Plan (including the Master Schedule, the Milestone Schedule, Project and Construction Budget, and Management Information Systems), changes in the character of construction or method of financing, and revising previously accepted studies, reports, design documents or Contract Documents when such revisions are required by changes in laws, rules, regulations, ordinances, codes or orders enacted subsequent to the preparation of such studies, reports or documents, or are due to any other cause beyond Design Professional's control.

6.1.6 Services in connection with visits to the site which are requested in writing by the Owner or CM for consultation and advice on specific aspects or parts of Contractors' Work prior to the CM's recommendation of acceptance and approval for payment, and consideration of whether or not such Work will produce a completed Project that conforms to the requirements of the Contract Documents and will be compatible with and not prejudice the integrity of the design concept of the completed Project as a functioning whole as indicated in the Contract Documents. Such services shall be treated as being in addition to visits necessary to enable the Design Professional to perform Basic Services under Paragraphs 5.3 through 5.7, inclusive. Such Additional Services shall include, but not be limited to, services identified as Additional Services in Paragraphs 5.10 and 5.11, but not services provided under Paragraphs 5.16 and 5.17.

CMAA Document No. A-4 (1990 edition)

6.1.7 Services to prepare Drawings and Specifications for incorporation into a change order to reflect design changes required to be responsive to changed conditions as described in Paragraph 5.7.

6.1.8 Services in connection with the preparation of Drawings, Specifications and other design documentation for alternate bids requested by the Owner or CM, or in connection with the preparation of additional or amended Drawings, Specifications and other design documentation to reflect changes in the Project's scope, extent, character or requirements as provided in Paragraph 3.5.2.

6.1.9 Services in connection with the preparation, review or assembly of maintenance manuals, warranties, guaranties, and the development of systems and procedures for control of operation and maintenance records for the Project.

6.1.10 Services to prepare a set of reproducible record prints of drawings showing those changes made during the construction process, based on marked-up prints, drawings and other data furnished by any Contractor or the CM to the Design Professional, and which the Design Professional considers significant.

6.1.11 Services to establish reference points on the site for construction.

6.1.12 Services in connection with any technical inspection or testing of any material or equipment prior to its incorporation in the Work, or of any aspect or part of the Work itself.

6.1.13 Services in connection with any dispute between the Contractor and the Owner, except as related to the Design Professional's services required by Paragraphs 5.3 and 5.5.

6.1.14 Consultation regarding replacement of Work damaged by fire or other cause during construction and furnishing services in connection with the replacement of such work.

6.1.15 Services made necessary by the default of a Contractor or CM.

6.1.16 Preparation for and serving as a witness in connection with any public or private hearing, or arbitration, mediation or legal proceeding.

6.1.17 Assisting the Owner in public relations activities, including preparing information for and attending public meetings.

6.1.18 Services related to occupancy of the Project, including preparing and soliciting responses to requests for proposals, preparing and coordinating the execution of contracts, conducting pre-moving conferences, administering the contract for moving activities in conjunction with occupancy of the Project and providing on-site personnel to oversee the relocation of furniture and equipment by the movers while actual move-in is in progress.

ARTICLE 7
OWNER'S RESPONSIBILITIES

7.1 The Owner shall not cause or permit the CM to take any action in violation of the Owner-CM Agreement that might be prejudicial to the interests or responsibilities of the Design Professional under this Agreement. The Owner shall require that the CM perform its services in cooperation with the Design Professional, consistent with this Agreement and in a timely manner in accordance with the Master Schedule so as not to delay the Design Professional in the performance of services. The Owner shall require that the CM show mutual respect for the authority and responsibility of the Design Professional under this Agreement. Whenever it is provided in this Agreement that the CM will or will not perform a certain act, the Owner shall take the necessary action to ensure that the CM complies with such provisions.

7.2. The Owner shall not amend the Owner-CM Agreement in any way inconsistent with this Agreement or that would be detrimental or prejudicial to the interests and obligations of the Design Professional under this Agreement. The Owner shall cause all agreements between the Owner and Contractor to be compatible and consistent with this Agreement. The Owner shall not authorize any change in the Construction Management Plan, including the

13

CMAA Document No. A-4 (1990 edition)

design requirements, design criteria, Master Schedule, Milestone Schedule, Project and Construction Budget and Management Information System without first receiving the written advice of the Design Professional.

7.3 The Owner shall not cause or permit the CM to authorize, accept or approve any Contractors' Work that varies from the design requirements, design criteria or the Contract Documents (except for minor changes referred to under Paragraph 5.5) without first having obtained the advice and written approval of the Design Professional in the form of a written addendum, interpretation, clarification, approval of a substitution, change order, shop drawing, sample, or other submittal.

7.4 The Owner shall furnish legal, accounting and insurance counseling services as may be necessary for the Project.

7.5 The Owner shall furnish insurance for the Project as specified in Article 11 and in the General Conditions [CMAA Document No. A-3 (1990 edition)].

7.6 If the Owner observes or otherwise becomes aware of any defect in design aspects of the Project, the Owner shall cause prompt written notice thereof to be given to the Design Professional.

7.7 The Owner shall furnish required information and approvals, render decisions and perform its responsibilities and activities in a timely manner and in accordance with the Master Schedule so as to facilitate orderly progress of the Design Professional's work in cooperation with the CM, consistent with this Agreement and in accordance with the Construction Management Plan. The Owner shall require the CM to do the same.

7.8 The Owner shall designate an officer, employee or other authorized representative to act on its behalf with respect to the Project who shall have authority to approve changes in the scope of the Project and be available during working hours and as often as may be required to render decisions and furnish information in a timely manner.

7.9 The Owner shall arrange for the Design Professional to have access to the site as necessary to carry out its services under this Agreement.

7.10 The Owner shall require that the Construction Contract (i) include waiver of subrogation provisions for the Design Professional's benefit, (ii) include provisions that negate the existence of any contractual relationship between the Design Professional and all Contractors, subcontractors and suppliers and (iii) state that the Design Professional's services are solely for the Owner's and CM's benefit. The Owner shall, at Owner's expense, furnish sufficient copies of the Contract Documents to the Design Professional.

7.11 The Owner shall require the CM to furnish to the Design Professional copies of the Construction Contracts and all written notices and communications sent to or received by the Owner or the CM which relate to design aspects of the Project, or the Design Professional's responsibilities under this Agreement, including all amendments to the Construction Contracts, Drawings, Specifications, approved submittals, change directives, Change Orders and other design documents referred to in Paragraphs 5.3 through 5.7, inclusive.

7.12 Owner shall furnish to the Design Professional as required for the performance of the Design Professional's services hereunder the following:

7.12.1 Reports of explorations and tests of surface and subsurface conditions at or contiguous to the site, and reports of explorations and tests of the conditions at the site (both surface and subsurface) in respect of the presence or absence of hazardous waste or similar materials (such as but not limited to asbestos, polychlorinated biphenyls, petroleum and radioactive materials), all of such reports and drawings to be based on appropriate borings, probings, examinations, surveys, tests, and samplings of the conditions involved, to be prepared by qualified persons, and to be accompanied by appropriate professional interpretations of all of the findings;

7.12.2 Environmental assessments and impact statements;

14

CMAA Document No. A-4 (1990 edition)

7.12.3 Property boundary, easement, right-of-way, topographical and utility surveys;

7.12.4 Property descriptions;

7.12.5 Zoning, deed and other land use restrictions; and

7.12.6 Other special data or consultation on similar subjects.

7.13 The Owner shall be responsible for the accuracy and completeness of all reports, data and other information furnished pursuant to Paragraph 7.12 and for the presence at the site of any asbestos, PCB's, petroleum, and radioactive materials, and the consequences of such presence. The Design Professional may use and rely on the same in performing services under this Agreement.

7.14 In the case of the termination of the CM's services, the Owner shall appoint a new CM who shall be acceptable to the Design Professional and whose responsibilities with respect to the Project and status under the new agreement with the Owner shall be similar to that of the CM under the Owner-CM Agreement and the Contract Documents.

7.15 The Owner shall, and shall cause the CM to give to the Design Professional all data of which each is aware concerning patents or copyrights for inclusion in Contract Documents.

7.16 The Owner shall in a timely manner secure, submit and pay for necessary governmental approvals, permits, easements, assessments and charges required for the construction, use or occupancy of permanent structures, or for permanent changes in existing facilities.

7.17 The Owner shall furnish evidence satisfactory to the Design Professional that sufficient funds are available and committed for the entire cost of the Project. Unless such reasonable evidence is furnished, the Design Professional shall not be required to commence services under this Agreement and may, if such evidence is not presented within a reasonable time, suspend such services upon fifteen (15) days' written notice to the Owner. In

such event, the Design Professional shall be compensated in the manner provided in Paragraph 12.2.

ARTICLE 8
DURATION OF DESIGN PROFESSIONAL SERVICES

8.1 The commencement date for the Design Professional's Basic Services shall be the date of the execution of this Agreement.

8.2 The duration of the Design Professional's Basic Services under this Agreement shall be _____ consecutive calendar days from the commencement date.

ARTICLE 9
COMPENSATION FOR DESIGN PROFESSIONAL'S SERVICES AND PAYMENT

9.1 The Design Professional shall receive compensation for its services in accordance with Paragraph 9.2 (Cost Plus Fixed Fee), Paragraph 9.3 (Lump Sum Fee) or Paragraph 9.4 (Personnel Expenses Times a Factor).

9.2 Cost Plus Fixed Fee

The Owner shall compensate the Design Professional on the basis of the Design Professional's cost plus a fixed fee in accordance with the terms and conditions of this Agreement and specifically as follows:

9.2.1 Compensation for Basic Services

The Design Professional shall be compensated for performing the Basic Services described in Articles 3, 4 and 5 as follows:

9.2.1.1 A Fixed Fee of _____
_____ Dollars
($).

9.2.1.2 The cost of employees working on the Project, other than principals, in an amount which equals the multiples as established in subparagraphs 9.2.1.2.1 and 9.2.1.2.2, multiplied by the personnel expense for each such employee. Personnel expense

15

SAMPLE AGREEMENT

CMAA Document No. A-4 (1990 edition)

for an employee shall be _____ times the base hourly wage. Personnel expense includes the base hourly wage, payroll taxes, employee benefits and Workers' Compensation Insurance. The cost of the Design Professional's principals shall be paid at the rate specified in subparagraph 9.2.1.3. The cost of engineers, architects and other consultants shall be paid at the rate specified in subparagraph 9.2.1.4. The specified multiples and rates shall remain constant for a twelve month period following the date of this Agreement. Thereafter, the multiples established in the referenced subparagraphs shall be adjusted by the Design Professional if the Design Professional's personnel expense changes;

9.2.1.2.1 Employees assigned to the Project and working at the construction site, or employees for which the Owner provides all office facilities and services, excluding the project manager and assistant project managers, a multiple of

_____ ($);

9.2.1.2.2 Employees assigned to the Project and working in the Design Professional's administrative office, including the project manager and assistant project managers, a multiple of_____

_____ ($);

9.2.1.3 Principals of the Design Professional who participate in the Project, a fixed rate of _____ ($) per hour. The principals to be compensated according to these terms are:

_____

_____

_____.

9.2.1.4 Independent professional engineers, architects and other consultants employed by the Design Professional and performing services related to the Project, a multiple of

_____ (   ) times the amount of the invoice for such services.

9.2.2 Direct Expenses

9.2.2.1 In addition to the compensation for Basic and Additional Services stated herein, the Design Professional shall be reimbursed for its direct expenses incurred in providing Basic and Additional Services. Direct expenses are those actual expenditures made by the Design Professional, its principals, employees, independent professional engineers, architects and other consultants in the interest of the Project, including, without limitation:

9.2.2.1.1 Long distance telephone calls, telegrams and fees paid for securing approval of authorities having jurisdiction over the Project;

9.2.2.1.2 Handling, shipping, mailing and reproduction of materials and documents;

9.2.2.1.3 Transportation and living expenses when traveling in connection with the Project;

9.2.2.1.4 Computer equipment rental or service fees;

9.2.2.1.5 Computer software purchased;

9.2.2.1.6 Electronic data processing service and rental of electronic data processing equipment;

9.2.2.1.7 Word processing equipment rental;

9.2.2.1.8 Premiums for professional liability insurance and other insurance beyond the limits normally carried by the Design Professional that are required by the terms of this Agreement;

9.2.2.1.9 Relocation of employees and families;

9.2.2.1.10 Temporary living expenses of employees who are not relocated, but assigned to the Project;

9.2.2.1.11 Gross receipts taxes, sales or use taxes, service taxes and other similar taxes required to be paid as a result of this Agreement;

16

CMAA Document No. A-4 (1990 edition)

9.2.2.1.12 Field office expenses, including the cost of office rentals, field telephones, utilities, field furniture, equipment and supplies; and

9.2.2.1.13 Premium time work.

9.2.3 Design Professional's Accounting Records

9.2.3.1 Records of the Design Professional's personnel expense, independent professional engineers', architects' and other consultants' fees and direct expenses pertaining to the Project shall be maintained on the basis of generally-accepted accounting practices and shall be available for inspection by the Owner or the Owner's representative at mutually convenient times for a period of two years after completion of the Construction Phase Basic Services.

9.2.4 Payments

Payments to the Design Professional shall be made monthly, not later than fifteen (15) days after receipt of the Design Professional's invoice by the Owner, as follows:

9.2.4.1 Payment of the Fixed Fee as indicated in Paragraph 9.2.1.1 shall be in amounts prorated equally over the duration of the Design Professional's Basic Services. The duration shall be as set out in Article 8;

9.2.4.2 Payment of personnel expense and the fixed hourly rate for principals shall be in amounts equal to the actual hours spent during the billing period on the Project multiplied by the rates and multiples stated in Paragraphs 9.2.1.2 and 9.2.1.3;

9.2.4.3 Payment of independent professional engineers', architects' and other consultants' services shall be in amounts equal to the invoice in receipt by the Design Professional for the billing period times the multiplier stated in Paragraph 9.2.1.4;

9.2.4.4 Reimbursement for direct expenses shall be in amounts equal to expenditures made during the billing period and during previous billing periods not yet invoiced;

9.2.4.5 No deductions shall be made from the Design Professional's compensation due to any claim by the Owner, Contractors or others not a party to this Agreement or due to any liquidated damages, retainage or other sums withheld from payments to the Contractors or others not a party to this Agreement; and

9.2.4.6 Payments due the Design Professional that are unpaid for more than thirty (30) days from the date of receipt by the Owner of the Design Professional's invoice shall bear interest at the legal rate from the due date, compounded annually. In addition, the Design Professional may, after giving seven (7) days' written notice to the Owner, suspend services under this Agreement until the Design Professional has been paid in full all amounts due for services, expenses and charges.

9.2.5 Compensation for Additional Services

The Design Professional shall be compensated and payments shall be made for performing Additional Services in the same amount and manner as provided in Article 9 for Basic Services. There shall be an increase in the fixed fee set out in Paragraph 9.2.1.1 in an amount which is mutually agreeable between the Owner and the Design Professional.

9.3 Lump Sum Fee

The Owner shall compensate the Design Professional on the basis of a lump sum fee in accordance with the terms and conditions of this Agreement and specifically as follows:

9.3.1 Compensation for Basic Services

The Design Professional shall be compensated for performing Basic Services described in Articles 3, 4 and 5 a total Lump Sum Fee in the amount of

_____

_____ ($), which amount shall be paid as follows:

_____

_____

_____

17

CMAA Document No. A-4 (1990 edition)

9.3.2 Direct Expenses

The cost of direct expenses incurred will be included in the Lump Sum Fee.

9.3.3 Payments

Payments shall be made monthly, not later than fifteen (15) days after receipt of the Design Professional's invoice by the Owner.

9.3.3.1 No deductions shall be made from the Design Professional's compensation due to any claim of the Owner, CM, Contractors or others not a party to this Agreement or due to any liquidated damages, retainage or other sums withheld from payments to Contractors or others not a party to this Agreement.

9.3.3.2 Payments due the Design Professional that are unpaid for more than thirty (30) days from date of receipt by the Owner of the Design Professional's invoice shall bear interest at the legal rate from the due date, compounded annually. In addition, the Design Professional may, after giving seven (7) days' written notice to the Owner, suspend services under this Agreement until the Design Professional has been paid in full all amounts due for services, expenses and charges.

9.3.4 Compensation for Additional Services

The Design Professional shall be compensated and payments shall be made for performing Additional Services in an amount and on terms mutually agreeable to the Owner and the Design Professional.

9.4 Personnel Expenses Times a Factor

The Owner shall compensate the Design Professional on the basis of personnel expenses times a factor in accordance with the terms and conditions of this Agreement and specifically as follows:

9.4.1 Compensation for Basic Services

The Design Professional shall be compensated for performing basic services described in Articles 3, 4 and 5 as follows:

9.4.1.1 The cost of employees working on the Project, other than principals, in an amount which equals the multiples of the employees' personnel expense as established in subparagraphs 9.4.1.1.1 and 9.4.1.1.2, multiplied by the personnel expense for each such employee. Personnel expense for an employee shall be _____ times the base hourly wage. Personnel expense includes the base hourly wage, payroll taxes, employee benefits and Workers' Compensation Insurance. The cost of the Design Professional's principals shall be paid at the rate specified in subparagraph 9.4.1.2. The cost of engineers, architects and consultants shall be paid at the rate specified in subparagraph 9.4.1.3. The specified multiples and rates shall remain constant for a twelve month period following the date of this Agreement. Thereafter, the multiples established in the referenced subparagraphs shall be adjusted by the Design Professional if the Design Professional's personnel expense changes;

9.4.1.1.1 Employees assigned to the Project and working at the construction site, or employees for which the Owner provides all office facilities and services, excluding the project manager and assistant project managers, a multiple of _____

_____

($);

9.4.1.1.2 Employees assigned to the Project and working in the Design Professional's administrative office, including the project manager and assistant project managers, a multiple of

_____

_____ ($);

9.4.1.2 Principals of the Design Professional who participate in the Project, a fixed rate of _____ ($) per hour. The principals to be compensated according to these terms are:

_____

_____

_____

9.4.1.3 Independent professional engineers, architects and other consultants employed by the Design Professional and performing services related

18

CMAA Document No. A-4 (1990 edition)

to the Project, a multiple of _____
_____ (   ) times the amount of
the invoice for such services.

9.4.2 Direct Expenses

9.4.2.1 In addition to the compensation for Basic
and Additional Services stated herein, the Design
Professional shall be reimbursed for its direct
expenses incurred in providing Basic and Additional
Services. Direct expenses for those actual
expenditures made by the Design Professional, its
principals, employees, independent professional
engineers, architects and other consultants in the
interest of the Project, including, without
limitation:

9.4.2.1.1 Long distance telephone calls, telegrams
and fees paid for securing approval of authorities
having jurisdiction over the Project;

9.4.2.1.2 Handling, shipping, mailing and
reproduction of materials and documents;

9.4.2.1.3 Transportation and living expenses when
traveling in connection with the Project;

9.4.2.1.4 Computer equipment rental;

9.4.2.1.5 Computer software purchased;

9.4.2.1.6 Electronic data processing service and
rental of electronic data processing equipment;

9.4.2.1.7 Word processing equipment rental;

9.4.2.1.8 Premiums for professional liability
insurance and other insurance beyond the limits
normally carried by the Design Professional that
are required by the terms of this Agreement;

9.4.2.1.9 Relocation of employees and families;

9.4.2.1.10 Temporary living expenses of employees
who are not relocated, but assigned to the Project;

9.4.2.1.11 Gross receipts taxes, sales or use
taxes, service taxes and other similar taxes
required to be paid as a result of this Agreement;

9.4.2.1.12 Field office expenses including the cost
of office rentals, field telephones, utilities,
field furniture, equipment and supplies; and

9.4.2.1.13 Premium time work.

9.4.3 Design Professional's Accounting Records

9.4.3.1 Records of the Design Professional's
personnel expense, independent professional
engineers', architects' and other consultants' fees,
and direct expenses pertaining to the Project shall
be maintained on the basis of generally-accepted
accounting practices and shall be available for
inspection by the Owner or the Owner's
representative at mutually convenient times for a
period of two years after completion of the
Construction Phase Basic Services.

9.4.4 Payments

Payments to the Design Professional shall be made
monthly, not later than fifteen (15) days after
receipt of the Design Professional's invoice by the
Owner, as follows:

9.4.4.1 Payment of personnel expense and the fixed
hourly rate for principals shall be in amounts equal
to the actual hours spent during the billing period
on the Project multiplied by the rates and multiples
stated in Paragraphs 9.4.1.1 and 9.4.1.2;

9.4.4.2 Payment of independent professional
engineers', architects' and consultants' services
shall be in amounts equal to the invoice in receipt
by the Design Professional for the billing period
times the multiplier stated in Paragraph 9.4.1.3;
9.4.4.3 Reimbursement for direct expenses shall be
in amounts equal to expenditures made during the
billing period and during previous billing periods
not yet invoiced;

9.4.4.4 No deductions shall be made from the Design
Professional's compensation due to any claim by the
Owner, Contractors or others not a party to this
Agreement or due to any liquidated damages,
retainage or other sums withheld from payments to
the Contractors or others not a party to this
Agreement; and

19

CMAA Document No. A-4 (1990 edition)

9.4.4.5 Payments due the Design Professional that are unpaid for more than thirty (30) days from the date of receipt by the Owner of the Design Professional's invoice shall bear interest at the legal rate from the due date, compounded annually. In addition, the Design Professional may, after giving seven (7) days' written notice to the Owner, suspend services under this Agreement until the Design Professional has been paid in full all amounts due for services, expenses and charges.

9.4.5 Compensation for Additional Services

The Design Professional shall be compensated and payments shall be made for performing Additional Services in an amount and on terms mutually agreeable between the Owner and the Design Professional.

ARTICLE 10
CHANGES IN DESIGN PROFESSIONAL'S
BASIC SERVICES AND
COMPENSATION

10.1 Owner Changes

10.1.1 The Owner, without invalidating this Agreement, may make changes in the Design Professional's Basic Services specified in Article 2, 3, 4 and 5 of this Agreement. The Design Professional shall promptly notify the Owner of changes that increase or decrease the Design Professional's compensation or the duration of the Design Professional's Basic Services or both.

10.1.2 If the scope or the duration of the Design Professional's Basic Services is changed, the Design Professional's compensation shall be adjusted equitably. A written proposal indicating the change in compensation for a change in the scope or duration of Basic Services shall be given by the Design Professional to the Owner with a copy to the CM within thirty (30) days of the occurrence of the event giving rise to such request. The amount of the change in compensation to be paid shall be determined on the basis of the Design Professional's cost and a customary and reasonable adjustment in the Design Professional's fixed, lump sum or factor fee consistent with the provision of Article 9.

10.2 Authorization

Changes in the Design Professional's Basic Services and entitlement to additional compensation or a change in duration of this Agreement shall be made by a written amendment to this Agreement executed by the Owner and the Design Professional. The amendment shall be executed prior to performing the Services required by the amendment. The Design Professional shall proceed to perform the services required by the amendment only after receiving written notice directing the Design Professional to proceed.

10.3 Invoices for Additional Compensation

The Design Professional shall submit invoices for additional compensation with its invoice for Basic Services.

ARTICLE 11
INSURANCE AND MUTUAL INDEMNIFICATION

11.1 Design Professional's Liability Insurance

11.1.1 General Liability

11.1.1.1 The Design Professional shall procure and maintain insurance for protection for claims under Workers' Compensation acts, claims for damages because of bodily injury including personal injury, sickness or disease or death of any or all employees or of any person other than such employees, and from claims or damages because of injury to or destruction of property including loss of use resulting therefrom.

11.1.2 Professional Liability

11.1.2.1 The Design Professional shall procure and maintain professional liability insurance for protection from claims arising out of the performance of professional services caused by a negligent error, omission or act for which the insured is legally liable; such liability insurance will provide for coverage in such amounts, with such deductible provisions and for such period of time

20

CMAA Document No. A-4 (1990 edition)

as required by the Owner. Certificates indicating that such insurance is in effect shall be delivered to the Owner.

11.1.2.2 The Design Professional shall also cause the independent professional engineers, architects and other consultants retained by the Design Professional for the Project to procure and maintain professional liability insurance coverage, for at least such amounts, deductibles, and periods as determined by the Owner.

11.2 Owner's Insurance

11.2.1 The Design Professional shall be named as an additional insured in any insurance policy obtained by the Owner for the Project.

11.3 Waiver of Subrogation

11.3.1 The Owner and the Design Professional waive all rights against each other and against the Contractor, CM, independent professional engineers, architects and other consultants, subcontractors, suppliers, agents and employees of the other for damages during construction covered by any property insurance as set forth in CMAA Document No. A-3, General Conditions of the Construction Contract, or the Supplementary Conditions. The Owner and the Design Professional shall each require similar waivers from their contractors, independent professional engineers, architects and other consultants, subcontractors, suppliers and agents.

11.4 Indemnity

11.4.1 The Design Professional hereby indemnifies and holds harmless the Owner, the CM and their employees, agents and representatives from and against any and all claims, demands, suits and damages for bodily injury and property damage for which the Design Professional is liable that arise out of the negligent acts or omissions of the Design Professional in performing professional services under this Agreement; provided, however, that the Design Professional does not assume any risk of damages to property that is incorporated in or shall be incorporated in or is located at the Project site which is not within the possession of the Design

Professional or under the Design Professional's direction or control. The total liability of the Design Professional arising by reason of this indemnity for all claims, demands, suits and damages that are not insured shall not exceed the amount of the total compensation actually paid to the Design Professional by the Owner pursuant to this Agreement.

11.4.2 The Owner shall cause the CM to indemnify and hold harmless the Design Professional, its employees, agents and representatives to the same extent and in the same manner that the Design Professional has provided indemnification for the CM under Paragraph 11.4.1.

11.4.3 The Owner hereby indemnifies and holds harmless the Design Professional and its employees, agents and representatives from and against any and all claims, demands, suits and damages for bodily injury and property damage for which the Owner is liable that arise out of the negligent acts or omissions of the Owner, its employees, agents, representatives, independent contractors, material suppliers, the Contractors and the CM.

11.4.4 The Owner shall cause each Contractor to indemnify and hold harmless the Design Professional from and against any and all claims, demands, suits and damages, for bodily injury or property damage, for which each Contractor is liable that arise out of negligent acts or omissions by such Contractor, its employees, agents and representatives in performing the Work.

ARTICLE 12
TERMINATION AND SUSPENSION

12.1 Termination

12.1.1 This Agreement may be terminated by the Owner for convenience after seven (7) days' written notice to the Design Professional.

12.1.2 This Agreement may be terminated by either party hereto upon seven (7) days' written notice should the other party fail substantially to perform in accordance with the terms hereof through no fault of the terminating party, or if the Project in whole

21

CMAA Document No. A-4 (1990 edition)

or substantial part is stopped for a period of sixty (60) days under an order of any court or other public authority having jurisdiction, or as a result of an act of government.

12.1.3 In the event of termination under Paragraph 12.1.1, the Design Professional shall be paid its compensation for services performed to the date of termination, services of independent professional engineers, architects and other consultants then due and all termination expenses. Termination expenses are defined as those expenses arising prior, during and subsequent to termination that are directly attributable to the termination, plus an amount computed as a percentage of the total compensation earned at the time of termination computed as follows:

12.1.3.1 Twenty (20) percent if the termination occurs during the Design Phase or Bidding Phase; or

12.1.3.2 Ten (10) percent if the termination occurs during the Construction Phase.

12.1.4 In the event of termination under Paragraph 12.1.2, the Design Professional shall be paid its compensation for services performed to the date of termination, services of independent professional engineers, architects and other consultants then due, and all termination expenses. No amount computed as provided in Paragraphs 12.1.3.1 and 12.1.3.2 shall be paid in addition.

12.2 Suspension

12.2.1 The Owner may in writing order the Design Professional to suspend all or any part of Design Professional's services for the Project for the convenience of the Owner or for Work stoppage beyond the control of the Owner or CM or Design Professional. If the performance of all or any part of the Design Professional's services for the Project is so suspended, an equitable adjustment in the Design Professional's compensation shall be made for the increase, if any, in the cost of the Design Professional's performance of this Agreement caused by such suspension, and this Agreement shall be modified in writing accordingly.

12.2.2 In the event the Design Professional's Services for the Project are suspended, the Owner shall reimburse the Design Professional for all of the costs of its staff assigned to the Project and other costs as provided for by this Agreement for the first thirty (30) days of such suspension. The Design Professional shall reduce the size of its staff for the remainder of the suspension period as directed by the Owner and, during such period, the Owner shall reimburse the Design Professional for all of the costs of its reduced staff. Upon cessation of the suspension, the Design Professional shall restore the staff to its former size.

12.2.3 Persons assigned to another project during such suspension periods and not available to return to the Project upon cessation of the suspension shall be replaced. The Owner shall reimburse the Design Professional for costs incurred in relocating previous staff persons returning to the home office or new persons assigned to the Project.

12.2.4 If the Project is suspended by the Owner for more than three (3) months, the Design Professional shall be paid compensation for services performed prior to receipt of written notice from the Owner of the suspension, together with direct expenses then due and all expenses and costs directly resulting from the suspension. If the Project is resumed after being suspended for more than six (6) months, the Design Professional shall have the option of requiring that its compensation, including rates and fees, be renegotiated. Subject to the provisions of this Agreement relating to termination, a suspension of the Project will not void this Agreement.

ARTICLE 13
DISPUTE RESOLUTION

13.1 The Owner and the Construction Manager shall submit all unresolved claims, counterclaims, disputes, controversies, and other matters in question between them arising out of or relating to this Agreement or the breach thereof ("disputes"), to mediation prior to either party initiating against the other a demand for arbitration pursuant to Paragraph 13.2 below, unless delay in initiating

22

CMAA Document No. A-4 (1990 edition)

or prosecuting a proceeding in an arbitration or judicial forum would irrevocably prejudice the Owner or the CM. The Owner and the CM shall agree in writing as to the identity of the mediator and the rules and procedures of the mediation. If the Owner and the CM submit the dispute to mediation it shall be under the then current Construction Industry Mediation Rules of the American Arbitration Association.

13.2 All disputes that the Owner and the CM are unable to resolve by mediation as aforesaid shall be decided by arbitration, subject to the limitations stated in Paragraph 13.4 below. The agreement to arbitrate, and any other agreement or consent to arbitrate entered into in accordance herewith shall be specifically enforceable under the prevailing law of any court having jurisdiction. The Owner and the CM shall agree in writing as to the identity of the arbitrator(s) and the rules and procedures of the arbitration. If the Owner and the CM do not so agree, then the Owner and the CM shall submit the dispute to arbitration under the then current Construction Industry Rules of the American Arbitration Association.

13.3 Notice of demand for arbitration must be filed in writing with the other party to this Agreement and with the arbitrator(s). The demand must be made within a reasonable time after the dispute has arisen, but not prior to or during the pendency of the mediation as agreed in Paragraph 13.1. In no event may the demand for arbitration be made after the date when institution of legal or equitable proceedings based on such dispute in question would be barred by the applicable statute of limitations.

13.4 No arbitration arising out of, or relating to, this Agreement may include, by consolidation, joinder or in any other manner, any person or entity who is not a party to this Agreement unless both parties agree otherwise in writing. No consent to arbitration in respect of a specifically described dispute will constitute consent to arbitrate any other dispute which is not specifically described in such consent or which is with any party not specifically described therein.

13.5 The award rendered by the arbitrator(s) will be final, judgment may be entered upon it in any court having jurisdiction thereof, and the award will not be subject to modification or appeal. In any judicial proceeding to enforce this Agreement to arbitrate, the only issues to be determined shall be those set forth in 9 U.S.C. Section 4 Federal Arbitration Act, and such issues shall be determined by the Court without a jury. All other issues, such as but not limited to, arbitratibility, prerequisites to arbitration, compliance with contractual time limits, applicability of indemnity clauses, clauses limiting damages and statutes of limitations shall be for the arbitrator(s), whose decision thereon shall be final and binding. There shall be no interlocutory appeal of an order compelling arbitration.

ARTICLE 14
OWNER'S RIGHTS IN DOCUMENTS AND REUSE

14.1 All documents including Drawings and Specifications prepared or furnished by the Design Professional (and the Design Professional's independent professional engineers, architects and other consultants) pursuant to this Agreement are instruments of service in respect of the Project, and the Design Professional shall retain an ownership and property interest therein whether or not the Project is completed. The Owner may make and retain copies for information and reference in connection with the use and occupancy of the Project by the Owner and others; however, such documents are not intended or represented to be suitable for reuse by the Owner, CM or others on extensions of the Project or on any other project. Any reuse without written verification or adaptation by the Design Professional for the specific purpose intended shall be at the Owner's sole risk and without liability or legal exposure to the Design Professional, or to the Design Professional's independent professional engineers, architects and other consultants, and the Owner shall indemnify and hold harmless the Design Professional and the Design Professional's independent professional engineers, architects and other consultants from all claims, damages, losses and expenses, including attorneys' fees arising out of or resulting therefrom. Any such verification or adaptation shall entitle the Design Professional

23

CMAA Document No. A-4 (1990 edition)

to further compensation at rates to be agreed upon by the Owner and the Design Professional.

ARTICLE 15
ADDITIONAL PROVISIONS

15.1 Limitations and Assignments

15.1.1 The Owner and the Design Professional each is hereby bound and the partners, successors, executors, administrators and legal representatives of Owner and Design Professional (and to the extent permitted by paragraph 15.1.2 the assigns of Owner and Design Professional) are hereby bound to the other party to this Agreement and to the partners, successors, executors, administrators and legal representatives (and said assigns) of such other party, in respect of all covenants, agreements and obligations of this Agreement.

15.1.2 Neither Owner nor Design Professional shall assign, sublet or transfer any rights under or interest in this Agreement without the written consent of the other, except that the Design Professional may assign accounts receivable to a commercial bank for securing loans.

15.2 Governing Law

15.2.1 This Agreement shall, unless otherwise provided be governed by the law of the state where the Project is located.

15.3 Extent of Agreement

15.3.1 This Agreement constitutes the entire agreement between the parties and incorporates all prior agreements and understandings in connection with the subject matter hereof. This Agreement may be amended only in writing signed by the party against whom enforcement is sought. Nothing contained in this Agreement is intended to benefit any third party other than the CM as specifically indicated herein. The Contractors, subcontractors, or suppliers are not intended third party beneficiaries of this Agreement.

15.4 Severability

15.4.1 If any portion of this Agreement is held as a matter of law to be unenforceable, the remainder of this Agreement shall be enforceable without such provisions.

15.5 Meaning of Terms

15.5.1 References made in the singular shall include the plural and the masculine shall include the feminine or the neuter.

15.5.2 The meaning of terms used herein shall be consistent with the definitions expressed in the CMAA Standard Form Agreements, Contracts and General Conditions.

15.6 Notices

15.6.1 All notices required by this Agreement or other communications to either party by the other shall be deemed given when made in writing and deposited in the United States Mail, first class, postage prepaid, addressed as follows:

To the Owner:

_____

_____

_____

_____

To the Design Professional:

_____

_____

_____

_____

24

CMAA Document No. A-4 (1990 edition)

This Agreement is executed as of the day and year first written above.

OWNER   DESIGN PROFESSIONAL

_____   _____

Title:_____   Title:_____

Attest:_____   Attest:_____

CHAPTER 5

WHAT WENT WRONG WITH THE ASCE AND NAAG DOCUMENTS?

Ralph L. Kaskell, Jr.

§ 5.1   The Kansas City Hyatt Regency Skywalk Collapse

ASCE MANUAL

§ 5.2   Overreaction of ASCE

§ 5.3   ASCE Manual of Professional Practice for Virtually Everybody

NAAG DOCUMENTS

§ 5.4   Overreaction of NAAG

§ 5.5   Agreement Between Owner and Design Professional

§ 5.6   Construction Contract

§ 5.7   Confusion Reigns

§ 5.1   The Kansas City Hyatt Regency Skywalk Collapse

Controversies over design professional publications do occur. The several generations of contract forms by the American Institute of Architects (AIA) have at times aroused comment.[1] But those disputes pale in the light of the controversies surrounding the *Preliminary Edition of the Manual of Professional Practice* by the American Society of Civil Engineers (ASCE)[2] and the *Model Design and*

---

[1] Sapers, *The new AIA General Conditions: A flawed document that architects will use at their peril,* Architectural Record 37 (Feb. 1988); Ellickson, *The AIA defends A201/1987,* Architectural Record, 36-42 (Mar. 1988).

[2] Preliminary Edition for Trial Use and Comment, Manual of Professional Practice, Quality in the Constructed Project, A Guideline for Owners, Designers and Constructors, Vol. 1, May, 1988 [hereinafter PE].

Construction Documents by the National Association of Attorneys General (NAAG).[3]

Many prominent and sober-minded civil engineers look upon the ASCE *Preliminary Edition* as a direct reaction to the Kansas City Hyatt Regency catastrophe of July 17, 1981.[4] Numerous manuals had been issued in the past for specific aspects of structural work.[5] No book like the *Preliminary Edition* (PE) had before been spawned. The PE sought to mold all building project thought into the confines of the PE.

It was fitting that the Hyatt Regency disaster shocked design professionals. The highest tribunal to consider the tragedy stated:

> On July 17, 1981, the second and fourth floor walkways of the Hyatt Regency Hotel in Kansas City collapsed and fell to the floor of the main lobby. Approximately 1500 to 2000 people were in the lobby. The walkways together weighed 142,000 pounds. One hundred and fourteen people died and at least 186 were injured. In terms of loss of life and injuries, the National Bureau of Standards concluded this was the most devastating structural collapse ever to take place in this country. That Bureau conducted an investigation of the tragedy and made its report in May 1982.[6]

The PE does not state, as it should, that the civil engineers are still trying to find an answer to the Hyatt Regency collapse. The true chronology, even in the PE, shows no "manual" prior to July 17, 1981.

The chronology begins with the 114 deaths and 186 injuries on July 17, 1981. The National Bureau of Standards (NBS) report of February 1982 found "insufficient load capacity, . . . inadequacy of the original design, . . . only 31 percent of the ultimate capacity expected . . . under the Kansas City Building Code," and, without shop drawing change, "the ultimate capacity would have been 60 percent of that expected under the Kansas City Building Code."

The final conclusion in the NBS abstract is that, with the shop drawing change, "the ultimate capacity of the walkways was so significantly reduced that, from the day of construction, they had only minimal capacity to resist their own weight and had virtually no capacity to resist additional loads imposed by people."[7]

---

[3] Model Design and Construction Documents, A Model Form of Agreement Between Owner and Design Professional, A Model Form of Agreement for Construction Between Owner and Contractor, and Standard Form General Conditions of the Contract for Construction, Dec. 1988.

[4] Jackson & Kaskell, *The Kansas City Hyatt Regency Disaster: What Went Wrong?*, 56 Def. Couns. J. 415 (1989).

[5] PE at 141.

[6] Duncan v. Missouri Bd. for Architects, 744 S.W.2d 524, 527 (Mo. Ct. App. 1988).

[7] NBSIR 82-2465 Investigation of the Kansas City Hyatt Regency Walkways Collapse, Abstract at iii (1982).

The Missouri Board for Architects, Professional Engineers and Land Surveyors filed its complaint against Daniel M. Duncan and Jack D. Gillum on February 3, 1984, for gross negligence, incompetence, misconduct, and unprofessional conduct.[8] The hearings began on July 16, 1984, and continued from time to time until September 17, 1984.[9] On November 15, 1985, Commissioner James B. Deutsch signed the 442-page decision, which stated "that cause for discipline exists . . . to suspend or revoke the certificates of . . . Duncan and . . . Gillum . . . for gross negligence, misconduct and unprofessional conduct in the practice of engineering."[10]

ASCE MANUAL

§ 5.2   Overreaction of ASCE

Apparently the first conference after the Hyatt collapse deemed significant by ASCE was the Structures Failure Conference of 1983.[11]

But it was in November 1984 that a Chicago workshop, of which ASCE was "the principal sponsor," designated ASCE as the organization to carry out the unanimous agreement "that the professionals of the design and construction industry should develop and be judged by their own standards of performance."[12] A number of state legislatures disagree. To them a civil engineer is licensed "to safeguard life, health and property."[13]

---

[8] Before the Administrative Hearing Commission, State of Missouri, Case No. AR-84-0239, at 1.

[9] *Id*. at 2.

[10] *Id*. at 442, *aff'd,* Duncan v. Missouri Bd. for Architects, 744 S.W.2d 524 (Mo. Ct. App. 1988), with the exception of a charge not set forth in the pleadings. *Id*. at 539, 542. But, although that charge was not pleaded, the court found that "the evidence is relevant and persuasive." *Id*. at 542.

[11] PE at 12.

[12] *Id*. But "courts will not permit an entire profession to absolve itself from liability by adopting negligent methods as its industry standard." Peek & Hock, *Liability of Engineers for Structural Design Errors; State of Art Considerations in Defining the Standard of Care,* 30 Vill. L. Rev. 403, 422-23 (1985).

[13] La. Rev. Stat. Ann. § 37:681 (West). The typical language concerning the regulation of the practice of engineering is "In order to safeguard life, health and property, and to promote the public welfare." *See* Ala. Code § 34-11-2(b); Cal. Bus. & Prof. Code § 6704 (West); Colo. Rev. Stat. § 12-25-101; Conn. Gen. Stat. § 20-299; Del. Code Ann. § 2802; D. C. Code Ann. § 2-1802(a); Ohio Rev. Code Ann. § 4733.01(B) (Baldwin); Tex. Occ. Code Ann. § 3271a (Vernon).

Before ASCE started its PE, a legal scholar commented in 1981 on the proper objective of the standard documents drafted for engineers:

> The Committee also feels strongly that it is undesirable and quite unprofessional to try by standard society-endorsed contract forms to relieve Engineers from liability for improperly performing those duties and responsibilities which their expertise and professional training qualifies them to perform and which, because of their being licensed to practice, they have a duty to the public to perform. In fact, such contractual endeavors may well provide no more than illusory legal protection since courts and juries are not likely to accept wholesale efforts to avoid professional responsibilities. . . .[14]

Faced with the worst building catastrophe in our history ASCE decided, not to reform itself, but to reform the entire construction industry and, apparently, the rest of society.

The ASCE devised a two-volume manual. "Volume 1 covers the entire design and construction process and states general and specific responsibilities, duties and limits of authority of the primary project team members through each phase of design and construction."[15]

The stated "Intent and Goals" of Volume 1, as set forth in the Preliminary Edition, are:

> The Manual is intended for anyone who is connected with or interested in the design and construction process. Interested readers will include owners, engineers, architects, constructors, developers, users, operation and maintenance personnel, and subcontractors. It is also intended for attorneys, government officials, university professors, students, judges and legislators. It is not in itself a technical document, not a guide strictly for design professionals. Its language, style, and format are intended for non-industry readers as well as for trade professionals.[16]

The PE covers all facets of construction in Volume 1, and relegates to Volume 2 "14 chapters covering recommended practices for specific disciplines."[17] Chapter 2 of the PE emphasizes Challenger, a space program failure in 1986. More attention is given to it than to the 114 deaths in the Hyatt Regency.[18] ASCE employed some 40 authors to do PE Volume 1.[19]

---

[14] Clark, *Commentary on Agreements for Engineering Services and Contract Documents*, EJCDC No. 1910-9 (1981). ASCE was part of EJCDC.

[15] PE at 13.

[16] *Id*.

[17] *Id*.

[18] *Id*. at 12, 17.

[19] *Id*. at 14. The list does not identify any author with the AIA.

ASCE states in chapter 2.3 that "This Manual is mainly concerned with defining the responsibilities and limits of authority of the primary members." This puts aside the great body of statutes, regulations, court decisions, and contracts used on most building projects of any size, for the homilies of the PE.[20]

In addition to drafts in 1987, ASCE issued over 15,000 copies of the PE beginning in May 1988.[21] The ASCE has continued on the course of revising and issuing the First Edition of the Manual's revised original PE.[22]

§ 5.3   ASCE Manual of Professional Practice for Virtually Everybody

This chapter cannot summarize in detail the 192-page PE.[23] But the chapter will suffice to show the reasons for the widespread adverse reviews of the ASCE bestseller. David R. Wittes, Senior Principal, Wittes and Associates, said: "The design professional who accepts as gospel the new ASCE Manual of Professional Practice for Quality in the Constructed Project is, in our opinion, a fool."[24]

Its temporary adverse press results from the PE's offering something to everybody in the construction industry field and elsewhere. ASCE does not, as it should, confine its guidelines to ASCE's constituents.[25]

The PE continued to divide groups of design professionals from other design groups and contractors from A/Es. The Board of Directors of the American Consulting Engineers Council accepted from its committee recommendations that "the publication should not be endorsed as a manual nor recognized as a standard of practice." The Board suggested that, if revised, "it could be used for educational purposes."[26]

---

[20] *Id.* at 18.

[21] *Id.* at 14; *AIA Drops ASCE Manual,* ENR, Apr. 20, 1989, at 15.

[22] PE at 14; ASCE Memorandum to Construction Team, May 1988, immediately after the title page. [Editor's note: The Manual finally was "unveiled" at ASCE's November 1990 annual convention. *ASCE Quality Gudie out AMid Praise and Pokes,* ENR, Nov. 15, 1990, at 16.]

[23] Copies may be purchased from ASCE, 345 East 47th Street, New York, NY 10017-2398. An engineer-client can probably get it for you at minimum cost.

[24] *The Case for a Construction Professional,* Civil Engineering, Mar. 1989, at 6. Apparently Wittes was not one of the "more than 1,000 professionals . . . involved in drafting and reviewing this document." PE at 1.

[25] *AIA Drops ASCE Manual,* ENR, April 20, 1989, at 15. "An important question raised by AIA's decision is whether a document describing quality practice can be universal in application. 'It's a laudable goal and a difficult one to achieve and we give ASCE high marks for trying,' says Ward [AIA group vice president for external affairs]. 'But how can any one association or group of experts decide what the process should be?' " The AIA announcement was confirmed by AIA President Benjamin E. Brewer to ASCE President Bud Carroll, saying, "We stated our conviction that the document was only relevant to a small percentage of architecture firms and an even smaller number of projects."

[26] *The Last Word,* Vol. IX, No. 15, Convention Highlights, May 19, 1989.

A senior contractor, W. O. Jones III, President of Kjellstrom and Lee, Inc., of Virginia, took Wittes to task for not recognizing the existence of "incompetent design professionals" who did not issue relatively complete plans and specifications. But Jones believed that "the manual fails because it is repetitive, elementary, subjective, verbose, arbitrary, and uninformed as to the construction business."[27]

Joseph Proctor, Jr., construction consultant in Oregon, said "that the engineering profession, and particularly ASCE, tends to minimize the importance of construction. Many engineers, it seems, feel the contractor is a body of dronelike laborers."[28]

On the fundamental responsibility of civil engineers, the profession is split over the apparent ambiguity of the PE. The American Institute of Steel Construction (AISC) "strongly objects to the crucial chapter on shop drawings" in the PE. The Institute sees it "as an unwarranted shifting of design responsibility from the designer to the subcontractor or steel fabricator." That means substituting the obligations of the engineer to the owner directly or indirectly (through the architect), with the non-contractual duty of a fabricator.[29]

Richard Tomasetti, co-author of the shop drawing chapter of the PE, distinguishes design responsibility for the shop drawings by comparing accepted civil engineering practice "on the West Coast" with "accepted practice on the East Coast."[30] In other words, responsibility for a Kansas City Hyatt Regency catastrophe depends on location and whether the locale allows the structural engineer to shift "full legal responsibility" to a fabricator by allowing him to design special or complex connections through his own engineer.[31]

AISC rebuts Tomasetti by retorting that "the fabricator and detailer are not the designers of the structure, they were not paid to design, and they are merely facilitating and implementing the design professional's original plan."[32]

In *Duncan v. Missouri Board for Architects,* the court held: "Design of connections is, under the statute, a matter for which the engineer is responsible. Custom, practice, or 'bottom line' necessity cannot alter that responsibility."[33] The court held that the law required the engineer to affix its seal to "all plans, and other documents prepared by him, or under his direction, *and he shall be personally responsible for the contents of all such documents.*"[34]

---

[27] *Readers Write*, Civil Eng'g, June 1989, at 31.

[28] *Id.*

[29] ENR, Dec. 1, 1988, at 11, 12.

[30] *Id.* at 12.

[31] *Id.*

[32] *Id.*

[33] 744 S.W.2d at 537.

[34] *Id.* at 535 (emphasis by court).

Without specific statutory provision for the affixing of the engineer's seal to shop drawings, nor for responsibility for shop drawings, the court concluded that the engineer had "a non-delegable duty of responsibility."[35]

Duncan made short shrift of the attempt to water down those duties and responsibilities of the engineer. In the face of the argument that "Duncan . . . intended for the fabricator to design the connection," the court stated: "The adequacy of the connection design remains the responsibility of the structural engineer;" that "[t]he primary reason is to provide assurance that the fabricator is conforming to the contract and that any engineering work conforms to acceptable standards;" that "[t]he structural engineer's duty is to determine that the structural plans which he designs or approves will provide structural safety because if they do not a strong probability of harm exists;" and that "[t]he purpose behind licensing statutes is to protect the public rather than punish the licensed professional."[36]

The statutory basis for sanctions against design professionals is even stronger in Louisiana and many other states. For example, under Louisiana Revised Statutes 37:141, Policy and Definitions, it is provided that: "In order to safeguard life, health and property and to promote the public welfare, the practice of architecture in this state is reserved for those persons who have the proper qualifications and who have been registered by the Board."[37]

The other problem area in the owner/engineer relationship becomes more of a problem under the PE. Under Standard Forms of Agreement published by the Engineers' Joint Contract Documents Committee (EJCDC), the engineer has some responsibility to look at the project while under construction.[38] The engineer has an ambiguously-worded contractual duty to visit the project to tell the owner that it is getting a project finished as called for by the plans and specifications. The owner/engineer contract reads:

> Visits to Site and Observation of Construction. In connection with observations of the work of Contractor(s) while it is in progress: 1.6.2.1. ENGINEER shall make visits to the site at intervals appropriate to the various stages of construction as ENGINEER deems necessary in order to observe as an experienced and qualified design professional the progress and quality of the various aspects of Contractor(s)' work. In addition, ENGINEER shall provide the services of a Resident Project Representative (and assistants as agreed) at the site to assist ENGINEER and to provide more continuous observation of such work. Based on information obtained during such visits and on such observations. ENGINEER shall endeavor to determine in general if such work is proceeding in accordance with the Contract

---

[35] *Id.* at 531, 534-37.

[36] *Id.* at 531, 533-40, *passim.*

[37] *Id.*

[38] Primarily under the 1983 and 1984 editions of the contracts.

Documents and ENGINEER shall keep OWNER informed of the progress of the work.[39]

Contrary to the engineer's comparatively watered down standard contract duties the PE counsels contradictory actions. Chapter 10.2 provides that "Design professionals . . . spend time in the field to observe that the design intent is being successfully transformed into a properly built project."[40] That is a higher degree of vigilance than required in AIA B141-1987, which provides for "visits" to "determine in general if the Work . . . will be in accordance with the Contract Documents . . . ." and to "endeavor to guard the Owner against defects and deficiencies in the Work."[41] The companion structural engineer duty provides for "visits" and that the Engineer "shall endeavor to determine in general if such work is proceeding in accordance with the Contract Documents."[42]

The PE's statements of the law governing all parties to the construction process are, in the main, not correct.[43]

NAAG DOCUMENTS

§ 5.4   Overreaction of NAAG

Against the turmoil of the drafting, preparation to print, and distribution of the PE from 1984 to April 1988, the NAAG apparently made a discussion draft of the NAAG model contracts in the fall of 1988. Although the NAAG prepared a third draft in October 1989, its issuance was postponed until March 1, 1990. NAAG printed and issued what was apparently the original NAAG draft under the date of December 1988.[44] Actually the NAAG documents became generally available to the public in March 1989, at $50 apiece.

The Attorney General of New York introduced the NAAG documents by stating:

> Public owners may use standard form contracts prepared by trade associations of architects, engineers or contractors which are not drafted with the interests of the state foremost. In a number of critical ways, public agencies may needlessly sign

---

[39] Standard Form of Agreement Between Owner and Engineer for Professional Services, EJCDC No. 1910-1 (1984 ed.).

[40] PE at 60.

[41] AIA B141-1987 ¶ 2.6.5.

[42] EJCDC No. 1910-1 ¶ 1.6.2.1.

[43] PE at 12, 65, 121-122, 125-126, 153, 155, 156, and an ill-advised mini-law textbook in Chapter 24 and Appendices 24-A and B.

[44] *Chronology of Arizona's Experience with NAAG Construction Documents Forms,* NAAG Construction Claims Seminar, Nov. 6-7, 1989, at 103-105.

away their rights and prejudice their interests by using these models as a starting point for contracts.[45]

This led to an account of heated exchanges between members of the construction industry. A/Es accused NAAG of "saddling designers with burdensome liabilities."[46] The Florida Department of Transportation stated: "We feel the design profession was protected too much by other model contracts. . . . We probably erred on the side of the owner. We'd rather start from their side than the other side."[47]

AIA stated "that the [NAAG] contracts are so biased that professional liability insurers will leave designers high and dry." AIA "would call it hostile. . . . [T]hey are distorting the bargaining so badly it leaves the other side harmed at the signing of the agreement and probably spiteful. . . . The contract form is not drafted in good faith, but is based on the premise that whatever we do will end in litigation, so let's [NAAG] protect the client and drive the contract (sic) to litigation."[48]

§ 5.5   Agreement Between Owner and Design Professional

NAAG countered the confusion created by the PE for the construction industry with NAAG's own brand of mistakes. In NAAG's adhesion agreement for design professionals NAAG provides: "ARTICLE 1 - GENERAL This Agreement incorporates the National Association of Attorneys General Standard Form General Conditions of the Contract for Construction." The incorporation clause would make the A/E a part of the contractor.[49]

Article 1 becomes more confusing in view of the NAAG comment[50] that the A/E's responsibility is "defined in the Owner-Designer agreement, not the Owner-Contractor agreement." Why then incorporate all of the General Conditions into the Owner-Designer agreement?

---

[45] NAAG President Robert Abrams, NAAG Model Documents, Introduction at 1.

[46] *Designers See a Threat in New Model Contract,* ENR, Mar. 23, 1989, at 12.

[47] *Id.*

[48] *Id.* "AGC has written NAAG President Tom Miller to restate its call for withdrawal of these documents." AGC National Newsletter, Vol. 11, No. 29, Nov. 16, 1989.

[49] The "administration" provisions of AIA B-141 ¶ 2.6.2 do not burden the design professional with the contractor's obligations which NAAG would fasten on the A/E with Article 1 of the NAAG form. *See also* EJCDC No. 1910-1, ¶ 1.6.1. Paragraph 1 of the NAAG Official Comment Owner/Designer Agreement (at 9 and 10) suggests that the NAAG document would be an "adhesion" contract. Under Design Development Phase subparagraphs (4) and (5), use of the term "include but not limited to" is a blank check which will inevitably lead to controversy. A sophisticated public owner knows what it wants.

[50] NAAG Standard Form General Conditions of the Contract for Construction [hereinafter General Conditions] at 64.

After the melange of Article 1, NAAG begins to lapse into the diffuse. From the vague, NAAG drifts into uninsurability. NAAG would not have an owner engage an A/E who had no insurance. But the NAAG documents accomplish that purpose by making it unlikely, if not impossible, for the A/E to have coverage for NAAG's uninsurable demands.[51]

The adhesion contract provisions lead the A/E into a guessing game. Under ¶ 2 the A/E agrees "to accept Owner's program and budget and further agrees to accomplish said Project within the intent of the program and established budget." At that stage of the matter the A/E could not possibly know that it can agree to this. It is contrary to ¶ 7 on page 13 which states that the A/E will furnish "a Statement of Probable Construction Cost." An A/E cannot intelligently or safely bind himself to meet the owner's guess.

In ¶ 3 on page 7, the A/E in effect agrees that it can redesign an over-budget job "so as not to exceed the Owner's construction budget." That is a guarantee by the A/E that the project will meet budget. The A/E would not have any insurance for that.

To the perpetual tug of war over bossing the superintendents and foremen on the job NAAG adds its contribution. Paragraph 4 on page 8 requires the A/E "to supervise the construction" and "to require that Contractor complies with Contract Documents." The contractor is bound to the owner to do that in 163 pages of the General Conditions, including "superintendence" through "a competent superintendent" and "such assistance with such individual specialized competencies as may be necessary to fully understand and oversee all aspects of the work."[52]

The Contractor gets about 95 percent of the cost of the project. That enables the contractor to "supervise" the work that has been the contractor's main responsibility for generations.

The public owner is really seeking a costly construction manager as an additional member of the construction team, without cost to the owner. At its usual fee, the A/E cannot afford the several expert superintendents needed to "supervise" a project. The A/E would need CGL and perhaps workers' compensation coverage because of the supervisory responsibilities thrust on the A/E,[53] in addition to substantially greater compensation.

---

[51] In some states public agencies cannot indemnify an A/E or contractor. A public indemnity for uninsurable claims would not protect the A/E or contractor. It could be void.

[52] General Conditions at 55.

[53] "Such SUPERVISION shall include, unless otherwise specified, the general administration of the Construction Contract; the issuance of Certificates of Payment; *the keeping of accounts;* the approval of specified materials, equipment, and apparatus used in WORK; and SUPERVISION of construction. General administration of the Construction Contract includes, but is not limited to, the performance of all acts, services, and responsibilities described, referred to, or implied in this Contract and to the performance of all acts, services, and responsibilities described, referred to, or implied in the General Conditions." (Emphasis in the original.) NAAG A/E agreement at 8.

§ 5.6 Construction Contract

NAAG treats construction with the same unreasonableness that it treats design. The Model Form of Agreement for Construction's Contract Document includes "modifications made after the execution of" the agreement "and the bid."[54] The "modifications" are not under the Change Order provisions. They are changes outside the scope of the contract and are a blank performance check.

The General Conditions are unfair to the contractor in demanding extra performance of unknown scope without compensation. The contractor cannot rely on the drawings and specifications.[55] If the public owner and its design professional give the contractor the wrong information, as long as they believe it is correct, there is no extra compensation to the contractor "unless the differing site condition provisions apply."[56]

Fifteen pages later the contractor declares that it "has carefully examined the site . . . and investigated and satisfied itself as to all conditions which can affect the Work or its cost, including but not restricted to, conditions bearing upon transportation, disposal, handling and storage of materials; availability of labor, water, electric power, and roads or other access to the site; uncertainties of weather, river stages, tides, water tables or other similar physical conditions at the site, the conformation and conditions of the ground; and the character of equipment and the facilities needed to perform the work."[57]

The contractor must agree that it has examined "the boring data and other subsurface data available . . . insofar as this information is reasonably ascertainable from an inspection of the site and analysis of the data furnished with the plans and specifications." The NAAG contract continues that this now puts "both Contractor and Owner . . . on an equal footing." The data given by the owner and his design professional are only "a general indication" of the material adjacent to the borings and "Contractor . . . shall base its bid on its own opinion of the conditions to be encountered."

To make matters worse for the contractor, the document goes on to state, "Reliance on any information provided with the plans does not relieve Contractor of its complete responsibility for all Work under this contract . . . ." Then the NAAG contract states that "Owner assumes no responsibility for any conclusions or interpretations made by Contractor on the basis of information made

---

[54] NAAG Construction Contract at 2.

[55] "In the event of a discrepancy between the drawings and specifications, the specifications shall be followed. Anything shown in one and not the other, and anything obviously necessary to complete the project and achieve the intended result although not shown or described in the one or the other, shall be brought to the attention of the DESIGN PROFESSIONAL, and if so directed by the DESIGN PROFESSIONAL shall be provided or performed by the CONTRACTOR as part of its Contract."

[56] General Conditions at 2.

[57] *Id.* at 15.

available by Owner. Contractor shall determine whether data is adequate for construction purposes and at its expense obtain additional information on which to base its bid."[58] Rarely are site condition provisions in a contract as one-sided as these.

It is impossible in the space of this chapter to discuss every NAAG miscue. A few additional highlights will suffice to warn attorneys representing design professionals or contractors to examine with microscopic closeness any contract based on the NAAG documents received from a public agency.

For example, if the public owner's design professional cites a standard like "ASTM" and the standard is in conflict with the owner's "written portion of the specifications," the standards shall govern. In fairness, the owner should straighten out its own contract documents before it issues them to those bidding on public works. At the very least, a contractor can argue that if the specifications are ambiguous or vague, the public bidding process for that job is invalid.[59]

NAAG requires also that the bidder be "familiar and comply with all Federal, State and local laws, ordinances and regulations which might affect those engaged in the work; the materials, equipment or procedures used in the work; or which in any way could affect the completion of the work." That would require, for example, that the contractor guarantee to the owner that the work does not violate zoning regulations or federal statutes on the protection of environment.[60]

The wording of NAAG's Model Bond Form is too broad and is an attempt to turn a performance bond into an insurance policy. To get a company to be surety for prompt and faithful performance of the prime contract does not require indemnities of all government employees of the owner as well as the owner, from all claims "whether in contract or in tort, whether imposed by law or in equity. . . ."

The word "strict" in connection with performance is completely unrealistic. Anybody who has watched a construction project in progress knows that the average American construction worker is not turning out a product like a fine antique reproduction. An owner could not afford that type of work in a multi-million dollar building or bridge.

Finally, the bond form states: "The Surety's liability of performance and damages for the cost shall not be limited to the penal sum of the bond." For the comment to say that "Surety will probably not agree to liability beyond penal sum of the bond" is gilding a cabbage. No officer of a surety could sign the model bond without exceeding his power. It would take a meeting of the board to permit execution of a CGL policy without limits. Experienced construction surety bond specialists will quickly give opinions that it is the worst performance bond they have seen. A public agency should do better than that.[61]

---

[58] *Id.* at 15-16.

[59] *Id.* at 7, 8.

[60] *Id.* at 13.

[61] *Id.* at 19-21.

The contractor's obligation for shop drawings is expanded to "coordination with connecting Work."[62] Whose work? The "Shop Drawings and Schedules shall indicate . . . engagements with Work of other trades or other separate contractors."[63] But coordination of separate contractors is the obligation of the owner or its construction manager, unless the owner pays an additional fee to the contractor for the added duty. The obligation that the "Contractor shall furnish prints of its approved Shop Drawings to all the Contractors whose work is in any way related to the Work,"[64] is again, overly broad. If, as I encountered in one project, the public owner issues 50 bid packages for separate contractors, the owner has to know the relationships.[65]

No contractor can get insurance for "claims . . . which may arise out of or result from the Contractor's operations under the Contract, whether . . . by the Contractor itself or by any Subcontractor or by anyone directly or indirectly employed by any of them or by anyone for whose acts any of them may be liable."[66]

Why should the owner be an "additional insured" unless it pays the premium? Is that to prevent the owner from paying its just share of a disaster liability because the owner furnished defective specifications, and the contractor's insurance carrier cannot sue its own insured for the damages?[67] If the public owner pays a big enough premium, it can be done.

Builder's risk insurance should be obtained by the owner at its expense, naming all those on the project as insureds.[68] Putting builder's risk insurance on the shoulders of the contractor, including, for example, fire caused by other separate contractors hired by the owner or collapse due to design defects, is inherently unfair. Neither a surety nor an insurance carrier will cover those risks.

If the state wishes to make its employees CGL-named insureds against claims of negligence, it can buy such insurance or indemnify them.[69]

NAAG requires that "the Contractor warrants to the Owner and the Design Professional that all materials and equipment furnished under this contract shall be new and of the most suitable grade for the purpose intended. . . ."[70] As a rule, equipment is specified by the owner's design professional. It would know whether the equipment was "the most suitable grade for the purpose intended." To require the contractor to warrant that is unreasonable.

---

[62] *Id.* at 59.

[63] *Id.* at 60.

[64] *Id.* at 61.

[65] *Id.* at 58-64.

[66] *Id.* at 69.

[67] *Id.* at 71.

[68] *Id.* at 73-74.

[69] *Id.* at 69-76.

[70] *Id.* at 86.

Many courts will not enforce the unreasonable burden placed on the Contractor by the "no damage for delay" clause.[71] If the owner or its separate contractor causes the delay, many courts, and rightly so, will hold the state liable.

By and large the NAAG documents are a disappointment to the construction industry.

§ 5.7   Confusion Reigns

Those who practice in the field of construction industry law know that there has been an explosive expansion of interest in the field. Statutes (regulatory and repose), court decisions (especially regarding contracts of adhesion), and activities of legal associations (ABA Forum on the Construction Industry) have involved practicing attorneys at an increasing rate. Any attorney in construction industry law receives several seminar brochures each day covering some phase of this work.

It is fair to say that the downpour among the contending parties became heaviest on November 6 and 7, 1989, in New Orleans at the NAAG Construction Claims Seminar. Attendees and speakers came from a couple dozen states and the District of Columbia.[72]

The prepared papers and much of the oral presentation made it plain that the parties were at complete loggerheads. In part, this may arise from the NAAG Introduction to the Model Documents, in which it is stated: "We believe public owners will reach more satisfactory final agreement if these models are used, in whole or in part, as local law and the circumstances of particular projects may require." The Foreword stated that "These documents are meant to be used as a tool for those representing public owners as they, in their wisdom, may see fit."

The trouble with this seeming reasonableness is that, if the attorney general of a state sends around copies of the NAAG documents and if the state agencies do not use those documents, how will the state agencies avoid criticism if something goes wrong? A good analogy would be a corporate official not following the recommendations of the corporation's general counsel.

Usually design professionals are the representatives of and the protectors of the interests of their client-owners. That is their usual role except when the design professionals are acting in a quasi-judicial function of making good-faith decisions between the owner and the contractor. Yet, in the controversy regarding NAAG documents, the A/Es and the contractors have fought shoulder-to-shoulder to get the NAAG Model Documents withdrawn.[73]

---

[71] *Id*. at 122-24.

[72] Conference manual at 1-6 and tentative attendance list. While AIA and AGC were represented, ASCE did not appear to be so.

[73] NAAG then temporarily put the use of its Model Documents on hold at its March 1990 meeting. At that meeting, NAAG extended the suspension until July 1990. On July 23, 1990, NAAG

The states and their agencies, having control of virtually all public work, have placed themselves in a position in which the courts must inevitably interpret all ambiguities against the public agencies. While insurance carriers have been concerned about decisions interpreting insurance contracts as "adhesion" contracts, their position with respect to their customers is not nearly as dominant as in the case of public agencies and their contractors.

Because the economy in the construction industry is flat, it is going to be more difficult for state agencies to get "lowest bidders" who are also "responsible." Counsel for contractors and design professionals undoubtedly will warn their clients that the contracts contain many objectionable and harmful features. Economic need will probably cause such clients to sign the contracts anyway. The unavoidable result will be something that the industry and public agencies do not need, namely protracted litigation.

Within reason a satisfied construction industry will make the states and public agencies satisfied. AIA, ASCE, and AGC have made evident their desire to try to satisfy all clients.

The insurance industry is aware of the needs of the owners as well as of their clients. It has been a most difficult period for insurance companies because of the increase in exposure to liability and damages. Insurance carriers cannot stay in business if their losses exceed their income. We have had some instances of carriers who cover design professionals and contractors going into liquidation in recent years. That does not help public or private owners.

It is fair to say that the elements of the construction industry that service owners are ready to confer thoughtfully and carefully to work out contract documents and performance that will take care of the rightful needs of the owners and provide fair conditions of service by the construction industry.

---

announced, "The construction documents are permanently suspended, and NAAG will no longer disseminate copies to the public." *See Attorneys General Permanently Suspend Model Contract Forms,* 30 NSPE Private Practice News, Vol. 30, No. 8, at 8.

PART II
MANAGEMENT OF CLAIMS

CHAPTER 6

KEYS TO SUCCESS IN AVOIDING AND MANAGING CLAIMS

Overton A. Currie
Neal J. Sweeney*

§ 6.1   Life in the Construction Industry: Avoiding Risks and Preserving Awards

§ 6.2   Involving Reputable and Reliable Participants in the Project

§ 6.3   Defining Rights, Responsibilities, and Risks

§ 6.4   Contract Framework

§ 6.5   Standard Contract Forms and Key Contract Provisions

§ 6.6   Interpreting and Applying Express and Implied Terms

§ 6.7   Contract Modification

§ 6.8   The Arbitration Alternative

§ 6.9   —Time and Costs of Arbitration

§ 6.10   —Selection of Arbitrators

§ 6.11   —Informality and Limited Appeals in Arbitration

§ 6.12   —Enforceability of Agreements to Arbitrate

§ 6.13   —Special Problems Involving Multiple Parties

§ 6.14   Avoiding and Preparing for Claims Through Proper Management and Documentation

§ 6.15   Prudent and Responsible Estimating

§ 6.16   Establishing Standard Operating Procedures

§ 6.17   Establishing Lines of Communication

§ 6.18   Project Documentation

§ 6.19   —Correspondence

§ 6.20   —Meeting Notes

---

* This chapter is adapted from a paper presented in December 1989 to the Fourth Annual Construction Litigation Superconference sponsored by Andrews Conferences.

§ 6.21   —Jobsite Logs or Daily Reports

§ 6.22   —Standard Forms and Status Logs

§ 6.23   —Photographs and Video Tapes

§ 6.24   Cost Accounting Records

§ 6.25   Monitoring the Work Through Scheduling

§ 6.26   Effective Claim Development

§ 6.27   Early Claim Recognition and Preparation

§ 6.28   Early Involvement of Experts and Attorneys

§ 6.29   Use of Demonstrative Evidence

§ 6.30   Components of a Well-Prepared Claim Document

§ 6.31   Importance of Calculating and Proving Damages

§ 6.32   —Basic Damage Principles

§ 6.33   Methods of Pricing Claims

§ 6.34   —Total Cost Method

§ 6.35   —Segregated Cost Method

§ 6.36   Project Cost Reviews and Audits

§ 6.37   Pursuing Negotiation and Settlement

§ 6.1   Life in the Construction Industry: Avoiding Risks and Preserving Awards

Construction is a large, volatile industry. It requires tremendous capital outlays but generally offers low rates of return, particularly in relation to the amount of risk imposed. The construction industry is affected by the same business cycles and economic influences that affect other industries. But construction carries an additional element of risk and volatility that generally does not exist in other major industries. That element is the manner in which disputes and claims are woven through the fiber of the construction process.

Construction is a dispute-prone industry, and claims are a fact of life. Even successful projects have claims. That does not mean there is something inherently wrong with the industry or its participants. Claims are a natural outgrowth of a complex and highly competitive process during which the unexpected often happens. Careful organization and coordination of numerous parties is required, and it may then be outside parties who control many of the circumstances and events that generate claims. The potential for claims cannot be ignored. It is naive and bad business to do so. The responsible owner, contractor, subcontractor, or designer, as part of doing business, recognizes the need to anticipate claims and to develop effective and affirmative strategies for dealing with them.

The best way to handle claims is to anticipate them and avoid them as much as possible. Despite the uniqueness of each project and its participants, there are certain recurring problems which generate disputes. The past is prologue and some of those recurring problems can be avoided, their impact mitigated, or, at a minimum, some preparation made for the dispute if it should occur. Of course, too much focus on eliminating all risks and anticipating claims and disputes can also create problems and a paralysis that can impair one's ability to do business effectively. A certain element of risk must be recognized and accepted. Risk can only be mitigated, not eliminated.

The successful prosecution of claims requires that foresight and planning be applied long before the facts and circumstances giving rise to the claim actually occur. This chapter focuses on those measures that can be taken at the outset of a project to avoid or effectively prepare for successful prosecution of claims when they cannot be avoided. Of course, there are no "sure things," and construction claims are no exception. Nevertheless, common sense, planning, skill, and experience can help identify those strategies for approaching construction claims that will increase the likelihood of success.

§ 6.2   Involving Reputable and Reliable Participants in the Project

Construction is a cooperative enterprise involving numerous entities and disciplines, from design professionals, the owner or developer, and lender through the prime contractor, subcontractors, and suppliers, each with an integral function. A failure by any participant to perform properly can mean disaster for the entire project and the rest of the participants.

The initial choice of project participants can dictate the destiny of the project and is one of the first steps in avoiding claims. Many headaches and possible losses can be avoided simply by investigating the past performance record of the other parties, rather than looking solely at the lowest price or the opportunity to obtain some work. By dealing with reputable companies and individuals with a proven ability to perform, by running credit checks, and by inquiring about the experience of others with that particular company, bad risks and big mistakes can be avoided.

Naturally, the owner is in the best position to control the selection of project participants because under most contracting schemes the owner selects the designer and the contractor. The owner can also have a significant impact on subcontractor selection. The prime contractor, who stands in a similar position to the owner, has the greater control over the selection of subcontractors, as does the architect or lead designer over the selection of its subconsultants. When the choice of a specific party would create a risk of claims or disputes to the extent that any reasonable return is jeopardized, that party should not be used on the project, regardless of price.

On the other hand, the prime contractor cannot select the owner or developer of a project. The contractor, however, does decide with whom it wants to do business, as do subcontractors. Sometimes the risks of a project or of doing business with a particular owner are simply too great, and prudence dictates that certain opportunities be foregone. Higher volume and backlog figures are meaningless if they engender unnecessary risks and do not translate to profit.

Despite the time crunch and euphoria often associated with the beginning of a project, everyone involved should consider certain key factors when selecting project participants: the financial condition of the parties, their qualification for bonds, evidence of their technical skills, and their reputation in the industry. Even a cursory investigation of potential project participants may yield clues to future problems.

Money, if not "the root of all evil," is the source of many disputes and claims that arise on a construction project. The financial resources of the owner are probably of paramount concern. An under-financed owner virtually dooms any project. Although the possibility of lien rights might provide comfort, if the owner goes under, the likelihood of full and complete payment to the contractor is pretty slim. Considering the preeminent influence of the owner on the success or failure of a project, contractors and architects are wise to subject the owner's background to an informal "prequalification" process, like that used on other project participants, to confirm that the owner has the capacity to meet its commitments.

In addition to other independent sources that may be available to obtain information about the owner's finances, ¶ 2.2.1 of the General Conditions published by the American Institute of Architects, AIA A201-1987, allows the contractor to demand reasonable evidence of the owner's ability to finance the work. Paragraph 2.1.2 also requires the owner to provide written information regarding title to the property as well as any changes in title, if requested by the contractor.

The financial condition of contractors and subcontractors is also extremely important. A subcontractor who has insufficient working capital may bring a myriad of problems, such as slow deliveries of materials as suppliers grow concerned about the subcontractor's ability to pay. This can have a ripple effect on other work. Similarly, a contractor needing cash flow may front-end load its bid and its pay requests. The early overpayment caused by front-end loading may result in the contractor's default on the latter part of the project as contract funds run out. Unfortunately, there are few, if any, effective remedies against an unbonded, insolvent contractor. The typical action to recover completion costs is often pointless when the default resulted directly from the contractor's financial problems.

An obvious source of financial protection for owners is to require payment and performance bonds. Bonding serves two purposes. First, the contractor's competence and financial well-being are endorsed by the surety's underwriting department, which is also trying to avoid bad risks. If a contractor is incapable of obtaining bonding, it means sureties have a grave concern about its ability to complete a project. That warning is probably best heeded. Second, and more directly, the bonds represent a financial guarantee. A performance bond usually

1991 WILEY CONSTRUCTION LAW UPDATE

Edited by Steven M. Goldblatt

As a subscriber to Wiley Construction Law publications, we are sending you this new related volume at a discount, on approval.

The *1991 Wiley Construction Law Update* is a collection of articles by the best construction law experts in the country. They have written on such timely topics as architect/engineer liability for asbestos; owner modifications to AIA A201; environmental liability documents; and pass-through clause enforcement. Many other articles covering the latest developments, strategies, and litigation pitfalls are included.

As a subscriber to our books, we are sending you this new volume at a special price of $75.00, a $20.00 savings off our regular price of $95.00.

If you are not thoroughly satisfied with this new volume, just return it to us within 30 days along with the enclosed invoice, and we will cancel the billing.

Sincerely,

WILEY LAW PUBLICATIONS
A Division of John Wiley & Sons, Inc.
One Wiley Drive
Somerset, NJ 08875

1-800-225-5945

means that, if the contractor defaults and fails to complete, the surety will complete performance or pay damages up to the limit of the penal sum of the bond. In contrast, a labor and material payment bond helps assure the owner that labor and materials will be paid for and creates alternatives to the filing of liens on the project.

Even if provided, payment and performance bonds are not a cure-all. It is also necessary to carefully consider the financial stability of the surety itself. In recent years, many sureties have themselves gone bankrupt. Moreover, even a solvent, well-financed surety is far from an automatic source of relief. Claims under the bond can themselves be the subject of lengthy disputes and litigation.

Of course, there are concerns about technical qualifications that go beyond money. For example, licensing requirements provide some protection from incompetent and inexperienced contractors, particularly in the skilled trades such as electrical and mechanical. Licensing should be deemed a bare minimum requirement, however, and not an endorsement of qualifications for any type of work authorized by a particular license. Inquiries into the contractor's experience on particular types and sizes of projects should also be pursued. There is a big difference between installing plumbing in a low-rise apartment building and installing the mechanical systems for a major health care facility. The owner's technical capabilities and qualifications to handle a particular type or size of project are also relevant. However, the owner's shortcoming may be offset by the association of capable consultants.

More subjective reports about other parties should also be considered, but perhaps be given lesser weight. For example, engaging a subcontractor with a reputation for shoddy or defective work may result in the prime having to remedy unsatisfactory work at its own expense. A particularly litigious owner may refuse to negotiate a settlement in the event of a dispute, forcing the contractor into more expensive arbitration or court battles.

Even if an owner, designer, or contractor appear to have the qualifications and established track record to pass muster as a company, it is important to consider the personnel they will devote to the particular project. Companies can be too successful, causing them to be stretched too thin, with all their capable and experienced personnel assigned to and consumed by other projects. The company is certainly important, but the individuals representing those companies and executing responsibilities and work in the field are no less important.

§ 6.3   Defining Rights, Responsibilities, and Risks

A written contract generally provides the foundation for each of the numerous relationships and binds the disparate project participants into a cohesive force to get the job built. Keeping those participants together requires in part anticipating issues and events that might create disputes and detract from the goal of prompt and cost-effective completion. This is done by a combination of allocating risks among the parties, so it is clear who will have to bear the burden if the risk becomes reality, and providing mechanisms for resolving disputes when the risk allocation is not clear or there is disagreement. A well-drafted contract is another important element in effectively managing a project and avoiding or efficiently dealing with claims.

Clarity, common sense, and precision should be employed in the drafting of contract language. Such efforts will hopefully limit later uncertainty and misunderstanding among the parties and the need to refer to some third-party decisionmaker, in court or arbitration, to determine how the contract will be interpreted. Unreasonable and overly burdensome terms should be avoided as they can unnecessarily drive up the cost of the work through uninflated contingencies and may be difficult to enforce.

On the other hand, such harsh terms cannot be ignored in an unrealistically optimistic view that they will not be enforced or that circumstances relating to those harsh terms will not arise on the project. The parties must grapple with the tough issues raised by their conflicting interests in the contract preparation stage or face the prospect of much more serious disagreements and disputes during the performance of the contract.

§ 6.4 Contract Framework

Establishing the contract framework for the project is a threshold decision that must be made by the owner. The selection depends on a variety of factors, including the owner's needs and its expertise and capabilities. Construction projects have traditionally been designed, bid, built, and paid for within a framework of strictly defined roles, relationships, and procedures. This has proven satisfactory for many construction projects, but perceived weaknesses in the traditional method have led to consideration and use of new, alternative methods, such as the various forms of construction management, multi-prime contracting and design/build.[1] The new methods have provided many advantages, but the manner in which they diverge from clearly defined practices and roles requires careful attention in the contract drafting phase to make certain that the advantages in use are not lost through unanticipated problems and disputes.

§ 6.5 Standard Contract Forms and Key Contract Provisions

There are a number of available standard contract forms which establish the various relationship on a construction project. The documents published by the

---

[1] *See generally Construction Management and Design-Build/Fast Track Construction from the Perspective of a General Contractor,* 46 Law & Contemp. Probs. (1983).

American Institute of Architects (AIA) are by far the most widely used and most generally accepted. The Associated General Contractors of America (AGC) and the Engineers Joint Contract Documents Committee (EJCDC) also publish contract documents. The provisions of the AIA documents, revised in 1987, are generally well understood by developers, architects, contractors, lenders, and others involved in the construction process. These common forms permit all parties to focus on critical variables when negotiating construction transactions and obviate the need to start from scratch with each new project.

The AIA documents are fairly well-integrated, with the terms of the various contracts coordinated with and complementing each other.[2] This consistency enhances the reliability of the AIA documents. The AIA documents have the advantage of familiarity and acceptance in the industry but do not necessarily meet the needs of each and every project, and some modification may be required for each specific situation. Moreover, it must be recognized that the AIA documents are drafted by an association which strongly promotes the interests of architect, often at the expense of the owner and contractor.

Whether reliance is placed on a standard form, a custom-drafted contract, or some combination of the two, certain contract provisions are of critical importance in anticipating, avoiding, and resolving claims. They are:

Payment

Time for Completion and Time Extensions

Damages for Delay

Changes in the Work

Termination for Default and for Convenience

Changed Conditions

Dispute Resolution

Insurance

Careful attention should also be paid to the use of liquidated damages or no damages for delay clauses as well as exculpatory and indemnity provisions, which can weigh heavily in the resolution of claims. It is also worthwhile to consider whether the parties intend for Article 2 of the Uniform Commercial Code, which governs the sale of goods, to apply to their construction contract. An extensive discussion of these provisions is beyond the scope of this chapter.[3] However, arbitration, as a means of resolving construction claims, is discussed separately in §§ 6.8 through 6.13.

---

[2] *See generally* J. Sweet, Sweet on Construction Industry Contracts (1987).

[3] *See generally* O. Currie, J. Stephenson, P. Beck, & R. Hafer, Construction Contracts, Negotiating Real Estate Transactions (1988).

§ 6.6   Interpreting and Applying Express and Implied Terms

Parties to a construction contract must recognize that the print within the four corners of the contract is not the limit of a contract's reach or application. The contract carries with it the baggage of industry trade and custom, the past dealing of the parties, and a set of principles for applying and interpreting the contract and further defining the relationships between the parties. Those considerations can have every bit as much consequence as the printed words on the contract document. Accordingly, whenever possible, a contract should be drafted and then performed with an understanding of the principles of contract interpretation.

One fundamental aspect of contract interpretation is that every contract contains implied obligations in addition to the obligations expressly enumerated in the contract. Perhaps the most important implied contract obligation in the construction context is the duty of cooperation. This duty to cooperate manifests itself in the form of an obligation on the part of the owner not to hinder or delay the contractor's performance.[4] It also encompasses the obligation to coordinate the activities of parallel prime contractors.[5]

Another very important implied obligation, known as the *Spearin* doctrine, is that the party furnishing the plans and specifications (that is, the owner) impliedly warrants their adequacy and sufficiency.[6] Under the *Spearin* doctrine, the contractor may recover for delays, extra work, disruption, and constructive changes when there are errors in the plans and specifications.[7]

§ 6.7   Contract Modification

Contracts typically provide that their provisions cannot be modified without the written agreement of both parties. Despite the presence of such a stipulation, parties can modify the terms of their written agreement orally or by their conduct.[8] The issue of modification frequently arises in situations in which formal written notice is required but, despite the contractor's failure to properly provide it, the owner repeatedly acts as if the notice had been given.

---

[4] *See, e.g.,* Coatesville Contractors v. Borough of Ridley, 509 Pa. 552, 502 A.2d 862 (1986).

[5] *See, e.g.,* Baldwin-Lima-Hamilton Corp. v. United States, 434 F.2d 1371 (Ct. Cl. 1970).

[6] *See, e.g.,* Ordinance Research, Inc. v. United States, 609 F.2d 462 (Ct. Cl. 1979); United States v. Spearin, 248 U.S. 132, 136 (1918).

[7] *See generally,* USA Petroleum Corp. v. United States, 821 F.2d 622 (Fed. Cir. 1987); La Crosse Garment Mfg. Co. v. United States, 432 F.2d 1377 (Ct. Cl. 1970); Chaney & James Constr. Co. v. United States, 421 F.2d 728 (Ct. Cl. 1970); Hollingshead v. United States, 111 F. Supp. 285 (Ct. Cl. 1953).

[8] Certified Corp. v. Hawaii Teamsters & Allied Workers, Local 996, 597 F.2d 1269 (10th Cir. 1979).

Similarly, when the contract states that written work or change orders are required before a contractor is entitled to additional compensation, an established pattern of payment without the contractor having first obtained a written order may serve to constitute a modification or waiver of this contract requirement.[9] Waiver of written notice and change order requirements, however, should never be presumed, and all efforts should be undertaken to comply with them.

§ 6.8   The Arbitration Alternative

The issue of arbitration is generally contemplated at the conclusion of the claims process. Arbitration is sought when the parties are unable to resolve the claim between themselves. The availability of arbitration as a means of resolving construction claims and disputes, however, must be planned and provided for at the outset of the project, in the contract itself. Otherwise, that alternative will not exist and if the parties cannot agree they will have to look to the courts. Generally, no particular form or special words are necessary to establish an agreement to arbitrate a dispute between the parties. However, there must be a clear indication from the contract language that the parties intended the disputed issue to be subject to arbitration.

To avoid any dispute about the scope of the agreement to arbitrate, it is best to state expressly that all disputes arising from the contract will be arbitrated. For example, the most widely used arbitration clause, contained in AIA A201-1987 ¶ 4.5.1 provides: "Any controversy or claim arising out of or related to the contract, or the breach thereof, shall be settled by arbitration in accordance with the Construction Industry Arbitration Rules of the American Arbitration Association."

Arbitration is not new to the construction industry. Contract clauses providing for arbitration of disputes have been commonplace in the construction industry for many years. Although arbitration is generally perceived as a way to avoid the delays and problems associated with litigation, time and many tests have demonstrated the drawbacks as well as advantages of relying on arbitration as a means of resolving construction claims.

§ 6.9   —Time and Costs of Arbitration

Avoiding delays normally associated with the courts and crowded dockets and trial calendars is one of the most often-cited benefits of arbitration. On balance, and particularly for smaller claims, arbitration does provide a faster resolution. Given the right set of circumstances, however, arbitration can also be excruciatingly time-consuming and expensive. A dispute over the existence, scope, or

---

[9] W.E. Garrison Grading Co. v. Piracci Constr. Co., 27 N.C. 725, 221 S.E.2d 512 (1975).

validity of an arbitration clause itself can engender a protracted court proceeding and appeal before there is a determination of whether and to what extent the parties should proceed with arbitration. In addition, arbitration of larger claims involving multiple parties can match the delays and complexity of the most arcane court proceeding.

Although ultimately dependent on the parties involved and the scope and complexity of the issues, the cost of arbitration may be less than that of a comparable court proceeding. Generally, a shortened period for resolution will keep costs down, but there are certain costs that cannot be avoided. These costs include those usually incurred in trial preparation, such as the examination and analysis of documents, legal research, the use of experts, and the development of demonstrative evidence.

The costs that can be avoided in arbitration usually involve certain trade-offs. For example, unless it is provided for by agreement or statute, discovery is often not available in arbitration.[10] The costs of discovery, which can be substantial, can thus be avoided. The lack of discovery, however, means less preparation for and knowledge of the opposition's case. It can also possibly lead to a less focused hearing, which may then require more time and increased costs. In addition, there are costs that are unique to arbitration, such as arbitrators' fees, which can be substantial, as well as administrative fees and the cost of meeting rooms.

§ 6.10   —Selection of Arbitrators

The qualifications and fairness of each arbitrator is essential to the viability of arbitration as a means of resolving disputes. From a partisan vantage point, the selection of arbitrators can be a major factor in the success or failure of a claim. Many factors must be considered in selecting the arbitrator or arbitration panel. Some of the most important considerations must be addressed long before any claim arises or construction begins, in the drafting of the arbitration clause. Some basic but fairly strategic considerations are the number of arbitrators and the manner in which they are selected.

The fact that arbitrators generally have more expertise in the construction industry than a judge or jury is generally cited as one of the major advantages of arbitration. Of course, this may not be an advantage if the arbitrator's experience and background are contrary to the claimant's. An engineer may view all contractor claims with a jaundiced eye, for example. Despite the expertise, that engineer is not desirable to the contractor-claimant. Conversely, a contractor-arbitrator may be reluctant to enforce a hefty liquidated damages provision as part of an owner's claim.

---

[10] *See* Tupman, *Discovery and Evidence In U.S. Arbitration: The Prevailing Views,* The Arb. J. (Mar. 1989).

In terms of numbers, the basic choice is between a single arbitrator and a three-member panel. A single arbitrator costs less and will probably simplify scheduling hearings. On the other hand, a three-member panel would probably be more balanced. The three-member panel generally decides by majority vote, that is, two of the three panel members can render a decision over the objection or dissent of the third member.

Parties to an arbitration are free to agree to their own procedures for arbitrator selection. The procedure is often set forth in the arbitration clause of the contract. Provided both sides agree, the procedures can also be established or changed at the time the claim is submitted to arbitration.

The method for selecting arbitrators set forth in the American Arbitration Association (AAA) Construction Industry Arbitration Rules is most widely employed. The AAA procedures provide for selection of one or three neutral and unbiased arbitrators either by mutual agreement between the parties or by administrative appointment if no agreement can be reached.

An alternative to the AAA procedures that is sometimes used to select a three-member panel allows each party to select an arbitrator sympathetic to their side. The third arbitrator is then appointed by the two partisan arbitrators and is expected to be neutral. As a practical matter, this process makes the neutral arbitrator the "swing vote" that decides the arbitration.

§ 6.11   —Informality and Limited Appeals in Arbitration

The emphasis on the technical expertise of arbitrators usually involves a substantial de-emphasis of legal principles, technicalities, and procedures, including the right of appeal. This aspect of arbitration is often cited as a positive, but the contrary can be argued as well.

In arbitration proceedings, strict rules of evidence do not apply and arbitrators are generally liberal in their acceptance of evidence. This permits an easier and faster presentation of records, correspondence, documents, photographs, and live testimony. In fact, the AAA rules encourage arbitrators to accept any and all evidence that may shed light on the dispute. In the more relaxed environment of arbitration, substantive defenses such as statute of limitations, no damages for delay clauses, and notice requirements may be given little weight.

In addition to the arbitrators being granted considerable latitude in their conduct of hearings and rendering of awards, the right of appeal by means of a challenge of an award is extremely limited in scope. This limited scope of judicial review of arbitration awards is yet another trade-off. Although it certainly curtails a party's rights as compared to the scope of an appeal of a jury verdict, the limited scope tends to reduce the number and length of appeals from arbitration awards. This is, of course, in contrast to the court system with its lengthy and expensive appellate procedures.

§ 6.12 —Enforceability of Agreements to Arbitrate

In addition to the arbitration clause in the contract, a party's right to arbitration depends upon its ability to go to court and enforce the agreement to arbitrate. At common law, the courts were jealous of their jurisdiction and protective of a person's right of access to the courts. Today, however, the overburdened court system has made alternative methods of dispute resolution a necessity, and most states have attempted to broaden the right to arbitration either by statute or by court decision.

In addition to state laws, construction arbitration agreements are often enforceable under the Federal Arbitration Act (FAA),[11] which is the expression of a strong federal policy favoring arbitration.[12] The FAA only applies if the arbitration clause is in a contract "evidencing a transaction involving commerce," meaning interstate commerce. Transactions of the type generally involved in a large construction project often satisfy this interstate commerce requirement and come within the scope of the FAA.[13]

If the interstate commerce requirement is met, the FAA must be enforced, even in state court, and it preempts and supersedes all contrary and inconsistent state law.[14] However, state law incorporated into the contract by a choice of law provision may still affect the manner in which the arbitration proceeds, even if the FAA were applicable.[15]

§ 6.13 —Special Problems Involving Multiple Parties

A recurring issue in the administration of construction arbitrations is the consolidation of a number of separate arbitrations and multiple parties on the same project into one proceeding. The potential for problems and the desirability of consolidation need to be considered at the time the arbitration clause is being drafted and the contract signed, long before any claim develops.

Although the consolidation of court proceedings involving numerous parties is common, few construction contracts presently provide for such consolidated proceedings in arbitration. Even without contractual authorization, however, some courts have required consolidation as an expeditious means to resolve

---

[11] 9 U.S.C. §§ 1-15 (1970 & Supp. 1989).

[12] J.S. & H. Constr. Co. v. Richmond County Hosp. Auth., 473 F.2d 212 (4th Cir. 1973).

[13] *See, e.g.,* Pennsylvania Eng'g Corp. v. Islip Resource Recovery Agency, 710 F. Supp. 456 (E.D.N.Y. 1986); Electronic & Missile Facilities, Inc. v. United States, 306 F.2d 554 (5th Cir. 1962), *rev'd on other grounds,* 374 U.S. 167 (1963); Metro Indus. Painting Corp. v. Terminal Constr. Co., 287 F.2d 382 (2d Cir. 1961).

[14] Perry v. Thomas, 482 U.S. 483 (1987); Southland Corp. v. Keating, 465 U.S. 1 (1984); Moses H. Cone Memorial Hosp. v. Mercury Constr. Corp., 460 U.S. 1 (1983).

[15] Volt Information Sciences v. Stanford Univ., 109 S. Ct. 1248 (1989).

construction disputes.[16] However, the traditional and majority rule appears to be that, without express contractual consent to multiparty arbitrations, courts will not require consolidation.[17] In *Stop and Shop Company v. Gilbane Building Company*,[18] the court insisted that "[if] multi-party arbitration is to become a standard procedure, arbitration clauses and the rules and procedures of the AAA and other concerned organizations should be redrawn to provide for it."

The arbitration clause contained in AIA A201-1987 ¶ 4.5.5 imposes strict limits on consolidation and prohibits consolidation of the owner's claim against the architect in any arbitration between the owner and the contractor. The AIA arbitration clause does, however, allow for consolidated proceedings involving parallel contractors. The prohibition against joining the architect can put the owner in the unenviable position of having to defend in arbitration the contractor's claim for the architect's defective design, without being able to compel the architect to join the same arbitration as a party. This places the burden of defending the architect's design or conduct on the owner.

The prohibition against consolidation also causes the owner to run the risk of inconsistent results as well as extra expenses from duplicative arbitration proceedings. For example, an owner could lose to a contractor's claim of defective design in one arbitration, only to fail to convince a separate arbitration panel that the design was defective and that the architect should therefore reimburse the owner for its loss to the contractor. If the owner wants to avoid this situation, the issue must be addressed in advance in the arbitration clauses of its contracts with the contractor and the architect.

§ 6.14   Avoiding and Preparing for Claims Through Proper Management and Documentation

The prudent and realistic contractor designs and utilizes systems and procedures to manage, monitor, and document the work and progress on the project. These systems serve two important functions. First, they ensure an adequate flow of information to facilitate proper project control and coordination, including adjustments needed to respond to unexpected circumstances. Second, they aid in the compilation of an accurate and complete record of job conditions and problems and their impact on the project.

The contractor certainly bears the bulk of responsibility during construction as it installs the work and generally controls the means and methods employed to

---

[16] *See* Episcopal Hous. Corp. v. Federal Ins. Co., 273 S.C. 181, 255 S.E.2d 451 (1979); Exber, Inc. v. Sletten Constr. Co., 92 Nev. 721, 558 P.2d 517 (1976); James Stuart Polshek & Assoc. v. Bergen County Iron Works, 142 N.J. Super. 516, 362 A.2d 63 (1976); Grover-Diamond Assoc. v. American Arbitration Ass'n, 297 Minn. 324, 211 N.W.2d 787 (1973).

[17] Consolidated Pac. Eng'g v. Greater Anchorage Area Borough, 563 P.2d 251 (Alaska 1979); Cumberland Perry Vocational Technical School Auth. v. Boyor & Bink, 261 Pa. Super. 350, 396 A.2d 433 (1978).

[18] 364 Mass. 325, 304 N.E.2d 429, 432 (1973).

do so. The architect and owner should not, however, abdicate all responsibility and oversight and totally remove themselves from the construction process in an effort to insulate themselves from liability. They cannot avoid all liability. Moreover, some interaction and monitoring of the construction is always required of the owner and architect and is in their interests. If the owner or the architect become too removed from the construction, they can neither anticipate nor promptly address problems requiring their assistance.

The level of activity and monitoring will vary depending on the type and terms of the contract involved, but should not be so active or intrusive as to constitute interference and disruption of the contractor's work. Although it may be somewhat unpleasant to begin a project with an eye to possible future claims, a failure to adopt such prudent management procedures almost ensures that disputes will develop.

§ 6.15   Prudent and Responsible Estimating

Efforts to effectively manage work on the project and avoid claims should begin for the contractor before it even mobilizes or reaches the site. Many risks and claims arise not in the field but in the estimating department. Prudent estimating and bidding can avoid a host of performance problems and claims. A project that starts out in the hole because of bad estimating generally cannot climb out. Instead, the hole gets bigger and deeper, expanding the problem and drawing more parties into it.

Failure at any level to accurately perceive and then price the scope of the work or the risks associated with it results in unnecessary losses and difficulties that tend to ripple throughout the project. Estimates and bids should be supported by worksheets and backup documentation of sufficient detail under the circumstances. Such backup and the entire estimating process should be subject to standard forms and procedures and management review to ensure their accuracy.

Overly optimistic estimates based on vague or incomplete designs should be avoided or at least clearly identified and qualified as such. Performance specifications which often entail much more responsibility and cost that is initially apparent is another soft-spot in the estimating effort. The zeal applied to selling the project or submitting an early guaranteed maximum price to satisfy the owner must be balanced with caution against establishing an unrealistic budget or inflated expectations which, regardless of any contractual significance, are bound to cause disappointment, distrust, and disagreement when they are not met.

This scrutiny must be applied to bids received from subcontractors as well as those generated in-house. It is not always the case that the contractor may have recourse against the subcontractor. More importantly, the contractor has its own obligations to the owner and other subcontractors and cannot evade that responsibility or liability simply by pointing to the subcontractor who is unable to perform because of an estimating error. Owners should likewise beware of a contractor bid which is too good to be true—it probably is! Success in initially enforcing a mistaken or reckless bid can reap bitter returns later in the project when the contractor's cash and capital run short.

§ 6.16 Establishing Standard Operating Procedures

Construction projects run by the seat of the pants are accidents waiting to happen. Every project should have formalized, standard operating procedures with which all project personnel are familiar. The procedures should identify the specific authority and areas of responsibilities for each project staff position. Ideally, these should be standardized within a company and consistent from project to project. Standard job descriptions can then be used to define the roles of the individuals on a particular project. The standard procedures should cover responsibility for processing change orders and extra work, purchasing and receiving, project documentation, and costs and accounting.

As the project team is being assembled and mobilized and the standard procedures are adjusted, defined, and implemented for the particular project, it is a good idea to reexamine the efforts on the project in terms of estimating, scheduling, procurement, cost accounting, and the like before construction begins. This reassessment can serve as an additional safeguard for the early identification and correction of problems that might otherwise have a serious impact on the project at some later date if left undetected.

§ 6.17 Establishing Lines of Communication

The ability of the parties on the project to establish and maintain constructive lines of communications is essential to the success of any project. Prosecution of the work must be recognized as a cooperative effort which demands a team approach rather than adversary conflict. The owner, architect, and contractor must establish some method both to discover what is going on at the jobsite (for example, what problems the subcontractors are having and the problems they anticipate) and to relay suggestions, recommendations, and requirements as to how these problems can be avoided or solved.

Satisfactory communications can be achieved only if the parties have personnel who can develop pleasant and confident working relationships with one another. The subcontractors' workers should have sufficient confidence in the prime contractor's on-site personnel so that they will not hesitate to report difficulties and seek the prime contractor's recommendations as to how those difficulties can be avoided or resolved. Efforts to develop this confidence should begin at the preconstruction conference and should continue throughout the contract period.

An important procedural aid to establishing and maintaining the required lines of communications is regular job meetings. Weekly, biweekly, or at least monthly meetings should be regularly scheduled and held. The participants and the frequency of the meetings will depend on their purpose and the status or level of activity on the job. Field coordination meetings should involve the project superintendent, subcontractor superintendents, and key foremen. Brief but regular meetings like this can aid the process of coordinating and scheduling the work on a firsthand basis. They can also help identify problem areas and information needed for progress before a situation becomes critical.

Regular meetings between the architect's staff and the contractor are helpful for keeping up on the status of submittals, shop drawings, and areas requiring clarifications. Meetings between the contractor, architect, and owner should also take place, but probably on a less frequent basis. These meetings can be used to apprise the owner of important developments and to work out contractual issues. Further, the parties can discuss problems that are not being worked out on a more operational level and require the owner's intervention. The contractor should be wary of allowing the owner to get too far removed from the construction effort.

§ 6.18 Project Documentation

Paperwork on a construction project can be overwhelming, but it is essential. The contractor typically generates and maintains the bulk of the documentation on a construction project, but all participants have an interest in it. Contracts often require that the contractor maintain certain documentation, with copies and/or access available to the owner and others.

Project documentation creates an accessible history of the project that serves two roles: (1) planning and managing the project, and (2) aiding in resolving claims and disputes. It must be organized and maintained in such a manner that it is a help and not a hinderance to effective project management and persecution or defense of claims. Routine and uniformity are two essentials to an effective system of project documentation. The procedures should not only be standardized for the project but for the company as a whole. Only with that level of emphasis and indoctrination can all the fruits and benefits of a system be reaped.

The system and procedures must be written down. The length and level of detail of the written description will vary with the size and complexity of the project. Some description may be obviated by the use of computerized tracking systems, such as for cost accounting and tracking submittals. Regardless of how extensive the procedures are, it is imperative that they be clear and specific. If they are vague and general, allowing for personal interpretation and selective application, there will be no system at all. Instead, a hodgepodge of personal record keeping and filing systems will result.

Just putting procedures on paper is not enough. The procedures must be reviewed with all levels of personnel who will be responsible for implementation so they are understood, used, and enforced. The critical importance of project documentation must be emphasized and that emphasis maintained throughout the project and from project to project.

The following checklist contains certain basic information that should be maintained and organized in separate files:

1. The contract, including all its components, and all change orders or amendments, including a bid or original set of project plans and specifications;

2. All documents, worksheets, and forms associated with the original bid estimate and subsequent revisions;

3. Subcontractor or vendor files, including bids, subcontracts, or purchase orders, together with changes, and correspondence;

4. Project schedules, including the original schedule and all updates;

5. Insurance requirements and information for all parties.

The standard procedures relating to documentation should also address the creation, maintenance, and orientation of certain specific types of documentation.

§ 6.19   — Correspondence

Procedures for date-stamping, copying, routing, filing, and indexing incoming and outgoing correspondence should be the responsibility of secretarial or clerical support staff to perform in accordance with standard procedures. A copy of all correspondence should go in a master correspondence file. The party responsible for responding to or acting on incoming correspondence should be identified.

As a matter of routine, the project management should be drilled on the importance of complying with technical notice requirements in the contract. Discussion with other parties should likewise be confirmed in writing to the involved parties with copies to the file. Such confirmation will help immediately resolve any misunderstanding that might exist and also preserve the substance of the discussion if there is a dispute at some later date.

§ 6.20   — Meeting Notes

Regular job coordination meetings between the various parties to the project, on a cumulative basis, probably cover more issues and contribute more to the exchange of information necessary to complete the work than all the correspondence on the project. What occurs at such meetings is therefore of great importance. Someone should be designated to maintain the minutes or notes for each meeting, preferably the same person at each meeting. That person should record the subjects covered, the nature of the discussion, the future actions to be taken and by whom. The name, title, and affiliation of each participant should be listed. The notes should be concise but informative. The items discussed should be indexed or designated in a manner so that they can be located for future reference. The notes should then be distributed to all participants and those affected on a regular basis.

A word processor or personal computer can be valuable for updating regular meeting notes, as certain items will likely remain open to discussion through several meetings. At the opening of each regular meeting, the notes from the previous meeting can be reviewed to confirm their accuracy and the mutual understanding of the participants. By identifying those items that remain outstanding, the previous week's minutes can also serve as an agenda for the current meeting.

§ 6.21   —Jobsite Logs or Daily Reports

Jobsite logs or daily reports are generally maintained by the project superintendent and can provide the best record of what happens in the field. They help keep management and office personnel informed of progress and problems. In the event of a claim, they are often among the most helpful documents in recreating the progress on the job and as-built schedules.

The daily log or report must be a part of the superintendent's daily routine. If it is too burdensome, it either will be ignored or will detract from the superintendent's primary function of getting the job built. Key information should be elicited briefly and concisely, requiring as little narrative as possible. The information covered should include: manpower, preferably broken down by subcontractors; equipment used and idle; major work activities; any delays or problems; areas of work not available; safety and accidents; oral instructions and informal meetings; a brief weather summary; and jobsite visitors.

The burden on the superintendent can be eased and the information maintained in a more organized manner by using a standard form. The process can be further expedited by simply allowing the superintendent to dictate entries and having the report typed up by office staff.

All key project personnel such as supervisors, project engineers, and project managers, should also be encouraged to maintain personal daily logs and procedures established to facilitate this effort. The information they should record should be similar to the job log or daily report but would not be as extensive or detailed.

These types of routine, contemporaneous descriptions of work progress, site conditions, labor and equipment usage and the contractor's ability (or inability) to perform its work can provide valuable information necessary to accurately reconstruct the events of the project in preparation of a claim. In maintaining these reports or logs, project personnel must be consistent in recording the events and activities on the job, particularly those relating to claims or potential claims.

Failure to record an event, once the responsibility of a daily report or log is undertaken, carries with it the implication that the event did not occur or was insignificant and also threatens the credibility of the entire log.

§ 6.22   —Standard Forms and Status Logs

There is a constant flow of information between the project participants by means of a variety of media. Drawings are revised, shop drawings are submitted, reviewed, and returned, field orders and change orders are issued, questions are asked, and clarifications are provided. Cumulatively and individually, these bits and pieces of information are essential for building the job and also for reconstructing the progress of events on paper in the event of a claim. The standard procedures must include the means for providing, eliciting, recording, and tracking this mass of data so that it can be used during the course of the job and efficiently retrieved in an after-the-fact claim setting.

Routine transmittal forms should be customized to address specific, routine types of communications in order to expedite the process, but also to ensure that required information is provided. For example, separate specialized forms can be prepared for transmittal of shop drawings and submittals, requests for clarifications, drawing revisions, and, of course, field orders and change orders. When possible, the forms should provide space for responses, including certain standard responses that simply can be checked off or filled in. At a minimum, the forms should identify the individual sender, the date issued, and specific and self-descriptive references to the affected or enclosed drawings, submittal, or specification. If a response is requested by a certain date, that date should be identified on the form.

Ideally, each discrete type of communication or specialized form should be numbered or somehow identified in a chronologically sequential manner based on the date it is initiated. Shop drawings and submittals, however, are best identified by specification section, with a suffix added to indicate resubmittals. This provides a basis for easy reference and orientation. Copies of the completed forms should be maintained in binders in reverse chronological/numerical order. Although various project staff members may require working copies, a complete master file should be maintained as a complete reference source and historical document.

In order to maintain the status of and track these numerous and varied communications, which can number many thousands, logs should be maintained. These logs need only address key information such as number assigned, date, and a self-descriptive reference. Proposed change orders and change order logs should also identify any increase or decrease in contract amount as well as time extensions. Such logs can be kept on personal computers using inexpensive, commercially available software or even on a word processor to expedite updating. Logs should be maintained for internal record-keeping and also for distribution to other parties on the project. The logs serve as a reminder of outstanding items and can highlight action required to keep the work progressing.

The contractor should use standard forms and procedures for communications with subcontractors as well as the owner and architect. Ideally, subcontractors should be encouraged to standardize their communications so there will be a more integrated approach for the entire project.

§ 6.23   —Photographs and Video Tapes

Photographs and videotapes are helpful, easy, and inexpensive means to monitor, depict, and preserve conditions of the work as those conditions change and the work progresses. They are particularly helpful in claims situations. One approach, incorporated in many contracts, is to accumulate a periodic pictorial diary of the job through a series of weekly or monthly photographs and pictures of significant milestones in the construction. This encourages personnel to take photographs of site conditions on a routine basis, perhaps concentrating on problem areas and those areas associated with crucial construction procedures and scheduling. Photographs are also the best evidence of defective work or problem conditions that are cured or covered up and cannot be viewed later.

A professional photographer may be needed at times or required by contract, but generally jobsite personnel with some instruction are more than capable of handling the photography chores. Cameras capable of producing quality photographs and negatives should be used. However, it is also a good idea to use as a backup a self-developing camera that allows the party responsible for taking pictures to check the content and clarity of the photos while at the site and before conditions are altered.

Pictures should always be identified on the back with a notation as to time, date, location, conditions depicted, personnel present, and the photographer. This should be done at the time the photograph is taken if a self-developing camera is used. Otherwise, a log should be kept as the photos are taken and the log immediately should be checked when the photos are developed and the appropriate entries made on the back of the prints. Without this information correlated to specific photographs, the utility of the entire photography effort can be substantially undermined. Negatives should also be retained in an organized, retrievable manner.

Videocassette recorders have become relatively inexpensive and easy to operate. In some situations, videotape can be considerably more informative than a still photograph, such as when attempting to depict an activity or the overall status of the project. Static conditions, however, are best photographed. The availability of a contemporaneous narrative as part of the video can give the after-the-fact viewer a much better idea of what is being depicted and why. A monthly videotape is an excellent way of preserving and presenting evidence.

Again, properly trained jobsite personnel can operate the video recorder and later testify in conjunction with the showing of the tape.

§ 6.24 Cost Accounting Records

The use of effective cost-accounting methods and the maintenance of appropriate cost records can minimize many of the proof problems inherently associated with construction claims. Unfortunately, even though a claimant may be able to prove that an event has occurred entitling it to additional compensation, it will be able to recover only that amount of damages that it can prove with reasonable certainty. Proving the actual dollars lost is crucial to any claim.

§ 6.25 Monitoring the Work Through Scheduling

The prime contractor should continuously monitor the work of all subcontractors to determine that each is meeting its deadlines so that the work of other trades can proceed as originally scheduled. The owner must perform the same task when multiple prime contractors are involved. Even when the contractor has primary scheduling responsibility, which is most often the case, the owner should nonetheless continuously monitor the progress of the work and the scheduling effort.

Most prime contracts require the preparation of a bar chart or progress schedule, which provides the easiest means of monitoring the work. The Critical Path Method (CPM) schedule required by the prime contract on many large projects can be even more valuable as a scheduling tool if properly developed, updated, and utilized.

The input of subcontractors and all project participants in the development and updating of any project schedule is critical to its usefulness. As a practical matter, a schedule that is developed without the input of the parties actually performing the work may result in an unworkable product, and the schedule as an instrument of coordination will be wasted. By getting the parties to participate in the preparation of the schedule, it becomes a much more meaningful and productive project management device. In addition, through its involvement, each party has in effect admitted what was reasonable and expected of it. If a party later fails to perform or follow the schedule, its ability to dispute the relevance of the project schedule and what was required of that party can be substantially reduced.

A project schedule can be a double-edged sword for the prime contractor, particularly if it is a CPM that shows the interrelationship of all activities and trades. A properly developed schedule can be used to demonstrate how a subcontractor is behind schedule and how its delayed performance is impacting the entire project.[19] Conversely, a subcontractor may also use a project schedule against the prime contractor to show how the subcontractor reasonably expected and planned to proceed with the work and how that plan was disrupted by the prime contractor, another subcontractor or the owner, for which the affected subcontractor is entitled to additional compensation.[20]

If the schedule is not properly maintained, updated and enforced, so that it bears little relationship to the actual progress of the work or the parties' contractual obligations, it may be dismissed by a court or arbitrators as merely representing "theoretical aspirations" rather than practical contract requirements.[21] The heavy use of scheduling information and analysis in resolving claims underscores the importance of preparing, and maintaining through updates, a realistic schedule that secures subcontractor involvement and agreement.

§ 6.26   Effective Claim Development

Construction claims, by their nature, are often tedious and complex. They generally involve facts and circumstances that stretch over months and years, rather than one catastrophic instant in time. The many facts and circumstances involved in the claim often ripple throughout the project in ways not so readily perceived, touching other parties and compounding the complexity of the situation. All these factors make the early formation and pursuit of a strategy an important step toward winning a construction claim.

The first step in developing a claim strategy is to decide upon the objective or goal the strategy will be geared to achieve. Simply identifying the goal as winning is not enough. What constitutes "winning" a construction dispute is a variable. Is a claim being pursued simply to recoup a pecuniary loss? Or is the claim being pursued to satisfy some principle or to set an important example or precedent so that the financial recovery may be of no importance? A practical and pragmatic approach generally prevails over thoughts of pursuing construction claims and litigation on principle. Most construction claims are best reduced to economic considerations of cost, risk, and potential recovery. Otherwise, a long and costly process of dispute and litigation can result.

Consequently, the amount of the claim or maximum likely recovery will dictate the level of effort and expense prudently invested in the claim effort. There is no exact formula for preparing for a successful claim, but there do exist useful procedures and fundamental techniques that provide a favorable basis for successful communication, documentation, negotiations, and, if necessary, arbitration or trial.

---

[19] Illinois Structural Steel Corp. v. Pathman Constr. Co., 23 Ill. App. 3d 1, 318 N.E.2d 232 (1974).
[20] *See* United States *ex rel*. R.W. Vaught Co. v. F.D. Rich Co., 439 F.2d 895 (8th Cir. 1971).
[21] *Id.*

§ 6.27 Early Claim Recognition and Preparation

Before there can be any preparation or prosecution of a claim, the claim must be recognized. Early recognition is required to ensure that notice requirements are met and evidence needed to support the claim. Familiarity with the contract requirements is needed to recognize claims and to avoid unknowingly providing or accepting a nonconforming quantity, quality, or method of performance. Consequently, all jobsite personnel should be familiar with the contract terms, including the plans and specifications, the general conditions, and special provisions so they can evaluate the performance actually demanded as compared to the performance specified in the contract. In-house educational programs to enhance this ability and better equip job personnel to identify and handle possible claim situations should also be considered.

Of course, a claim should not be asserted for every minor incident or disagreement. Conversely, trying too hard to get along and never filing a claim is not good business either. Part of an effective program of identifying claims requires targeting those incidents that are sufficiently meritorious and substantial to justify the cost of preparing and prosecuting them. Filing claims with little merit or significance will merely waste resources and squander credibility.

Once a determination is made that a claim merits prosecution, comprehensive preparation and organization should be promptly undertaken. The facts, evidence, and documents bearing on the claim should be assembled, organized, and reviewed when they are fresh and before they are lost or forgotten. This preparation should be undertaken with an eye toward resolving the claim in the formal setting of an arbitration or litigation, while still seeking early resolution through informal and less onerous means. If early resolution is not achieved, complete preparation at an early stage provides important insight for developing a claim strategy and a factual foundation that can be relied upon, but subject to revision, as prosecution of the claim continues.

The first step in claim preparation should be an exhaustive investigation of the claimant's own records and sources of information about the project and the claim. Project records are generally voluminous. Although the review of the records must be sufficient in scope to cover the documents relevant to the claim and anticipated defenses, it must also be sufficiently focused and specific to avoid inundating the claim preparation process with unnecessary and irrelevant documents.

There are certain categories of documents that almost always merit some consideration, such as the contract and all change orders, pay applications, daily logs or reports, bonds and insurance policies, correspondence files, and internal memoranda. Some further organization of the documents may be required beyond that used during construction in order to make individual documents relating to the claim more readily accessible.

Although documentation is certainly critical in any construction claim, it is not everything. At trial, although the documents will be admitted into evidence, the witnesses and their words, perceptions, and recollections will also gain considerable attention. Those individual resources should not be overlooked in the claim preparation process, but they often are. The more remote claim preparation is from the people actively involved in the field, the more likely there will be unpleasant surprises and inconsistencies as the claim is subjected to greater scrutiny in discovery or at trial.

Consequently, the project staff and field personnel involved should be interviewed to confirm that management's secondhand understanding about the facts and circumstances of the claim is accurate and complete. To the extent possible, project staff should be utilized to staff and assist in the claim preparation effort. At a minimum, project personnel should be given the opportunity to review the claim at various stages of preparation, and certainly before it is submitted, to confirm they can vouch for its accuracy.

§ 6.28 Early Involvement of Experts and Attorneys

Construction claims often require the assistance of experts to help solve problems and to assemble and analyze the facts. Part of a program of prompt and cost-effective claim preparation requires considering involving attorneys experienced with construction claims and other technical experts at an early stage. Of course, the use of outside assistance will depend on the size and complexity of the claim, but in most claims such early involvement will facilitate prompt resolution or better preparation for trial and will be worth the investment. Scrimping on experienced and qualified legal and technical support for a claim can prove very costly in the long run.

An attorney experienced in construction claims and litigation can be deemed an "expert" whose advice and guidance at the early stages of a claim is often desirable. The construction attorney who would ultimately be charged with presenting the claim to judge, jury or arbitrators should be consulted to ensure that the claim and supporting documentation and evidence is being assembled and preserved in a manner consistent with favorable resolution of the claim in such a formal proceeding. The construction attorney need not take over the claim effort, but should be consulted to ensure that the claim effort will not be wasted or undercut the claimant's position in any proceeding which may ensue.

An experienced construction attorney can also often suggest competent technical consultants in specialized areas such as accounting and scheduling, and thereby help avoid the expense and frustration of relying on an individual who does not have the proper qualifications to testify in the case.

Involvement of an attorney does not presuppose resort to litigation or arbitration. On the contrary, it is simply another element of comprehensive preparation which hopefully contributes to the early resolution of claims. Early involvement of technical and accounting expertise will likewise enhance claim preparation efforts and hopefully the claimant's leverage in negotiation of persuasiveness at trial.

If it is possible to involve an expert during the actual construction phase, when a claim is merely a probability, that option should be considered. At such an early stage, the expert may be able to suggest ways of mitigating damages or reducing the impact of an injurious condition. The expert may also be able to recommend methods of preserving evidence and of creating demonstrative evidence for use during negotiation, arbitration, or trial.

Further, testimony based on firsthand observation of the construction will generally be more credible and persuasive than testimony based solely on secondhand input. There is the risk, however, that an expert's involvement in the project may rise to such a level that the credibility of any testimony the expert might provide in the future is compromised as the expert goes from neutral observer to active and adversary participant. This risk can only be weighed on a case-by-case basis.

Construction is a complex process, involving a broad spectrum of scientific and technical disciplines. Resolution of construction claims likewise may require a variety of experts to serve as consultants in the claim preparation or to testify as expert witnesses. There is neither the space nor the need to enumerate here the various technical specialties or subspecialties which are often called upon in claim situations. It is important, however, to note and recognize such specialization and to ensure that the right expert is consulted for the particular problem at hand. If a claim merits prosecution, it also merits the best and most qualified technical expert in that subject who is reasonably available.

The immediate concern with technical qualifications must be balanced with need to have a witness who is capable of persuasive testimony in the formal forum selected for resolution of claims. A technical expert respected in its field may be understood by a technically-oriented arbitration panel, but be incomprehensible to a lay jury. It is this type of counterbalancing concerns which must be considered and addressed early in the claim preparation process to avoid difficult surprises and dramatic adjustments in the later stages of the claim, immediately before or during trial.

Delay is a frequent subject of construction claims. Hence, scheduling analyses and scheduling experts are often involved in resolution of claims. Beyond their scheduling expertise, scheduling consultants must have a detailed, working knowledge of the construction process so their analysis reflects the practical problems and difficulties experienced on the construction site and not merely a computer-generated abstraction. Likewise, it is essential that the scheduling expert involved in a claim be provided access to contemporaneous project documentation which accurately reflects the manner in which the work proceeded.

Costly and complex "as-built" scheduling analyses presented in support of claims can be severely undermined if the dates used in the analysis conflict with those contained in project documentation, such as daily reports or monthly schedule updates. The scheduling expert's task and effectiveness can be substantially enhanced and such problems avoided through the maintenance of project documentation as described in § **6.18**.

Certified public accountants who are familiar with the construction industry and its financial and accounting practices can also contribute significantly to quantifying and proving the financial consequence of the technical problems that generated the claim. Their involvement is discussed separately in § **6.36**.

§ 6.29   Use of Demonstrative Evidence

Demonstrative evidence has the special advantage of presenting in pictorial form abstract, complicated, and extensive facts. It can clarify or explain oral testimony or documentary narrative in concrete terms. In addition, demonstrative evidence adds interest and avoids the tedium of a relentless one-dimensional recitation of facts. The simplicity and clarity demonstrative evidence can provide is particularly effective in large, highly technical, and complex construction claims. However, the utility of demonstrative evidence should not be overlooked in smaller, more straightforward disputes.

Demonstrative evidence can range from photographs and videos to charts summarizing facts or making comparisons, such as a chart comparing as-planned manpower to as-built manpower in order to graphically depict an overrun. Charts and graphs are often used in connection with scheduling presentations, again usually comparing the as-planned schedule to the as-built schedule, with a focus on those problems which created problems or delays. By displaying this information in an attractive visual way in combination with other written and oral presentations, the claim can be advanced in a more compelling and persuasive manner. The goal of the demonstrative presentation is lost if it is not clear and understandable and firmly supported by the facts.

Discussions of the importance and usefulness of demonstrative evidence as a means of persuasion generally are found in trial advocacy materials. But there is no need to hold such a powerful and effective tool in reserve until trial. Demonstrative evidence should be developed and used to simplify the claim and persuade the other side as soon as possible.

§ 6.30   Components of a Well-Prepared Claim Document

Simplicity to promote prompt understanding, while making the claim interesting and appear to be well supported, is the key to effective claim preparation and presentation. One means by which to synthesize the claims and this approach is to use a *claim document*, a written synopsis of the claim that can be presented to the opposition at the early stages of the dispute. Like essentially every other aspect of claim preparation, the claim document serves two alternate purposes. First, its immediate and primary goal is to bring about a prompt and satisfactory resolution of the claim. Failing that, the second purpose of the claim document is to provide a blueprint or plan for further prosecution of the claim.

The claim document provides an opportunity for the claimant to explain its grievance in a complete and comprehensive fashion. The process of preparing the claim document is an important step in developing a claim strategy because it requires the claimant to refine and synthesize the claim from beginning to end. The claim document should be viewed as telling a story. It should have a clear and definite theme that can be readily communicated, understood, and remembered. The theme should be the strongest argument supporting the claimant's theory of recovery.

There will certainly be a considerable quantity of facts gathered in support of the claim, but trying to present and argue each and every one of these facts will simply overwhelm and confuse the reader, and the claim document as a tool of persuasion will be a failure. When multiple and unrelated claims are presented in one document, the document must be structured to emphasize the strongest claim.

The primary communicative component of the claim document is the factual narrative. Although this narrative will certainly focus on the claimant's point of view, it should not be expressed in overly argumentative or combative terms. Instead, to the extent possible, the facts presented should be permitted to speak for themselves. The writing style should be clear and precise, but should not read like technical specifications. It is, after all, a story and not simply a recital of a string of facts. The narrative should be comprehensive and logically organized, so it can be used as a resource throughout negotiations and further prosecution of the claim. If the complexity of the matter is such that the narrative is exceedingly long, an executive summary should be prepared.

The factual narrative is often followed by a written discussion of the applicable legal principles that support and illustrate the theories on which the claim is based. Assistance from an experienced attorney in construction claims is generally required to fashion the legal arguments and otherwise to ensure that the factual narrative is presented in a manner consistent with the applicable legal principles. The need for or extent of a legal discussion is generally geared to the expertise or experience of the ultimate decision maker for the opposition. For example, in federal construction contracts, certain theories of entitlement are so firmly established and recognized on all levels that little or no legal discussion is required.

In other situations, the legal discussion may be a crucial element in causing the other side to recognize its liability and exposure. A one-time owner may have no idea of what a differing site condition is or why the contractor should be paid for it. On the other hand, claims against local governmental entities which contract regularly may be ruled upon by elected officials who also require an education about construction law before they can be expected to recognize the need to settle a claim.

As discussed in greater detail in §§ **6.31** through **6.36**, pricing the claim and supporting such calculations is every bit as important as establishing liability for the claim. The claim document must recognize the importance of damages and include a specific dollar figure and fairly detailed cost analysis and breakdown.

Supporting information and sources should be identified and appended if not too voluminous.

Finally, the claim document should be used to showcase and highlight the most persuasive and impactive documentary and demonstrative evidence. The most potent documents should be quoted or even reproduced in their entirety in the body of the narrative. Those documents that do not merit incorporation into the text, but which are referenced and support the claim, can be included in an indexed appendix that is cross-referenced with and organized like the factual narrative. In this manner, the narrative can be reviewed without having to sift through every bit of paper, but that backup is readily available should further review be desired.

In addition to documents, charts, graphs, drawings, and photographs, other demonstrative and visual evidence should be incorporated into the claim document to the extent practical. Similarly, all consideration should be given to including relevant reports by experts as attachments to the claim document as exhibits, with appropriate references to and quotes from the reports in the narrative.

In certain situations, the nature of the claim or the character or capacity of the opposition may counsel against submitting an extensive claim document. The opposition may not have the financial resources or genuine interest in resolving the claim by negotiation, which is a primary goal of the claim document. Instead, the opposition may seek a one-way flow of information, it being willing to receive a detailed presentation of the claim, but unwilling to explain or document any response, defense, or counterclaim until trial. The claimant must evaluate whether pursuing the "race for disclosure" by providing a claim document will ultimately eliminate the roadblocks to negotiation and settlement, or simply better equip the opposition to defend the claim, without a commensurate benefit to the claimant.

Generally, but not always, a sound, well-documented and prepared claim should be able to withstand and be improved through feedback from the opposition's scrutiny. Moreover, even if the judgment is made that an extensive claim document should not be submitted, that conclusion does not necessarily mean that a claim document should not be prepared for internal use to better synthesize the claim and prepare for whatever proceeding may follow. Of course, if formal claim submission is mandated by the contract, such a requirement should be followed, although the extent of the submission may vary.

§ 6.31 Importance of Calculating and Proving Damages

The issue in construction disputes that generally receives the most attention and focus is liability. Does a differing site condition exist? Who caused the delay and is it compensable? However, the issue of damages or costs flowing from the events that give rise to liability is no less important. Too often, the issue of calculating and proving damages is given a back seat, with little precision or scrutiny applied until the eve of trial. That approach can result in an entirely misguided claim effort, missed opportunities for settlement, and loss at trial or in arbitration. An early analysis of damages can help determine whether a claim really exists and the best means of preparing and positioning the claim for the affirmative recovery sought.

The problem of calculating and proving damages can be substantially reduced by initiating proper cost accounting at the time the claim is identified. Accounting measures can be established to segregate and carefully maintain separate records. If such a procedure is followed, proof of damages can be reduced to little more than the presentation of evidence of separate accounts.

Unfortunately, this ideal situation seldom exists; either the problem is not recognized in time to set up separate accounting procedures, the maintenance of separate accounts is simply not possible because of an inability to isolate costs, or no attempt is made to establish the requisite procedures. These circumstances necessitate the development of some formula which is sufficiently reliable to permit the court or arbitrators to allow its use as proof of damage. If settlement is being sought, the claimant must likewise convince the other side of the validity and reliability of its damage calculations. There are many specific approaches and alternatives for pricing claims. However, certain principles and possible approaches are common to all construction claims.

§ 6.32   —Basic Damage Principles

The law of damages is compensatory in nature. In contracts, the goal is to reimburse the claimant for all "losses caused and gains prevented" by the other party's breach.[22] Tort claims, which in construction generally involve allegations of negligence and misrepresentation, may offer a broader scope of damages, but many courts have limited tort damages to cases involving either personal injury or property damage, denying recovery for the purely economic loss that is typically the subject of construction claims.[23]

Damages in construction claims, like other contract claims, are of two basic types: direct and consequential. Although punitive damages may also be available in the extreme case, they are by far the exception. Direct damages are those which result from the direct, natural, and immediate impact of the breach and are recoverable when proven.[24] In the contractor's case, such damages may include the cost of items such as idle labor and machinery, material and labor escalations, and extended jobsite and home office overhead associated with

---

[22] J. Calamari & J. Perillo, The Law of Contracts § 327 (1970).

[23] See, e.g., State v. Mitchell Constr. Co., 198 Idaho 335, 699 P.2d 1349 (1985).

[24] Spang Indus. v. Aetna Casualty & Sur. Co., 512 F.2d 365 (2d Cir. 1975).

delay. The owner's direct damages are generally those costs incurred in completing or correcting the contractor's work and the cost of delay, which is either its actual costs in terms of lost rent, loss of use, or liquidated damages.

Consequential damages do not flow directly from the alleged breach but are an indirect source of losses. The most frequently sought types of consequential damage in connection with delay claims are lost profits (stemming from reduced bonding capacity), interest on tied-up capital, and damage to business reputation. These are more difficult to prove because the causal link between such damages and the act constituting the breach is often tenuous and uncertain.

§ 6.33 Methods of Pricing Claims

There are two basic methods for pricing construction claims. The simplest method is the total cost method. The other, more complicated but more widely accepted, method is the discrete or segregated cost method.

§ 6.34 —Total Cost Method

A total cost claim is simply what the name implies. It essentially seeks to convert a standard fixed-price construction contract into a cost-reimbursement arrangement. The contractor's total out-of-pocket costs of performance are tallied and marked up for overhead and profit. Payments already made to that contractor are deducted from that amount, and the total cost price is achieved. Of course, this approach can be refined or adjusted to meet particular needs and circumstances, but the basic components and approach remain: costs associated with the basis for the claim are not segregated. The total cost method is well suited for impact disruption claims when the segregation of costs is virtually impossible.

The total cost approach, although preferred by claimants because of the ease of computation, is generally discouraged by the courts because it requires the contractor to be virtually fault-free and is fraught with uncertainties. Numerous court decisions have therefore established fairly rigorous requirements for the presentation of total cost claims. In order for the total cost method to yield an accurate and reliable figure, the contractor's original price must have been accurate and correct, overruns in performance cannot be the result of any performance problems caused by the contractor or its subcontractors, and those costs actually incurred must be reasonable. Even when these conditions are met, the contractor must demonstrate that the use of a segregated cost approach was not feasible.

Of course, if another approach is not feasible because of the contractor's own poor record keeping, the validity of the total cost approach is further questioned. Owners probably view contractor total cost claims with even greater suspicion and distrust than the courts do, so much so that the credibility of the entire claim and the claimant can be undermined. The difficulties of establishing the prerequisites for use of a total cost calculation in court combined with the skepticism it can generate counsel against use of the total cost method whenever possible.

§ 6.35   —Segregated Cost Method

The segregated cost method of pricing claims is certainly more difficult than the total cost method, but it is a far more accurate, reliable, and persuasive way of presenting damages. Under this approach, the additional costs associated with the events or occurrences that gave rise to the claim are segregated from those incurred in the normal course of performance of the contract. For example, on an extra work claim, the pricing would reflect an allocation (actual or estimated) for the additional labor, materials, and equipment used in performing the extra work. If the project was delayed, costs of field overhead and home office overhead would also be calculated.

§ 6.36   Project Cost Reviews and Audits

Even if the segregated cost method is to be employed to price and prove the claim, a good starting point is to summarize the project from a financial standpoint by making a total cost calculation. This will establish the contractor's overall profit or loss position on the entire project. Although the overall profit or loss may not ensure or bar recovery on a discrete claim issue, it is nonetheless important. As a practical matter, a claimant's out-of-pocket loss can be the most compelling evidence to support recovery, whether through settlement or at trial. Conversely, if a substantial profit was earned on the project but an overrun was incurred in one area as a result of some action by the other party, it may not make sense to pursue the claim.

Once the overall profitability of the project has been evaluated, it is a good idea to audit the contract. The size of the claim dictates whether an internal audit by accounting personnel is adequate or if an outside certified public accountant is required. Generally, it is best to get outside, specialized accounting expertise involved early. Allowing an outside CPA to perform the audit provides a number of significant benefits. The scrutiny of an audit will identify any problems in the contractor's accounting that can be corrected or at least taken into account without the embarrassment of a surprise discovery by the other side. An outside audit will further refine and organize the contractor's cost information so that it is more readily usable in developing a segregated cost approach to the claim.

The CPA doing the audit should be the one to testify, if necessary, in support of damages, so the audit will give that CPA greater credibility and also allow the CPA to provide greater assistance in the development of the claim. Depending on the size and complexity of the claim and the condition of the project records, such audit exercises are relatively inexpensive and generally extremely cost-effective.

If the initial audit confirms the accuracy and reliability of the claimant's accounting records, the claim should be priced and presented in a format consistent with those records and audit results. This will limit the opportunity for inconsistency and confusion. The endorsement of an outside CPA will also lend considerable credibility to the claim. In addition, this level of preparation and organization allows the claimant to invite an audit of the job and claim costs by the opposition. Construction contracts with the federal government and most public contracts provide for audits of claims, as do some private contracts. An audit can be used offensively by the claimant if it will confirm that the costs were actually incurred. That confirmation will give the claimant greater credibility and hopefully limit the scope of the dispute.

§ 6.37 Pursuing Negotiation and Settlement

Although claims and disputes are a part of the construction process, they need not and should not dominate the process. When claims and disputes cannot be avoided, efforts should be redoubled to resolve them as quickly as possible. The complexity, time, and cost of arbitration and litigation naturally favor negotiation and settlement.

An approach favoring prompt resolution should be part of a claims policy and project personnel and management should be indoctrinated and trained along those lines. Although contract provisions regarding notice of claims and other technical requirements should be complied with, other lines of communication on the project should not be overlooked as a means of bringing a claim to quick settlement and avoiding the need to have the dispute process run its full course. It is far easier and less expensive to resolve problems in the field, where they arise, than in the courtroom. Even if early settlement is not achieved, the negotiations force the claimant to seriously examine the merits of its claim and also reveal the strengths and weaknesses of the claim at an early stage.

Comprehensive and careful preparation greatly enhances the likelihood of early resolution and settlement. A party attempting to settle a claim should know its own case intimately and should have anticipated as many of the opposing party's points as possible without the benefit of discovery. Use of a well-prepared claim document, as discussed in § 6.30, is helpful both as a starting point and as a reference during settlement discussions. People with firsthand, detailed knowledge of the underlying facts are also an essential part of any negotiating effort. There is simply no substitute for the person who lived with the project's problems on a daily basis.

CHAPTER 7

PROGRESS PAYMENTS AS CLAIM WAIVERS, TRUST FUNDS, AND PARTIAL LIEN RELEASES

Kerry C. Lawrence
Jeff A. Hellinger

§ 7.1   Introduction

§ 7.2   Establishing the Ground Rules

§ 7.3   Prompt Identification of Claims

§ 7.4   Waiver of Claims for Extra Cost or Time Extension

§ 7.5   Release of Lien Rights

§ 7.6   Trust Funds

§ 7.7   Restrictive Indorsements

§ 7.8   Form—Contractor's Application for Payment

§ 7.9   Form—Conditional Release/Unconditional Release of Lien

§ 7.1   Introduction

The genesis of this chapter was the request several years ago by a client for some system whereby it could: 1) require the prompt identification and presentation of claims, 2) obtain a waiver of all claims not promptly made, 3) obtain lien releases as work progressed, and 4) obtain greater assurances that monies paid were applied to satisfy potential lien claimants on its projects.

The client was somewhat unusual in that it operated both as a developer for its own account and as a general contractor for other developers. Because of this dual role, the client wanted a system which was fair to owners, general contractors, and subcontractors. This chapter is intended only to provide an example of one approach which may be taken, and is not intended to be an exhaustive analysis of alternatives.

The path we ultimately chose to take centered around the contractor/subcontractor application for payment and the actual payment itself. Refer to § **7.8** for the Contractor's Application for Payment, to § **7.9** for the Conditional Release/Unconditional Release of Lien, which is submitted with the payment application, and to § **7.7** for the restrictive indorsement form.

§ 7.2   Establishing the Ground Rules

Although the application for payment, release of lien, and restrictive indorsement are essential to the approach utilized, the ability to require that these forms be utilized and to establish their effectiveness requires that there be some contractual term in the initial contract which mandates their use. We insert the following provisions in the payment terms of the owner/contractor agreement:

> CONTRACTOR shall make application for payment on OWNER Forms, Contractor's Application for Payment and Partial Release of Lien. Terms and conditions set forth on these Forms are hereby incorporated into this agreement by this reference as if set forth in full. CONTRACTOR acknowledges that it has read and fully understands the forms and agrees to act as a fiduciary for all funds received from OWNER, which shall be held as trust funds for the benefit of all potential lien claimants claiming by or through CONTRACTOR, including, but not limited to, subcontractors, laborers, material suppliers, equipment suppliers, employee benefit plans, and all taxing authorities.

A similar provision is inserted in all subcontracts.

§ 7.3   Prompt Identification of Claims

Almost all modern contracts and subcontracts contain requirements that extra or changed work be ordered in writing. Similarly, most of these forms require that notice of any claims be made in writing within a certain time period. For example, the American Institute of Architects' (AIA) A201-1987 ¶¶ 7.2.1 and 7.3.1 address these issues.

Similarly, ¶¶ 4.3.3 and 4.3.7 address the requirement for notice of claims. Paragraph 4.3.3 provides, "Claims by either party must be made within 21 days after occurrence of the event giving rise to such Claim or within 21 days after the claimant first recognizes the condition giving rise to the Claim, whichever is later. Claims must be made by written notice." Paragraph 4.3.7 provides, "If the

Contractor wishes to make Claim for an increase in the Contract Sum, written notice as provided herein shall be given before proceeding to execute the Work."

A construction contract provision requiring a written order for alterations or extras will normally be enforced.[1] Likewise, clauses relating to time limits for bringing forth claims will also be enforced.[2] Time limits may vary in length depending upon the particular contract. The court in *Batson-Cook Co. v. Loden & Co.*[3] held that provisions as to notice must be reasonably construed.

Although these clauses are commonly enforced, courts in this country have almost uniformly held that a contractual requirement that alterations for additional work be ordered in writing can be avoided through waiver, modification, rescission, abandonment, estoppel, or other theories.[4] Generally the courts have done a very poor job of keeping distinct the different theories for avoiding the effect of the contract term and frequently use these theories interchangeably.[5]

It is the authors' experience that frequently many small claims accumulate during the course of the construction project and may form the basis for one composite claim at the end of the project. This accumulation of claims creates several difficulties. By the time the project is complete, memories are poor, documentation of the events and costs is generally not good, and the claim is extremely difficult to effectively present or defend against. A large claim composed of numerous small items takes an inordinate amount of time to prepare, present and defend.

Similarly, it is our experience that other times there is a single significant claim item, and the attitude becomes, "Well, if I have to sue him for one item, I might as well sue him for a whole bunch of things." Many times these claims are the fulfillment of the old construction definition of a claim as "the amount of money needed to transform a net loss into a gross profit."

---

[1] 13 Am. Jur. 2d *Building and Construction Contracts* § 22 (1964); Whitfield Constr. Co. v. Commercial Dev. Corp., 392 F. Supp. 982 (D.V.I. 1975); United States v. Centex Constr. Co., 638 F. Supp. 411 (W.D. Va. 1985) [hereinafter *Centex*].

[2] *Centex*, 638 F. Supp. 411; Novak & Co. v. New York City Hous. Auth., 125 Misc. 2d 647, 480 N.Y.S.2d 403 (Sup. Ct. 1984), *modified on other grounds*, 108 A.D.2d 612, 485 N.Y.S.2d 68 (1985); *In re* Board of Educ., 122 A.D.2d 421, 505 N.Y.S.2d 233 (1986).

[3] 129 Ga. App. 376, 199 S.E.2d 332 (1973).

[4] *See* Swenson v. Lowe, 5 Wash. App. 186, 486 P.2d 1120 (1971); Moorhead Constr. Co. v. City of Grand Forks, 508 F.2d 1008 (8th Cir. 1975) [hereinafter *Moorhead*]; Biltmore Constr. Co. v. Tri-State Elec. Contractors, 137 Ga. App. 504, 224 S.E.2d 487 (1976); Moore Constr. Co. v. Clarksville Dep't of Elec., 707 S.W.2d 1 (Tenn. Ct. App. 1985), *aff'd*, 707 S.W.2d 1 (Tenn. 1986); Central Iowa Grading v. UDE Corp., 392 N.W.2d 857 (Iowa Ct. App. 1986) [hereinafter *Central Iowa*].

[5] For greater discussion of this issue, see Annotation, *Effect of Stipulation, in a Private Building or Construction Contract, That Alterations or Changes Must be Ordered in Writing*, 2 A.L.R.3d 620 (1965).

§ 7.4   Waiver of Claims for Extra Cost
or Time Extension

The waiver section of the contractor's application for payment requires that the contractor, for each payment period, identify the value of contract work completed, change order work completed, and field directive work completed. If the contractor wishes to make any claim for work which is outside of these three categories, the contractor must identify the claim item and the amount for which it will be seeking recovery.

If the contractor does not identify a claim, its application for payment expressly waives all rights to compensation for any costs incurred during the period covered by the application which are not identified as a claim. If the contractor does identify a claim and its amount, the claim is immediately placed into the dispute resolution process of the contract. Under AIA A201-1987 ¶ 4.4.1, an architect has five choices of action.

While acceptance of payment would effect a waiver of claims not identified, it would not bar recovery of claims identified and submitted for resolution under ¶ 4.4.1.[6]

Where a similar form is used as a subcontractor's application for payment, the contract between the general contractor and the owner typically would have a flow down clause for subcontractor disputes which involve the owner or the owner's agents. Typically, a subcontractor is not entitled to recover for extra work performed pursuant to the general contractor's verbal change which the owner has not approved.[7] Therefore, the general contractor would need to provide its own dispute resolution mechanism in the subcontract to ensure that claims were promptly dealt with.[8]

This is, we believe, the most crucial juncture in the use of this system. If the sole purpose of utilizing this process is to obtain a waiver of claims, but the owner (or general contractor) then does not take steps to force the prompt resolution of claims that are made, much of the value of the process is lost. In the several years that our client has been using this process, it has resolved a large number of disputes (most without involving counsel) in a prompt, economical, and fair manner. If claims are allowed to be identified and then remain unresolved, much of the benefit of this system is lost.

Although the issue has never been raised against our client, my greatest concern is that a court would be tempted to find that there is no consideration for the waiver of a claim. However, no additional consideration is required for a

---

[6] *See* Cape Fear Elec. Co. v. Star News Newspapers, 22 N.C. App. 519, 207 S.E.2d 323, *cert. denied*, 285 N.C. 757, 209 S.E.2d 280 (1974) [hereinafter *Cape Fear*].

[7] *Central Iowa*, 392 N.W.2d 857.

[8] *See* Sime Constr. Co. v. Washington Pub. Power Supply Sys., 28 Wash. App. 10, 621 P.2d 1299 (1980).

release at the time of final payment which is required in the original contract.[9] The United States Supreme Court, in *William Cramp & Sons Ship & Engine Building*,[10] held that the contract itself supplied sufficient consideration. The Washington Appellate Court, in *Yakima Asphalt v. Department of Transportation*,[11] held that a release required by the provisions of a contract is supported by the same consideration that supports the contract itself.

Therefore, by analogy, if the contractor's application for payment requirements are part of the original contract, no consideration should be required for the waiver at each progress payment period.[12] Consideration would be present in the original contract which sets out the use of the contractor's application for payment forms, as well as the conditions of progress and final payment. AIA A201 has long had a similar waiver upon final payment, which currently is ¶ 9.10.4.

Courts have uniformly held similar contractual provisions for waiver by the making of final payment to be effective.[13] However, we have found no case law which directly addresses the type of interim waiver we are utilizing.[14] Waivers of claims upon final payment are generally effective as to all claims except those claims previously made in writing and identified in writing as still unsettled at the time of final payment.[15] Also, the final payment does not waive pending lawsuits at the time of final payment.[16]

The idea of requiring the contractor's application for payment at the end of each progress payment period serves a function similar to the final payment at the end of the project.

§ 7.5   Release of Lien Rights

As an additional protection, the client has typically obtained release of lien rights as part of the application for payment process. The lien release form

---

[9] United States v. William Cramp & Sons Ship & Engine Bldg. Co., 206 U.S. 118, 27 S. Ct. 676 (1907) [hereinafter *William Cramp*]; Inland Empire Builders, Inc. v. United States, 424 F.2d 1370 (Ct. Cl. 1970) [hereinafter *Inland Empire*]; Yakima Asphalt v. Department of Transp., 45 Wash. App. 663, 726 P.2d 1021 (1986) [hereinafter *Yakima*].

[10] *William Cramp*, 206 U.S. 118.

[11] *Yakima*, 726 P.2d 1021.

[12] *See Inland Empire*, 424 F.2d 1370.

[13] *See Moorhead*, 508 F.2d 1008; John E. Fisher Constr. Co. v. Town of Onondaga, 115 A.D.2d 993, 497 N.Y.S.2d 557 (1985); Centerre Trust Co. v. Continental Ins. Co., 167 Ill. App. 3d 376, 521 N.E.2d 219 (1988).

[14] *But see* McMerit Constr. Co. v. Knightsbridge Dev. Co., 367 S.E.2d 512 (Va. 1988) [hereinafter *McMerit*]; *Inland Empire*, 424 F.2d 1370 (addressing interim releases as applied to completion of individual lease areas within one project).

[15] *Cape Fear*, 207 S.E.2d 323.

[16] Zion's Coop. Mercantile Inst. v. Jacobsen Constr. Co., 27 Utah 2d 6, 492 P.2d 135 (1971).

appears in § **7.8**. This form is executed as a release of lien rights through the closing date of the pay period. If the contractor or subcontractor is uneasy about giving the unconditional release without having received payment, our client allows the option of using the "conditional" release versions on the page. We originally observed a similar form submitted by a construction materials supply company in Seattle and adapted it to the needs of our clients.

Although the waiver provisions of the application for payment which waive all claims for labor, materials, or equipment also waive the right to file a mechanic's lien based on such claims, we chose to include the lien release form to expressly provide for a waiver of lien rights for the period of the application for payment. Contract provisions waiving lien rights are generally enforced by the courts where the clauses are clear and unambiguous.[17]

In *McMerit Construction Co. v. Knightsbridge Development Co.*,[18] the contract in dispute provided for interim lien waivers and releases. The court held that the waiver and lien release provision was not effective because the waiver provision in the contract did not constitute an express waiver of lien rights. The court implied that, had the language in the contract constituted an express waiver of lien rights, the interim lien waiver and release would have been effective.

Whether a waiver and release of lien rights by the contractor waives and releases lien rights of lower-tiered subcontractors and suppliers is a question of state law.[19] Several states have statutes precluding enforcement of such blanket waivers of lien rights.[20]

Clauses in the principal contract prohibiting the assertion or attachment of liens upon the owner's property are not effective waivers of lien rights of subcontractors where such liens have already attached or where state law provides a separate and independent lien in favor of each party.[21] In our scheme, the lien release form that accompanies the contractor's application for payment waives only the lien rights of the named contractor on the waiver and release of lien rights.

As discussed previously with regard to consideration, the agreement for use of the interim release form must be contained in the principal contract to supply the consideration for enforcement. We have found no cases that specifically address this issue of consideration as it applies to interim waivers and releases.[22]

---

[17] *McMerit,* 367 S.E.2d 512; Pero Build. Co. v. Smith, 6 Conn. App. 180, 504 A.2d 524 (1986) [hereinafter *Pero*]; Formigli Corp. v. Fox, 348 F. Supp. 629 (E.D. Pa. 1972).

[18] 367 S.E.2d 512.

[19] *See Yakima,* 726 P.2d 1021; Wavetek Ind., Inc. v. K.H. Gatewood Steel Co., 458 N.E.2d 265 (Ind. Ct. App. 1984); Trustees of C.I. Mortgage Group v. Staga of Huntington, Inc., 484 Pa. 464, 399 A.2d 386 (1979); VNB Mortgage Corp. v. Lone Star Indus., Inc., 215 Va. 366, 209 S.E.2d 909 (1974).

[20] *See Pero,* 504 A.2d 524; Bentz Plumbing & Heating v. Favaloro, 128 Cal. App. 3d 145, 180 Cal. Rptr. 223 (1982).

[21] *See* 53 Am. Jur. 2d *Mechanics Liens* § 296 (1990).

[22] *But see Pero* 504 A.2d 524; Torres v. Meyer Paving Co., 423 N.E.2d 692 (Ind. Ct. App. 1981).

The release form is an additional measure to provide notice to the contractor that not only is it waiving its right to claims not identified for the application period it also is releasing any lien rights for that period. The release form clearly and unambiguously expresses the contractor's voluntary intention to relinquish its lien rights for the particular pay period.

§ 7.6   Trust Funds

Although the lien release form submitted with the contractor's application for payment will be effective as to that applicant, in those states which have "direct" lien statutes (also commonly known as "Pennsylvania" systems), there many times are problems with unpaid subcontractors and suppliers asserting lien rights. A number of states have statutes providing criminal penalties for failure of contractors or subcontractors to pay their bills.[23]

The concept behind the construction trust fund statute is that monies received by a general contractor or subcontractor earmarked for a specific project are to be held in trust for the subcontractors and suppliers on those projects. A trustee-beneficiary relationship is created.

More recently, Maryland enacted a construction trust statute which provides for personal civil liability of officers, directors, or employees of any contractor/subcontractor who participates in the diversion of trust funds.[24] This statute rejects criminal sanctions.[25]

A similar approach is currently being considered in Washington. However, at the time the forms discussed in this chapter were originally drafted, Washington did not have a construction trust statute and none was being considered. For that reason, the client was seeking a way to impose personal liability upon contractors and subcontractors who did not apply payments to the project for which they were received. The infamous "robbing Peter to pay Paul" all too often ultimately led to a bankrupt contractor or subcontractor, with no assets and a significant number of unpaid labor and material lien claimants, which the client would have to pay twice because the original funds had been diverted to other purposes.

In the absence of a statutory trust fund, the trust fund provision in the contractor's application for payment was intended to create civil liability with the

---

[23] For a more thorough discussion, see W. Habeeb, *Validity and Construction of Statute Providing Criminal Penalties for Failure of Contractor who has Received Payment from Owner to Pay Laborers or Materialmen,* 78 A.L.R.3d 563 (1977), discussing the laws of Arkansas, California, Delaware, Florida, Georgia, Minnesota, Nebraska, New Jersey, New York, South Carolina, South Dakota, Tennessee, Virginia, Washington, and Wisconsin.

[24] Md. Real Prop. Code Ann. §§ 9-201, 9-204 (1988).

[25] For a discussion of the Maryland construction trust statute, see, Albright, *Maryland Construction Trust Statute: New Personal Liability, Its Scope and Federal Bankruptcy Implications,* 17 U. Balt. L. Rev. 482 (1988). Several other states have enacted express construction trust statutes, including Georgia, Kentucky, Louisiana, Michigan, New York, Oklahoma, Texas, and Wisconsin.

possibility of criminal prosecution being present. The possibility of criminal prosecution was based upon the decision of the Washington Court of Appeals in *State v. Oglesbee.*[26] In that case, the contractor executed a contract document which provided, in part:

> Owner shall make progress payments, on account, of the contract price to Contractor, on the basis of applications for payment submitted to Owner by Contractor as the work progresses, and in accordance with the requirements for financing as set forth by [the bank]. The progress payments may be withheld if: . . . Contractor does not make prompt and proper payments for labor, materials, or equipment furnished by him. . . .[27]

Oglesbee, the contractor, was paid by the owner, and then issued a check to his supplier (who knew the source of the funds it was receiving from the contractor). The supplier applied the funds to the oldest accounts receivable, rather than to the invoices for materials supplied to the project which was the source of the funds. Oglesbee was unable to make payment on the invoices for materials supplied in the construction of the residence and was charged with criminal theft. The trial court found him guilty, and the Washington Court of Appeals affirmed.

Absent any construction trust provision, unpaid subcontractors and suppliers have recourse either under the mechanic's lien statutes or via criminal complaints for embezzlement against the general contractor. However, these two remedies often do not afford the subcontractor or supplier sufficient remedy and, where they do, an innocent owner often is forced to pay twice for the same work. Perfecting lien rights often proves inadequate, and criminal prosecutions raise obstacles in the area of proving intent to defraud.[28]

In most states with express construction trust statutes, absent express language in the statute, traditional common law trust principles apply.[29] Under traditional trust law, the trustee of an express trust may not commingle trust funds with its general funds and it must treat beneficiaries of the same class impartially.[30] The act of diverting funds creates liability the instant the trustee uses the funds for other than their stated purpose.[31]

---

[26] 24 Wash. App. 769, 603 P.2d 1275 (1979).

[27] 24 Wash. App. at 770.

[28] *See* Lewis, *Criminal Misapplication of Construction Funds—Myth and Reality,* 63 Fla. B. J. 4 (Apr. 1989); Annotation, *Validity and Construction of Statute Providing Criminal Penalties for Failure of Contractor Who has Received Payment from Owner to Pay Laborers or Materialmen,* 78 A.L.R.3d 563 (1977).

[29] *See* Note, *Liens: Mechanic's and Materialmen's Liens: Oklahoma's Trust Fund Provisions,* 31 Okla. L. Rev. 199 (1978) [hereinafter *Liens*] (discussing the nature of the statutory trust vs. the traditional trust); *see also* Frates, *Mechanic's and Materialmen's Lien Claims, Recovery under Oklahoma's Trustee Statutes,* 47 Okla. B. A. J. 125 (1976) (addressing various questions and concerns associated with mechanic's liens and trust statutes).

[30] *Id.*

[31] *Id.*

Because this has placed an undue burden upon the general contractor, many states have set out exceptions to their trust statutes allowing for commingling of funds; removal of trust fund money, provided they are promptly repaid; and allowing the favoring of certain beneficiary claimants over others.[32] However, the general contractor remains under a duty to account for the funds in the account when they become due to the subcontractors and suppliers.[33]

In addition to the general contractor or subcontractor being accountable for funds in the trust account earmarked for specific subcontractors and suppliers, these subcontractors and suppliers, as beneficiaries, are afforded additional protection. Under traditional trust law principles, the beneficiaries have the right to demand disbursement of the particular funds held by the general contractor and earmarked for them.[34] The beneficiaries have a right to demand an accounting of the funds held by the general contractor or subcontractor as trustee.[35]

It is also well established under traditional trust law principles that persons to whom trust property is transferred take the property subject to the trust in the event the recipient had notice that the property was trust property.[36] Under this principle, the beneficiary would have the right to pursue funds in the hands of third parties in the event the funds were misapplied by the trustee and were disbursed to a third party who had notice that they were trust funds.[37]

Under circumstances where the general contractor is a corporation, the subcontractor and supplier beneficiaries would have the right to hold the officers or agents of the corporation personally liable when they have participated in the conversion of the trust funds; they would also have a cause of action against the corporation.[38] This provides additional protection to the beneficiaries, especially in cases where the corporation is insolvent. Where the general contractor is an individual, the conversion would provide an additional cause of action to a subcontractor or supplier who already has a cause of action against the general contractor for breach of contract.[39]

If an individual is liable pursuant to a contractual trust agreement or a construction trust statute, the individual generally will not be able to evade responsibility for the debt by filing for bankruptcy. The Bankruptcy Code provides: "A discharge under section 727, 1141, 1228(a), or 1328(b) of this title

---

[32] See Meyer, *Trust Fund Provisions of the New York Mechanics Lien Law,* 10 Buffalo L. Rev. 314 (1961).

[33] 76 Am. Jur. 2d *Trusts* § 505 (1975).

[34] See McGuire, *Construction Contract Proceeds as Trust Funds,* 63 Fla. B.J. 30 (Oct. 1989) [hereinafter McGuire].

[35] *Id.*

[36] 76 Am. Jur. 2d *Trusts* § 257 (1975).

[37] See *Liens,* 31 Okla. L. Rev. 199 (1978).

[38] 18 Am. Jur. 2d *Conversion* § 73 (1985); *see* 31 Okla. L. Rev. 199 (1978).

[39] *Liens,* 31 Okla. L. Rev. 199 (1978).

does not discharge an individual debtor from any debt . . . for fraud or defalcation while acting in a fiduciary capacity, embezzlement, or larceny. . . ."[40]

It is generally held that, where a construction trust statute expressly creates a trust, a fiduciary relationship is established.[41] Under a contract or statute which expressly creates a fiduciary relationship, an individual's debt resulting from the diversion of trust funds would be nondischargeable under § 523(a)(4).[42]

In interpreting the Texas construction trust statute, the Fifth Circuit held that debts created through diversion of trust funds would be nondischargeable under § 523(a)(4) only if intent to defraud was shown.[43] Where the statute does not expressly create a trust, but instead is a criminal statute which imposes penalties for diversion of funds, there generally is no fiduciary relationship created. In the absence of a fiduciary relationship, any debt resulting from the diversion would probably be dischargeable in bankruptcy. In cases involving misappropriation of funds subject to criminal statutes, the Fifth, Eighth, and Ninth Circuits have held that no fiduciary relationship exists absent a statutory provision expressly creating one.[44]

In the event of bankruptcy, the subcontractors and suppliers would have the right to claim identifiable trust proceeds in the hands of the bankruptcy trustee as their property not subject to the unsecured claims of the general contractor/debtor.[45]

§ 7.7 Restrictive Indorsements

The final step in this process is the restrictive indorsement on the checks for the progress and final payments. A release is also included with the check that is presented for each progress payment period. The restrictive indorsement reads:

> In full satisfaction of all liability of OWNER to CONTRACTOR for the pay period for which this check is issued. This check is issued in trust for all laborers,

---

[40] 11 U.S.C. § 523(a)(4).

[41] *See, e.g., In re* Thomas, 729 F.2d 502 (7th Cir. 1984); *In re* Johnson, 691 F.2d 249 (6th Cir. 1982); Carey Lumber Co. v. Bell, 615 F.2d 370 (5th Cir. 1980); *In re* Weedman, 65 Bankr. 288 (W.D. Ky. 1986); *In re* Polidoro, 12 Bankr. 867 (E.D.N.Y. 1981); *In re* Kawczynski, 442 F. Supp. 413 (W.D.N.Y. 1977); *see also* McGuire, 63 Fla. B.J. 30; 17 U. Balt. L. Rev. 482 (1988); 31 Okla. L. Rev. 199 (1978).

[42] 17 U. Balt. L. Rev. 482 (1988).

[43] *In re* Boyle, 819 F.2d 583 (5th Cir. 1987).

[44] *In re* Angelle, 610 F.2d 1335 (5th Cir. 1980); *In re* Cross, 666 F.2d 873 (5th Cir. 1982); *In re* Pedrazzini, 644 F.2d 756 (9th Cir. 1981); *In re* Dloogoff, 600 F.2d 166 (8th Cir. 1979).

[45] *See* Selby v. Ford Motor Co., 590 F.2d 642 (6th Cir. 1978); 9 Am. Jur. 2d *Bankruptcy* § 261 (1980); *see* McGuire, 63 Fla. B.J. 30; *Liens,* 31 Okla. L. Rev. 199 (1978).

suppliers, subcontractors, taxing authorities and other potential lien claimants taking by or through CONTRACTOR.

When dealing with restrictive indorsements on checks, two issues arise. First, does the state follow the common law rule of accord and satisfaction? Second, has the state adopted the Uniform Commercial Code (UCC)?

The common law rule of accord and satisfaction prevents a person from reserving rights simultaneously with cashing the check, while UCC § 1-207 may allow a person to reserve rights upon the cashing of the check. Some jurisdictions have adopted § 1-207 to replace the common law rule of accord and satisfaction, while other jurisdictions have adopted § 1-207 and also retained the common law rule of accord and satisfaction.

In jurisdictions that have adopted UCC § 1-207, the question then becomes what transactions fall within the coverage of this section. For example, New York's highest court has held that § 1-207 applies to all situations where a check has been used irrespective of the underlying transaction. This holding, in *Horn Waterproofing Corp. v. Bushwick Iron & Steel Co.,*[46] basically eliminates the common law rule of accord and satisfaction with respect to UCC-covered transactions. Previously in New York the courts were divided as to the application of § 1-207 to transactions for services in addition to transactions in goods. *Horn Waterproofing* settled this issue by applying § 1-207 to all transactions involving a check.

Some jurisdictions distinguish between transactions involving services and transactions involving goods. A majority of courts hold that UCC § 1-207 is not applicable to service contracts. The court in *Van Sistine v. Tollard,*[47] as well as in several other jurisdictions, found that § 1-207 cannot apply unless the underlying transaction is subject to the UCC.

However, where there is a mixed contract for both goods and services, these jurisdictions apply a balancing test to determine whether the predominant factor is the furnishing of services or the furnishing of goods. If the furnishing of goods is predominant, then § 1-207 applies. In these jurisdictions, common law accord and satisfaction rules apply to service contracts where the conditional check has been used.[48]

In other jurisdictions the courts have found that § 1-207 has not displaced the common law rule of accord and satisfaction. By interpreting another section of the UCC, § 1-103, the courts have found that accord and satisfaction are not displaced unless done so explicitly.[49] In addition, courts are divided on the issue of whether the common law rule of accord and satisfaction or § 1-207 applies

---

[46] 66 N.Y. 2d 321, 488 N.E.2d 56, 497 N.Y.S.2d 310 (1985).

[47] 95 Wis. 2d 678, 291 N.W.2d 636 (1980).

[48] *See id.*

[49] *See* Department of Fisheries v. J-Z Sales Corp., 25 Wash. App. 671, 610 P.2d 390 (1980); Milgram Food Stores, Inc. v. Gelco Corp., 550 F. Supp. 992 (W.D. Mo. 1982); Connecticut Printers, Inc. v. Gus Kroesen, 134 Cal. App. 3d 54, 184 Cal. Rptr. 436 (1982).

with respect to liquidated as well as unliquidated claims and disputed as well as undisputed claims.[50]

With respect to final payment, a reservation in the claimant's indorsement of the check constituting final payment will not alter the legal status of that payment under the terms of the contract.[51] Therefore, with each progress payment having the effect of final payment for each individual payment period, a reservation in the claimant's indorsement of the progress check would not alter the legal status of that payment under the terms of the contact. The consequences of a waiver and release are imposed by virtue of the contractor's application for payment, the lien release form, and, finally, the acceptance of the payment.

---

[50] For a greater discussion of this issue involving restrictive indorsements on checks and whether the common law rule of accord and satisfaction or UCC § 1-207 applies, see Walter, *The Rise and Fall of UCC Section 1-207 and the Full Payment Check—Checkmate?*, 21 Loy. L.A.L. Rev. 81 (1987).

[51] Buffalo Elec. Co. v. State, 14 N.Y.2d 453, 201 N.E.2d 869, 253 N.Y.S.2d 537 (1964).

§ 7.8   Form—Contractor's Application for Payment

CONTRACTOR'S APPLICATION FOR PAYMENT

TO :_____

FROM:_____

PROJECT:_____

PAYMENT REQUEST NO.:_____

PERIOD:_____, to _____

STATEMENT OF CONTRACT ACCOUNT:

1.	Original Contract Amount	$_____
2.	Approved Change Order Nos._____ (per attached breakdown)(Net)	$_____
3.	Adjusted Contract Amount	$_____
4.	Value of Contract Work Completed to Date (per attached breakdown)	$_____
5.	Value of Approved Change Order Work Completed (per attached breakdown)	$_____
6.	Value of Field Directed Work Completed (per attached breakdown)	$_____
7.	Materials Stored on Site (per attached breakdown)	$_____
8.	TOTAL TO DATE	$_____
9.	Less Amount Retained (____%)	<_____>
10.	Total Less Retainage	$_____
11.	Total Previously Paid (Deduct)	<_____>
12.	AMOUNT DUE THIS REQUEST	$_____

WAIVER OF CLAIMS FOR EXTRA COST OR TIME: Except for field directives or approved change orders listed herewith, or claims in the amounts reserved below, Applicant has incurred no costs during the period covered by this Application for extra or changed work, nor delays or accelerations, and will make no claim therefor; hereby specifically waiving any and all rights to any claims for costs or time extensions arising out of or relating to extra or changed work or delays or accelerations not specifically identified and reserved in the amounts identified below:

_____

_____

_____

Contractor shall submit all claims reserved herein for resolution as provided by the Contract no later than _____ days from the date of this Application for payment.

CONTRACTOR'S APPLICATION FOR PAYMENT: Page 1 of 2
[da]g3/payment.app

PROGRESS PAYMENTS

CERTIFICATE OF THE CONTRACTOR: I hereby certify that the work performed and the materials supplied to date, as shown on the above, represent the actual value of accomplishment under the terms of the Contract (and all authorized changes or field directives) between the undersigned and _____, relating to the above-referenced project, and that the remaining contract balance is sufficient to cover all costs of completing the contract work in accordance with the contract documents.

I also certify that payments, less applicable retention, have been made through the period covered by previous payment received by the contractor, to (1) all my subcontractors; and (2) for all materials, equipment and labor used in or in connection with the performance of this Contract. I further certify that I have complied with all Federal, State and Local tax laws, including Social Security laws and Unemployment Compensation laws and Workmen's Compensation laws, insofar as applicable to the performance of this Contract, and have paid all such taxes or assessments arising out of the performance of contract work.

All funds received from owner arising out of or relating to this Application for Payment shall be held as trust funds for the payment of all subcontractors, labor, material, equipment and taxes.

Within five (5) days of receipt of payment upon this request, all payments, less applicable retention, will be made through the period covered by this pay request to all my subcontractors and for all materials, equipment, labor, taxes and assessments arising out of the performance of his contract.

DATED:_____

_____
CONTRACTOR

SUBSCRIBED AND SWORN to before me this _____ day of _____, 19___.

_____
NOTARY PUBLIC, in and for the State of Washington, residing at _____. My Comm. Expires:_____.

§ 7.9 Form—Conditional Release/Unconditional Release of Lien

RELEASE

(Mechanic's Lien, Stop Notice, Equitable Lien and Material Bond Release)

FROM:_____   PROJECT:_____
(Name of person or firm giving Release)   (Name and Tract No.)

_____   _____
(Street Address)   (Address of Project)

_____   _____
(City, State, Zip)   (City, State, Zip)

TO:

FULL RELEASE

The undersigned has been paid in **FULL** for all labor, subcontract work, equipment and materials supplied to the above-described project and hereby releases all mechanic's lien, stop notice, equitable lien and labor and material bond rights on the project for all materials, supplies, labor, services, etc., purchased, acquired or furnished by or for us and used on above premises, up to and including (Date)_____.

This Release is for the benefit of, and may be relied upon by the owner, the prime contractor, the construction lender, and the principal and surety on any labor and material bond posted for the project.

FIRM NAME:_____
_____
_____
(Firm furnishing, labor, etc.)

By:_____

Date:_____

**CONDITIONAL RELEASE
(Full Payment)**

The undersigned does hereby release all mechanic's lien, stop notice, equitable lien and labor and material bond rights against the above-described project for all materials, supplies, labor, services, etc., purchased, acquired or furnished by or for us and used on above premises up to and including (Date)_____ _____. This Release is for the benefit of, and may be relied upon by, the owner, the prime contractor, the construction lender, and the principal and surety on any labor and material bond.

This Release is **CONDITION-AL**, and shall be effective only upon payment to the undersigned in the sum of $_____.

If payment is by check, this Release is effective only when the check is paid by the bank upon which it is drawn.

FIRM NAME:_____
_____
(Firm furnishing labor, etc.)

By:_____
Date:_____

**CONDITIONAL RELEASE
(Progress Payment)**

The undersigned does hereby release all mechanic's lien, stop notice, equitable lien and labor and material bond rights against the above-described project for all materials, supplies, labor, services, etc., purchased, acquired or furnished by or for us and used on above premises up to and including (Date)_____ _____, excluding retainage, unpaid change orders, unpaid field directives, or claims for additional compensation not waived. This Release is for the benefit of, and may be relied upon by, the owner, the prime contractor, the construction lender, and the principal and surety on any labor and material bond.

This Release is **CONDITION-AL**, and shall be effective only upon payment to the undersigned in the sum of $_____.

If payment is by check, this Release is effective only when the check is paid by the bank upon which it is drawn.

FIRM NAME:_____
_____
(Firm furnishing labor, etc.)
By:_____
Date:_____

[da]g3/release.cnd

CHAPTER 8

QUANTUM MERUIT

Bradley H. Bagshaw

§ 8.1   Introduction

§ 8.2   A Source of Payment When There Is No Contract

§ 8.3   A Source of Payment When the Contract Is Silent about a Particular Aspect of the Work—Extra Work

§ 8.4   —Work Done under Unanticipated Conditions

§ 8.5   —Owner Interference

§ 8.6   Owner Control of Methods and Materials

§ 8.7   Payment for Work Despite the Contract

§ 8.8   Recovery Despite a Clause Limiting or Controlling Recovery

§ 8.9   —The No Damages for Delay Cases

§ 8.10   —The Cardinal Change Cases

§ 8.11   Recovery Despite Inequitable Contract Provisions That Purport to Cover the Changed Work

§ 8.1 Introduction

Imagine that you are the painting subcontractor on the new county jail and that the project is well behind schedule before you get on the job. The owner and the prime contractor try to make up for lost time by accelerating your work and the work of the other finish trades. With a herculean effort you do your work in a third of the planned time, despite having to work side by side with the drywall contractor and the plasterer. But the cost of this effort is that you spend three times as many labor hours as you had planned to spend; and now you want to be paid. You do not think this is a problem, because your contract says you are entitled to an equitable adjustment as compensation for your extra effort.

However, when you send your bill you discover that the prime contract, to which you are not a party but to which your subcontract refers, says that all equitable adjustments are calculated at your direct cost, plus 15 percent for overhead and profit. Unfortunately, your real cost of doing business is much higher than that. You routinely bid your jobs assuming $35 per labor hour, which is the going rate and which results in a reasonable profit most of the time. But you pay your painters only $17 per hour plus incidentals, so the formula in the prime contract pays you only $22 per hour, not nearly enough to pay all your costs, let alone make a profit. What can you do, short of filing bankruptcy and cursing your partner who should have discovered this problem before the contract was signed?

What you would really like to do is just throw away the contract and get fair compensation for the work you actually did. What you want is a recovery in quantum meruit, and twenty years ago that is probably what you would get. However, two recent cases will make it more difficult for you to succeed on a quantum meruit claim. Before discussing these cases, this chapter will look at what quantum meruit is and how it is used.

§ 8.2   A Source of Payment When
There Is No Contract

Quantum meruit is a means for compensating someone who has done work but whose compensation is not governed by a contract. *Quantum meruit* is a Latin phrase that means "as much as he deserved."[1]

Here is a simple example of how quantum meruit works: Suppose at dinner one evening I mention to my teenage daughter that I need my fence repaired, and that I would like her to do the repair. She agrees to do the work, but the conversation turns to other matters before we settle on a price. The next day my daughter, in a state of high ambition and with nothing better to do, goes ahead and makes the repairs. What do I pay her for the work, or more precisely, what will I have to pay her if she sues me?

If you have an owner's perspective, you will probably say she has nothing coming because we never agreed on a contract price. Since I made no contract, you will reason, I have no obligation to pay. If, on the other hand, you have a contractor's perspective, you will undoubtedly say that my daughter is entitled to time, materials, overhead and profit. After all, I asked her to do the work, she did it, and now I have a repaired fence.

Neither viewpoint reflects exactly what a court would do. My daughter is entitled to quantum meruit—which is to say she should get as much as the fence repair is worth.[2] How much that is would be a question for the jury. The facts that the jury would look at include how much I would have to pay on the open market for the repair, how many hours my daughter spent, whether she was efficient in the use of her time, what materials cost, and any other factor that her lawyer or mine thought would influence the jury's opinion of the value of her work. If my daughter could prove that she worked with the same efficiency as a professional

---

[1] Losli v. Foster, 37 Wash. 2d 220, 233, 222 P.2d 824, 831 (1950).

[2] Which, of course, could be more, or less, than it cost my daughter to do the work.

and did the job in the same eight hours it would have taken him, she should get the same $15 an hour or so that he would charge. If the pro could have done the job in half the time, my daughter should not get the pro's rate for the full eight hours that she spent.

This simple example has little application in the real world because no contractor today starts a job without a contact that sets forth how much it will be paid. Nevertheless, quantum meruit lives today when the unexpected happens on the job. Although contracts almost always set out what the contractor will be paid for doing the work that the parties anticipate, they usually do a less complete job of setting pay for the unexpected. After all, it is virtually impossible to forecast the cost of resolving the myriad problems that can arise in a complex construction project. Add to this the difficulty of predicting how a change on one part of the job will affect the costs and time of performance on other unchanged parts of the project, and it is easy to appreciate the formidable task facing anyone trying to set compensation ahead of time for every contingency. Quantum meruit, which is determined with the benefit of hindsight, can be the most accurate method for setting fair compensation when a job runs into unanticipated conditions that materially alter the scope of the work.

§ 8.3   A Source of Payment When the Contract Is Silent about a Particular Aspect of the Work—Extra Work

The clearest example of the application of the quantum meruit doctrine is when the contractor does unanticipated extra work while on site. For example, suppose I had a contractor out at my house constructing a deck for a fixed price. After my site is cleared I decide I want a bigger deck than I originally planned, but with the cement truck coming that morning to pour the foundation there is no time to plan the job properly and get a bid from my contractor. I will probably have the contractor go ahead with the expansion anyway and quantum meruit will provide the basis for its pay (unless the contractor was smart enough to negotiate a favorable time and materials contract).

§ 8.4   —Work Done under Unanticipated Conditions

Perhaps the most common application of the quantum meruit doctrine occurs when the work is changed due to undiscovered site conditions, or due to some other condition not known by the parties at the time of the contract. The key to application of the doctrine here is that the parties did not anticipate the conditions for which extra compensation is sought. The rule is well set forth in a case from the Washington Supreme Court: "[Quantum meruit] provides an appropriate basis for recovery when substantial changes occur which are not covered by the contract and were not within the contemplation of the parties, if the effect is to require extra work or materials or to cause substantial loss to the contractor."[3]

The key in applying the doctrine is that the conditions were unanticipated at the time by the parties to the contract. The reason for this rule is simple: If the contractor knew or should have known what it would encounter when it bid the contact, it should have adjusted its bid price to allow for the expense of dealing with the condition. But if the condition could not be anticipated, then the contractor should be allowed extra compensation for dealing with it. Since a contractor does not bargain to perform work it does not know will be needed, it should not have to do the work unless it is paid extra.[4]

§ 8.5   —Owner Interference

The same rationale supports a contractor's quantum meruit recovery when the owner interferes with the contractor's performance. Since the contractor has a right to expect that the owner will not interfere, owner interference is an unanticipated condition that entitles the contractor to additional compensation. The contractor's extra compensation can be equal to its extra costs if the interference is a breach of contract. But if the contract gives the owner the right to order changes in the work, the compensation can be measured by quantum meruit; i.e., the court determines what the contractor's performance is worth, giving due consideration to the unexpected conditions under which it worked.

§ 8.6   —Owner Control of Methods and Materials

Unless the contract states to the contrary, it is the contractor's option to do the job by whatever means it sees fit. After all, it is the expert at what it does and should be able to do it most efficiently. It also knows how it bid the job, so it would not be fair for the owner to be able to force the contractor to do the work in a way that may be more expensive than the way it bid it. When the owner takes control of the contractor's methods by making it perform in a way different from the way it planned, the contractor is entitled to additional compensation, either in quantum meruit, or for a breach of contract, depending on whether the contract gives the owner the right to make changes.

---

[3] Bignold v. King County, 65 Wash. 2d 817, 826, 399 P.2d 611, 617 (1965).

[4] It could be argued that the contractor, by agreeing to do the work for a fixed price, has agreed to do the work regardless of what it encounters. That argument has not been successful, unless the unanticipated condition should have been discovered beforehand by the contractor.

§ 8.7   Payment for Work Despite the Contract

Experienced contractors and owners try to anticipate the unexpected and to provide for it in their contracts. Most modern construction contracts recognize that the parties often do not know in advance everything that will be required, and establish the method for dealing with at least some otherwise unanticipated situations.

The first and most influential of such contract provisions is the federal government with its "changes" clause. The changes clause requires a contractor to perform such extra work as may be ordered by the government, and it provides for an "equitable adjustment" to the contract price in payment for the extra work ordered. Before long the various Boards of Contract Appeals and the Court of Claims were construing the changes clause to cover much more than one would normally think of as extras. Soon equitable adjustments were being handed out to compensate the contractor for extra expenses caused by unanticipated site conditions, for owner interference with the scope of the work and for essentially every other event for which the original contract did not provide fair compensation.[5]

The difference between an award of an equitable adjustment and a recovery in quantum meruit can be real or it can be little more than a matter of semantics. When the parties fail to define the term "equitable adjustment" the court determines what is fair and equitable compensation for the extra work, much the same as it would do in quantum meruit.

The distinction between recovery in quantum meruit and an equitable adjustment can have real meaning when the contract sets forth how the equitable adjustment will be calculated, generally by providing for unit pricing, or by setting the equitable adjustment equal to direct costs plus a percentage for overhead and profit. Clauses that establish a formula for calculating an equitable adjustment make the scope of the recovery for extra work more predictable than it is under quantum meruit. These clauses can sometimes favor the contractor, because generally it will get reimbursed for every hour it spends on the job, even if it does not perform efficiently. But almost always such clauses will favor the owner, because the overhead percentage will almost always fall short of compensating the contractor for its true overhead expense.

Another example of the way in which contracts now deal with situations that used to be covered by quantum meruit is contained in AIA A201-1987. Article 7 covers changes to the work. In the absence of agreement between the parties, the owner can order the contractor to perform a change by issuing a construction change directive. The contractor then must perform the changed work with compensation to be determined either (1) by agreement, (2) according to unit prices set forth in the contract or later agreed to, (3) in some other manner agreed to by the parties, or (4) in the absence of any of the foregoing, by the architect's

---

[5] *See* Nash, Government Contract Changes (1981).

determination of certain contractor costs, plus an allowance for overhead and profit.[6]

§ 8.8   Recovery Despite a Clause Limiting or Controlling Recovery

Quantum meruit lives in two types of cases where at first blush it seems that the contract provides a complete remedy. In contracts that contain no damages for delay clauses, courts are reluctant to enforce the clauses in circumstances where the delays increase the contractor's costs in a major way. Similarly, some courts refuse to hold contractors to contractually stated remedies when there has been a "cardinal change" to the contract. In both cases courts refuse to enforce unambiguous contractual provisions on the theory that the parties did not really mean for the contract to cover everything it seems to cover.

§ 8.9   —The No Damages for Delay Cases

The most familiar remedy-limiting clause is the no damages for delay clause. This clause provides that a contractor is not entitled to any additional compensation for its increased costs due to delay, regardless of whether the delay was caused by an increased scope of the work, by unanticipated conditions, or by any other condition that the contractor could not anticipate at the time of contract formation. All that the contractor is entitled to is an extension in the deadline for completing its contract. In other words, it will not be compensated for its extra expenses that the delay causes, but it will not be assessed liquidated damages either.

A strong no damages for delay clause sets out all causes of delay and expressly brings them within reach of the clause's provision. For example, the following clause was at issue in *Nelse Mortensen v. Group Health:*

> If . . . the contractor is delayed at any time in the progress of the work by any of the following causes, the contract time shall be extended for such reasonable time as the architect shall determine. . . . *[The extension] shall not be ground for claim by the contractor of damages or for additional costs, expenses, overhead or profit or other compensation.*
>
> 1.   Floods, fires, strikes, war, acts of the public enemy, acts of God.
> 2.   Change Orders.
> 3.   Acts of performance or delays in performance by other contractors employed by the owner or their subcontractors.
> 4.   *Causes beyond the control of the contractor. . . .*[7]

---

[6] ¶¶ 7.3.3, 7.3.6.

[7] 17 Wash. App. 703, 707-08, 566 P.2d 560, 562 (1977) (emphasis added).

Contractors have signed thousands of contracts that contained provisions like this. If strictly enforced, this clause eliminates a quantum meruit (or other) recovery for delays, because delays are no longer unanticipated events; on the contrary, the contract acknowledges the possibility of delay and sets out how delays are to be handled. The contractor gets a time extension but no more money.

At first these clauses were routinely enforced, and on some occasions they still are today. The state of Washington has now legislated these clauses out of existence on the theory that they are contrary to public policy, but the *Nelse Mortensen* case, which inspired the legislation, is still a good example of how these clauses operate in states where they are permitted.[8] In *Nelse Mortensen* the contractor performed a difficult, two-year $6,000,000 hospital addition. During the course of construction it encountered some 146 different delaying events.

The trial court awarded it $600,000 in delay costs, holding that the no damages for delay clause did not foreclose such an award because the contract covered only reasonable delays, and these were unreasonable, hence beyond the scope of the contract: "[I]n my judgment this action is not founded upon the contract. It is founded upon the 'unreasonable delay' which is a semi-tortious action outside the expressed terms of the contract. . . ."[9]

The court of appeals reversed. It held that the no damages for delay clause "was intended to foreclose damage claims based on owner-caused delay."[10] But the court left open the possibility that such clauses would not be enforced in a case where the delays were more severe than in *Nelse Mortensen:*

> [T]he sort of delays for which damages were awarded by the trial court were contemplated by the contracting parties and should be controlled by the contractual remedies, unless the delays can be said to be so excessive and unreasonable as to fall outside the scope of the contract and warrant additional recovery in quantum meruit.[11]

Courts strictly construe no damages for delay clauses because they take away the contractor's remedy. Enforcement is generally avoided by applying the clause only to certain delays, namely delays that were "contemplated" by the parties: "[D]amages resulting from uncontemplated delays caused by the contractee may be recovered despite the existence of a broad exculpatory clause relieving the contractee from liability."[12]

---

[8] The Washington statute reads: "Any clause in a construction contract . . . which purports to waive, release, or extinguish the rights of a . . . subcontractor . . . to damages or an equitable adjustment arising out of unreasonable delay in performance, which delay is caused by the acts or omissions of the contractee . . . is against public policy and is void and unenforceable." Wash. Rev. Code § 4.24.360.

[9] 566 P.2d at 569-70.

[10] *Id.* at 571.

[11] *Id.* at 572.

[12] Cortino Civetta Constr. v. City of New York, 67 N.Y.2d 297, 493 N.E.2d 905, 908 (1986).

The theory adopted by courts that find an exception to the unambiguous language of the clauses is that the parties did not really mean what they said:

> The exception is based on the concept of mutual assent. Having agreed to the exculpatory clause when he entered into the contract, it is presumed that the contractor intended to be bound by its terms. It can hardly be presumed, however, that the contractor bargained away his rights to bring a claim for damages resulting from delays which the parties did not contemplate at the time.[13]

This exception to enforcement of the clause runs head on into the rule that there usually is no room for interpretation of an unambiguous contract. The no damages for delay clause is hardly ambiguous. By its terms it purports to deal with all delays, not just delays that a reasonable contractor might have foreseen.

Courts have not done a good job harmonizing their treatment of no damages for delay cases with the rule that unambiguous contractual language will not be questioned. That courts fail to enforce no damages for delay clauses from time to time probably results not so much from a cold-headed analysis of the law as from a conviction that such clauses are unfair.

§ 8.10   —The Cardinal Change Cases

The cardinal change doctrine has been developed over many years by the Court of Claims to determine when a contractor may recover in quantum meruit outside of the remedy set forth in the changes clause found in most federal construction contracts. The changes clause permits the government to order the contractor to do additional work on the contract, for which it must pay an "equitable adjustment" to the contract price.[14]

The Court of Claims has held that the contractor is not bound to the remedy set forth in the changes clause if there is a "cardinal change," which "occurs when the government effects an alteration in the work so drastic that it effectively requires the contractor to perform duties materially different from those originally bargained for."[15]

The inquiry focuses on the magnitude of the effect that the changed circumstances has on the contractor:

> If plaintiff's allegations are true, then it performed work that was not "essentially the same work as the parties bargained for when the contract was awarded" [citation omitted]. Our decision on this point is based on the sheer magnitude of reconstruction work caused by the alleged defective specifications.[16]

---

[13] 493 N.E.2d at 910.

[14] *See, e.g.,* Saddler v. United States, 287 F.2d 411, 412-13 (Ct. Cl. 1961).

[15] Allied Materials & Equipment Co. v. United States, 569 F.2d 562, 563-64 (Ct. Cl. 1978).

[16] Edward R. Marden Corp. v. United States, 442 F.2d 364, 370 (Ct. Cl. 1971).

The cardinal change doctrine can apply even if the contractor winds up doing the same work it originally contracted to do. The critical factor is whether the circumstances were dramatically different from those the contractor anticipated encountering. For example, in *Marden* the contractor was building a hangar for the Air Force. During construction the partially completed hangar collapsed due to faulty design. The government corrected the design and it ordered the contractor to rebuild. The contractor did so, and sought recovery outside the contract, in quantum meruit, arguing that the contract was no longer a fair measure of the performance. As a result of the faulty design the contractor spent twice as many labor hours on the project as it had anticipated spending.

The government attempted to hold the contractor to payment under the changes clause of the contract. The principal government argument was that the job was really not changed very much because the contractor wound up building almost the exact same hangar that it had contracted to build. The court disagreed, holding that the change, which required a virtual rebuilding of the hangar, was a cardinal change that entitled the contractor to recover outside the contract:

> Admittedly this case differs from the usual cardinal change case in at least one important respect. In the present case the reconstructed hangar was, presumably, the identical hangar called for in the original specifications. In other words, in directing reconstruction of the hangar, the Government did not alter the design or other physical characteristics of the structure. We do not view this as a crucial difference, however. Where a cardinal change is concerned, it is the entire undertaking of the contractor, rather than the product, to which we look.[17]

Quantum meruit is an appropriate remedy, even for a contractor with a contract containing a changes clause, if "the totality of the change" that occurred was well beyond the changes that could have been anticipated when the parties bid the job: "Our opinions have cautioned that the problem 'is a matter of degree varying from one contract to another' and can be resolved only 'by considering the totality of the change and this requires recourse to its magnitude as well as its quality.' "[18]

The cardinal change doctrine is based on the proposition that the contract cannot be the basis for resolving changes that drastically alter the contractor's undertaking because such changes are not anticipated by the contractor when it signs the contract. It is not fair to say that the contractor agreed to do the work for the compensation set forth in the contract, if it could not foresee at bid time that the work would be required.

This proposition runs into some of the same difficulties that plague cases giving a quantum meruit recovery for delay despite a no damages for delay clause. It can be argued that "cardinal changes" should be treated the same way

---

[17] *Id.* at 370.

[18] Air-A-Plane Corp. v. United States, 408 F.2d 1030, 1033 (Ct. Cl. 1969) (quoting Saddler v. United States, 287 F.2d at 413).

as other changes because the changes clause is unambiguous. It gives the owner the power to order changed work and sets the basis for compensation. On the other hand, it cannot be convincingly argued that any meeting of the minds occurs on work that is beyond the scope of what all parties believe the contract will be. In *Marden,* for example, the contractor agreed to build a hangar, and it agreed to do other related work that may be required by the government under the authority given it by the changes clause. But it did not agree to build the hangar twice.

The cardinal change doctrine places sensible limits on the extent of a party's power to contract. The limits are justified because contractors do not bid a job with the expectation of massive disruption. When disruption is massive, it is only fair that the contract be disregarded in favor of a recovery in quantum meruit.

§ 8.11   Recovery Despite Inequitable Contract Provisions That Purport to Cover the Changed Work

Contracts more and more purport to provide a detailed remedy for every contingency, as owners try to draft quantum meruit out of existence. What does a contractor do when it finds itself in a contract that contains a compensation formula that fails to compensate it for its real costs? In a case where the quantity of the extra work is small, it just does the work and takes the pay that the contract provides for it. But what if, as in *Marden,* the extra work took as much time and effort as the bid work? In that case the formula falls short of reimbursing the contractor's real cost, which could result in a financial disaster for the contractor, even if it did everything right. The contractor's solution is to try to convince a court that the extra work is outside the contract, so that it is entitled to a recovery in quantum meruit.

That is what the subcontractor tried unsuccessfully to do in *Hensel Phelps Construction Co. v. King County.*[19] In that case Phoenix Painting was the painting subcontractor on the new 18-story King County jail that was being constructed in downtown Seattle by prime contractor Hensel Phelps. The project was delayed by numerous problems prior to the interior painting getting underway. When King County and Hensel could not agree on who was responsible for the delay, the County ordered the work finished according to the original schedule, and Hensel accelerated the finish trades, all of whom had started late due to the earlier delays.

As a result Phoenix was required to paint upper floors in 19 days, instead of the contractually allowed 45, and it was required to paint while plasterers and electricians continued to work, rather than after they were done. The acceleration had a significant effect on Phoenix's work:

---

[19] 57 Wash. App. 170, 787 P.2d 58 (1990).

Stacking [of the trades] impacted Phoenix's performance by substantially increasing the amount of touch-up work it performed, due to a large number of tradespeople working in the same area. In addition, the working environment was chaotic, causing work to proceed inefficiently; at points Phoenix had to pull out and wait for a section to be built before the painters could do their work. Finally, Phoenix bid the job intending to spray paint it, but because of the stacking of trades it ended up going through the building a second time brushing and rolling many of the surfaces.[20]

As a result of the acceleration, Phoenix's labor hours on the project ballooned from a pre-bid estimate of 9,725 hours to an actual expenditure of 25,500 hours.

The subcontract between Phoenix and Hensel contained a changes clause modeled after the federal government changes clause. It gave Hensel the power to order changes to the work, such as an unlimited acceleration of the contract, subject to its obligation to pay an equitable adjustment. The changes clause purported to cover all the types of changes encountered by Phoenix. The subcontract also incorporated the prime contract between Hensel and the County, which contained a clause that limited a subcontractor's equitable adjustment to direct labor costs, plus a fixed percentage for overhead and profit. In Phoenix's case, application of the formula meant that it would receive about $22 per hour for a journeyman painter. However, its rate, and the standard rate around town for that work at that time, was $35 per hour. The additional $13 per hour that Phoenix might have recovered in quantum meruit was crucial in Phoenix's case where the overrun was over 15,000 hours.

At trial Phoenix sought a recovery in both quantum meruit and under the contract. The quantum meruit claim was dismissed by the trial judge, and the verdict on the contract claim was in favor of Hensel.[21] On appeal Phoenix argued that the trial court should not have dismissed the quantum meruit claim because the scope of the acceleration was well beyond what a reasonable contractor could have anticipated when bidding the job.

In a decision with ominous overtones for anyone seeking a quantum meruit recovery, the appeals court affirmed, finding that the breadth of the contractual language was the dispositive factor. The court distinguished earlier quantum meruit cases by their lack of any remedy-granting clause, and it placed heavy reliance on the comprehensive provisions of the contract at issue. Since the contract unambiguously purported to grant a remedy for every conceivable eventuality, the court held that there was no room for quantum meruit. According to the court, whether a party anticipated changes was a question to be determined from an examination of the contract alone:

---

[20] 787 P.2d at 60.

[21] The jury verdict does not disclose why Hensel won, but a number of contractual defenses were argued, such as failure of notice and release, one of which obviously was adopted by the jury.

The fact that Phoenix used nearly three times the amount of labor hours to perform its contract obligations, or that it used 26 painters instead of 9, is irrelevant. *As long as the nature of the problem encountered was contemplated by the contract, and we hold that is so, there is no basis to abandon the contract in favor of quantum meruit.*[22]

The Washington court did leave the door open a crack for contractors claiming relief under the cardinal change doctrine by holding that the court will look to the "magnitude as well as the quality of the changes involved" to determine whether the doctrine applies.[23] The court stated that the case before it did not involve the magnitude of the changes that existed in the federal cases, implying that it might treat a more extreme case differently. However, the court also stated that none of the Phoenix changes reflected a fundamental alteration of the project, because all of the types of changes were anticipated in the contract, and because none of them resulted in a change in the "shape or square footage of the surfaces painted."[24]

It is difficult to know what the court was saying here. It may have been reaffirming its earlier statement that there is no room for quantum meruit if the contract covers the types of changes for which relief is sought. On the other hand, there may still be some opening for quantum meruit on a cardinal change theory—but only in a very extreme case.

Another decision that seems to virtually eliminate a contractor's prospect of abrogating its contract in favor of a quantum meruit recovery is *Costanza Construction Corp. v. City of Rochester.*[25] In *Costanza* the contractor on a public improvement project had made a unit price bid of $25 per yard for removing what it thought was a small quantity of rock, estimated to be 20 yards on the plans and 100 yards in the specifications. The contractor's rock removal bid amounted to $2500 on a $936,000 contract. However, it turned out that the contractor ran into 600 yards of solid rock that was six-feet thick in places. The unexpected solid rock layer ultimately cost $800,000 to remove, over $1300 per yard. The City paid the contractor the $25 per yard specified in the contact, and the contractor sued, contending that a cardinal change had occurred that entitled it to payment in quantum meruit.

The court rejected the contractor's claim, based on what the dissent called a "now common exculpatory clause" that disclaimed any warranty in the plans and specifications and that obligated the contractor to inspect the site and to determine site conditions for itself. The principle followed in *Costanza* is the same as that followed in *Hensel Phelps*. If the contract limits the remedy, that is the end of the discussion. There will be no quantum meruit recovery.

---

[22] Hensel Phelps v. King County, 787 P.2d at 65 (emphasis added).

[23] *Id.*

[24] *Id.* at 66.

[25] 147 A.D.2d 929, 537 N.Y.S.2d 394 (1989).

Owners can applaud *Hensel Phelps* and *Costanza* as they appear to furnish a simple, straightforward, deterministic rule of changes compensation. If the contract has a clause that unambiguously deals with the changed work of the type for which claim is made, the claim will be governed by that clause. *Hensel Phelps* and *Costanza* probably mean that the court will not resort to quantum meruit, regardless of how severe conditions become on the job. Owners (and contractors in their dealings with their subs) can take advantage of these cases by drafting all inclusive changes clauses that control, i.e., limit, the compensation their contractors get for changed work.

Contractors have little in the way of effective defense. They can refuse to sign contracts that contain unfair changes provisions or one-sided exculpatory clauses. But making that difficult choice will often mean sacrificing the job. Many contractors have a bit of the gambler in them, and there will often be one bidder willing to take the job despite harsh contractual language. If there are few changes, a stringent compensation clause would cost little. If it turns out that there are a lot of changes, then the bet is lost, and the gambling contractor must lick its wounds and go on — if the experience has not propelled it into bankruptcy.

With the *Hensel Phelps* and *Costanza* cases the pendulum has swung way into the owner's corner, probably too far for any single contractor to take effective counter-action. If those cases are followed by other courts, life will be more difficult for all contractors. For now, federal contractors at least have the cardinal change doctrine to rely on, and contractors in some states can rely on statutory protection from certain onerous provisions, such as no damages for delay clauses. Perhaps future legislation will protect contractors from the strict enforcement of overreaching remedy provisions.[26]

---

[26] Legislation could be modeled after the way requirements contracts are handled. A changes clause is very much like a requirements contract that is tacked onto the end of a regular construction contract. In effect the contractor agrees to do the specified construction work, plus all the other work that the owner requires done in connection with its project. Requirements contracts in most states are governed by the UCC § 2-306: "A term which measures the quantity by the output of the seller or the requirements of the buyer means such actual output or requirements as may occur in good faith, except that no quantity unreasonably disproportionate to any stated estimate or in the absence of a stated estimate to any normal or otherwise comparable output or requirements may be tendered or demanded." This provision contains two limits on the literal enforceability of a requirements contract. First, the buyer must act in good faith. The analogue in the construction contract area would be that the changed work must relate to the original contract, and it must have been unanticipated. Second, the quantity required cannot be disproportionate to what the parties could reasonably expect. In construction parlance this might mean that the changes could not be so large that the volume of changed work is disproportionate to the size of the project as a whole.

CHAPTER 9

RECOVERY FOR JOINTLY-CAUSED DELAY

Thomas W. Hayton

§ 9.1   Introduction

§ 9.2   Both Parties Must Prove Causation and Delay to Whole Job

§ 9.3   Concurrent Cause Rule

§ 9.4   —Apportionment Still Possible under Liberal Rule

§ 9.5   —Other Criteria Not Useful in Concurrent Cause Rule Analysis

§ 9.6   —Breach versus Price Adjustment

§ 9.7   —Suspension of Work and Government Delay of Work Clauses

§ 9.8   —Hopelessly Intertwined Causes

§ 9.9   —Concurrent Cause Rule Used to Analyze Government Claims of Delay

§ 9.10   —No Apportionment Possible under Conservative Version of Concurrent Cause Rule

§ 9.11   Presumed Sharing Rule

§ 9.12   —Application of Presumed Sharing Rule to Costs Not Time-Related

§ 9.13   —Application of Presumed Sharing Rule to Delay

§ 9.14   —Criteria Used in Apportioning under Presumed Sharing Rule

§ 9.15   Consequence of Choosing Particular Rule

§ 9.1   Introduction

This discussion considers delay to a construction project which is attributable to a number of causes, at least some of which are the responsibility of different parties. This circumstance, of course, is far from rare; the rules which control it should be appreciated.

Most of the cases deal with federal construction projects. As usual, however, their rules seem applicable to other settings.

For simplicity, the original complainant will be called the "plaintiff," the respondent will be called the "defendant" and multiple causes of this type will be called "joint causes." The underlying questions, put in their most basic terms, are whether and how the responsibility for delay can be apportioned. The cases show that apportionment is often possible, but that disparate rules exist as to when and how apportionment might occur.

The plaintiff must first prove the defendant caused any delay; this is true both in claims of breach of contract[1] and equitable adjustment under a contract.[2] Regardless of whether the plaintiff is the government or the contractor, if the defendant's rebuttal thereafter is that things which were not its fault also precipitated the delay, the issue of apportionment arises.[3]

While often a court or board gives the plaintiff the burden of segregating the various causes of delay, upon pain of having its relief eliminated altogether,[4] there actually are alternate rules with widely varying results available in this situation.

Under one rule (called here the "concurrent cause" rule), the plaintiff's failure to segregate the causes usually is fatal to its entitlement to monetary relief. Under the second rule (called here the "presumed sharing" rule), however, the parties are presumed to share equally the responsibility for the plaintiff's loss, and that is what happens unless the parties prove that some different ratio is more appropriate.

§ 9.2   Both Parties Must Prove Causation and Delay to Whole Job

Regardless of what rule is employed, each party still (under most circumstances) must prove that the other actually caused delay to the job as a whole. In this respect, cases dealing with joint causes are similar to any other delay claim.

---

[1] Commerce Int'l Co. v. United States, 167 Ct. Cl. 529, 338 F.2d 81 (1964) [hereinafter *Commerce*] (cannot infer impact to job by government's slow performance of its duty to supply property); Montgomery-Ross-Fisher, PSBCA 1033, 84-2 B.C.A. (BNA) ¶ 17,492 (cannot infer entitlement to more time from authorized increases to price); G.M. Shupe, Inc. v. United States, 5 Cl. Ct. 662 (1984) [hereinafter *Shupe*]; Bruno Law v. United States, 195 Cl. Ct. 370 (1971) [hereinafter *Bruno*].

[2] Fischbach & Moore Int'l Corp., ASBCA 18146, 77-1 B.C.A. (BNA) ¶ 12,300, *aff'd*, 223 Ct. Cl. 119, 617 F.2d 223 (1980) [hereinafter *Fischbach*]; Utley-James. Inc., GSBCA 5370, 85-1 B.C.A. (BNA) ¶ 17,816 [hereinafter *Utley*]; Ultra Constr. Co., VABCA 1873, 85-2 B.C.A. (BNA) ¶ 18,007 [hereinafter *Ultra*]; R-W Contracting, Inc., ASBCA 25459, 85-1 B.C.A. (BNA) ¶ 17,785 [hereinafter *R-W*].

[3] Cedar Lumber, Inc. v. United States, 5 Cl. Ct. 539 (1984) [hereinafter *Cedar*] (contractor must apportion delay if government defends with proof that contractor caused some delay); *Fischbach*, ASBCA 18146, 77-1 B.C.A. (BNA) ¶ 12,300. *Cf.*, Wilner Constr. Co., ASBCA 26621, 84-2 B.C.A. (BNA) ¶ 17,411 (contractor must sort causes where government was at fault but there also were non-compensable delays); *Utley*, GSBCA 5370, 85-1 B.C.A. (BNA) ¶ 17,816; Arntz Contracting Co., EBCA 187-12-81, 84-3 B.C.A. (BNA) ¶ 17,604 [hereinafter *Arntz*].

[4] William F. Klingensmith, Inc. v. United States, 731 F.2d 805 (Fed. Cir. 1984) [hereinafter *Klingensmith*]; *Cedar*, 5 Cl. Ct. 539; *Arntz*, EBCA 187-12-81, 84-3 B.C.A. (BNA) ¶ 17,604.

A defendant's proof of causation should be of comparable quality to the plaintiff's proof.[5] Accordingly, both claims should be measured against a critical path (CPM) schedule. It is frequently held, for example, that any alleged joint cause (whether it is proffered as the fault of the plaintiff or of the defendant) is material only to the extent that it itself impeded the work on the critical path,[6] notwithstanding the fact that there are also other factors which are equal candidates as causes of delay.

Authorities trying to sort through alleged joint causes of delay have expressed a preference for an "as-built critical path" over the original schedule so as to picture how the job was really performed,[7] and also have accorded less import to simple start and stop dates on any schedule than to its logical sequence.[8]

At least when the contract does not say otherwise, proof in an apportionment-type case that any particular act or omission caused delay need not be through a formal CPM analysis. Boards occasionally even devise their own informal concept of the work sequence for use in judging claims of delay.[9]

For example, after finding the contractor's schedule was useless because of its inaccuracies and wild conclusions, the board in *William Passalacqua Builders* settled upon this ad hoc formula to segregate the causes: (1) hypothecate when the completion date would have been if there had been no changes (by plotting productivity of work without change against work with change), (2) subtract the hypothecated completion date from the actual completion date, and (3) give the contractor relief for the difference.

There is an interesting counterpoint to this "delay to the whole job" concept; each joint cause actually must cause delay, rather than itself be the product of delay. If it appears that the plaintiff deliberately backed off its schedule because

---

[5] *Bruno,* 195 Ct. Cl. 370; *Fischbach,* ASBCA 18146, 77-1 B.C.A. (BNA) ¶ 12,300. *See, e.g., Arntz,* EBCA 187-12-81, 84-3 B.C.A. (BNA) ¶ 17,604; Blinderman Constr. Co., ASBCA 2445, 84-3 B.C.A. (BNA) ¶ 17,527 [hereinafter *Blinderman*] (liquidated damages); Blackhawk Plumbing & Heating Co., GSBCA 2432, 76-1 B.C.A. (BNA) ¶ 11,649, *aff'g* 75-1 B.C.A. (BNA) ¶ 11,261 [hereinafter *Blackhawk*] (contractor's delays were to work on the critical path, government's delays were to work off that path; contractor is liable for all of the liquidated damages); *Fischbach,* ASBCA 18146, 77-1 B.C.A. (BNA) ¶ 12,300 (alleged joint cause must have had an impact on the job as a whole); Dawson Constr. Co., GSBCA 3998, 75-2 B.C.A. (BNA) 11,563 [hereinafter *Dawson*]; United States *ex rel.* Thorleif Larsen & Son, Inc. v. B.R. Abbot Constr. Co., 466 F.2d 712 (7th Cir. 1972) [hereinafter *Thorleif Larsen*]. *Cf.* Titan Mountain States Country Corp., ASBCA 23095, 85-1 B.C.A. (BNA) ¶ 17,931 [hereinafter *Titan*] (it is insufficient merely to compare original and as-built schedules). *But see,* Chaney & James Constr. Co. v. United States, 190 Ct. Cl. 699, 707-708, 421 F.2d 728 (1970) [hereinafter *Chaney*] (because suspension of work clause permits recovery where any part of the job is delayed, the contractor need not show delay to overall job).

[6] On CPM analysis generally, see *Shupe,* 5 Ct. Cl. at 677, n. 5.

[7] *Blackhawk,* GSBCA 2432, 76-1 B.C.A. (BNA) ¶ 11,649.

[8] *Shupe,* 5 Ct. Cl. 662.

[9] *Utley,* GSBCA 5370, 85-1 B.C.A. (BNA) ¶ 17,816. *See also,* William Passalacqua Builders, Inc., GSBCA 4205, 77-1 B.C.A. (BNA) ¶ 12,406 [hereinafter *Passalacqua*]; *R-W,* ASBCA 25459, 85-1 B.C.A. (BNA) ¶ 17,785.

the defendant's earlier acts or omissions made going forward futile, that should not be charged as a concurrent cause. It, rather, is a consequence of the defendant's delay.[10]

There are at least two distinct rules addressing this problem of joint causation: (1) the "concurrent cause" rule, wherein joint causes will entirely dispose of a remedy for delay unless the moving party can segregate sufficiently the impact of the causes, and (2) the "presumed sharing" rule, which assumes that both parties will equally share in the moving party's delay costs where both are partly responsible for the delay. The concurrent cause rule is the one most frequently employed by courts and boards in this situation.

Envisioning the case law as being controlled by two separate rules helps to explain the divergent results. In many of these decisions, however, it is unlikely that the trier of fact deliberately picked one rule over the other—or was even conscious of that other rule. One case which at least implicitly recognizes the two rules is *Ultra Construction Co.,*[11] where the apportionment of delay costs was done under one rule and the apportionment of out of pocket repair costs was done under the other. More commonly, one finds courts and boards characterizing one or the other rule as quite well established—while completely ignoring the competing rule.[12]

§ 9.3   Concurrent Cause Rule

What rule a court or board chooses to employ in this situation is obviously important to both parties. The concurrent cause rule promises the draconian prospect of loss of all affirmative relief where causes of the delay are shared between the defendant and the plaintiff. There are cases evidently applying this rule to bar apportionment automatically, and there are cases of a less restrictive bent, where apportionment can still occur under certain circumstances. When apportionment is not possible, the joint causes are often referred to as "concurrent" or "intertwined."[13]

---

[10] *See, e.g.,* Stephenson Assocs., Inc., GSBCA 6573, 863 B.C.A. (BNA) ¶ 19,071 at 96,341 [hereinafter *Stephenson*]; John Driggs Co., ENGBCA 4926, 87-2 B.C.A. (BNA) ¶ 19,833 (government's delay affected related work, and contractor may properly adjust work plan to reach the delay rather than "slavishly" following original schedule).

[11] VABCA 1873, 85-2 B.C.A. (BNA) ¶ 18,007.

[12] *Compare Passalacqua,* GSBCA 4205, 77-1 B.C.A. (BNA) ¶ 12,406 (concurrent cause rule is "well settled") *with* ACS Constr. Co., ASBCA 28488, 84-1 B.C.A. (BNA) ¶ 17,179 [hereinafter *ACS*] (presumed sharing rule is "well established").

[13] One case, E.H. Marhoefer, Jr. Co., DOTCAB 70-17, 71-1 B.C.A. (BNA) ¶ 8791 [hereinafter *Marhoefer*], proffers a suggestion for meshing the two rules, but there is no evidence that it either is trying to explain prior cases or predict the results of later ones. *Marhoefer's* coalescence is this: there can be no apportionment of damages caused by joint causes, but there can be where there is but one cause for which the two parties are jointly at fault.

There is language in two standard federal construction clauses, the suspension of work and government delay of work clauses, which has been interpreted to call for the application of the concurrent cause rule. But, as we shall see, they more record the law than create it.

§ 9.4 —Apportionment Still Possible under Liberal Rule

The liberal and most prevalent view by this rule is that the plaintiff can recover if it can segregate the effects of the various causes.[14] Apportionment, under this view of the rule, requires presentation of credible proof that delays caused by separate causes did not overlap. For any part of the overall delay for which this segregation is not possible, all affirmative right to monetary relief is lost for both parties.

The case stating this liberal variant most clearly is *Fischbach & Moore International Corp.*[15] Here the government's erroneous rejection of material (and equally erroneous orders to correct the problem) affected steel members to be used in radio towers. Also affecting the steel work, however, were (1) financial difficulties of the contractor's steel supplier and (2) a reasonable period of time accorded the government for checking steel which had failed to pass the initial inspection. Although these causes all interfered with the same items of work, at roughly the same time, the board thought the contractor sufficiently segregated the periods of delay caused by at least some problems so as to prevent some recovery.

What passes, however, as sufficient proof of segregation under this rule is not necessarily limited to the mathematically precise. In this respect, proof of segregation is not radically different than proof of the quantum of damage. While the *Fischbach and Moore* board praised the relative degree of precision possible

---

[14] *See, e.g., Fischbach,* ASBCA 18146, 77-1 B.C.A. (BNA) ¶ 12,300 (explanation of difference between cases like it permitting apportionment and those like *Commerce,* 167 Ct. Cl. at 543, 338 F.2d at 90, with a contrary result, is simply the availability of proof permitting segregation of cause). *See also* Cox, *Owner's Damages,* 83-3 Construction Briefings (Fed. Pub.).

[15] ASBCA No. 18146, 77-1 B.C.A. (BNA) ¶ 12,300. *See also, Blinderman,* 695 F.2d 552 (remanding to determine if contractor can separate delays to which he "contributed"); *R-W,* ASBCA 25459, 85-1 B.C.A. (BNA) ¶ 17,785 (most causes found to be concurrent, so no contractor relief; for remainder of causes, small delays were assigned evidently on the basis of common sense); *Bruno,* 195 Ct. Cl. 370. *Cf. Commerce,* 167 Ct. Cl. at 543, 338 F.2d at 90 (contractor's failure to satisfy proof requirements relative to apportionment given as a reason to hold that it failed to prove causation); EJT Constr. Co., ASBCA 22795, 83-2 B.C.A. (BNA) ¶ 16,712 [hereinafter *EJT*] (segregation by cause found possible where separate omissions by each party affected the same item of work—roof insulation—but sequentially; award here attempts to follow Coath & Goss, 101 Ct. Cl. 702 (1944) [hereinafter *Coath*], one of the very earliest cases discussing the consequence of concurrency of causes of delay).

within a CPM analysis, it did not require anything so precise. Instead, it relied upon a "jury verdict" approach for part of the delay period at issue.[16]

There are, of course, cases where the contractor failed to sufficiently segregate the effects of the various causes even though only a reasonable basis for segregation was demanded by the court or the board. Cases displaying a contractor's failed efforts include the early case of *Vogt Bros. v. United States*[17] and the fairly recent opinion of *Utley-James, Inc.*[18]

Regardless of the standards for the needed degree of mathematical precision in making this segregation, the cited cases show that allocation under the concurrent cause rule is generally done on the basis of causation.[19] (As we shall see, this is a principal area where the concurrent cause rule differs from the presumed sharing rule.)

§ 9.5   —Other Criteria Not Useful in Concurrent Cause Rule Analysis

It is interesting to note that some things which naturally suggest themselves as factors which might be useful in apportioning have been held not to be; they should not be offered to a court or board by a party attempting to establish how to apportion losses. Examples of the things which have been held to be irrelevant in the apportionment process include: (1) whether the claim is one in breach of contract as opposed to a claim for an equitable price adjustment under the contract, and (2) whether there exists in the contract a suspension of work clause or some other clause specially addressing the concept of apportionment.

§ 9.6   —Breach versus Price Adjustment

It does not matter whether the debate takes place over a type of relief granted by the contract itself for a delay (i.e., an equitable price adjustment) or over a claim

---

[16] *Fischbach,* ASBCA 18146, 771 B.C.A. (BNA) 12,300, at 59,224. *See also,* Raymond Constructors of Africa, Ltd. v. United States, 188 Ct. Cl. 147, 411 F.2d 1227, 1236 (1969) [hereinafter *Raymond*]; Specialty Assembly & Packing Co. v. United States, 174 Ct. Cl. 153 (1966) [hereinafter *Specialty*]; Steve P. Rados, AGBCA 77-130-4, 82-1 B.C.A. (BNA) ¶ 15,624 [hereinafter *Rados*]; J.R. Pope, Inc., DOTCAB 78-95, 80-2 B.C.A. (BNA) ¶ 14,582; *Marhoefer,* DOTCAB 70-17, 71-1 B.C.A. (BNA) ¶ 8791; *Stephenson,* GSBCA 6973, 86-3 B.C.A. (BNA) ¶ 19,071.

[17] 160 Ct. Cl. 687 (1963). *See also, Passalacqua,* GSBCA 4205, 77-1 B.C.A. (BNA) ¶ 12,406; Wexler Constr. Co., ASBCA 23782, 84-2 B.C.A. (BNA) ¶ 17,408.

[18] GSBCA 5370, 85-1 B.C.A. (BNA) ¶ 17,816.

[19] *Fischbach,* ASBCA 18146, 77-1 B.C.A. (BNA) ¶ 12,300; *Rados,* AGBCA 77-130-4, 82-1 B.C.A. (BNA) ¶ 15,624; *Raymond,* 188 Ct. Cl. 147, 411 F.2d at 1236; *Bruno,* 195 Ct. Cl. 370; *EJT,* ASBCA 22795, 83-2 B.C.A. (BNA) 16,712; *Specialty,* 174 Ct. Cl. 153; *R-W,* ASBCA 25459, 85-1 B.C.A. (BNA) ¶ 17,785.

to the effect that the contract terms were breached. The concurrent cause rule applies in both settings. Indeed, it was held sometime ago that:

> This principle [of allowing apportionment only where it is possible to "ascertain the true balance"] applies equally to delays attributable to the change [i.e., one basis for an equitable price adjustment] as to ordinary damages for delay.[20]

It, thus, is not surprising to find cases using the concurrent cause rule in the context of breach of contract claims[21] and in the context of demands for equitable adjustment.[22]

§ 9.7 —Suspension of Work and Government Delay of Work Clauses

These two standard federal contract clauses explicitly discourage apportionment.[23] Similar phrases exist in the state and even private construction contracts. While these clauses, where they are shown to apply to the specific facts, may well discourage the use of the presumed sharing rule, they do not appear to be a precondition for the use of the concurrent cause rule.

The section of the current federal suspension of work clause which is important for this purpose says:

> However, no adjustment shall be made under this clause for any suspension, delay, or interruption to the extent that performance would have been so suspended, delayed, or interrupted by any other cause including the fault or negligence of the Contractor, or for which an equitable adjustment is provided for or excluded under any other term or condition of this contract.[24]

---

[20] Hardman-Monier-Hutcherson, AJV, ASBCA 11869, 67-2 B.C.A. (BNA) ¶ 6522 [hereinafter *Hardman*]. Second, Acme Missiles & Constr. Corp., ASBCA 11794, 68-1 B.C.A. (BNA) ¶ 6734 ("calling such [delay] damages by another name such as "impact" costs does not alter the principle [regarding concurrent delay]").

[21] *Coath*, 101 Ct. Cl. 702; *Cedar*, 5 Cl. Ct. 539; John McShain, Inc. v. United States, 412 F.2d 1281 (Ct. Cl. 1969).

[22] *Klingensmith*, 731 F.2d 805.

[23] *See* FAR §§ 52.212-12 (Suspension of Work) and 52.212-15 (Government Delay of Work). The suspension of work clause is to be inserted in firm fixed price construction and A/E contracts. FAR § 12.505(a). The government delay of work clause is to be used in firm fixed price non-commercial supply contracts, and may be used when the contract is for firm fixed price services or firm fixed price commercial or modified commercial supplies. FAR § 12.505(d).

[24] FAR § 52.212-12. The delay of work clause sentence is identical with this but for the deletion of the word "suspension." In contrast, the firm fixed price construction contract Changes clause

The case dealing with this language in most detail (although also in dicta) is *Merritt-Chapman & Scott Corp. v. United States,*[25] where the modern version of the suspension of work clause was said to be an outright bar to apportionment where the plaintiff was itself responsible for some of the delay.

The *Merritt-Chapman & Scott* opinion also says that if this special language is absent, apportionment of delay costs should occur as in most other circumstances where there is a confluence of causes, i.e., some sharing of costs unless one party is responsible for some superseding cause:

> A contractor is entitled to recover, under the pre-1960 clause if the government's delay is the proximate cause of the contractor's additional loss, even if some other occurrence might have hypothetically caused a like delay during that time. A contractor would be denied recovery here only if it could be shown that the government's delay did not cause the additional loss because some other factor caused the loss independent of the government's actions.[26]

In sum, fair implications to be drawn from this case include the idea that the concurrent cause rule applies only where it is specifically called for by the suspension clause and, where this rule is brought to bear by the clause, no apportionment whatsoever is possible. It is important to note that neither implication has attracted a following in the cases. Later cases have cited *Merritt-Chapman & Scott* and allowed apportionment anyway.

In *William F. Klingensmith. Inc. v. United States*[27] for example, the *Merritt-Chapman & Scott* rule was specifically said to embrace the possibility of a contractor recovering by proving that the government's cause of delay was "separate and apart from that chargeable to the contractor." There are a number of other cases to a like effect, i.e., cases permitting apportionment, or at least expressing willingness to do so, if the contractor would segregate the causes of

---

simply provides for an adjustment where the "change causes an increase or decrease in the contractor's cost of, or the time required for, the performance of the work." FAR § 52.243-4(d). Likewise, the contractor's entitlement to an extension of time under the default clause provides for such relief simply when the "delay . . . arises from unforeseeable causes beyond the control and without the fault or negligence of the contractor." FAR § 52.249-10 (firm fixed price construction contract).

[25] 528 F.2d 1392 (Ct. Cl. 1976) [hereinafter *Merritt*].

[26] *Id.* at 1398.

[27] 731 F.2d 805 (Fed. Cir. 1984). The *Klingensmith* opinion cites one of the earliest opinions on joint cause of delay, *Coath,* 101 Ct. Cl. 702. Since it concerned a 1934 construction contract, *Coath* presumably did not deal with a suspension of work clause. Note, however, that the *Klingensmith* case itself, though specifically refining *Merritt's* rule, does not talk about the suspension clause. And the government's delay-causing act there also was answerable under the changes or the differing-site-conditions clauses.

delay.[28] There also are cases disallowing apportionment only after it was determined that segregation would not or could not be done.[29]

Cases also have disassociated the concurrent cause rule from the suspension of work clause, in that the rule itself has been employed notwithstanding the absence of such a clause. We have already seen a number of cases which impose the concurrent cause rule without reliance upon that clause. This was the case both before the suspension of work clause added its special language[30] and after that change.[31] As noted in more detail later, there are cases applying the concurrent cause rule to government claims for liquidated damages, where there is no special language on apportionment.[32]

§ 9.8   —Hopelessly Intertwined Causes

Under the concurrent cause rule, irretrievably and truly concurrent causes of delay cancel monetary relief which otherwise would be available to either party.[33] Apart from the obvious propositions that in these cases there must be a number of causes of delay, and that the plaintiff need be responsible for some (but only some) of them, there appear to be no universally applicable criteria defining truly concurrent or intertwined causes. Given the intensely fact-oriented nature

[28] *See, e.g.,* Toombs & Co. v. United States, 4 Ct. Cl. 549 (1984) [hereinafter *Toombs*]; Capitol Elec. Co., GSBCA 5316, 83-2 B.C.A. (BNA) ¶ 16,548, *reversed on other grounds,* 729 F.2d 743 (Fed. Cir. 1984); *Blinderman,* 695 F.2d 552. *But see,* Blake Constr. Co., ASBCA 24356, 82-1 B.C.A. (BNA) ¶ 15,688 (contractor not permitted to apportion under suspension of work clause because (1) contractor's cause of delay was just as significant as government's cause, and (2) although separate causes and separate time periods, these delays affected the same item of work); *Marhoefer,* DOTCAB 70-17, 77-1 B.C.A. (BNA) ¶ 8791 (suspension of work clause held to bar apportionment where [as here] the situation involved one delay with shared fault.)

[29] *See, e.g.,* Utley, GSBCA 5370, 85-1 B.C.A. (BNA) ¶ 17,816; *Chaney,* 190 Ct. Cl. at 717, 421 F.2d 728; *Passalacqua,* GSBCA 4205, 77-1 B.C.A. (BNA) ¶ 12,406; Riveria Gen. Contracting, ASBCA 25888, 85-2 B.C.A. (BNA) ¶ 18,094.

[30] *See Commerce,* 167 Ct. Cl. at 543, 338 F.2d at 90; *Coath,* 101 Ct. Cl. 702; *Toombs,* 4 Cl. Ct. at 550, n. 14. (*Commerce* said to require segregation if possible).

[31] *See, e.g.,* Pittman Constr. Co. v. United States, GSBCA 4897-R, 81-1 B.C.A. (BNA) ¶ 15,111, *aff'd,* 2 Cl. Ct. 211 (1983); *Rados,* AGBCA 77-130-4, 82-1 B.C.A. (BNA) 15,624; *Fischbach,* ASBCA 18146, 77-1 B.C.A. (BNA) 12,300; *Stephenson,* GSBCA 6573, 86-3 B.C.A. (BNA) ¶ 19,071 (suspension of work clause makes concurrent cause rule explicit; it has been implicit in the Changes clause). As in *Rados, Fischbach* dealt with claims under both the suspension of work clause and the changes clause. It also seemingly made no difference which clause was used.

[32] *See, e.g., Passalacqua,* GSBCA 4205, 77-1 B.C.A. (BNA) 12,406; *Utley,* GSBCA 5370, 85-1 B.C.A. (BNA) 17,816; Powell's Gen. Contracting Co., DOTCAB 77-27, 79-1 B.C.A. (BNA) ¶ 13,694, *reh'g denied,* 79-1 B.C.A. (BNA) ¶ 9,606 [hereinafter *Powell*]. *See also,* Engineered Sys., Inc., DOTCAB 76-12, 78-1 B.C.A. (BNA) ¶ 13,074 [hereinafter *Engineered*].

[33] *Commerce,* 338 F.2d at 90.

of this inquiry, it is perhaps naive to expect detailed definitions. In any case, one must be content with broad statements that an intertwined or truly concurrent causes are those the effects of which are impossible of segregation, i.e., during the time when one such cause is delaying the job the other is also delaying it.

Further, the government's field of delay-causing events which will dilute or refute liability for independent acts of government fault goes beyond acts which merely are the contractor's fault. At least when the contractor is suing the government for delay, the government can take advantage of not only the contractor's delay causing acts, but also a number of other things such as (1) problems which are the responsibility of third parties and (2) acts of God.[34] Some cases extend this concept to the contractor's benefit as well: where the government seeks delay damages, it may not recover for periods wherein there was a contractor-caused problem but also one which was the responsibility of neither party.[35]

Finally, there is even a difference in the cases as to precisely what should be the principal objective of proof that the joint causes had segregable impact. Some authorities concern themselves with whether the two causes affect different items of work and others focus on whether they occur during different time periods. There are cases saying that the key concern is the item of work,[36] and there are cases saying that the key is the time period during which the cause was afoot.[37] Under the critical path method of analysis, however, this distinction should be largely one without a difference; for each time period there should be only one or a very limited number of items of work the delay of which would also delay the entire job.

§ 9.9 — Concurrent Cause Rule Used to Analyze Government Claims of Delay

Government claims for liquidated damages and actual damages for delay are often analyzed by boards and courts using the concurrent cause rule. As with

---

[34] *Rados,* AGBCA 77-130-4, 82-1 B.C.A. (BNA) ¶ 15,624 (contractor cannot recover for government-caused delay where intertwined with any delay for which government was not responsible); *Fischbach,* ASBCA 18146, 77-1 B.C.A. (BNA) ¶ 12,300 (causes for which government was not responsible, including a reasonable period of suspension and financial difficulty of subcontractor); *Arntz,* EBCA 187-12-81, 84-3 B.C.A. (BNA) 17,604 ("other delays for which the government was not responsible"); *Dawson,* GSBCA 3998, 79-2 B.C.A. (BNA) ¶ 11,563 (weather delays).

[35] *See, e.g., Powell,* DOTCAB 77-27, 79-1 B.C.A. (BNA) ¶ 17,694.

[36] Santa Fe, Inc., VABCA 1943 et seq., 84-2 B.C.A. (BNA) ¶ 17,341. *Cf. Arntz,* EBCA 187-12-81, 84-3 B.C.A. (BNA) ¶ 17,604.

[37] *Fischbach,* ASBCA 18146, 77-1 B.C.A. (BNA) ¶ 12,300; *R-W,* ASBCA 25459, 85-1 B.C.A. (BNA).¶ 17,785; Robert L. Rich, d/b/a Unitranco, DOTCAB 1026, 82-2 B.C.A. (BNA) ¶ 15,900; Active Fire Sprinkler Corp., GSBCA 5461, 85-1 B.C.A. (BNA) ¶ 16,868. *See also, Dawson,* GSBCA 3998, 79-2 B.C.A. (BNA) ¶ 11,563.

cases cataloged above, it is not unusual for these cases to give the government the opportunity to salvage some of its delay claim even though the contractor has demonstrated that the government caused a portion of the delay.

For a recent case holding that liquidated damages can be apportioned upon proof of segregation of cause, in a fashion comparable to that permitted contractors, see *Santa Fe, Inc.*[38] The flexibility accorded the government by *Santa Fe* shows that it, no less than contractors, needs to pay close attention to its ability to prove what items are critical to the job progress, and when and how specific problems affected such critical items.

Just as is the case where a contractor is the plaintiff, nothing about the proposition that the government might sufficiently segregate its causes says that it has done so in any particular case. *Computer Science Corp.*[39] for example emphasizes the difficulty facing the government even if it is given the same chance to segregate causes. In this latter case, the concurrent cause rule was applied symmetrically to the disadvantage of both the government (regarding its liquidated damages assessment) and the contractor (regarding its delay claim); both parties shared fault for the delay, but neither could sufficiently prove segregation.

Just as *Computer Science Corp.* is not alone in saying the rule is both perilous and symmetrical, *Santa Fe, Inc.* is not alone in apportioning liquidated damages.[40] As the *Santa Fe* board itself recognized, however, there are also cases automatically and unthinkingly barring apportionment of liquidated damage assessments.[41]

---

[38] VABCA 1943 et seq., 84-2 B.C.A. (BNA) ¶ 17,341 at 86,411.

[39] ASBCA 27275. 84-3 B.C.A. (BNA) ¶ 17,671. *Accord, Klingensmith,* 731 F.2d 805; *Cedar,* 5 Ct. Cl. 539; *Coath,* 101 Ct. Cl. 702; *Blinderman,* ASBCA 24445, 84-3 B.C.A. (BNA) 17,527 (liquidated damages assessment void because segregation of responsibility for delay found to be hopeless); *EJT,* ASBCA 22795, 83-2 B.C.A. (BNA) ¶ 16,712; ETS-Hokin Corp. AECBCA 70-5-70, 72-2 B.C.A. (BNA) ¶ 9,606 (1972) [hereinafter *Hokin*]; *Hardman,* ASBCA 11869, 67-2 B.C.A. (BNA) ¶ 6522; Midstate Constructors, Inc., PSBCA 913, 81-1 B.C.A. (BNA) ¶ 14,898; *Ultra,* VASCA 1875, 85-2 B.C.A. (BNA) ¶ 18,007; *Titan,* ASBCA 24184, 87-1 B.C.A. (BNA) ¶ 19,626. Some of these cases merely express the rule in terms equally applicable to the government as the contractor; others explicitly apply the rule to government claims. *But see,* Dewey Schmoll, Assignee v. United States, 91 Ct. Cl. 1 (1941) [hereinafter *Schmoll*] (court refused to attempt to apportion liquidated damages and also noted this relieved the contractor of its obligation to complete on time, presumably relieving it of assessment for actual damages too; also denied the contractor's delay costs, but on the basis of particular facts not concurrent cause rule).

[40] *See, e.g., Toombs,* 4 Cl. Ct. 549; Lawrence D. Krause, AGBCA 76-18-4, 82-2 B.C.A. (BNA) ¶ 16,129 (giving the contractor the burden of allocation where the government has assessed liquidated damages). *See also, Powell,* DOTCAB 77-27, 79-1 B.C.A. (BNA) ¶ 13,964; *Thorleif Larsen,* 466 F.2d 712 (owner's liquidated damages assessment against apportioned between prime and sub); *Blackhawk,* GSBCA 2432, 76-1 B.C.A. (BNA) ¶ 11,649 (no apportionment where government problem did not affect work then on critical path).

[41] *See, e.g.,* Acme Process Equip. Co. v. United States, 171 Ct. Cl. 324, 347 F.2d 509 (1965), *rev'd on other grounds,* 385 U.S. 138 [hereinafter *Acme*]; *Schmoll,* 91 Ct. Cl. 1; *Engineered,*

The idea of apportionment has likewise been applied to reduce government claims of actual damages for delay. In *Freuhauf Corp. v. United States*,[42] the Court of Claims reduced the contracting officer's assessment of actual damages (namely, wasted rent on a new facility which was not entirely useful because the contractor was late with equipment needed to fully utilize the building) by prorating those damages. The ratio used was the contractor's entitlement to time extensions (for change order work) compared to the total delay on the job.

Finally, apportionment of a sorts was done recently in the context of a special price reduction clause in *Space Age Engineering, Inc.*[43] but with a significant new twist. This clause keyed contract price to the actual date of delivery, reducing price for late delivery. The rule for apportionment concocted by this board permitted the government to take its reduction of price, but also permitted the contractor to roll back some of that price reduction for the period of delay which the contractor could show was caused solely by the government. In other words, the government got its relief even for days of delay for which it was partly responsible and only suffered a reduction of recovery for days it was found to be the only guilty party.

§ 9.10   —No Apportionment Possible under Conservative Version of Concurrent Cause Rule

The concurrent cause rule is occasionally expressed in a way which appears to absolutely prohibit apportionment. The ability to segregate causes logically does not matter if this variant is used. This more conservative view is certainly in the minority—but it cannot be dismissed as an anachronism.

One recent opinion apparently expressing this view is *Cline Construction Co.*[44] Here, there were three distinct periods of delay. The government's delays ran from September 24 until January 18 and again from February 25 until April 1. The contractor's delay occurred from February 2 until March 2. In sum, there was only partial overlap between the contractor's delay and the government's delay. The board nevertheless called all delays "concurrent" and, citing *Commerce International*, denied all affirmative relief to the contractor.

The *Cline* opinion is not completely unique. At least one earlier opinion, *Acme Missiles & Construction Corp.*,[45] makes a similar statement. The *Acme* board

---

DOTCAB 76-12, 78-1 B.C.A. (BNA) ¶ 13,074. *See also,* SOG v. Missouri Pac. Ry. Co., 658 F.2d 562 (8th Cir. 1981) (Arkansas law).

[42] 24 CCF, 81,992 (Ct. Cl. 1978), *rev'g in part* PSBCA 197, 76-1 B.C.A. (BNA) ¶ 11,771 and PSBCA 478, 74-1 B.C.A. (BNA) ¶ 10,399. *Accord, Hokin,* 70-5-7, 72-2 B.C.A. (BNA) ¶ 9,606; *Acme,* 171 Ct. Cl. 324, 347 F.2d 509 (rejecting apportionment of liquidated damages, but permitting it for actual damages).

[43] ASBCA 25761, 83-2 B.C.A. (BNA) ¶ 16,607.

[44] ASBCA 28600, 84-3 B.C.A. (BNA) ¶ 17,594.

[45] ASBCA 11794, 68-1 B.C.A. (BNA) ¶ 6,734.

disallowed a contractor's demand for compensation for costs for delay to radio tower installation, finding its causes to be "concurrent" with government delays even though the contractor's causes neither occurred at exactly the same time nor affected the same materials.

We have already noted that some cases hold that any joint cause dispatches completely the government's right to liquidated damages. Those cases are actually applying the conservative view of the concurrent cause rule to government claims.

§ 9.11   Presumed Sharing Rule

This rule pays less heed to segregation of the effect of joint causes and more attention to finding some way to grant compensation notwithstanding them. The rule is not necessarily hostile to the idea of isolating the parts of the overall delay which were caused by each party; it, however, does not make so much depend upon the plaintiff's ability to segregate. Even where some or all of a delay is the product of irretrievably intertwined causes, some apportionment of the cost will be ordered. Where no other division presents itself,[46] costs incurred because of joint causes are apportioned 50/50.[47]

In this respect, the presumed sharing rule is reminiscent of the tort law principles of comparative negligence and contribution by multiple tortfeasors. Indeed, authorities using the presumed sharing rule have sometimes said that they are simply adopting tort principles.[48]

Another distinction between the first and second rules is how common it is to see them employed. In delay claim cases, courts more commonly employ the concurrent cause rule. The presumed sharing rule, on the other hand, is more commonly employed where costs at issue are not time related.[49] (The concurrent cause rule, of course, only applies to delay claims.)

---

[46] E.C. Ernst, Inc. v. Manhattan Constr. Co., 551 F.2d 1026 (5th Cir. 1977) [hereinafter *Ernst*] (for concurrent delays, apportionment on the basis of comparative negligence; cites United States v. Reliable Transfer Co., which disposes of earlier rule requiring a 50/50 split in casualty loss claims in admiralty). *See also,* National Presto Indust., Inc. v. United States, 338 F.2d 99, 167 Ct. Cl. 749 (1964), *cert. den.,* 380 U.S. 962 [hereinafter *National Presto*].

[47] *ACS,* ASBCA 28488, 84-1 B.C.A. (BNA) ¶ 17,179, at 85,570; Frank Briscoe Co., GSBCA 6169 (5145)-REIN, 81-2 B.C.A. (BNA) ¶ 15,456 [hereinafter *Briscoe*]; Dynalectron Corp. (Pac. Div.) v. United States, 207 Ct. Cl. 349, 366-369 (1975) [hereinafter *Dynalectron*]; Environmental Growth Chambers, ASBCA 25845, 83-2 B.C.A. (BNA) ¶ 16,609 [hereinafter *Environmental*]; Circle Elec. Contractors, Inc., DOTCAB 76-27, 77-1 B.C.A. (BNA) ¶ 12,339 [hereinafter *Circle*].

[48] *See, e.g., Ultra,* VABCA 1873, 85-2 B.C.A. (BNA) ¶ 18,007; *Environmental,* ASBCA 25845, 83-2 B.C.A. (BNA) ¶ 16,609; United States v. Seckinger, 397 U.S. 203, 212-216 (1970) [hereinafter *Seckinger*].

[49] *See, e.g., Seckinger,* 397 U.S. 203; *Dynalectron,* 207 Ct. Cl. at 366-369; Bruce-Anderson, Inc., PSBCA 1000, 83-2 B.C.A. (BNA) ¶ 16,733 [hereinafter *Bruce*]; Richard A. Wand d/b/a Dick

§ 9.12 — Application of Presumed Sharing Rule to Costs Not Time-Related

Looking at how the presumed sharing rule has been applied to non-delay damages is instructive on how it could be applied to delay claims. *ACS Construction Inc.*[50] is one relatively recent example of the application of this second rule to costs incurred because of poor, but not untimely, performance. Here, the contractor did two things wrong in installing exterior walkways, both of which were held to have contributed to undesirable ponding of water. The government, however, also contributed to the drainage problem by giving inaccurate specifications for the walkway's elevation. When the contractor relied upon those elevations to fabricate steel columns, the inaccuracies reduced the drainage slope of the walkways.

As with cases applying the concurrent cause rule, the *ACS* board was very careful to assure that each alleged fault actually caused some extra cost.[51] It is what happened after the board decided that both parties were responsible for extra costs that distinguishes the *ACS* analysis: In *ACS* it was not fatal that the individual causes could not be shown to have isolated impacts. It was not essential to the *ACS* board that relative responsibility be assigned; instead, that board used the following hierarchy: (1) apportion according to a relative degree of "responsibility," if this can be done, and (2) if not, force both parties to share equally:

> Where government-responsible and contractor-responsible causes operate jointly to create defects, damage or injury, the costs of compensation, repair or correction will be shared by the parties. Where possible the shares will be prorated according to the degree of responsibility for the end result that each side bears.

> From the present record, we are not able to determine whether any of the aforesaid causes was predominantly responsible for the ponding condition, nor do the facts offer any basis for apportionment. . . . In such circumstances it is proper that the parties should share such costs equally.[52]

There have been a number of cases with similar approaches and results. The United States Supreme Court, for example, interpreted the federal permits and responsibility clause to endorse comparative negligence in *United States v. Seckinger*.[53] In *Seckinger* the government was permitted to get contributions

---

Wand Contractor, AGBCA 83-215-3, 83-2 B.C.A. (BNA) ¶ 16,820 [hereinafter *Wand*]; *Environmental*, ASBCA 25845, 83-2 B.C.A. (BNA) ¶ 16,609.

[50] ASBCA 28488, 84-1 B.C.A. (BNA) ¶ 17,179.

[51] There are examples, however, where this presumed sharing rule is applied without such careful attention to causation. *See, e.g., Briscoe*, GSBCA 6169 (5145)-REIN, 81-2 B.C.A. (BNA) ¶ 15,456.

[52] *ACS*, ASBCA 28488, 84-1 B.C.A. (BNA) ¶ 17,179, at 85,570. *See also, Briscoe*, GSBCA 6169 (5145)-REIN, 81-2 B.C.A. (BNA) ¶ 15,456.

[53] 397 U.S. 203, 212-16 (1970).

from a contractor for damages assessed for injuries sustained by a contractor's employee who touched an electrical wire the government negligently left energized. The government was held to be entitled to the participation by the contractor to the extent of the contractor's relative fault in the accident.

Similarly, the Court of Claims in *Dynalectron Corp. (Pacific Division) v. United States*[54] rewarded an antenna manufacturer one-half of its costs where its default termination was precipitated by both bad government design and the contractor's own poor management. A number of more recent board cases are to a like effect.[55]

§ 9.13   —Application of Presumed Sharing Rule to Delay

There are cases applying this second rule to delay claims, but they are bereft of any substantial explanation of what persuaded that authority to pick this rule over the more common concurrent cause rule. For contractor claims, another confounding factor would be the presence of the suspension of work or government delay of work clauses, both of which, as we saw earlier, are antithetical to apportionment. While this second rule has much to recommend itself over the concurrent cause rule, it only occasionally is employed in a delay cost setting.

A case implying that the presumed sharing rule does not apply to delay costs is *Ultra Construction Co.*,[56] where the Veterans Administration Board applied the presumed sharing rule to a contractor's claim for reimbursement of repair costs but the concurrent cause rule to its related claim for delay. In *Ultra,* steam escaping from an uncapped steam line ruined the contractor's interior finish work. The contractor was found to be negligent in leaving the line uncapped but the government also was negligent since it failed to warn the contractor before turning on the steam.

On the other hand, there have been a number of cases which have employed the presumed sharing rule to apportion even delay-related costs. Given the pedigree of the rule, this really should not be surprising. The case which was one of the first to express this rule, *National Presto Industries, Inc. v. United States,*[57] actually dealt in large measure with delay costs (i.e., extended overhead and inefficiency during the delay period).

---

[54] 207 Ct. Cl. 349, 366-69, 518 F.2d 594 (1975).

[55] *See, Bruce,* PSBCA 1000, 83-2 B.C.A. (BNA) ¶ 16,733; *Wand,* AGBCA 83-215-3, 83-2 B.C.A. (BNA) ¶ 16,820; *Environmental,* ASBCA 25845, 83-2 B.C.A. (BNA) ¶ 16,609; *Ultra,* VABCA 1973, 85-2 B.C.A. (BNA) ¶ 18,007.

[56] VABCA 1973, 85-2 B.C.A. (BNA) ¶ 18,007.

[57] 338 F.2d 99, 167 Ct. Cl. 749 (1964), *cert. denied,* 380 U.S. 962. The Supreme Court in *Seckinger,* 397 U.S. 203, calls *National Presto* the progenitor of this line of cases.

Probably the most recent case applying this idea to a delayed project is *Reese Industries,*[58] where the contractor's one-week delay in installation of a roof occurred at the same time that the government was taking too long to deliberate over the contractor's production submittal. The protective coating was not installed in time to beat two substantial snow storms. The storms, in turn, ruined roof installation. The board, expressing an inability to more scientifically divide responsibility for repair costs, divided them 50/50.

Another recent case which, in effect, applied the presumed sharing rule to claims of time-related costs is *Frank Briscoe, Inc.*[59] The *Briscoe* case also involved a building construction project wherein a period of delay (and the attended unabsorbed overhead and increased labor costs) resulted from failures by both the government (improper dimensions in one drawing) and the contractor (inefficient coordination). Notwithstanding the obvious fact that these causes of delay affected the same item of work and were effective at the same time (i.e., the classic circumstance where delay-related costs are forfeited under the concurrent cause rule), this board simply split the costs 50/50:

> Since what the parties want from us is some resolution of their dispute over who is responsible for the delay, and since they have been unable to shed enough light on the delay period to permit us to assign the responsibility firmly to either party, we must have recourse to a jury verdict. . . . [F]or lack of anything else to do we simply split the entire delay down the middle.[60]

An earlier opinion apportioning delay costs on this basis is *Mershon-Gimeno Construction Co.,*[61] where a construction contractor was awarded one-half of its delay costs. The government was late with drawings needed for installation of plumbing lines, but the contractor was also late finishing the walls in which those plumbing lines were to be placed. Relief was apportioned even though there was no good way to segregate the impacts of these two causes.

The presumed sharing rule also has been applied in the context of private owner claims for liquidated damages. This was the case in *E.C. Ernst, Inc. v.*

---

[58] ASBCA 27741, 85-3 B.C.A. (BNA) ¶ 18,358.

[59] GSBCA 6169 (5145)-REIN, 81-2 B.C.A. (BNA) ¶ 15,456 (1981). See also 80-2 B.C.A. (BNA) ¶ 14,476 (on entitlement).

[60] *Briscoe,* GSBCA 6169 (5145)-REIN, 81-2 B.C.A. (BNA) ¶ 15,456 at 76,584. *See also Marhoefer,* DOTCAB 70-17, 77-1 B.C.A. (BNA) ¶ 8791 (apportionment by relative fault where one delay caused by two separate acts).

[61] GSBCA 4524, 77-1 B.C.A. (BNA) ¶ 12,317. *See also, Circle,* DOTCAB 76-27, 77-1 B.C.A. (BNA) ¶ 12,339. For a case applying the concept to a contractor's claim and against a subcontractor, see Sam Macri & Sons, Inc. v. United States *ex rel.* Oaks Constr. Co., 312 F.2d 119 (9th Cir. 1963). A recent case supporting the concept of flexible apportionment in the context of non-federal public construction contracts was Novak & Co. v. Facilities Dev. Corp., 489 N.Y.S.2d 492 (App. Div. 1986).

Manhattan Construction Co.[62] where the Fifth Circuit Court of Appeals apportioned the liquidated damages assessment between the project owner (a hospital) and its construction contractor using a two-step process: (1) dividing liability for discrete periods of delay caused by one party or the other, and then, (2) for those periods of delay for which there is joint, intertwined fault, apportioning costs on the basis of "proportional fault" and the principle of comparative negligence.

Finally, however, it must be noted that none of these cases applying the presumed sharing rule to delays explain away the apparently contrary impact of the suspension of work and government delay of work clauses. Given the language in these clauses dispensing with apportionment, it legitimately may occur only where the suspension clause can be distinguished. Suspension clauses do not claim to apply to government demands for relief and they do not apply even to contractor claims if some other clause pertains.

The inapplicability of such clauses to government claims may explain some of the cited cases: *Bowen Construction, Inc.,* considered a government claim in the form of a credit change order, and *E.C. Ernst* dealt with the government assessment of liquidated damages for delay. (Further, the *Ernst* opinion concerned a non-federal public construction contract, where there may not even have been a suspension of work clause.)

As to contractor claims, we have seen above that the changes clause, in certain circumstances, provides for an equitable adjustment for governmental delay and, thus, a mechanism to escape the suspension clause's prohibition. The changes clause can be relied upon by a contractor where the government's delay was associated with new or changed work which the contractor had to perform, and even with government failures falling within the amorphous boundaries of "constructive changes."

§ 9.14   —Criteria Used in Apportioning under Presumed Sharing Rule

The criteria used by "presumed sharing" cases to apportion damages is by no means uniform. Some authorities (especially those saying that they are engrafting the concept of comparative negligence into the federal common law of contracts) maintain that the proper criterion is relative fault.[63] Other courts,

---

[62] 551 F.2d 1026 (5th Cir. 1977), *reh'g granted in part,* 559 F.2d 268, *cert. denied,* 434 U.S. 1067 (applying Alabama law; see particularly n. 33-34, p. 1039).

[63] *See, e.g., Dynalectron,* 207 Ct. Cl. at 366-369; *Ultra,* VABCA 1873, 85-2 B.C.A. (BNA) ¶ 18,007; *Ernst,* 551 F.2d 1026. *See also,* Restatement (Second) of Torts § 886A, Comment h (majority rule is just to split loss by the number of participants, but the trend is to divide on the basis of relative fault); *Environmental,* ASBCA 25845, 83-2 B.C.A. (BNA) ¶ 16,609 (citing as authority United States v. Reliable Transfer Co., 421 U.S. 397 (1975), an admiralty case apportioning casualty losses on the basis of fault).

however, apportion on the basis of relative cause.[64] Still others appear to keep their options open to use either or both.[65] The landmark case of *National Presto*[66] apportioned losses on the basis of neither fault, nor cause, but rather mutual mistake.[67] All in all, the presumed sharing rule cases exhibit much more variety in this area than concurrent cause rule cases.

§ 9.15   Consequence of Choosing Particular Rule

The presumed sharing and concurrent cause rules have some similarities and some important differences. Both rules usually are held to be limited to causes which retard progress on the entire job. When it comes time to actually allocate delay costs, cases under either rule may proceed on an equitable, jury verdict basis. The rules part company where, when trying to segregate causation, the effort proves impossible. Segregation of cause is not necessary under the presumed sharing rule, but failing to segregate the impact of multiple causes can, and often does, result in the total loss of the moving party's entitlement under the concurrent cause rule.

This difference is important in many cases; it presents the moving party with the prospect of losing entirely its right to relief where segregation of cause is not possible. Even when modern scheduling techniques are used, the concurrent cause rule more than occasionally results in such a forfeiture. The presumed sharing rule, on the other hand, does not present this risk. In sum, the plaintiff should normally attempt to get the court or board to think in terms of the presumed sharing rule, while the defendant should press the concurrent cause rule.

---

[64] *Environmental,* ASBCA 25845, 83-2 B.C.A. (BNA) ¶ 16,609; *Bruce,* PSBCA 1000, 83-2 B.C.A. (BNA) ¶ 16,733. *See also, ACS,* ASBCA 28488, 84-1 B.C.A. (BNA) 17,179, at 85,570 (since board could not ascertain whether any cause was predominant, apportioned on the basis of 50/50; board interchanged the terms "responsibility" and "cause"); *Briscoe,* GSBCA 6169 (5145)-REIN, 81-2 B.C.A. (BNA) ¶ 15,456 (where cannot attribute cause to specific delay, apportion at 50/50; interchanged the terms "attribution" and "responsibility"); *Wand* AGBCA 83-215-3, 83-2 B.C.A. (BNA) ¶ 16,820.

[65] *Seckinger,* 397 U.S. 203 (apparently trying to allocate on the basis of relative cause and fault); *Circle,* DOTCAB 76-27, 77-1 B.C.A. (BNA) 12,339 (emphasized cause and fault).

[66] 338 F.2d 99, 167 Ct. Cl. 749 (1964), *cert. denied,* 380 U.S. 962.

[67] National Presto, however, required first the proof of causation. The parties' mutual mistake led to some of the contractor's loss, but there was no showing that it led to all of the loss. The parties were held to share 50/50 in only the percentage of the total loss on the job which was caused by that mutual mistake.

CHAPTER 10

LANDMARK CPM DECISIONS FROM 1980 TO 1990

Jon M. Wickwire
Lance J. Lerman
Mark R. Berry

§ 10.1   Introduction

§ 10.2   What Is CPM?

§ 10.3   Use of CPM for Delay Analysis and Contract Claims

§ 10.4   Delay Claim Analysis

§ 10.5   —The Parameters

§ 10.6   Acceleration Claim Analysis

§ 10.7   Loss of Productivity Analysis

§ 10.8   The Decisions

§ 10.9   —*Fortec Constructors versus United States*

§ 10.10 —*Gulf Contracting, Inc.*

§ 10.11 —*Weaver-Bailey Contractors, Inc. versus United States*

§ 10.12 —*Williams Enterprises versus Strait Manufacturing & Welding, Inc.*

§ 10.13 The Major Cases and Issues

§ 10.14 —*Utley-James, Inc.*

§ 10.15 —*Haney versus United States*

§ 10.16 —The *Santa Fe* Decisions

§ 10.17 —*Ealahan Electric Co.*

§ 10.18 —*Titan Pacific Construction Corp. versus United States*

§ 10.19 State Recognition of CPM Principles

§ 10.1   Introduction

"Except in the middle of a battlefield, nowhere must men coordinate the movement of other men and all materials in the midst of such chaos and with such limited certainty of present facts and future occurrences as in a huge construction project."[1]

The weapon of choice for combatting such chaos on huge construction projects, and not so huge projects, has increasingly become the Critical Path Method (CPM) of scheduling project performance. Network analysis techniques such as the CPM were first introduced into the construction field in the early 1960s. The federal government now requires network analyses on most, if not all, major construction projects.[2]

Use of CPM techniques for planning and scheduling work has become the accepted standard in the construction industry for private contracts as well. Federal boards and courts have indicated their willingness to utilize network analysis techniques to identify delays and disruptions and their causes.[3] With the increased use of CPM techniques in scheduling, state courts are increasingly recognizing this tool in the scheduling process.[4]

This chapter briefly examines the basic principles of CPM techniques used in the construction industry for scheduling, delay analysis, and proof. The chapter then examines in detail significant decisions relating to CPM techniques from 1980 to 1990 and their impact on CPM principles. In addition, a survey of the use of CPM techniques in state actions from 1980 to 1990 is included.

§ 10.2   What Is CPM?

CPM techniques provide an efficient way of organizing and scheduling a complex project that consists of numerous interrelated separate small projects. Subprojects are identified and classified as to duration and precedence of the work. For example, an area cannot be carpeted until the flooring is in place and the flooring cannot be completed until the underlying electrical and telephone conduits are installed. The data is then analyzed, usually by computer, to determine the most efficient schedule for the entire project.

Subprojects can be performed at any time within a given period without any effect on the completion of the entire project. However, some items of work are given no leeway and must be performed on schedule or they will delay the entire project. Items that must be performed timely to prevent delay to the project are deemed to be on the "critical path." Delays or acceleration of work along the critical path will affect the entire project.[5]

---

[1] Blake Constr. Co. v. C.J. Coakley Co., 431 A.2d 569 (D.C. 1981).

[2] *See, e.g.,* FAR 36.515, 52.236-15.

[3] *See* Utley-James, Inc. v. United States, 14 Cl. Ct. 804 (1988); Santa Fe, Inc., GSBCA No. 2168, 87-3 B.C.A. (BNA) ¶ 20,104; Blackhawk Heating & Plumbing Co., GSBCA 2432-R, 76-1 B.C.A. (BNA) ¶ 11,649.

[4] See § **10.19.**

[5] Haney v. United States, 230 Ct. Cl. 148, 676 F.2d 584 (1982).

§ 10.3   Use of CPM for Delay Analysis and Contract Claims

The basic technique used to evaluate the CPM schedule for contract claims and delay analysis is to compare the as-planned CPM with the as-built CPM. After determining how construction of the project was planned, the comparison is then made by answering the following questions:

1. How is the project actually constructed?
2. What are the differences between the project as planned and as constructed with respect to activities, sequences, durations, manpower, and other resources?
3. What are the causes of the differences or variances between the project as planned and the actual performance?
4. Finally, what are the effects of the variances and activities, sequences, durations, manpower, and other resources, as they relate to the costs experienced by both the contractor and the owner?[6]

§ 10.4   Delay Claim Analysis

To prepare a CPM, initial determination of all activities necessary to complete the work in accordance with the plans and specifications must be made. Once identified, the interrelationship between the activities must be determined. Preparation of the original CPM and all subsequent analyses require determination of which activities must begin before others, which activities can be performed concurrently, and which activities must be completed before a separate activity is commenced.

Once project activities are plotted, the contract's "critical path" requires identifying time duration for various activities. Assessment of time durations required for activities requires consideration of resource loading, material and equipment needs and availability. A project's critical path is the longest chain (in terms of time) of interrelated activities through the diagram from the beginning to the end of the project.

The "critical chain of activities" takes the longest to complete. Accordingly, if one of the critical activities is delayed by one day and no pressure is applied to the

---

[6] For a more detailed discussion of the preparation and use of a CPM schedule in contract claims, see Wickwire & Smith, *The Use of Critical Path Method Techniques in Contract Claims,* 7 Pub. Cont. L.J. 1 (1974) and Wickwire, Hurlbut, & Lerman, *Use of Critical Path Method Techniques in Contract Claims: Issues and Development, 1974-1988,* 18 Pub. Cont. L.J. 338 (1989).

schedule or critical activity by resequencing, additional resource loading, or acceleration, the entire project will be delayed.

Certain activities are excluded from the critical path of performance because they contain excess time for performance, referred to as *float* or *slack*. A side-path activity that is not initially critical may become critical if its completion is a condition precedent to commencement or completion of an activity on the critical path. If the side-path activity requires more time than that allocated for normal completion and available float time for the activity, it will become critical because it will affect the completion of the activity on the critical path.

§ 10.5   —The Parameters

Performing a delay claim analysis requires examination of expenses resulting from an extended performance time. Examples of such expenses include: extended field expense, wage escalation, extended home office expense, and extended or standby equipment expenses. Longer project duration can result from a number of causes with responsibility attributable to the owner (suspensions of work or changes), the contractor (delayed submittals or labor inefficiency), or neither (strikes or acts of God).

Use of CPM in claim presentations permits visual and numerical segregation and identification of delays that are the direct responsibility of the different parties. The CPM claim presentation should also display the effect of these delays on project completion. Proving an extended duration claim requires a showing of when the contractor actually completed its work and when the contractor would have completed its work absent owner-caused delays. The difference in time represents the measure of delays. After giving credit for all excusable and noncompensable delays, the difference in dates determines when the contractor would have finished, absent owner-caused delays.

One method for proving a delay claim involves the preparation of four CPM schedules:

1. A reasonable as-planned CPM
2. An as-built CPM
3. An as-built CPM reflecting all delays—owner, contractor, and excusable and
4. An adjusted CPM to establish completion of the project absent owner delays.

Each CPM chart should be supplemented with analysis establishing that the data reflected meets CPM and any estimates contained therein are grounded in the actual records for the project.

§ 10.6 Acceleration Claim Analysis

Use of CPM diagrams and accompanying analysis to establish an acceleration requires preparation of the same four diagrams discussed in § **10.5**. Because acceleration claims focus primarily on the status of the project at the time of the acceleration order, all of the diagrams and analyses should highlight this point. Unlike the delay claim CPM, the adjusted CPM used in acceleration presentations should reflect not only delays that the owner is responsible for, but also all other excusable delays that would entitle the contractor to a time extension, such as strikes and unusually severe weather. Such delays are included because the contractor may be entitled to a time extension even where its own delay is concurrent with an owner-caused or other excusable delay.

The adjusted CPM for an acceleration claim seeks to demonstrate that at the time the acceleration directive was issued, the contractor's performance was on or ahead of a properly adjusted schedule. This requires identification and consideration of the effect of all excusable delays. Consideration of all such delays enables the contractor to prove that at the time of an owner's acceleration directive, the contractor was entitled to finish after the actual completion date or the date stated in the acceleration order.

The adjusted CPM for acceleration claims must take into account actual durations of activities as indicated on an as-built diagram and include any time extensions previously granted. Determining the total amount of excusable delay a contractor is entitled to requires consideration of any disruption and loss of productivity resulting from both excusable and compensable delays. Time extensions for a particular delay, therefore, should take into account not only delay to the operation immediately affected, but also any disruption delays to any subsequent operations.

§ 10.7 Loss of Productivity Analysis

CPM presentations can be used to prove loss of productivity. Approaches in conjunction with a CPM presentation can be used to prove the effect loss of productivity has on a contractor's performance. Such approaches include the development of engineering estimates, comparisons of disrupted versus undisrupted periods utilizing graphs, manpower costs, loaded CPMs, summary diagrams, and time-expand matrices.[7]

---

[7] *See* Wylie Bros. Contracting Co., IBCA No. 1175, 841 B.C.A. (BNA) ¶ 17,078 (where CPM analysis was relied on in conjunction with a productivity claim). In addition, the 1979 Corps of Engineers Modification Impact Evaluation Guide, EP 415-1-3, provides specific cost curves for performance problems such as acceleration, crowding, excess resource loading, and loss of morale. These costs curves can be utilized in conjunction with CPM impact analyses with respect to changes in sequence and durations and in developing documentation supporting the additional costs experienced by a contractor.

§ 10.8   The Decisions

The recognition and refinement of CPM in analyzing construction claims advanced greatly in the 1980s. The following cases, in the authors' opinion, represent landmark decisions that significantly advance the state of the law and answer key questions on the use of CPM analysis.

Fortec Constructors v. United States[8] stresses the requirement that the CPM diagram be current, accurate, and forward-looking.

Gulf Contracting, Inc.[9] demonstrates that a contractor must recognize the effect of its own delays in CPM analysis, and evaluate such delays contemporaneously, thereby rejecting the use of a hindsight approach.

Weaver-Bailey Contractors, Inc. v. United States[10] recognizes the availability of "float" to the contractor as a resource, and that the contractor's progress is to be evaluated as found at the inception of delay.

Williams Enterprises, Inc. v. Strait Manufacturing & Welding, Inc.[11] provides that prior delay is no bar to recovery if the delay does not affect the critical path as found at the time the project is impacted by a later delay, thus affirming the contemporaneous evaluation of delay and use of float as a project resource. The case also recognizes that a prime contractor may recover against a subcontractor that prevents its early completion as projected by the CPM, if the subcontractor agreed to adhere to the CPM.

§ 10.9   *—Fortec Constructors versus United States*

Because of the dynamic and ever-changing nature of a construction project, a CPM diagram must be dynamic and current to accurately portray contract performance and assess the impact of changes. In *Fortec*, the Claims court recognized that project control is lost if the CPM diagram is not properly updated to reflect delays and time extensions. Knowledge of the project's actual critical path is also vital for determining delay damages and proper time extensions due as a result of performance problems. As the court noted in *Fortec:*

> The reason that the determination of the critical path is crucial to the calculation of delay damages is that only construction work on the critical path had an impact on the time in which the project was completed. If work on the critical path was delayed, then the eventual completion date of the project was delayed. Delay involving work not on the critical path generally had no impact on the eventual completion date of the project.[12]

---

[8] 8 Cl. Ct. 490 (1985) [hereinafter *Fortec*].

[9] ASBCA Nos. 30195, 89-2 B.C.A. (BNA) ¶ 21,812, *on reconsid.*, 90-1 B.C.A. (BNA) ¶ 22,393 [hereinafter *Gulf*].

[10] 19 Cl. Ct. 474 (1990), *reconsid. denied*, 20 Cl. Ct. 158 (1990) [hereinafter *Weaver-Bailey*].

[11] 728 F. Supp. 12 (D.D.C. 1990) [hereinafter *Williams*].

[12] *Fortec* at 505 (quoting from G.M. Shupe, Inc. v. United States, 5 Cl. Ct. 662, 728 (1984)).

A CPM schedule used to evaluate delay on a project must be kept current and reflect delays as they occur. In *Fortec*, the CPM schedule was only updated once and did not consider delays in the work performed prior to or subsequent to the update. Because the critical path is subject to change, items not originally critical can become critical and items that were once critical may become no longer critical. Because there was no effort to keep the CPM in *Fortec* current, the critical path of performance was no longer an actual depiction of project progress.

The government in *Fortec* claimed the contractor was not entitled to a time extension because the additional work claimed did not appear on the critical path or the CPM schedule. In fact, the court found that the parties did not rely on the CPM to schedule the project or evaluate performance. Changes to the actual critical path of performance were not acknowledged and the government refused to grant the contractor timely and adequate time extensions. Based on this information, the court concluded that the CPM could not be used by the government to assert that a particular activity was critical or noncritical, on schedule or behind.

Because the changes in contract performance were not integrated into the CPM, it was impossible to determine which activities were on the critical path. Accordingly, the court rejected the government's attempt to rely on an incomplete CPM to bar recovery, noting that the "Corps failure to act in a timely fashion should not now be used as a sword against Fortec."[13] The court, recognizing that the utility of a CPM schedule requires that it be as dynamic as the project it is portraying, further noted:

> Reliance upon an incomplete and inaccurate CPM to substantiate denial of time extensions is clearly improper. While the contract states that the CPM shall be used to evaluate the impact on the contractor's work in determining the allowance of time extensions, it also states that the CPM to be so used must include time revisions. . . . Consequently, the contract requires the use of a properly revised and updated CPM to evaluate claims for time extensions.[14]

§ 10.10   — *Gulf Contracting, Inc.*

A CPM schedule can only be a useful tool to the extent that the as-planned schedule is modified and updated periodically to indicate actual changes to performance. In *Gulf*, the Armed Services Board of Contract Appeals considered approaches used by two consultants in compiling information for a claim. The claim arose from a contract for construction of a barracks complex for Fort Gordon, Georgia. The contractor's CPM expert provided a CPM presentation that compared a reconstructed as-planned schedule with an as-built schedule

---

[13] *Id*. at 506.

[14] *Id*.

and then adjusted the CPM schedule to reduce the durations of actual time taken for concrete and masonry work for those of the fastest concrete and masonry durations experienced in construction. The contractor's expert analyzed the impact of the owner's changes to the project by excluding all contractor disruptions from the project analysis.

On the other side, the government's expert developed a CPM evidenced by a chronological approach, starting with a reasonable as-planned schedule and then moving forward through the project chronologically, incorporating the time impacts into the schedule as they occurred on the project. Under the government expert's method, once a time impact was identified, the original schedule dates were revised to create an adjusted schedule incorporating the time impact. The adjusted schedule was then revised to incorporate the next chronological time impact. Thereafter, the project schedule was periodically updated to incorporate the new time impacts.

The board rejected the methodology used by the contractor's expert and accepted the presentation of the government's expert. The board reasoned that the government expert's methodology more accurately reflected the events that occurred during contract performance, stating as follows:[15]

> In support of its claim, Gulf relied on the analysis of its expert, Vinson. Vinson claimed to have performed an in-depth review of all correspondence and data pertinent to the progress of the project (Finding 81). If this was indeed the case, we do not believe that Vinson could have missed the well documented performance problems that existed between Gulf and Hughes. Vinson said that he was in-structed to "exclude other disruptions from the claim" (Finding 92). We have found that Vinson's analysis systematically excluded all delays and disruptions except those allegedly caused by the government (Finding 92). We conclude that his analysis was inherently biased, and could lead to but one predictable outcome. For all purposes therefore, we deem Vinson's analysis to be totally unreliable. To be credible, a contractor's CPM analysis ought to take into account, and give appropriate credit for all of the delays which were alleged to have occurred.[16]

On reconsideration, the board reaffirmed its rejection of the contractor's incomplete analysis, noting that the contractor must assume responsibility for all its faults during performance. The board noted:

> More plausible would have been for Vinson to assess against Gulf the longest masonry and concrete durations for each barracks. It was easy to gloss over Gulf's and Hughes' problems by shifting the focus to the contractor's best performance model, but we must be persuaded that Gulf has taken full responsibility for its faults, and that the government was only being asked to pay for what was its responsibility.[17]

---

[15] *Gulf* at 109, 758-109, 759.

[16] (citing Haney v. United States, 676 F.2d 584 (Ct. Cl. 1982); Pathman Constr. Co., ASBCA No. 23392, 85-2 B.C.A. (BNA) ¶ 18,096 (CPM analysis with "built in bias" rejected)).

[17] 90-1 B.C.A. (BNA) ¶ 22,393 at 112,521.

Gulf indicates that the preferred methodology in using CPM analysis in claims requires that delays and impacts on performance be viewed contemporaneously with their performance context. Accordingly, the government expert's methodology of evaluating delays to the project as they occur chronologically, commencing with the as-planned schedule and then moving forward to evaluate each delay through the various project updates, is the most accurate and preferred method of tracking and determining the impact of delays on a project.

§ 10.11   — *Weaver-Bailey Contractors, Inc. versus United States*

In *Weaver-Bailey,* the chief judge of the Claims Court provided us with a detailed exposition on float which implicitly recognizes the availability of float to the parties to the project for use as an expiring resource. This landmark decision further confirmed the increasing sophistication of the courts in working with CPM techniques.

Weaver-Bailey involved a contract for the construction of beaches, breakwaters, boat ramps, and other items improving the recreational areas surrounding Arcadia Lake in Oklahoma. The Corps of Engineers substantially underestimated the amount of excavation required under the contract, a fact that did not become evident until well into the project. Weaver-Bailey disrupted its work schedule and concentrated its efforts on completing the increased earthwork, as later tasks were dependent on the earthwork. The increased effort pushed the schedule into the winter months, when much of the required grading and sloping could not be undertaken. As a result, project completion was delayed, and Weaver-Bailey sought compensation for the delay.

The court in this case totally rejected the government's argument that the contractor's failure to prosecute work during earlier time frames when float was available excused the government from its responsibilities for changes resulting from the increased excavation required later in the project after the float had expired on the project.[18] The court provided an insightful essay on the meaning of "float" and its application:

> To reiterate, a critical path activity is one which, if allowed to grow in duration at all, will cause the overall time required to complete the project to increase. By contrast, an activity with float time may grow in duration up to a certain point, without an adverse impact on the time required to complete the project. Consider the example of a contractor who committed himself to building a house, beginning on January 1, 1989. The contractor has determined that he will need one year to complete the job. Pouring the foundation is a critical path activity because any increase in the amount of time required to complete the foundation will cause an increase in the amount of time needed to complete the house; work on the walls, floors, roof, and utilities cannot begin until the foundation is complete.

---

[18] *Weaver-Bailey* at 482.

Suppose that as part of the job, the contractor promised to build a fence along two edges of the property, and that building the fence will take 20 days. No other work depends upon the completion of the fence, so delaying the work on the fence until December 11, 1989 will not put the contractor in danger of late completion. In other words, building the fence is an activity with a lot of float time. However, float time is never unlimited. If on December 20 the contractor has yet to begin the fence, or if there is more than 11 days' worth of fencing work to be done as of December 20, then the contractor will not finish the job on time. From the foregoing, one can make the following generalization: regardless of whether an activity is on the critical path of a project, if the time required to complete the activity is greater than the time remaining to complete the project, then project completion will be delayed.

Consider now the effect on our hypothetical contractor if on December 1, before fencing work had begun, the buyer of the house told the contractor that he would like all four sides of the property to be fenced, thereby doubling the fencing work. Clearly the contractor could not complete the entire project by the end of the year, but through no fault of his own. The time required for the fencing portion of the job is now 40 days, and the contractor has only 31 days left. Weaver-Bailey was in much the same position as our hypothetical contractor when it discovered in October that the unclassified excavation portion of the project had increased. It was progressing toward a late November or early December completion, until the work was increased by 41%.[19]

The court then considered which party should be held responsible for delay when delay occurs after all float time is utilized:

Mr. Berkey's critical path analyses merely distract from defendant's real argument concerning the effect of the 41% underestimate of unclassified excavation. At trial, J.D. Stahlman testified that rip-rap replacement can and should follow closely behind unclassified excavation, in a technique known as phased construction. If this technique is used, the slope is protected from deterioration almost as soon as it is cut. Defendant seems to be arguing that Weaver-Bailey should have spent more time in the fall protecting the already-excavated areas from erosion, and less time trying to complete the unclassified excavation.

The court does not see how Weaver-Bailey can be faulted for the way it handled the unclassified excavation. The government does not even allege that plaintiff would not have completed the project by early December, in the absence of the 41% increase in unclassified excavation. Furthermore, the government does not allege that the contract required Weaver-Bailey to use the phased construction technique. The reason Weaver-Bailey did not use the phased construction technique from the outset is because it did not have to. It was not until early October that plaintiff had any indication that the earthwork portion of the project would be increased, and Mr. Stephenson, an experienced and successful earthwork contractor, had no reason to anticipate through the late summer and early fall that the slopes would need the protection from the effects of winter weather. Once the Corps' underestimate was revealed, Weaver-Bailey acted reasonably under the newly-imposed time

---

[19] *Id*. at 481.

constraints. Weaver-Bailey does not have unlimited resources, and it concentrated its manpower in the areas which it thought needed the earliest attention.[20]

The decision recognizes that the CPM analyses for delays must take the project as it finds it at the time that the delay is occurring. Thus, if a delay occurs when the project still has significant float available on the activities that have been delayed, no delay to the entire project is encountered and the party is not going to be charged for extending the project duration. However, if the delay pushes the activity onto the critical path and the entire project is extended, then the party responsible for that particular delay will be held to have proximately caused delays to the project.

§ 10.12   — *Williams Enterprises versus Strait Manufacturing & Welding, Inc.*

In *Williams,* the United States District Court for the District of Columbia considered the issue of the quantification of delays resulting from a structural collapse encountered during structural steel erection by a subcontractor on the modernization and construction of a new high school gym.

The court accepted the methodology provided by the prime contractor's expert that compared the planned completion of steel erection with the actual erection of the steel which was then checked against an analysis of the same period of delay by evaluating each period of delay chronologically in three phases. Under both methods, the length of project delay was determined to be the same.

The court next considered the subcontractor's defense of concurrent delay against the contractor's delay claim. The structural steel subcontractor responsible for the steel collapse on the project argued that a delay in approving structural steel shop drawings that occurred in the very first month of the project presented a concurrent delay with the delay caused by the collapse much later in the life of the project. The court, describing this particular argument as the assertion of "pre-collapse" issues, found that the owner's delays arising from late approval of shop drawings had no impact on the critical structural steel activities, as the steel erection began on the date scheduled for commencement. The court stated as follows:

(12) It is obvious that the critical path delay occurred from the date of the collapse until the steel was re-erected. Williams did not deny that this did not occur, but rather asserted that other events created a "concurrent delay." To avoid confusion, particular care is required in use of the word "concurrent." For example, Williams does not assert that it was delayed by Smoot or any other party in its work in erection of structural steel. Williams began work on August 13, 1984, and continued unimpeded until the day of the collapse. Further, no argument is made

---

[20] *Id.* at 481-82.

that any party interfered with the re-erection work; that process was completed on or about January 30, 1985. Thus, this delay was of Williams' making.

(13) Stated otherwise, Williams' defense of "concurrency" was that other events canceled out the delay resulting from the collapse and therefore absolved Williams of liability. These arguments are affirmative defenses and should be examined closely. Williams' arguments are best analyzed by dividing the project into three distinct periods: (1) pre-collapse issues; (2) the immediate impact period (September 25, 1984 to January 30, 1985); and (3) post-January 30 events. The Court concludes that the arguments are not meritorious.

(14) Williams pointed to delays in the approval of shop drawings for structural steel and shop drawings for precast fabrication which occurred in the first months of the Project. Both Williams and Strait argued strenuously that a delay in approval of structural steel shop drawings presented a concurrency with the delay caused by the collapse.

The testimony and evidence, however, is to the contrary. Structural steel erection could not begin until shop drawings had been completed and the structural erection began in fact on August 13, 1984. Williams continued unimpeded until the September 25 day of the collapse. Similarly, it is clear that any delays in approval of precast shop drawings had no impact on the beginning or performance of structural steel erection in the period prior to the collapse. Any delays of other parties prior to August 13 could not be charged to defendants. The Court finds that there was no "concurrent" delay in this period.[21]

Thus, the delay in approvals only impacted the available float time, and did not affect the work on the critical path. This decision is in accord with the principle that a party takes the project "as it finds it" at the inception of the delay. Earlier occurrences are unimportant in the context of evaluating a later delay at a later point of time. The key inquiry is the status of the project at the time it is impacted by the delay.

The *Williams* case is also important as it clearly breaks new ground by permitting the prime contractor to recover from a subcontractor that deprives the prime contractor of the ability to complete at a date earlier than the date specified in the contract with the owner. The prime contractor specifically consulted the subcontractors to verify the timing and duration of the sub-elements of their work and the subcontractor specifically agreed to be bound to the CPM scheduling requirements. Pertinent sections of the court's decision state:[22]

(3) Section 6 of the subcontract specifically provides that the subcontractor will prosecute the work efficiently and promptly; further, that subcontractor agrees to pay to the Contractor such other or additional damages as the Contractor may sustain by reason of delay by the Subcontractor. This provision is an express

---

[21] *Williams* at 16.

[22] *Id*. at 22-23.

statement of the generally recognized common law obligation of parties not to hinder or interfere with one another's performance.[23]

(4) In an action between private parties, it suffices to show that a subcontractor caused a substantial delay in performance, that the contract terms forbade such a delay, and that the plaintiff was injured as a result.[24] Smoot has proved each of these elements.

(5) The steel erection activity was an activity on the critical path of the Project. By definition, a delay to a critical path activity will result in a delay to the entire project resulting in compensable costs.[25]

(6) Smoot may properly commit its resources and those of its subcontractors to its projected CPM completion date—even if that date is earlier than the final date required by the contract with the owner—and may recover damages from a subcontractor which causes delay.[26]

Accordingly, *Williams* permits the prime contractor to recover from a subcontractor that prevents the prime from meeting its projected completion date, even if the date projected in the CPM is earlier than its contract completion date. It is important to note, however, that the subcontractor in *Williams* was consulted on, and agreed to, adherence to the CPM schedule.

§ 10.13   The Major Cases and Issues

During the 1980s the courts and boards have shown an increasing level of knowledge and sophistication in using CPM scheduling concepts to assist their decisions. A plethora of major CPM decisions by the boards of contract appeals and federal courts have demonstrated their acceptance of CPM as a preferred method of claim analysis. Below is a review of the major decisions.

§ 10.14   —*Utley-James, Inc.*

The significant level of understanding of CPM analysis that developed in the 1980s is evinced in the 1985 *Utley-James* decision. *Utley-James, Inc.*[27] provides

---

[23] (citing Fuller Co. v. United States, 69 F. Supp. 409, 411, 108 Ct. Cl. 70 (1947)). *See also* United States *ex rel.* Heller Elec. Co. v. Klingensmith, Inc., 670 F. 2d 1227 (D.C. Cir. 1982); Luria Bros. v. United States, 369 F.2d 701, 177 Ct. Cl. 676 (1966).

[24] (citing United States *ex rel.* Gray-Bar Elec. Co. v. J.H. Copeland & Sons, 568 F.2d 1159, 1160 (5th Cir. 1978); District Concrete Co. v. Bernstein Concrete, 418 A.2d 1030, 1038 (D.C. 1980)).

[25] (citing S. Siegfried, Introduction to Construction Law, Ch. 12 at 243 (ALI-ABA, 1987); Bramble & Callahan, Construction Delay Claims 9-10, 145 (1987)).

[26] (citing District Concrete Co. v. Bernstein, 418 A.2d 1030, 1038 (D.C. 1980); Grow Constr. Co. v. State, 56 A.D.2d 95, 391 N.Y.S.2d 726, 728 (1977); Canon Constr. Co., ASBCA 16142, 72-1 B.C.A. (BNA) ¶ 9404 (1972)).

[27] GSBCA No. 5370, 85-1 B.C.A. (BNA) ¶ 17,816.

an essay on CPM scheduling that includes consideration of such important concepts as the critical path, resource leveling, acceleration and buy-back time and recognizes the importance of the concepts in project scheduling:

> 17. These and other considerations affect the preparation of a CPM schedule. The way in which the schedule reflects these considerations is called the "logic" of the schedule. The closer the logic of the schedule is to reality, the better we say it is, and vice versa.

> 20. During job performance, CPM schedules are adjusted to reflect: (a) actual events in the performance of the contract and (b) contractual events in the form of time extensions. If the actual finish date of a given activity does not match the scheduled date, the schedule is adjusted to reflect actual finish, and the early start of all activities downstream from that one is adjusted accordingly. If delays pile up, as noted, early start dates can become later than late start dates. At this point, the float becomes negative and the job is behind schedule. As we have noted, one cure for this is to accelerate the performance of job activities, thereby pulling the early start dates back toward those originally scheduled and wringing out some of the negative float. The other solution, which again requires an adjustment to the CPM schedule, is to extend the time for completion. This makes the late start dates later and has the same sort of effect on negative float. If there is neither an extension of time nor an acceleration of performance, the negative float stays there, and it finally shows up at the end of the job as a late completion.[28]

In applying critical path methodology, the GSA board in *Utley-James* demonstrated a willingness to apportion or discriminate between concurrent delays to determine the actual delays to the critical path. The board specified that the finder of fact should not assess the contractor with responsibility for delays that would not have affected the critical path. Such instances arise where the contractor's progress is delayed on scheduled work not falling on the critical path. This circumstance of delay is appropriately called "why hurry up and wait." Consider the following passage:

> [S]trictly speaking, there can be but a single delay over a given period of time, and when that delay has multiple, indivisible causes, it is attributable not to either party but to both. Hence it would probably be more accurate to speak not of concurrent delays but of a single delay with concurrent causes. We note this even though, for convenience, we will use the standard terminology for the most part. . . . To take an easy example, if the job schedule was originally such that the contractor needed certain widgets on hand by January 1, but because of a six-month delay attributable to the Government, the contractor rescheduled the delivery for July 1, the Government cannot be heard to say the delays were concurrent because the contractor would have had to wait six months for the widgets anyway. In such a situation there is no reason to doubt that the contractor could have had the widgets on January 1 and proceeded on schedule absent the

---

[28] *Id*. at 89,062.

Government-caused delay. Such a simplistic example poses no problem at all. The problem lies not in reaching the right conclusion, given such an example, but in determining whether a given fact situation is an example of such an occurrence or is instead an example of a true concurrent delay.[29]

Consequently, where the government causes delays to the critical path, it is permissible for the contractor to relax its performance of non-critical work to the extent that it does not impact project completion. Based on *Utley-James,* we know that where the owner causes delays to the critical path, it is permissible for the contractor to relax its performance of non-critical work to the extent that it does not impact project completion (and still avoid the defense of concurrent delay).

This concept is the same basic principle as that presented in *Weaver-Bailey,* the Claims Court landmark decision on float. There the court found that the contractor had the right to plan its work in accordance with its own plans or reasonable resource usage (regardless of the fact that this utilized float).

§ 10.15   —*Haney versus United States*

The Court of Claims recognized the value of CPM in evaluating contractor claims in *Haney v. United States.*[30] This case involved the construction of a 450,000 square foot "build and lease" office construction project. A claim was brought by Haney, the developer, on behalf of its general contractor and subcontractors, seeking delay damages caused by ordered changes and late plan approvals. The claims utilized CPM analysis to demonstrate the effects of delay on overall job completion. The court noted its favor with the method, providing the following description of the CPM process:

> The normal construction procedure as anticipated by Haney was to start the construction, then finish the work from the bottom up in accordance with a "critical path method" (CPM) of construction. The government welcomed Haney's use of CPM as a planning and management tool. Essentially, the critical path method is an efficient way of organizing and scheduling a complex project which consists of numerous interrelated separate small projects. Each subproject is identified and classified as to duration and precedence of the work. (E.g., one could not carpet an area until the flooring is down and the flooring cannot be completed until the underlying electrical and telephone conduits are installed.) The date is then analyzed, usually by computer, to determine the most efficient schedule for the entire project. Many subprojects may be performed at any time within a given period without any effect on the completion of the entire project. However, some items of work are given no leeway and must be performed on

---

[29] *Utley-James,* 85-1 B.C.A. (BNA) at 89,109.

[30] 230 Ct. Cl. 148, 676 F.2d 584 (1982).

schedule; otherwise, the entire project will be delayed. These latter items of work are on the "critical path." A delay, or acceleration, of work along the critical path will affect the entire project.[31]

The court in *Haney* found that the original CPM was realistic, as the contractor periodically revised and updated the CPM schedule to reflect work in progress and account for delays. The board found that these computerized revisions reflected that the work could have been performed in accordance with that schedule but for the government-caused delays.[32]

The contractor's technical staff provided a technical analysis using the CPM schedule to establish a ten month impact and delay on job performance. The contractor used this CPM analysis at trial to show the cumulative effect of each delay. While the government disputed liability, it conceded that the contractor's CPM methodology was acceptable and the events described would cause a delay to the job's critical path as demonstrated by CPM analysis. The court noted:

> The CPM analysis of delay presented on behalf of plaintiff took into account, and gave appropriate credit for all of the delays which were alleged to have occurred, including the results of plaintiff's acceleration by expediting equipment and materials, working out-of-sequence, weather delays, and the strike by the operating engineers. (Haney did not seek compensation for the latter event.)[33]

The *Haney* decision emphasized that the CPM schedule needs to be continually updated to provide accurate proof of the effect of delays in changes and its effect on the entire project, with adequate notation of the precipitating causes of these interruptions in the schedule as planned. By applying the CPM analysis, the court reached the conclusion that the delays were caused by the government's actions, thus entitling Haney to delay damages, and excusing Haney's late delivery of the premises for occupancy.

§ 10.16 —The *Santa Fe* Decisions

A preference for contemporaneous evaluation of the effects of delay upon the project schedule is illustrated in the two *Santa Fe* cases before the Veterans Administration's Board of Contract Appeals.

In the first case, *Santa Fe, Inc.*,[34] the contractor sought time extensions and corresponding remissions of liquidated damages for various change orders issued by the Veterans Administration in connection with the construction of a VA replacement hospital. The board considered a VA clause that required delays

---

[31] 676 F.2d at 595.

[32] *Id.*

[33] *Id.* at 595-96.

[34] VABCA No. 1943, 84-2 B.C.A. (BNA) ¶ 17,341.

to be evaluated in connection with the current CPMs to determine if the delays affected the "extended and predicted" completion dates for the contract. The clause's procedures required the VA to process monthly updated job reports and generate computerized cost and schedule reports necessary for monitoring job progress, while placing responsibility on the contractor for the accurate and timely submittal of updated reports and CPM data necessary to produce the cost and schedule reports. The VA utilized these current updates to evaluate the effect of delays for purposes of its presentation to the board. The board implicitly approved the use of current CPM updates to evaluate delays:

> At best, Appellant has shown only that the change orders "could have delayed" the contract completion work. The available CPM data and narrative reports which are based on information submitted by the Contractor not only fail to support Appellant's claim that the change orders extended its contract completion date, but demonstrate to the contrary because of available float time that they had no adverse impact on the Contractor's predicted contract completion date. . . .

> Nor do we find merit in Appellant's contention that because some of the change orders (i.e., VABCA-1943-45) were issued after the scheduled contract completion date it is automatically entitled to a time extension because all such work becomes "critical" or because the CPM provisions are inapplicable in such situations.

> We observe first that NAS-13.A provides that delays which "do not affect the extended and predicted contract completion dates shown by the critical path in the network will not be the basis for a change to the contract completion date."

> It should be acknowledged, however, that Boards generally appear ready to give a contractor the benefit of the doubt in liquidated damages cases which involve changes ordered after the scheduled completion date. But no close question is presented in these appeals where the parties agreed to use a sophisticated CPM network analysis which reflects available float time, and where the appellant has offered little evidence that the change orders extended its performance period.[35]

Any doubts that remained after the 1984 *Santa Fe* decision on whether the VA board would look to CPM updates that are current at the time delays occurred in evaluating the effect of such delays on the critical path were removed in a 1987 decision under the same contract.[36] The relevant provisions in the contract required use of current updates to evaluate delays.[37] The board discussed the need to use contemporaneous CPMs to measure delays, stating:

> Nor will we totally disregard the October CPM in favor of the November CPM, as the Government suggests, notwithstanding that significant revisions to the CPM were mutually effected by the parties in November 1981. We do not find that the November revisions were necessary to "correct" the October CPM. Rather, the November CPM merely reflected a different plan for further prosecution of the

---

[35] *Id*. at 86,411-412.

[36] Santa Fe, Inc., VABCA No. 2168, 87-3 B.C.A. (BNA) ¶ 20,104.

[37] *Id*. at 101,749.

work which differed from the previous plan. However, the adoption of an alternate method of performance in the later CPM does not, of itself, contradict the existence of a delay as shown in the preceding CPM. There is a rebuttable presumption of correctness attached to CPM's upon which the parties have previously mutually agreed. In the absence of probative evidence, not present in this appeal, that the delay shown was not in fact sustained we will rely on the October CPM for the period it was in effect, i.e., through the end of November 1981. For the subsequent period, we will rely on the November CPM. To put it another way, in the absence of compelling evidence of actual errors in the CPM's, we will let the parties "live or die" by the CPM applicable to the relevant time frames.

Thus, we will apply the October CPM to the eleven-day period from the time the suspension commenced, November 19, 1981, until November 30, 1981, at which time the November CPM became effective. Under the earlier October CPM, the suspended AHU work was critical and we find that the first eleven days of the suspension entitles the Contractor to an eleven-day extension to the contract completion date. Under the November CPM, the balance of the suspension applied to non-critical work and no time extension is warranted.[38]

This decision underscores the importance of using current CPM updates as reference points during the life of the project to assess the location of the critical path and amount of float available for specific activities. The contractor may successfully pursue delay claims for periods that exceed the number of days project completion was actually extended beyond the contract completion date. This principle appears to apply even where the contractor meets the scheduled completion date.

§ 10.17   — *Ealahan Electric Co.*

The use of CPM in analyzing claims involving concurrent delay is illustrated in *Ealahan Electric Co.*[39] The contractor sought a time extension for its renovation work at an existing Coast Guard facility at the Montauk Station. The board rejected the CPM analyses of both the government CPM expert and the contractor's CPM expert. The contractor's expert was faulted for failing to consider Ealahan's actual performance in the development of its analysis:

> [H]e solely considered the impact of various change orders on Ealahan's completion schedule, without regard to the actual performance of appellant of the original contract work. . . . In other words, this witness took the critical activities from Ealahan's progress schedule and added the time it actually took Ealahan to perform the Coast Guard change, beginning with the date of each request for proposal. . . . According to appellant, by using this method the appellant would

---

[38] *Id*. at 101,760.

[39] 1990 DOT BCA Lexis 31 (July 27, 1990).

retain the benefit of any float built into the original schedule. This method did not take into account Ealahan's own delays during performance.[40]

In addition, the board also rejected the analysis of the Government expert because of similar deficiencies. Like the contractor, the owner's analysis failed to consider the impact of the client's delays to the project. The board stated:

> We reject the analysis of both appellant's and respondent's experts. Mr. Stoker, for appellant, failed to consider the impact of Ealahan's own delays on the completion date. This must be considered as Ealahan is not entitled to a time extension if it delayed performance during the same period of time that Coast Guard actions delayed work. Mr. Beach's analysis is rejected because his analysis failed to consider the impact of the Coast Guard changes on actual performance. Further, Mr. Beach did not consider actual periods of time during which Ealahan delayed performance, but instead rounded any delay by Ealahan into weekly periods.[41]

The board also faulted Ealahan's evidence as to the actual amount it spent on each change, as it attempted to simply add up the time taken for each change, not accounting for overlapped periods during which the changes were performed. The court stated:

> Since the work on many changes was performed at the same time, Ealahan is entitled to a time extension only from the date the first change impacted its performance, to the day the final change was completed. In other words where two or more changes are performed during the same time, a contractor is only entitled to a contract extension for the calendar time taken in performing the changes, absent evidence of acceleration.[42]

In addition to accounting currently for current delays, the contractor must also demonstrate that the government-caused delay fell upon the critical path.

The board considered an argument presented by the defendants to the effect that certain delays that occurred in an earlier time frame in the project were the basis for offsetting concurrences for delays encountered in later time frames of the project.

The board deemed invalid this attempt to move delays from one time frame to another, stating in pertinent part:

> Certain of the delays caused by Ealahan occurred in an earlier time frame than the change orders issued by the Coast Guard. Such delays are not concurrent. Though Ealahan may have delayed completion by its actions early in the project, we find that these delays are independent of delays caused by the Coast Guard in a later time period. A contractor is entitled to a time extension for government-caused delays although it also has delayed performance, where such delays have occurred

---

[40] *Id*. at 128.

[41] *Id*. at 131.

[42] *Id*. at 132.

in a different time period than the government-caused delays, assuming the actions delayed the job completion.[43]

Thus, although Ealahan had caused earlier delays affecting the critical path, those which were not concurrent with the Coast Guard delays did not affect its right to a time extension for the Coast Guard's delays. This decision affirms the modern trend favoring contemporaneous evaluation of time in CPM analysis.

§ 10.18   — *Titan Pacific Construction Corp. versus United States*

In *Titan Pacific Construction Corp. v. United States,*[44] the court rejected a "like-time" analysis of delay for failure to attribute the cause of delay among the parties. The Claims Court decision concerned a Naval contract for the relocation of ordinance facilities in the State of Washington. The work involved the construction of several new buildings, a reservoir, and extensive roadwork and earthwork. The work was to be performed in three phases. The contractor at the inception of performance provided the owner with an as-planned CPM which was then corrected and approved.

The contractor, in its presentation to the Board of Contract Appeals, attempted to avoid the effect of liquidated damages which had been assessed against its performance. In its presentation, the contractor sought to substantially revise the as-planned schedule to adjust it for wet and dry season restraints, to provide a much later projected completion date. In addition, in providing the analysis of the impact of delays upon the approved as-planned schedule or the adjusted as-planned schedule for what the expert described as "like-time" analysis, the contractor's expert totally failed to take into account the actual activities occurring on the project and the contractor's responsibility for the durations of the activities which occurred on the project. The Claims Court decision stated the following:

> Plaintiff's "like-time" argument assumes that the final approved as-planned CPM network delineates procedures that are fixed and contractually binding without regard to actual operations on the project. The approved CPM network diagram is an administrative tool that is useful in organizing and directing work, reporting progress, and for requesting progress payments for work accomplished. Analyses made after project completion, however, that make adjustments to attain new and revised projected scheduling depend on theoretical contingencies. They are of limited value.
>
> Plaintiff's delay/impact claims expert did not present a comparison of either the October 17, 1977 as-planned schedule, or his as-planned schedule adjusted for wet

---

[43] *Id.* at 133.

[44] 17 Cl. Ct. 630 (1989), *aff'd without opinion,* 899 F.2d 1227 (1990).

and dry season restraints, with actual activities on the project as-built schedule. The Board had before it the records that reflect actual field operations and was in a position to relate the as-built schedule to the expert's theoretically adjusted as-planned schedule.

Plaintiff's calculations in application of its "like-time" theory disregard the facts found by the Board as to the sequence of work, the quality of work, and the effects of weather on the Phase III work in the years 1977, 1978 and 1979. The calculations reflect a theoretical application to a CPM as-planned schedule that was not intended to be followed. The calculations disregard the facts that actually existed in the on-site operations.[45]

Thus, in *Titan Pacific,* the Claims Court once again affirmed its preference for delay analysis that reflects the status of the project at the time of delay impact and addresses the impact of all causes of delay.

§ 10.19   State Recognition of CPM Principles

The state courts have yet to develop the degree of sophisticated CPM analysis currently possessed by the federal courts and boards of contract appeals. However, the widespread recognition of CPM as a valuable tool of construction claim analysis is evident by the numerous state court opinions employing critical path evaluations of contractor claims. The following briefly summarizes examples of these opinions:

Connecticut.   In *Walter Kidde Constructors, Inc. v. State,*[46] the court utilized CPM in examining the causes of delay and calculating damages.

District of Columbia.   In *Blake Construction Co. v. C.J. Coakley Co.,*[47] the court evaluated the contractor's performance by comparison with a CPM.

Florida.   In *Florida Power Corp. v. Cresse,*[48] the court discounted the use of a post-construction CPM, as it failed to address causation or enable as-planned comparison.

Indiana.   In *Attlin Construction, Inc. v. Muncie Community Schools,*[49] the court recognized the usefulness of CPM in construction management.

---

[45] *Id.* at 637-38.

[46] 37 Conn. Supp. 50, 434 A.2d 962 (1981).

[47] 431 A.2d 569 (D.C. 1981).

[48] 413 So. 2d 1187 (Fla. 1982).

[49] 413 N.E.2d 281 (Ind. Ct. App. 1980).

Michigan.　In *Walter Toebe & Co. v. Department of State Highways,*[50] although the contractor commenced work late, the court utilized the CPM to find the delay reasonable, as it did not impact the critical path.

In *Walter Toebe & Co. v. Yeager Bridge & Culvert Company,*[51] the court used a critical path diagram to gauge delayed delivery dates and found those not on the critical path not to be "late." The court also used the CPM to date contractual milestones and measure the period of delay.

New Jersey.　In *American Sanitary Sales Co. v. State Department of Treasury,*[52] the court remanded the case to locate CPM data for assistance in determining delay damages.

In *Utica Mutual Insurance Co. v. DiDonato,*[53] the court briefly described the function of CPM and noted the failure of the contractor to keep the CPM current.

In *Broadway Maintenance Corp. v. Rutgers,*[54] the contractors on a multi-prime contract agreed to adhere to a CPM, and the court recognized basic CPM principles.

In *P.T.&L. Construction Co. v. State Department of Transportation,*[55] the court recognized the CPM process and its usefulness.

Ohio.　In *Mount Olivet Baptist Church, Inc. v. Mid-State Builders, Inc.,*[56] the court recognized that construction delays can occur on two paths, those critical and those not, and the effect of the delay changes accordingly.

---

[50] 144 Mich. App. 21, 373 N.W.2d 233 (1985).

[51] 150 Mich. App. 386, 389 N.W.2d 99 (1986).

[50] 187 N.J. Super. 30, 453 A.2d 559 (App. Div. 1982).

[52] 178 N.J. Super. 429, 429 A.2d 403 (App. Div. 1981).

[53] 187 N.J. Super. 30, 453 A.2d 559 (App. Div. 1982).

[54] 90 N.J. 253, 447 A.2d 906 (N.J. 1982).

[55] 108 N.J. 539, 531 A.2d 1330 (N.J. 1987).

[56] No. 84AP-363, slip op. (Ohio Ct. App., October 31, 1985).

PART III

DESIGN PROFESSIONALS' LIABILITY

ADMINISTRATIVE, REGULATORY, AND REGISTRATION PROCEEDINGS INVOLVING DESIGN PROFESSIONALS

David J. Hatem*

§ 11.1   Introduction

§ 11.2   Case Study

GENERAL DISCUSSION AND BACKGROUND

§ 11.3   OSHA Proceedings

§ 11.4   Board of Registration Proceedings

§ 11.5   —Kansas City Hyatt Case

§ 11.6   Civil Actions Arising Out of Construction Accidents

IMPACT OF DETERMINATIONS IN ADMINISTRATIVE AND REGISTRATION PROCEEDINGS ON SUBSEQUENT CIVIL LIABILITY

§ 11.7   Issue Preclusion Generally

§ 11.8   Issue Preclusion in Case Study

§ 11.9   Admission of Findings into Evidence

§ 11.10   Effect of Professional Practice Standards

§ 11.11   Guidelines

* This chapter is adapted from a paper presented in May 1990 to the 29th Annual Meeting of Invited Attorneys sponsored by AIA, NSPE, and Victor O. Schinnerer & Company.

§ 11.1 Introduction

This chapter explores in the context of a case study the relationship between and potential impact of administrative, regulatory, and/or registration proceedings involving design professionals on the adjudication of their liability in subsequent civil actions arising out of the same acts, errors, or omissions which gave rise to the prior proceedings.

This subject is important and timely in view of the ever-increasing number, frequency, and different types of administrative/registration proceedings which are being initiated against design professionals by, for example, the Department of Labor and state boards of registration which involve complaints against design professionals based upon acts, events, or circumstances which may also result in (1) the commencement of civil actions for damages against the design professional for claims arising out of the same acts, events or circumstances, and/or (2) some preclusive effect or other impact on the ability of the design professional to defend or otherwise contest in a subsequent civil action some or all of the issues which were in controversy and actually, necessarily, and finally determined in the prior administrative or registration proceeding.

This chapter discusses these issues in the context of a case study involving administrative proceedings which may be initiated against design professionals by the Department of Labor involving alleged violations of the Occupational Safety and Health Act of 1970 (OSHA)[1] and by state boards of registration responsible for the regulation and disciplining of design professionals.

§ 11.2 Case Study

The application and interaction of these concepts may be demonstrated by the following case study:

An owner engaged a design professional to provide architectural and engineering services in connection with the design and construction of a multi-story office building (the Project). The owner engaged Careless Construction as general contractor for the Project and, in turn, Careless engaged a number of subcontractors to do the specialty trade work required for the construction of the Project. The agreement between the owner and the design professional contained provisions equivalent to those found in AIA B141-1987 ¶¶ 2.6.5, 2.6.6, and 2.6.12. The general conditions of the construction contract between the owner and Careless contained the provisions equivalent to those found in AIA A201-1987 ¶¶ 3.3.1, 4.2.2, and 4.2.3.

Section 1.04 of Section 03300, Cast-in-Place Concrete, incorporated by reference the American Concrete Institute's Classifications for Structural Concrete for Buildings.[2] Chapter 4, Form Work, provide that "[t]he design and

---

[1] 29 U.S.C. §§ 651-678.

[2] ACI 301-84.

engineering of the form work, as well as a construction, shall be the responsibility of the Contractor."[3] That same chapter require that "[s]hop drawings for form work including the location of shoring and reshoring shall be submitted for review as required by the contract documents."[4]

On January 2, 1990, Careless sent to the design professional a submittal which was stamped by a registered professional engineer and set forth the design for the temporary form work for the concrete to be placed on the project. The design professional reviewed and approved the submittal on January 4, 1990. On January 5, 1990, during the first pour of the concrete, the temporary form work gave way resulting in injuries to six construction workers. No representative of the design professional firm was on site at the time of the accident and no employee of the design professional firm was injured in the accident.

The local building inspector immediately issued a cease work order. On January 8, 1990, an inspector from the Occupational Health and Safety Administration (the Agency) arrived at the site and began taking statements from various individuals, including the structural engineer employed by the design professional firm who reviewed and approved the temporary concrete form work submittal and was also responsible for performing periodic site visits, as required by the agreement between the owner and design professional firm.

The Department of Labor issued citations against Careless, some of its subcontractors, and, the design professional firm. The citations against the design professional firm alleged violations[5] on the basis that "the temporary concrete form work was not designed, erected, supported/braced and maintained so that it was capable of supporting without failure all vertical and lateral loads that were applied to it" and, further, upon the grounds that the design professional firm "was negligent in the supervision of construction work." After an unsuccessful attempt to resolve the citations through an informal conference with the Agency, the Department of Labor commenced an OSHA action against the design professional firm based upon the same complaints set forth in the citations previously issued against that firm.

Shortly thereafter, the six injured construction workers commenced civil actions against, among others, the design professional firm seeking recovery of damages due to alleged negligence of the design professional firm in (1) the design of the temporary concrete form work and (2) the supervision of construction means, methods, procedures, techniques and sequences. In addition, one of the injured construction workers filed a complaint with the state board of registration for architects and engineers alleging gross negligence, incompetency and unprofessional conduct of the design professional in the performance of services on the Project.

While the civil actions were pending, an administrative law judge, after a trial in the OSHA action, adjudicated in the form of specific findings of fact and

---

[3] *Id*. at § 4.21.

[4] *Id*. at § 4.1.4.

[5] 29 C.F.R. 1926.703(a)(1).

conclusions of law, that the design professional firm was negligent in the design of the temporary concrete form work and in the supervision of construction and that the latter negligence was a contributing factor of the collapse which occurred and resulted in the injuries to the construction workers.

While the civil actions were pending, the board of registration, after conducting an adjudicatory hearing, determined that fines should be imposed upon the design professional firm due to its gross negligence and incompetency in the design of the temporary concrete form work and in the supervision of construction. In making its determination, the board was especially impressed by a standard of practice manual which counsel for the board introduced into evidence and which generally and unqualifiedly stated that an architect/engineer of record on a project may not delegate to a contractor responsibility for the design of "any component" of a project. In addition, conflicting expert testimony as to the standard of care required under the circumstances was introduced during the course of the board hearing.

In the civil actions, counsel for the respective construction workers filed motions for summary judgment against the design professional firm[6] on the basis that the design professional firm should be precluded from contesting (relitigating) its negligence with respect to (1) the design of the temporary concrete form work and (2) the supervision of construction, on the basis of (1) the findings of fact and conclusions of law of the administrative law judge in the OSHA action and (2) the determination of the board of registration.

GENERAL DISCUSSION AND BACKGROUND

§ 11.3   OSHA Proceedings

In the last two years, the Department of Labor has more aggressively initiated and pursued complaints against design professionals in the context of a variety of alleged acts or omissions involved in construction accidents.[7] As a general matter, OSHA was enacted by Congress to encourage employers and employees in their efforts to reduce the number of occupational safety and health hazards at their places of employment, and "to stimulate employers and employees to institute new and to perfect existing programs for providing safety and helpful working conditions."[8] OSHA requires an employer to "furnish to each of *his*

---

[6] Pursuant to Fed. R. Civ. P. 56.

[7] Korman, *OSHA Testing Designers Over Role at the Jobsite,* ENR, Apr. 27, 1989, at p. 13; M. Lunch, Architect and Engineer Exposure For Project Safety: A Relatively New Hazard, Guidelines For Improving Practice, Volume XXII No. 1 (Victor O. Schinnerer & Company, 1990).

[8] 29 U.S.C. § 651(b)(i).

employees employment and a place of employment which are free from recognized hazards that are causing or likely to cause death or serious physical harm to *his employees*" and to "comply with Occupational Safety and Health standards promulgated under this chapter."[9]

The secretary of labor is authorized[10] to issue a citation to an employer who, after inspection or investigation, is believed to have violated a requirement of § 654 or any standards and regulations promulgated pursuant to OSHA. Pursuant to OSHA, the secretary has promulgated regulations regulating health and safety standards in the construction industry.[11]

The secretary is authorized to commence enforcement proceedings against persons alleged to have violated OSHA. The Occupational Safety and Health Review Commission (the Commission) has promulgated Rules of Procedure of the Occupational Safety and Health Review Commission (the Rules).[12] The Rules provide for the service and filing of complaints[13] and answers[14] and motions,[15] and for a broad range of traditional discovery, i.e., document requests and inspections, requests for admissions and interrogatories,[16] and for depositions "by agreement of all the parties, or on order of the Commission or Judge following the filing of a motion of a party stating good and just reasons."[17]

The Rules provide for a "fair and impartial hearing" before an administrative law judge "to assure that the facts are fully elicited, to adjudicate all issues and avoid delay."[18] The parties have the right to cross-examine witnesses and have other procedural and evidentiary rights[19] which normally exist in the civil trial setting.[20] The parties may file, at the close of the hearing, proposed findings of fact and conclusions of law.[21] The decision of the administrative law judge "shall be in writing and shall include findings of fact, conclusions of law, and the

---

[9] 29 U.S.C. § 654(a) (emphasis added).

[10] Pursuant to U.S.C. § 658(a).

[11] *See generally* 29 C.F.R. §§ 1910.12, 1926. These regulations apply to employers and employees engaged in "construction work" which is defined as "work for construction, alteration, and/or repair." 29 C.F.R. 1926.12(b).

[12] 29 C.F.R. pts. 2200 and 2204. § 22.2 (b) of the Rules provides that, in the absence of a specific provision in the rules, the procedure shall be in accordance with the Federal Rules of Civil Procedure.

[13] 29 C.F.R. § 2200.35.

[14] *Id.* § 2200.36.

[15] *Id.* § 2200.40.

[16] *Id.* § 2200.52(a)(i).

[17] *Id.* § 2200.56(a).

[18] *Id.* § 2200.67.

[19] The Federal Rules of Evidence apply. 29 C.F.R. § 2200.71.

[20] *See, e.g.,* 29 C.F.R. §§ 2200.69 (examination of witnesses), 2200.70 (admission of exhibits), 2200.71 (evidentiary rules), and 2200.72 (procedure for objections).

[21] *Id.* § 2200.74.

reasons or bases for them, on all the material issues of fact, law or discretion presented in the record."[22]

A party adversely affected or aggrieved by the decision of the administrative law judge may seek review by the Commission by the filing of a petition for discretionary review.[23] However, review by the Commission is not a matter of right.[24] In those situations in which the Commission does not direct review of the administrative law judge's decision, the judge's decision becomes a final order of the Commission thirty days after it has been filed. In either event—by a final order of the judge or by written decision of the Commission upon granting direct review—further appeal may be taken to a United States Court of Appeals.

Until recently, the Department of Labor had not typically initiated citations or proceedings against design professionals with any degree of frequency in circumstances arising out of construction accidents. The case law on the subject of design professionals and OSHA is relatively sparse.[25] More recently, the Department has taken a far more aggressive stance in the initiation and prosecution of complaints against design professionals.[26]

§ 11.4   Board of Registration Proceedings

The legislatures of the various states have enacted statutes which generally regulate and establish criteria and standards for the practice of architecture and

---

[22] *Id.* § 2200.90(a).

[23] *Id.* § 2200.91(b).

[24] *Id.* § 2200.91(a).

[25] *See generally* Secretary of Labor v. Skidmore, Owings & Merrill, 5 O.S.H. Cas. (BNA) 1762 (1977) (the Commission held that an architectural and engineering firm that was responsible for observing the work of contractors was not engaged in "construction work" and therefore was not subject to construction industry standards of 29 C.F.R. § 1926); Secretary of Labor v. Kaiser Eng's Inc., 6 O.S.H. Cas. (BNA) 1473 (1978) (The Commission vacated the citations for various construction safety violations at a nuclear power plant construction site because the engineering firm's own employees were not exposed to a hazard at the jobsite and the firm did not have supervisory control or authority over the contractors or the physical progress of the construction work.); Bertrand Goldberg Assocs., 4 O.S.H. Cas. (BNA) 1587 (1977) (the Commission held that the architect/construction manager at a multi-employer worksite was an "employer" within the meaning of 29 U.S.C. § 652(5) since as manager of the project there existed a duty to see that the builders complied with the terms of their contract which included matters of safety, and that the construction manager had the authority to stop the work if the circumstances warranted); Evans v. Lockwood-Greene Eng's, Inc., 13 O.S.H. Cas. (BNA) 1985 (1988) (the Commission granted a motion for summary judgment in favor of a construction manager/architect at a multi-employer worksite in the absence of a duty owed under the contract documents to provide a safe working environment or assumed by the construction manager/architect's independent actions).

[26] M. Lunch, Architect and Engineer Exposure For Project Safety: A Relatively New Hazard, Guidelines For Improving Practice, Volume XXII No. 1 (Victor O. Schinnerer & Company, 1990).

engineering.[27] These statutes typically define criteria and standards for admission to the practice of the architectural and engineering professions, but also provide standards for the regulation and control of post-admission practice standards, compliance with those standards, and the imposition of sanctions or other appropriate disciplinary action based upon a finding that those standards have been violated.

Many of these regulatory statutes authorize disciplinary action on the grounds of "gross negligence," "incompetency," "unprofessional conduct," and/or "misconduct" in the practice of the profession.[28] Typically, the statutes do not define the terms "unprofessional conduct," "gross misconduct," "gross negligence," or "incompetence" and, in determining whether to impose disciplinary action on those grounds, administrative tribunals generally will consider evidence as to the standard of care prevailing in the profession and reasonably required under the circumstances. Expert testimony and recognized (published) professional practice standards or ethical codes are certainly and typically considered relevant in this regard.

Generally speaking, these statutes provide for (or authorize) adjudicatory-type hearings before an administrative tribunal in the first instance, with "substantial evidence" review of fact findings and a broader review of "legal" determinations or rulings of the administrative tribunal. Typically, the adjudicatory-type hearing provides for various procedural opportunities and safeguards, including the right to call and cross-examine witnesses, the right to submit rebuttal evidence, the requirement that the administrative determination be based "on the record" of the proceeding, and that the decision be in writing and include a statement of reasons for the decision (including determinations of each subsidiary factual and legal issue necessary to the ultimate, final decision).[29] In the latter regard, the relevant Massachusetts statute and case law require that the administrative tribunal make such specific, clear and definitive subsidiary findings of fact as may be warranted by the evidence in the record.[30]

The penalties and sanctions generally available to a registration board include reprimands, license suspension and license revocation. In reviewing a decision of a registration board, a court will generally not reverse the decision in the absence of some determination that the decision was unsupported by the

---

[27] *See generally* J. Sweet, Legal Aspects of Architecture, Engineering, and the Construction Process, Chapter 13 (4th ed. 1989).

[28] *See generally* Wright v. State Bd. of Eng'g Examiners, 250 N.W.2d 412 (Iowa 1977); Annotation, *Revocation or Suspension of License to Practice Architecture,* 58 A.L.R. 3d 543, § 6 (1974); Annotation, *Revocation or Suspension of License of Professional Engineer,* 64 A.L.R. 3d 509, § 4 (1975).

[29] *See, e.g.,* Mass. Gen. L. ch. 30A, § 11.

[30] *Id.* § 11(8); Costello v. Department of Pub. Utils., 391 Mass. 527, 462 N.E.2d 301 (1984).

evidence, arbitrary or capricious, or that the board exceeded its statutory or constitutional authority.[31]

§ 11.5 —Kansas City Hyatt Case

The decision of the Missouri Court of Appeals in *Duncan v. Missouri Board for Architects, Professional Engineers & Land Surveyors,*[32] which affirmed disciplinary action imposed by a Missouri registration board on the structural engineers involved in the design of the Hyatt Regency Hotel in Kansas City, is illustrative in this regard.[33] The background and holding of the *Duncan* case provides a useful context to demonstrate the relationship and potential impact of findings and determinations in registration proceedings upon the adjudication of the civil liability of a design professional in subsequent civil litigation.

The *Duncan* case involved an appeal from a determination of the Missouri Board for Architects, Professional Engineers and Land Surveyors (the Board) revoking the licenses of certain structural engineers involved in the design of the walkways for the Hyatt Regency Hotel in Kansas City which collapsed on July 17, 1981, killing 114 people and injuring many other persons. A Commission of the Board conducted an adjudicatory proceeding which involved 27 days of hearings. The Commission received substantial testimony, and the parties (the Board and the engineers) were afforded rights of examination and cross-examination of the various witnesses, as well as other rights typically afforded in a civil litigation.

After the hearings concluded, the Commission issued its 442-page "Statement of the Case, Findings of Fact, Conclusions of Law and Decision" and found that one of the engineers had committed: (1) "gross negligence" in the preparation of a structural drawing and in failing to review shop drawings, and (2) "misconduct" in misrepresenting to the architect the safety of a certain double hanger rod-box beam connection. Furthermore, the Commission found the second engineer to have engaged in: (1) "gross negligence" in failing to personally review or assure that someone had reviewed a certain structural drawing prior to his affixing his seal to that drawing; (2) "unprofessional conduct" in failing and refusing to take responsibility for the entire engineering project; and (3)

---

[31] *See, e.g.,* Maiman v. Allen, 295 N.Y.S. 2d 760 (1968); Lorance v. Colorado Bd. of Examiners of Architecture, 35 Colo. App. 177, 532 P.2d 382 (1974).

[32] 744 S.W.2d 524 (Mo. Ct. App. 1988).

[33] For general commentary on the Hyatt Regency case, see Jackson & Kaskell, *The K.C. Hyatt Regency Disaster: What Went Wrong,* 56 Def. L. J. 415 (No. 4 Oct. 1988); Hatem, *Impact of Professional Practice Standards on Liability of Engineers,* 5 J. of Mgmt. in Eng'g 249 (No. 3 July 1989).

"misconduct" for his failure to perform a review of the Hyatt atrium design following specific requests for such a review by the architect, and for continuous misrepresentations to the owner and architect concerning the atrium design review.[34]

In reaching its decision, the Commission considered, among other things, (a) the terms of the agreement regarding the structural engineers' services to be performed on the Hyatt Regency project; (b) testimony of various fact and expert witnesses concerning the custom and practice in the engineering profession with respect to the responsibility for the design of connections for steel columns and beams; and (c) the actual conduct, interaction and communications of the respondent engineers and other members of the design team with and in relation to other participants in the construction process. A transcript or record of the testimony and evidence was maintained.[35]

Subsequent to the Commission's decision (by an administrative law judge), the Board, after conducting a hearing, decided to revoke the certificates of registration of both respondent engineers.[36]

§ 11.6   Civil Actions Arising Out of Construction Accidents

Unfortunately, and much too frequently, design professionals are sued by injured construction workers and/or members of their families or, in the event of death, their estates. The case study presented in § 11.2 involves a fact pattern somewhat typical of the generic claims made against design professionals by

---

[34] The Commission defined the term "gross negligence" as "an act or course of conduct which demonstrates a conscious indifference to a professional duty," *Duncan* at 533. In finding no error in this definition, the Missouri Court stated: "The very nature of the obligations and responsibility of a professional engineer would appear to make evident to him the probability of harm from his conscious indifference to professional duty and conscious indifference includes indifference to harm as well as to the duty. The structural engineer's duty is to determine that the structural plans which he designs or approves will provide structural safety because, if they do not, a strong probability of harm exists. Indifference to the duty is indifferent to the harm. We find no error in the definition utilized by the Commission. It imposes discipline for more than mere inadvertence and requires a finding that the conduct is so egregious as to warrant an inference of a mental state unacceptable in a professional engineer."

[35] *See generally* Note, *Defining the Engineer's Scope of Responsibility: The Missouri Adjudicatory Commission Hands Down a Decision on the Hyatt Case,* 55 U.M.K.C. L. Rev. 108 (1986) [hereinafter Note, *Hyatt*].

[36] The scope of judicial review over the administrative law judge's findings, conclusions, and decisions and the order of the Board regarding the appropriate disciplinary action involved, under Missouri law, an inquiry into whether those determinations violated constitutional

construction workers arising out of construction accidents. In general terms, injured construction workers in this type of claim allege that the design professional was either negligent in the design of the project and/or in the administration of the construction contract.[37]

In determining whether in this type of claim context to impose liability upon the design professional on the theory of negligence, a court will generally consider expert testimony, as well as the relevant provisions of the owner/design professional agreement and other pertinent provisions of the contract documents (as well as other actual conduct of the design professional on the project).[38]

The recent case of *Rodriguez v. Universal Fastenings Corp.*[39] is illustrative and instructive in this regard. In *Rodriguez,* the wife and children of a construction worker who was killed when he fell from a concrete slab brought suit against, among others, the engineering firm responsible for the design of the project. After a trial, the jury rendered a verdict in favor of the engineering firm. Under its agreement, the engineering firm was responsible for the preparation of plans and specifications and for observing construction of the project to provide the owner with greater confidence that the completed project would conform to the requirements of the contract documents.

The plaintiffs alleged that the engineering firm was negligent in the design of the project as well as in the performance of construction administration duties. The decedent construction worker was in the process of pouring concrete from the slab of the lift station when the accident occurred. At trial, the jury considered (among other things) conflicting expert testimony as well as the relevant provisions of the engineer's agreement and the contract documents. The contract documents made clear that the engineering firm was not responsible for the means, methods, techniques, sequences, or procedures of construction, or for the safety precautions and programs incident to them. According to the contract documents, the contractor and not the engineering firm was responsible for the design and construction of temporary form work, and for insuring that the form work was adequately braced and supported.

The appellate court, after reviewing the evidence introduced at trial, affirmed the jury verdict in favor of the engineering firm.

---

provisions and/or statutory authority, exceeded the jurisdiction of the agency, were unsupported by competent and substantial evidence, or involved an abuse of discretion. Mo. Rev. Stat. § 536.140 (1978).

[37] *See generally* Annotation, *Liability to One Injured in Course of Construction, Based Upon Architect's Alleged Failure to Carry Out Supervisory Responsibilities,* 59 A.L.R. 3d 869 (1974); Annotation, *Architect's Liability for Personal Injury or Death Allegedly Caused by Improper or Defective Plans or Design,* 97 A.L.R.3d 455 (1980).

[38] Hatem, *Liability of Design Professionals to Non-Clients: Impact and Influence of Contract Documents,* 4 Constr. L. Advisor (Apr. 1984).

[39] 777 S.W.2d 513 (Tex. Ct. App. 1989).

IMPACT OF DETERMINATIONS IN ADMINISTRATIVE AND REGISTRATION PROCEEDINGS ON SUBSEQUENT CIVIL LIABILITY

§ 11.7   Issue Preclusion Generally

Having discussed in general terms the nature of the claims, procedures and decision-making processes involved in OSHA, board of registration, and civil actions against design professionals, the focus will now shift to an analysis of the extent to which findings, decisions, or other determinations made in a prior OSHA (or related administrative) or board of registration proceedings involving a design professional may preclude, impair, or otherwise affect the design professional's ability to defend claims for damages made in a subsequent civil action arising out of the same facts, events, and circumstances giving rise to the prior proceeding.

This topic necessarily requires a discussion of the principle of collateral estoppel, or issue preclusion.[40] Under the affirmative defense of issue preclusion, "[o]nce an issue is actually and necessarily determined by a court of competent jurisdiction, that determination is conclusive in subsequent suits based on a different cause of action involving a party to the prior action."[41]

---

[40] Generally speaking, the related principle of res judicata (or claim preclusion)—which requires an identity of parties and claims—is not strictly applicable in this context since the prior administrative and/or board proceeding against the design professional typically would involve a different complainant (for example, the Secretary of Labor in the case of OSHA or the particular board of registration) and does not technically involve the same claim as would be involved in a subsequent civil action for damages by a private party against a design professional (despite the potential commonality or identity of issues in the prior and subsequent proceedings). However, the principle of res judicata may arguably be applicable in those circumstances in which the complainant in a prior board of registration proceeding is the same person (or in privity with the plaintiff) who subsequently commences a civil action against the design professional. For a discussion of the application of claim and issue preclusion in the context of claims against design professionals, see Hatem, *Survey of Defenses Available to Design Professionals Based Upon Prior Adjudication or Settlement of Claims Involving the Owner and Other Parties,* 11 Constr. L. Advisor (Nov. 1984); Associated Constr. Co. v. Camp, Dresser & McKee, 646 F. Supp. 1574 (D. Conn. 1986); Wellons, Inc. v. T.E. Ibberson Co., 869 F.2d 1166 (8th Cir. 1989); McReynolds & Welch, *Res Judicata and Collateral Estoppel: New Defenses in Construction Litigation,* 21 Ga. State B.J. 108 (No. 3, Feb. 19, 1985).

[41] Montana v. United States, 440 U.S. 147, 153 (1979). Under the mutuality requirement of collateral estoppel, only a person bound by a prior judgment may preclude another party from litigating issues or claims based on that judgment. Thus, as a general rule, under the mutuality requirement "a judgment was binding only on parties and persons in privity with them, and a judgment could be invoked only by parties and their privies." 18 C. Wright, A. Miller & E.

May a finding, decision, or other final determination on certain issues by an administrative agency in a prior proceeding involving a design professional be used as the basis for precluding (under the principle of issue preclusion) the design professional from (re)litigating some or all of those issues in a subsequent civil action brought against the design professional?[42]

The case study presented in § **11.2** squarely raises this issue. More particularly, can (should) the design professional in the case study be precluded from relitigating in the subsequent civil actions brought by the injured construction workers the findings and determinations of negligence made, respectively, by the administrative law judge in the OSHA action and by the board in the registration proceeding?

Although the Hyatt Regency collapse presented a somewhat "ideal" and concrete context within which to raise and address these questions,[43] it is probable that these questions will be raised, confronted, and addressed by courts in the future in actual circumstances in which related and successive OSHA (or other administrative), disciplinary, and civil proceedings are instituted against design professionals arising out of and involving the same alleged acts, errors or omissions, or other alleged misconduct.

The general rules on the subject of the applicability of issue preclusion (or collateral estoppel) in this context are set forth in § 83 of the Restatement (Second) of Judgments (1982) and have been summarized as follows:

Cooper, Federal Practice and Procedure, § 4463, at 559 (1981). The federal courts and an increasing number of state courts have abandoned the mutuality requirement. *See generally* Annotation, *Mutuality of Estoppel as Prerequisite of Availability of Doctrine of Collateral Estoppel to a Stranger to the Judgment,* 31 A.L.R.3d 1044 (1970). As a general principle, courts permit nonmutual preclusion only if the party against whom the estoppel is asserted had a full and fair opportunity to litigate in the prior action which resulted in the judgment upon which the estoppel is predicated. The various applications of nonmutual preclusion include the "defensive" assertion of collateral estoppel by a defendant against a plaintiff who had been a plaintiff in the prior action; and the "offensive" assertion of collateral estoppel by a plaintiff against a defendant who was a non-prevailing party in the prior action. In determining whether the party sought to be precluded had a full and fair opportunity to litigate in the prior action, courts will consider a variety of factors. *See* Restatement (Second) of Judgments, § 29 (1981); 18 C. Wright, A. Miller & E. Cooper, Federal Practice and Procedure § 4465. The offensive assertion of collateral estoppel against nonparties to the prior adjudication raises due process issues which caution against the indiscriminate utilization of collateral estoppel in that context. *See generally* Pielemeiere, *Due Process Limitations on the Application of Collateral Estoppel Against Nonparties to Prior Litigation,* 63 Bos. Univ. L. Rev. 383 (1983). *In re* John F. Harck, 70 Bankr. 18 (Bankr. 9th Cir. 1987) is instructive in this regard.

[42] This question is also generally discussed in Hatem, *Impact of Professional Practice Standards on Liability of Engineers,* 5 J. of Mgmt. in Eng'g, No. 3, p. 249 (July 1989).

[43] These questions were not raised or addressed in the context of the Hyatt Regency collapse because both of the known civil actions arising out of the collapse were settled prior to the Commission's issuance of its findings, conclusions, and decisions against the respondent engineers. In the first action commenced against the engineers by personal injury and wrongful

Administrative . . . decisions can foreclose judicial proceedings as a result of either claim preclusion or issue preclusion. . . . The Supreme Court has put it simply in *United States v. Utah Construction & Mining Co.*:[44] "When an administrative agency is acting in a judicial capacity and resolves disputed issues of fact properly before it which the parties have had an adequate opportunity to litigate, the courts have not hesitated to apply res judicata to enforce repose."

Two major qualifications limit the use of administrative decisions to preclude judicial decision. The first is reflected in the passage quoted above, and draws from the same concerns that once combined to deny any preclusion. An administrative decision commands preclusive effects only if it resulted from a procedure that seems an adequate substitute for judicial procedure. This qualification is a general one that applies to proper relations between courts and administrative agencies. The second qualification draws from concerns that are much more specific to particular regulatory schemes. Any particular scheme may contemplate that administrative decisions are not meant to preclude independent judicial action, or to the contrary may contemplate that courts extend special deference to an agency.

. . . Whether or not a general formula can be found, it is clear that some specific differences between administrative and judicial procedure do not defeat preclusion. Preclusion has been accepted despite the absence of jury trial, limitations on discovery, and general arguments that more evidence could be produced in a second proceeding. More drastic procedural differences do defeat preclusion. An administrative decision based on a written record, without opportunity for examination or cross-examination of live witnesses, for example, is not likely to support preclusion in a subsequent judicial action.

Apart from the procedures provided by the agency itself, the opportunity for judicial review may prove important in determining the availability of preclusion. If review is sought but denied as to a particular issue, preclusion may well be denied. Failure to seek an available opportunity for review, on the other hand, does not defeat preclusion; preclusion may indeed be extended to low-level administrative decisions for reasons akin to the policies that require exhaustion of administrative remedies before seeking judicial review.[45]

§ 11.8   Issue Preclusion in Case Study

Applying the foregoing principles to circumstances similar to those presented in the case study, a court, in determining whether to give issue preclusion or

---

death claimants, all of the defendants, including the engineers, declined to contest liability; and the second action commenced by the Hyatt Corporation against certain members of the design and construction team was likewise settled. *See* Note, *Hyatt* at 108-09 and nn. 4-7 (1986).

[44] 384 U.S. 394, 421-22 (1966). *See also* University of Tenn. v. Elliott, 106 S. Ct. 3220 (1986); Kremer v. Chemical Const. Corp., 102 S. Ct. 1883 (1982).

[45] 18 C. Wright, A. Miller & E. Cooper, Federal Practice and Procedure, §§ 762-67, at 462-67 (1981). *See also* 4 David on Administrative Law, §§ 21:1, 21:2, 21:3 (1983); Note, *The*

collateral estoppel effect to a determination made in a prior administrative proceeding, will certainly focus on at least the following factors:

1. Whether the party sought to be estopped (i.e., the design professional in the case study) had a full, fair, and adequate opportunity to contest the issues which were in controversy and which were actually, necessarily, and finally determined in the prior OSHA or board proceeding.

2. Whether the administrative agency had jurisdiction or authority to make the findings or determinations in question.[46]

3. Whether the nature of the prior proceeding was adjudicatory in nature.

4. Whether the design professional in the prior proceeding had a full, fair, and adequate opportunity to adjudicate the issues actually, necessarily, and finally determined (for example, the right to call and cross-examine live witnesses, and fair and reasonable notice of the issues and claims in controversy).

5. Whether the issues necessarily, actually, and finally determined in the prior proceeding can be reasonably identified on the basis of the record and, if so, whether the determination on those issues was essential and necessary to the ultimate decision in that prior proceeding.

6. Whether the issues necessarily, actually, and finally determined in the prior proceeding are identical to some or all of the essential issues in controversy in the subsequent civil action.[47]

7. Whether the standards for imposing fault, discipline, or liability in the prior proceeding are the same or substantially similar to those which would be utilized to determine liability in the subsequent civil action, and whether there are any significant differences in the applicable burdens of proof in the prior and subsequent proceedings.

Collateral Estoppel Effect of Administrative Agency Actions on Federal Civil Litigation, 46 Geo. Wash. L. Rev. 65 (1977); Note, *Collateral Estoppel Effects of Administrative Agency Determinations: Where Should Federal Courts Draw the Line,* 73 Corn. L. Rev. 817 (1988); A. Cella, Administrative Law and Practice, § 431, at 775 (1986).

[46] *See, e.g.,* Lightsey v. Harding, Dahm & Co., 623 F.2d 1219 (7th Cir.), *cert. denied,* 449 U.S. 1077 (1980). In *Lightsey,* the Seventh Circuit reversed an order of the district court granting summary judgment in favor of a real estate brokerage firm in a subsequent civil action on the grounds that a prior decision of the Indiana Real Estate Commission had collateral estoppel effect in that it resolved the issue presented by the plaintiff in the subsequent civil action against the brokerage firm as to whether the brokerage firm had breached its agreement with the plaintiff.

[47] In determining whether to apply issue preclusion in the context of prior administrative determinations, courts also examine whether the standard of proof in the subsequent proceeding is identical or substantially similar to that applicable in the prior proceeding. If the burden of proof differs significantly, a court may well be persuaded to reject the applicability of issue preclusion. *See generally* Note, *The Collateral Estoppel Effect of Administrative Agency Actions in Federal Civil Litigation,* 46 Geo. Wash. L. Rev. 65, 86 (1977).

Applying these criteria, courts have recognized that issue and claim preclusion principles may generally be applicable based upon prior OSHA proceedings.[48] Clearly, the determination whether issue preclusion or collateral estoppel will be applied in the circumstances posed in the case study must be made on a case by case basis (in accordance with the criteria and factors generally discussed above).

The decision whether to apply issue preclusion in a subsequent civil action (involving a design professional) based upon the prior determination of a board of registration proceeding will, in general, be based upon the same general analysis as governs in the context of the application of issue preclusion based upon a prior administrative proceeding (such as OSHA). Although this precise issue has not been considered by any appellate court in a reported decision involving design professionals, the same generic issue has been presented to one federal district court in the context of an attorney malpractice claim.

In *Kuehn v. Garcia*,[49] the Eighth Circuit declined to affirm a district court's order allowing summary judgment against an attorney on the basis that a prior determination of a board of registration against the attorney precluded the attorney from relitigating the issue of his negligence in the civil action subsequently commenced against the attorney. However, in the *Kuehn* case, the Eighth Circuit declined to affirm the district court's allowance of summary judgment on the basis of collateral estoppel solely due to the failure to satisfy the mutuality requirement (which exists under North Dakota law for the offensive use of collateral estoppel).[50] Of course, in a jurisdiction in which the mutuality requirement is not so strictly enforced, the potential applicability of issue preclusion may certainly be available under appropriate circumstances, such as those presented in *Kuehn*.[51]

---

[48] *See generally* International Harvester Co. v. Occupational Safety & Health Review Comm'n, 628 F.2d 982, 984-86 (7th Cir. 1980) (declining, however, to apply res judicata based on particular circumstances presented); Continental Can Co. v. Marshall, 603 F.2d 590, 593-96 (7th Cir. 1979) (holding that requirements of collateral estoppel were satisfied).

[49] 608 F.2d 1143 (8th Cir. 1979).

[50] *See generally* Annotation, *Mutuality of Estoppel as Prerequisite of Availability of Doctrine of Collateral Estoppel to a Stranger to the Judgment,* 31 A.L.R.3d 1044 (1970).

[51] One authority in the field of legal malpractice, commenting on the *Kuehn* decision, has stated:

> Although the court's ruling appears to rest upon the North Dakota privity requirement for collateral estoppel, estoppel under any circumstances is questionable. Disciplinary rules are not intended to provide standards for civil liability. Codified disciplinary rules are not always the same as common-law rules defining civil liability. Moreover, in a disciplinary proceeding, evidence is not offered based upon a standard of care, nor do the parties usually offer expert testimony as is common in civil litigation. While it may be tempting to infer civil liability because of discipline for the same wrongful conduct, the problems created by the procedural and substantive differences between the proceedings make collateral estoppel and res judicata inappropriate.

Mallen & Levitt, Legal Malpractice, § 27.12 at p.662 (3d ed. 1989). Although this commentary on the *Kuehn* decision may be accurate, given the character in general of disciplinary

In the circumstances presented in the case study, the design professional may well be precluded from relitigating issues relating to its negligence if a court in the subsequent civil actions is satisfied that: (1) the factual and legal issues involved in the subsequent civil actions are identical to the issues involved, and necessarily, actually, and finally determined in the prior administrative proceedings; (2) the administrative agency had jurisdiction or authority to make the findings or determinations in question; (3) the design professional had adequate notice of the issues to be determined in the prior administrative proceeding and had a full, fair, and adequate opportunity to present its position (defense) with respect to those issues; (4) the design professional had a full, fair, and adequate opportunity to present evidence and legal argument in support of its defense in the prior administrative proceeding and had a full, fair and adequate opportunity to rebut evidence (including the right of cross-examination of opposing witnesses) and arguments of its opponent in that proceeding; and (5) the record in the prior administrative proceeding provides a reasonable and reliable basis to support the conclusion that the engineer was afforded these rights and that the administrative board or agency specifically, actually and necessarily determined the same issues as are in dispute in the subsequent civil actions.

Although, admittedly, there may be distinctions between issues that may be determined in a registration proceeding against a design professional involving a particular claimed error or omission and the issues which are in dispute in a subsequent civil action (such as the issue of damages, which typically are not presented in the registration proceeding), these distinctions do not necessarily negate the application of issue preclusion as to those issues which were specifically, necessarily, and actually at issue and finally determined in the prior registration or administrative proceeding.[52]

§ 11.9   Admission of Findings into Evidence

Short of collateral estoppel or other preclusive effect, may findings issued in a prior administrative adjudicatory proceeding involving a design professional be

---

proceedings, the nature of the issues, hearings, and the evidence involved in the proceedings before the Commission in the *Hyatt Regency* case may lead to a conclusion contrary to that suggested in the above quote.

[52] In this regard, one authority has stated:

There are several significant differences between a civil malpractice action and a disciplinary proceeding. First, a lawyer may be disciplined even if the misconduct does not cause any damage. The rationale is the need for protection of the public and the integrity of the profession. Second, although the severity of the breach may affect the nature of the discipline, the prophylactic purpose of the ethical rules may result in a sanction even if the conduct would not otherwise constitute a civil wrong. Third, even if the injured party initiates a disciplinary complaint, that individual is not a party to the

admitted into evidence in a subsequent civil action against the same design professional arising out of the same events or circumstances at issue in the prior proceeding? Although as a general rule a prior judgment entered in a judicial proceeding is inadmissible hearsay in a subsequent civil action,[53] the common law evidentiary rules of several states, as well as the Federal Rules of Evidence,[54] allow for the admission into evidence of factual findings issued in administrative proceedings as an exception to the hearsay rule, provided that the finding is a "factual finding," the factual finding has resulted from an investigation authorized by law, and the finding (and circumstances giving rise to the finding) indicates no lack of trustworthiness.[55]

Federal Rule of Evidence 803(8) provides a hearsay exception for: "Records, reports, statements, or data compilations, in any form, of public offices or agencies setting forth . . . in civil actions and proceedings and against the Government in criminal cases, factual findings resulting from an investigation made pursuant to authority granted by law, unless the sources of information or other circumstances indicate a lack of trustworthiness."

Thus, even though factual findings of an administrative agency issued in an adjudicatory proceeding may not be entitled to collateral estoppel or other preclusive effect, those findings may be admitted into evidence (in some jurisdictions) as an exception to the hearsay rule, subject to the requirements set forth above. One commentator, noting the distinction between the use of administrative factual findings as the basis for preclusion and solely for evidentiary purposes, has stated:

> The net result is that after *Utah Construction*,[56] administrative findings can affect subsequent litigation in two different ways. If they are not given preclusive effect through the application of collateral estoppel, they can still be given evidentiary effect as an exception to the the rule against hearsay. This continuum of effect, and the choice that it gives courts, has certain appeal to common sense. But it effectively gives administrative findings greater influence on later litigation than other types of findings exercise. Administrative findings that do not qualify for collateral estoppel may be admitted into evidence. Judicial findings, on the other hand, are not admissible under Rule 803(8)(C), so a judicial finding that is not collateral estoppel is ignored completely. Neither case law nor commentary

---

proceeding. These differences often mean that a rule promulgated for discipline is inappropriate as a principle of law or standard for defining proper civil conduct.
Mallen & Levitt, Legal Malpractice, § 1.9 (3d ed. 1989).

[53] *See generally* Motomora, *Using Judgments as Evidence,* 70 Minn. L. Rev. 979, 980-81 (1986) [hereinafter Motomora].

[54] Fed. R. Evid. 803(8)(C).

[55] *See* Beech Aircraft Corp. v. Rainey, 109 S. Ct. 439, 446 (1988) (holding that factually based conclusions or opinions are not on that account excluded from the scope of Fed. R. Evid. 803(8)(c)).

[56] 384 U.S. 394 (1966).

adequately explains why administrative findings should enjoy this greater range of subsequent effect.[57]

The same commentator has also noted that similar concerns underlie the application of collateral estoppel and the use of prior administrative factual findings as evidence, in stating that:

> Whether any deference will be given to a prior judgment depends largely on our confidence that it is "reliable," in the sense that we believe it accurately ascertains historical truth. A leading commentary observes "hearsay is excludable because it is generally less reliable than live testimony." The exceptions to the rule against hearsay are justified on grounds that substitute assurances of reliability or "trustworthiness" are present.

> Collateral estoppel shares this basic concern with reliability, and the requirements that must be met to use a prior judgment as collateral estoppel are similar but often stiffer than those necessary to use a judgment as evidence. For example, an administrative finding that lacked a hearing or other procedural protections, or that was not necessary to the outcome of the case, cannot be used as collateral estoppel, although it still may be sufficiently trustworthy to be admissible as evidence under Rule 803(8)(C). . . . Administrative collateral estoppel is also more difficult to obtain because its proponent must prove that all of the requirements are met, while the opponent of admission into evidence must prove a finding is not trustworthy.[58]

Although the case law concerning the use of prior administrative factual findings in the context of subsequent liability claims involving professionals is relatively sparse,[59] in those circumstances in which Rule 803(8)(C) or similar state evidentiary rules apply, a court may admit such findings into evidence (assuming that the evidentiary requirements described above are satisfied) even though those findings may not be entitled to collateral estoppel effect.

---

[57] Motomora at 986-87.

[58] Motomora at 1006-08. Generally speaking, litigants opposing the admission of a factual finding issued in an administrative proceeding argue that the finding was not "factual," that the finding is not "trustworthy," or that, in any event, the finding is unduly prejudicial under, for example, Fed. R. Evid. 403. Professor Motomora also discusses a number of practical concerns associated with the admissibility and use of administrative factual findings in subsequent civil litigation, such as the potential for undue jury deference to those findings, the necessity of proper cautioning or limiting instructions to the jury, and other concerns and protections relevant in this context. Motomora at 1037-51.

[59] *See, e.g.,* Brown v. Sierra Nev. Memorial Miners, 849 F.2d 1186 (9th Cir. 1988). In *Brown,* the Ninth Circuit held that the district court erred in refusing to admit into evidence, in a subsequent civil action involving a doctor, findings previously made by a State Board of Medical Quality Assurance that the doctor's care was adequate. In the subsequent civil action, the doctor sought to testify as to the Board's findings, but the district court ruled that such testimony would be irrelevant. The Ninth Circuit disagreed on the basis of Fed. R. Evid. 803(8)(C), but held that the district court's exclusion of that evidence did not constitute reversible error.

§ 11.10   Effect of Professional Practice Standards

A final, but related issue presented by the case study is the extent to which professional practice standards may impact upon the determination of civil liability of design professionals. Design professionals, like other professionals, are guided, governed, and regulated in their professional practice not only by statutes and contracts, but also by standards, ethical codes, and other forms of regulations at the local, state and national levels. These standards, ethical codes and regulations ("professional practice standards") may or may not have the force of law. The issue is what effect, if any, such professional practice standards may have on the determination whether a design professional is liable for civil damages with respect to claims that invoke the applicability of those standards.

The consideration of this issue is especially timely in view of ASCE's May 1988 issuance of the Quality in the Constructed Project Manual of Professional Practice, Preliminary Edition (the Manual). The Manual is intended to provide guidelines and recommendations reflecting a consensus of opinion among design professionals, owners and contractors who are involved in the construction process, the goal of which is to "lead to quality in constructed projects."

Although there is no case law directly on point, it is likely that a court in a civil action involving a design professional may receive into evidence all or pertinent portions of the Manual as evidence relevant to the issues of the appropriate standard of care (or duty) owed by the design professional and whether the design professional breached any such standard. Recognizing that the admissibility of this type of evidence may vary from jurisdiction to jurisdiction, courts, as a general principle, will permit the introduction of evidence such as the Manual if some foundation has been established to the effect that the Manual represents a consensus of opinion in the profession and otherwise constitutes reliable evidence for the trier of fact to consider with respect to the issues of standard of care and the design professional's alleged departure from that standard.

In related professional liability contexts, courts have demonstrated a willingness to admit such evidence. For example, in *Fishman v. Brooks*,[60] the Supreme Judicial Court of Massachusetts addressed the issue of the effect of an attorney's alleged violation of a canon of ethics or disciplinary rule upon the determination whether the attorney would be liable for damages in a civil action. The court held that while a violation of an ethical rule, standing alone, does not itself constitute a breach of duty to a civil claimant, such a violation may provide some evidence of the attorney's negligence or civil liability.

Equally significant, the court in *Fishman* held that a plaintiff need not introduce any expert testimony to explain to a trier of fact (judge or jury) the meaning, intent, or application of the ethical rule or standard, and that the

---

[60] 396 Mass. 643, 487 N.E.2d 1377 (1986).

ethical rule or standard may simply be read to the jury or otherwise available for the jury's review along with other evidence. Specifically, the court stated:

> We add a brief comment about the relationship between the canons of ethics and an attorney's duty of care to his client. A violation of canon of ethics or a disciplinary rule . . . is not itself an actionable breach of duty to a client . . . as with statutes and regulations, however, if a plaintiff can demonstrate that a disciplinary rule was intended to protect one in his position, a violation of that rule may be some evidence of the attorney's negligence. . . . Expert testimony concerning the fact of an ethical violation is not appropriate, any more than expert testimony is appropriate concerning the violation of, for example, a municipal building code. . . . A judge can instruct the jury (or himself) concerning the requirements of ethical rules. The jurors need no expert testimony on legal ethics to assess whether a disciplinary rule is violated. A jury would not be aided and their function could be infringed upon by expert testimony in such a circumstance. . . . Of course, an expert on the duty of care of an attorney properly could base his opinion on an attorney's failure to conform to a disciplinary rule.

Fishman and related case law in other professional malpractice contexts suggest that, under appropriate circumstances, ethical rules and professional practice standards may well be admissible as evidence in civil actions involving a design professional—both as evidence against and in support of the design professional's level of performance. In *Taylor, Thorn, Thompson & Peterson v. Canaday,*[61] the Supreme Court of Montana upheld the trial court's admission into evidence of the AIA's *Architect's Handbook of Professional Practice,* and held that the handbook standards were to be considered as evidence with respect to the duty owed by the architect.

Beyond any doubt, this case law should serve to emphasize the importance of clear, concise, understandable, fair, and realistically achievable professional practice standards, especially when those standards are promulgated by members of one's own profession. In this regard, it is important to keep in mind that ethical rules and other professional practice standards can provide a defensive shield as well as an offensive sword against the design professional; however, the extent to which such standards and rules may be utilized successfully as a defense to the design professional depends, in material part, on the clarity and comprehensibility (to persons other than design professionals) of the particular standards or rules.

§ 11.11   Guidelines

Although the case law is relatively sparse and evolving, it would appear that a court, if satisfied that the requirements of issue preclusion and the other factors

---

[61] 749 P.2d 63 (Mont. 1988).

discussed in this chapter are satisfied, may preclude a design professional from (re)litigating in a subsequent civil action issues which were presented and necessarily, actually, and finally determined in a prior administrative or board of registration proceeding involving the design professional.

Also, although the law is relatively sparse, it would appear that courts (depending on the law of the jurisdiction) will (subject to certain foundation requirements) admit into evidence factual findings of an administrative agency and admit into evidence ethical or other professional practice standards as relevant to the issues of defining the standard of care (custom and practice in the profession) required under the circumstances and whether the design professional adhered to that standard.

These guidelines, albeit tentative given the absence of substantial or definitive case law on this subject, suggest the importance of insuring that: (1) an adequate, competent, and comprehensive defense is provided and presented by the design professional in the context of the prior administrative proceeding; and (2) ethical and other professional practice standards be fair, clear, comprehensible, and realistically achievable by the design professional.

Undoubtedly, given the apparent emerging and increasing interest of the Department of Labor in initiating citations and complaints against design professionals and the more active role of professional registration boards in regulating and disciplining professionals (as well as the increasing public awareness of that process and the availability of that process to private parties as a means of presenting grievances against professionals), it would appear reasonably certain that the issues discussed in this chapter will be raised and adjudicated more frequently in the next several years.

CHAPTER 12

CONSTRUCTION ADMINISTRATION SERVICES AND THE ARCHITECT'S LIABILITY DILEMMA

John A. Knutson*

§ 12.1 Introduction

§ 12.2 Background

§ 12.3 Supervision

§ 12.4 —Early Case Law

§ 12.5 —AIA Standard Form Contract

§ 12.6 —*Moundsview*

§ 12.7 —Modern Statutes

§ 12.8 —Recent Cases

§ 12.9 Limiting Liability by Contract

§ 12.10 Recommendations

§ 12.1 Introduction

As society has become increasingly complex, so too have the tasks of the architect.[1] Today's architect must take into account a myriad of differing and often conflicting demands. Often, the architect's response to these demands will play a significant role in whether the architect will later be subject to potential liability.

---

* This chapter is adapted from a paper presented in May 1990 to the 29th Annual Meeting of Invited Attorneys sponsored by AIA, NSPE, and Victor O. Schinnerer & Company.

[1] The word *architect,* as used in this chapter, refers to both architects and engineers.

The two primary sources of the architect's potential liability are design and supervision of construction.[2] This chapter will examine the duty of the architect to provide construction administration services, the scope of those services, and the potential liability incurred by providing such services.[3] After briefly establishing the appropriate legal background, the various attempts to limit the architect's scope of work and attendant liability will be discussed. These include limits imposed by statute in some states, as well as exculpatory language in the AIA form contracts.

Additionally, several recent cases will be examined in an effort to discern whether imposition of liability upon architects signifies an expansion of the architect's duty of supervision during construction. Finally, some recommendations to reduce the chances of incurring unanticipated liability will be set forth.

§ 12.2   Background

Generally, the law relating to an architect's liability distinguishes between liability in tort for negligence and liability for breach of contract.

Negligence in the context of an action against an architect is often referred to as professional malpractice. However, the general concept does not vary from common law principles of negligence. The elements of actionable negligence against an architect involve a legal duty to use due care, a breach of such legal duty, and a breach as a proximate or legal cause of resulting injury.[4]

An action for breach of contract may rest either upon breach of an express provision of the contract or on some implied obligation arising out of the contract. Clearly, the signing of a contract obligates the architect to provide those services specified in the contract. However, the architect may also incur contractual obligations derived not only from the express language of the contract, but from conduct implied in fact or law.[5]

§ 12.3   Supervision

Traditionally, supervision of the construction process was automatically the responsibility of the architect. However, divisions of labor and construction

---

[2] The term "construction supervision" has now been replaced in the form contracts by the term "observation." For simplicity and consistency, the term "construction supervision" will be used herein.

[3] Liability arising from design is beyond the intended scope of this chapter and will not be discussed.

[4] Sanbutch Properties Inc. v. United States, 343 F. Supp. 611 (N.D. Cal. 1972); United States Liability Ins. Co. v. Haidinger-Hayes Inc., 1 Cal. 3d 586, 463 P.2d 770, 83 Cal. Rptr. 418 (1970).

[5] An *implied contract* is one in which the existence and terms are manifested by conduct. *See* Cal. Civil Code § 1621.

responsibility and the complexity of modern construction have curtailed this responsibility.[6] In fact, it would appear that "supervision" is a term which no longer accurately describes the architect's obligations in connection with the observation of construction. Supervision implies control and direction, which the architect often does not have in the typical construction setting.

As discussed in more detail below, the architect is not required to direct or inspect the performance of the work unless an explicit term in the architect's contract with the owner requires the architect to assume this role and direct construction. However, the nature and extent of the supervision required of the architect is anything but clear and what is required has varied over time and by jurisdiction. Nevertheless, it is possible to discern trends in the types of obligations being imposed on the architect at a given point in time.

§ 12.4   —Early Case Law

Many of the early cases which held the architect liable for failure to supervise predated the transfer of the power to stop work from the architect to the owner, a provision which became standard in the AIA form contract. For instance, the following quote from the court in *United States ex rel. Los Angeles Testing Lab v. Rogers and Rogers*[7] aptly illustrates the important effect of the architect's ability to stop work on the imposition of liability:

> Considerations of reason and policy impel the conclusion that the position and authority of a supervising architect are such that it ought to labor under a duty to the prime contractor to supervise the project with due care under the circumstances. . . . Altogether too much control over the contractor necessarily rests in the hands of the supervising architect for him not to be placed under a duty imposed by law to perform without negligence his functions as they affect the contractor. *The power of the architect to stop work alone is tantamount to a power of economic life or death over the contractor.* It is only just that such authority, exercised in such a relationship, carry commensurate legal responsibility.[8]

However, in the prior case of *Paxton v. County of Alameda,*[9] the court did not base its decision on the architect's ability to stop work, but instead, held that the architect had the duty to: (1) direct and supervise the erection and completion of the construction work to the end that such work be completed in strict conformity with the drawings and specifications and in good and workmanlike manner; (2) to order the correction or removal of all defective work and materials not strictly conforming to the plans and specifications; (3) to see that the said work be

---

[6] Architect-Engineer Liability Under California Law (1987) at 14-6.

[7] 161 F. Supp. 132 (S.D. Cal. 1958).

[8] *Id.* at 136 (emphasis added).

[9] 119 Cal. App. 2d 393, 259 P.2d 934 (1953).

constructed and completed in strict accordance with the plans and specifications adopted therefor; and (4) to make such inspections as were necessary to enable it to properly advise the county.[10]

Clearly, the *Paxton* court implied some duty to supervise and was willing to hold the defendant liable for any failure to meet the appropriate standards of care in this regard. The decision was apparently not based on the architect's ability to stop work.[11]

The early New York Court of Appeals case of *Clemmons v. Benzinger*[12] was an action for wrongful death against a cement contractor, the contractor who directed the structural steel work, and the architect. The decedent was killed by a steel column which fell as a result of the use of the wrong type of anchor bolt. Judgment was rendered against all three defendants.

The court affirmed the judgment as to the architect, stating that a finding of negligence against the architect could be based upon its supervisory activities in failing to notify the structural steel contractor of the effect of the use of the wrong type of anchor bolts in this situation.

Perhaps the most significant case imposing liability upon the architect for failure to supervise was *Miller v. DeWitt*.[13] In *Miller,* the architect used the standard form architect's agreement that was in use until 1969. According to the owner/architect contract, the architect had the duty of general supervision of the work and had authority to stop work when necessary to ensure the proper execution of the contract. During construction, the contractor's workers suffered injuries during the removal of some existing structural supports that were to be temporarily replaced during renovation of a school.

The *Miller* court held the architect liable for failing to exercise its authority to stop the work. The court reasoned that the architect had supervised the project and therefore had the duty to exercise its right to stop the work before injury resulted.

The *Miller* opinion attracted a great amount of attention at the time it was published.[14] However, it should be noted that the architect in *Miller* was found to be "in charge" of the work within the meaning of the Illinois Structural Work Act.[15] That Act, in fact, did not require proof of negligence for imposing liability. This may at least partially explain the *Miller* court's departure from the general view that architects will be held responsible for results, not for the methods used.

---

[10] 119 Cal. App. 2d at 409.

[11] *See also* Carey, *Assessing Liability of Architects and Engineers for Construction Supervision,* 1979 Ins. L. J. 147, 152, n. 34 [hereinafter Carey] where the author perceptively notes that the right to reject work, still retained by the architect, is hardly less of a power than the right to stop work.

[12] 211 A.D. 586, 207 N.Y.S. 539 (1925).

[13] 37 Ill. 2d 273, 226 N.E.2d 630 (1967).

[14] *See also* Carey at 154.

[15] *Id.; see* Ill. Rev. Stat. ch. 48, ¶¶ 60, 69 (1963).

However, perhaps the most significant aspect of the *Miller* decision can be found in the fact that in addition to examining and interpreting the owner/architect agreement, the court also considered the owner/contractor agreement. It was the owner/contractor agreement that provided for broad rights of the architect to approve work performed and even to stop work if it were being performed unacceptably. In reading these two contracts together, the court seemed to be saying that the architect in this case had such pervasive rights that corresponding duties would also be imposed.

§ 12.5   —AIA Standard Form Contract

Perhaps one of the most prevalent areas of dispute between owner and architect is that of the provision of site services during construction. In fact, many of the contracts that predated the 1977 edition of AIA B141 gave the architect a general supervisory power such as the power to stop work. Accordingly, plaintiffs brought lawsuits against architects alleging that the architect had a duty to supervise construction and therefore was liable for injuries resulting from defective work and/or unsafe conditions.[16]

In 1977, a revised AIA B141 was drafted, disclaiming responsibility for the architect to provide supervision and, in fact, transferred the power to stop work to the owner. The obvious purpose of this provision was to attempt to preclude the architect from incurring any liability for unsafe conditions or defective work. This, of course, assumes that no actual exercise of control by the architect takes place. Where the architect goes beyond the contract and actually assumes control of the project, the fact that the architect no longer has the power to stop work will not insulate the architect against liability.

Further, when the architect goes beyond merely providing the architectural services and acts as a builder, construction manager, or any capacity other than as an architect, the architect will incur liability if these tasks are not performed up to the appropriate standard of care. In short, the best advice to the architect is to avoid assuming roles for which it is either not qualified or for which it is not being compensated under the contract with the owner.

The latest edition of AIA document B141 is the 1987 version. The use of this architect/owner contract has now become extremely prevalent. As illustrated in the following, this form allows the architect to clearly define the scope of work and hopefully limit liability for services outside of those set forth in that contract.

In B141-1987, ¶ 2.6 deals with the administration of the construction contract. Under ¶ 2.6.5, the architect does continue to have the responsibility to visit the site and observe the work. However, it is significant that this obligation is

---

[16] *See* United States *ex rel.* Los Angeles Testing Lab v. Rogers & Rogers, 161 F. Supp. 132 (S.D. Cal. 1958); Pancoast v. Russell, 148 Cal. App. 2d 909, 307 P.2d 719 (1957); Montijo v. Swift, 219 Cal. App. 2d 351, 33 Cal. Rptr. 133 (1963).

limited to completed work and to a determination that the work is being performed in a manner indicating that, when the work is completed, it will be in accordance with the contract documents. However, it is clearly stated that more extensive site representation may be agreed to as an additional service.

Paragraph 2.6.10 states that the issuance of a certificate for payment shall *not* be a representation that the architect has: "(1) made exhaustive or continuous on-site inspections to check the quality or quantity of the Work, (2) reviewed construction means, methods, techniques, sequences or procedures. . . .

Further, ¶ 2.6.11 makes it clear that neither the architect's authority to reject non-conforming work or require additional inspection or testing of the work nor "a decision made in good faith either to exercise or not to exercise such authority shall give rise to a duty or responsibility of the Architect to the Contractor . . . or other persons performing portions of the Work."

The use of an on-site project representative by the architect is contained in B141-1987 ¶ 3.2. However, this is an optional provision. Obviously, where the owner/architect contract calls for use of an on-site project representative to provide supervisory services, the architect may be held liable if negligent supervision causes harm.

§ 12.6 — *Moundsview*

Moundsview Independent School District No. 621 v. Beutow & Associates, Inc.[17] provides an excellent illustration of the effectiveness of a contract limiting the architect's liability to the owner.[18] In *Moundsview,* the owner brought suit against the architect when portions of a roof were torn off during a windstorm after construction was completed. The architect had offered the owner three options for the level of supervision it would provide during the construction process: (1) no supervision, (2) general supervision, and (3) continuous on-site inspection by a full time project representative or "clerk of the works."

The owner opted for the general supervision option, which was specifically described in a periodic inspection clause similar to that set forth in B141 ¶¶ 2.6.5 and 2.6.6. As described above, these clauses in the contract expressly disclaimed any liability of the architect for the contractor's failure to properly perform the work so long as the architect performed the required periodic inspections.

The architect in *Moundsview* performed 90 site inspections during the 79-week construction period. After the damage to the roof had occurred, it was determined that the roof had not been properly secured to one of the walls of the school, as required by the architect's plans and specifications. The owner

---

[17] 253 N.W.2d 836 (Minn. 1977).

[18] See Architect-Engineer Liability Under California Law (1976) at 4-3.

claimed, therefore, that the architect had breached its contractual obligation to provide supervision.

The trial court granted summary judgment for the architect and the Minnesota Supreme Court affirmed, stating that:

> It is the general rule that the employment of an architect is a matter of contract, and consequently, he is responsible for all the duties enumerated within the contract of employment. . . . An architect, as a professional, is required to perform his services with reasonable care and competence and will be liable in damages for any failure to do so. . . . *Moundsview cannot be allowed to gain the benefit of the more detailed clerk-of-the-works inspection service while in fact contracting and paying for only a general supervisory service.*[19]

A similar result was reached in *Waggoner v. W&W Steel Co.,*[20] where the court interpreted that the contract provision requiring site visits did not call for "exhaustive or continuous on-site inspections to check . . . the work."[21] Again, these cases demonstrate the value of precise contract drafting and a clear understanding of the scope of the site services to be performed by the architect. However, as will be shown in § **12.8**, even this precise language may not be interpreted by some courts as sufficient to warrant summary judgment for the architect.

§ 12.7 —Modern Statutes

Despite some of the previously cited decisions which imposed liability on architects for failure to supervise, B141 clearly reflects the AIA's preference for imposition of responsibility upon the architect only where the architect has specifically contracted to assume these responsibilities. In California this modern preference is also reflected in California Business & Professions Code § 5536.25(b), adopted in 1985, which provides:

> The signing of plans, specifications, reports or documents which relate to the design of fixed works shall not impose a legal duty or responsibility upon the person signing the plans, specifications, reports or documents to observe the construction of the fixed works which are the subject of the plans, specifications, reports or documents. However, nothing in this section shall preclude an architect and a client from entering into a contractual agreement which includes a mutually acceptable arrangement for the provision of construction observation services. Nothing contained in this subdivision shall modify the liability of an architect who undertakes, contractually or otherwise, the provision of construction observation services for rendering those services.

---

[19] 253 N.W.2d at 839 (emphasis added).

[20] 657 P.2d 147 (Okla. 1982), *reh'g. denied* (1983).

[21] *Id.* at 152.

A recent addition to the statute, § 5536.25(c), defines *construction observation services* as follows:

> "Construction observation services" means periodic observation of completed work to determine general compliance with the plans, specifications, reports or other contract document. However, construction observation services does not mean the superintendence of construction processes, site conditions, operations, equipment or personnel, or the maintenance of a safe place to work or any safety in, on, or about the site. For purposes of this subdivision, "periodic observation" means visits by an architect, or his or her agent, to the site of the work of improvement.[22]

As the above-quoted statutes indicate, the architect's duty to "supervise" a construction project, other than those services specified by statute, should arise only out of specific provisions in the contract between the architect and the owner. In fact, in the absence of contractual provisions to the contrary, the duty is more appropriately described as a duty of "periodic observation," not supervision.

However, it should be kept in mind that, if the architect undertakes duties which go beyond the scope of those imposed by the explicit terms of the contract, the architect will be held to have an implied duty of reasonable care in the supervision undertaken. Further, the above-cited statutes do not relieve the architect from its duty to insure that the work performed is in compliance with the plans and specifications prepared by the architect.

Clearly, architects in California are protected by these statutes. However, architects in states where no such legislation exists would be well-advised to incorporate the language of these California statutes into all owner/architect contracts.

§ 12.8   —Recent Cases

Despite statutes such as the California legislation discussed above, and the severe limiting of the architect's duties under the standard AIA form contract, there continue to be many cases involving an alleged duty of the architect to supervise construction. The most significant of these many cases, for purposes of this chapter, are those that may indicate a trend toward imposition of liability upon the architect for failure to provide supervision. Interestingly enough, these decisions impose liability despite the clear and unequivocally exculpatory language discussed above.

In *W.H. Hunt v. Ellison & Tanner, Inc.,*[23] the owner brought an action against the architect for breach of contract. Specifically, the owner alleged that the

---

[22] *See also* Business & Professions Code § 6703.1 affording the same protection to engineers.
[23] 739 S.W.2d 933 (Tex. Ct. App. 1987).

architect breached its obligation under the contract with the owner to observe the progress of the work and to endeavor to guard the owner against defects in the work. The critical paragraph in the owner/architect contract read:

> The architect will make periodic visits to the site to familiarize himself generally with the progress and quality of the work and to determine in general if the work is proceeding in accordance with the contract documents. On the basis of his on-site observations as an architect, he will keep the owner informed of the progress of the work and will endeavor to guard the owner against defects and deficiencies in the work of the contractor. The architect will not be required to make exhaustive on-site inspections to check the quality and quantity of the work. Further, the architect will not be responsible for the construction means, methods, techniques, sequences or procedures, or for the safety precautions and programs in connection with the work, and he will not be responsible for the contractor's failure to carry out the work in accordance with the contract documents.

The architect in *Hunt* sought to utilize these exculpatory defenses, relying on *Moundsview*. In fact, the contract provisions at issue in *Hunt* involved contract provisions identical to those in *Moundsview*. Recall that the architect was exculpated from any liability occasioned by the acts and omissions of the contractor, where the failure of a contractor to follow the plans and specifications caused a roof mishap. The court in *Moundsview* further held that "by virtue of the aforementioned contractual provisions, [the architect] is absolved from any liability, as a matter of law, for a contractor's [failure] to follow the contract documents."[24]

In spite of this clear language, the *Hunt* court declined to follow *Moundsview*. The *Hunt* court stated that the exculpatory language in the owner/architect contract was nothing other than an agreement that the architect was not the insurer or guarantor of the general contractor's obligation to carry out the work in accordance with the contract documents. However, in spite of this exculpatory language in the contract, the court held that the contract did not exculpate the architect's liability for the general contractor's failure to carry out the work in accordance with the contract documents.

In *Magnolia Construction Co. v. Mississippi Golf Engineers, Inc.*,[25] the court addressed the question of what legal duty the project design professional owed the project contractor. The trial court concluded that the project design engineer did not assume any duties to supervise or inspect by its conduct on the job. However, the contractor presented evidence in the form of testimony of its project supervisor that the engineers checked certain pipes several times per day and, when specific problems arose, the engineers were notified and made decisions to change the plans. Additionally, the engineer engaged in other conduct which could be construed as inspection of the work. Further, the certificates attached to pay requests stated that "work and materials have been inspected and comply

---

[24] 253 N.W.2d at 839.

[25] 518 So. 2d 1194 (Miss. 1988).

with the standards of the contract." This certificate was signed by the field engineer and its supervisor.

Thus, the court concluded that there was clearly a factual dispute as to whether or not the contractor could reasonably rely upon the engineer to inspect its work on a consistent basis as a result of the conduct of the engineer and the engineer's field representative on the jobsite. Because this dispute involved factual issues, the appellate court reversed the trial court's granting of the summary judgment and held that these factual determinations should be made by the trier of fact at a trial.

In *Rian v. Imperial Municipal Services Group*,[26] a construction employee injured on the construction site brought suit against the site's owner and architect. The court held that the architect did not have the duty to supervise construction. Interestingly, the court in *Rian* left open the possibility that the architect could be liable for negligence in failing to supervise if such supervision, even absent a contract provision, was required by the ordinary standards of the architectural community.

In this case, the architect submitted an affidavit of another licensed architect with its motion for summary judgment which stated that, absent a contractual provision, it was not the custom or practice of an architect to supervise construction. Because plaintiff failed to refute this contention, summary judgment was granted. However, had plaintiff submitted an affidavit by a licensed architect stating that, despite the absence of a contract provision, supervision is required by the ordinary standards of the architectural community, then presumably plaintiff could have survived the architect's motion for summary judgment and the case would have gone to the jury on the question of whether the architect failed to meet the appropriate standard of care.

In the recent case of *Watson, Watson, Rutland Architects, Inc. v. Montgomery County Board of Education*,[27] the Supreme Court of Alabama had occasion to address the issue of whether exculpatory clauses such as those discussed in the cases above were effective to preclude the liability of the architect for failure to supervise.

In *Watson,* the school board alleged negligence and breach of contract against the architect. At trial, the court granted the architect's motion for directed verdict as to the school's negligence claim on the ground that the statute of limitations had expired. However, the breach of contract claim was submitted to the jury, and the jury returned a verdict of $24,813 against the architect.

The issue on appeal was whether the exculpatory language in the owner/ architect agreement absolved the architect from liability for damages arising from the failure of the contractor to follow the plans and specifications. The architect argued that the exculpatory language in the contract absolved the architect from liability to the school board because all of the damages were

---

[26] 768 P.2d 1260 (Colo. App. Ct. 1989).

[27] 559 So. 2d 168 (Ala. 1990).

attributable to the faulty workmanship of the contractor. Here again, like the owner in the *Moundsview* case, the owner elected to receive only general site inspections by the architect rather than pay an additional fee for continuous on-site inspections ("clerk of the works").

The architect contended on appeal that the imposition of liability upon it would be nothing short of holding the architect as a guarantor of the contractor's work. The school board responded to this argument by stating that it never contended the architect should be a guarantor of the contractor's work, but where a contract is for work and services, there is an implied duty to perform with an ordinary and reasonable degree of skill and care. Further, the school board argued that the claim was covered under the terms of the agreement because its claim was limited to those deviations from the plans and specifications that should have been obvious to one skilled in the construction industry.

In construing these exculpatory clauses, the court clearly recognized that the architect's duty to inspect was somewhat limited. However, the court did not agree with the argument that there could never be an imposition of liability under an agreement containing such exculpatory clauses. In support of this conclusion, the *Watson* court looked to the case of *First National Bank of Akron v. Cann*,[28] where the court stated:

> That exhaustive, continuous on-site inspections were not required, however, does not allow the architect to close his eyes on the construction site, refrain from engaging in any inspection procedure whatsoever, and then disclaim liability for construction defects that even the most perfunctory monitoring would have prevented.[29]

Thus, the *Watson* court held that:

> Although the contract here clearly made the architect's inspection duty a limited one, we cannot hold that it absolved the architect from all possible liability or relieved it from the duty to perform reasonably the limited contractual duties that it agreed to undertake. . . . While the agreement may have absolved the architect of liability for any negligent acts or omissions of the contractor and subcontractors, it did not absolve the architect of liability arising out of its own failure to inspect reasonably. Nor could the architect close its eyes on the construction site and not engage in any inspection procedure, and then disclaim liability for construction defects that even the most perfunctory monitoring would have prevented, or failed to advise the owner of a known failure of the contractor to follow the plans and specifications.[30]

---

[28] 503 F. Supp. 419 (N.D. Ohio 1980), *aff'd*, 669 F.2d 415 (6th Cir. 1982).

[29] 503 F. Supp. at 436.

[30] *See* Board of Educ. v. Sargent, Webster, Crenshaw & Foley, 146 A.D.2d. 190, 539 N.Y.S.2d 814, 817-18 (1989) (despite exculpatory clauses, where the trier of fact could find architect was aware of defect and failed to notify owner, liability is not precluded).

It is not yet clear whether these cases reflect a trend away from judicial enforcement of these exculpatory causes in the owner/architect agreement. However, it is clear that some courts are now recognizing that, despite the inclusion of these exculpatory clauses, the architect will be required to provide at least some minimum supervision of the construction process and will be held liable in damages for any failure to do so.[31]

§ 12.9   Limiting Liability by Contract

As the above discussion should indicate, the architect's objective in drafting a contract with the owner should be to minimize exposure to unexpected risks. By clearly and explicitly defining the architect's responsibilities in the contract with the owner, the architect can define the outer limits of liability to both the owner and, very often, to third parties as well.[32]

An appropriately drafted contract can limit the architect's duties and thereby limit the architect's potential liability for negligence. This is aptly illustrated in *Waggoner,* where the Oklahoma Supreme Court held that the clause in AIA A201 limiting the review of shop drawings to verification of conformance with design criteria precluded imposition and responsibility for tasks such as control of the work, construction methods and site safety, which were explicitly allocated to the contractor. In that way, the architect limited, and in this case avoided, liability by allocating specific tasks to other parties. The architect simply cannot be held liable for failing to perform duties not set forth in the contract. This also has the great benefit of avoiding a battle regarding what was or was not part of the architect's scope of work.

Again, it must be emphasized here that the contract can only limit liability to those activities explicitly set forth in that contract so long as the architect does not undertake, by conduct, to perform services not embodied in the contract. Where the architect does so, the architect will potentially incur liability for any negligence in performing those duties.

Additionally, some states will allow the architect, by contract, to limit liability to the owner for certain types of damages or may limit recovery to a maximum amount. In *Florida Power & Light Co. v. Mid-Valley, Inc.,*[33] the court, applying Florida law, held that a limitation of liability clause could be used to exculpate the engineers from their own negligence. However, these provisions were held to bind only the parties to a contract, or their intended third party

---

[31] It should be noted that there are at least as many cases giving effect to the exculpatory clauses and refusing to impose liability upon the architect based thereon. *See, e.g.,* Mayor & City Council v. Clark-Dietz & Assocs. Eng'rs, Inc., 550 F. Supp. 610 (N.D. Miss. 1982); Shepard v. City of Palatka, 414 So. 2d 1077 (Fla. Dist. Ct. App. 1981); Vonasek v. Hirsch & Stevens, Inc., 65 Wis. 2d 1, 221 N.W.2d 815 (1974).

[32] *See* Hensler v. City of Los Angeles, 124 Cal. App. 2d 41, 268 P.2d 12 (1954).

[33] 763 F.2d 1316 (11th Cir. 1985).

beneficiaries. Further, there are many states in which these attempts to limit or entirely preclude liability for the architect's own negligence will not be given effect as they are interpreted to be against public policy.

In *W. William Graham, Inc. v. City of Cave City*[34] the court held that a clause limiting liability, while valid and enforceable, was to be strictly construed against the party relying on such clause, and limited to its exact language. The clause at issue in *Graham* limited recovery for damages based upon professional negligence, errors, or omissions. No mention was made of liability for breach of contract. Thus, the court held that liability was limited only insofar as plaintiff sought damages for malpractice. Because breach of contract was not mentioned in the clause limiting liability, no such limitation applied to the breach of contract cause of action. Thus, *Graham* is an excellent illustration of just how strictly courts may construe clauses limiting liability.

In *Lincoln Pulp Paper Co. v. Dravo Corp.,*[35] the court noted that, although Pennsylvania law permitted private parties to contract validly to relieve themselves from the consequence of negligent acts, there must be a "clear and unequivocal" expression of the intent to limit liability for negligence. Again, the court notes that contracts limiting liability for negligence are not favored by the law and will be construed strictly, with every doubt resolved against the party seeking protection under the clause. This is particularly so where the party seeking such protection has drafted the contract.

In California, Civil Code § 2782.5 provides that an owner or other party to a construction contract may agree with respect to allocation, release, liquidation, exclusion, or limitation as between the parties of any liability (a) for design defects, or (b) of the promisee to the promisor arising out of or relating to the construction contract. Additionally, the architect may require that the owner purchase insurance or limit the architect's liability to the amount of the architect's insurance, the amount of the fee, or to the architect's proportional share of any joint and several liability.

However, when an architect fails to notify the owner of a known defective condition, the architect cannot hide behind an exculpatory clause in the owner/architect contract. In *Board of Education v. Sargent, Webster, Crenshaw & Foley,*[36] the court stated that:

> The underlying rationale for exonerating an architect under the exculpatory clause does not apply to defects known by the architect. . . . When, as a result of period inspection, an architect discovers defect in the progress of the work which the owner, if notified, could have taken steps to ameliorate the imposition of liability upon the architect for failure to notify would be based upon breach of his own contractual duty, and not as a guarantor of the contractor's performance. . . .

---

[34] 209 Ark. 105, 709 S.W.2d 94 (1986).

[35] 436 F.2d 262 (1977).

[36] 146 A.D.2d 190, 539 N.Y.S.2d 814 (1989).

Thus, the architect's knowledge of the existence of defective or dangerous conditions will not be protected under an exculpatory provision in the architect/owner contract.

§ 12.10 Recommendations

The foregoing authority and analysis demonstrate that the role of the architect is one that is dynamic and ever-changing. The nature and extent of the duties imposed will depend on the contract and the prevailing judicial attitude toward the role of the architect in the construction process. The use of sound business practices can enable the architect to avoid liability arising out of any implied duty to supervise construction. When the architect determines to provide construction supervision services, the nature and extent of these services must be clearly and explicitly set forth in the owner/architect contract.

However, as shown by the recent cases examined in § **12.8**, even careful drafting of the architect/owner contract will not always guarantee that the architect will prevail on a motion for summary judgment. It remains to be seen whether these cases constitute a new trend toward imposition of liability on the architect despite exculpatory provisions now in widespread use.

A few recommendations to the architect are possible. First, those architects practicing in states that do not have the type of protective legislation enacted in California would be wise to incorporate the text of these California statutes into a contract with the owner.

Second, when the architect determines to provide construction supervisory services, the architect should make every effort to obtain insurance protection for this additional risk. For instance, as a condition to providing such services, the architect might demand that the owner and/or contractor name the architect as an additional insured on any policy of insurance. This may enable the architect that is sued for damages allegedly arising out of these services to tender the defense and receive indemnification for any liability which falls upon the architect.[37] Where no such tender and indemnification occurs, the architect's own policy will usually cover the defense and liability. However, with the enormous deductibles applicable to most professional liability policies, this may mean that the architect must spend a large amount of its own funds.

Third, the architect must always remember that undertaking activities which are not considered architectural are not covered by the architect's liability insurance. Thus, before acting in the capacity such as the construction manager or project manager for the construction project, it would be prudent for the architect to verify that the liability insurance carried will cover the services which the architect intends to render. It has also been suggested by one commentator that the architect who intends to supervise construction should be

---

[37] *See The Liability of the Architect in his Supervisory Function,* 1 Forum 28, 39 (1966), where suggested language of such an indemnity agreement is set forth.

required to adequately prepare for that role through appropriate training in that area.

Fourth, regardless of the nature and extent of the construction administrative services provided by the architect, it is essential that the architect keep detailed records regarding the project.[38] In this way, the architect can later demonstrate that all supervisory obligations have been met. Recall that the architect in *Moundsview* visited the site 90 times over a 79-week construction period under a "general supervision" clause and was found to have no liability, as a matter of law, for failure to properly supervise.

Fifth, it has been suggested that the architect should receive training as to the legal consequences of the various construction roles so that needless liability can be avoided.[39] The reasoning here is that, because the architect plays such a large role in the contract formation process, some education will assist the architect in negotiating a contract that more precisely allocates the rights and obligations of the parties. Although this suggestion has some merit, the effect of various contract provisions will be different in each jurisdiction and will change over time. Therefore, the education process would need to be continuing. Further, where the issues become more legally sophisticated, it would behoove the architect to obtain the assistance of an attorney knowledgeable in this area.

Finally, the primary and overriding goal of the architect should be to avoid unexpected and unanticipated liability. Through careful contract drafting, knowledge of the effectiveness of various exculpatory provisions and strict adherence to the letter of the contract during the construction process, the architect can minimize potential exposure to unanticipated liabilities.

---

[38] *See also* Carey at 164.
[39] *Id.* at 169.

CHAPTER 13

IMPACT OF CONSTRUCTION SAFETY ON DESIGN PROFESSIONALS

Milton F. Lunch

§ 13.1   Introduction

§ 13.2   The Master Builder Concept

§ 13.3   Early Supervision Cases

§ 13.4   Stop the Work Cases

§ 13.5   Current Document Language

§ 13.6   Relationship of Workers' Compensation Laws

§ 13.7   Labor Laws

§ 13.8   Impact of OSHA

§ 13.9   Pending Safety Legislation

§ 13.10 Defense by Indemnification

§ 13.11 Construction Safety Guidelines

§ 13.1   Introduction

Construction is the second most dangerous activity in the United States. (Mining is first.) According to various estimates, construction accidents led to over 3000 deaths in 1988 and a substantially higher number of injuries. One of the significant developments of the 1980s for design professionals was a series of initiatives to deal with construction industry fatalities and injuries, a number of which suggested a greater involvement of engineers and architects in the construction phase of a project.

The major developments in this regard are summarized in this chapter, but before these recent developments can be put into proper perspective, it is necessary to look at some of the historical background relative to the role of the design professional in construction safety issues.

§ 13.2 The Master Builder Concept

In an earlier and simpler time the design professional was regarded as the *master builder*. It was the design professional's project from start to finish, including not only the basic design, but also the overall control of the construction of the project. That control in the original concept of the master builder entailed the supervision of the construction as set forth in the plans and specifications.

The struggle to change from that master builder philosophy on the part of architects in particular is set forth in Joseph Dundin's interesting review of the development of the standard documents of the American Institute of Architects over a 100-year period.[1] The author notes that abandonment of the "supervision" standard was made over the strong objection of William Stanley Parker, the recognized "father" of the AIA documents "who ran the documents program more or less as a one-man show until the early 1950s."

§ 13.3 Early Supervision Cases

In the 1950s several key court decisions led to the realization on the part of design professionals that the use of "supervision" in the context of a construction project meant something quite different from what was intended by the architect or engineer (A/E).

In *Day v. National U.S. Radiator Corp.,*[2] a subcontractor worker had been killed in a boiler explosion. The subcontractor employing the worker had installed the boiler without the thermostat and pressure relief valve called for in the specifications, and had mistakenly installed these devices on a hot water storage tank instead. He then test-fired the boiler without notifying the architect, and the boiler exploded. The architect, whose contract called for his supervision, was held responsible for the accident by the trial court under the supervision duty in the contract.

On appeal, however, the Louisiana Supreme Court reversed the judgment against the architect, holding that he had no duty to supervise the installation of the hot-water system or inspect it during its installation. Nevertheless, as noted in Dundin's paper, this was an "explosive" case, giving rise to the effort to remove the architect from any duty to supervise the construction.

In another leading example during that same general period,[3] an engineering firm undertook to design an air-conditioning system for a race track clubhouse.

---

[1] Dundin, *A Hundred Years (Or So) of AIA Standard Documents,* Architecture, Oct. 1988.

[2] 128 So. 2d 660 (La. 1961).

[3] Pastorelli v. Associated Engr's, Inc., 176 F. Supp. 159 (D.R.I. 1959).

After the work was completed an employee of the race track was injured by a falling heating duct. In the subsequent suit against the engineering firm, which had contracted to supervise the construction, the court held that the firm was liable because it failed to see that the ducts were properly installed, and took no steps after their installation to ascertain how and by what means they were secured. "He was not an insurer that the contractors would perform their work properly in all respects; but it was his duty to exercise reasonable care to see that they did so."

§ 13.4   Stop the Work Cases

Closely related to the supervision cases are the "stop the work" cases (sometimes both issues are involved in the same case) under which the early standard documents provided that the design professional was authorized to stop the work of the contractor. The intention was to provide the design professional the means to assure the owner that the completed construction would comply with the plans and specifications. But the courts did not see it that way.

In the leading case of *Miller v. DeWitt*,[4] suit was against the architect by injured workers when a gymnasium roof collapsed during construction, asserting common law negligence and violation of the Illinois Structural Works Act. Under the contract, the architect had "general supervision and direction of the work," as well as "authority to stop the work."

Ruling in favor of the plaintiffs, the court said that "if the architects knew or in the exercise of reasonable care should have known that the shoring was inadequate and unsafe, they had the right and corresponding duty to stop the work until the unsafe condition has been remedied."

Earlier, the Arkansas Supreme Court held an architect liable when a 17-foot-deep basement excavation collapsed because it had not been shored in accordance with the requirements of the building code.[5] The court construed the architect's contract as giving him the authority to stop the work, thereby creating a duty to do so.

In short, these cases, as examples of a number of others of like import, stand for the proposition that the growth of liability exposure over the years on the part of architects and engineers had to lead to substantial changes in standard contract language in an effort to restrict that liability exposure to the professional services originally contemplated on the part of the design professional, namely, to participate in the construction phase only for the limited purpose of determining that the project was being built in accordance with the plans and specifications.

---

[4] 226 N.E.2d 630 (Ill. 1967).

[5] Erhart v. Hammonds, 334 S.W.2d 869 (Ark. 1960).

§ 13.5   Current Document Language

The documents currently published by the American Institute of Architects (AIA) and the Engineers Joint Contract Documents Committee (EJCDC) go to some pains to make as clear as possible that the contractor alone is responsible for construction means, methods, techniques and sequences of construction as well as the safety of construction workers.

In the agreement between the design professional and owner, the language states that the design professional will visit the site at appropriate intervals based on the state of construction to determine that the work is being performed pursuant to the contract documents.[6] Likewise, the general conditions state that the contractor "shall supervise and direct the Work, using the Contractor's best skill and attention."[7]

And with specific regard to safety, in addition to repetition of the language regarding the contractor being solely responsible for construction means and methods, etc., another provision adds "or for safety precautions and programs in connection with the Work, since these are solely the Contractor's responsibility as provided in Paragraph 3.3."[8]

There was a recent effort to return to the use of "supervision" in stating the role of the design professional during the construction phase, but the apparent intention of the authors was to express the idea that the design professional should do a more adequate job of inspecting the construction for compliance with the plans and specifications.[9]

§ 13.6   Relationship of Workers' Compensation Laws

More than 75 years ago, workers' compensation laws were enacted in all of the states. Under such laws, an injured worker is entitled to compensation for an injury (or the estate of a worker to death benefits) in accordance with a schedule of benefits established by the state. Efforts over the years to establish a single national schedule of benefits have been resisted strongly, and there appears to be no likelihood that a national standard will be established in the foreseeable future.

For architects and engineers, however, the problem arising from these laws has not been related to workers' compensation benefits payable to their own employees. Under the state laws the injured worker's benefits paid from the employer's workers' compensation insurance policy prevents that employer's

---

[6] AIA B141-1987 ¶¶ 2.6.5 and 2.6.6; EJCDC Document 1910-1 (1984 ed.) ¶ 1.6.2.3.

[7] AIA A201-1987 ¶ 3.3.1; EJCDC Document 1910-8 (1983 ed.) ¶ 6.1.

[8] AIA A201-1987 ¶ 4.2.3.

[9] *Model Design and Construction Documents,* National Association of Attorneys General, Dec. 1988. The NAAG document, which drew extensive criticism from all elements of the design and construction community was withdrawn in July 1990. See **Ch. 5.**

liability exposure to any other claims from the injured worker. That arrangement does not prevent the injured worker, or the deceased worker's estate, from seeking additional compensation for the injury from third parties allegedly responsible for the injury due to negligence.

Thus, architects and engineers increasingly have been charged with negligent conduct in connection with their services prior to or during the construction phase, leading to injury of the construction workers. A review of some of the more recent cases dealing with those kinds of claims demonstrates, but not conclusively, that the contract document language alluded to above has become a key factor in the disposition of such construction worker suits.

In *Hanna v. Huer, Johns, Neel, Rivers & Webb,*[10] a construction worker sued an architectural firm for injuries he sustained when a structural roof bar joist fell, alleging that the design firm had contractual responsibilities for safety precautions, and was negligent in performing onsite services by not making observations or inquiries regarding safety. The state supreme court ruled in favor of the architects, commenting on the basic issue of the duty of a design professional for safety of workers during construction:

> [T]he great weight of authority supports the rule that an architect does not, by reason of his supervisory authority over construction, assume responsibility for the day-to-day methods utilized by the contractor to complete the construction. The architect's basic duty is to see that his employer gets a finished product which is structurally sound and which conforms to the specifications and standards. Any duty that the architect may have involving safety procedures of the contractor must have been specifically assumed by the contract or must have arisen by actions outside the contract. In determining whether the architect's contractual duty to supervise the construction includes the safety practices on the jobsite, the architect may intentionally, or impliedly by his actions, bring the responsibility for safety within his duty of supervision.

By pure coincidence, essentially the same issue was considered by the same court within months of the *Hanna* decision, this time following the death of a construction worker who was killed when a trench caved in on him while working at the construction site. The engineering firm in *Balagna v. Shawnee County & Van Doren-Hazard-Stallings,*[11] as in *Hanna,* had not contracted to be responsible for safety precautions, and the technical specifications stated that the contractor would assume full responsibility for safety of workers.

In a decision which generated extensive publicity in engineering circles, the court reached an opposite conclusion, holding that the engineering firm was liable because under the facts of the case the firm's resident engineer had seen the open and unshored trench, in violation of federal and state safety laws, and had not taken any action to correct the dangerous condition:

---

[10] 662 P.2d 243 (Kan. 1983).

[11] 668 P.2d 157 (Kan. 1983).

In Hanna, Justice Holmes stated that, if the architect-engineers had actual knowledge of unsafe practices, they should have taken some action in that case. However, in Hanna all the evidence disclosed that they had not been advised of such practices. Huer, Johns were held not responsible for safety on the jobsite since that duty was placed upon the general contractor as specifically spelled out in the contract. . . . We have considered the record in this case and concluded that there is evidence to show that the Engineers, Van Doren, through their employee, Freeborn, had actual knowledge of the safety standards requiring shoring in trenching operations and, furthermore, had actual knowledge that the prescribed safety precautions were not being followed by the contractor at the time the tragic accident occurred. In our judgement, this created a duty in the Engineers to take some reasonable action to prevent injury to the contractor's employee. . . .

The court did not state, or even intimate, what action the engineering firm's representative should have taken. The obvious action might be to immediately notify the contractor of the dangerous conditions, but in this case the contractor's supervisor stood side by side with the resident engineer, and both saw the same condition. Since this case there has been repeated discussion at engineering meetings as to what kind of action a design firm should take in such circumstances.

Waggoner v. W&W Steel Co.[12] was one of the more significant cases involving the question of liability of the design professional, and in a general sense might be regarded as a turning point in how the courts came to regard the issue in light of the contract language in the AIA and EJCDC contract forms.

In this case two workers were killed and a third injured while working on guy lines to secure the portion of steel framework on which they were standing. A gust of wind hit the unsecured, unbraced steel, causing it to collapse. The subsequent suit contended that the A/E was negligent in approving shop drawings that did not provide for temporary connections on the expansion joints.

The trial court directed a verdict for the architect, but the appellate court reversed, determining that the architect owed a duty to the workers in that it "undertook to supervise the construction project." The state supreme court vacated the appellate decision and affirmed the trial court's judgment. The basis for the supreme court's decision was the language in the general conditions, alluded to above, and particularly the part which states that the contractor is solely responsible for all construction means and methods, etc. Further, it was the duty of the contractor, not the architect, to see that the shop drawings included provisions for temporary connections which are part of the field construction criteria.

More recently there have been a series of decisions exonerating the design professional for worker injury claims, particularly where the architect or engineer had used the standard contract document language alluded to above.

---

[12] 657 P.2d 147 (Okla. 1982), *reh. denied* (1983). *Compare* Jaeger v. Henningson, Durham & Richardson, Inc., 714 F.2d 773 (8th Cir. 1983), in which the A/E firm was liable for approving shop drawings which were erroneous and in conflict with the specifications, resulting in worker injuries.

In *Young v. Eastern Engineering & Elevator Co.*,[13] the court, after noting the earlier decisions in *Miller* and *Erhart v. Hammonds*,[14] in which the professional firms had either implicit or explicit authority to stop the work regarding unsafe working conditions, stated that such a condition did not prevail under the facts of the case:

> We therefore hold that absent an undertaking by an architect, by contract or conduct of the responsibilities of the supervision of construction and the maintenance of safe conditions on a construction project, an architect is not under a duty to notify workers or employees of the contractor or subcontractors of hazardous conditions on the construction site.

And where the allegation against the design firm is general negligent performance of the contract and a corresponding failure to observe unsafe working conditions, the courts will generally turn to the issue of whether the design firm had undertaken a duty in that regard. In *Pugh v. Butler Telephone Co.*,[15] the court observed that the engineer's contract stated that its obligations were to run to and only for the benefit of the client. Further, the construction contract required the contractor at all times to take all reasonable precautions for the safety of its employees on the project, and to comply with all applicable provisions of federal, state and municipal safety laws and building construction codes.

> Fundamental to the maintenance of a negligence action is the existence of a legal duty of care owed by the defendant to the plaintiff. Plaintiffs place great emphasis upon the contractual undertaking of Fail [the engineer] in its contract with Butler. While a party's negligent performance of a contract may subject the party to liability in tort for physical harm to others . . . the scope of that duty, i.e., the persons to whom the duty runs, must be ascertained. . . . In this case, efforts to prove the existence of a duty towards Pugh must fail, because plaintiffs are necessarily relying on nonfeasance, as opposed to misfeasance, in Fail's performance of the contract, i.e., plaintiffs contend that Pugh was killed because of the failure of Breland [Fail's resident engineer] to be at the bore site at the time of the accident.

In describing the role of the design professional during the construction phase, both the AIA and EJCDC documents specify that the design professional will generally "observe" the construction in endeavor to protect the interests of the owner. The use of "observe" has been extensively criticized for its lack of specificity, leading one noted authority to comment that it is intended that the

---

[13] 554 A.2d 77 (Pa. Super. 1989).

[14] Miller v. DeWitt, 226 N.E.2d 630 (Ill. 1967); Erhart v. Hammonds, 334 S.W.2d 869 (Ark. 1960).

[15] 512 So. 2d. 1317 (Ala. 1987). Along similar lines, see Rodriguez v. Universal Fastenings Corp., 777 S.W.2d 513 (Tex. Ct. App. 1989); Davis v. Lenox School, 541 N.Y.S.2d 815 (App. Div. 1989).

design professional will do something more during the process than "enjoy the scenery and sniff the air."

To date efforts to find a better or more definitive word or phrase has not found universal acceptance in the design community. The potential danger in finding a substitute for "supervise" is illustrated in *Marshall v. Port Authority of Allegheny County*.[16] There the engineering firm agreed to provide field personnel to "monitor" the construction. A worker injury occurred during the performance of ultrahazardous demolition work at night under unsafe conditions. The reference to "monitor" was ambiguous, the court said because it appeared to require the engineering firm to monitor construction "methods," whereas the owner-contractor agreement specified that the contractor would be solely responsible for all construction means and methods (employing the language in the standard contract forms of AIA and EJCDC).

The court construed that language to mean that the engineering firm's oversight function ran only to determining whether the project conformed to the design specifications. To impose a duty on the engineering firm to inspect demolition procedures for safety compliance would conflict with the sole responsibility of the contractor under the general conditions.

One might comment that the engineering firm was lucky in that situation. Other courts might well take a different tack in equating "monitor" to something very close to "supervision." Other suggestions to replace "supervision" have included "oversee," or "inspect," or "review." Any of these words, or others of similar import, leave large question marks. But that leaves for further refinement what would be appropriate language to describe the role of the design professional during the construction phase.

One idea that has been advanced, but not generally accepted to date, is to define the role of the design firm in terms of "provide professional services during the construction phase for the purpose of determining that the construction is being performed in accordance with the contract documents." That wording leaves for another day the broader question of the ability of the design firm to check each and every item of construction set forth in the specifications. How many field personnel of the firm would be required to achieve that degree of oversight, and would the owner be willing to pay for that more-extensive field operation?

Following the decision in *Waggoner* those who were impacted by the high costs associated with the defense of the design firm undertook to seek legislative relief to deal with that kind of problem. They were successful in having the legislature enact an amendment of the worker compensation law to restrict injured worker suits against design professionals except for negligent preparation of design plans and specifications.

To date, ten other states have enacted similar revisions to their worker compensation laws: Hawaii, Connecticut, Florida, Kansas, Maine, Nebraska,

---

[16] 525 A.2d 857 (Pa. Commw. Ct. 1987).

North Dakota, Oregon, South Dakota, and Washington. The Kansas law, which is typical of the several statutes, is set out below:

> Except as provided in the workmen's compensation act, no construction design professional who is retained to perform professional services on a construction project or any employee of a construction design professional who is assisting or representing the construction design professional in the performance of professional services on the site of the construction project, shall be liable for any injury on the construction project for which compensation is recoverable under the workmen's compensation act, unless responsibility for safety practices is specifically assumed by contract. The immunity provided by this subsection to any construction design professional shall not apply to the negligent preparation of design plans or specifications.[17]

The foregoing comment on the relationship between the potential liability exposure of the design professional and the exclusive remedy rationale of the workers' compensation laws is predicated on the understanding that the injured worker (or its estate) is free to sue the design professional, as a third party alleging negligence in the plans or specifications, causing the injury. That has been the pattern in all of the worker injury cases.

However, a notable exception was declared in a recent decision of the Supreme Court of Virginia.[18] In what appears to be the only decision of its kind, the Virginia court declared that the architect was covered by the contractor's workers' compensation policy, and therefore immune from suit by a third party.

Under the court's reasoning, the workers' compensation act covers all persons engaged in work that is part of the trade, business or occupation of the party who undertakes to perform the work, but a common law action may be brought against an "other party" who is a "stranger" to the work. On that line of distinction, the court ruled that the architect was not a "stranger" and therefore not an "other party" because of his relation to the project. This is akin to the "common enterprise" theory of the extent of coverage under the worker compensation laws.

Whether other courts will follow this kind of analysis is problematical. None others have done so to date.

§ 13.7   Labor Laws

Special attention must be paid to state labor laws which may impact professional firms, over and above the ordinary negligence cases of the type discussed above.

The New York state law,[19] for example, calls for all construction work to be performed in a manner that will provide reasonable and adequate protection and

---

[17] Kan. Stat. Ann. § 44-508 (Supp. 1984).

[18] Evans v. Hook, 387 S.E.2d 777 (Va. 1990).

[19] New York Labor Law §§ 240 and 241.

safety to persons employed in the process. A separate part of that law, however, mandates that no liability for noncompliance with any of the provisions of the law or regulations shall be imposed on consulting engineers or architects "who do not direct or control the work for activities other than planning and design." But it is further provided that "this exception shall not diminish or extinguish any liability of professional engineers, architects or landscape architects arising under the common law or any other provision of law."

The quoted language will be interpreted on a case-by-case basis, but presumably means the design professional may be liable upon proof of the negligent preparation of plans and specifications leading to injury of workers. A recent New York decision[20] dealing with this issue exonerated an engineer who was retained to inspect and test a refuse compactor supplied and installed by the contractor. The court commented: "It is well settled in New York that liability may not be imposed upon an engineer who is engaged to assure compliance with construction plans and specifications, for injury sustained by a worker, unless the engineer commits an affirmative act of negligence or such liability is imposed by a clear contractual provision."

In Illinois, there have been mixed results from the Structural Works Act, sometimes referred to as the "Scaffolding Act,"[21] under which the person "in charge" of construction is strictly liable for worker injuries. The words "in charge" have been construed in different ways in various fact situations. One of the more recent decisions[22] holds that an engineer with authority to stop the work and who also had a "supervisor" at the job site each day was "in charge" and therefore liable when a worker was injured while laying pipe. In an earlier case, an architect was held liable because he had the authority to stop the work, harking back to *Miller.*[23]

But in an earlier case the Illinois court held that the engineering firm was not "in charge" of the work when the allegation was that the engineering firm had failed to prepare plans and specifications for a safe ladder.[24]

A number of other states have similar "safe place" statutes, requiring that in each instance it is necessary to review the cases under those state laws to determine the circumstances which may lead the court to relate the activities of the design firm to control of construction. Again, the standard document wording alluded to above is the safest course to follow with regard to control of the construction process.

---

[20] Brooks v. A. Gatty Serv. Co., 511 N.Y.S.2d 643 (App. Div. 1987).

[21] Ill. Rev. Stat., ch. 48, para. 60-69 (1981).

[22] Bisset v. Joseph A. Schult & Assocs., 478 N.E.2d 911 (Ill. App. Ct. 1985).

[23] Emberton v. State Farm Mut. Auto. Ins. Co., 373 N.E.2d 1348 (Ill. 1978).

[24] Robinson v. Greeley & Hansen, 408 N.E.2d 723 (Ill. App. Ct. 1980); Diomar v. Landmark Assocs., 401 N.E.2d 1287 (Ill. App. Ct. 1980); Fruzyna v. Walter C. Carlson Assocs., Inc., 398 N.E.2d 60 (Ill. App. Ct. 1979).

§ 13.8   Impact of OSHA

The Occupational Safety and Health Act (OSHA)[25] declares that each employer shall furnish a place of employment free from recognized hazards that are causing or are likely to cause death or serious physical harm. The key word is "employer," as related to the liability concerns of architects and engineers. In a construction setting the employer would be assumed to be the construction company. But there is presently an open question of the extent to which OSHA may seek to apply the law to design professionals engaged in providing services during the construction phase of the project designed by the A/E.

In the 1970s there were a series of cases along related lines, dealing mainly with the question of whether a construction manager was an employer, subject to penalties for nonconformance with OSHA standards. On the question of whether a construction manager was such an employer the results were mixed. In one case[26] an architectural firm serving as the design architect and construction manager was held "engaged in construction" work, and therefore subject to construction safety standards even though the firm had contracted to provide normal professional services and performed no construction work. The Occupational Safety and Health Review Commission (OSHRC) said that the architect was within the scope of the law because his agreement to "coordinate" the construction was inextricably intertwined with the actual physical labor at the site and his position was more akin to that of a general contractor.

Shortly thereafter the OSHRC reached an opposite result in a closely related case.[27] The architectural firm had contracted to provide field representative to "observe" the construction, review tests, and direct correction of improper work. The contract disclaimed authority to direct the work of the contractors or supervise construction methods or techniques. Proving that labels can sometimes make a difference, the Commission noted that the architect was not identified as a "construction manager," as in *Bertrand Goldberg*. In this case, the Commission concluded that "an employer must perform actual construction work or exercise substantial supervision over actual construction." In ruling in the design firm's favor, the OSHRC concluded, "Although the architect exercises some supervision over construction we would not characterize it as substantial."

The issue of the application of OSHA to design firms remained quiet after the 1970 cases, but has come to life in a significant way in the late 1980s. At the present time there are two cases against A/E firms filed by OSHA, assessing fines in one case for alleged safety violations during construction following an explosion, and in the other case a fine for the alleged negligence of the design firm in designing unsafe materials for use in the construction. At least one of the cases has been appealed to the OSHRC.

---

[25] 29 U.S.C.A. § 651.

[26] Bertrand Goldberg Assocs., 4 O.S.H. Cas. (BNA) 1587 (1976).

[27] Skidmore, Owings & Merrill, 5 O.S.H. Cas. (BNA) 1762 (1977).

While the exact details of these cases remain to be developed in the further proceedings, the significant issue for A/Es is whether they will be treated by OSHA as the employer of construction workers exposed to hazards, or whether OSHA intends to apply the construction safety standards to employees of the A/E firm at the site without regard to which party created the condition.

In that regard, a recent decision of the Third Circuit[28] is pertinent, even though not involving a design firm, in that the court ruled that a subcontractor was subject to penalty for a violation created by the general contractor, and over which situation the subcontractor had no control. The court said:

> Since the petitioner's employees were exposed to the hazardous condition and since petitioner was aware, actually or constructively, that the condition was hazardous, the only avenue open to the petitioner to prove its defense was to show that its employees working on the second floor were protected by other realistic means.

The court suggested that "other realistic means" might be filing a complaint with the general contractor, attempting to have the party responsible for the hazard correct it, or instructing its employees to avoid the area of the hazard. A similarity will be seen here to the situation in the *Balacna* decision where the engineering firm was liable when it saw a dangerous condition and did not take any corrective action.

The current OSHA regulations[29] dealing with multi-employer work sites state that if employees of more than one employer are exposed to a hazard, it may be deemed appropriate to issue citations to each of the employers, although the basic rule is to cite the employer primarily responsible for the health and safety of the employees. But the regulation further states that an employer, although not creating the hazard, may be cited if he knew or reasonably should have known of the hazard before permitting his employees to work in the hazardous area or with hazardous equipment.

For A/Es a number of questions come to mind. If the A/E has personnel at the site, to what extent should the A/E employees be instructed to report apparent violations to the responsible contractor? To what extent should A/E representatives at the site be expected to know the OSHA construction safety standards? How will the A/E's representatives at the site determine what is a dangerous condition? If the A/E representative sees what he believes to be a dangerous condition, should he withdraw from further inspection or observations of that part of the site until the condition is corrected?

---

[28] D. Harris Masonry Contracting, Inc. v. Dole, 876 F.2d 343 (3d Cir. 1989).

[29] OSHA Instruction CPL 2.45B (1988).

§ 13.9   Pending Safety Legislation

Following the collapse of the L'Ambiance Plaza building in Connecticut in 1987 in which 28 construction workers were killed, and 16 injured, legislation was introduced in Congress to try to deal with construction safety.

The original bill (S. 2518) would have required the owner of a construction project to retain a state-registered engineer to provide oversight of the construction to ensure workers' safety, and would have imposed substantial requirements for preparation of safety plans and detailed reporting requirements. The A/E community promptly noted that the requirement for a P.E. to be in charge of construction safety raised serious liability implications, and that P.E.s as a rule are not adequately trained in safety techniques to serve that function. Also, professional liability insurance would not cover such activities.

In 1989 the legislation was substantially revised. Under the 1989 bill (S. 930) the requirement for an engineer to be responsible for construction safety was dropped. In its place, the bill would require that the contractor employ a certified safety specialist (CSS) for the safety function, with authority for the CSS to stop the work in situations in which there is imminent danger to workers. The CSS would be qualified by the Office of Construction Safety and Health and Education of the Department of Labor on the basis of completing a 40-hour course of study on construction safety, or, in the alternative, have received on-the-job training with a certified CSS for a minimum of 18 months.

At a hearing on the bill in 1989, representatives of the A/E societies, as well as the construction industry, raised objection to the minimum requirements to achieve CSS status, and said, in general, that if the concept is to be adopted a much more extensive and formal educational process and examination would be required. The bill, as it stands, however, would authorize the CSS to require the employer to obtain the advice of a qualified design professional if he determines that a particular phase of the work involves special safety hazards. That aspect of the bill, if enacted, also raises liability questions and insurance coverage for A/Es serving in that kind of role.

§ 13.10   Defense by Indemnification

The most obvious way for an A/E to protect himself from liability claims related to injured construction workers, to the extent that such protection is available at all, is through the use of indemnification provisions in the general conditions. The standard indemnification language in both the AIA and EJCDC documents stipulate that the contractor will indemnify the design professional and the owner for all claims, losses, expenses, etc., arising out of the performance of the work caused in whole or in part by the contractor, except that the contractor indemnification does not apply if the injury was the result of the preparation of maps, drawings, opinions, reports, surveys, change orders, designs or specifications by the design professional.[30]

These provisions have been subject to numerous interpretations by the courts under the facts and circumstances of each case.[31]

Many of the indemnification cases turn on the principle that the courts look with disfavor on provisions which indemnify a person for that person's own negligence. In that connection, note should be taken of the anti-indemnification statutes which have been adopted in a large number of states.[32]

These anti-indemnification laws have received little judicial notice to date, but of particular interest with regard to A/Es, a Florida court, applying the anti-indemnification law of the state, ruled that the statute did not prevent enforcement of the indemnification clause against the contractor when the architect was found not negligent in a prior proceeding.[33]

And in a more recent case, a court has ruled that indemnification provisions in a construction contract required the contractor to indemnify the owner's engineer, even if the safety problem in question should have been detected by the engineer.[34]

§ 13.11   Construction Safety Guidelines

Based on the above review, perhaps some fairly obvious guidelines should be kept in mind by design professionals concerned with the potential impact of worker safety possibilities:

1.   The A/E should not contract to "supervise," "monitor," or "inspect" the construction.

2.   The contract documents should clearly state that the contractor is solely responsible for construction means, methods, sequences of construction, and the safety of workers.

3.   The A/E should not, by its conduct, become involved in safety aspects of the construction; but

---

[30] EJCDC 1910-8 (1983 ed.) ¶ 6.30; AIA A201-1987 ¶ 3.18.

[31] Board of Trustees v. RTKL Assocs., 559 A.2d 805 (Md. App. 1989); Disdier v. Woodbridge Preservation Group, 257 Cal. Rptr. 535 (Cal. Ct. App. 1989); Burns & Roe, Inc. v. Central Maine Power Co., 659 F. Supp. 141 (D. Me. 1987); South Dakota Bldg. Auth. v. Geiger-Berger Assocs., 414 N.W.2d 14 (S.D. 1987); Grossman & Bliss v. Sea Air Towers, Ltd., 513 So. 2d 686 (Fla. Dist. Ct. App. 1987).

[32] For an overview of such statutes and a state-by-state listing, see Guidelines for Improving Practice, Vol. XIX, No. 8 (1989), Office for Professional Liability Research, Victor O. Schinnerer & Co., Inc.

[33] Cuhaci & Peterson Architects, Inc. v. Huber Constr. Co., 516 So. 2d 1096 (Fla. Dist. Ct. App. 1987).

[34] Apel Mach. & Supply Co. v. J.E. O'Toole Eng'g Co., 548 So. 2d 445 (Ala. 1989).

4. If the A/E sees a dangerous condition it should take some action to try to prevent the accident. Just what action it should take is not clear, but at a minimum it should notify the contractor or state authorities, time permitting.

5. Special attention must be paid to states having a structural works act, such as Illinois, in which case the A/E can be held liable for being "in charge" of the work if the court can find any basis to prove A/E involvement.

6. The A/E may be held liable for a worker injury if the worker can make out a case that the injury occurred because of defective plans and specs, or failure to check shop drawings correctly.

THE DEFENSE OF QUALIFIED PRIVILEGE IN DEFAMATION AND COMMERCIAL TORT CLAIMS AGAINST ARCHITECTS

Christopher L. Noble*

§ 14.1   Introduction

§ 14.2   Defamation

§ 14.3   Tortious Interference

§ 14.4   Privilege Defenses

§ 14.5   Communications

§ 14.6   —Communications with Owner

§ 14.7   —Communications with Persons Other than Owner

§ 14.8   Case Summaries

§ 14.9   —*Riblet Tramway Co. versus Ericksen Associates, Inc.*

§ 14.10 —*Somers Construction Co. versus Board of Education*

§ 14.11 —*Joba Construction Co. versus Burns & Roe, Inc.*

§ 14.12 —*Conway Corp. versus Construction Engineers, Inc.*

§ 14.13 —*Kecko Piping Co. versus Town of Monroe*

§ 14.14 —*Vojak versus Jensen*

§ 14.15 —*Certified Mechanical Contractors, Inc. versus Wight & Co.*

§ 14.16 —*Dehnert versus Arrow Sprinklers, Inc.*

§ 14.17 —*George A. Fuller Co. versus Chicago College of Osteopathic Medicine*

* This chapter is adapted from a paper presented in June 1989 to the 28th Annual Meeting of Invited Attorneys sponsored by AIA, NSPE, and Victor O. Schinnerer & Company. The assistance of Maureen McGee, Esq., and Clare McGorrian in its preparation is gratefully acknowledged.

§ 14.18   — *V.M. Solis Underground Utility & Paving Co. versus City of Laredo*

§ 14.19   — *Alfred A. Altimont, Inc. versus Chatelain, Samperton & Nolan*

§ 14.20   — *Santucci Construction Co. versus Baxter & Woodman, Inc.*

§ 14.21   — *Ballou versus Basic Construction Co.*

§ 14.22   — *Waldinger Corp. versus CRS Group Engineers, Inc.*

§ 14.23   **Guidelines to Protect Architects**

§ 14.1   Introduction

A contractor who has suffered a loss on a project, or who believes itself to have been harassed or unfairly treated, is likely to seek relief not only against the owner of the project but also against the architect or engineer. Since the contractor does not have a contract with the design professional, it must seek to collect under a noncontractual theory. Third-party beneficiary of the contract and negligence theories have been commonly called into service by contractors for this purpose. However the former theory is often negated by an express exclusion of third-party rights in the agreement between the owner and the design professional, and the latter theory is countered with increasing success by the economic loss doctrine.

A contractor seeking a more effective noncontractual cause of action against an architect or engineer is likely to consider the theories of defamation and/or tortious interference with contractual relations.

There are a number of defenses to each of these causes of action. (Truth, for instance, is an absolute defense to a defamation claim.) For architects and engineers, however, their most effective shield is likely to be the defense of privilege. This chapter will summarize the elements of the subject causes of action, review cases in which privilege was asserted by design professionals as a defense, and suggest strategies which design professionals can employ in their contracts and their professional practices in order to strengthen the protection which can be afforded to them by the privilege defense.

§ 14.2   Defamation

Defamation is a communication that tends so to harm the reputation of another as to lower it in the estimation of the community or to deter third persons from associating or dealing with it.[1] In general, the plaintiff must prove: (1) defamatory language by the defendant which identifies the plaintiff to a reasonable reader, listener, or viewer; (2) publication of the defamatory language by the

---

[1] Restatement (Second) of Torts § 559 (1977).

defendant to a third person; (3) damage to the plaintiff's reputation; and (4) fault on the defendant's part.

If the defamatory language is in writing or some other permanent medium, the defamation constitutes libel. Damages on account of libel are presumed and need not be proven by the plaintiff. Spoken defamation constitutes slander. Injury to reputation is not presumed in the case of slanderous statements, and special damages must thus be alleged and proven with specificity by the plaintiff. If the defamatory statement adversely reflects on the plaintiff's abilities in its business, trade or profession, it constitutes libel or slander per se, and malice, falsity, and damage to reputation are presumed without pleading or proof.

§ 14.3   Tortious Interference

Tortious interference consists of intentional and improper interference with the performance of a contract—or prospective contractual relation—between the plaintiff and a third person through inducing or otherwise causing the third person not to perform or enter into the contract. The interfering defendant is subject to liability to the plaintiff for the plaintiff's pecuniary loss resulting from the failure of the third person to perform or enter into the contract.[2]

The elements required for a prima facie case of tortious interference with a contractual relationship are: (1) the existence of a valid contractual relationship or business expectancy; (2) knowledge of the relationship or expectancy on the part of the interferor; (3) intentional interference inducing or causing a breach or termination; and (4) resultant damage to the plaintiff.

§ 14.4   Privilege Defenses

There are similar, but not identical, privilege defenses to the two causes of action. The defamation privilege arises when circumstances lead any one of several persons having a common interest in a particular subject matter correctly or reasonably to believe that facts exist which another sharing such common interest is entitled to know.[3] The tortious interference privilege arises in a number of circumstances, including legitimate business competition, financial interest, responsibility for the welfare of another, directing business policy, and

---

[2] *Id.* §§ 776, 766B (1977).

[3] *Id.* § 596 (1977).

the giving of requested advice.[4] It also can arise, as discussed in cases summarized below, from an interest on the part of the interfering party which is equal or superior to the interest of the plaintiff in the same subject matter.[5]

As will be observed below, different appellate courts have defined these privileges in different ways, although similar general principles apply in most cases. The court decisions also illustrate several other legal characteristics of the privilege defense:

1. The privilege is not absolute, but is conditional. It can be lost in a number of ways, the most common being when the person asserting the privilege has been found to have acted maliciously or in bad faith.

2. Whether or not a communication is privileged is a question of law for the court to decide.

3. Whether or not malice or bad faith existed so as to defeat the privilege is a question of fact for the trier of fact (judge or jury, as the case may be) to decide.

4. The burden of establishing the existence of the privilege is on the party asserting it.

5. Once the privilege has been established, the burden of proving that it has been lost rests with the plaintiff.

§ 14.5   Communications

Architects and engineers are the "great communicators" of the construction process. They produce a constant stream of advice, information, instructions, interpretations, opinions, and other communications to owners, contractors, and others. The following types of communications have generated defamation or tortious interference claims which have resulted in the court decisions discussed in this chapter.

§ 14.6   —Communications with Owner

1. Advice regarding rejection of a low bidder: *Riblet Tramway* (see § **14.9**), *Somers Construction* (see § **14.10**), *Joba Construction* (see § **14.11**), and *Conway* cases (see § **14.12**).

2. Advice regarding rejection of proposed subcontractors: *Kecko Piping* (see § **14.13**) and *Vojak* cases (see § **14.14**).

---

[4] *Id.* §§ 768-772 (1977).

[5] An issue related to the defense of qualified privilege in tortious interference and defamation actions is the assertion of absolute privilege for advice given by architects or engineers in preparation for or in anticipation of litigation. Although detailed discussion of this issue is

3. Advice regarding stopping or rejection of work: *Certified Mechanical Contractors* case (see § **14.15**).

4. Advice regarding termination of a contractor: *Dehnert* (see § **14.16**), *George A. Fuller* (see § **14.17**), and *Solis* cases (see § **14.18**).

§ 14.7 —Communications with Persons Other than Owner

1. Direct communications with surety: *Altimont* case (see § **14.19**).

2. Communications with suppliers: *Santucci Construction* case (see § **14.20**).

3. Insistence upon full compliance by subcontractor with contract requirements: *Ballou* (see § **14.21**) and *Waldinger* cases (see § **14.22**).

§ 14.8 Case Summaries

The following case summaries describe in greater detail the circumstances under which these claims arose, the theories on which the claims were based, and the applicability and effectiveness of the design professionals' privilege defense.

§ 14.9 —Riblet Tramway Co. versus Ericksen Associates, Inc.[6]

The State of New Hampshire engaged Ericksen as an engineering consultant to renovate and repair ski lifts. Ericksen's duties included reviewing bids for compliance with specifications. At a public hearing before the governor and executive council, a councilor asked the engineer, "Are you saying there is a risk to the public safety if the state was to go with Riblet [the low bidder]?" The engineer answered, "That's correct." Riblet claimed that the engineer, through the exchange at the public hearing, slandered it and tortiously interfered with its prospective agreement.

---

outside the scope of this chapter, reference may be made to two particularly relevant cases: Western Technologies, Inc. v. Sverdrup & Parcel, Inc., 154 Ariz. 1, 739 P.2d 1318 (1987) (critical statements in report by consulting engineer held absolutely privileged where engineer was engaged by owner who was actively contemplating litigation, and who relied on such statements in bringing suit); and Middlesex Concrete Prods. & Excavating Corp. v. Carteret Indus. Ass'n, 68 N.J. Super. 85, 172 A.2d 22 (1961) (engineer's investigation, report, and advice held absolutely privileged when furnished during and in preparation for litigation).

[6] 665 F. Supp. 81 (D.N.H. 1987).

The court ruled that the engineer was entitled to summary judgment as a matter of law on both the defamation and intentional interference claims. The statements were held to be the nondefamatory opinion of an expert consultant based upon fully disclosed, undisputed facts. On the intentional interference count, the court found that the facts alleged by Riblet were sufficient to make out a claim of tortious interference with Riblet's prospective agreement with the State.

The issue then became whether the engineer's statements were privileged or otherwise justified. The court[7] stated that: (1) the defendant's advice was requested by the terms of its contract and by the councilor's specific question; (2) the response was within the scope of the request; and (3) there was no dispute as to the honesty of the advice.

§ 14.10   —Somers Construction Co. versus Board of Education[8]

The architect tabulated the bids and alternates for a public construction contract and determined that a contractor other than Somers was the low bidder. After a notice to proceed was issued and work had been commenced, Somers advised the architect that there was an error in the tabulation, and Somers was in fact the low bidder. The awarding authority then met, rescinded the award, and proposed to reconsider the previously selected alternates. By declining one previously selected alternate for which the price of the other contractor exceeded Somers's price, the Board reinstated the award to the other contractor as new "low" bidder.

Somers alleged that the architect's initial mistabulation of bids and the architect's subsequent advice to the awarding authority constituted tortious interference with prospective economic advantage. In ruling on the architect's summary judgment motion, the court held that, under the governing law of New Jersey, malice is an essential element of this tort. Somers had failed to allege that the mistabulation was malicious, and that count was dismissed. However, Somers did allege that the architect's advice was maliciously given, and the court declined to grant summary judgment on the factual issue of whether or not malice existed.[9]

---

[7] Applying Restatement (Second) of Torts § 772, Comment c (1979).

[8] 198 F. Supp. 732 (D.N.J. 1961).

[9] Note that, under the New Jersey law, malice was held to be an element of the cause of action, not an element by which a claim of privilege could be defeated. The analysis is substantially the same, however.

§ 14.11   —*Joba Construction Co. versus Burns & Roe, Inc.*[10]

Joba, a contractor specializing in underground and heavy-duty construction, sued a firm of consulting engineers retained by the City of Detroit Public Lighting Commission for tortious interference with prospective advantageous economic relations. The engineer's main responsibilities were to prepare construction specifications, evaluate bids made by contractors, and make recommendations to the commission as to which contractor should be awarded contracts.

Joba alleged that the engineer had wrongfully persuaded the commission not to award Joba the general contract on one project, for which Joba submitted the lowest bid, and to have Joba removed as excavation and piling subcontractor on another project. The court of appeals affirmed the judgment for Joba, finding that the trial judge had properly instructed the jury as to the requisite elements of qualified privilege and the burden of proof.

The court of appeals upheld the trial judge's instruction to the jury that, under Michigan law, the defendant had the burden of raising and proving qualified privilege as an affirmative defense. The court further found proper the jury instruction that a presumption of good faith and proper motive arose once qualified privilege was established, but that the presumption could be overcome if the plaintiff produced evidence of bad faith or dishonest purpose. In addition, the court upheld the inclusion of "reasonableness" as an element of the qualified privilege defense, stating that the determination of whether the defendant's conduct is privileged is a factual issue to be decided upon all the circumstances, including whether the conduct was fair and reasonable.

Finally, the court of appeals upheld the trial judge's charge to the jury to the effect that, if the underlying purpose of the defendant's advice was malevolent, instead of to protect a legitimate interest, the defendant is liable for the harm done regardless of the apparent existence of privilege.

The jury had found against the defendant engineer on the facts of this case, and, although the privilege defense was applicable as a matter of law, it failed to protect the engineer from the consequences of its own actions.

§ 14.12   —*Conway Corp. versus Construction Engineers, Inc.*[11]

Construction Engineers, Inc. (CEI), the low bidder on a municipal construction contract, sued Conway Corporation, the nonprofit corporation which operated

---

[10] 329 N.W.2d 760 (Mich. Ct. App. 1982).

[11] 300 Ark. 225, 782 S.W.2d 36 (1989).

the City of Conway's utilities, along with the corporation's directors, general manager, and the engineer on the construction project. The complaint, seeking injunctive and declaratory relief as well as damages, alleged that the contract was awarded to the second lowest bidder in violation of the law, and that defendants had conspired to interfere with CEI's business expectancy.

In reversing the lower court's entry of judgment for CEI, the Supreme Court of Arkansas held that the utility had rejected CEI's bid in good faith, and that the actions of the individual defendants, including the project engineer, were privileged from liability for the claim of tortious interference with business expectancy.

When the corporation solicited bids on the expansion of Conway's water treatment plant, the general manager asked the project engineer to contact CEI and dissuade it from bidding on the project. The general manager's concern arose from reports of serious problems in CEI's performance as general contractor on another local project. The project engineer contacted CEI's principals to express the general manager's reservations about their ability to perform the work but was unable to dissuade them from submitting a bid.

Upon opening the bids and discovering that CEI's was lowest, the general manager ordered the project engineer to conduct a post-bid investigation of both CEI and the second lowest bidder, Limbaugh Construction Company. The engineer's investigation uncovered excellent reports on Limbaugh but, at best, mixed reviews of CEI. The results of the engineer's investigation were presented to the corporation's board, which voted unanimously to award the contract to Limbaugh.

On appeal, the state supreme court found clearly erroneous the lower court's findings that the defendants acted with improper motives or bad faith. The court concluded that, where the general manager and project engineer acted without bad faith in the interest of those to whom they were responsible, their interference was privileged and they were therefore not liable.

§ 14.13   —*Kecko Piping Co. versus Town of Monroe*[12]

A prospective subcontractor who was not accepted for a school construction project after being named as a preferred sub in the general contractor's successful bid brought suit against the town and the architect. The sub sought damages for the architect's tortious interference with the making of a contract between it and the general contractor.

The architect's duties included obtaining bids and awarding and preparing construction contracts. The architect notified the sub that it was named by the general contractor. But the sub, despite urging by the architect, never provided information to substantiate its qualifications to perform the work. The architect

---

[12] 172 Conn. 197, 374 A.2d 179 (1977).

and the town became concerned about the sub's ability to perform, and the architect advised the town to require the general contractor to select a different sub.

The trial court held that the architect acted under a qualified privilege, and that the architect did not exceed the limits of such privilege. The Connecticut Supreme Court confirmed that the trial court had correctly stated the law and applied it to the facts which it found. On the issue of privilege, the court stated, "Pursuant to its contract with the town, the architect was under an obligation to advise the town as to the suitability of contractors and subcontractors and accordingly enjoyed a qualified privilege as noted in *Restatement (Second) of Torts*, § 772: 'One is privileged purposely to cause another not to perform a contract, or enter into or continue a business relation, with a third person by giving honest advice to the other within the scope of a request made by him.' There was clearly no error in the court's conclusion that the defendant architect in this case did not exceed the limits of its qualified privilege."[13]

§ 14.14   — *Vojak versus Jensen*[14]

The plaintiff, doing business as United Roofing Company, sought to be employed as a subcontractor on a school construction contract for which the defendant was the architect. Several years before, United had installed a roof on another school project designed by the architect, and the roof had failed.

The architect wrote letters to the general contractor and the awarding authority, rejecting United as a subcontractor unless the general contractor would "assume complete responsibility" for the roofing work and give the awarding authority "complete protection." The general contractor thereupon cancelled its contract with United. United sued the architect for libel and obtained a jury verdict in its favor. The trial judge sustained the architect's motion for a new trial which United appealed.

The Iowa Supreme Court summarized the applicable law in the following terms: "(1) A statement attributing business incompetence or lack of skill to another is libelous per se, from which a presumption of malice, falsity, and damage arises; (2) if made under a qualified privilege, such libelous statement is rendered innocuous and nonactionable; (3) actual malice nullifies the immunity of a qualified privilege."[15]

The court held that the architect's letters to the contractor and owner were libelous per se. On the issue of privilege, the court adopted the following definition from 33 Am. Jur., *Libel and Slander*, § 126:

---

[13] 172 Conn. at 202.

[14] 161 N.W.2d 100 (Iowa 1968).

[15] *Id*. at 105.

A communication made in good faith on any subject matter in which the person communicating has an interest, or in reference to which he has a duty, is privileged if made to a person having a corresponding interest or duty even though it contains matter which, without this privilege, would be actionable and although the duty is not a legal one. . . . The essential elements of a conditionally privileged communication may accordingly be enumerated as good faith, an interest to be upheld, a statement limited in its scope to this purpose, a proper occasion and publication in a proper manner to proper parties only. The [qualified] privilege arises from the necessity of full and unrestricted communication concerning a matter in which the parties have an interest or duty and is not restricted within narrow limits.[16]

The court held that the defendant architect had pleaded and proven a qualified privilege. The next issue was actual malice, which the court defined and discussed:

Actual malice is defined as ill-will, hatred, or desire to do another harm. It may also result from a reckless or wanton disregard of the rights of others. Actual malice maybe shown by the libelous statement itself or by extrinsic facts and circumstances. Here there was evidence from which the jury might find the defendant was seeking to relieve its own failures by falsely accusing plaintiff of incompetence; that defendant unreasonably refused to give consideration to suggestions submitted by plaintiff concerning the cause and possible cure of the [prior] roof trouble; that defendant recklessly accused plaintiff of incompetence without making any bona fide investigation to determine the basis for such charges.[17]

The court found, therefore, that the jury properly had before it the issues of privilege and malice. However, the court found the trial judge's instructions with respect to these issues to be so confusing, inconsistent, and misleading as to justify the granting of a new trial.[18]

§ 14.15 — *Certified Mechanical Contractors, Inc. versus Wight & Co.*[19]

A general contractor claimed that an architect wrongfully, maliciously, and in bad faith interfered with its contract with an owner by causing the owner to halt the project in order to permit the architect to test the general contractor's work.

---

[16] *Id.*

[17] *Id.* at 107.

[18] On the subject of a proper instruction, the Iowa Supreme Court stated, "The jury should have been told unequivocally that the letters were libelous per se; that they were written under a qualified privilege; and that plaintiff could recover only upon proving actual malice on the part of defendant." *Id.* at 109.

[19] 515 N.E.2d 1047 (Ill. App. Ct. 1987).

The architect's report of the test results outlined problems with the poured-in-place concrete work, and was critical of the general contractor's performance. A six-month delay ensued, for which the contractor sought damages.

The trial court granted summary judgment for the architect on the intentional interference count, on the ground of privilege. The contractor appealed. It claimed that the record raised a reasonable inference that the architect desired to injure it for reasons unrelated to a desire to advise the owner properly. In particular, the contractor asserted that the architect attempted to have it removed from the project to cover up the architect's own mistakes and omissions. The court analyzed this claim by the contractor in the following terms:

> A plaintiff can state a cause of action for tortious interference with a contract against a third party who is conditionally privileged if the plaintiff can set forth factual allegations from which actual malice may reasonably be said to exist. Actual malice means a positive desire and intention to annoy or injure another person. To demonstrate malice, more than ill will must be shown, and the evidence must establish the defendant acted with a desire to harm which was unrelated to the interest he was presumably seeking to protect by bringing about the contract breach. If an architect induces a breach of contract, not to further its principal's best interest, but with the intent to harm the other party to its principal's contract or to further its personal goals, the architect is liable for tortious interference.[20]

The court found that there was no factual support for a reasonable inference that the architect was motivated by a desire to harm the contractor or to further its own personal goals, and it therefore affirmed summary judgment for the architect.

§ 14.16 — *Dehnert versus Arrow Sprinklers, Inc.*[21]

A school district entered into a construction contract with Arrow Sprinklers, which specified the use of brass sprinkler heads or an approved equal. The contract further required that any changes in the work, including the substitution of an equal, had to be approved by the district pursuant to a formal written change order prepared by the architect and signed by the district.

Without obtaining prior approval or a written change order, Arrow installed plastic sprinkler heads. (The plastic heads had been indicated on a shop drawing approved by the architect, on which the architect did not take specific exception to the substitution.) The architect directed Arrow to replace the heads after they had been installed. When Arrow refused, the architect recommended that the school board terminate the contract. Five months later, upon the architect's certification that sufficient cause existed, the board terminated the contract.

---

[20] *Id.* at 1053-54 (citations omitted).

[21] 705 P.2d 846 (Wyo. 1985).

Arrow sued the architect for intentional interference with a contractual relationship.

The court noted that the architect had a contractual duty to reject nonconforming work and to advise and protect the school district with respect to the construction project. The court held that no liability attaches where an individual charged with protecting the interests of a third person justifiably acts to cause that person not to perform a contract. An architect who acts within the scope of its employment is not liable for advising an owner to terminate unless it acts with malice or bad faith.

The court distinguished malice or bad faith from "negligence, poor judgment or inflexibility," and stated that "[the architect's] failure to reject the plastic heads at the outset and his resolution of the resulting impasse may reflect negligence and poor judgment, but such conduct does not amount to malice or bad faith necessary to hold [the architect] liable."[22] Finding no malice or bad faith, the Wyoming Supreme Court reversed the decision of the trial court.

§ 14.17   —George A. Fuller Co. versus Chicago College of Osteopathic Medicine[23]

A general contractor who had contracted to build a new clinic brought an action for tortious interference with contract against the owner, two of its officers, and the project architect because it was terminated before the clinic was completed.

With regard to the claim against the architect the court concluded that, under Illinois law, an architect would be afforded a conditional privilege to interfere in a construction contract of its principal. The acts of interference alleged by the contractor were all held to fall within the architect's contractual duties, and there was no allegation that the architect acted contrary to the owner's best interest. The architect's motion to dismiss, which had been granted by the trial court, was affirmed.

§ 14.18   —V.M. Solis Underground Utility & Paving Co. versus City of Laredo[24]

Solis agreed to construct a storm sewer system for the city. Following several months of "continuing delays and disputes concerning the quality of the work," the project engineer recommended that the city order Solis to suspend work. Shortly thereafter, Solis filed for bankruptcy. The city terminated the contract and completed the project using city employees.

---

[22] *Id*. at 852.

[23] 719 F.2d 1326 (7th Cir. 1983).

[24] 751 S.W.2d 532 (Tex. Ct. App. 1988).

The engineer's contract required it to inspect the contractor's work "continuously" and to report any failure of the work or materials to conform to project specifications. Solis's contract with the city stated that the engineer's duties included inspection of Solis's work.

Solis sued the engineer for tortious interference with its contractual relationship with the city. The court affirmed a directed verdict for the engineer, stating, "An important element in a right of recovery for contract interference is that the interference must be without right or justification. Interference with contractual relations is privileged where it results from the bona fide exercise of a party's own rights or where the party possesses an equal or superior interest to that of the plaintiff in the subject matter. . . . The consulting engineer . . . was not liable because the recommendation to terminate the contract with Solis was based on the engineer's superior contractual rights with the City."[25]

§ 14.19   — *Alfred A. Altimont, Inc. versus Chatelain, Samperton & Nolan*[26]

When construction of a church project was far behind schedule and far from completion, the architect wrote to the contractor's surety expressing distress at the slow construction process. The letter indicated that there were many days when no one was on the job and that the contractor was not promptly and faithfully performing the contract and might be in default. In a second letter the architect blamed the contractor for the delays and stated that it considered it "extremely negligent." At a subsequent meeting, a representative of the architect refused to retract the statements and stated that it thought the contractor should get out of the construction business.

On the basis of the architect's letters and statement, the contractor sued the architect for defamation, interference with its business with bonding companies, and intentionally or maliciously interfering with its contract with the church.

The court upheld a directed verdict on the defamation claim because it found that the architect's statements to the bonding company were subject to a qualified

---

[25] *Id.* at 537. Recently, a New York trial court decided a case similar to the foregoing three cases involving advice regarding the termination of a contractor. N.S. Elec. Corp. v. Procida Constr. Corp., N.Y.J. T, p. 24, col. 1 (Dec. 13, 1989) (N.Y. Sup. Ct., Kings County). The New York case involved an action for slander and tortious interference with contract rights by a subcontractor against the construction manager of a building project. The court granted summary judgment to the defendant construction manager, finding that the defense of qualified privilege applied to the defendant's actions in recommending that the plaintiff's contract be terminated. In support of its conclusion, the court specifically found that the construction manager's actions were taken pursuant to its contract with the project owner, in furtherance of its interest shared with the project owner in seeing the project completed in a timely and proper manner, and without malice.

[26] 374 A.2d 284 (D.C. 1977).

privilege as defined in § 596 of the *Restatement (Second) of Torts,* and that the architect acted in good faith and within the scope of its duty in communicating with the bonding company. That the architect "undoubtedly felt antagonistic and resentful" toward the contractor was not enough to submit the evidence to the jury where it was as consistent with the non-existence of malice as with its existence.

The court recognized the existence of privilege as a defense to the interference claims, but did not reach this issue because it found that the contractor failed to establish a prima facie case of interference with contractual relations.

Even assuming the church was the party in breach, there was no evidence that the architect intentionally induced the church to breach its contract with the contractor. Nor was there a prima facie case of interference with business relations with the bonding companies. Most had rejected the contractor before the letters were written based upon the contractor's past history and financial background.

§ 14.20 — *Santucci Construction Co. versus Baxter & Woodman, Inc.*[27]

A municipality brought suit against Santucci Construction, general contractor on a sewer project. Santucci filed a third-party complaint against Baxter & Woodman, who had entered into a separate contract with the municipality to serve as project administrator, design engineer, and supervising engineer for the project.

Santucci alleged negligent and intentional interference with a contractual relationship and interference with prospective advantage from the continuing relationship it would otherwise have had with the municipality.

Santucci claimed that Baxter communicated directly with Santucci's suppliers, purportedly to determine the status of their accounts with Santucci, and encouraged the suppliers to terminate delivery of materials and provision of services. Santucci further claimed that Baxter abused its responsibility to supervise and administer the project by persuading the municipality to treat the actions of the suppliers as grounds to terminate Santucci's contract. Santucci alleged that these actions were done with malice (to deliberately cause injury to Santucci) or negligently and carelessly in violation of Baxter's duty to administer and supervise Santucci's work.

The appellate court followed the United States Court of Appeals for the Seventh Circuit[28] in holding that Illinois would allow an engineer or an architect a conditional privilege to interfere with the construction contract of its principal.

---

[27] 502 N.E.2d 1134 (Ill. App. Ct. 1986).

[28] George A. Fuller Co. v. Chicago College of Osteopathic Medicine, 719 F.2d 1326 (7th Cir. 1983); Waldinger Corp. v. CRS Group Eng'rs, Inc., 775 F.2d 781 (7th Cir. 1985).

Such a privilege would justify an interference which otherwise would be improper interference with a contractual relationship.

To establish the privilege, two factors must be considered. First, a third party may purposely bring about a breach of plaintiff's contract with another when it is acting to protect a conflicting interest that is considered under the law to be of a value equal to or greater than plaintiff's contractual rights. Second, the third party's acts that bring about the breach must be legal acts and must not be unreasonable in the circumstances. Because the full extent of the duties of Baxter had not been developed below, the court remanded for determination whether the actions complained of fell within the engineer's conditional privilege.

§ 14.21   *—Ballou versus Basic Construction Co.*[29]

The architect for a hospital project insisted upon literal compliance with a contract specification requiring a certain thickness of concrete covering over the reinforcing steel in certain concrete columns. The architect rejected 41 of the first 50 columns fabricated and installed by the subcontractor. In the course of the ensuing dispute and delay, the sub went bankrupt. The trustee of the bankrupt sub claimed that the architect's rejection of the columns constituted tortious interference with the contract between the sub and the general contractor.

The architect's defense was that of quasi-judicial immunity, under contract provisions giving the architect the right to determine the acceptability of work, to reject defective work, and to have defective work replaced without charge. The court treated this defense as a qualified privilege, adopting the trial court's finding that the architect was immune from suit in this case unless the plaintiff could show that fraud or bad faith motivated the decision. The court stated, "The architects' decision to enforce literal compliance with the contract may have reflected poor judgment or excessive rigidity, but there is no evidence or even suggestion that they were motivated by malice or bad faith."[30]

---

[29] 407 F.2d 1137 (4th Cir. 1967).

[30] The concept of quasi-arbitral immunity, which was used interchangeably with the privilege defense in the *Ballou* case, was first clearly recognized in Corey v. Eastman, 166 Mass. 279, 44 N.E. 217 (1896) (when resolving a dispute the architect is immune from liability; when advising the owner pursuant to contractual obligations, however, the architect must show reasonable care and professional judgment). *See also* Wilder v. Crook, 34 So. 2d 832 (Ala. 1948) (engineer cannot be held liable for failure to use skill and care in discharge of its duty to decide all questions relating to quality or acceptability of work); Craviolini v. Scholer & Fuller Associated Architects, 357 P.2d 611 (Ariz. 1960) (architect charged with negligent, willful, and malicious conduct toward contractor in matters "wholly unconnected with any owner-contractor dispute" had no defense of immunity because architect is immune only when performing as arbitrator); City of Durham v. Reidsville Eng'g Co., 255 N.C. 98, 120 S.E.2d 564 (1961) (engineer's decisions on any matter of dispute arising under the contract were within its capacity as arbitrator, and therefore immune from liability in the absence of bad faith); Lundgren v.

§ 14.22 — *Waldinger Corp. versus CRS Group Engineers, Inc.*[31]

An engineer prepared the specifications for two waste water treatment facilities. When a subcontractor was unable to supply sludge dewatering equipment as specified in its subcontract, the project's mechanical contractor sued the sub for breach of contract. In defense, the sub claimed impracticability of performance due to the engineer's intentional or negligent drafting of inordinately restrictive specifications.

The mechanical contractor also sued the engineer for intentional interference with the subcontract. The basis of the interference claim was the engineer's allegedly unreasonable insistence on strict compliance by the subcontractor with the restrictive specifications.

The mechanical contractor argued that the engineer, while performing its contractual duties, was not conditionally privileged to interfere with sub-contracts. The court disagreed, finding "little sense" in recognizing an engineer's or architect's conditional privilege to interfere with the principal's contract by enforcing compliance with contract specifications but declining to recognize a conditional privilege to enforce compliance with the same specifications in a subcontract.

While holding that the engineer was conditionally privileged to interfere with the subcontract, the court remanded to determine whether the engineer's insistence on strict compliance with the restrictive specifications was intended to injure the sub or to further the engineer's personal goals. If so, liability would attach.

§ 14.23 Guidelines to Protect Architects

From these decisions, design professionals' defense attorneys can take heart that their clients are likely to be afforded the protection of privileged status when they

---

Freeman, 307 F.2d 104 (9th Cir. 1962) (as quasi-arbitrator, architect should be protected when acting in good faith, however erroneously; if acting fraudulently, or with willful and malicious intent to injure, however, architect should be liable); Johnson v. Construction Co., 292 F. Supp. 300 (D.C. 1968), *aff'd*, 429 F.2d 764, 777 (D.C. Cir. 1970) (architectural duties of design and supervision properly can be delegated but judicial responsibilities cannot) (dictum); E.C. Ernst, Inc. v. Manhattan Constr. Co., 551 F.2d 1026 (5th Cir. 1977), *cert. denied,* 434 U.S. 1067 (1978) (architect not immune from liability for delays caused in its quasi-judicial arbitral role where the "tentative, incongruous and often contradictory nature of its actions constituted a default to all parties"; the architect's procrastinations and equivocations defeated its immunity, which would not have been so defeated had it made a clear statement that it would not or could not decide some issue put to it during the construction project); Blecick v. School Dist. No. 18, 406 P.2d 750 (Ariz. Ct. App. 1965) (architect immune from suit for refusal to issue a completion certificate; in its capacity as arbitrator, an architect cannot be held liable in damages for failure to exercise care or skill).

[31] 775 F.2d 781 (7th Cir. 1985).

are charged with defamation or tortious interference. The law will probably be on their side. As often happens, however, the problem will be the facts. The plaintiff will seek to overcome the legally established privilege by attempting to show that it has been lost through malice or bad faith.

Those of us who advise architects and engineers in their contracts and in the conduct of their professions can also extract a number of lessons from these decisions. Our clients can apply these lessons to their own practices, thus strengthening their defenses in case of attack. These guidelines include the following:

1. Because the privilege defense rests on the duties owed by the design professional to its client, a written contract which defines and confirms these duties can be helpful in establishing the defense.

2. Both the design professional's contract and the construction contract should confirm that the design professional's duty runs to the owner, not to the contractor, and that the proper discharge of that duty could result in cost or expense to the contractor for which neither the owner or the design professional will be responsible.

3. In some circumstances a mutual covenant not to sue running between the design professional and the contractor may be achievable, especially if the owner perceives that such a covenant is advantageous to it and requires its insertion in both contracts.

4. AIA A201-1987 ¶¶ 2.4.1 and 14.2.2 provide that an "approval" or "certification" by the architect is a precondition to the owner's exercise of its rights to take a portion of the work away from the contractor or to terminate the contract. These provisions should be deleted. Although the architect may well respond to the owner's request for professional advice on the advisability of taking the proposed action, the "certification" requirement puts altogether too much pressure on the architect to make statements which may not be fully supportable and which will expose the architect to liability to contractors.

5. Advice and communication with the owner or others which is critical of the contractor should not be offered gratuitously, but should be given in fulfillment of a contractual duty or in response to an express, documented request. The advice should be based upon observable facts which are subject to independent verification. It should be expressed in temperate terms, without inflammatory generalizations or characterizations.

6. The design professional should restrict its communications to those who have a need to know and should avoid unnecessary public statements, media exposure, and "wall-to-wall" copies of communication which are critical of the performance of a contractor or subcontractor. When appropriate, communications should be made directly by the owner or owner's legal counsel—for instance, notices to the contractor's surety that the contractor is in default.

7. The design professional should build a record of actions and documentation which clearly demonstrate that its activities are motivated by a fiduciary concern for the interest of the owner. This is not only the hallmark of professionalism, but, as the cases demonstrate, it is the most effective response to allegations of malice which, if proven, could deprive the design professional of the defense of privilege.

CHAPTER 15

LIABILITY OF ARCHITECT/ ENGINEERS FOR ERRONEOUS SOFTWARE AND COMPUTER DATA

Michael J. Ladino*

§ 15.1   Introduction

TRADITIONAL AREAS OF A/E LIABILITY

§ 15.2   Legal Background and Development of the Concept of Malpractice

§ 15.3   Liability to Persons with Whom the A/E Is in Privity of Contract

§ 15.4   Negligence

§ 15.5   Third-Party Beneficiary

§ 15.6   Indemnification

§ 15.7   Tortious Interference with Contractual Relations

§ 15.8   Implied Warranty

LIABILITY OF SOFTWARE DESIGNER FOR DEFECTIVE SOFTWARE

§ 15.9   Scope of Problem

§ 15.10 Sale of Goods versus Sale of Services: Rights and Responsibilities of Software Designer to Software User and Third Parties

§ 15.11 UCC Problems Facing Software Dealers

§ 15.12 —Express Warranties

§ 15.13 —Implied Warranties

§ 15.14 —Limitation on Remedy Provisions

§ 15.15 Software Manufacturer's Exposure to Professional Malpractice Liability

§ 15.16 Substantive or Mechanical Errors

§ 15.17 CADD Use Guidelines

---

* This chapter is adapted from a paper presented in June 1989 to the 28th Annual Meeting of Invited Attorneys sponsored by AIA, NSPE, and Victor O. Schinnerer & Company.

§ 15.1   Introduction

Computer Assisted Drafting and Design (CADD) was born in the 1980s. It represents a technological advance for all design professionals and their employers. As new as the technology is, the law surrounding the use of CADD equipment and software has not yet materialized. Indeed, there may never be any "CADD law," per se.

Most of the commentators that have examined liability implications involved in the use of CADD concern themselves with the standard of care and precautions that design professionals (A/E) should take when using the technology. This analysis views CADD in the same manner as other design tools used by A/Es in rendering professional services. Since few court decisions have been reported that would give design professionals or their legal counsel clear guidelines to follow, most commentators counsel A/Es to exercise the same degree of skill and care in using CADD technology as they do in using other design tools.

Indeed, most of the advice to CADD users in the liability area has been general in nature and oriented towards the duties of responsible care that design professionals owe to their employers and third parties. Yet, the technology itself has many contexts and each context raises different questions. Some software is developed in-house. Other software is purchased from well-established vendors. Some employers insist that their design professionals have CADD capacity in-house.

Some A/Es pool their software. Other A/Es are concerned with desk-top computers used by project personnel. All in all, the industry is discussing a new and developing collection of tools that have many applications in all areas of the design professional's business.

The purpose of this chapter is to explore potential areas of liability to which an A/E may be exposed when using, or electing not to use, CADD. Traditional areas of A/E liability will be reviewed to explain how they may be applied to the CADD user. We will also discuss aspects of CADD technology which may involve A/Es in areas of legal exposure with which they have not concerned themselves in the past.

TRADITIONAL AREAS OF A/E LIABILITY

§ 15.2   Legal Background and Development of the Concept of Malpractice

American law distinguishes between liability in tort for negligence and liability for breach of contract. The breach of a general duty which the law imposes on one party towards another, such as the duty to act with due care, is called a tort. Judicial construction of most agreements between owners and A/Es, however, has blurred the distinction between tort and breach of contract. Since such agreements generally address only those services which the A/E is specifically required to provide to the owner, contracts between an owner and an A/E are said to imply a duty of ordinary care and skill owed by the A/E when performing these services. An A/E's failure to provide services in accordance with this implied contractual duty of care has been held to be both a breach of contract and negligence (sometimes called *professional malpractice*).

A growing number of disputes between owners and A/Es concern the A/E's liability for additional construction costs paid by employers to third parties which allegedly result from the A/E's negligence or breach of contract. Some of these disputes arise from risk shifting clauses found in most A/E-owner contracts under which the A/E assumes liability for damages and loss incurred by the employer and/or contractors resulting from defective specifications. If an A/E negligently designs or supervises a project, and such negligence causes damage to the contractor or third parties, the A/E will be responsible at law for such damage. Such liability is often termed "negligence" or "malpractice."

The law in this area has been described in general terms by the courts:

> Architects, doctors, engineers, attorneys and others deal in somewhat inexact sciences and are continually called upon to exercise their skilled judgment in order to anticipate and provide for random factors which are incapable of precise measurement. The indeterminable nature of these factors makes it impossible for professional service people to gauge them with complete accuracy in every instance. . . . Because of the inescapable possibility of error which inheres in these services, the law has traditionally required, not perfect results, but rather *the exercise of that skill and judgment which can be reasonably expected from similarly situated professionals.*[1]

> The law imposes upon every person who enters upon an active course of conduct the positive duty to use ordinary care so as to protect others from harm. A violation of that duty is negligence. It is immaterial whether the person acts in his own behalf or under contract with another.[2]

> One who undertakes to render professional services is under a duty to the person for whom the service is to be performed to exercise such care, skill, and diligence as men in that profession ordinarily exercise under like circumstances.

> The circumstances to be considered in determining the standard of care, skill and diligence to be required in this case include the terms of the employment agreement, the nature of the problem which the supplier of the service represented himself as being competent to solve, and the effect reasonably to be anticipated from the proposed remedies upon the balance of the system.[3]

> It is the general rule that the employment of an architect is a matter of contract, and consequently, he is responsible for all the duties enumerated within the contract of

---

[1] Mounds View v. Walijarvi, 263 N.W.2d 420 (Minn. 1978) (emphasis added).

[2] Shoffner Indus., Inc. v. W.B. Lloyd Constr. Co., 42 N.C. App. 259, 257 S.E.2d 50 (1979).

[3] Eveleth v. Ruble, 302 Minn. 249, 253, 225 N.W.2d 521, 524 (1974).

employment. . . . An architect, as a professional, is required to perform his services with reasonable care and competence and will be liable in damages for any failure to do so.[4]

In essence, an A/E who designs a project owes a duty of care to any person who foreseeably and with reasonable certainty may be injured or damaged by the A/E's failure to exercise reasonable care.[5] American courts have found the contractor to be such a foreseeable party, and have permitted recovery not only for resulting personal injuries, but for economic loss as well.[6]

The past twenty years have seen tremendous expansion of liability of design professionals to employers, contractors and third parties. The entire construction industry is watching in anticipation to see how far this expansion will extend and how it will affect the relationship between the traditional parties to construction projects. It is likely that this expansion will include liability for failure to use CADD.

§ 15.3   Liability to Persons with Whom the A/E Is in Privity of Contract

The fifth edition of *Black's Law Dictionary* defines *breach of contract* as

Failure, without legal excuse, to perform any promise which forms the whole or part of a contract. Prevention or hinderance by a party to a contract of any occurrence or performance requisite under the contract for the creation or continuance of a right in favor of the other party or the discharge of a duty by him. Unequivocable, distinct and absolute refusal to perform agreement.

An A/E's potential liability for breach of contract is well known to most design professionals. If an A/E fails to provide satisfactorily the services agreed upon in a contract with its employer, it will be liable for such failure under a breach of contract theory of law.

Liability for breach of contract has many applications with regard to CADD technology. For instance, if an A/E is required to utilize CADD hardware or software as part of the design process and fails to do so, the A/E will be liable for breach of contract. Similarly, an A/E may be found liable for breach of contract if it is unable to perform, or is late in completing, contract work because it has defective or inadequate CADD equipment.

---

[4] Moundsview Indep. School District No. 621 v. Buetow & Assocs., Inc., 253 N.W.2d 836, 839 (Minn. 1977).

[5] Inman v. Binghamton Hous. Auth., 3 N.Y.2d 137, 143 N.E.2d 895, 164 N.Y.S.2d 699 (1957).

[6] Davidson & Jones, Inc. v. County of New Hanover, 41 N.C. App. 661, 255 S.E.2d 580 (1979), *cert. denied,* 259 S.E.2d 911 (1979); W.H. Lyman Constr. Co. v. Village of Gurnee, 84 Ill. App. 3d 28, 403 N.E.2d 1325 (1980).

A new development in the design field is the requirement that design professionals develop CADD software packages themselves. With increasing frequency, owners require A/Es to develop software packages or programs which can be used for maintenance or expansion of a project. For instance, A/Es who design transportation networks are commonly asked to produce a software package which can be used by the owner to maintain the system. Obviously, if the A/E fails to produce a workable software package, it will be liable for breach of contract. Additionally, if the software program fails to satisfy the owner's specifications and requirements, the A/E may face any express or implied warranty problems which arise later.

The issues surrounding a transaction involving the exchange of a software package or computer program, including the issue of whether such an exchange constitutes the sale of goods or services, will be discussed below. Design professionals should be aware, however, that failure to satisfy contract specifications for software packages can constitute breach of contract. Additionally, a design professional may have legal exposure for malpractice when acting simply as a professional computer programmer.

Another aspect of A/E-employer agreements with which A/Es are regularly concerned are the numerous risk shifting provisions which assign responsibility for contract losses among the parties in advance of performance. A number of risk shifting provisions addressing CADD technology can be imagined which may have implications in the design field.

For instance, an A/E who produces a software package for an owner may be required to provide an express warranty concerning the quality or function of the software as part of its contract with an owner. Such warranties may be deemed to be in addition to implied warranties assumed by the design professional in producing the software package. Such warranties often go beyond simply indemnifying the owner against potential loss or damage incurred by the owner as a result of defects in the software.

If an A/E purchases a software or hardware package from a company specializing in producing computer products for design professionals, the A/E should consider the implications of indemnity provisions in its contract with the supplier. Moreover, the design professional who produces a design software package which is released to the owner should consider including some sort of an exculpatory provision in its contract to shield it from potential liability if the software package proves defective.

§ 15.4 Negligence

A/E liability to third parties has expanded in recent years. The theory of liability which third parties have used with the most success to recover against design professionals has been negligence. Although few, if any, reported negligence cases involve CADD, it is foreseeable that the basic elements of a negligence claim will be applied to the use of CADD technology. They are:

1. The A/E owed the contractor a duty of care in the performance of its contracted for services (i.e. the contractor's [or other third parties'] reliance on the A/E's work product was foreseeable)
2. The A/E breached its duty of care
3. The breach caused the contractor damage and
4. The A/E's breach was the proximate cause of the contractor's damage.[7]

A claim against an A/E for negligence is remarkably similar to one for malpractice. For instance, the standard duty of care which an A/E has to satisfy to avoid liability for negligence has been stated as follows:

> [A]n architect's efficiency in preparing plans and specifications is tested by the rule of ordinary and reasonable skill usually exercised by one of that profession. [I]n the absence of a special agreement it does not imply or guaranty a perfect plan or satisfactory result.[8]

This standard was stated a bit differently in *Shoffner Industries, Inc. v. W.B. Lloyd Construction Co.:*[9]

> [T]he law imposes upon every person who enters upon an active course of conduct the positive duty to use ordinary care so as to protect others from harm. A violation of that duty is negligence. It is immaterial whether a person acts in his own behalf or under contract with another. . . . An act is negligent if the actor intentionally creates a situation which it knows, or should realize, is likely to cause a third person to act in such a manner as to create an unreasonable risk of harm to another.

It has become increasingly easy for third parties to recover from A/Es for negligence. Indeed, many states have eliminated the requirement of privity all together. For example, in a Massachusetts decision, *Craig v. Everett M. Brooks,*[10] a contractor brought suit against an A/E for erroneously locating certain stakes which were needed to direct construction. In addressing the A/E's liability to a third party contractor for negligently locating the stakes, the court stated:

> The requirement for a contractual relationship for injury to the person due to negligent performance of a contractual duty was done away with in [a previous

---

[7] Gravely v. Providence Partnership, 549 F.2d 958 (4th Cir. 1977); Prosser, Law of Torts, § 30 (14th ed.).

[8] Mississippi Meadows, Inc. v. Hodson, 13 Ill. App. 3d 24, 26, 299 N.E.2d 359 (1973).

[9] 42 N.C. App. 259, 257 S.E.2d 50, (1979).

[10] 351 Mass. 497, 222 N.E.2d 752 (1967).

case]. In the case at bar, where the defendant was under a contract with the owner to perform professional services, where the plaintiff was under another contract with the owner which contemplated reliance on those services, where the identity of the only possible plaintiff and the extent of its reliance were known to the defendant, and where damages are not remote, it is reasonable to reach an analogous result.

In light of this case and others, it will not be surprising if negligence emerges as the predominate theory of A/E liability for using CADD technology. It is plain that an A/E's failure to exercise reasonable care in using CADD will expose the A/E to claims for negligence as well as breach of express contract requirements (defective specifications, design defects, express warranties) and professional malpractice. For instance, an A/E may find itself liable for the negligent use of CADD in any of the following situations:

1. Where the A/E fails to select the proper computer or software package to perform necessary tasks

2. Where a computer is used to perform a complex calculation and the A/E fails to select the proper formula(ae) and/or assumption(s) for properly completing this task

3. Where the A/E fails to accurately assess and consider the margin of error inherent in the task which it has asked the computer to perform

4. Where the A/E does not obtain adequate training in the use of computers prior to incorporating CADD technology into a project

5. Where the A/E employs an unqualified computer operator or programmer

6. Where improper data is entered into the computer for any of a number of reasons, including the following:

    a. The data is gathered improperly

    b. The A/E fails to verify the data prior to entering it into the computer or

    c. The A/E fails to review and verify the data after it has been entered into the computer.

7. Where the A/E uses the computer to perform a task which is properly performed by other means or

8. Where the A/E fails to detect errors in the program or software package used in performing the design work.

This is not an inclusive list of situations where design professionals could be found liable for negligent use of CADD. It demonstrates, however, the importance of exercising reasonable care when using CADD technology to avoid liability for negligence.

A/Es are not the only ones who are potentially liable for design defects resulting from the use of CADD. Item 8 above gives a situation where an action may be appropriate against the programmer personally for negligence. This is especially true if it is assumed that a computer programmer is a professional for purposes of malpractice liability.

Additionally, if the program or software package was obtained from an outside software design firm (a company which designs computer programs or software packages for design professionals to use in rendering professional services), the outside source may be ultimately liable for losses which result from defects in the software package under a number of theories, including negligence, indemnity, implied and express warranties, or tortious interference with contractual relations. Most software design companies are aware of this potential and include exculpatory and/or "hold harmless" provisions in their contracts to limit their exposure to such claims. The design professional should likewise consider including such provisions in any contracts which involve the use of CADD.

§ 15.5   Third-Party Beneficiary

Third parties have achieved limited success in recovering losses against design professionals as third-party beneficiaries of the contract between an employer and the A/E. In general, a third party must show it is a specifically *intended* beneficiary of the A/E's contract to be successful under this theory. Generally, contractors are considered only incidental beneficiaries of such contracts. Therefore, many of these claims have failed.

For instance, in *A.P. Mover, Inc. v. Graham,*[11] the Supreme Court of Florida held that a third-party beneficiary relationship does not exist unless specific contract language expresses that a specific third party is the intended beneficiary of the contract between the A/E and the employer. Courts in other states have reached the same conclusion.

In *Peter Kiewit Sons' Co. v. Iowa Southern Utilities Co.*[12] the United States District Court for the Southern District of Iowa rejected a contractor's argument that portions of an A/E-owner contract which required the A/E to perform "in accordance with the highest standards of the engineering profession" was sufficient to establish a third-party beneficiary claim because the contractor was not specifically named as the intended beneficiary of the contract.[13]

The potential liability to third parties arising out of the use of CADD can be demonstrated by a hypothetical scenario. Assume that an owner contracts with an A/E to design a structure which is unique, requires the A/E to implement an innovative and technically complex idea, or necessitates the use of highly complex calculations. To design this structure properly, the A/E must incorporate CADD into its design plan.

---

[11] 285 So. 2d 397, 65 A.L.R.3d 238 (Fla. 1973).

[12] 355 F. Supp. 376, 392-94 (S.D. Iowa 1973).

[13] *See also* C.H. Leavell & Co. v. Glantz Contracting Corp., 322 F. Supp. 779, 783-84 (E.D. La. 1971).

Assume further that the A/E enters into a subcontract with a software design firm to provide a software package to perform these difficult tasks. If the software package produced by the subcontractor is defective and directly (or proximately) causes errors in the A/E's design, the software contractor may find itself liable to third parties, including the owner, contractor and any subcontractors, who are damaged as a result. This probability is increased if the contract between the A/E and the software subcontractor specifically references and incorporates the owner's requirements or names the owner as an intended beneficiary.

If the A/E has an in-house programmer who is responsible for using an existing software package to develop a specific design, the software contractor may be successful in claiming the programmer's activities shield the company from liability. Moreover, if the A/E's in-house programmer is not a professional, the A/E may bear full liability for the programmer's mistakes. If the programmer is unlicensed in the profession and it is unable to check the programs as written, there may even be a question of unauthorized practice by the programmer, not to mention malpractice by the A/E. This is especially true if the alleged design defect was caused by the in-house programmer or the in-house programmer should have discovered the error during the course of the design process.

§ 15.6   Indemnification

In situations where a contractor is held vicariously liable for the negligent acts of an A/E, the law may imply an obligation on the part of the A/E to indemnify the contractor from liability. (This principle may also apply where an owner is held vicariously liable for the A/E's negligence.) Under such circumstances, it is not always necessary that the A/E's duty to indemnify be derived from contract provisions; it may be implied by law even where the contractor is negligent.

For example, in *McCloskey & Company v. Wright,*[14] the United States District Court for the Eastern District of Virginia held that a contractor's claim alleging that an A/E's negligent supervision and directives to the contractor during construction constituted "active" negligence by the A/E and stated a valid cause of action for indemnification even though the contractor was "passively" negligent itself. To date, the indemnification theory advanced in *McCloskey* has not been widely reported in the United States. Nevertheless, the *McCloskey* decision could have a significant future impact on A/E liability.

The utility of the indemnification theory is demonstrated in *Fidelity Casualty Co. v. J.A. Jones Construction Co.*[15] In this case, the A/E's insurer sought indemnity from a contractor for a judgment awarded against an A/E and a contractor for negligence arising out of injury to the contractor's employees

---

[14] 363 F. Supp. 223 (E.D. Va. 1973).

[15] 325 F.2d 605 (8th Cir. 1963).

during a cave-in at a work site. The court noted that there was no express contract right requiring the A/E to indemnify the contractor because there was no privity of contract between them. Additionally, the court found that no common law right to indemnity existed. Since both the A/E and the contractor were "actively" negligent, neither had a right to be indemnified by the other.

It is interesting to observe that had an AIA owner/contractor agreement been used in the previous case, the A/E would have succeeded in its indemnification claim. The AIA's owner/contractor agreements are generally used in conjunction with the standard AIA A201 General Conditions of the Contract for Construction. The 1987 version of A201 provides both the owner and A/E with an express contractual right to indemnification from the contractor for any bodily injury or property damage caused, in whole or in part, by a negligent act of the contractor. This type of clause has been construed to provide for indemnity by the contractor even where the A/E participates in the negligent act or acts which create liability.[16]

The hypothetical scenario setting forth the A/E's potential liability to third parties also illustrates potential indemnity obligations arising from the use of CADD. For example, if the software subcontractor discussed in the foregoing hypothetical fails to provide a product which is adequate for the design of a particular project, it may be liable to the A/E for contractual or common law indemnity if the A/E is found liable to the owner for a design error which was caused by the defective software. Likewise, if an A/E creates an in-house program which is defective or negligently uses CADD in designing the project and thereby exposes the owner to liability to a contractor or other third party, the owner may have the right to indemnification from the A/E.

An A/E may also find itself liable under the theory of indemnity if it produces a software package which is released to the owner. If there are defects in the software package which causes the owner to incur liability to third parties when the owner subsequently uses the software, the owner may seek indemnification from the A/E for such losses.

§ 15.7   Tortious Interference with Contractual Relations

A new and potentially dangerous development for A/Es is the increasing frequency with which claims have been brought by contractors alleging that an A/E's interpretation of contract documents constitutes an intentional, tortious interference with the contractor's contractual relationship with the owner.

For example, in *Waldinger Corp. v. Ashbrook-Simon-Hartley, Inc.,*[17] a federal judge held an A/E liable in tort for the extra costs a contractor incurred to install substitute mechanical equipment in an EPA funded sewer project. The court held

---

[16] *See, e.g.,* Shea v. Bay State Gas Co., 383 Mass. 218, 418 N.E.2d 597 (1981).

[17] 564 F. Supp. 970 (C.D. Ill. 1983).

that the A/E was liable for tortiously interfering with the contractor's agreement with the owner because the A/E wrote anti-competitive and restrictive specifications for the equipment and refused to accept substitute equipment without adequate justification.

The United States Court of Appeals for the Seventh Circuit heard the case on appeal.[18] In its decision, the circuit court recognized that an A/E possesses a conditional privilege to interfere with a contractor-owner agreement in its fiduciary capacity to the owner. Nevertheless, the court affirmed the district court's award of damages under the theory of intentional interference with contract. In reaching this decision the court stated:

> Where a conditional privilege exists, the plaintiff, to succeed on a claim for tortious interference with contract, must allege and prove that the agent's intentional acts were not taken to further its principal's best interests, but to further its personal goals or to injure the other party to the contract.[19]

The court further stated:

> The plaintiff may defeat the privilege by establishing that the defendant was acting other than in accord with his contractual obligations to his principal. Where an architect's action in enforcing literal compliance with contract specifications was not justifiable in that it was not necessary to protect his principal's conflicting interests, but rather was taken with an intent to further his personal goals or to injure the party which is thereby forced to breach its contract with the plaintiff, the element of actual malice exists and the architect is liable for tortious interference.[20]

The decision and rationale used in *Waldinger* is likely to give rise to additional claims against A/Es under similar circumstances. Such circumstances may arise from the use of CADD.

Assume an A/E enters into a contract with an owner. The owner, in turn, enters into a contract for construction with a prime contractor. The A/E includes certain assumptions in a computer program used in the design of the project which are invalid; the invalidity stemming from the designer's desire to include a specific manufacturer's product in the structure. As a result of this error, the contractor installs improper material into the project. If the error is later discovered and the contractor is forced to remove and replace the inadequate material, the contractor may be able to recover directly against the A/E. This will be considered the "equitable" result since the designer's actions caused the defective material to be installed. Of course, it is also possible that the contractor could recover its losses

---

[18] Waldinger v. CRS Group Eng'rs, Inc., 775 F.2d 781 (7th Cir. 1985).

[19] *Id.* at 790 (citing George A. Fuller Co. v. Chicago College of Osteopathic Medicine, 719 F.2d 1326, 1335 (7th Cir. 1983)).

[20] *Id.* at 790-91.

directly from the owner. In that situation, the A/E may be required to indemnify the owner for such losses.

The foregoing hypothetical can be taken one step further to illustrate a more remote possibility of liability. Assume that there are multiple prime contractors involved in the hypothetical project. Assume further that the prime contractor who must remove and replace the inadequate material, Contractor A, is delayed in completing its contract because of this error. A parallel prime contractor, Contractor B, is also delayed by this error because it can not proceed with its work until Contractor A has completed performance. Since Contractor B's delay was caused by the A/E's negligence, the A/E may be liable for tortiously interfering with Contractor B's contract.

§ 15.8   Implied Warranty

A few courts have held that an A/E impliedly warrants that its work is fit for its intended purpose.[21] Some courts have limited such warranties to situations that involve routine work similar to that involved in the mass production of consumer goods.[22]

A Minnesota case declined to follow that approach. The court stated:

> The finder of fact will be forced in every case to determine, as a preliminary matter, whether the alleged architectural error was made in the performance of a sufficiently simplistic task. Defects which are found to be more esoteric would presumably continue to be tried under the traditional [negligence] rule. It seems apparent, however, that the making of any such threshold determination would require the taking of expert testimony and necessitate an inquiry strikingly similar to that which is presently made under the prevailing negligence standard. We think that the net effect would be the injection of substantive ambiguity into the law of professional malpractice without a favorable trade-off in procedural expedience.[23]

In other circumstances, the courts have said that warranty claims are so similar to actions in tort that they are subject to the same statutes that expressly govern tort claims.[24]

In what appears to be an implied warranty decision, a court held that a contractor may sue an A/E directly for foreseeable economic loss resulting from

---

[21] *See, e.g.,* Hill v. Polar Pantries, 219 S.C. 263, 64 S.E.2d 885, 25 A.L.R.2d 1080 (1951).

[22] *See* Schipper v. Levitt & Sons, Inc., 44 N.J. 70, 82, 90, 92, 207 A.2d 314 (1965). *Cf.,* Broyles v. Brown Eng'g Co., 275 Ala. 35, 40, 151 So. 2d 767 (1963).

[23] *Moundsview* at 425.

[24] *See, e.g.,* Wolfe v. Ford Motor Co., 386 Mass. 95, 98-99, 434 N.E.2d 1008 (1982) (implied warranty); Salem Orthopedic Surgeons, Inc. v. Quinn, 377 Mass. 514, 386 N.E.2d 1268 (1978) (express warranty).

the breach of an A/E's duty of reasonable care in the performance of the A/E's contract with the employer.[25] Because of the peculiarities of North Carolina law, the court held that neither the contractor nor subcontractors had a good cause of action against the A/E based upon the negligent performance of the A/E's contract with the employer.

A number of courts have, however, expressly rejected implied contract theory. For example, in *C.H. Leavell Co. v. Glantz Contracting Corp.,*[26] a contractor argued that provisions in its contract with an owner which referred to the A/E's authority over the work also established implied contractual duties on the part of the A/E towards the contractor. The court held that the A/E was not a party to the contractor/employer agreement and dismissed the contractor's claim. This appears to be the likely result for implied contract claims involving the use of CADD.

The example used to illustrate potential liability of a software contractor to third-party beneficiaries can also be used to illustrate the potential liability of the software contractor under an implied warranty theory. For instance, if the software contractor (or the A/E itself) tailors a new program for a specific project, or advertises that the program or software package will perform a specific task which is inherent in the type of work performed, an implied warranty may be created. An A/E's liability for such warranties, both express and implied, will be discussed in more detail later in this chapter.

LIABILITY OF SOFTWARE DESIGNER
FOR DEFECTIVE SOFTWARE

§ 15.9   Scope of Problem

The analysis of a computer software designer's potential liability in the construction design area can be divided into two segments. First, software vendors face potential liability to software users with whom the vendor has a written contract. The contract generally governs the rights and liabilities between the contracting parties. Second, the software supplier may be obligated to third parties who are injured as a result of the use of defective computer software which it produces. In both situations, the injuries which may arise are not strictly economic or monetary. Physical damage to property or injury to persons can result from design defects. The type of injury involved is important since it may govern or limit the vendor's potential liability.

---

[25] Davidson & Jones, Inc. v. County of New Hanover, 41 N.C. App. 661, 255 S.E.2d 580, *cert. denied,* 298 N.C. 293, 259 S.E.2d 911 (1979).

[26] 322 F. Supp. 779 (E.D. La. 1971).

§ 15.10   Sale of Goods versus Sale of Services: Rights and Responsibilities of Software Designer to Software User and Third Parties

Virtually all computer software contracts include provisions which limit the vendor's liabilities and the buyer's remedies. These clauses include disclaimers which attempt to shield the vendor from all warranty claims except those expressly included by the parties to the agreement. Limitation of remedies clauses include provisions which limit the users remedies to repair or replacement of defective software.

Additionally, software vendors commonly include provisions in their agreements which preclude the buyer from enforcing claims for consequential or special damages. These clauses, coupled with the *integration clause*, which provides that the written contract constitutes the entire agreement between the parties, are used throughout the computer industry to protect software vendors from future claims.

Several factors will determine the effectiveness of such provisions. Perhaps the most important factor is whether the transaction is considered the sale or licensing of "goods," thereby subjecting transaction to the requirements of the Uniform Commercial Code (UCC), or "services," which is outside the scope of the UCC. A/Es are generally familiar with the sale of "services," the product design professionals usually provide. Most design professionals, however, have little experience with the sale of goods or the legal implications involved in such transactions. Therefore, the proper classification of a transaction involving the exchange of software raises significant implications which A/Es have generally not had to consider in the past.

Most states have statutes which are very similar to the UCC and create implied warranties that attach to the sale of goods. Such warranties will generally be effective unless disclaimed in writing in accordance with the statute. No implied warranty implications attach to service contracts.

Courts traditionally have had difficulty applying legal concepts to computers and properly characterizing computer services. While computer hardware resembles many other manufacturers' products from a legal standpoint, software is more complicated. Most courts have held that a contract involving the exchange of software alone is a sale of goods which falls within the scope of the UCC.[27] Indeed, software may appear to be more like a manufactured product when brought to market. Matters become more confusing when hardware and software make up varying degrees of a computer package.

The difficulty in properly defining a software package as a "good" or a "service" has led most courts to determine the applicability of the UCC to a contract for computer programs on a case-by-case basis. The court must examine

---

[27] *See generally* Rodau, *Computer Software: Does Article 2 of the Uniform Commercial Code Apply?*, 35 Emory L.J. 853 (1986).

the elements of the computer package to determine whether the sale or service aspects of the transaction predominate. For instance, the sale of computer hardware is almost always defined as a contract for the sale of goods under the UCC.[28] On the other hand, an agreement solely to perform data processing services is almost always considered a service which is outside the scope of the UCC. The difficulty of definition occurs in the grey area created by software packages which include elements of both goods and services.

The courts generally look to "the essence of the agreement" to determine whether a contract involves goods or services. For instance, when a sale of goods predominates, incidental services provided do not alter the basic transaction.[29]

In one decision, a computer data processing services company brought an action under a state statute prohibiting companies engaged in the selling of "goods or commodities" from participating in a monopoly. The plaintiff alleged that a software package provided by the defendant was governed by the statute because the package not only included services such as computerized data processing, record keeping, and billing, but also goods such as printed records of fiscal conditions, statements of account, statistical reports, management reports, accounts receivable reports, and billing reports.

The court rejected this argument and found that, although tangible goods were involved in the product produced by the defendant, "rarely is an intangible service performed without the involvement of some tangible."[30] The court also found that "the analysis and processing of customers' records are the heart of the matter, the reports rendered to the customers being the embodiment of the services."[31] This analysis has been followed in other courts.[32]

Other courts have declined to follow this rationale. For instance, the United States Court of Appeals for the Second Circuit, in the *Triangle* case, held that a contract involving the exchange of a software package consisting of both hardware and software was a contract for the sale of goods as a matter of law.[33] In this decision, rather than holding that the sale of goods was incidental to the services provided, the court determined that the services were merely incidental to the sale of goods.[34]

---

[28] *See* Triangle Underwriters, Inc. v. Honeywell, Inc., 604 F.2d 737 (2d Cir. 1979) [hereinafter *Triangle*].

[29] *See* R.R.X. Indus., Inc. v. Lab-Conne, 772 F.2d 546 (9th Cir. 1985).

[30] SDK Medical Computers Servs. Corp. v. Professional Operating Management Group, 371 Mass. 117, 354 N.E.2d 852, 858 (1978).

[31] *Id.* at 858.

[32] *See, e.g.,* Computer Servicenters, Inc. v. Beacon Mfg. Co., 328 F. Supp. 753 (D.S.C. 1970), *aff'd*, 443 F.2d 906 (4th Cir. 1971) (data processing services were held not to be the sale of goods because the contemplated payment was for the analysis, collection, storage, and reporting of certain data supplied to the plaintiff by the defendant).

[33] *Triangle*, 604 F.2d 737.

[34] *Id.* at 742 (*citing* Dynamics Corp. of Am. v. International Harvester Co., 429 F. Supp. 341, 347 (S.D.N.Y. 1977)).

Triangle involved a defendant who was contractually obligated to develop and deliver a completed computer system for the plaintiff to operate. The defendant was not obligated to actually run a data processing service for the plaintiff. Moreover, the defendant's compensation was limited to the purchase price for the hardware. The defendant did not bill for the services prior, during or subsequent to installation. The court believed that these were recognized conditions of a contract for the sale of goods, and not the rendition of professional services.[35]

From a computer software supply company's perspective, the Second Circuit's decision in *Triangle* may be disturbing. Software manufacturers generally limit their services to providing software or software packages which are used by consumers on an independent basis. The manufacturer's obligations, both before and after the sale, are generally limited to training the buyer's personnel in use of the system and routine upkeep and maintenance.

Nevertheless, the law in this area is far from clear. For instance, courts often draw analogies to the typical A/E contract as an example of a contract for services. A/E services are generally limited to design and construction services and A/E work product is virtually always considered a service. This is true even in the government contract context where the A/E only produces drawings, plans and specifications.

If an A/E produces a software package which is released to the owner, it may face UCC problems. Obviously, the A/E's design effort is considered a "service" and is outside the scope of the UCC. Nevertheless, an A/E is potentially obligated to provide UCC-type warranties with regard to the software package actually released. While this potential may be less than that faced by software design companies, the A/E should be aware of UCC implications inherent in such an exchange and attempt to limit exposure through exculpatory provisions.

The United States District Court for the District of New Jersey's decision in *Chatlos Systems* demonstrates the importance of classifying a transaction as the sale of goods or the sale of services. In *Chatlos Systems,* the court, after finding the contract in question was one for the sale of "goods," held the defendant liable for violations of both express and implied warranty provisions. Since the UCC remedies were applicable, the defendant was liable for breach of warranty damages equal to the difference between the value of the goods accepted and the value of the goods had they performed as warranted.[36] If the contract had been viewed as one for services, the court would have limited the plaintiff's remedies to those found in traditional contract law.

---

[35] *See also* Chatlos Sys., Inc. v. National Cash Register Corp., 479 F. Supp. 738 (D.N.J. 1979), *aff'd,* 635 F.2d 1081 (3d Cir. 1980) [hereinafter *Chatlos Systems*].

[36] *Id.* at 744; UCC §§ 2-714(2) and (3).

§ 15.11   UCC Problems Facing Software Dealers

Once a transaction is found to be a sale of goods under the UCC, the seller should turn its attention to its UCC rights and obligations. Through careful planning and foresight, a seller can avoid many of the UCC's problem areas.

§ 15.12   —Express Warranties

One of the most important UCC problems facing vendors is the creation of warranties under the Code. Indeed, many software dealers create express warranties without even knowing it. Section 2-313 of the UCC provides that an express warranty may be created orally or in writing. Even general statements regarding performance level or product demonstrations have been held to constitute express warranties.[37] Vendors should be aware that advertisements, product documentation, and employee statements may also constitute express warranties.[38] Therefore, vendors should review their product literature and instruct their employees to avoid responsibility for unlimited warranties.

Perhaps the best way to avoid express warranty liability is to address the issue in the contract itself. The seller should avoid generalized and ambiguous statements and provide clear specifications concerning the functioning of the software. Contractual provisions limiting warranties to specifically identified functions in clear and concise statements are helpful. Use of words such as "defects" or "errors" should be avoided. Provisions which limit the buyers' remedies and/or time within which the buyer must bring an action should also be included in the software contract.

§ 15.13   —Implied Warranties

The UCC creates two implied warranties which attach to the sale of goods. An implied warranty of merchantability, which requires that goods be fit for the ordinary purpose for which they are used, is created by UCC § 2-314(2). An implied warranty of fitness for an intended purpose is created by UCC § 2-315. Where a seller has reason to know that the buyer will use the goods for a particular purpose, and the buyer relies on the seller's opinion that the goods will be adequate for that purpose, the latter warranty will be implied.

Both implied warranties may be disclaimed through careful contract language.[39] Since contractual ambiguities are generally resolved against the

---

[37] *See, e.g.,* Sierra Diesel Injection Serv., Inc. v. Burroughs Corp., 874 F.2d 653, 657 (9th Cir. 1989).

[38] *See, e.g.,* Overstreet v. Norden Laboratories, Inc., 669 F.2d 1286, 1290 (6th Cir. 1982).

[39] UCC § 2-316.

warrantor, disclaimers should be clear, conspicuous, and unambiguous. They should not be lost in the fine print of a contract document.

§ 15.14 —Limitation on Remedy Provisions

Software manufacturers may be able to limit their UCC liability by including remedy limitation provisions in their contracts. Typical remedies which are included in such clauses include repair or replacement of specifically designated items. The UCC permits modification and limitation of remedies provided that the seller makes it clear such remedies are exclusive.[40] Consequential damages may also be excluded provided that such limitations are not unconscionable.[41] Nevertheless, where contractual remedies fail their "essential purpose," the buyer may be able to obtain excluded UCC remedies.[42]

§ 15.15 Software Manufacturer's Exposure to Professional Malpractice Liability

Two questions arise when analyzing the liability and malpractice implications which face a software manufacturer. First, is a computer programmer a professional for the purposes of malpractice liability? Second, if the programmer is considered a professional, how does this status affect the manufacturer's liability for negligent preparation of software?

The courts have recognized the computer programmer's duty to exercise reasonable skill and care in using computers. Nevertheless, the determination of whether a programmer should be treated as a professional for purposes of liability is not clear. Indeed, the distinction between professional and nonprofessional services has traditionally been vague.[43]

The issue of whether a computer programmer is considered a professional when programming services are rendered in the design and engineering field is not yet clear either. The issue has been addressed, however, by the courts for the purpose of determining whether programmers are professionals as defined in the Fair Labor Standards Act (FLSA). In *Pezzillo v. General Telephone & Electric Information Systems, Inc.*,[44] the court found that computer programmers were not professionals with regard to the FLSA's provisions concerning exemptions from overtime requirements.

---

[40] UCC § 2-719.

[41] UCC § 2-719(3).

[42] UCC § 2-719(2).

[43] *See* Pezzillo v. General Tel. & Elec. Information Sys. Inc., 414 F. Supp. 1257 (M.D. 1976), *aff'd per curiam*, 572 F.2d 1189 (6th Cir. 1978).

[44] *Id.*

To be included within the definition of "professional capacity" under the FLSA, the employee's work must require "the constant exercise of discretion and judgment in its performance." The court held that programmers are not professionals under this standard since 100 percent of their time is involved in purely mechanical and highly skilled work which does not require the use of discretion or the exercise of independent judgment.[45]

It is interesting that the court in *Pezzillo* drew an analogy to the A/E field to explain its decision. The court likened the duties of a programmer to those performed by a drafter working for an architect. The court noted that both drafters and programmers generally perform mechanical functions while architects and computer analysts act as professionals.[46] This distinction may be carried over to the malpractice area. If this type of distinction is raised, it would appear that the "exercise of discretion and skilled judgment" would be the determining factor in assessing whether a programmer or software developer is considered a professional. Of course, this analysis still leaves confusion since many persons employed by design firms are assigned hybrid duties which include both mechanical and discretionary functions.

Perhaps it is this ambiguity which has led some courts to reject the concept of "computer malpractice" altogether. For instance, the United States District Court for the District of New Jersey addressed the issue of computer malpractice as follows:

> The novel concept of a new tort called "computer malpractice" is premised upon a theory of elevated responsibility on the part of those who render computer sales and service. Plaintiff equates the sale and servicing of computer systems with established theories of professional malpractice. Simply because an activity is technically complex and important to the business community does not mean that greater potential liability must attach. In the absence of sound precedential authority, the Court declines the invitation to create a new tort.[47]

§ 15.16   Substantive or Mechanical Errors

Another distinction which may affect liability is whether errors in the computer software are substantive or merely mechanical. *Substantive errors* are errors in the instructions or advice which are normally given by professionals with respect to matters with which professionals deal. For example, in an IRS ruling, a developer of a computer program for use in preparing income tax returns was found to be potentially responsible for errors in the tax law which were incorporated into the program.[48]

---

[45] *Id.* at 1270.

[46] *Id.*

[47] *Chatlos Systems,* 479 F. Supp. 738.

[48] Rev. Rul. 85-189, 1985-48 I.R.D. 8 (Dec. 2, 1985).

Computer programs which incorporate substantive guidance based on human judgment from disciplines as diverse as medicine, law, accounting, engineering and architecture may have liability beyond mere arithmetic or mechanical calculations in the computer software programs. Design professionals should take note of this development in implementing CADD technology or creating software packages to be turned over to owners.

Potential liability for errors in substantive guidance increases potential liability for software developers. Several tort theories are potentially available to impose liability for damages caused by substantive errors in computer software programs. These include negligence, misrepresentation and product liability.

If a computer program incorporates substantive engineering or architectural guidance, then the established legal standards of care applicable to the engineering and architectural communities may be applicable to the software program. If the substantive guidance does not measure up to the required standard of care, then the logical rule will be that the computer software developer may sustain liability which is not unlike that for professional negligence on the part of an architect or engineer. Therefore, the design professional should exercise reasonable care when using or developing software in the design process.

§ 15.17   CADD Use Guidelines

The use and misuse of CADD in the 1990s will in very large part be governed by traditional notions of A/E negligence and other theories of liability. The design professions should anticipate no new emerging CADD law, per se.

While it is no doubt true that the applications of CADD will continue to expand, professionals must endeavor to maintain the requisite standard of care. In a world of ever-increasing complexity, the chances for error or omission only increase. This is the new environment for design professionals and it is a matter best left to the professions rather than the courts, judges and juries.

The traditional role of the A/E as service provider can only blur with the many new and novel applications of CADD hardware and software. Owners are keenly aware of the advantages inherent in the new technologies and are asking their design professionals to experiment with software design and development for the ultimate use and benefit of the owners themselves. This not only creates new opportunities for the design professionals but also creates new relationships which the law has yet to address in full.

CHAPTER 16

REVIEW OF RECENT SIGNIFICANT CASES INVOLVING DESIGN PROFESSIONALS

John J. Lynch*

CONTRACTUAL LIABILITY

§ 16.1   Architect's Contract and Poor Work

§ 16.2   Exculpatory Clause Does Not Absolve Architect

§ 16.3   Contract Disclaimer

§ 16.4   Engineering Firm Liable for Failure to Detect Fraud

§ 16.5   Excess Cost of Construction Does Not Defeat Architect's Fee Claim

CONTRIBUTION AND INDEMNITY

§ 16.6   Contribution or Indemnity from Designer

§ 16.7   Architect Not Entitled to Contribution or Indemnity

§ 16.8   Equitable Indemnity Not Available from Engineer

§ 16.9   Architect Allowed Indemnity for Attorneys' Fees

§ 16.10 Indemnification of Joint Tortfeasor

§ 16.11 Defendant Can Maintain Contribution Action

§ 16.12 Engineer Not Entitled to Contribution or Implied Indemnity

§ 16.13 Design Engineer Could Not Obtain Contribution from EPA

§ 16.14 Indemnity or Contribution from Design Drawing Company

§ 16.15 Apportioned Fault Verdict Upheld

ECONOMIC LOSS

§ 16.16 Negligent Misrepresentation Case Requires Functional Equivalent of Privity

---

* This chapter is adapted from a paper presented in May 1990 to the 29th Annual Meeting of Invited Attorneys sponsored by AIA, NSPE, and Victor O. Schinnerer & Company.

§ 16.17   Tort Recovery for Economic Loss Not Allowed Regardless of Relationship Between Parties

§ 16.18   Tort Recovery for Economic Loss Not Allowed Even to Supplier of Services

§ 16.19   Claim for Negligent Review of Shop Drawing

ENVIRONMENTAL LAW

§ 16.20   Waste Disposal Problems

EXPERT WITNESS LITIGATION

§ 16.21   Expert Witness Immune from Suit

§ 16.22   Expert Opinion Necessary to Prove Negligence

§ 16.23   Non-Architect as Expert Witness Against Architect

§ 16.24   Statute Requires Filing of Expert's Affidavit with Complaint Against Architects

§ 16.25   Surveyor Liable as a Matter of Law

§ 16.26   Architect's Own Expert Establishes Architect's Negligence

MEASURE OF DAMAGES

§ 16.27   Cost to Repair

§ 16.28   Consequential Damages from Engineer

PATENT AND LATENT DEFECTS

§ 16.29   Question of Fact

§ 16.30   Owner's Allegation of Latent Defect

§ 16.31   Subsequent Owner Could Not Recover

PRIVITY

§ 16.32   Condominium Owner Third-Party Beneficiary

PUBLIC OFFICIAL IMMUNITY

§ 16.33   Suit Against State Employee Engineer Barred

RACKETEERING

§ 16.34   Engineering Firm Supplying Reports and Studies

SAFETY ON THE JOBSITE

§ 16.35   No Duty to Notify Workers

§ 16.36   Architect Not Liable to Injured Worker

§ 16.37   No Duty to Supervise

STATUTES OF REPOSE

§ 16.38   Wisconsin's Statute of Repose Held Unconstitutional

§ 16.39   Utah's Statute of Repose Held Unconstitutional

§ 16.40   Ohio's Statute of Repose Held Constitutional

§ 16.41   Oklahoma's Statute of Repose Held Constitutional

STATUTES OF LIMITATIONS

§ 16.42   **A/E Firm Estopped from Asserting Statute of Limitations**

§ 16.43   **Damage Claim Did Not Change Contract Action Into Tort Action**

§ 16.44   **Economic Loss Action Governed by Tort Statute of Limitations**

§ 16.45   **Suit by Governmental Agencies Not Barred by Statute of Limitations**

CONTRACTUAL LIABILITY

§ 16.1   Architect's Contract and Poor Work

U.R.S. Co. v. Gulfport-Biloxi Regional Airport Authority[1]

The defendant architectural firm's contractual responsibilities included design, preparing construction documents, assisting and obtaining bids, administrating the construction contract, and providing a full-time resident inspector for administration of the construction contract for a new airport terminal building. During the construction of the roof, a roofing expert warned the airport commissioner that the roof was not being put on in accordance with contract specifications. The airport personnel checked with the resident inspector who found nothing wrong. The architectural firm certified that construction was sufficiently completed in accordance with the contract documents. A few months later, the roof began to leak.

The architect contended that it was not liable to the airport authority because the construction contract absolved the architect from any liability because of poor work on the part of the contractor. The court found that the deficiencies were pointed out to the resident inspector and the architectural firm had a duty to inspect the roof construction and to protect the airport authority against defects and deficiencies in the work of the contractor and the architectural firm would therefore be liable for negligently performing that duty.

§ 16.2   Exculpatory Clause Does Not
Absolve Architect

Board of Education v. Sargent, Webster, Crenshaw & Folley[2]

Although the architect's contract contained exculpatory language that the architect was not required to make "exhaustive or continuous on-site inspections

---

[1] 544 So. 2d 824 (Miss. 1989).

[2] 146 A.D.2d 190, 539 N.Y.S.2d 814 (1989), *appeal denied*, 75 N.Y.2d 702, 551 N.Y.S.2d 906 (1990).

to check the quality or quantity of the work and will not be responsible for the Contractor's failure to carry out the construction work in accordance with the Contract Documents," the architect was not exonerated where it knew of construction defects during the course of construction and where the trier of fact could find that it was aware of the defect and failed to notify the owner.

The architect was aware that the roofing contractor had failed to protect the layers of roofing material from exposure to precipitation during construction and had failed to attach a vapor barrier to the poured gypsum deck. The architect had engaged an outside roofing expert to inspect the installation and, based on the expert's report, the architect had directed the general contractor to remove and replace the defective roofing. The general contractor refused to do so and the architect agreed to several less severe remedial measures. Once these were completed, the architect issued certificates of payment for the roofing. The school building's roof began leaking two months after the building's completion and the school district was forced to consider replacing the entire roof within seven years.

§ 16.3   Contract Disclaimer

Costanza Construction Corp. v. City of Rochester[3]

The low-bid contractor on a public improvement contract sued the city and designer of the job drawings after encountering substantially more rock than was shown in the job drawings and specifications. The job drawings showed only 20 cubic yards of rock while the specifications estimated 100 cubic yards, and 600 cubic yards were actually encountered.

The appellate court held that the contractor's cause of action was properly dismissed because the contract included a disclaimer by the city of any responsibility for the accuracy or completeness of information on the drawings concerning existing conditions, including rock, and obligating the contractor to satisfy itself as to site conditions and the work required. In view of the contract language, the contractor could not have justifiably relied on any information in the documents regarding the quantity of rock to be excavated. The New York Court of Appeals dismissed the appeal without opinion on the basis that the order appealed from did not finally determine the action.

---

[3] 147 A.D.2d 929, 537 N.Y.S.2d 394 (1989), *appeal dismissed*, 74 N.Y.2d 715, 543 N.Y.S.2d 400 (1989).

§ 16.4   Engineering Firm Liable for Failure to Detect Fraud

City of Houma v. Municipal & Industrial Pipe Service, Inc.[4]

An engineering firm hired by a city to oversee rehabilitation of the sewage system was required by contract "to make periodic site visits to determine in general if the work was progressing in accordance with the contract documents." The engineering firm was alleged to have breached its contractual duty by certifying inaccurate or deficient records which purported to verify compliance with the contract specifications. The engineering firm argued that it was not liable because the contractor required to inspect, test, and seal the joints between sections of sewage piping covered by the contracts had developed a sophisticated scheme whereby the engineers and their representatives could not possibly detect skillfully hidden defects. The project was one of the last worked on by the contractor before its principals were indicted in over 40 counts of criminal fraud based on activities in projects spanning the southern United States.

The trial court noted that the engineering firm's field representatives were for the most part untrained, unskilled personnel who employed no reasonable, analytical method calculated to spot performance deficiencies. The engineering firm's project engineer testified that the sealing process took three to four minutes per joint. Based on this estimate it would take a crew ten hours to seal 150 joints. The logs however indicated that there were eight days when 175 to 200 joints were sealed, 15 days when 250 joints were sealed, and 13 days when 250 to 300 joints were sealed. On some of the heavy days, the field representative supervisor billed only five to seven hours of work. The court noted that although the contractor's deceit was skillfully executed in some regards, the deceit regarding the joints should have been apparent and obvious to any well trained and observant representative.

Therefore the Fifth Circuit affirmed the conclusion that the engineering firm was negligent in the performance of its contractual inspection duties.

§ 16.5   Excess Cost of Construction Does Not Defeat Architect's Fee Claim

Getzschman v. Miller Chemical Co.[5]

In a suit by an architect for his fee for designing a family home, the court affirmed a jury verdict in favor of the architect in the full amount of his fee and

---

[4] 884 F.2d 886 (5th Cir. 1989), *reh'g denied.*

[5] 232 Neb. 885, 443 N.W.2d 260 (1989).

against the homeowners on their counterclaim. Where an architect has no express contractual obligation to design a structure within a specified budget or to estimate the construction costs of a proposed project, construction at a cost greater than anticipated by or acceptable to the owner is no defense to an architect's action to recover fees even when the cost is more than double what the owner anticipated.

CONTRIBUTION AND INDEMNITY

§ 16.6   Contribution or Indemnity from Designer

Village of Cross Keys, Inc. v. United States Gypsum Co.[6]

A condominium developer and architect sued USG claiming they relied upon USG's design specifications for the construction of the exterior walls and that the design and certain representations concerning it were faulty. The developer and architect produced evidence which would permit the trier of fact to find that a curtainwall system built to USG's specifications with USG's materials would not perform adequately. However, the evidence was clear that the information published by USG clearly applied to USG products.

In the construction involved, USG products were neither specified nor used in the structural portions of the curtain wall system. This fact was not in dispute and the court held that the developer's and architect's claimed reliance upon the information contained in the USG publication was not reasonable within the meaning of the "reasonable reliance" requirement of the tort of negligent misrepresentation. The court stated the same result could be expressed in terms of the absence of a duty. Assuming the possible existence of a tort duty upon USG as a result of the publication of the specifications, that duty should extend to those who seek to challenge a system they have actually used and not to those who do not use it.

The court did note that in some circumstances it is the practice of the industry for architects and engineers to depend upon technical information supplied by manufacturers and the court doubted that industry standards require that each architect and engineer reinvent the wheel for each project. The court, however, did not have to reach the issue of whether a manufacturer may be responsible for negligent publication of technical information because the fact that the product had not been used in this case permitted a ruling on a narrower basis.

---

[6] 315 Md. App. 741, 556 A.2d 1126 (1989).

§ 16.7   Architect Not Entitled to
Contribution or Indemnity

SSDW Co. v. Feldman-Misthopoulos Associates[7]

A dispute arose over the design and construction of windows which had to be replaced. The plaintiff sued the architect for breach of contract. The architect brought a third-party action against the general contractor and the suppliers of the windows and glass used in the building, seeking either indemnity or contribution from these third-party defendants.

Since the basis of the lawsuit brought by the plaintiff against the architect was breach of contract, and since contribution was limited to actions sounding in tort, contribution was unavailable. Since the architect had no contractual relationship with the third-party defendants, the architect could not maintain an indemnity action. Nor could the architect rely on an implied indemnification theory. The third-party complaint did not predicate the architect's liability on the basis of the negligence of the third-party defendants, or on the basis of vicarious or imputed liability. The architect was not alleged to be vicariously responsible for defects in the materials supplied by the third-party defendants, but was charged with directly causing those defects by breaching its contract to design windows for the structure. Since the predicate of common law indemnity is vicarious liability, a party which actually participated to some degree in the wrongdoing cannot receive the benefit of the doctrine.

§ 16.8   Equitable Indemnity Not Available
from Engineer

Woodward-Gizienski & Associates v. Geotechnical Exploration, Inc.[8]

The developers of a condominium project who were sued by homeowners for damages arising from the settlement of balconies, buildings, and pools brought an action based on equitable indemnity and negligence against the forensic soils engineers who allegedly caused the homeowners to make excessive repairs to their subsidence-damaged property. Relying on the recommendations of the soils engineers, the homeowners had implemented repairs at a cost of about $1 million. The developers settled with the homeowners for $731,400 and alleged in their equitable indemnity suit that the soils engineers breached their duty of professional care and were negligent in obtaining and relying on inadequate

---

[7] 151 A.D.2d 293, 542 N.Y.S.2d 565 (1989).

[8] 208 Cal. App. 3d 64, 255 Cal. Rptr. 800 (1989).

engineering information, and in failing to consider recommending less expensive alternative repair measures. It was also alleged that the repairs recommended by the soils engineers were not reasonably necessary.

The court noted that the excess repairs alleged could not have caused detriment to the developers because, under the fundamental principles of damages, the developers were only liable in the first instance for reasonable costs of repair and not for excessive costs of repair. If the soils engineers' recommended repairs were excessive, the developers were not liable for the excess and the developers could assert their claim regarding the soils engineers' negligence in the context of challenging the reasonableness of the costs of repair damages. Fairness would not require resorting to the doctrine of equitable indemnity.

§ 16.9 Architect Allowed Indemnity for Attorneys' Fees

Hillman v. Leland E. Burns, Inc.[9]

The owner and contractor entered into a standard AIA short form construction agreement containing a clause requiring the contractor to indemnify the architect against all claims, damages, losses and expenses including attorneys' fees attributable to death caused in whole or in part by the contractor's negligence. The indemnity obligation did not extend to the liability of the architect arising from professional negligence. After a jury verdict finding the owner's and contractor's negligence to be the cause of the plaintiff's death and also finding that the architect was not liable, the architect moved for attorneys' fees from the contractor based on the indemnification provision of the contract.

The court held that, since the architect had been found not liable by the jury, the exclusionary provision relating to professional negligence was not triggered and the architect was entitled to indemnification for the attorneys' fees in defending the plaintiff's lawsuit even though the plaintiff's lawsuit was based on allegations of professional negligence. The court noted that if it were to accept the contractor's argument that the indemnity provision of the contract excluded all actions against the architect based upon professional negligence claims, regardless of the architect's liability, it would essentially eliminate the indemnity agreement.

§ 16.10 Indemnification of Joint Tortfeasor

Apel Machine & Supply Co. v. J.E. O'Toole Engineering Co.[10]

---

[9] 209 Cal. App. 3d 860, 257 Cal. Rptr. 535 (1989).

[10] 548 So. 2d 445 (Ala. 1989).

The court noted that, although the general rule in Alabama is that joint tortfeasors are not entitled to indemnity, when one joint tortfeasor agrees in writing to indemnify the other, even for claims based on the other's own negligence, the agreement can be upheld and the joint tortfeasor can receive indemnification. The language of the indemnity provisions of the contract involved was clear and unequivocal. The general contractor agreed to indemnify the engineer against all claims based on damage, injury, or death arising out of or connected with the work covered by the contract, regardless of how it may have been caused. The general contractor further agreed to indemnify the engineer for loss on account of or in consequence of any negligence in safeguarding the work.

§ 16.11   Defendant Can Maintain Contribution Action

Robinson Redevelopment Co. v. Anderson[11]

The plaintiff developer engaged an architectural firm to provide services in connection with a rehabilitation project. The architectural firm retained a structural engineer, a mechanical engineer, a landscape architect, and a supervising architect. The plaintiff sued the architect for economic losses alleging breach of contract and professional malpractice. The defendant filed third-party claims for contribution and indemnity. The third-party defendants argued that since the gravamen of the plaintiff's complaint was breach of contract and not professional malpractice, the defendant was precluded from obtaining contribution. The defendant argued that the negligent performance of contractual services can give rise to a cause of action in contract or tort and that the architect-client relationship gave rise to an independent legal duty owed by defendant to plaintiff, the breach of which could form the basis of a viable tort claim.

The court found that the complaint sufficiently alleged that a legal duty independent of the contract had been violated and sufficiently set forth a cause of action in malpractice for which the third-party defendants may be responsible in contribution to the defendant. The defendant's duty of care to the plaintiff sprang from the professional relationship the defendant had with the plaintiff and was extraneous to the contract, although connected to and dependent on the contract.

§ 16.12   Engineer Not Entitled to Contribution or Implied Indemnity

Hennepin Drainage & Levee District v. W.H. Klingner[12]

---

[11] 155 A.D.2d 755, 547 N.Y.S.2d 458 (1989).

[12] 187 Ill. App. 3d 710, 543 N.E.2d 967 (1989).

The plaintiff brought a breach of contract suit against an engineering firm which had prepared construction plans for a new pumping plant, alleging that the defendant had recommended the purchase of a pump which was incompatible with the anticipated range of hydraulic field conditions in which it was to operate. The defendant engineering firm filed a third-party complaint against the pump manufacturer seeking contribution and indemnity.

The court held that since contribution is a statutory remedy available to parties who are subject to liability in tort arising out of the same injury, and since the damages suffered by the plaintiff were purely economic in nature and recoverable only on a contract theory, the defendant engineering firm could not maintain a contribution action. Since there was no contractual relationship between the defendant engineering firm and the pump manufacturer, an implied indemnity theory would not be permitted.

§ 16.13 Design Engineer Could Not Obtain Contribution from EPA

City of Garland v. Zurn Industries, Inc.[13]

A city sued the design engineer of a physical chemical treatment plant which incorporated a technologically innovative carbon absorption system. The city had received a substantial grant from the EPA, which financed 75 percent of the cost of the project and which had reviewed and approved the engineer's design before the city was awarded the grant. The EPA had rejected the city's funding request for a pilot plant so that the physical chemical process could be tested.

After operation began, the system ruptured and could not be repaired to operate as originally intended. The plant did not meet the permit requirements and the EPA filed suit against the city for violations of the Clean Water Act. The city then filed suit against the design engineer in order to recoup the costs it had incurred under a consent decree entered into in settlement of the EPA's action. The city alleged that the design engineer's novel physical chemical process could never have produced the required effluent quality and that the design engineer had failed to recommend and perform essential pilot scale testing and sufficient waste water testing before recommending the process.

The design engineer filed a third-party action against the EPA for contribution as a joint tortfeasor alleging that the EPA's acts or omissions in its review and approval process were negligent and a proximate cause of any injury the city had suffered. The design engineer alleged that it had relied heavily on the EPA's input in making its final recommendation to the city.

The court held that the misrepresentation exception to the government's waiver of sovereign immunity under the Federal Tort Claims Act barred the engineer's

---

13 870 F.2d 320 (5th Cir. 1989).

claim for contribution from the EPA as a result of the engineer's reliance on data the EPA generated or collected on the physical chemical process and shared with the design engineer. The court found that the applicable regulations of the Clean Water Act imposed no duty on the EPA to warrant to the city that its plant would meet its permit requirements, which would suspend the application of the misrepresentation exception.

§ 16.14 Indemnity or Contribution from Design Drawing Company

Higgins Erectors & Haulers, Inc. v. E.E. Austin & Son, Inc.[14]

An engineering firm was added as a fourth-party defendant by the owner who was a third-party defendant in a suit brought by a subcontractor against a prime contractor arising out of damages alleged to have been caused by delayed construction. The engineering firm in turn brought a fifth-party complaint against the company which had a separate contract with the owner for design drawings and conveyor belts. The engineering firm alleged that the design firm's negligent delays in providing the drawings and conveyor belts to the owner led to the engineering firm's own delays in providing drawings and specifications for the foundation supports for the conveyors.

The court granted the motion to dismiss the fifth-party complaint noting that the engineering firm's alleged liability arose solely out of its contract with the owner and was not secondary to the wholly unrelated alleged liability of the design drawing company which was based upon an entirely separate contract. The owner's claim against the engineering firm was based upon a contract between the two and no cause of action sounding in tort was pleaded. Contribution would not be permitted in such a case.

§ 16.15 Apportioned Fault Verdict Upheld

Eventide Lutheran Home for the Aged v. Smithson Electric & General Construction, Inc.[15]

The Iowa Supreme Court upheld the trial court's apportionment of 14 percent of the comparative fault to the defendant engineering firm and 86 percent to the defendant general contractor in spite of unrebutted testimony regarding the engineering firm's professional negligence. On appeal, the plaintiff sought a finding that at least 50 percent of the fault was attributable to the engineering

---

[14] 714 F. Supp. 756 (W.D. Pa. 1989).

[15] 445 N.W.2d 789 (Iowa 1989).

firm so as to create joint and several liability for the engineering firm which apparently had a greater ability to pay the judgment.

The court held that the apportionment of liability among defendants was for the trier of fact and unrebutted expert testimony was only one of many factors to be weighed. The court concluded that a defendant's financial ability to pay damages is irrelevant to the apportionment of damages.

ECONOMIC LOSS

§ 16.16   Negligent Misrepresentation Case Requires Functional Equivalent of Privity

Ossining Union Free School District v. Anderson LaRocca Anderson[16]

The plaintiff school district retained an architectural firm to provide an evaluation and feasibility study of the plaintiff's buildings. The architectural firm retained engineering consultants, who tested the concrete at various locations throughout the school building and reported serious weaknesses in the building. The school district then closed the annex building. Later a third independent expert checked the results and concluded that the structure had been constructed with a lightweight concrete rather than the 2,500-pound-per-square-inch cement defendants had assumed in their report.

The school district sued the consulting engineers for negligence alleging that the defendant engineers were aware that the plaintiff would rely on their findings and that the intended purpose of the defendants' reports was to enable the school district to determine what measures should be taken to deal with structural problems in the buildings. The trial court dismissed the complaint and the appellate division affirmed based on the long-standing general rule that recovery will not be granted to a third person for pecuniary loss arising from the negligent misrepresentations of a professional with whom there was no contractual relationship.

The New York Court of Appeals was faced with the issue of whether, in a negligent misrepresentation case which produces only economic loss, privity of contract is required in order for the plaintiff to state a cause of action. The court concluded that a cause of action requires that the underlying relationship between the parties be one of contract or a bond between the parties so close as to be the functional equivalent of contractual privity.

The court found that the defendant engineers could not possibly have failed to be aware that the substance of the reports they furnished would be transmitted to and relied upon by the school district. The bond between the parties was so close

---

[16] 73 N.Y.2d 417, 539 N.E.2d 91, 541 N.Y.S.2d 335 (1989).

as to be the functional equivalent of contractual privity and the school district stated a case of action against the engineers.

§ 16.17   Tort Recovery for Economic Loss Not Allowed Regardless of Relationship Between Parties

Tolona Pizza Products Corp. v. Davy McKee Corp.[17]

While recognizing the differences of opinion in other divisions, the Illinois Appellate Court held that a professional malpractice action cannot be sustained under Illinois law if the plaintiff seeks damages for economic loss due to defeated commercial expectations. The plaintiff, a manufacturer and seller of pizza crusts, retained the defendant A/E firm to design, procure, and supervise the installation of an automatic pizza crust line that would achieve the plaintiff's automation objectives.

The plaintiff's breach of contract and negligent misrepresentation claims against the A/E remained pending in the trial court. The professional malpractice counts were dismissed by the trial court.

The appellate court noted that the relevant inquiry is the type of loss sustained, not the nature of the relationship between the parties which resulted in the alleged damage. The court found the distinction between providing services and products not to be determinative as to when economic loss may be recovered in tort. A professional malpractice action could not be maintained where the plaintiff sought damages for economic loss due to defeated commercial expectations.

§ 16.18   Tort Recovery for Economic Loss Not Allowed Even to Supplier of Services

Carmania Corp. v. Hambrecht Terrell International[18]

Applying New York law the court held that a New York plaintiff can recover economic losses only in a contract action. Recognizing that New York law allows concurrent recovery in tort and contract as long as the defendant violates distinct legal duties, the court stated that the plaintiff's tort claim must allege a breach of a duty that springs from circumstances extraneous to, and not constituting elements of, the contract, although it may be connected with and dependent upon the contract.

Damages in a breach of contract action seek to place the plaintiff in the position the plaintiff would have enjoyed had the parties' expectations been

---

[17] 187 Ill. App. 3d 365, 543 N.E.2d 225 (1989).

[18] 705 F. Supp. 936 (S.D.N.Y. 1989).

realized. Tort law has the goal of deterring people from inflicting harm when they behave unreasonably and compensating those injured by restoring them to the state they occupied before they suffered harm. The law preserves these distinctions by restricting a plaintiff who has suffered economic loss but not personal or property injury to a contract action for the benefit of the bargain. If the damages suffered are of the type remediable in contract, a plaintiff may not recover in tort.

The court rejected the plaintiff's argument that the economic loss rule only applies in the absence of contractual privity and that the rule never applies in an action against a supplier of services. The court found that there is no reason for any distinction between a supplier of goods and a supplier of services.

§ 16.19   Claim for Negligent Review of Shop Drawing

Malta Construction Co. v. Henningson, Durham & Richardson[19]

In a case involving a general contractor's claim against an engineering firm for damages caused by the preparation and approval of plans and shop drawings, the court discussed the Georgia economic loss rule which bars recovery in tort where the parties are not in privity and where the plaintiff's damages are purely economic. The court noted the Georgia exception to this rule relating to one who supplies information during the course of its business or its profession.

The court had previously held that an allegation of failing to review shop drawings promptly and adequately does not fall within the exception to the economic loss rule because a claim for negligent review of shop drawings is not like a claim for negligent misrepresentation, supply, or omission of information. The court then rejected the plaintiff's contention that shop drawings provide construction requirements and their approval constitutes a negligent misrepresentation.

ENVIRONMENTAL LAW

§ 16.20   Waste Disposal Problems

Strauss Veal Feeds, Inc. v. Mead & Hunt, Inc.[20]

An A/E firm specializing in designs for the dairy industry provided services relating to the construction of a processing facility for a client which had

---

[19] 716 F. Supp. 1466 (N.D. Ga. 1989).

[20] 538 N.E.2d 299 (Ind. Ct. App. 1989).

developed and implemented a liquid veal feed production process. The A/E was sued after the client had been ordered to shut its plant down by the Indiana Stream Pollution Control Board because the industrial waste produced by the plant had an excessive biochemical oxygen demand level. The client maintained that the A/E breached its contract when it failed to warn the client about possible industrial waste disposal problems associated with the production of liquid veal feed and also alleged the A/E breached its tort duty of due care when it did not independently investigate and warn the client about potential industrial waste problems.

The evidence indicated that the client did not specifically ask for consulting or design services from the A/E with respect to waste treatment or waste disposal and that, when the A/E questioned the client regarding its ability to meet the requirements imposed by the waste water treatment regulations, the client indicated that its operation would be a clean one and that direct discharge of effluent into the sewage and waste system would create no problem. The court held that the violations of state environmental laws caused by the client's innovative process did not constitute a breach of the A/E's implied agreement to design a suitable processing facility. The plant had been designed in compliance with applicable building and zoning codes.

The trial court had accepted the client's argument that the A/E had an independent tort duty to independently investigate and warn the client about potential waste disposal problems and had found that the A/E did have a duty to advise the client that it might have a waste disposal problem. The appellate court held that such a duty went beyond the scope of the parties' agreement. An architect does not owe a fiduciary duty to its employer but rather the architect's duties to its employer depend upon the agreement that is entered into with that employer. The contract between the A/E firm and the client stated that the A/E would provide consultation upon request. The client never asked for consulting services from the A/E regarding waste disposal or treatment.

The appellate court noted that the client in this case occupied a unique position in the veal feed production industry as the developer and the first to implement the liquid veal feed production process. The A/E's reliance upon the client's statement concerning waste disposal did not fall below the requisite standard of care for architects, given the client's expert knowledge of the production process.

EXPERT WITNESS LITIGATION

§ 16.21 Expert Witness Immune from Suit

Bruce v. Byrne-Stevens & Associates[21]

---

[21] 113 Wash. 2d 123, 776 P.2d 666 (1989).

Property owners retained an engineering firm to calculate and testify as to the cost of stabilizing soil on their land. At a trial against a neighbor they obtained a judgment in the amount of the expert engineer's testimony. Later they learned it would cost double the amount of the expert engineer's trial estimate to resolve the problem.

The owners filed suit against the engineer alleging that but for the expert engineer's low estimate of the cost of restoring lateral support, they would have obtained a judgment for the true cost of the restoration. The expert engineer's motion to dismiss based on the witness immunity rule was granted by the trial court.

The Washington Supreme Court noted that the purpose of the witness immunity rule is to preserve the integrity of the judicial process by encouraging full and frank testimony. Even a privately retained and compensated expert is immune because experts, as a matter of law, serve the court. The court further noted that imposing civil liability on expert witnesses would discourage anyone who is not a full-time professional expert witness from testifying because only professional witnesses would be in a position to carry insurance to guard against such liability. The immunity granted the witness extends to the actions forming the basis of the testimony and the witness cannot be sued for negligent engineering rather than negligent testifying. The court held that absolute immunity extends to acts and statements of experts which arise in the course of or preliminary to judicial proceedings.

§ 16.22   Expert Opinion Necessary to Prove Negligence

Board of Education v. Sargent, Webster, Crenshaw & Folley[22]

A school district's claim against the architect based upon the architect's failure to notify the district of a known defective roof installation asserted the breach of a specific contractual undertaking by the architect, similar to the failure to achieve a particular promised result, which does not require proof of professional negligence. Therefore expert testimony that the architect's performance fell short of accepted professional standards of architectural practice was not necessary.

To the extent that the relationship between the school district and the architect created a duty on the architect's part sufficiently independent of the contract which would give rise to an action in tort for negligent misrepresentation or concealment, expert testimony would be necessary to establish the architect's negligence. The failure to produce expert testimony would justify the dismissal of the tort cause of action.

---

[22] 146 A.D. 190, 539 N.Y.S.2d 814 (1989), *appeal denied,* 75 N.Y.2d 702, 551 N.Y.S.2d 906 (1990).

§ 16.23 Non-Architect as Expert Witness Against Architect

Prichard Brothers, Inc. v. Grady Co.[23]

In a negligence case against an architect, the court allowed the plaintiff to present testimony from a person who was a professional estimator and certified engineering technician that the shop drawings presented to the architect were proper and appropriate and should have been approved. The witness had worked as a draftsman for two architectural firms and had an ownership in a consulting firm and worked with architects on a regular basis.

The trial court indicated that to the extent plans and specifications are to be read and responded to by non-architects, the trial court would permit a non-architect to express an opinion as to those plans and specifications regarding whether they say what they purport to say and whether they are adequate for a non-architect to respond to and provide the services and materials that are required. The appellate court agreed with the trial court that the professional estimator and certified engineering technician was qualified to testify regarding the architect's interpretation of specifications and responses to shop drawings.

§ 16.24 Statute Requires Filing of Expert's Affidavit with Complaint Against Architects

Housing Authority of Savannah v. Greene[24]

The Supreme Court of Georgia held that a statute requiring that, in any action for damages alleging professional malpractice, the plaintiff shall be required to file with the complaint an affidavit of an expert competent to testify and setting forth specifically at least one negligent act or omission and a factual basis for each claim, applies to architects as well as other professionals even though the remainder of the act was enacted as part of a medical malpractice act.

§ 16.25 Surveyor Liable as a Matter of Law

Spainhower v. B. Aubrey Huffman & Associates[25]

A surveyor sued a landowner for the unpaid balance of his fee. The landowner counterclaimed for damages arising from the surveyor's alleged negligence. The

---

[23] 436 N.W.2d 460 (Minn. Ct. App. 1989), *review denied.*

[24] 259 Ga. 435, 383 S.E.2d 867 (1989).

[25] 377 S.E.2d 615 (Va. 1989).

landowner's expert alleged error in disregarding a recorded distance, relying on an unrecorded fence line observed in the field, and depending on acreage computations. Expert witnesses called by the surveyor testified that the surveyor's methods met the locally prevailing standards of skill, care, and diligence. The case was submitted to a jury which found in favor of the surveyor.

The appellate court reversed and found that the trial court erred in submitting the case to the jury. While the question of whether a professional departed from the standard of care is ordinarily an issue of fact to be resolved on the basis of expert testimony, exceptions exist which have become rules of law. Such exceptions fix binding standards which are not left to the exercise of professional judgment. As rules of law, they are not subject to expert opinions regarding local practices. Land surveyors are governed by certain standards which have ripened into rules of law. A natural monument or landmark should prevail over measurement of acreage. The appellate court concluded that the surveyor was negligent as a matter of law in ignoring this rule.

§ 16.26   Architect's Own Expert Establishes Architect's Negligence

D&O Contractors, Inc. v. Terrebonne Parish School Board[26]

The appellate court affirmed the trial court's finding of negligence against an architect for the design of a resurfacing plan for running tracks which later cracked. The plaintiff school board's expert had conceded that the defendant's plans and specifications were competent, but the trial court concluded that expert testimony was unnecessary because a lay person could infer negligence in the resurfacing of already cracked tracks without corrective work on the base and without specifying an herbicide to prevent grass growth.

The appellate court affirmed, but found the trial court's reliance on the exception to the requirement of expert testimony to prove architectural negligence unnecessary because the co-defendant contractor's expert and the architect's own expert established a deviation from the standard of care.

MEASURE OF DAMAGES

§ 16.27   Cost to Repair

Council of Unit Owners v. Carl M. Freeman Associates[27]

---

[26] 545 So. 2d 588 (La. Ct. App. 1989).

[27] 564 A.2d 357 (Del. Super. Ct. 1989).

A condominium association filed suit against the designer, contractor, and others alleging defects in the design and construction of the condominium complex. The plaintiff filed a motion in limine to preclude the defendants from introducing evidence at trial of any diminution of value and useful life theories as a means of reducing the plaintiff's damage award. The defendants argued that diminution or loss in value of the condominium was the appropriate measure of damages or in the alternative an adjusted cost of repair or replacement measure could be utilized taking into account the already expired useful life of the condominium and any increase in condominium value created by such repairs or replacement.

The court assumed that the cost of repairs would be in the $13 million to $15 million range. The defense experts expressed the position that there was no discernable difference or decrease in the property's appreciation attributable to the defects alleged by the plaintiff. The court noted that the cost of repair rule is generally preferred over the value rule and held the cost of repair rule to be the appropriate measure of damages. The court then rejected the defendants' argument that the application of the cost of repair rule could give the plaintiff a windfall by extending the useful lives of those components repaired beyond what was reasonably expected at the time of construction.

The defendants argued that, if the cost of repair or replacement rule was used, it should be prorated for the already expired useful lives of the allegedly defective building components. The court decided the case was not appropriate for implementation of the useful life theory as the measure of damages. The court noted that such an approach has the potential of giving the defendants too much of a benefit and has the potential to create significant proof problems and substantial jury confusion. The court therefore granted the plaintiff's motion in limine.

§ 16.28 Consequential Damages from Engineer

Lochrane Engineering, Inc. v. Willingham Realgrowth Investment Fund, Ltd.[28]

The plaintiff purchaser of five residential duplex units sued the developer, general contractor, civil engineer, and septic tank subcontractor for damages relating to an inadequate septic tank sewage disposal system. The developer cross-claimed against the engineer and septic tank contractor. The trial court found the developer liable to the buyer on theories of negligence and implied warranty. The trial court also held the engineer and septic tank installer, neither of whom had contractual privity with the plaintiff buyer, jointly and severally liable with the developer to the buyer for the entire amount awarded the buyer for damages.

---

[28] 552 So. 2d 228 (Fla. Dist. Ct. App. 1989).

The appellate court held that the engineer should not have been held jointly and severally liable with the developer for the full damages for which the developer was liable to the buyer under the theory of implied warranty. The appellate court noted that the engineer should not be liable to the plaintiff buyer for more money damages than the engineer would have been liable for to the developer. The appellate court affirmed the buyer's judgment against the developer, reversed the buyer's judgment against the engineer and entered judgment in indemnity in favor of the developer and against the engineer based only on the consequential damages resulting from the necessity of pumping the septic tank to make the system useful until fully repaired.

PATENT AND LATENT DEFECTS

§ 16.29   Question of Fact

Kala Investments, Inc. v. Sklar[29]

The appellate court reversed summary judgment in favor of an architect on the present building owner's crossclaim holding that there was a question of fact whether a window design which violated the building code by being too low without a guard rail was a patent or latent defect.

A child fell through a fourth story screened window and was injured. There was no dispute that there was a building code violation, but the court held there was a question of fact whether the low window without a guard rail or special screen was a patent, or obvious, defect. The court noted the Florida rule that if the defect was patent, then the architect would not be liable for injuries occurring after acceptance of the building by the owner since the owner could have discovered and remedied the defect. However, if the defect was latent, the owner could pursue a claim under the doctrine of equitable subrogation.

§ 16.30   Owner's Allegation of Latent Defect

W.P. Johnson Properties, Inc. v. Miller[30]

The plaintiff brought suit against a hotel owner alleging that a patent defect in the stairs caused his fall. The owner in a cross-claim against the designer alleged a latent defect in the failure to allow sufficient distance between an exit door and the first step down the stairway. The appellate court reversed the trial court's dismissal of the cross-claim and held that the plaintiff's allegations of a patent

---

[29] 538 So. 2d 909 (Fla. Dist. Ct. App. 1989).

[30] 549 So. 2d 213 (Fla. Dist. Ct. App. 1989).

defect in a stairway design were not binding on the owner's cross-claim against the designers alleging a latent defect. The court noted the Florida rule that if the defect was patent rather than latent, the owner could not recover against the designer because the error could have been discovered and remedied by the owner. The appellate court noted that it is generally a question of fact whether a design defect is patent or latent.

§ 16.31 Subsequent Owner Could Not Recover

Eastover Corp. v. Martin Builders[31]

The Louisiana Appellate Court held that a subsequent building owner could not recover damages from the architect for a sewer system failure because the alleged defect in the design of the sewer system was patent and the building had been accepted by the original owner without objection. In constructing the sewer system, pipe hangers had been placed every ten feet, rather than every five feet as required, which resulted in the system's failure. The court found that the architect knew or should have known of this obvious defect. Because the architect was a general partner of the original owner, the architect's knowledge of the patent defect was imputable to the original owner.

PRIVITY

§ 16.32 Condominium Owner Third-Party Beneficiary

R.H. Sanbar Projects, Inc. v. Gruzen Partnership[32]

Where the owner retained a developer to build a condominium building and the developer hired two architectural firms, the owner was the third-party beneficiary of the contract between the developer, who was sufficiently alleged to be the owner's agent, and the architects. The court noted that it was almost inconceivable that professional employees who render their services in connection with a major construction project would not contemplate that the performance of their contractual obligations would ultimately benefit the owner of that development.

The court distinguished the situation where a subcontractor seeks payment from an owner by virtue of its contract with the general contractor. The

---

[31] 543 So. 2d 1358 (La. Ct. App. 1989).

[32] 148 A.D.2d 316, 538 N.Y.S.2d 532 (1989).

subcontractor there is not a foreseeable beneficiary of the contract between an owner and a general contractor. The court held that the property owner's complaint stated a cause of action against the architects.

PUBLIC OFFICIAL IMMUNITY

§ 16.33   Suit Against State Employee Engineer Barred

Keene v. Bierman[33]

The plaintiff auto accident victim sued the engineer who designed the roadway. The engineer was an employee of the State of Illinois. The court rejected the plaintiff's argument that the defendant as a registered professional engineer was obligated to meet a standard of care required of all those in the profession and concluded that the engineer had no relationship with the plaintiff as an individual and therefore his status as a professional would not give rise to any basis for liability. Any duty owed by the engineer was to the public generally and the engineer's activity was clearly governmental in nature and protected by the doctrine of public official immunity.

RACKETEERING

§ 16.34   Engineering Firm Supplying Reports and Studies

Beauford v. Helmsley[34]

The plaintiffs brought suit alleging RICO and state violations in connection with the conversion of an apartment complex to condominiums. The defendants were the partners in the real estate partnership sponsoring the conversion, the sponsor's sales agent, and an engineering firm and an individual engineer who supplied reports and studies as part of the conversion.

The plaintiffs alleged that the defendants made material misrepresentations in the conversion offering plan and subsequent plan amendments relating to the concealment of serious structural defects in the buildings, the presence of asbestos in the insulation, and the need to replace plumbing and electrical

---

[33] 184 Ill. App. 3d 87, 540 N.E.2d 16 (1989).

[34] 865 F.2d 1386 (2d Cir. 1989).

systems. The alleged means of concealment included statements by the engineering defendants, failures to disclose by the sponsoring defendants, and absorption by the sponsoring defendants of certain repair costs in order to set forth artificially low maintenance levels for the apartments. The conversion plan had been mailed to more than 8000 tenants of the apartments and other potential buyers.

The trial court granted a motion to dismiss which was affirmed by the Second Circuit. However, upon rehearing en banc, the Second Circuit reviewed its prior RICO rulings and held that the amended complaint sufficiently pleaded the RICO enterprise element and then the court examined the issue of whether the amended complaint adequately alleged a pattern of racketeering activity.

The court noted that racketeering activities include any act which is indictable as mail fraud. The amended complaint alleged that since 1984 there had been several amendments to the original offering plan and that the amendments were also mailed to tenants and potential buyers. The court also noted that there could be no question that the thousands of alleged mail frauds had the necessary interrelationship to be considered a pattern. All the mailings were made to groups of persons related by their tenancy in the apartments or their potential interest in purchasing the apartments. All the frauds had as their goal the inflation of profits to be made by the defendants. The court concluded that the amended complaint did not fail to satisfy the pattern requirement.

The court noted that it recognized that its decision would open the door to more civil RICO cases. The dissenting opinion indicated that any real estate conversion involving the mailing of an offering plan with one misrepresentation to apartment house tenants, coupled with the mailing of an amendment to the plan that fails to remedy the fraud, is now subject to civil RICO charges.

SAFETY ON THE JOBSITE

§ 16.35   No Duty to Notify Workers

Young v. Eastern Engineering & Elevator Co.[35]

The plaintiff was injured when he fell through a 20-inch-wide opening in the drywall enclosure surrounding an elevator shaft. The architect's contract required periodic visits to the jobsite to determine whether the work was proceeding in accordance with the contract documents. The contract had no provisions requiring the architect to supervise or control job safety or to implement safety precautions for the employees of the general contractor or subcontractor. The contract did not impose on the architect the responsibility for

---

[35] 381 Pa. Super. 428, 554 A.2d 77 (1989).

safety on the construction site, but rather the general contractor and the subcontractors had the duty to protect the workers from hazards on the construction site.

The court noted that there is a split of authority as to whether an architect is liable to workers for injuries or death resulting from hazardous working conditions on the construction site. The court stated that although there is no clear majority it would appear that the weight of authority is on the side of nonliability. The court discussed the leading cases imposing liability and also denying liability.

The court held that, absent an undertaking by an architect, by contract or conduct, of the responsibilities of the supervision of construction and the maintenance of safe conditions on the construction project, an architect is not under a duty to notify workers or employees of the general contractor or subcontractors of hazardous conditions on the construction site.

§ 16.36   Architect Not Liable to Injured Worker

Davis v. Lenox School[36]

The architect's contract with the school district provided that he was not to have any control or responsibility "for construction means, methods . . . or for safety precautions and programs in connection with the work, for acts or omissions of the contractor, subcontractor or any other persons performing any of the work." The court noted that the architect lacked the authority to halt the work for unsafe conditions or to control or determine on-site working conditions. In the absence of a contractual right to supervise and control the construction work or site safety, the architect cannot be held liable in negligence for a plaintiff's injuries.

Before a statutory duty is imposed upon a party to provide a safe work place it must have the authority to control the activity bringing about the injury to enable it to avoid or correct an unsafe condition. Only upon having the authority to supervise and control does an architect have a nondelegable statutory duty to provide a safe work place.

§ 16.37   No Duty to Supervise

Jones v. Gateway Realty, Inc.[37]

The architect was retained based on an oral agreement to prepare plans for an office building. The owners bought the plans from the architect and then only

---

[36] 151 A.D.2d 230, 541 N.Y.S.2d 814 (1989).

[37] 550 So. 2d 388 (La. Ct. App. 1989).

consulted the architect regarding a problem involving bricks on the building. The plaintiff was injured when she struck a barrier curb while riding her bike through the building's parking lot. After the architect's plans had been drawn, a survey revealed different dimensions for the property which meant that the architect's parking lot plan would not work. The architect was not asked to do a revised plan nor was the architect consulted about a change which consisted of the installation of barrier curbs. The architect did visit the site monthly to inspect the construction for the limited purpose of allowing the contractor to make its periodic monetary draw.

The appellate court reversed the finding of the trial court that the architect breached a duty to supervise construction at least minimally and permitted a deviation from his original plan. The appellate court could find no basis in law or contract for the obligation to supervise the project when the architect did not agree to supervise and the alleged defect was not designed by the architect.

STATUTES OF REPOSE

§ 16.38   Wisconsin's Statute of Repose Held Unconstitutional

Funk v. Wollin Silo & Equipment, Inc.[38]

The Wisconsin Supreme Court held that Wisconsin's six-year statute of repose for actions for injuries resulting from improvements to real property was unconstitutional because its classification scheme violated the equal protection clauses of the United States and Wisconsin constitutions. A former Wisconsin statute had previously been held unconstitutional because the statute afforded special protection to persons who perform and furnish the design, planning, supervision of construction, or construction of improvements to real property, but not to other classes such as suppliers, owners, and occupants.

The second statute included protection for persons performing land surveying services or furnishing materials but still did not include owners and occupiers of land. The court noted that the arbitrary exclusion of property owners and tenants results in a statute that still affords protection and favors without a reasonable and rational basis and is unconstitutional.

---

[38] 148 Wis. 2d 59, 435 N.W.2d 244 (1989).

[39] 782 P.2d 188 (Utah 1989).

§ 16.39   Utah's Statute of Repose
Held Unconstitutional

Sun Valley Water Beds v. Herm Hughes & Son, Inc.[39]

The Utah Supreme Court held that the seven-year architects and builders statute of repose violated the open courts provision of the Utah constitution by failing to provide an injured person with an effective and reasonable alternative remedy and by being arbitrary and unreasonable. The court noted that the statute did not protect the industry from a significant number of lawsuits since the evidence before the court indicated that nationally only 2.1 percent of all claims are initiated subsequent to the seventh year from completion, and that since the number of claims affected by the statute was insignificant, it was highly unlikely that lower insurance rates were inextricably tied to the existence of the statute.

§ 16.40   Ohio's Statute of Repose
Held Constitutional

Sedar v. Knowlton Construction Co.[40]

The Ohio Supreme Court held that the Ohio ten-year statute of repose which cuts off the tort liability of architects and builders, but does not so limit the liability of owners and suppliers, does not violate the equal protection guaranties of the Ohio and United States constitutions.

§ 16.41   Oklahoma's Statute of Repose
Held Constitutional

St. Paul Fire & Marine Insurance Co. v. Getty Oil Co.[41]

The Oklahoma Supreme Court held that a statute which bars tort actions against builders, architects, owners, and the like for damages by reason of defective design or construction for injuries occurring more than ten years after completion of construction of an improvement to real property is constitutional. The court upheld the constitutionality of the statute as a reasonable legislative measure, finding that the statute does not disturb vested rights, it treats equally an entire class of similarly situated persons or things, and it bears a reasonable relation to the objective to be accomplished. The statute of repose involved had broadened the classifications from a prior statute which had previously been

---

[40] 49 Ohio St. 3d 193, 551 N.E.2d 938 (1990).

[41] 782 P.2d 915 (Okla. 1989).

ruled unconstitutional. The current statute includes owners and lessees and expands the limitation period from five to ten years.

STATUTES OF LIMITATIONS

§ 16.42 A/E Firm Estopped from Asserting Statute of Limitations

Senior Housing, Inc. v. Nakawatase, Rutkowski, Wyns & Yi, Inc.[42]

The plaintiff and the defendant A/E firm entered into a contract for the development of a multi-unit residential building for the elderly. After substantial completion, the plaintiff notified the A/E firm that there were certain problems resulting in numerous water and air leaks at windows and heat/vent/air conditioning units when it rained or when the wind blew. The A/E firm instructed the contractor to recaulk the windows in accordance with the drawing.

During a 21-month period further measures were undertaken. The plaintiff then retained an independent masonry consultant who concluded that the original drawings did not allow water drainage and the plaintiff then commissioned additional work to correct the problems. When the plaintiff demanded payment from the A/E for the repair costs, the A/E firm failed to respond. When suit was brought, the A/E firm alleged that the complaint had not been filed within the applicable two-year limitations period.

The plaintiff argued that the A/E firm's conduct in both investigating the leakage and attempting to correct the problem by instructing the contractor as to what remedial steps to take estopped the architectural firm from asserting the statute of limitations as a defense. The court indicated that the A/E was responsible and took responsibility to direct the repair work. The court rejected the A/E's argument that its actions consisted of mere investigation and held that the A/E firm was the intermediary between the plaintiff and the contractor and acted in an apparent acknowledgment of its responsibility under the contract.

The court found it reasonable for the plaintiff to have refrained from filing its lawsuit in reliance on the A/E firm's representations that remedial measures would be taken, observed and further corrected if necessary.

§ 16.43 Damage Claim Did Not Change Contract Action Into Tort Action

Flint Ridge Development Co. v. Benham-Blair & Affiliates, Inc.[43]

---

[42] 192 Ill. App. 3d 766, 549 N.E.2d 604 (1989), *reh'g denied.*
[43] 775 P.2d 797 (Okla. 1989).

The plaintiff development company sued the defendant A/E firm for breach of contract to provide architectural, engineering, and construction supervision services in connection with the construction of a subdivision. The A/E defendant argued that the plaintiff's claims were tort-based resulting from the A/E firm's negligent performance of duties arising out of the contract relationship. The trial court agreed with the A/E defendant that the plaintiff's action was brought in tort and governed by the two-year statute of limitations rather than the five-year contract statute of limitations.

The Oklahoma Supreme Court disagreed with the A/E's contention that, since the plaintiff had alleged only breaches of duties implied as a result of the contractual relationship and had sought damages recoverable only in a tort action, the action should properly be held to have been brought exclusively in tort. The court noted that, even assuming that the plaintiff had sought damages normally recoverable only in tort, the plaintiff had also made claims for damages clearly recoverable under the contract theory. The court noted that it was for the trial court to appropriately limit the scope of the damages available under the appropriate theory.

§ 16.44   Economic Loss Action Governed by Tort Statute of Limitations

Merchants National Bank & Trust Co. v. Smith, Hinchman & Grylls Associates, Inc.[44]

The assignee of a subcontractor sought recovery against the defendant architect for economic losses incurred as a result of defects and deficiencies in architectural plans and specifications for an army hospital. The Fifth Circuit noted that the courts have recognized that under Louisiana law a contractor or subcontractor may bring an action in tort for economic loss caused by an architect's failure to provide adequate plans or specifications. The court held that the Louisiana one-year prescriptive period for torts governed claims against architects for economic loss rather than the ten-year period for personal actions and certain suits against architects and contractors.

§ 16.45   Suit by Governmental Agencies Not Barred by Statute of Limitations

New Jersey Educational Facilities Authority v. Conditioning Co.[45]

---

[44] 876 F.2d 1202 (5th Cir. 1989).

[45] 237 N.J. Super. 310, 567 A.2d 1013 (App. Div. 1989).

The New Jersey facilities authority and a state college brought suit arising out of the design and construction of a student union building, alleging that the firm retained to supervise the design and construction of the building breached its contract and was negligent in failing to ascertain that the contractor was performing the construction in an improper matter, that the work performed did not conform to the plans and specifications, and that the firm failed to design and prepare plans and specifications properly. The trial court dismissed the case on the basis that it was barred by the six-year statute of limitations.

The appellate court reversed and held that the doctrine of *nullum tempus occurrit regi* (time does not run against the king) applied and the case was not barred by the statute of limitations. The court noted that it is settled in New Jersey that statutes of limitations do not run against any civil action brought by the state or any of its agencies and subdivisions unless the legislature so allows by express language or necessary implication. The appellate court concluded that the authority and the college were engaged in a governmental function and that as state agencies they were entitled to the same statute of limitations which is afforded to the state itself.

PART IV

STRATEGIES, TECHNIQUES, AND OBSERVATIONS

CHAPTER 17

THE WORK FORCE SHORTAGE AND ORGANIZED LABOR'S AGENDA FOR THE 1990S

Judd H. Lees

§ 17.1   Introduction

§ 17.2   Agenda Item 1: Continue the Apprenticeship Battle

§ 17.3   Agenda Item 2: Employ More Sophisticated Top-Down Organizing Techniques

§ 17.4   Agenda Item 3: Engage in More Aggressive Bottom-Up Organizing

§ 17.5   Agenda Item 4: If All Else Fails, File an Unfair Labor Practice Charge

§ 17.1   Introduction

Most labor law practitioners are aware of the startling shift of construction employees from union to nonunion status which marked the 1980s. Twenty years ago 80 percent of all construction in the United States was performed by union construction workers. Today organized labor represents only 22 percent of the total construction work force. An even more startling fact is that the total number of trained construction workers—both union and nonunion—is shrinking and getting older. The average age of a carpenter is 48. The average age of a tool and die maker is 52. Construction is perceived by young people as an unsafe, cyclical profession which cannot effectively compete with the more glamorous opportunities in the high-tech industries. In addition, young people's expectations are affected by a society which puts a premium upon a college education and a desk job.

The increase in the numbers of merit shop construction employees which marked the 1980s was not the result of an increase in construction applicants but merely a shift by union construction employees to the greater opportunities for employment offered by the open shop sector. While the nonunion sector has been making laudable efforts to train its employees, a large percentage of these employees were already trained by the unions. However, the 1990s will be marked by a shift of these employees back to the union ranks as a result of the increase in construction work and the resulting shortage in available, trained construction workers. In addition to "stealing back" its members, organized labor will attempt to gain a choke-hold upon the open shop's source of personnel in order to provide a major incentive for nonunion contractors to voluntarily sign collective bargaining agreements.

It is this battle for bodies which will guide construction labor law in the 1990s as organized labor utilizes the National Labor Relations Board (NLRB), federal and state law, and the various state agencies involved in work force training and apprenticeship in order to obtain and maintain a monopoly on the shrinking numbers of young people coming into construction.

§ 17.2   Agenda Item 1:
Continue the Apprenticeship Battle

Before examining organized labor's agenda in the area of existing construction personnel, one needs to examine the recent efforts of organized labor to monopolize the source of trained construction employees. In order to understand this agenda fully, one needs to understand the apprenticeship system, both at the federal and state level. It is this system which organized labor has so artfully controlled in order to control the incoming ranks of construction employees. It is also this apprenticeship system which has been earmarked by nonunion contractors as the object of legal challenge to wrest control from the unions over the training of construction employees.

On the federal level, federal policy regarding apprenticeship is set by the Bureau of Apprenticeship and Training (BAT), a branch of the Department of Labor. The laws governing BAT are set forth in the Fitzgerald Act. That Act states in part:

> The Secretary of Labor is authorized and directed to formulate and promote the furtherance of labor standards necessary to safeguard the welfare of apprentices, to extend the application of such standards by encouraging the inclusion thereof in contracts of apprenticeship, to bring together employers and labor for the formulation of programs of apprenticeship, to cooperate with the State agencies engaged in the formulation and promotion of standards of apprenticeship, and to cooperate with the Office of Education under the Department of Health, Education and Welfare in accordance with Section 17 of Title 20. For the purposes of this chapter the term "State" shall include the District of Columbia.[1]

BAT has the authority to register apprenticeship training programs.[2] For those states which have no state apprenticeship council, BAT approval allows the

---

[1] 29 U.S.C. § 50 (1988).

[2] The requirements for approval of such programs are set forth in 29 C.F.R. § 29.

employer-participants to pay apprentice wage rates on both state and federal public works. In states which do have a state apprenticeship council (SAC), BAT sees that state standards conform with the secretary of labor's published standards to ensure that the state program is also eligible for federal purposes. However, SAC approval is necessary before a program sponsor will be allowed to pay apprentice wage rates on state prevailing-wage projects.[3]

The problem arises when the SAC standards are more rigorous than the BAT standards. In the SAC states, organized labor has mounted a legal and political campaign to discourage the state approval of nonunion apprenticeship programs. By preventing or discouraging such state approval, organized labor has been successful in discouraging open shop penetration of state public works since the employer-participant in the unapproved apprenticeship training program must pay apprentices the journeyman wage rate.

Direct legal challenges have taken place in three SAC states—Washington, California, and Nevada. In all three states, the federal BAT has approved nonunion apprenticeship programs. Yet, in all three states, few if any of these nonunion programs have been approved by the state councils. The basis for SAC rejection of the programs has varied but generally turns on the alleged absence of need for the proposed program, the failure to conform with the state's more rigorous wage requirements, and the absence of eligible employee representatives in the nonunion sector for membership on the monitoring joint apprenticeship training council. The parties challenging this system to open up state approval for nonunion programs have employed a variety of legal theories.

In the state of Washington, the SAC had an outright ban on nonunion or "parallel" programs until 1978. In that year, the SAC succumbed to pressure from BAT to modify this practice. However, the SAC passed a regulation requiring program sponsors to pay union wage rates to apprentices even if they were nonunion.

This was challenged in 1983 by a number of nonunion contractors and contractor organizations in a lawsuit entitled *Washington State Electrical Contractors Association v. Forrest.*[4] The plaintiffs alleged that the SAC's action constituted price-fixing in violation of federal antitrust law. The plaintiffs lost before the federal district court which determined that the "state action" exemption to antitrust liability, which protects anticompetitive conduct carried

---

[3] For example, the Public Works Act for the State of Washington states in part:

> Apprentice workmen employed upon public works projects for whom an apprenticeship agreement has been registered and approved with the state apprenticeship council pursuant to Chapter 49.04 RCW, must be paid at least the prevailing hourly rate for an apprentice of that track. Any workman for whom an apprenticeship agreement has not been registered and approved by the state apprenticeship council shall be considered to be a fully qualified journeyman and, therefore, shall be paid at the prevailing hourly rate for journeymen.

RCW 39.12.021.

[4] 839 F.2d 547 (9th Cir.), *cert. granted*, 109 S.Ct. 38 (1988), *on remand*, 880 F.2d 247 (9th Cir. 1989).

out pursuant to state policy and under state supervision, applied to the SAC's action.

The plaintiffs appealed and lost before the Court of Appeals but filed a successful petition for writ of certiorari to the United States Supreme Court. The basis for the Supreme Court's vacating the ruling and remanding the case was its determination in the case of *Patrick v. Burget*[5] that the "state action" exemption to antitrust liability did not apply unless the state actively supervised the anticompetitive conduct at issue. The case is now pending before the Court of Appeals.

A successful challenge was mounted in California to the state apprenticeship council's refusal to approve a nonunion apprenticeship program. *In re Riverside & San Bernardino Electrical*[6] was filed after a nonunion program was turned down because it would allegedly "lower or adversely affect existing prevailing conditions, including wages, benefits and training in the area and industry." A superior court issued a writ of mandate that the program be approved since the court found that the determination of illegal substandard conditions was not supported by the evidence. The court specifically held:

> The present record, while reflecting a much greater downward differential in wages and benefits, contains no evidence that the wage and benefit disparity will have any type of adverse effect on Real Parties' existing programs or on the apprentices in those programs; in this respect all of the evidence is to the contrary [citations omitted]. There is no suggestion that apprentices will leave the existing programs to join the parallel program. While such a movement would not be anticipated because the wages in the parallel program are lower than those of the existing program, there is also no evidence that there are insufficient applicants to fill all of the programs; indeed, there appears to be a great shortage of apprenticeship positions for potential applicants in the area. . . . Nor is there any evidence that apprentices in the existing programs would be threatened with a reduction of their apprenticeship wages if the parallel program were approved.

The plaintiffs also asked that the council's action be set aside based upon preemption of the SAC's actions by the Employee Retirement Income Security Act (ERISA).[7] The plaintiffs pointed out that § 514(a) of ERISA states that the Act shall "supersede all state laws insofar as they may now or hereafter relate to an employee benefit plan." The court, however, disagreed and held that the ERISA "savings" clause[8] applied to protect the state's regulation in this area.

---

[5] 486 U.S. 94 (1988).

[6] California Superior Court, Department 8, Cause No. 900-162 (1989).

[7] 29 U.S.C. §§ 1001, 1144.

[8] Section 514(d) of ERISA provides that "[n]othing in this subchapter shall be construed to alter, amend, modify, invalidate, impair, or supersede any law of the United States . . . or any rule or regulation issued under any law." 29 U.S.C. § 1144(d).

A different preemption analysis was utilized by the plaintiffs in Nevada in the case of *Associated Builders & Contractors, Inc., v. MacDonald.*[9] The state council refused to approve an open-shop program despite the fact that its program had federal approval pursuant to the Fitzgerald Act and the corresponding federal regulations. Pursuant to BAT approval, a program sponsor is normally allowed to pay apprentice wage rates on public works jobs. However, as a result of the state council's refusal to approve the federally-approved program, the state, by its regulation, was not allowing the program sponsor to pay apprentice wage rates on state prevailing wage jobs. According to the plaintiffs, this interfered with federal law and federal oversight and therefore was preempted. The Nevada federal district court agreed and held as follows:

> The state law governing wages on public works in Nevada . . . allows apprenticeship programs authorized by SAC. Inasmuch as the general field of apprenticeship training has been preempted by the [Fitzgerald] Act [citation omitted] and the delegation of authority to state apprenticeship councils is controlled by federal law, state laws affecting wages paid to apprentices must apply equally to BAT approved and SAC approved apprenticeship programs. A state law which grants a significant benefit only to SAC approved programs is discriminatory and unconstitutional.

In addition, the federal court held that ERISA preempted the application of inconsistent state regulations to federally-approved trust fund programs.

All three challenges are being watched with a great deal of attention by both state legislators and organized labor. In addition, BAT is informally lobbying these states to modify their procedures in order to conform with the federal practices. Until such modification occurs, however, nonunion contractors have been successfully frustrated by the state apprenticeship councils who, with the active support of organized labor, have blocked state approval for nonunion training programs.

In addition to this battle over control of the state approval process for construction laborers, several states require that an apprenticeship training program be approved by the state apprenticeship council before employer contributions to those programs can be credited against prevailing wage requirements. Such contributions to a training trust fund can normally be credited to reduce the labor force costs on state prevailing wage work. However, by removing this credit, this benefit to construction employers is lost.

This union-supported position by the state legislatures and stage apprenticeship agencies has two significant impacts on employees for nonunion contractors. First, those contractors who do train employees and finance that training do not receive credit for this funding and are therefore at a competitive disadvantage against those union contractors who either do not train or who receive credit for these monies. Second, without this financial incentive, funding for nonunion

---

[9] Nevada District Court, Cause No. CV-N-89-409 BRT (1989).

programs dries up. Many nonunion training trusts have experienced a significant decrease in employer contributions as a result of successful lobbying by organized labor to obtain these laws.

Several challenges have been mounted to this scheme, resulting in significant decisions which will impact employee training in construction well into the 1990s. In *Hydrostorage v. DAS*,[10] a contractor challenged a requirement in the California labor code which required that contractors on state prevailing wage work participate in an existing union apprenticeship training program and contribute to a specific union trust. The contractor already had an existing training program and the trust fund contributions were governed by ERISA. The contractor claimed that its training trust constituted an "employee benefit welfare plan" under ERISA and that the state of California could not favor or disfavor its plan over another. According to the contractor, the legislation was preempted by ERISA.

The court agreed. According to the court, any state statute regulating participation in the funding of a training fund would be preempted by federal law. The court also ruled that the state law which required that a nonunion employee join a union in order to participate in a union training plan, was preempted by the National Labor Relations Act (NLRA).

In *Local Union 598 v. J.A. Jones*,[11] the Ninth Circuit similarly held that the State of Washington could not mandate payment levels to an apprenticeship program as part of its prevailing wage laws. In that case, the contractor met the federally-prescribed level of training contributions. However, this amount was lower than the level set by the state prevailing wage laws. The court held that a state regulation requiring that the difference be made up by the contractor was preempted by federal law.

Finally, the federal Wage Appeals Board (WAB) has become involved in this issue. In a case involving Miree Construction, WAB held that voluntary employer contributions to a nonunion training trust could not be credited in their entirety against prevailing wage liability. Instead, these amounts had to be prorated to reflect actual hours spent by the apprentice on the prevailing wage job in question. In addition, the contributions had to be mandatory and not voluntary. The case is now pending before a federal district court.

These challenges to both direct and indirect state and federal regulations in the area of employee training indicate that the 1990s may be frustrating for labor. After exercising so much control over state approval for apprenticeship training, unions will find their grip being loosened by the courts with resulting competition by nonunion contractors to train the future construction employee.

---

[10] 685 F. Supp. 718 (N.D.Cal. 1988), *aff'd*, 891 F.2d 719 (9th Cir. 1989).

[11] 846 F.2d 1213 (9th Cir.), *aff'd*, 109 S. Ct. 210 (1988).

§ 17.3 Agenda Item 2: Employ More Sophisticated Top-Down Organizing Techniques

The NLRA allows employers in construction to sign a union agreement without the benefit of a certification election. So-called "prehire agreements" are allowed under § 8(f) of the NLRA due to the cyclical and sporadic nature of employment in this field. As a result, organized labor can directly approach construction management to sign a union agreement in what is known as "top-down" organizing.

In the 1980s organized labor markedly decreased its reliance on top-down organizing efforts. This decrease was largely the result of increasing reluctance by construction contractors to be saddled with either union wages or union work rules which impact their competitiveness. In addition, employers were either aware of, or themselves had participated in, disputes arising out of the trust fund obligations which accompanied the collective bargaining agreements.

Another obstacle to top-down organizing was the NLRB's *Deklewa* decision.[12] This decision, which changed the rules governing prehire agreements, offered long-time union employers an opportunity to repudiate their collective bargaining agreements and start over. Thus, while top-down organizing was still the favored organizing tool for unions because of the cyclical nature of employment in construction, it was not meeting with the type of success it had enjoyed 20 years ago.

However, in the 1990s organized labor has become more sophisticated in its "sales pitch" to both contractors and owners and may successfully stem the decline in success of top-down organizing. Again, it is the labor force shortage which offers the key element for these renewed efforts. After the recession which marked the 1980s, construction in many parts of the country has enjoyed a resurgence. With this resurgence has come the need for trained employees. Open shop contractors are facing a critical shortage of trained employees.

Organized labor has exacerbated this problem by recruiting qualified employees from the nonunion ranks to obtain employment with union contractors. Nonunion employers have seen wholesale defections of long-term employees to their union competitors based upon union promises of high wages and fringe benefits. As a result, many nonunion contractors will be forced to enter into collective bargaining agreements voluntarily in order to obtain access to the union hiring hall.

Nonunion employers will also face top-down organizing efforts based upon so-called "corporate campaign" strategies. This strategy, which was successfully utilized in the famous 1986 campaign at the Saturn plant in Tennessee, involves a broad appeal to the public, state legislators, and pressure groups to assist the union in its efforts to obtain a collective bargaining agreement with the

---

[12] 282 N.L.R.B. No. 184 (1987).

reluctant owner. Rather than responding with the traditional dual gate system, the employer will have a harder time responding to adverse publicity, consumer boycotts, targeting of financial institutions that do business with the employer, and political lobbying. These campaigns will increase as the unions repair their tattered public image.

"Job targeting" will be another controversial form of top-down organizing which will place competitive pressure upon the nonunion contractor. In order to set up a job targeting program, the union must set aside funds or ask its members to participate in a voluntary assessment to create such funds. The union employer, when competing against a nonunion contractor, can then petition the union to have access to these funds. If successful, the union employer will be allowed to bid the project at the nonunion wage rate and the employees will be paid the difference between the union wage rate and the nonunion wage rate from the reserve fund. In some cases, the funds go directly from the union to the employees. In others, funds are funnelled through the employer.

The legality of the job targeting program will be subject to attack on several grounds because of the source and nature of the funding. One such challenge may come from the Internal Revenue Service (IRS) which may treat the monies as "wages" for which the requisite tax deduction must be made. Apparently, several of the union job targeting programs are sloppy in explaining employer requirements under the Internal Revenue Code (IRC) and have been subject to attack. A second basis for IRS challenge is that such funding programs may deprive the union of its tax-exempt status under § 501(c)(5) of the IRC.

Union job targeting programs may also be challenged before the federal Department of Labor's Wage and Hour Division. According to the challengers, the differential funds constitute wages under the Fair Labor Standards Act and therefore must enter into overtime computations. In addition, such contributions may constitute deductions under the federal Copeland Anti-Kickback Act.[13] As such, these deductions must conform to several statutory requirements including individual employee approval of these assessments.

Finally, the job targeting program may be subject to attack under the federal Davis-Bacon Act. Those who challenge the union program may allege that direct payments by the union to employees cannot be credited toward satisfying the "prevailing wage" obligation under the Act. Time will tell whether job targeting programs will be a lawful union tool in the 1990s.

Finally, organized labor's traditional tool for top-down organizing— picketing—will continue. In the recent case of *Laborers Local Union No. 1185 (NVE Constructors),*[14] the NLRB held that a union could picket for the object of inducing an employer to sign a prehire agreement under § 8(f) of the NLRA. Employers had argued that prehire agreements were exempt from recognitional picketing since, by law, the § 8(f) agreements must be entered into voluntarily.

---

[13] 18 U.S.C. § 874.
[14] 296 N.L.R.B. No. 165 (1989).

The NLRB disagreed and held that there was no statutory exemption for prehire construction contracts and that the union could picket for a reasonable period of time in order to obtain such a contract. Had the NLRB ruled otherwise, organized labor would have been dealt a grievous blow to their already weakened top-down organizing strategies.

§ 17.4   Agenda Item 3: Engage in More Aggressive Bottom-Up Organizing

As a result of the decrease in open shop receptivity to the top-down organizing strategy, unions will be forced to beef up their bottom-up organizing campaigns. The unique characteristics of the construction employee and the construction industry make successful bottom-up organizing difficult. Construction projects are short-lived, the complement of employees varies on a daily basis, the management-to-work crew ratio is typically high, and the construction employee tends to be relatively independent and therefore not subject to peer pressure. In addition, because of the blurred distinction between management and rank-and-file prevalent among open shop contractors, organizing efforts can typically be spotted at an early stage.

Even if the organizing campaign has been successfully carried through to the petition stage with a resulting election, the construction employer can utilize the NLRB process to obtain more time prior to the election, to limit or expand the scope of the bargaining unit in the employer's favor, and to effectively prepare a campaign which will address employee concerns. Despite these obstacles and long odds, construction unions have no choice. They must either organize or disappear. Based upon the following phenomena which will increase into the 1990s, the unions are doing their best to adapt to an increasingly hostile environment in the construction industry. Again, the key element to successful bottom-up organizing in the 1990s will be the labor force shortage.

First, unions will engage in widespread "salting" of nonunion projects. "Salting" refers to the phenomenon of planting union supporters among the ranks of nonunion contractors. Contrary to the traditional practice of convincing an existing nonunion employee to spearhead a union campaign, organized labor is taking advantage of the nonunion contractor's desperate need for trained employees. The application process offers the union ready access to the nonunion contractor's work situs and its employees. Realizing this, unions have trained their apprentices in organizing techniques so that they may spearhead bottom-up organizing efforts once they obtain employment in the nonunion construction industry.

In addition, business agents are obtaining application forms from unsuspecting nonunion employers and distributing these forms to out-of-work union construction workers. These applicants are able to survive the relaxed scrutiny of nonunion employers desperate for applicants and commence a successful organizing campaign. Even if these applicants are revealed as union adherents in the application process or after they have commenced an organizing campaign, it is too late. The union then has the opportunity to file an unfair labor practice (ULP) charge in the event the applicant is rejected or the employee terminated.

An even bolder phenomenon has been the directive by organized labor to its business agents to apply for work with nonunion contractors. In contrast to the usual "salting" strategy of slipping union sympathizers past unsuspecting employers, the business agent openly announces that he or she is seeking employment in order to organize the employer. The strategy has received a boost from the NLRB but has been rejected by a federal court of appeals in *H.B. Zachry Co. v. NLRB*.[15]

In *Zachry*, the business agent applied for his old position with a nonunion company. The employer refused to hire him and based its refusal on the applicant's concurrent employment with the union as a business agent. The business agent filed an ULP charge and the employer claimed that a union employee did not constitute a protected "employee" under the NLRA. The NLRB disagreed. The Board affirmed the administrative law judge's finding that the NLRA prohibits any distinction between an applicant employed by the union or an applicant employed by anyone else. According to the judge:

> This principle has been specifically applied to full-time paid union organizers who, although their ulterior purpose may be to organize the unorganized, are merely applying for a job just like any other employees, are to be judged on their abilities as employees, and are forbidden by the Act to be judged on their union sympathies.

The Court of Appeals for the Fourth Circuit, however, disagreed. According to the court: "The Board's argument exalts form over substance. Though, if hired, Edwards would undoubtedly share some of the external characteristics of a Zachry employee, at core he would remain an employee of the union."

Since the job applicant in *Zachry* was still employed by the union and since he sought employment at the union's direction, the court determined he was not an "employee" subject to protection under the NLRA. The court emphasized that an employer has a right to expect loyalty from the applicants: "A decision to hire only those applicants who will, without question, answer to only one employer is so peculiarly a matter of management prerogative, that it must be protected as an employer's right as long as it is not applied in a manner which discriminates against union employees."

Until the dispute between the NLRB and the courts of appeals is resolved, however, one can expect continued use of business agents as applicants in order to organize employees.

---

[15] 886 F.2d 70 (4th Cir. 1989) (denying enforcement of 289 N.L.R.B. No. 117 (1988)).

§ 17.5   Agenda Item 4: If All Else Fails, File an Unfair Labor Practice Charge

In the mid- to late-1980s, construction employers rarely found themselves subject to investigation by the NLRB. This was simply because organized labor expressly swore off the Board as an organizing tool based upon the widely-held perception that the Board was pro-management. While this may have been true during the Reagan years, the sympathies of the Board have shifted. In addition, as Mike Lucas, Director of Organizing for the International Brotherhood of Electrical Workers, pointed out in an interview, ULP charges cost the nonunion employer a great deal of money:

> We need some NLRB elections, simply because we were adding very expensive, nonproductive "journeymen" in the form of lawyers to the nonunion contractor's payroll and, therefore, improving our employers' competitive ability. We did a lot of unfair labor practice charges because ULPs are common in the construction industry. I believe the NLRB told us that the average ULP charge costs the employer $12,000. We did a lot of those, and in the course of doing those, we educated folks as to what the union was all about.

As a result, in 1989, ULP complaints were up nearly seven percent. More importantly, the percentage of ULP charges deemed to show probable cause for a violation of the NLRA has been the highest in 19 years.

The labor force shortage is the most compelling reason the unions will increasingly utilize the NLRB as a means of organizing the nonunion contractor. Nonunion contractors who have been used to turning away applicants will be forced to recruit and hire applicants on a large scale. In addition, the nonunion contractor will have to replace employees who have been successfully enticed away by the union. This widespread hiring by the employer who is unschooled in the restrictions on hiring practices of the NLRA will result in a great many potential violations of the Act. If the violations are extreme enough, the union may be able to obtain a bargaining order which would obviate the need for an election. More realistically, the union can file election objections or blocking charges which will counteract the employer's careful orchestration of the Board's processes.

Unions are increasingly finding that ULPs are easy to come by in the hiring process. Violations of the NLRA not only occur in informal interrogations of applicants but can be solicited by the applicant in one of two common ways. The applicant may profess to dislike the union and ask for assurance that the employer will never "go union." The unsuspecting nonunion employer will often give such assurances.

The second successful approach is the applicant who professes to actively support the union, has worked for union contractors in the past, and who wishes to know whether this will present a problem. The common response by the majority of employers is to refuse to hire the applicant. The well-schooled applicant has, by virtue of his or her open disclosure, created the requisite prima facie for an ULP charge since the employer now knows of the applicant's pro-union beliefs and has refused to hire the applicant. The NLRB can be easily convinced to issue a complaint thereby requiring the employer to prove at hearing that the applicant was not hired based upon bona fide business reasons.

Employers who seek to avoid this liability by delegating the hiring process to third parties are not immune from this union strategy. In *Westward Hotel,*[16] an employer was held jointly liable with a "headhunting" firm retained by the employer based upon unlawful questions asked by the firm in its screening of applicants. Such liability may be avoided if the employer does not expressly or impliedly request that the screening firm keep out union adherents. However, such antiunion biases can often be imputed to the employer.

In summary, in the 1990s organized labor will utilize the increasing labor force shortage in order to limit the supply of trained applicants to the nonunion contractor, to bolster its sagging top-down organizing efforts, to obtain egress to job sites for bottom-up organizing, and to generate costly ULP litigation. As a result, nonunion employers will have to become increasingly sophisticated in governing laws in order to obtain, train, and retain construction employees.

In addition, the employer will have to educate its interviewers and management in order to respond lawfully to both top-down and bottom-up organizing campaigns. Finally, the open shop contractor will have to devote the kind of money usually spent by organized labor in training and recruitment programs in order to ensure its continued success in the precarious and cyclical world of construction.

---

[16] F & D Enterprises, Inc. d/b/a Westward Ho Hotel, 251 N.L.R.B. 1199 (1980).

CHAPTER 18

THE RIGHT TO STOP WORK

Laurence Schor
Richard C. Walters*

§ 18.1   Introduction

§ 18.2   Impossibility and Commercial Impracticability

§ 18.3   The *McCarthy* Case

§ 18.4   The New AIA Clause

§ 18.5   Observations

§ 18.1   Introduction

It is rare that a construction contractor will be able to cease or abandon contract performance without incurring substantial liability to an owner. Normally, the only circumstance justifying cessation of work on a project is where the owner has materially breached the contract's payment terms.[1]

Standard contract language[2] requires a contractor to proceed with extra work pending resolution of any dispute over whether an owner's directive to perform the work may amount to a so-called "constructive change order" which entitles the contractor to additional compensation.[3] Similarly, boilerplate clauses[4] will only provide a contractor with additional compensation (money and/or time extension) for concealed or differing site conditions, i.e., those which are materially different from conditions shown or indicated on contract drawings or boring log data provided at bid time. They do not authorize a contractor to cease

---

* This chapter is adapted from an article in the August 1990 issue of AGC of *America's Constructor* and is used with AGC's permission.

[1] *See, e.g.,* Texas Bank & Trust Co. v. Campbell Bros., 569 S.W.2d 35 (Tex. Civ. App. 1978). *See also* H.E.&C.F. Blinne Contracting Co., ENGBCA No. 4174, 83-1 B.C.A. (BNA) ¶ 16,388; Charles H. Siever, ASBCA No. 24814, 83-1 B.C.A. (BNA) ¶ 16,242 at 80,726.

[2] *See* AIA A201-1987 ¶¶ 4.3.4, 7.1.3, and 7.3.4; FAR §§ 52.233-1, 52.243-1.

[3] *See* Tester Corp., ASBCA No. 21312, 78-2 B.C.A. (BNA) ¶ 13,373 at 65,372.

[4] *See* AIA A201-1987 ¶¶ 4.3.4 and 4.3.6; FAR 52.236-2.

work, except for the time necessary to allow the owner to observe the conditions before they are disturbed and to provide any desired direction to the contractor.[5]

§ 18.2   Impossibility and Commercial Impracticability

On the other hand, when unanticipated conditions render performance impossible or so financially onerous as to be commercially impracticable, the law allows a contractor to stop performance. The doctrine of commercial impracticability has long been recognized to apply in cases involving both government and private contracts.[6]

The Uniform Commercial Code (UCC) likewise incorporates the doctrine of commercial impracticability and has been referenced in many of the above-cited case decisions. UCC § 2-615(a) reads as follows:

> Delay in delivery or non-delivery in whole or in part by a seller who complies with paragraphs (b) and (c) is not a breach of his duty under a contract for sale if performance as agreed has been made impracticable by the occurrence of a contingency the non-occurrence of which was a basic assumption on which the contract was made or by compliance in good faith with any applicable foreign or domestic governmental regulation or order whether or not it later proves to be invalid.

Thus, under UCC § 2-615, a contractor will be excused from performance in the event that three prerequisites are met: (1) a contingency has occurred, the non-occurrence of which was a basic assumption of the parties; (2) the promisor has not assumed the risk of such a contingency; and (3) the occurrence of the contingency has rendered performance commercially impracticable.[7]

In *In re XPLO Corp.*[8] (a case which the authors tried for the contractor), the Department of Transportation Board of Contract Appeals found a contractor justified on the basis of commercial impracticability when it abandoned performance of a contract for concrete bridge pier demolition after encountering unanticipated steel caissons. The caissons there were so structurally massive that

---

[5] *Id.;* FAR § 52.233-1.

[6] *See* Clark Grave Vault Co. v. United States, 178 Ct. Cl. 52 (1967); Tombigbee Constructors v. United States, 190 Ct. Cl. 615 (1970); GTE Sylvania, Inc., DOT CAB No. 78-57, 79-2 B.C.A. (BNA) ¶ 14,069; Morrison-Knudsen-Perini-Hardeman, Inc., ENG BCA No. 2857, 68-2 B.C.A. (BNA) ¶ 7106; L.J. Casey Co., AGBCA 75-148, 76-2 B.C.A. (BNA) ¶ 12,196; E.W. Bliss Co., ASBCA No. 11297, 68-2 B.C.A. (BNA) ¶ 7090; Johnson Elecs., Inc., ASBCA No. 9366, 65-1 B.C.A. (BNA) ¶ 4628. *See also* Transatlantic Fin. Corp. v. United States, 363 F.2d 312 (D.C. Cir. 1966); Ocean Salvage, Inc., ENG BCA Nos. 3485, 3547, 76-1 B.C.A. (BNA) ¶ 11,905, and cases cited therein at 57,905 n.7; Ascani Constr. & Realty Co., VABCA No. 1572, 83-2 B.C.A. (BNA) ¶ 16,635.

[7] *See also* Restatement of Contracts § 454 (1932).

[8] DOTCAB 1289, 86-3 B.C.A. (BNA) ¶ 19,125.

they could not be removed by the government's replacement contractor, even with the use of the largest dredge bucket in the world, a 100-ton (25 cubic yard) capacity bucket having a squeeze capability of 1200 tons which was imported specially from Bremerhaven, Germany. The Board ruled the government's default termination improper under those circumstances. Such cases are by no means common, however.

§ 18.3   The *McCarthy* Case

Perhaps even rarer are those cases where contractors cease performance when the unexpected conditions they encounter pose a substantial threat to life and limb. One such case was recently decided in the contractor's favor by an American Arbitration Association (AAA) panel of arbitrators in Washington, D.C. In the *Arbitration of McCarthy Construction Co. & Fair Oaks Phase II*[9] (in which the authors represented the contractor, McCarthy), raw asbestos was encountered in its natural rock form (asbestiform actinolite) as the contractor's earthwork subcontractor and second-tier blasting subcontractor excavated for the foundation of an office building in Fairfax County, Virginia.

The Fair Oaks Phase II project was among the first to be built in an area of western Fairfax County containing a vein of rope-like asbestiform actinolite and the very first construction project on which the carcinogenic material was known to be encountered either in Virginia or elsewhere. Neither the pre-bid soil and boring information nor the contract general or special provisions contained any asbestos warning, and knowledgeable contractors and geotechnical consultants in the area had never before dealt with asbestos in its natural rock form. Accordingly, it came as a complete surprise when airborne asbestos fibrils were first released during drilling and blasting operations. The situation came to the attention of the contractor and owner when the blaster's employees began to complain of itchy skin rashes which seemed to correlate with their exposure to those fibrils.

McCarthy's general liability insurance (CGL) policy contained the following iron-clad asbestos exclusion which precluded McCarthy not only from doing any asbestos removal itself, but from subcontracting out for or otherwise supervising any work in connection with sampling, testing, or removal of asbestos:

Asbestos Liability Exclusion: This Endorsement Modifies Insurance Provided Under the Following:

Commercial General Liability Coverage Part

Owner's and Contractor's Protective Liability Coverage Part

Products/Completed Operations Liability Coverage Part

Railroad Protective Liability Coverage Part

---

[9] Am. Arb. Ass'n. Case No. 1611000349875.

Provisions: This Insurance Does Not Apply to "Bodily Injury" or "Property Damage" Arising Out of or Caused By:

1. Asbestos, Asbestos Fibers or Products Containing Asbestos or to Any Obligation of the Insured to Indemnify or Contribute with Another Because of Damages Arising Out of Such Injury or Damage; Or

2. Any Supervision, Instructions, Recommendations, Warnings or Advice Given or Which Should Have Been Given in Connection Therewith.

There were at the time (and still are) no EPA or OSHA regulations specifically governing removal of asbestos rock. Furthermore, neither Fairfax County nor the Commonwealth of Virginia had previously dealt with asbestiform actinolite through rules or regulations, and it was not known (at that time at least) whether the kinds of asbestos abatement procedures normally applied in removal of asbestos from existing closed structures would prove effective in coping with asbestiform actinolite in the open air environment of a construction site. Under these circumstances and in light of the clear and all-encompassing asbestos exclusion in its liability policy, McCarthy concluded that the risk of its completing the excavation simply could not be quantified and hence could not be assumed.

McCarthy, with the authors' advice, also concluded that the life-threatening aspects of asbestos made encountering it beyond the scope of the standard American Institute of Architects (AIA) "concealed conditions" clause of its contract, and thus beyond any obligation it may have assumed to proceed with the work. Therefore, McCarthy asked the owner to undertake the balance of the excavation work (including foundation and utility trench excavation). McCarthy assured the owner that it would resume performance of all remaining office building construction once the owner completed excavation and advised that the site was safe. It was understood that the owner would be allowed to adjust the contract price to reflect the deletion of the remaining excavation from McCarthy's contract.

Initially, the owner indicated its agreement with this approach, but later it chose to terminate McCarthy's contract for alleged default and to bring in another general contractor to finish the balance of construction after a separate excavation contractor completed excavation and asbestos removal. Although the owner argued at the arbitration proceedings that McCarthy gave it cause to terminate by materially varying the scope of the remaining work it was agreeing to perform, it is apparent from the arbitrators' award to McCarthy that this argument was without merit.

§ 18.4   The New AIA Clause

A clause is now contained in Article 10—Protection of Persons and Property— of the 1987 version of AIA Document A201, General Provisions.[10] This clause

---

[10] *See* AIA A201-1987 ¶ 10.1.2.

makes it clear that the contractor cannot be forced to proceed when either asbestos or PCBs are encountered at a jobsite.

> and provides that "Work in the affected area shall not thereter be resumed except by written agreement of the Owner and Contractor if in fact the material is asbestos or polychlorinated biphenyl (PCB) and has not been rendered harmless. The Work in the affected area shall be resumed in the absence of asbestos or polychlorinated biphenyl (PCB), or when it has been rendered harmless, by written agreement of the Owner and Contractor, or in accordance with final determination by the Architect. . . .

Significantly, the new AIA clause was not included in McCarthy's contract, which incorporated AIA A201-1976. Nevertheless, through the expert testimony of Robert Lathlaen, President of W.J. Barney Company, and formerly AGC's liaison to the AIA/AGC Task Group of the AIA Documents Committee and Chairman of AAA's National Construction Industry Arbitration Committee (NCIAC), McCarthy was able to establish that even before the above clause was formulated, the practice of a number of owners had been for them to deal directly with their own asbestos consultants and to assume responsibility for removal of unanticipated asbestos in the absence of insurance coverage available to general contractors.

A commentary issued in December 1989 by AIA's California Council[11] indicates that the new AIA clause language contemplates that any asbestos (or PCB) specialists and abatement contractors be separately employed by the property owner rather than by the general contractor: "Presumably, a specialist would be employed by the Owner to investigate the problem and, if abatement activities were necessary, the Owner would employ an abatement Contractor to remedy the problem."[12]

Just to be sure that there is no misunderstanding that it is the property owner who is to bear responsibility for testing to determine the presence or absence of asbestos, PCBs, and so forth, the AIA in 1989 also issued an *Additions to Guide for Supplementary Conditions*[13] containing supplementary paragraphs for use in conjunction with the new clause in its AIA A201. One paragraph makes that obligation explicit: "The Owner shall be responsible for obtaining the services of a licensed laboratory to verify a presence or absence of the material or substance reported by the Contractor and to verify that it has been rendered harmless."

That supplementary paragraph goes on to require the owner to present to the contractor and project architect lists of "persons or entities proposed by the Owner" and whom the owner will engage for such testing or to perform the task of removal or safe containment. Both the contractor and architect have the unconditional right to "object" to any proposed abatement contractor, since their

---

[11] *Professional Liability Reports, AIA Document A201 Commentary* (Dec. 1989) [hereinafter *Commentary*].

[12] *Id.* at 49.

[13] AIA A512-1989 ¶ 10.1.6.

work could be affected by the presence and activities of other contractors or entities.[14]

Notably, the 1987 AIA clause does not include hazardous materials other than asbestos and PCBs.[15] This omission appears to have been purposeful on the part of the AIA/AGC Task Group which formulated the clause because of the difficulties inherent in defining precisely what a "hazardous material" might include. By the same token, the supplementary paragraphs which AIA has even more recently issued for use with the new A201 clause are intentionally couched in language sufficiently broad to allow the parties to expand the coverage of that clause to include harmful "materials or substances" other than asbestos or PCBs.[16]

§ 18.5   Observations

Stopping work on a construction project is almost invariably a risky proposition, since it can and often does entail the creation of substantial additional costs. From the owner's perspective, delays in construction and project completion can mean not only higher construction and construction management costs but significant lost rental or sales income. From the contractor's perspective, in addition to exposure to the financial risks of default termination, it can mean labor and material cost escalation for any delayed performance, as well as the incurrence of extended field and home office costs. Perhaps most important, it will mean the loss of momentum so critical to establishing and maintaining productivity on a project.

Therefore, when deciding whether or not to cease work or abandon a project when encountering unexpected potentially life-threatening conditions, it is imperative that a contractor carefully assess the degree of risk posed by such conditions with the aid of technical experts. Also, it is essential under those circumstances that it review with competent legal counsel the terms of its insurance policies to determine the extent, if any, of insurance coverage available for the particular risk or hazard. Not every policy has an exclusion as broadly worded as the *McCarthy* provision quoted above, although notably, some companies have attempted to read clauses excepting coverage of hazardous materials to include asbestos.

Finally, it is important to recognize that the *McCarthy* arbitration presented a case of first impression, and that its result may not necessarily be repeated. Even if a contractor finds itself confronted with a situation which is similar to that in *McCarthy,* it must realize that the AAA arbitration award in *McCarthy* will not have the status of binding legal precedent. Therefore, any course of action under

---

[14] *Id.,* notes.

[15] *Commentary* at 49.

[16] AIA A512-1989 ¶¶ 10.1.5 and 10.1.6 notes.

such circumstances must be governed by an evaluation of the particular facts of the case and the terms of the particular contract involved.

In this regard, close attention should be paid to the general or special provisions of the contract, and such provisions and any existing precedents should be reviewed with legal counsel in order to determine whether any contract terms already cover the condition encountered and how the contractor should handle it. Only by careful evaluation and reasoned balancing of the risks involved will a contractor be able to reach a decision appropriate to the specifics of its case.

CHAPTER 19

ASBESTOS LIABILITY STRATEGIES

Philip R. Croessmann

§ 19.1   Introduction

REGULATORY HISTORY OF ASBESTOS IN BUILDINGS

§ 19.2   Federal Regulatory History

§ 19.3   State Regulation

§ 19.4   Criminal Enforcement

COST RECOVERY

§ 19.5   Strict Liability

§ 19.6   Product Liability

§ 19.7   Negligence

§ 19.8   Warranty

§ 19.9   Miscellaneous Theories

COST RECOVERY DEFENSES

§ 19.10   Economic Loss versus Property Damage

§ 19.11   Statute of Limitations

§ 19.12   Safe Product Defense

§ 19.13   Product Identification

LIABILITY AND ASBESTOS ABATEMENT

§ 19.14   Owner

§ 19.15   Architects and Engineers

§ 19.16   Asbestos Consultants

§ 19.17   Asbestos Contractors

§ 19.18   Other Groups

PROTECTION AND ALLOCATIONS OF LIABILITY

§ 19.19   Contracts

§ 19.20   Supervision

§ 19.21   Recordkeeping

§ 19.22   Workers' Training

§ 19.23   Worker Release

§ 19.24   Liability Insurance

§ 19.25   Incorporation

§ 19.26   Legislation

§ 19.1   Introduction

The person developing appropriate asbestos liability strategies for the 1990s, without a doubt, faces great challenges. However, he or she holds the distinct advantage over his or her counterpart at the beginning of the 1980s of having clearer guidelines with which to work. Building owners, asbestos consultants, abatement contractors, architects and engineers, and other real estate professionals now can draw on twenty years of regulatory history of asbestos in buildings.

Despite the fact that each building and situation brings its own unique set of problems and considerations and that the laws of states vary widely on many of the issues affecting the ultimate outcome of any litigation, a survey of regulatory history, recent court decisions, and available risk management techniques remains a valuable first step toward defining a strategy that meets the specific need at hand. It is hoped that this chapter will serve as such a survey and as an impetus for all those in need of such strategies to succeed in tailoring a suitable one.

REGULATORY HISTORY OF ASBESTOS IN BUILDINGS

§ 19.2   Federal Regulatory History

Although knowledge of the dangers associated with asbestos can be attributed to the asbestos manufacturing industry as early as the mid-1930s,[1] it was not until the 1960s that the medical profession in the United States recognized that a potential health hazard arose from the use of insulation products containing asbestos. Before that time, the danger from asbestos was believed to be limited to workers in asbestos textile mills, who were exposed to much higher concentrations of asbestos dust than were the workers at other sites.[2]

---

[1] *See* Hardy v. Johns-Manville Sales Corp., 509 F. Supp. 1352, 1355 (E.D. Tex. 1981) [hereinafter *Hardy*]; Borel v. Fibreboard Paper Prods. Corp., 493 F.2d 1076 (5th Cir. 1973).

[2] Beshada v. Johns-Manville Prod. Corp., 447 A.2d 539 (N.J. 1982).

The March 31, 1971, publication by the United States Environmental Protection Agency (EPA) of an initial list naming asbestos as one of the three air pollutants to be targeted for regulation under § 112 of the Clean Air Act[3] began a long history of federal and state regulation. Shortly thereafter, on December 7, 1971, proposed standards for the regulation of asbestos during demolition or renovation of existing buildings and the banning of asbestos in spray-on fire-proofing were submitted for public comment.[4] In addition, the Occupational Safety and Health Administration (OSHA) began targeting asbestos for regulation in 1971 by adopting a rather liberal standard of twelve fibers per cubic centimeter as a maximum for work place exposure.

In 1972, OSHA reduced the standard to two fibers per cubic centimeter.[5] In 1973, under §§ 112 and 301(a) of the Clean Air Act,[6] the EPA finalized its regulations prohibiting asbestos in spray-on materials for insulation, fire protection, and soundproofing and regulating asbestos removal during demolition and renovation.[7] During this time, architects recognized the problems associated with the use of asbestos in building products and, through their specifications, limited the use of asbestos in accordance with the law in spray-on materials for insulation, fire protection, and soundproofing.

In 1975, the EPA banned molded and wet-applied insulation containing asbestos if the materials would crumble easily when dried. In 1977, the Consumer Product Safety Commission banned patching compounds containing asbestos.[8]

> The Commission noted that in the scientific literature, there is general agreement that there is no known threshold level below which exposure to respirable free-form asbestos would be considered safe. Further on the basis of such scientific opinion, it appears to the Commission that children are particularly vulnerable to carcinogens because of their longer potential lifetime and their rapid rate of growth.
>
> The Commission concluded on the basis of these factors that consumer patching compounds containing respirable free-form asbestos present an unreasonable risk of injury to the public.[9]

In 1980, Congress got into the act. Recognizing that asbestos posed a particular danger to young children, it took the first step to require inspection and abatement of asbestos in school buildings. Under the Asbestos School

---

[3] 36 Fed. Reg. 5931, Mar. 1, 1971.

[4] 40 C.F.R. § 61, Proposed Rules, 36 Fed. Reg. 23239, Dec. 7, 1971.

[5] 29 C.F.R. § 1910.1101; 87 Fed. Reg. 11318, June 1972.

[6] 42 U.S.C. §§ 7412, 7601(a).

[7] 38 Fed. Reg. 8820, Apr. 6, 1973.

[8] 16 C.F.R. § 1304; 42 Fed. Reg. 63362, Dec. 15, 1977.

[9] 16 C.F.R. § 1304.5.

Hazard Detection and Control Act of 1980,[10] technical guidance and assistance was to be offered to schools. Lack of funding, however, caused the effort to languish. In 1984, Congress responded with the Asbestos School Hazard Abatement Act,[11] an act which provides a loan and grant program to help needy schools finance abatement actions.

By this time, asbestos was a well-known carcinogen. As one court stated in 1981:

> So comfortable are we with that assertion, that a former Secretary of Health, Education and Welfare estimated that more than 67,000 human lives are taken each year by asbestos-related cancers. Thus far in the litigation, asbestos has been found to be a competent producing cause of asbestosis and mesothelioma.

> Pulmonary asbestosis can best be described as a non-malignant scarring of the lungs. Asbestosis is generally cumulative; the continued exposure to asbestos dust and fibers increases both the risk and the severity of the disease. . . . Mesothelioma is a form of malignant tumor of the chest and lungs; it may also affect the abdomen. Extraordinarily painful and always fatal, it is a relatively rare form of cancer whose relationship to asbestos has been generally known since the late 1930's. Like asbestosis, mesothelioma has a long latent period. Rather unlike asbestosis, mesothelioma may result from one exposure to asbestos dust or fibers.[12]

In April 1984, the EPA amended its regulations regarding asbestos by revamping the national emission standard for asbestos.[13]

The year 1986 saw a new flurry of activity. Congress, displeased with the efforts at voluntary inspection and abatement under the 1980 laws, mandated deadlines and stiff penalties, along with detailed guidelines for school inspection and abatement plans.[14] The EPA issued its final regulations pursuant to the Asbestos Hazard Emergency Response Act of 1986 (AHERA) on October 30, 1987.[15] In addition to regulating the asbestos in schools, Congress directed the EPA to investigate the feasibility of inventorying private and public buildings and the impact of regulation on liability insurance.

In February 1988, the EPA issued its report to Congress, entitled *EPA Study of Asbestos-Containing Materials in Public Buildings*. In recommending that a comprehensive regulatory inspection and abatement program, such as was implemented for the nation's schools, not be implemented for public and commercial buildings for at least three years, the EPA Administrator stressed the importance of enforcement. He made the following comments:

---

[10] Pub. L. No. 96-270.

[11] Title V of Pub. L. No. 98-377.

[12] *Hardy,* 509 F. Supp. 1351.

[13] 40 C.F.R. §§ 61.1451 & 61.148; 49 Fed. Reg. 13661, Apr. 5, 1984.

[14] Asbestos Hazard Emergency Response Act of 1986 (AHERA), Pub. L. No. 99-519.

[15] 40 C.F.R. § 733; 52 Fed. Reg. 41826, Oct. 30, 1987.

If we are not careful we will stimulate more asbestos removal actions in public and commercial buildings during the next few years than the infrastructure of accredited professionals and governmental enforcement can effectively handle. For example, as public and commercial buildings are sold, investors are increasingly insisting that the asbestos in the buildings be removed, as a condition of the purchase. Unless such removals are done correctly, exposure of asbestos to the public may actually be increased. We already have anecdotal information which leads us to believe that irresponsible and potentially dangerous removal action is taking place outside of carefully monitored programs, and we do not want to exacerbate this problem by our actions.

I therefore strongly recommend that we take steps now to focus our attention on assessing and improving the QUALITY of the asbestos-related actions that currently take place in public and commercial buildings.[16]

More recently, EPA has banned the use of asbestos in all building products.

§ 19.3 State Regulation

Maryland became one of the leaders in state regulation in 1982 when it passed its law requiring the licensing of contractors for the safe handling of asbestos-containing materials. The Maryland General Assembly found that "exposure to asbestos, a known carcinogenic agent creates a significant hazard to the health of the people of this state."[17]

Since 1984, state regulation has been extensive. In 1986, a survey of state asbestos statutes conducted by the Bureau of National Affairs found a plethora of provisions with little consistency of standards among the states. Two-thirds of the states had enacted more than 60 asbestos-related laws. More than 75 percent of these provisions were passed from 1984 to 1986.[18] This activity still continues as states enact and revise these asbestos laws to stay current with the technology. Most laws fall into two categories: (1) those that require licensed contractors to handle asbestos-containing materials,[19] and (2) those that mandate the inspection of buildings before renovation or demolition.[20]

---

[16] EPA Study of Asbestos-Containing Materials in Public Buildings.

[17] Md. Environment Code Ann. § 6-402 (1982).

[18] Asbestos Abatement, Risk & Responsibilities, A BNA Special Report, The Bureau of National Affairs, Inc. (1987).

[19] Md. Environment Code Ann. § 6-401 (1982).

[20] See generally Wash. Rev. Code § 49.26 (19 ___) & Va. Code Ann. §§ 36-99.7, (Uniform Statewide Building Code) (19 ___).

§ 19.4   Criminal Enforcement

Criminal enforcement actions have become the hallmark of the EPA and state environmental policies of the 1990s. The numbers speak for themselves.

> The Environmental Protection Agency has referred 286 cases to the DOJ; as of 1 July, 1989, the Federal Bureau of Investigation had 211 environmental crime cases pending in federal courts. Between the start of fiscal year 1983, when the DOJ Environmental Crimes Section began its prosecutions program and 30 June, 1989, the DOJ indicted 540 defendants, winning pleas or convictions from 412. More than 254 years of jail time were meted out, nearly 88 years of which have already been served. And, if the figures through June of this year are any indication, 1989 will see a higher percentage of actual jail time imposed than any year thus far.[21]

On December 29, 1988, Terrel E. Hunt, EPA Associate Enforcement Counsel for Air Enforcement, announced that the Air Enforcement Office will focus its criminal prosecution on asbestos removal cases where contractors or building owners fail to follow asbestos removal regulations. He added that penalties for asbestos violations are expected to be increased under EPA's penalty policy to better reflect the economic benefit violators gain through noncompliance.[22]

On December 8, 1989, William K. Reilly, EPA's Administrator, stated that:

> [O]ur emphasis on enforcement produced a record or near-record year for every majority category of enforcement in the fiscal year that just ended. The Agency referred 364 civil judicial cases addressing violations of environmental laws to the Department of Justice for prosecution—just short of the Agency record set in Fiscal Year 1988. Our criminal enforcement program referred a record total of 60 criminal cases to Justice last year, and we issued 4,017 administrative orders— also an Agency record. As these figures indicate, I'm working hard to instill an "enforcement first" ethic in all of EPA's major regulatory programs.[23]

The EPA's actions are also drawing upon the resources and cooperation of the states. Hubert G. Johnson, Senior Environmental Counsel for the National Association of Attorneys General, stated on December 30, 1988, that state and EPA cooperation has been strong, especially in the area of criminal enforcement. He indicated that the states have tried to forge a more cooperative approach by sharing information, enforcement experience, and resources. He predicted at that time that cooperation would continue in 1989 as the states become more concerned with environmental problems and federal budgetary problems persist.

He observed that states are continuing to get more involved as maturity and sophistication at the state level allow for more state-initiated enforcement

---

[21] Rich, *Getting Tough on Environmental Crime,* Resources (Oct. 1989).

[22] 19 Env't Rep. (BNA) 1882, (1990) [hereinafter E.R.].

[23] Reilly, *The Turning Point: An Environmental Vision for the 1990's,* 20 Env't Rep. (BNA) 1386.

actions. States will be doing more in the enforcement area because they have a vested interest in taking care of their environment and there is popular support for improving the environment.[24]

Indeed, many states are increasing their enforcement capabilities. Maryland, for example, has instituted a state program with a significant enforcement element in the hazardous waste area, including a strike force comprised of three attorneys general and five state police officers dedicated specifically to hazardous waste regulation enforcement.[25]

Criminal convictions in 1989 demonstrate that these agencies are dedicated to backing up the rhetoric with action. On June 5, 1989, a Kentucky demolition contractor was indicted on what federal prosecutors said were among the first felony charges for alleged violations of federal asbestos regulations and superfund laws. The owner of the company, Charles A. Donahoo, was charged with violation of the federal Clean Air Act's National Emission Standards for Hazardous Air Pollutants (NESHAP) and under The Comprehensive Environmental Recovery, Compensation and Liability Act (CERCLA) felony provisions.

The two CERCLA felony counts allege that Donahoo twice failed to notify government authorities as required under § 103(b)(3) that reportable quantities of asbestos were released both before and after he was apprised of requirements by the government officials. Donahoo was also charged with violating NESHAP requirements to provide enforcement authorities with ten days' advance written notice of a project to demolish or to renovate a structure. Felony charges further specified that when the defendant finally submitted the required notification forms to the county air pollution authority, he did so, "knowing the same to contain a false, fictitious, or fraudulent statement." According to the indictment, a site inspector revealed work was already underway to remove asbestos before the date Donahoo specified in writing that it would begin.

While the agency viewed the nature of Donahoo's actions as so egregious that they warranted criminal prosecution, Donahoo stated in an interview that the government was over-reacting. "I did not even know I was being indicted until someone showed me the [news] paper," he said, noting that he had been unaware of the actions taken by federal officials. On December 12, 1989, Donahoo was sentenced to serve one year in prison for illegally abating asbestos in violation of the Clean Air Act. In addition, he was sentenced to serve a three-year term for failure to report an unpermitted release of asbestos in violation of CERCLA. The court, however, suspended all but six months of the prison term. Following his time in prison, Donahoo will have to spend three years on probation. The court did not impose a fine for the violations.[26]

In the same time period (May-June 1989), two employees of a defunct Philadelphia waste disposal company were sentenced to one year in prison each,

---

[24] 19 Env't Rep. (BNA) 1882.

[25] 17 Env't Rep. (BNA) 1903.

[26] United States v. Donahoo, No. 89-00057-01-L, 20 Env't Rep. Cas. (BNA) 1437 and 20 Env't Rep. Cas. (BNA) 477 (W.D. Ky. 1989).

for violations of asbestos disposal regulations under the Clean Air Act. Gregory Boone and Alex Fineman pleaded guilty to the violations. The employees of HMC Recycling were charged with disposal of asbestos in early 1986 in an unauthorized site in Maryland. The defendants were also charged with failure to notify federal and state authorities of release of a hazardous substance into the environment.[27]

In another action, three New York City businessmen were indicted on June 15, 1989, on federal racketeering and mail fraud charges in connection with their alleged operation of an illegal landfill on Staten Island. The three men were executives of eight related waste disposal and real estate companies. The indictment described a criminal enterprise to operate a landfill that illegally accepted 5000 tons per day of asbestos waste, other construction waste, ordinary trash and garbage, and medical waste. The landfill allegedly accepted waste from companies operated by the defendants and from approximately 50 other companies. The landfill operated for a four-month period, ending in September 1988, when a search warrant was executed at the site.

Prosecutors said the defendants collected nearly $2.5 million in profits from unaffiliated companies and saved more than $4.6 million in fees that they would have had to pay to legally dispose of waste hauled by their own companies. According to U.S. attorneys, each of the individual defendants faces a possible penalty of 70 years in prison, fines totalling $2 million, and forfeiture of assets derived from alleged racketeering enterprise. Each of the companies faces criminal fines of up to $4 million, except for one of the companies, which faces a fine of up to $1 million. The companies also face possible forfeiture of their assets.[28]

Another instance of criminal convictions is the April 7, 1989, sentencing of a contracting firm and one of its supervisors under the Clean Air Act for violating federal asbestos removal and handling regulations at a project in New York City. The supervisor was sentenced to serve 90 days in jail after being convicted by a jury in December 1988. The contracting firm, D.A.R. Construction, Inc., pleaded guilty to three counts in December, and was ordered to pay a total of $50,000 in fines payable over two years and $600 in special assessments. The trial centered on a 1986 asbestos removal, conducted by D.A.R. at the New York City Department of Sanitation garage in Manhattan, in which dry asbestos was removed from pipes and dropped 25 feet to the ground below. The supervisor was acquitted of charges that he violated federal superfund laws by failing to report the release of a hazardous substance into the environment.

This case is of particular interest because the building owner, the New York City Department of Sanitation, was also involved. The Department of Sanitation reached an agreement on December 14, 1988, with federal prosecutors, to settle charges against the City agency stemming from the D.A.R. removal job. The

---

[27] United States v. Fineman, C.R. No. 88-543, 20 Env't Rep. Cas. (BNA) 497 (E.D. Pa. 1989).

[28] United States v. Paccione, C.R. No. 89-446, 20 Env't Rep. Cas. (BNA) 605 (S.D.N.Y. 1989).

agreement requires the Sanitation Department to ensure that NESHAP rules are followed in the future on all abatement jobs under the agency's jurisdiction.[29]

COST RECOVERY

§ 19.5   Strict Liability

Seeking to defray the cost of asbestos removal or abatement, many building owners have brought cost recovery actions. Among the most prominent legal theories which form the basis of a claim of this type are strict liability, product liability, negligence, and warranty.

To understand the theory of both strict liability and product liability (discussed below), we must review the historical context in which strict liability developed in American jurisprudence. Strict liability arose out of a series of cases involving injuries resulting from ultra-hazardous activities. Typical examples were the injuries resulting from the building of reservoirs, blasting, manufacturing of explosives, and fumigating. In these cases, the courts held the plaintiff party engaged in such activities liable without regard to fault because the activities carried a substantial risk of serious harm to persons or property.

In defining ultra-hazardous activities, the courts set up a three-pronged test. First, the activity must involve a serious risk of harm to persons or property; second, the activity must be one that cannot be performed in complete safety no matter how much care is taken; and third, the activity must be one not commonly engaged in the community.

§ 19.6   Product Liability

Product liability is actually not a distinct theory of liability but incorporates the three other theories of negligence, strict liability, and warranty. It was the codification of strict liability into Section 402A of the *Restatement (Second) of Torts* that brought product liability into the limelight of American law. The *Restatement*, which has been adopted by the majority of state courts, provides that one who sells any product in a defective condition which renders it "unreasonably dangerous" to the user or the consumer or his or her property, is subject to liability for any physical harm that results from it. The seller must be engaged in the business of selling the product and the product must be one that is expected to and does reach the user or consumer without substantial change. These theories emphasizes the unreasonably dangerous nature of the product and not the defendant's conduct.

---

[29] United States v. D.A.R. Constr., Inc., No. 88 C.R. 65, 20 Env't Rep. Cas. (BNA) 21 (S.D.N.Y. 1989).

§ 19.7 Negligence

Most of us are familiar with negligence. To establish negligence, four elements must be proved. First, there must be an existence of a duty on the part of the defendant (the actor) to conform to a specific standard of conduct for the protection of the plaintiff (the injured party) against unreasonable risk or injury. This is commonly known as the standard of care. Second, there must be a breach of that duty by the defendant. Third, the breach must have been the proximate cause of the injury to the plaintiff's person or property. The fourth element that must be proved is damages. Under this theory, it is not sufficient merely to prove that the injury was caused by the defendant. The plaintiff must prove that the defendant's actions were not in accordance with the standard of care exercised by a "reasonable" person or in the case of professionals a "reasonable" professional. In other words, negligence requires the proof of some degree of fault, although the level of fault does not require culpability or intentional wrongdoing.

§ 19.8 Warranty

The Uniform Commercial Code (UCC), which has been adopted in almost every state in the United States, sets forth the applicable law in this area. The UCC provides for two types of warranties, *express warranties* which are actual representations made by a seller or supplier, and *implied warranties* which are implied by law for the protection of the consumer.

Under the UCC, an implied warranty of fitness for a particular purpose exists where the seller had reason to know the purpose for which the product was purchased, had represented that the product was suitable for such purpose, and the buyer relied upon the seller's skill and knowledge. The courts also will imply a warranty of merchantability. In some states the warranty of merchantability is a substitute theory, for the strict liability theory. Under this theory the seller in effect warrants that the goods are fit for the ordinary purpose for which they are used. An unreasonably dangerous product by definition cannot be fit for the ordinary purpose.

§ 19.9 Miscellaneous Theories

The previously mentioned theories are the heart and soul of any asbestos litigation; however, because of the particular facts involved and the degree of culpability, cases have been brought on other theories, such as fraud, negligent misrepresentation, conspiracy, CERCLA, RICO,[30] and intentional tort.

---

[30] Racketeering Influenced and Corrupt Organizations Act, 18 U.S.C. § 1961.

When dealing with manufacturers, the courts have often been liberal in their findings of liability because of evidence of outrageous misconduct.[31] In cases based on fraud or misrepresentation, the plaintiff must show reliance on representations of safety or suitability.[32]

One of the more interesting but unsuccessful theories has been the application of CERCLA to buildings containing asbestos. So far, courts have been unwilling to extend CERCLA superfund liability to a building containing asbestos. The issue was recently brought before the U.S. Supreme Court, but the Court denied review, making it unlikely that this theory will meet with success in the future.[33]

On the other hand, claims brought under the organized crime statutes, alleging RICO violations, have survived initial motions to dismiss.[34] Whether this theory will be successful at trial remains to be seen.

COST RECOVERY DEFENSES

§ 19.10   Economic Loss versus Property Damage

As building owners have vigorously pursued cost recovery, manufacturers have just as vigorously, and often successfully, defended these actions. The major theories of defense used by manufacturers are as follows.

In bringing an action for negligence or strict liability, an owner has to convince the courts that the cost of removal and replacement was not merely an "economic loss," but constituted property damage. Generally, tort liability is not applicable to mere economic loss. One must prove actual damage to the property.

Some courts have held that asbestos problems constitute a merchantability defect and are covered only by contract and not tort law.[35]

The traditional rule is exemplified by the early Alaska ruling in *Cloud v. Kit Manufacturing Co.*[36] In this case, the Alaska Supreme Court focused on the manner in which the injury occurred in deciding whether the application of strict

---

[31] *See generally* Brodeur, Outrageous Misconduct, 1985.

[32] Hebron Public School Dist. No. 13 v. United States Gypsum Co., No. Al-86-184 (D.N.D. 1988); *see also* earlier decision at 690 F. Supp. 866 (D.N.D. 1988) [hereinafter *Hebron*]; Federal Reserve Bank v. Carey Canada, Inc., No. 3-86-185 (D. Minn. 1988).

[33] First United Methodist Church v. United States Gypsum Co., No. 88-1612 (4th Cir. 1989), *rev. denied*.

[34] Prudential Ins. Co. v. United States Gypsum Co., No. 87-4227 (D.N.J. 1989); Helmsley v. Beauford, 650 F. Supp. 548 (S.D.N.Y. 1986), *aff'd*, 843 F.2d 103 (2d Cir. 1988), *vacated and remanded on reh'g en banc*, 865 F.2d 1386 (1989), *cert. denied*, 110 S. Ct. 539.

[35] Other courts for policy reasons have allowed strict liability. *Products Liability Issues in School Asbestos Litigation,* 10 Am. J. of L. & Med. 467 (1985).

[36] 563 P.2d 248 (Alaska 1977).

liability policies was warranted. The Court found that "sudden and calamitous" accidents were likely to result in direct property damage while deterioration, internal breakage, and depreciation would constitute an economic loss.

However, like Alaska, most jurisdictions have retreated from this rigid test.[37] Many courts reject the sudden and calamitous events test and focus on the potential danger posed to the product user. The court distinguished between merely disappointed users and endangered ones.

Now, most jurisdictions, including those which strictly adhere to the economic loss doctrine, allow recovery in tort for the cleanup and abatement of asbestos in buildings.[38]

In *City of Greenville v. W.R. Grace Co.*,[39] the court stated:

> The issue of whether asbestos contamination of buildings is actionable in tort has generated a large number of opinions, mostly unreported, by trial courts around the country. In support of their respective positions, the parties have favored the court with copies of many of these opinions. After considering the issue in detail, the court believes that the vast majority of these rulings, which have found such asbestos contamination actionable in tort, represent the correct view.

In arriving at this conclusion the courts have uniformly followed the same line of reasoning, as recently expressed by a federal district court in North Dakota.

> Gypsum argues that Hebron's loss, if any, is therefore an "economic loss" which is not recoverable at tort. This is an interesting argument, and one which has, on its face, some persuasive force. However, this court's own analysis of the law and facts is in accord with the dominant line of cases rejecting this position. Without reiterating the lengthy deliberations set out in the case law, this analysis is in brief as follows: The asbestos in this case is apparently found in a acoustical ceiling coating. If this coating had failed in its purpose—if it had fallen off, or failed to muffle reverberations—that would have given rise to an action sounding in contract for an economic loss. However, it appears that the coating functioned satisfactorily in its intended role except that, Hebron alleges, it released harmful asbestos fibers into the building, poisoning it and rendering it unfit for use. This is damage to property on which a tort claim can be founded: the building's physical structure was unharmed, but it was damaged in its utility, in its function as a building.[40]

---

[37] Northern Power & Eng'g Corp. v. Caterpillar Tractor Co., 623 P.2d 324 (Alaska 1981).

[38] *See generally* Board of Educ. v. A, C, & S, Inc., 171 Ill. App. 3d. 737, 525 N.E.2d 950 (1988); City of Greenville v. W.R. Grace & Co., 827 F.2d 975 (4th Cir. 1987) (interpreting South Carolina law); *Hebron*, 690 F. Supp. 866; City of Manchester v. National Gypsum Co., 637 F. Supp. 646 (D.R.I. 1986) [hereinafter *Manchester*].

[39] 640 F. Supp. 559 (D.S.C. 1986).

[40] *Hebron*, 690 F. Supp. 866.

This principle was firmly established in the landmark case of *City of Manchester v. National Gypsum Co.*[41] The court stated:

> Thus, the focus in this case in determining whether the plaintiff has stated a claim for physical harm is not exclusively on the measure of the plaintiff's damages — for abatement program costs and consequential expenditures — but, more properly, is on the nature of the defect and the manner in which the damages occurred. What the City of Manchester alleges about the defendants' products is not that it did not perform its function in the ceiling plaster, but rather that it posed a grave risk of personal injury to those in contact with it. . . . The case does not primarily involve a problem with the product which mandates its replacement or repair in order to perform its function, or a loss of profit stemming from a defect in the product's performance, but rather the replacement of the product because of a grave personal safety risk.

§ 19.11   Statute of Limitations

The second major hurdle that property owners face is the statute of limitations. The statute of limitations period and, of even greater importance, the time at which the period begins to run, varies from state to state depending on the legal theory applied.

Under a breach of contract claim, the statute typically runs from the time of delivery or at the time the breach occurs. In products liability and negligence cases, the statute generally begins to run at the time the defective product is delivered or when the act causing the breach is committed.

An asbestos claim for breach of contract will be barred in most jurisdictions because the period begins to run at a definite point established early in the contractual relationship. However, under the tort theories, the statute of limitations begins to run at the time the act was committed or, in some jurisdictions, if the injury is not obvious, the time that the injury is discovered. The "discovery rule" can extend the statutory period for an indefinite period of time.

The application of these rules has varied from state to state in asbestos cases. Some courts have held that the date of installation controls.[42] Others have strictly applied a discovery rule against plaintiffs.[43] Still other courts have adhered to the traditional discovery rule.[44]

While many statutes of limitation may have run their course, a manufacturer should not depend on this defense as the courts may find a way around the statute

---

[41] *Manchester*, 637 F. Supp. 646.

[42] Corporation of Mercer Univ. v. National Gypsum Co., 877 F.2d 35 (11th Cir. 1989); St. Joseph Hosp. v. Celotex Corp., 874 F.2d 764 (11th Cir. 1989) (interpreting Georgia law).

[43] Kansas City v. W.R. Grace & Co., No. CV86-19615 (Cir. Ct. Jackson Cty. Mo. Aug. 1988).

[44] University of Vt. v. W.R. Grace & Co., No. 88-181 (Vt. Aug. 4, 1989); Archbishop of Baltimore v. United States Gypsum Co., No. 71693 (Md. Cir. Ct. Hartford Cty. Aug. 2, 1989).

of limitations problem or legislatures may decide to pass revival statutes which establish new deadlines for filing asbestos lawsuits. Many states now have such revival statutes.[45] While these statutes are under constitutional attack by asbestos manufacturers, courts are upholding their validity.[46]

§ 19.12   Safe Product Defense

Asbestos manufacturers continue to contend that their materials, if properly used, are not unreasonably dangerous. A jury, in a recent Washington case involving the Highline School District, rendered a defense verdict where manufacturers alleged the safe product defense. In addition, the mere presence of asbestos may not be sufficient to trigger liability. Some courts require showings of an actual release of fibers,[47] whereas others require a showing of personal injury or property damage.

§ 19.13   Product Identification

While market share theories, which hold manufacturers liable on the basis of their share of the market, have been successful in holding manufacturers liable when the product manufacturer cannot be identified, these theories have not been upheld in the asbestos arena.[48] It is therefore essential that owners be able to establish the origin of the asbestos. Identification through historical evidence, plans and specifications, and scientific analysis of samples must be carefully considered. Some courts have required the preservation of samples even on small abatement jobs.[49]

---

[45] City of Boston v. Keene Corp., No. 5060 (Sup. Jud. Ct. Mass).

[46] Wesley Theological Seminary v. United States Gypsum Co., No. 88-7144 (D.C. Cir. 1989); Hymowitz v. Eli Lilly & Co., 73 N.Y.2d 487, 541 N.Y.S.2d 941 (1989). In addition, some states, such as Washington, have longer product liability statutes (twelve years) that typically run from the date of the sale.

[47] Catasauqua Area School Dist. v. Eagle-Picher Indust., Inc., No. 85-3743 (E.D. Pa. 1988).

[48] Mullen v. Armstrong World Indus., Inc., No. A036661 (Cal. Ct. App. Mar. 30, 1988). *Cf.* Vigiolto v. Johns-Manville Corp., 643 F. Supp. 1454 (W.D. Pa. 1986), *aff'd,* 826 F.2d 1058 (3d Cir. 1987) (rejecting market share under Pennsylvania law); Case v. Fibreboard Corp., 743 P.2d 1062 (Okla. 1987).

[49] City of New York v. Aaer Sprayed Insulations, Inc., No. 19288187 (Sup. Ct. N.Y. Cty. July 1989).

LIABILITY AND ASBESTOS ABATEMENT

§ 19.14 Owner

With respect to the asbestos abatement process, key members of the team face potential liability in different ways.

An owner owes a general duty to the public to provide a building which is reasonably safe for human occupancy, and a survey, of course, begins with the owner. Obviously, a building containing friable asbestos or airborne asbestos levels beyond federal standards would violate this duty, and subject the owner to liability.[50]

At present, there is little evidence that the levels of exposure experienced in the occupancy of buildings is sufficient to cause asbestos-related diseases.[51] However, as public awareness of asbestos increases we will see more attempts in the future to litigate these issues. Cases are already appearing throughout the country of building service employees, including office workers, developing asbestos-related diseases and claiming against the building owner.[52]

In addition, increased pressure from unions is likely to result in stricter standards for general exposure of workers in public and commercial buildings.[53]

In personal injury cases, plaintiffs sometimes seek recovery for "cancerphobia" or the fear of developing cancer. One court has recognized that the inhalation of asbestos fibers is a physical impact. It does not matter how large or small, visible or invisible the substance, or whether it immediately causes harmful effects: imbedding of asbestos fibers in the lungs is an impact.[54] While most jurisdictions have not extended recovery for fear of injury where there is not a substantial physical manifestation of the injury,[55] the courts are becoming more liberal in allowing recovery for fear of cancer or asbestosis.[56]

Courts are recognizing that fear of cancer from asbestos exposure constitutes actual injury; policy concerns regarding recognition of this "injury" are satisfied by evidence that shows that a person exposed to a substantial amount of

---

[50] Brooklyn Law School v. Raybon, Inc., 143 Misc. 2d 237, 540 N.Y.S.2d 404 (1989).

[51] See Guidance for Controlling Asbestos-Containing Materials in Buildings, EPA, 1985.

[52] See, e.g., Layne v. GAF Corp., No. 84-07194 (Cuyahoga Co., Ohio Ct. of Comm. Pleas, Oct. 6, 1987) ($400,000 judgment, later reduced to $338,300), see also comments of Hon. James J. McMonagle (presiding judge in Layne) at N.Y.U. Conference on Asbestos Management in Public, Commercial and Residential Real Estate in New York City, Oct. 18, 1988 reprinted in Nat. J. Asb.-in-Bldgs. Lit., Vol. I, No. 6 (Oct. 28, 1988).

[53] Service Employees Int'l Union v. Reilly, No. [_____] (filed D.D.C. Mar. 30, 1989).

[54] Eagle-Picher Indus., Inc. v. Cox, 481 So. 2d 517, 526-27 (Fla. Dist. Ct. App. 1985).

[55] Tysenn v. Johns-Manville Corp., 517 F. Supp. 1290 (E.D. Pa. 1981).

[56] See Devlin v. Johns-Manville Corp., 202 N.J. Super. 556, 495 A.2d 495, 498 (1985).

asbestos has a more than 50 percent chance of developing cancer.[57] Of more immediate concern to the owner, however, will be the issue of economic loss. Although there may be questionable evidence that the asbestos levels in a building are actually injuring people, asbestos has been recognized by Congress and the EPA as a potentially hazardous condition. As a result, a building owner who owns an asbestos-containing building faces a number of very real economic problems.

First, the presence of asbestos will create a dramatic decrease in the building market value upon discovery.[58] This decrease is often greater than the economic impact on the net operating income generated by abatement and maintenance costs.

Second, owners should disclose the existence of asbestos to future tenants.[59] Such disclosure will undoubtedly decrease rental values and inflate vacancy factors.

Third, if the owner decides to sell its building, in many states it has an obligation to put the purchaser on notice that the building contains asbestos.[60]

Fourth, in commercial markets, with continual renovation of space common-place during the building's useful life, the presence of asbestos will greatly inflate the cost of routine renovation.[61]

Finally, as indicated by recent criminal enforcements, owners may face liabilities under the Clear Air Act, CERCLA, and the Resource Conservation and Recovery Act (RCRA) during the abatement process. Environmental risk assessments or audits will become as common as title insurance. Furthermore, the owner runs the risk of future changes in the regulations. In some cases, courts have held owners liable for changing regulations.[62]

§ 19.15   Architects and Engineers

Most owners, when they decide to renovate or when they are aware of an asbestos problem, first approach an architect. The architectural profession has generally taken a hands-off approach to this problem, suggesting that architects not get involved in the abatement process. Unfortunately, no matter how hard these professionals try, they cannot avoid some involvement.

---

[57] Jackson v. Johns-Manville Sales Corp., 781 F.2d 394, 413 (5th Cir. 1986). *But see* Pollack v. Johns-Manville Sales Corp., 666 F. Supp. 489 (D.N.J. 1988) (43% chance deemed insufficient).

[58] Jefferson Assoc. Ltd. v. Prudential Ins. Co., No. 441 712 (filed Jan. 1989 Tex. Dist. Ct. Travis Cty.).

[59] Gurman Kurtis & Blask v. Charles E. Smith Management, Inc., No. 88-CA11228 (D.C. Super. Ct. 1989); ARZ Acres v. Satellite Business Sys., No. 106608 (Cuyahoga Cty. [Ohio] Ct. C. P.).

[60] 195 Broadway Co. v. 195 Broadway Corp., 199 N.Y. L.J. No. 72 (1988); Kinsey v. Jones, No. CV 87-2959 (E.D.N.Y. 1989).

[61] Chase Manhattan Bank N.A. v. Turner & Newall PLC, 87 Civ. 4436 (ULB) (S.D.N.Y.).

[62] Kaufman v. City of New York, No. 89-7621 (2d Cir. 1989).

[63] RCD v. Sherertz, No. L. 11889 (filed Cir. Ct. Alexandria Cty, VA).

To begin with, any building that was built or renovated during a period of time when asbestos building products were prevalent should be inspected for asbestos. The architect, as the owner's professional advisor, may have a duty at least to warn the unsophisticated owner that it should take necessary precautions.[63]

Failure to warn the owner adequately creates one of the most dangerous situations in the asbestos abatement process: A situation in which an unknowing contractor enters the building and begins demolition of asbestos-containing materials without any of the necessary precautions.

Assuming the architect properly warns the owner and at this point leaves the site until the asbestos has been fully removed, it can re-enter the project, perform its architectural duties, and remain well insulated from liability. However, as we all know, asbestos abatement is not simply the removal of asbestos, and when encapsulation, enclosure, or operation and maintenance procedures are recommended, the architect will find it difficult to remove itself totally from the situation.

If asbestos materials remain on the site during construction, the architect may have some obligation to ensure that proper warnings are given, that the asbestos remains undisturbed, and that the activities of the asbestos contractor and general contractor are coordinated.

In Texas, 166 construction workers claimed that they were exposed to asbestos and filed suit against the owner of the project, the contractor, and the professional firm involved. Although the workers merely claimed exposure and could show no actual injury (due to the long manifestation period of asbestos-related diseases), the workers' claims were settled for $1.6 million.[64]

§ 19.16   Asbestos Consultants

Although asbestos consultants come from a variety of backgrounds, many are industrial hygienists. When asked about their potential liability in asbestos removal, many industrial hygienists feel they are fairly safe since they tend to view themselves as scientists who historically have had few liability problems. As newcomers to the construction industry, however, they will undoubtedly be a target for claims. Consequently, in this litigious environment they must exercise extreme care in undertaking any form of construction supervision.

At this point, it is not known if the standard for asbestos liability during construction will be strict liability, because ultra-hazardous activity is involved, or whether the courts will limit the liability to a negligence standard. So far, some courts have found strict liability inapplicable to the construction process.[65]

---

[64] Fox, *The Impact of Asbestos on Real Estate Ownership* (unpublished paper presented to the World Congress II Exposition on Asbestos Abatement, Asbestos Abatement Council — AWCI).

[65] J & S Enterprises, Inc. v. RREEF USA Fund-III, No. 87-CV-16900, and RREEF USA Fund-III v. W.R. Grace & Co., No. 88-CV-1516 (Denver Dist. Ct. 1988).

§ 19.17   Asbestos Contractors

The asbestos contractor, like all contractors, bears the brunt of liability. Contractors are normally insulated, however, from personal injury claims of workers. Under the workers' compensation laws, the contractor's liability is statutorily limited and, therefore, insurance is readily available for this protection. Although some legal scholars have suggested that workers' compensation laws will not withstand pressure to compensate injured victims fully, to date they have adequately limited the contractors' liability.[66] Of greater concern is the threat of contamination from improper procedures. Once a release has occurred, economic losses can skyrocket. Decontamination is extremely expensive and time consuming.

§ 19.18   Other Groups

Other real estate professionals are also becoming entangled in the asbestos issue. Brokers face potential liability for failing to advise purchasers to investigate for asbestos and for negligent or fraudulent misrepresentations. Appraisers are now required by ethical standards to take into consideration hazardous materials in the appraisal of buildings. Also, real estate syndicators are being sued by investors for failure to discover or disclose the existence of asbestos, as are banks and construction lenders.[67]

PROTECTION AND ALLOCATIONS
OF LIABILITY

§ 19.19   Contracts

While methods of maintaining reasonable limits on liability exposure will vary with the circumstances, the major strategies embraced have been contracts, supervision, recordkeeping, workers' training, worker releases, liability insurance, incorporation and legislation.

Contracts are the first step in allocating liability. Although contracts are not very effective in abolishing liability, they are useful in shifting the burden to other parties. As an example, architectural contracts such as AIA B141 allocate

---

[66] *Hazardous Waste and Workers' Compensation: Some Evolving Concerns,* 2 ABA Tort & Ins. L. J. 90 (Fall 1985).

[67] Steiner v. J.F. Baxter, No. 89-809 (D. Colo. May 9, 1989); Bank W. Fed. v. W. Office Partners, No. 86-CV-13417 (Denver Dist. Ct. Feb. 8, 1989); LaPlacita Partners v. Northwestern Mut. Life Ins. Co., No. C88-2824 (N.D. Ohio).

the responsibility of abatement to the owner and seek indemnification. In addition, many owners' contracts seek to obtain indemnification from parties involved in the abatement process. While indemnification agreements sound great on paper, they are fraught with pitfalls and are often found void for public policy reasons.

A more important aspect of a contract is the allocation of duties between the parties. At this point there are no standard contracts for the industry and these allocations are the result of negotiations, or the lack thereof. There are many conflicts, particularly when the contracts flow between the owner and the various team members without proper coordination.

§ 19.20   Supervision

In the field of architecture "supervision" is a dirty word, but no matter what it is called in the contract, careful review of each phase is the best way to ensure that the procedures are carried out properly. Obviously, it is safer to have everything reviewed and rechecked to discover problems before they result in injuries. Although it may not be desirable in a contract to outline this level of supervision, a team that works together and has members who try to assist each other will be more effective and safer.

§ 19.21   Recordkeeping

As is typical of federal legislation, EPA regulations and guidelines have placed a strong emphasis on recordkeeping. This strategy cuts two ways, since liability can be established as well as disproven through recordkeeping. Recordkeeping, however, is an essential part of asbestos abatement and well-kept records will be the best defense for abatement professionals in controlling liability. Formalizing the recordkeeping process also focuses an employee's attention on its importance and the potential liability that accompanies it.

The litigation process demonstrates over and over again the downside of inadequate recordkeeping since problems in existing records tend to arise from gratuitous statements or from sloppily kept records. An employee who believes that its records, often only a scrawl on a scrap of paper, will not be seen by others is more likely to make damaging statements. When such informal and perhaps unclear, incomplete, and ambiguous records exist, they are still admissible in court and can be damaging in the absence of other, better organized records.

§ 19.22   Workers' Training

The level of workers' training must obviously be balanced against the economic concerns of providing asbestos abatement at an affordable cost. However, better educated and trained workers will perform their task more safely. Employers may wish to establish training programs beyond those required by law.

§ 19.23   Worker Release

The National Institute of Building Sciences Model Guide Specifications—Asbestos Abatement in Buildings, 1986, contains various form letters to be signed by employees documenting the fact that they had been adequately warned as to the hazards of asbestos work and have been adequately trained in the use of respirators and other safety procedures. The more direct and alarming the language used in these forms the better, since, in past asbestos litigation, courts consistently focus on the level of warnings that have been given to the worker and have consistently ruled that the worker's general knowledge of the hazards of asbestos exposure was not sufficient to relieve employers' or manufacturers' liability.

In *Borel v. Fibreboard Paper Products,*[68] the court specifically held that warnings that stated working with asbestos "may" be hazardous to one's health were inadequate to shift the responsibilities from the product manufacturer to the worker. In addition, these signed statements should include a general release of the various parties involved in the asbestos abatement team. Although such statements may or may not be effective in court, they are certainly worth the trouble to obtain and may provide some level of protection.

§ 19.24   Liability Insurance

After getting stung in the past, insurance companies dropped asbestos insurance in the 1980s like a hot potato. However, more recently, some major insurance companies have been willing to insure specific risks associated with asbestos projects. While most policies place severe limitations on coverage, as the market softens major coverage improvements can be expected. As ever, careful scrutiny of policies is essential to understanding your coverage.

§ 19.25   Incorporation

Although incorporation offers little protection to a licensed professional, it can effectively limit liability of asbestos consultants and contractors. There is no reason to believe that the courts will pierce the corporate veil and find personal liability in the case of asbestos. Organizational structure and asset management

---

[68] 493 F.2d 1076.

become important parts of any asbestos consultant's or contractor's liability program.

§ 19.26 Legislation

At this point in time, legislation offers one of the most important tools for limiting liability in the future. Congress has opened the door to examination of the state's standards for liability in asbestos abatement cases. Under AHERA the federal government has taken the approach that it will not interfere with the states' rights to establish their own standards of tort liability. Furthermore, some states, such as New Jersey, have taken the lead in limiting asbestos removal liability to a negligence standard.

CHAPTER 20

DISCOVERY IN CONSTRUCTION LITIGATION

John B. Tieder, Jr.
Julian F. Hoffar
David C. Romm*

INTRODUCTION

§ 20.1   **Purposes of Discovery**

§ 20.2   **Defending Against Discovery**

OTHER SOURCES OF INFORMATION

§ 20.3   **Client Sources**

§ 20.4   **Third Parties**

§ 20.5   **Former Employees or Representatives of Opponent**

§ 20.6   **Experts**

§ 20.7   **Published Materials**

ORGANIZING CLIENT INFORMATION

§ 20.8   **Basic Case Established from Client Data**

§ 20.9   **Gathering Documents**

§ 20.10   **—Indexing**

§ 20.11   **—Identification and Removal of Privileged or Exempt Documents**

§ 20.12   **Witness Interviews**

AVAILABLE METHODS OF AFFIRMATIVE DISCOVERY

§ 20.13   **Document Requests: Identifying the Records**

§ 20.14   **—Organizing the Documents**

§ 20.15   **—Analyzing the Documents**

§ 20.16   **Interrogatories**

§ 20.17   **Depositions**

§ 20.18   **Requests for Admissions**

§ 20.19   **Discovery Through Negotiations**

---

* This chapter is adapted from a paper presented in December 1989 to the Fourth Annual Construction Litigation Superconference sponsored by Andrews Conferences.

409

NONCOMPLIANCE OR OBJECTIONS TO DISCOVERY

§ 20.20 Motion Practice

§ 20.21 Sanctions

§ 20.22 Duty to Preserve Documents

§ 20.23 Attorney Liability

DEFENSIVE DISCOVERY

§ 20.24 General Considerations

§ 20.25 Interrogatories: When and How to Object

§ 20.26 —Preparation of Responses

§ 20.27 Requests for Production of Documents

§ 20.28 —Responding to a Request

§ 20.29 Depositions: Preparing the Witness

§ 20.30 —Objections

§ 20.31 —Memory of Witnesses

§ 20.32 —Designating Witnesses

§ 20.33 —Requests for Admissions

§ 20.34 —Duty to Supplement

EXPERT DISCOVERY

§ 20.35 Who Is an Expert?

§ 20.36 Discovery of Nontestifying Experts

§ 20.37 Discovery of Testifying Experts

§ 20.38 Impeachment of the Trial Expert

INTRODUCTION

§ 20.1 Purposes of Discovery

The primary purpose of discovery is to learn the opposition's case so a realistic determination can be made of whether to settle, and if so at what level, or to proceed to trial. It should be remembered that this includes learning both the strengths and the weaknesses of the case. On too many occasions, it appears that the attorneys only want to learn the weaknesses in their opponent's case, not the strengths. This is not a prudent approach. In order to assess the opposition's case, one must know it in its entirety. In addition, by failing to learn the strengths of the opposition's case, it will not be possible to address and minimize those strengths at trial.

One should not forget, however, to ascertain the weaknesses in the opposition's case as well. Internal documents in which the opposition disparages its own position are obviously helpful and can be of particular use in negotiations and cross-examination at trial.

Another purpose of discovery is of course to assist in the building of the client's case. One area in particular where discovery can assist in the building of the client's case is daily reports and similar documents maintained by the opposition. For example, a contractor who is performing an as-built schedule analysis or a loss of productivity analysis can use the owner's or engineer's raw data to perform its analysis. This will prevent or at least limit attacks on the validity of the underlying data, which would be the case if the client used its own data to perform the analysis. It is also possible to find documents in the opposition's files which constitute admissions, establish that information was concealed during the course of the construction project, or assess the client's case in a favorable light.

It should be remembered, however, that discovery is no substitute for building an affirmative presentation. In many cases it appears that discovery becomes an end in itself, a tactic to force the other side to settle. Although this tangential benefit may arise in certain cases, it should not be a substitute for preparing the client's affirmative position. Discovery can be used to strengthen the affirmative case, but it is only very rarely that a case is won by information revealed in discovery.

§ 20.2 Defending Against Discovery

Responses to discovery requests from the opposition are typically regarded as an exercise in damage control. Virtually every case has at least some weaknesses, and it is the job of the opposition to unearth those weaknesses during the course of the discovery. Responses to discovery can, however, serve to strengthen the client's case. Timely and complete answers to discovery requests indicate to the opposition that the client is organized, committed to the case, and prepared to substantiate its position. The weaknesses, which are bound to be revealed at some time, can be far outweighed by revelation of the strengths.

One of the side benefits of responding to discovery requests is that it forces the attorney to learn its own case. In this regard, responses to discovery requests should be a continuation of an attorney's preparation for trial. Proper discovery requests frequently require the attorney to gather information which will be needed for trial. They also identify weaknesses in the case which will need bolstering for trial and which should be taken into consideration in assessing settlement.

Another side benefit of responding to discovery requests is that it teaches the client its case. This is particularly useful when there are weaknesses in the case which the client may not be prepared to face. By responding to discovery requests these weaknesses are brought to the client's attention and a more realistic settlement position may evolve.

OTHER SOURCES OF INFORMATION

§ 20.3   Client Sources

Although discovery is an extremely useful method of gathering information on the case, it is only one of several. The primary source of information still remains the client.

The client's records of the project will form the basis of any case. As set forth above, documents gathered during discovery may supplement the client's materials, but the internal records will remain the primary source.

In addition to the documents, the other and perhaps even more valuable source of information is the client's employees or other representatives. The attorney's first exposure to a case is usually through one or more of the project personnel and it is only these persons who can properly explain the operative events.

Another source of information is former employees or representatives of the client. Although current employees and representatives can be freely interviewed and the case discussed with some candor, former employees or representatives present certain difficulties. Since they are no longer employed they are free to talk to anyone including the opposition. Perhaps even more fundamentally, former employees are not even obliged to consult with the attorneys for their ex-employers. One method of dealing with this difficulty is for the employer to enter into a consulting agreement whereby the ex-employee assists in the preparation of the case and cooperates with the firm's attorneys in exchange for some compensation. It is important, however, that these arrangements be such that there is no appearance of the former employee being paid for factual testimony.[1]

§ 20.4   Third Parties

Another source of information is other parties who were involved on the project. This could include other contractors, the engineer, and others. There is no requirement that information from third parties be gathered by formal discovery proceedings. It is frequently possible to gather such information through informal means, such as interviews. This is usually less expensive and time consuming than formal discovery. In addition, there is no requirement to notify the opposition when informal means are used. One should be sure, however, that information gathered informally can be used at trial by subpoenaing the persons or records. Interviews are not introducible into evidence as are transcripts of depositions.

Public entities which are either parties or participated in some other way in the project can also be informally interviewed or made subject to formal third-party

---

[1] *See, e.g.,* Model Rules of Professional Conduct Rule 7-107 (1983).

discovery. In many jurisdictions, however, formal discovery can be disregarded. Instead, the client can rely on the various freedom of information act statutes which apply in the various jurisdictions.[2] These freedom of information act statutes allow access to most information which can be gathered through discovery. Except in those cases where the public entity is an opposing party, the opposition does not need to be notified that the information is being sought.

§ 20.5 Former Employees or Representatives of Opponent

On some occasions one of the most valuable sources of information is former employees or representatives of the opponent. Since they are no longer employed and, assuming there is no consulting or other arrangement with their prior employer, an attorney is free to interview or talk to any such person without notice to the opposition. It is recommended that such approaches be made with caution. If former employees retain a good relationship with the opposition, they may well discuss the attorney's conversations with him and reveal whatever information or assessment may have been provided.

On the other extreme are former employees who have some dispute with their former employer. Such employees can frequently overstate the case or their position can be undermined by the mere fact of their dispute. It is always recommended that such disaffected former employees' statements of fact be verified by other sources.

§ 20.6 Experts

Most significant construction cases require the use of at least one expert. Experts in such matters as structural engineering, soils, schedule analysis, labor inefficiency, etc. are widely used. Experts, of course, are retained by the client and there are special rules dealing with discovery from them.[3] The attorney, of course, has free access to the expert for whatever information it may provide in connection with the case. There is a distinction between the discoverability of information from testifying experts versus non-testifying experts. The attorney should bear this distinction in mind in connection with what information the expert reduces to writing during the investigatory stages of the case.

---

[2] *See, e.g.,* Freedom of Information Act, 5 U.S.C. § 552; Freedom of Information Act, Ark. Stat. Ann. §§ 25-19-101 to -107 (1988); Public Records Act, Cal. Govt. Code § 6250; Public Records Act, Fla. Stat. Ann. § 119. 01; Freedom of Information Act, Ill. Rev. Stat. ch. 116, ¶ 201; Md., Ann. Code, Title 10, Part III Access to Public Records (1984); Freedom of Information Law, N.Y. Public Officers Law, Chap. 47, Art. 6 (McKinney).

[3] *See* §§ **20.35-20.38.**

§ 20.7   Published Materials

There are two categories of published materials which are useful in the preparation of a case. The first and perhaps most common is published data dealing with empirical data which may be of use to the case. This would include, for example, learned treatises on engineering, soils mechanics, etc. The second and less common type of published data deals directly with the particular project in dispute. Both local news publications and national publications such as ENR (formerly Engineering News-Record) occasionally contain statements by one or more of the parties to a case which may not be wholly consistent with the position being taken in a lawsuit. A review of at least the local newspapers in connection with a case is usually worth the limited investment of time. In a similar fashion, information provided in connection with seminars and meetings of professional societies can provide useful information about a particular project.

ORGANIZING CLIENT INFORMATION

§ 20.8   Basic Case Established from Client Data

As mentioned above, the basic case should be established from the client's own materials. Thus, the first step in the discovery process by the attorney should be the organization of information which is available from the client and a review of that information in order to be aware of all its contents. It is very difficult to prepare a case properly and to conduct meaningful discovery from other parties until one knows what is available in his or her own files.

§ 20.9   Gathering Documents

The first step in the organization of documents is, of course, to gather them all. Although this may sound like a simple process most attorneys have suffered at least some embarrassment when new documents appear late in the discovery process. In addition to gathering the obvious jobsite materials, there are several other potential sources of documents which should be investigated.

In addition to the basic project records, many reports at higher levels in the company deal with the particular project. This can be something as simple as a financial statement of the profit/loss situation on the project to a detailed analysis of why the project is performing as it is. These management records are frequently not made available to the jobsite personnel and, therefore, not included in the jobsite files.

In addition to the records that are maintained at the jobsite, many supervisory and management personnel maintain personal diaries or other records which they do not consider part of the overall company documents. This is particularly true of diaries and journals maintained by superintendents, supervisors, and even direct laborers. Although there may be an issue as to whether these documents are within the possession, custody, or control of the client, it is always possible for the opposition to obtain copies of them through a subpoena of the individual. It is best to learn of the existence of these personal records during the early stages of the case so any adverse data can be properly addressed during the deposition of the individual who maintained the records.

It is widely accepted that computer data is discoverable.[4] This includes not only the data which has already been printed, but data which can be reconfigured in some fashion. Thus, most discovery requests seek the materials on which computer data is stored: tapes, floppy disks, and so forth.

§ 20.10   —Indexing

After the documents have been gathered, the next step is to organize and index them. The documents should be retained in their original format. The reason for this is that the department or division of the company which originally maintained the document may be of some significance during the course of the case. Also, it facilitates the location of documents by the persons who originally prepared them. If the documents are reorganized in a fashion to suit the attorneys, it is often difficult for company personnel to relocate their files.

The documents need to be indexed by the attorneys and their assistants to ascertain what information is available. The index should identify the date, author, addressee, other recipients and subject matter categories.

A determination must be made early in the litigation process as to whether a manual or computer indexing system is most appropriate. The issue of whether to maintain a manual or computer index is dictated by two factors. The first is the volume of documents. In cases where there are 50,000 documents or less, many of which are repetitive (e.g., inspection reports, invoices, etc.) computer indexing is usually not necessary. If there are a large number of documents (e.g., in excess of 1,000,000), computer indexing may be the only feasible means of gaining access to the information.

The second factor is the expense. If the client has its own computer resources, both equipment and personnel, computer indexing can be economical even in a relatively small case. If an outside entity must be retained, the expense can be quite significant. There are several organizations which specialize in this business.[5] In addition, there are software packages which can be purchased for the organization of materials.[6]

---

[4] *See, e.g.,* Fed. R. Civ. P. 26(b)(1); Dunn v. Midwestern Indem., 88 F.R.D. 191 (S.D. Ohio 1980).

[5] Two of them are American Legal Systems®, (800) 221-3076 and Quorum Litigation Services, (800) 328-4454.

[6] Two of the more commonly used ones are dBase III Plus® by Ashton-Tate, Inc., and Paradox® by Borland International Company.

The keys to computer or manual indexing are the preparation of reasonable subject matter categories and the accurate classification of documents into these categories. The main problem with indexing seems to be that the categories are either too gross or too finite. In the former case the subject matter categories are so large that individual documents cannot be located. In the latter case, the subject matter categories are so specific that they cannot be readily indexed except by someone who is totally familiar with the case. The number of subject matter categories should depend, therefore, on the quality of the indexers and their familiarity with the case.

§ 20.11 — Identification and Removal of Privileged or Exempt Documents

As set forth below, there are certain categories of documents which are exempt from discovery. If such documents are revealed either intentionally or inadvertently, the party who revealed the document will be deemed to have waived any claim of privilege or exemption from discovery not only as to that particular document but as to any other document which deals with the same subject matter.[7]

It is important, therefore, that during the indexing process, all such documents are identified and removed from the files. A list should be prepared of all documents removed so they can be identified for the opposition. The persons who are actually indexing the files should be instructed to remove any documents which appear to be even colorably exempt or privileged. The attorney in charge of the case should then review all such documents and finally decide which will be withheld from discovery and which will be left in the files.

In identifying possibly privileged or exempt documents, it is recommended that documents which are potentially harmful but which will probably have to be produced at some time not be withheld. The identification and attempt to withhold such documents only highlights their significance. The documents which are actually withheld should only be ones which will survive a motion to compel by the opposition.

Documents which are subject to the attorney/client privilege are not discoverable.[8] This includes all documents wherein any information is provided to an attorney or an attorney provides advice or recommendations to the client. This would include not only specific letters and memoranda but records of telephone conversations, diaries, daily logs and similar type documents. When a document contains both privileged and nonprivileged information the privileged data should be redacted and the remainder of the document made available.

---

[7] Commodity Futures Trading Comm'n v. Weintraub, 471 U.S. 343 (1985); Permian Corp. v. United States, 665 F.2d 1214, 1215 (D.C. Cir. 1981).

[8] *See, e.g.,* Fed. R. Civ. P. 26(b)(1).

Documents which are prepared in anticipation of litigation are generally exempt from discovery. This means there is no privilege which attaches to them but as a matter of policy they are only discoverable upon the showing of extraordinary circumstances.[9] Such extraordinary circumstances mean that the party cannot obtain the information or its substantial equivalent without a showing of "undue hardship."[10] Furthermore, if such materials are to be produced, "the mental impressions, conclusions, opinions or legal theories" of attorneys and other representatives of the party concerning the litigation shall be deleted.

As a practical matter, all documents which arguably belong to the trial preparation phase or, as sometimes termed, prepared "in anticipation of litigation," should be removed. There is frequently a question as to when documents fit within the trial preparation phase as compared to the normal course of business. At least in the initial phases of a complex case the term "anticipation of litigation" should be expansively construed.

The discovery of information prepared by a testifying expert is usually required to be produced. Pursuant to Federal Rule of Civil Procedure 26(b)(4)(A), for example, information regarding an expert is first provided by answers to interrogatories and then, upon motion, by other means. As a practical matter, however, any information prepared by a testifying expert will usually be produced. The same is not true of a nontestifying expert.[11] Information regarding such experts is only discoverable when it would be "impracticable for the party seeking discovery to obtain facts or opinions on the same subject by other means."[12]

In practice it is best initially to withhold all information regarding experts from discovery. Once it is decided which experts will testify, it can be determined which materials must be produced.

In addition to the documents which are exempt from discovery as trial preparation or expert materials, there is often information which companies consider "confidential." This means information about their business practices, finances, etc. which they consider to be proprietary. There is no rule which allows the withholding of such documents from discovery if it is otherwise relevant to the dispute. It is possible, however, to obtain a protective order to limit the access to such "confidential information."[13] Such documents should be identified and removed from the files prior to discovery. They must, however, be identified and arrangements made to obtain a protective order before their disclosure.

---

[9] *See, e.g.,* Fed. R. Civ. P. 26(b)(3).

[10] *Id.*

[11] *See, e.g.,* Fed. R. Civ. P. 26(b)(4)(B).

[12] *Id.*

[13] *See, e.g.,* Fed. R. Civ. P. 26(c).

In preparing a construction case for litigation, summaries are frequently prepared, such as labor hours, equipment hours, and so forth. As the case is being prepared for trial these summaries are certainly exempt from discovery as trial preparation materials.[14] If, however, they are eventually going to be used in the case, they must be provided to the opposition at some time prior to trial. Failure to provide information which a party intends to rely upon trial can, of course, result in exclusion of that material from evidence.[15] Thus, drafts of such materials should be identified as trial preparation materials and withheld from discovery. It must be remembered, however, that discovery responses should be supplemented to assure that such information is provided.

§ 20.12   Witness Interviews

A final source of information is interviews of potential witnesses in the case. In this regard the distinction must be made between witnesses who are current employees or representatives of the client, those who are no longer employees or representatives, and those who are totally unrelated to the parties to the case. For current employees or representatives, the information which is gathered during an interview should be deemed trial preparation materials and thus be exempt from discovery without a showing of undue hardship. Possibly the only such time when such documents could be discovered is if the witness were to become impaired or otherwise unavailable and the opposition had no other alternative means of learning the information.[16]

If the person interviewed is no longer an employee of the company, he has an absolute right to any statement that he may have made.[17] Likewise an opposing party has an absolute right to any statement he may have made.[18]

AVAILABLE METHODS OF
AFFIRMATIVE DISCOVERY

§ 20.13   Document Requests:
Identifying the Records

Inevitably, the first formal step toward discovery in a large complex construction case will be a request for documents. This is important as an immediate first step

---

[14] *See, e.g.,* Fed. R. Civ. P. 26(b)(3).

[15] Weiner King, Inc. v. King Corp., 615 F.2d 512 (C.C.P.A. 1980).

[16] *See, e.g.,* Hickman v. Taylor, 329 U.S. 495, 511-12 (1947).

[17] *See, e.g.,* Fed. R. Civ. P. 26(b)(3).

[18] *Id.*

since certain categories of documents, usually maintained in a construction trailer, are prone to be altered, lost, destroyed, or mutilated. This is particularly the case where the parties have not contemplated litigation during performance.

Often critical documents such as schedules, shop drawings, change orders, requests for information, meeting minutes, and even the contract documents themselves are not maintained in their original, pristine state. Therefore, an initial discovery step involves determining the types of records maintained on a construction project during construction and their present location and/or custodian. This can be accomplished one of two ways: an initial deposition of the custodian of documents; or by a few, very brief interrogatories designed to ferret out the extent and nature of documents maintained.

Under most circumstances documents should be produced, analyzed, categorized and perhaps computerized before depositions are taken and substantive interrogatories are posed. This can prove to be quite expensive in a large construction case which often involves tens of thousands of documents, multiple parties, and scores of issues. And, no matter how well thought out the issue identification process is at the start of a case, the issues will change and grow — right up to trial.

Thus, it is extremely important that the lead counsel at the very start of a case devote enough time to formulating lists of critical issues, witnesses and parties to immediately begin the process of educating the litigation team (including paralegals and project assistants). If the document review team is sufficiently well versed in the issues, the drastic expense of "going in and copying everything" should be avoided.

§ 20.14   —Organizing the Documents

Once documents have been obtained they must categorized, analyzed and, if necessary, computerized. Construction contractors, architect/engineers and owners seldom maintain one unified master chronology of project correspondence or other forms of communication. Construction industry entities communicate by a great variety of vehicles—all of which must be pieced together to understand the flow of a project and the sequence of events. These typically involve the following categories of documents: correspondence, field memos, requests for proposals, requests for information, meeting minutes, telephone notes, shop drawing transmittals and returns, nonconformance reports, change orders, schedules (both project-wide and short-term), inspection reports, time extension requests, and pay requests.

The construction industry is wedded to the concept of keeping these categories of documents in separate and distinct files and further dividing them as to sender/ sendee (i.e., correspondence "to the architect," correspondence "from the architect"). Considerable wasted energy will be saved by developing a master project chronology initially and maintaining its integrity throughout litigation.

§ 20.15   — Analyzing the Documents

Once the lead counsel has surveyed the documents and developed the factual and legal issues, the attorney is ready to prepare a list of key phrases identifying (for the litigation team) the important factual and legal issues. The next step is to create an indexing system which identifies every document as to its area of importance. The index form should include information for each document as follows: number of the document, source of the document (party and file), date, deposition exhibit number, significance rating (e.g., numerical rating system),[19] description of document (i.e., field memo, letter, meeting minutes), short abstract of document, author, recipients (including copies), and key phrases. As stated earlier, with the inevitable emergence of new issues, parties, and facts the system must be periodically updated.

§ 20.16   Interrogatories

Once the documents are obtained, reviewed, and analyzed, the next phase of discovery usually involves written interrogatories. They should initially be used to fill significant gaps in the written record. A great deal of thought must go into determining the nature and extent of interrogatories to be posed. Most federal courts and several state courts limit the number of interrogatories a litigant can ask (including subparts). The United States District Court for the Eastern District of Virginia, for example, limits the number of interrogatories that one party can serve on another to 30.[20] This limitation cannot be expanded by agreement of counsel; it requires permission of the court for "good cause."

Generally these are utilized to determine basic facts, pertinent parties, personnel and records relating to the construction project, such as the identification of project diaries, internal cost reports, subcontractors, suppliers, key personnel down to the foreman level, photographs, recordings, location of ex-employees, consultants, experts and investigation reports, bids and budgets, profit/loss projections, revisions to estimates, and file indices.

A second set is often designed to define disputed facts, obtain the particulars of vague pleadings, gather damage calculations and generally set the groundwork for depositions. Absent court-imposed limitations in construction cases they are often abusively long and, as a result, evasively answered. The second set should not be a "shotgun", the use of canned interrogatories usually motivate the other side to devote their energy toward the meticulous drafting of non-answers.

---

[19] One system used in a recent case rated documents as follows: ". . . warm, hot, very hot and scorchers." This type of significance rating is cautiously recommended by the authors as documents can grow and diminish in importance throughout a case.

[20] Local Rule 11.1(a) (E.D. Va.).

§ 20.17   Depositions

It is common in construction cases to respond to even the most carefully drafted interrogatories requesting the particulars of damages or delays by reference to Federal Rule of Civil Procedure 33(c). As a result it is only through depositions that the real particulars of defenses, theories of relief and damage calculations can be obtained. As corporations are usually the parties in a construction dispute, pursuant to Rule 30(b)(6) the corporation must designate individuals with knowledge as to specific areas of the case. Hence Rule 30(b)(6) is typically used to elicit competent testimony in the areas of damage calculation bases, the bases for time extension requests, the original estimate, profit/loss projections, and specific general and affirmative defenses.

The number of potential witnesses on a construction case is usually imposing. Therefore, prior to the commencement of substantive depositions the attorney ideally should have developed complete and separate files in the following areas: issue files, witness files, the original set of contract documents, shop drawing history, change order files, scheduling history, RFI logs, cost reports and projections, and estimate and budget files.

It is only through the development of those working files can the important deponents be identified and linked to critical issues. Nevertheless, no matter how prepared one is at the start of depositions on a complex construction case inevitably new "embarrassing" documents will surface; previously understood documents will take on new and often frightful meaning; previously unheard of, but suddenly material, witnesses will emerge. As with interrogatories, certain courts, for example, the United States District Court for the Eastern District of Virginia and Virginia Circuit Courts, limit the number of depositions.

§ 20.18   Requests for Admissions

Like interrogatories the number of requests to admit may be limited by court rule. Nevertheless, some counsel use requests as a supplement to the number of permissible interrogatories. However, their primary benefit is to shorten and simplify the trial process by authenticating documents, determining costs and identifying facts not in dispute. The requests must be short and clear to avoid evasive answers. Even then the requests may have to be supplemented with interrogatories seeking detailed facts supporting the particular response obtained. Note, for example:

> Request: Admit that the electrical drawings (Nos. E-1 through E-25) do not refer to or otherwise depict galvanized rigid steel conduit as part of the electrical distribution system.

Response: Defendant admits the allegations of this request only to the extent supported by the documents cited, which are the best evidence of their contents. The defendant otherwise denies the allegations stated above.

The drafter of the above request has gained nothing from this response. Thus a party may want to supplement this request with the following interrogatory:

If your response to this request for admission is not an unqualified admission: (a) state in detail the reasons for the lack of such an admission; (b) state each and every fact and/or contract provision upon which you base your response; (c) identify each and every contract section, drawing or specification paragraph discussing or related to the requirement that plaintiff provide galvanized rigid steel conduits.

§ 20.19   Discovery Through Negotiations

Every attorney in a major construction case owes his or her client a full exploration of settlement possibilities. Several organizations have emerged in recent years that specialize in providing formalized settlement and/or mediation services to the construction industry.[21] While it is essential that the parties have a basic level of good faith and intent to resolve the dispute by negotiation, a failure to resolve the dispute rarely means that the parties' effort is wasted, for the following reasons:

1. One's approach to an understanding of a complex construction case tends to crystallize while preparing for mediation;

2. A party's decision makers and key witnesses are often all together for the first time while preparing for the mediation. This forces all parties to focus on the theory of the case and the factual issues involved. Thus certain strengths and weaknesses may emerge which may alter one's approach to the case in the event mediation proves futile;

3. Obviously, one can learn a great deal about the other side's view of its own strengths and weaknesses during the mediation process; and

4. The statements or views of the mediator during the process can prove a real eye-opener to the parties' decision makers, who are often isolated from the litigation process until mediation.

---

[21] Some national firms involved in the mediation process for the construction industry are AIS, One Montgomery Suite 2100, San Francisco CA 94101, (415) 788-6253; Center for Public Resources, 366 Madison Avenue 14th Floor, New York NY 10017, (212) 949-6490; Judicate, 1608 Walnut Street Suite 1200, Philadelphia PA 19103, (215) 546-6200; Endispute, 222 South Riverside Drive, Chicago IL 60606, (312) 648-4343; American Arbitration Association, 140 West 51st Street, New York NY 10020, (212) 484-4000; Americord, 512 Nicolette Mall Suite 375, Renaissance Square, Minneapolis MN 55402, (612) 344-1999; and United States Arbitration & Mediation, 83 South King Street Suite 806, Seattle WA 98104, (206) 467-0794.

NONCOMPLIANCE OR OBJECTIONS
TO DISCOVERY

§ 20.20 Motion Practice

Because of the volumes of documents and numerous witnesses involved in construction disputes, a large amount of time and energy is spent on motion practice during the discovery phase. Discovery disputes are generally brought to the courts via two mechanisms: motions for protective orders[22] and motions to compel.[23]

If a party wants to object to some form of discovery, the proper procedure should be, immediately upon receipt of the interrogatories, to contact the other side in writing and to state specific objections, for example, irrelevant, too burdensome, too broad, too numerous, and so forth. Most local rules require a conference between the parties prior to seeking the court's participation in the dispute. In addition, Federal Rule of Civil Procedure 26(f) provides that a court "may direct . . . the parties to appear before it for a conference on the subject of discovery."

The court may also order a discovery conference on the motion of either party so long as the motion includes the following: statement of the issues, a proposed discovery plan, any limitations proposed for discovery, any other proposed discovery orders, and a statement showing that the attorney making the motion has made a good faith effort to reach an agreement with the other side as to a discovery plan.

On large cases it may be necessary to start this process immediately after the parties are at issue. This can be commenced by a letter to opposing counsel outlining a discovery plan suggesting milestone dates as follows: requests for production filed, general depositions for the purpose of identifying documents, interrogatories, deposition periods, requests for admission, audits/finalization of damages, expert identification, expert witness deposition, motions for summary judgment, and pre-trial conference.

Then, if the opposing party is nonresponsive, the assistance of the court can be sought. Some federal courts will automatically issue a schedule immediately after the parties are at issue. These orders are typically computer generated and often contain very limited time periods. The parties should respond to these orders by proposing an alternative schedule to the other side and then seeking a conference pursuant to Federal Rule of Civil Procedure 26(f) if an agreement can not be reached.

---

[22] *See, e.g.*, Fed. R. Civ. P. 26(c).

§ 20.21 Sanctions

Pursuant to Federal Rule of Civil Procedure 37(c), upon failure to comply with court-ordered discovery the court can order sanctions including finding contempt of court, an order establishing facts against the recalcitrant party, preclusion of evidence, an order striking defenses or causes, and the rendering of judgment by default. The court's authority in discovery abuses can be quite broad. In one interesting case, a New Jersey court disqualified an owner's attorney from participating further in a large construction arbitration where that attorney inadvertently came into possession of the other side's privileged documents (and reviewed those documents).[24]

§ 20.22 Duty to Preserve Documents

Unfortunately, questions arise regarding actions by the parties as to the preservation of documents arising out of a construction project. Although a potential litigant has no duty to preserve every document, it must retain what it knows or reasonably should know as it may be evidence relevant to litigation. A court may impose sanctions for prelitigation document destruction and may allow negative inferences to be drawn against the destroying party.

A potential litigant is not under a duty to preserve every document in its possession prior to the commencement of a lawsuit.[25] The test that has been applied concerning the propriety of destroying documents is whether the potential litigant, with knowledge that this lawsuit would be filed, willfully destroyed documents which it knew or should have known would be evidence relevant to this case.[26]

The standard created in *Bowmar* prohibits intentional destruction of documents.[27] Generally, courts will not impose penalties against a party if evidence is destroyed negligently rather than intentionally or in bad faith.[28] When an attorney reviews documents for the purpose of destroying them, however, it is an intentional act. If the attorney is reviewing and destroying documents in good faith, rather than seeking to keep potentially discoverable and relevant documents from future adversaries, there may be no impropriety.

---

[23] Fed R. Civ. P. 37.

[24] Perini Corp. v. Great Bay Hotel & Casino, Civ. Action No. A-3075-8577, slip op. (N.J. App. 1987).

[25] United States v. IBM, 66 F.R.D. 189, 194 (S.D.N.Y. 1974).

[26] Bowmar Instrument Corp. v. Texas Instruments, Inc., 25 Fed. R. Serv. 2d 423, 427 (N.D. Ill. 1977) [hereinafter *Bowmar*]; Struthers Patent Corp. v. Nestle Co., 558 F. Supp. 747, 765 (D.N.J. 1981) [hereinafter *Struthers*].

[27] *Bowmar* at 427.

[28] Universe Tankships, Inc. v. United States, 388 F. Supp. 276, 286 (E.D. Pa. 1974), *aff'd*, 528 F.2d 731 (3d Cir. 1975) [hereinafter *Universe*]; Vick v. Texas Employment Comm'n, 514 F.2d 734, 737 (5th Cir. 1975) [hereinafter *Vick*].

Documents that are destroyed as a matter of routine maintenance or according to a practice of document disposal are considered to be destroyed in good faith.[29] However, be aware that many construction contracts have document retention provisions that require a contractor to maintain certain types of documents for a period of time.

The Rules of Professional Conduct provide, "A lawyer shall not . . . unlawfully obstruct another party's access to evidence or unlawfully alter, destroy or conceal a document or other material having potential evidentiary value or assist another person to do any such act. . . ."[30]

This rule prohibits document destruction that is unlawful. Some states make destruction of evidence a misdemeanor of the second degree when a person "alters, destroys, conceals or removes any record, document or thing with intent to impair its verity or availability" in any official proceeding or investigation which the person believes is pending or about to be instituted.[31]

As previously stated, Federal Rule of Civil Procedure 37(d) authorizes sanctions for failure to cooperate only during discovery. However, document destruction before discovery and prior to the commencement of a lawsuit can also be sanctioned. Federal courts have held that they have inherent authority to sanction litigants for prelitigation destruction of evidence.[32] This inherent authority is an exercise of the court's power to preserve and protect its jurisdiction and the integrity of proceedings before it.[33]

Courts have applied a variety of sanctions to parties who have wrongfully destroyed relevant documents. In *Radiation Survivors,* the defendants were required to pay the plaintiff's costs and fees and $15,000 to the court for expenditure of unnecessary time and resources.[34] There have been several cases of prelitigation destruction of documents that did not result in sanctions. In *Bowmar,* the court found that it had not been clearly proven that the legal department was aware of pending litigation at the time the evidence was destroyed. Although there had been rumors of litigation, this did not prove the legal department had actual knowledge.[35]

---

[29] *Vick* at 737.

[30] *E.g.,* Pa. Rules of Professional Conduct Rule 3.4 (1988).

[31] *See, e.g.,* 18 Pa. Const. Stat. Ann. § 4910(1) (Purdon 1983).

[32] Wm. T. Thompson Co. v. General Nutrition Corp., 593 F. Supp. 1443 (C.D. Cal. 1984) [hereinafter *Thompson*]; *Bowmar,* 25 Fed. R. Serv. 2d 423; National Ass'n of Radiation Survivors v. Turnage, 115 F.R.D. 543 (N.D. Cal. 1987) [hereinafter *Radiation Survivors*].

[33] *Radiation Survivors* at 554.

[34] *Id.* at 558-59. *See also Thompson,* 593 F. Supp. at 1456 (imposing monetary sanctions and "ultimate" sanction of default judgment and dismissal).

[35] 25 Fed. R. Serv. 2d 423. *See also Struthers,* 558 F. Supp. at 766 (denying sanction when no injury to opposing party and other documents were sufficient); Independent Petrochemical Corp. v. Aetna Casualty & Sur. Co., 654 F. Supp. 1334, 1364 (D.D.C. 1986) (denying sanctions when opposing party failed to show relevant documents willfully destroyed and duplicates not in existence).

Another sanction imposed by courts is the negative inference rule.[36] Bad faith destruction of a document gives rise to a strong inference that it would have been unfavorable to the destroying party.[37] Some courts have not required a showing of bad faith before drawing this inference against the destroying party.[38]

§ 20.23 Attorney Liability

A litigant will probably not escape sanctions or negative inferences by claiming that its attorney was responsible for document destruction or that evidence was destroyed upon the attorney's advice.[39] The attorney may subject himself or herself to tort liability to the client or sanctions from the bar association including reprimands, suspension or disbarment.[40] Any decision to destroy documents should be made only after considering the possibility of such sanctions.

As one court described the obligation of counsel in such matters:

> The heart of the legal profession is sustained with the blood of ethical conduct. If public confidence in the legal profession is to be maintained, the lawyer's conduct must be at the highest ethical level. Such a level precludes the partisan type evaluation of . . . privileges and protections.[41]

DEFENSIVE DISCOVERY

§ 20.24 General Considerations

Defending against your adversary's discovery plan is largely an exercise in damage control. In responding to discovery requests, one must remember that

---

[36] Coates v. Johnson & Johnson, 756 F.2d 524 (7th Cir. 1985).

[37] *Id.* at 551. *See also Vick,* 514 F.2d 734, 737 (stating in dicta that destruction before request for the documents may weigh against negative inference); Haas v. Kasnot, 371 Pa. 580, 92 A.2d 580 (1952) (stating inference may be drawn by jury against party failing to produce witness); Hertz Corp. v. Hardy, 197 Pa. Super. 466, 178 A.2d 833 (1962) (rule not invoked unless the parties' interests would be furthered by production of evidence).

[38] NationWide Check Corp. v. Forest Hill Dist., Inc., 692 F.2d 214 (1st Cir. 1982). *But see, Universe,* 388 F. Supp. 276, 286 (finding government negligence in failing to preserve evidence not enough to draw inference).

[39] Berkey Photo, Inc. v. Eastman Kodak Co., 603 F.2d 263 (2d Cir. 1979) (prior attorney's concealment of document a factor in determining scope of permissible cross examination).

[40] *See, e.g.,* Bar Ass'n v. Cassaro, 61 Ohio St. 2d 62, 399 N.E. 2d 545 (1980).

[41] Perini Corp. v. Great Bay Hotel & Casino, Civ. Action No. A-3075-8577, slip op. (N.J. App. 1987).

civil discovery under the Federal Rules is broad.[42] The applicable Federal Rules are liberally construed to foster a full disclosure of the facts and opinions underlying each party's case.[43]

As previously stated, the sanctions under Federal Rule of Civil Procedure 37 (for parties) and Rule 45 (for nonparties) can be severe for providing incomplete or evasive responses, refusing to respond, failing to appear for deposition, or failing to admit a matter requested under Rule 36. The sanctions can include an award of the attorneys' fees and costs of bringing a motion to compel, an order designating that certain facts shall be taken as established, an order that prohibits the disobedient party from supporting or opposing certain claims, or an order that strikes all or part of the pleadings.

Therefore, the risks in evading your adversary's discovery must be carefully considered in light of the federal courts' increased willingness to sanction violations of the discovery rules. Most courts' local rules now require that counsel first meet to resolve in good faith any objections to discovery.[44] Unresolved disputes may then be brought before the court on a motion to compel or for a protective order. As a practical matter the burden is usually on the defending party to overcome a presumption that the requested information is discoverable. It is a truism that judges dislike discovery disputes. An obstructionist party will quickly alienate the court.

In defending against your opposition's discovery, the better practice is to make complete disclosures of the information that has been fairly requested. However, the Federal Rules do not require that you be a volunteer or fill in the gaps of your opponent's discovery request. Simply stated, if your adversary did not pose an obvious interrogatory or request a plainly relevant document, you are not obligated to disclose that information. As discussed herein, under the Federal Rules and local rules, there are some limitations on your opponent's discovery of the facts and opinions underlying your case. Through well-founded objections, assertions of valid privileges, and early preparation, one can "control the damage."

§ 20.25   Interrogatories: When and How to Object

Objections to interrogatories, signed by counsel, must be made within the time specified by the Rules.[45] However, local rules can often shorten the time to

---

[42] *See* Fed. R. Civ. P. 26(b)(1).

[43] *See* Blankenship v. Hearst Corp., 519 F.2d 418 (8th Cir. 1975).

[44] *See* Local Rule 190-1(f)(2) (D. Nev.).

[45] *See, e.g.,* Fed. R. Civ. P. 33(a).

object.[46] Failure to object timely can constitute a waiver of all objections, including a valid privilege.[47]

Objections should be applied to specific interrogatories. General objections to definitions and instructions accompanying the interrogatories are appropriate. However, "catch-all" objections to all interrogatories may result in a waiver of all objections.[48]

A court's local rules often place limitations on the number of interrogatories, including subparts, your adversary is allowed.[49] Typically, such limitations are strictly enforced.

Under the Federal Rules and the decisional case law, the following are *valid* objections to interrogatories as well as to other forms of discovery such as requests for documents and depositions:

1. Discovery sought is unreasonably cumulative or duplicative

2. Discovery sought is obtainable from another source that is readily available, and it is equally or less burdensome for your opponent to obtain that information

3. Discovery sought is unduly burdensome or expensive

4. Discovery sought is not admissible evidence and is not reasonably calculated to lead to admissible evidence

5. Discovery request violates an existing or developing rule of law

6. Discovery request is motivated by an improper purpose (harassment, delay, embarrassment).

7. The requesting party has already had ample opportunity to discover the information;

8. Discovery sought is irrelevant and immaterial[50]

9. Discovery request is overly broad, vague or ambiguous

10. Discovery sought calls for a conclusion of law or counsel's theory of the case

11. Discovery request seeks information from a non-testifying expert or consultant retained by counsel

12. Discovery seeks identification of witnesses and exhibits for trial[51]

---

[46] *See, e.g.,* Local Rule 11.1(D) (E.D. Va.) (fifteen days).

[47] *See* Fonsecu v. Regan, 98 F.R.D. 694, 701 (E.D.N.Y. 1983).

[48] *See In re* Folding Carton Antitrust Litig., 83 F.R.D. 260, 264 (N.D. Ill. 1979).

[49] *See, e.g.,* Local Rule 190-1(c) (D. Nev.) (forty interrogatories including subparts) and Local Rule 11.1(A) (E.D. Va.) (thirty interrogatories including subparts).

[50] Although Fed R. Civ. P. 26 does not specifically state irrelevancy as grounds for objection, it does use "relevant" as a test in defining the scope of permissible discovery. As a practical matter, discovery is seldom prohibited solely on this basis. *See* Buffington v. Gillette Co., 101 F.R.D. 400 (W.D. Okla. 1980). Moreover, the burden is generally on the objecting party to demonstrate irrelevancy. *See* Home Ins. Co. v. Bellenger Corp., 74 F.R.D. 93 (N.D. Ga. 1977).

[51] *See* E.E.O.C. v. Metropolitan Museum of Art, 80 F.R.D. 317, 319 (S.D.N.Y. 1978).

13.   Discovery sought is protected by a recognized privilege or the attorney work product immunity.

The following are *invalid* objections to discovery:

1.   Discovery sought calls for hearsay
2.   Discovery sought is inadmissible in evidence
3.   Discovery request calls for an opinion or contention[52]
4.   Best evidence rule
5.   Discovery request will require an investigation[53]
6.   Discovery request seeks proprietary or sensitive business information.[54]

By far the most used, abused and litigated objection to interrogatories and other discovery is that of privilege and attorney work product. It is beyond the scope of this chapter to discuss all the nuances of these privileges. Excellent treatises and law review articles are readily available.[55] However, the basic considerations are set forth below.

The most commonly involved privilege is attorney-client communication. The privilege applies to communications, and belongs to the client but is invoked by the attorney. The privilege can also be extended to unprivileged information if its disclosure would necessarily reveal confidential communications.[56] Similarly, the privilege extends to representatives of the attorney and the client.[57] The privilege can be waived if the communication is made in the presence of or subsequently disclosed to a third person.[58]

---

[52] However, Fed. R. Civ. P. 33 provides that the court may order that such an interrogatory need not be answered until after completion of discovery or the pretrial conference.

[53] A party's obligation to conduct research to answer an interrogatory is decided on a case-by-case basis. Generally, an interrogatory that would require information not in a party's possession or control is objectionable. *See* La Chemise La Coste v. Alligator Co., 60 F.R.D. 164, 171 (D. Del. 1973). Otherwise, the interrogatory is usually valid. *See* Flour Mills of Am. v. D.F. Pace, 75 F.R.D. 676, 680-81 (E.D. Okla. 1977) [hereinafter *Flour Mills*].

[54] Assuming the information requested is relevant and not privileged, discovery cannot be resisted merely on grounds that the information is proprietary or sensitive. In typical construction claims, damages are often calculated on bid information and include claims for profit, extended home office overhead, and loss of capital. As a result, a party's bidding documents and techniques are fair game for discovery. Likewise, a party's corporate overhead accounts, profit/loss statements, return on investments information, loans, and the like are usually discoverable. For particularly sensitive data, one can request the court to "seal" the information to prevent further dissemination.

[55] Recommended are J. Weinstein & M. Berger, Weinstein's Evidence ¶¶ 501-513 (1986) and Developments in the Law, *Privileged Communications*, 98 Harv. L. Rev. 1450-1666 (1985).

[56] *See* Baird v. Koener, 279 F.2d 623, 627 (9th. Cir. 1960).

[57] *See In re* LTV Security Litig., 89 F.R.D. 595 (N.D. Tex. 1981).

[58] *See generally,* Marcus, *The Perils of Privilege: Waiver and the Litigator,* 84 Mich. L. Rev. 1605 (1986).

When there is a partial waiver, often all other related communications become discoverable.[59] Likewise, selective disclosure has the same result.[60] An inadvertent disclosure may or may not lead to a waiver depending upon the factual circumstances and the applicable law.[61] Documents pre-existing the privilege do not become privileged when subsequently provided to the attorney.[62]

A recent area of controversy is the application of the privilege to communications between in-house legal counsel and other corporate employees. The leading case is *Upjohn Co. v. United States*,[63] which sets forth a test that considers the purpose and circumstances surrounding the communication and the scope of its dissemination. The privilege in a corporate setting appears to cover both current and former employees who meet the *Upjohn* test.[64] In-house counsel should set up advance written procedures to identify and protect privileged communications. Such communications should be maintained in legal files in the custody of counsel, clearly marked as privileged, and not randomly accessible.

Related to the attorney-client privilege is the attorney work product immunity. This immunity traces its origins to *Hickman v. Taylor*[65] and has been largely codified in Federal Rule of Civil Procedure 26(b)(3).[66] The essence of the immunity is to protect from discovery the attorney's mental impressions, opinions and theories of the case. Also protected are an attorney's notes of interviews with witnesses and consulting experts and any investigations. The communications and work papers of any experts or consultants made at the direction of counsel are also protected provided that such expert is not designated as a testifying expert.

The immunity also extends to the party and its representatives as to any materials prepared in anticipation of litigation or for trial.[67] To strengthen this immunity, it is advisable that investigations or materials prepared by the party be undertaken at the request and under the direction of an attorney.

When an objection will likely be tested before the court by your adversary, it is often advantageous to initiate the issue through a motion for a protective order.[68] By so doing, the defending party will be the one who first frames the issue and makes its argument. Generally, this tactic puts the objecting party in the strongest posture before the court.

---

[59] *See* United States v. Tunes, 696 F.2d 1069, 1672 (4th Cir. 1982).

[60] *Id.*

[61] *See generally* Note, *Inadvertent Disclosure of Documents Subject to the Attorney-Client Privilege,* 82 Mich. L. Rev. 598 (1983).

[62] *See* Fisher v. United States, 425 U.S. 391, 403-05 (1976).

[63] 449 U.S. 383, 395-96 (1981).

[64] *Id.* at 394 n.3, 397 n.6.

[65] 329 U.S. 495 (1947).

[66] *See generally* Special Project, *The Work Product Doctrine,* 68 Cornell L. Rev. 760 (1983).

[67] Fed. R. Civ. P. 26(b)(3).

[68] *See* Fed. R. Civ. P. 26(c).

§ 20.26   —Preparation of Responses

Upon receipt of the opponent's interrogatories, the attorney should promptly send them to the client. This is necessary, if for no other reason, because the client must sign the responses to those interrogatories.[69] As a more practical matter, the issues raised in complex construction litigation will undoubtedly require substantial assistance and information from the client's employees in order to respond adequately to the interrogatories. In transmitting the interrogatories, the attorney should specifically identify questions which the client should focus on and the type of information which must be accumulated.

Also, if the attorney intends to object to certain interrogatories, the client should be informed so as to avoid wasting resources. Time is of the essence because a party has only thirty days, or forty-five days if interrogatories are served with the complaint, to respond.[70] Recently, courts have become increasingly stingy with time extensions.

It is advisable for the client to designate one capable employee with some knowledge of the project as its liaison with the attorney. Although clients initially resist committing such a person, it will reduce legal costs and contribute to a better overall discovery plan. The liaison should assist the attorney in ensuring that all the requested information which is discoverable has been identified and accumulated from the various sources within the company.

Since a party is obligated to furnish all information available to it, current and former employees must be contacted.[71] Sometimes research is necessary in order to answer an interrogatory. Generally, the research must be done if it relates to facts alleged in the pleadings or if the defending party would have to do the research to prepare its case.[72]

In complex construction cases, attorneys should be mindful of the option of producing business records which contain the information requested by an interrogatory.[73] Simply stated, where the answer to an interrogatory can be ascertained from the business records of a party (such as daily inspection reports, equipment logs, certified payrolls, voluminous cost records, and the like) and the burden of ascertaining the answer is substantially the same, the records can be produced in lieu of a lengthy answer. This option is particularly attractive since it substantially reduces the defending party's efforts and the documents will likely be produced anyway pursuant to a request for production.

While the range of interrogatories are as varied as construction projects, some questions are common to all cases. Considerations in responding to those types

---

[69] Fed. R. Civ. P. 33(a).

[70] Fed. R. Civ. P. 33(c).

[71] *See* General Dynamics Corp. v. Selb Mfg. Co., 481 F.2d 1204, 1210-11 (8th Cir. 1973).

[72] *See Flour Mills*, 75 F.R.D. 676.

[73] Fed. R. Civ. P. 33(c).

of interrogatories are discussed below. For example, in responding to an interrogatory to identify all persons with personal knowledge, the attorney should identify any person whose testimony may be relied upon. However, an attorney should be cautious in identifying persons with superficial knowledge because their identification will only encourage unnecessary depositions. Also, an attorney is not obligated to ascertain persons who may have personal knowledge who are not current or former employees or otherwise subject to the control of the client.

In response to interrogatories to identify documents or conversations, the same considerations apply. If the attorney knows that a particular document or conversation will be relied upon at trial, it should be identified. With respect to conversations, it is often sufficient to respond that, absent a written record, the conversations are too numerous to identify.

An interrogatory to identify specific elements of damages or the manner in which they were calculated requires particularly close scrutiny. A written response to this type of interrogatory is advisable rather than solely relying on the option of producing the cost records under Federal Rule of Civil Procedure 33(c). Often the response necessarily involves the legal theories on which the damages are based. Failure to make an adequate response or the making of an erroneous response to a damage interrogatory can result in a loss of recovery.

Another common interrogatory which requires careful consideration is one which applies facts to contentions of law. An example is an interrogatory that asks the party to identify all facts on which it bases its contention that there was a constructive acceleration. The contention interrogatory is permissible under Federal Rule of Civil Procedure 33(b). The attorney's first response should be to delay an answer until after the completion of discovery or until the pretrial conference, as allowed under Federal Rule of Civil Procedure 33(b). This will enable the attorney to see how the case progresses before responding. When a response is drafted, the attorney must ensure that it does not incorporate any inadvertent admission or inconsistent facts. An answer which is conclusive and self-serving will usually guarantee that your opponent will never use it to your detriment.

§ 20.27 Requests for Production of Documents

Similar to interrogatories, under Federal Rule of Civil Procedure 34 your adversary is entitled to discover any document or other tangible thing within the scope of Rule 26(b) that is in your custody or control. The discovery is made by a written request for the production of the document. A response must be made within thirty days, or forty-five days if the request is served with a complaint. Objections which may be interposed to a request for production are essentially the same as for interrogatories.

§ 20.28   — Responding to a Request

As with interrogatories, upon receipt of an adversary's request for production, the attorney should determine which requests are objectionable on their face and advise the client accordingly. In some instances, the attorney must consult with the client to determine whether a request is objectionable. To illustrate, the client's input is necessary to determine if a request is overly burdensome, requires disclosure of sensitive business documents, or encompasses a prior consultant's work done in anticipation of litigation. If you know that an objection to a particular request will be tested, a preemptive motion for a protective order pursuant to Rule 26(c) is usually advisable.

The client's liaison should coordinate the effort to identify and accumulate all the records responsive to the requests which are in the client's possession, custody or control. This would include records retained by a subsidiary company, records provided to a consultant or expert, and perhaps records retained by a subcontractor if the subcontract entitles the party to those records.

Once the records have been accumulated, the attorney must review them to ensure that no privileged documents, work product, or other undiscoverable documents have been inadvertently included. An internal record should be kept that identifies documents which are responsive to a request, but that have been withheld under an objection. Should the objection be tested by your adversary, a description sufficient to identify the withheld documents will usually be required.

A written response to each of your opponent's requests for production is required.[74] The response should note any objections and state whether the requested documents are to be produced for inspection. On construction projects, the responsive documents are typically voluminous. Therefore, the common practice for physically producing the documents is to allow your opponent's counsel to inspect them at a central location and identify the documents to be copied.

Under Federal Rule of Civil Procedure 34(b), the documents must be produced as they are kept in the usual course of business or must be organized to correspond to the requests. This rule was intended to curtail past practices of mixing-up the files to confuse and frustrate the adversary's inspection or to obscure damaging documents. Nonetheless, the manner in which documents are produced can impact the outcome of a case, particularly if your adversary is not diligent. For example, the production of a voluminous original file which contains irrelevant material is permissible even though it may obscure the relevant documents.

Also, if the organization of the original files would give your adversary new insight to the case, these files should be reorganized to correspond to the

---

[74] Fed. R. Civ. P. 34(b).

requests. For example, on construction projects separate files are often maintained on specific claims, potential claims, and backcharges against subcontractors. Production of these files in their original condition may only fuel your opponent's case.

When producing the documents identified by your adversary, you should keep an exact "shadow" copy for your records. Also, each page produced should be stamped with a serial number to avoid later disputes as to whether the documents identified for copying were actually provided.

§ 20.29 Depositions: Preparing the Witness

The most effective defense to your opponent's discovery depositions is a well-prepared, knowledgeable witness. To prepare a witness properly, counsel must first anticipate the purposes for which the deposition is being taken. In construction litigation, a particular witness's personal knowledge will typically apply to one or more of the claims. Counsel should preliminarily interview the witness to determine the exact scope of his or her personal knowledge and involvement in the project. Thereafter, the witness should be prepared for the deposition procedures and the substance of his testimony.

As to deposition procedures, it should be explained to the witness that his obligation is to testify truthfully as to his personal knowledge of the facts in response to the questions by his adversary. The witness is not obligated to guess, speculate or remember every fact. The witness should be informed as to the setting of a deposition and generally the manner in which it will proceed. Set forth below are considerations the defending attorney should make a witness aware of in answering questions:

Always answer truthfully

Understand the question asked. If not, ask that it be restated

Answer only the question asked. Do not volunteer or anticipate the next question

Recognize inaccurate and misleading assumptions in the question

Take time in answering. The transcript does not reflect pauses

If in doubt on a matter, consult your attorney

If a document is needed to answer more accurately and fully, state so

If you do not know the answer, or cannot remember, state so

Answer based only on your personal knowledge

Do not argue or spar with the examining attorney

Remain calm, unemotional, and civil

Allow your attorney time to state objections for the record.

After the witness is prepared for the procedural aspects, he must be prepared for his substantive testimony. The defending attorney must balance the need to prepare the witness on the issues and facts pertaining to his testimony against the risks of over preparing. A witness who is given too much material ancillary to his testimony is more likely to confuse his personal and acquired (hearsay) knowledge and to play lawyer. With that consideration in mind, the witness should be given an overview of the basic theories and issues of the case.

For the specific areas of his testimony, the witness will require a more detailed preparation. A notebook of all documents that the witness wrote or received should be assembled for his review. Any documents identified as damaging or troublesome should be discussed in detail to determine the witness's response. Determine whether the witness has any specific areas of concern or negative views of his involvement in the project. It is not unusual for some witnesses to feel guilt or responsibility for an unsuccessful project even though there may be no factual basis for that feeling. Provide the witness with deposition transcripts, interrogatory answers, and other discovery materials related to his substantive testimony. Finally, test the witness with a mock deposition.

§ 20.30   —Objections

Before the deposition even begins, the defending attorney may be able to limit or prevent the inquiry through timely objections. For example, the notice of deposition may be materially defective. It may request the production of a party's documents in less than the time allowed under Federal Rule of Civil Procedure 34(c).[75] Also, although a notice of deposition has the effect of a subpoena on a party, former employees and present employees who are not officers must be properly subpoenaed.

If a subpoena is issued, it must conform to the requirements for notice and service.[76] If the deposition will likely cover matters protected by a valid objection or privilege, the defending attorney would be wise to obtain a protective order limiting the scope of the inquiry. Also, local rules may place limitations on the number of depositions allowed.[77]

Once the deposition actually begins, the defending attorney's primary weapon is the timely objection. The objections that can be properly made are the same as at trial. The principal objections are typically lack of foundation, hearsay and speculation. Under Federal Rule of Civil Procedure 32(d)(3)(B) objections are waived unless seasonably made during the deposition.

---

[75] *See* Fed. R. Civ. P. 30(b)(5).

[76] *See* Fed. R. Civ. P. 45(c) and (d).

[77] Local Rule 11.1(B) (E.D. Va.) (five non-party depositions).

By making appropriate objections, the defending attorney accomplishes several goals: the admissible deposition record is limited to the witness's personal knowledge; the witness is alerted[78] to defects, pitfalls and erroneous assumptions in the question before answering; examining attorneys tend to become more conservative when confronted by valid objections; and the witness will become more relaxed and confident if he believes he has an advocate in the room. If it becomes apparent during the deposition that it is being taken in bad faith, for an improper purpose, or the adversary's conduct is objectionable, the defending attorney can move to terminate or limit the deposition.[79]

Depositions of fact witnesses in complex construction cases typically involve large numbers of documents. Where appropriate, the defending attorney should: (1) ensure that the record clearly identifies the specific document the witness is testifying about; (2) note that a certain document is needed for the witness to provide a more accurate answer; (3) clarify that the witness has no personal knowledge regarding a particular document; and (4) insist that the examining attorney state the purpose for which the document is being used. Most of the pitfalls inherent in document questions can be avoided by careful preparation.

On occasion, even the best prepared witness can get into some trouble. However, consultation between the witness and defending attorney should be kept to a minimum. If there is no question pending, it is appropriate to confer with the witness. Consultation while a question is pending will look like coaching and should be avoided if possible. If the witness is getting into more serious trouble, initiate a short recess. Unless the witness is particularly strong, the defending attorney should adjourn the deposition at the end of the normal work day. Witnesses invariably become more mentally fatigued, and subject to confusion, as the evening progresses.

§ 20.31   —Memory of Witnesses

The memory of the witness will, to an extent, be stimulated by the pre-deposition preparation. Nonetheless, some witnesses find it easier to take refuge by saying, "I cannot remember," than to give a substantive answer. The defending attorney's concern will turn on the extent to which he or she will rely on that witness at trial. If the witness will not be used at trial, a memory loss only results in a useless deposition for your adversary. On the other hand, a witness who will be relied upon risks losing credibility if his memory returns just in time for the trial. Also, a good recollection of the facts by key witnesses may assist in promoting a settlement or to oppose a future depositive motion.

---

[78] If the principal purpose of an objection is to forewarn the witness, the defending attorney should provide some elaboration rather than merely stating, "lack of foundation."

[79] *See* Fed. R. Civ. P. 30(d).

§ 20.32   — Designating Witnesses

Under Federal Rule of Civil Procedure 30(b)(6), your adversary can make the company designate witnesses to testify on specific subjects. While there is little case law defining the Rule 30(b)(6) deponent's obligations, there is some authority that, once named, the representative is responsible for answering all questions regarding the designated subject.[80]

In defending a Rule 30(b)(6) deposition, the prudent response is to designate your primary witness for that subject area and to ensure that the witness is thoroughly prepared. While a Rule 30(b)(6) notice shifts the burden to the defending attorney to identify his primary spokesperson, it also gives him more ability to control his adversary's inquiry.

§ 20.33   — Requests for Admissions

When faced with requests for admissions under Federal Rule of Civil Procedure 36, the defending attorney's primary consideration should be the severe consequences of failing to respond properly. These consequences are: an unanswered request is deemed admitted; a defective answer or objection may be taken as admitted at trial; and an improper denial may result in an assessment of attorney fees under Federal Rule of Civil Procedure 37(c).[81] Although the burden is on the requesting party to demonstrate the insufficiency of the answers and objections, Rule 36 places stringent requirements on the answering party. In short, there is no safety in clever answers and borderline objections.

In responding to requests for admissions, the defending attorney should consider the following:

Admit any requests where the subject matter is not in issue

Explain and qualify any admission or denial where necessary

Respond to every sub-part of a request

If only part of a request is objectionable, answer the rest

Even objectionable requests should be answered on alternative grounds if possible

Reasonable inquiry must be made to determine the truth or falsity of the subject matter

If a request contains undisputed facts and inferences drawn from those facts, admit the facts and deny the inferences.

---

[80] *See* Mitsui & Co. (U.S.A.) v. Puerto Rico Water Resources Auth., 93 F.R.D. 62 (D.P.R. 1981).

[81] *See* Fed. R. Civ. P. 36(a).

§ 20.34   —Duty to Supplement

A typical instruction accompanying discovery requests is that they are continuing in nature. The defending attorney should always object to this instruction. Generally, under Federal Rule of Civil Procedure 26(e) a party "is under no duty to supplement the response" with information acquired later, provided the response was complete when made. However, there are some exceptions to the general rule of no duty to supplement. A party must seasonably[82] supplement a response: (1) to questions asking the identity of fact and expert witnesses; (2) when he obtains information that the response was inaccurate when made; and (3) when he obtains information that the response, though true when made, is no longer true and that a failure to supplement would be a knowing concealment.

As a practical matter, the defending attorney should supplement discovery responses for newly obtained evidence if he intends to use it at trial and if a discovery request arguably seeks that information.

EXPERT DISCOVERY

§ 20.35   Who Is an Expert?

Major construction litigation necessarily requires reliance on expert witnesses. Often, expert testimony is the primary proof to establish a differing site condition, a loss of labor efficiency, the productivity of equipment and work crews, and damages. Nearly every case involves at least one expert on each side and most cases require multiple experts. The attorney's reliance on the expert extends beyond the trial testimony. Experts typically assist the attorney in investigating and evaluating the bases of a particular claim, to prepare the claim, and to prepare for affirmative and defensive discovery.

Generally, any person who will give technical or specialized opinion testimony or assistance is considered an expert, as opposed to a fact witness. Experts fall into three general categories: testifying experts, nontestifying experts retained in anticipation of litigation, and nontestifying experts not retained in anticipation of litigation.

Discovery of these experts is now controlled by Rule 26(b)(4) and is discussed in more detail below. The importance of discovering the testifying expert's opinions and the bases for them is particularly great considering the Federal Rules of Evidence. Under Rule 702, it is relatively easy to qualify someone as an expert provided the person has specialized knowledge that will assist the finder of fact. Since specialized knowledge can be obtained through work experience,

---

[82] The duty is triggered when the new information is discovered and not when the attorney realized its significance.

the spectrum of experts in a construction case is almost unlimited. Rule 703 allows an expert to base his opinion on information that is not admissible provided that it is of the type reasonably relied upon in the field. Under Rule 704, the expert can testify on the ultimate issue in the case. Under Rule 705, the expert does not have to reveal the basis for his opinion on direct examination.

As discussed below, discovery of experts in federal court is fairly restrictive. By comparison many state courts, such as California,[83] allow depositions and disclosure of reports as a matter of discovery right. Similarly, some federal district courts' local rules[84] and standard pretrial orders allow more discovery than that initially permitted by Federal Rule of Civil Procedure 26(b)(4).

§ 20.36   Discovery of Nontestifying Experts

Under Federal Rule of Civil Procedure 26(b)(4)(B), discovery of a nontestifying expert retained "in anticipation of litigation or preparation for trial" is restricted. The party seeking discovery must demonstrate exceptional circumstances which make it impractical for them to obtain the facts and opinions by other means. The underlying principle is one of basic fairness. One party will not be allowed to build its case based on the other party's work. The two key tests are whether the expert was retained in anticipation of litigation or exceptional circumstances exist.

Whether the nontestifying expert was retained in anticipation of litigation is a question of fact for the judge to decide.[85] Factors considered in determining whether an expert was retained in anticipation of litigation include: (1) circumstances surrounding the initial engagement, (2) the scope of the experts' review, (3) the duration of the relationship to the party or attorney, and (4) the terms of the engagement.

There are some common situations where experts are prone to fail this test. First, experts who were merely occurrence observers during the events are fully subject to discovery. For example, a soils engineer who happens to observe subsoils conditions during excavation is subject to discovery like any other ordinary witness.

Second, regular company employees who are assigned to provide expertise in the initial investigation or development of claims are also suspect.[86] Third, work by outside claims consultants can be discovered if litigation was not reasonably anticipated at the time it was undertaken. For example, a productivity expert who studies work crew performance to determine whether a meritorious loss of

---

[83] *See* Cal. Civ. Proc. Code ¶¶ 2034(g) and (i).

[84] *See* Local Rule 9.4.6. (C.D. Cal.).

[85] *See* Healy v. Counts, 100 F.R.D. 493, 496 (D. Colo. 1984).

[86] *See* Kansas-Nebraska Natural Gas Co. v. Marathon Oil Co., 109 F.R.D. 12, 16 (D. Neb. 1985); Virginia Elec. & Power Co. v. Sun Shipbuilding & Dry Dock Co., 68 F.R.D. 397 (E.D. Va. 1975).

efficiency claim exists is probably subject to discovery. The most effective manner to protect expert work related to the preliminary analyses and claim development is to conduct those efforts through outside counsel.

Even an expert within the scope of Federal Rule of Civil Procedure 26(b)(4)(B) can be discovered if exceptional circumstances exist. Complex construction claims can present such circumstances. For example, the high cost to duplicate the discovery where a party has limited resources can be an exceptional circumstance.[87] To illustrate, a major and costly subsurface investigation undertaken by an expert using exotic equipment might be discoverable.

As another example, the unavailability of an object subsequent to an expert's analysis can be an exceptional circumstance. To illustrate, if a nontestifying expert examines a piece of equipment whose performance is in dispute (tunneling devices, dredges, and so forth) and that equipment is then rebuilt or altered on the expert's recommendation, the expert's evaluation is probably discoverable. Similarly, in a differing site conditions case, if subsurface conditions have been disturbed (that is, excavated), a nontestifying expert's prior analysis is likely to be discoverable.

An expert protected by Federal Rule of Civil Procedure 26(b)(4)(B) can be quite useful and even essential to the attorney. The following are some of the advantages to retaining such experts:

1. Their work is usually protected from discovery
2. They can assist the attorney in meeting the reasonable inquiry required under Federal Rule of Civil Procedure 11
3. They can evaluate technical documents obtained from the client and through discovery
4. They can assist in framing discovery requests and preparing for depositions of opposing experts
5. They can explore creative theories and analyses without risk of disclosure
6. They can be more of an advocate than a testifying expert
7. They can be present at deposition and trial because they are not subject to Federal Rule of Evidence 615 (sequestration of witnesses).

§ 20.37 Discovery of Testifying Experts

Under Federal Rule of Civil Procedure 26(b)(4)(A)(i), some limited discovery of testifying experts is permitted. Often, attorneys assume that full civil discovery is allowed, including production of the expert's work papers and depositions. However, Rule 26(b)(4)(A)(i) allows, as a matter of right, only the following

---

[87] *See In re* Agent Orange Prod. Liab. Litig., 105 F.R.D. 577, 581 (E.D.N.Y. 1985).

inquiry through written interrogatories: (1) the identity[88] of each expert; (2) the subject matter on which he is expected to testify; (3) the substance of the facts and opinions on which he is expected to testify; and (4) a summary of the grounds for each opinion.

Once the interrogatories have been answered,[89] a party can then move for further discovery pursuant to Rule 26(b)(4)(A)(ii). Typically, the attorney should request leave to serve a request for production of documents to obtain all the expert's work papers and to depose the expert.

The test of whether further discovery will be allowed is in the court's discretion and varies with jurisdictions. Some courts apply the substantial need test under Federal Rule of Civil Procedure 26(b)(3).[90] Other courts apply the Rule 34 standard.[91] The expert's costs to prepare for and attend a deposition are assessed to the requesting party.[92] As a practical matter, an attorney who is considering opposing further discovery of his expert should consider his need to discover fully the opposition's expert. Often, the most efficient method is a stipulation between counsel as to the scope of further expert discovery.[93]

If further discovery is allowed by local rule, court order, or stipulation, the following areas should be thoroughly probed:

Investigate the expert's qualifications. Often a party will attempt to minimize the number of trial experts by "stretching" one expert's expertise into other areas

Examine the basis of the expert's engagement including his fee

Identify his testimony on similar issues in other cases

Identify all publications by the expert

Identify all the facts and materials provided to the expert by the opposing party

Identify all notes, files, reports and other work papers generated by the expert

Identify all codes, statutes or industry standards relied upon by the expert

Determine all the facts, documents and other circumstances which form the bases for each separate opinion by the expert

Identify all persons that the expert consulted in forming his opinion

Determine whether and when the expert personally inspected the jobsite or condition at issue.

---

[88] The expert's identity includes its qualifications. *See* Clark v. General Motors Corp., 20 F.R. Serv. 2d 679 (D. Mass. 1975).

[89] Interrogatories under Rule 26(b)(4)(A)(i) are a condition precedent to a request for further discovery. United States v. IBM, 72 F.R.D. 78, 81 (S.D.N.Y. 1976).

[90] *See* Wilson v. Resnick, 51 F.R.D. 510 (E.D. Pa. 1970).

[91] *See* Quadrini v. Sikorsky Aircraft Div., 74 F.R.D. 594, 595 (D. Conn. 1977).

[92] Fed. R. Civ. P. 26(b)(4)(C).

[93] *See* Fed. R. Civ. P. 29.

§ 20.38   Impeachment of the Trial Expert

The primary purpose of further discovery under Federal Rule of Civil Procedure 26(b)(4)(A)(ii) is to prepare for effective cross-examination at trial. However, in certain circumstances, impeachment of the expert during deposition may be useful. If a case is dominated by expert testimony, or the opposition is relying heavily on a particular expert, effective impeachment at deposition can disrupt the opposition's case and promote a settlement.

The following are the most common areas for possible impeachment:

The expert's qualifications are being molded to fit the case, or he or she is unqualified

The expert's opinions rest on faulty assumptions

The expert did not consider material facts, or relied on erroneous facts

The expert's opinion is inconsistent with his own publications

The expert's opinion is inconsistent with his own prior testimony in other, similar cases

The expert's opinion is inconsistent with a learned treatise, recognized industry standard, statute, regulation, or other authority

The expert's opinion actually relies exclusively on the work or opinions of others

The expert always testifies the same way on a particular issue (an "industry" hired gun)

The expert is a full-time witness (that is, a hired gun)

The expert has a past history of testifying for the opposing party or attorney

The expert is biased because of his fee arrangement

The expert is an employee of the party or a related party.

As a general rule, however, impeachment should be saved for trial. Impeachment during the depositions allows the expert to be prepared for trial.

INDEX

ABANDONMENT
Price considerations in private contracts
§ 1.7
Progress payments as claim waivers, trust
funds, and partial lien releases § 7.3
Stoppage of work § 18.5
Substantive terms, incorporation of
§ 3.15

ACCELERATION CLAIM ANALYSIS
Critical Path Method (CPM) decisions
from 1980 to 1990 § 10.6

ACCIDENTS
See PERSONAL INJURIES

ACCOUNTING
See CERTIFIED PUBLIC
ACCOUNTANTS (CPAS); COST-
ACCOUNTING RECORDS

ACTS OF GOD
AIA Document A201 modifications, 1987
edition § 2.10
ASCE and NAAG documents, problems
regarding § 5.6
Claims, avoiding and managing § 6.21
Critical Path Method (CPM) decisions
from 1980 to 1990 §§ 10.5, 10.15,
10.18
Quantum meruit § 8.9
Recovery for jointly-caused delays
§§ 9.8, 9.13

ACTUAL COST
Claims, avoiding and managing § 6.32
Competitive bidding and competitive
negotiation § 1.12

ACTUAL MALICE
Defense of qualified privilege in
defamation and commercial tort claims
against architects § 14.14

"ADMINISTRATION OF CONTRACTS"
AIA Document A201 modifications, 1987
edition § 2.7

ADMINISTRATIVE FEES
Claims, avoiding and managing § 6.9

**ADMINISTRATIVE, REGULATORY,
AND REGISTRATION PROCEEDINGS
INVOLVING DESIGN PROFESSIONALS**
Generally § 11.1

**ADMINISTRATIVE, REGULATORY,
AND REGISTRATION PROCEEDINGS
INVOLVING DESIGN PROFESSIONALS**
(*Continued*)
Administrative and registration
proceedings on subsequent civil
liability
–Generally, issue preclusion § 11.7
–Admission of findings into evidence
§ 11.9
–Issue preclusion in case study § 11.8
–Professional practice standards, effects
§ 11.10
Case study § 11.2
General discussion and background
–Board of registration proceedings § 11.4
–Civil actions arising out of construction
accidents § 11.6
–Kansas City Hyatt case, board of
registration proceedings § 11.5
–Occupational Safety and Health Act
(OSHA) proceedings § 11.3
Guidelines § 11.11

AFFIDAVITS
Construction administration services and
the architect's liability dilemma § 12.8
Design professionals, significant cases
§ 16.24

**AFFIRMATIVE DISCOVERY,
AVAILABLE METHODS**
Depositions § 20.17
Discovery through negotiations § 20.19
Document requests, identifying the
records
–Generally § 20.13
–Analyzing documents § 20.15
–Organizing documents § 20.14
Interrogatories § 20.16
Requests for admissions § 20.18

AGREEMENTS
See PREHIRE AGREEMENTS;
WRITTEN AGREEMENTS

**AIA DOCUMENT A101 (BASIC
AGREEMENT)**
Standard trade association contracts
§ 1.23

443

AIA DOCUMENT A201 (GENERAL
CONDITIONS)
Claims, avoiding and managing
§§ 6.8, 6.13
Defense of qualified privilege in
defamation and commercial tort claims
against architects § 14.23
Progress payments as claim waivers, trust
funds, and partial lien releases § 7.4
Quantum meruit § 8.7
Standard trade association contracts
§ 1.23
Stoppage of work § 18.4
Substantive terms, incorporation of
§ 3.14
AIA DOCUMENT A201
MODIFICATIONS, 1987 EDITION
Generally § 2.1
New clause § 18.4
Owner's exposure to claims and how to
protect against them
–Defective plans § 2.12
–Delay damages § 2.10
–Differing site conditions § 2.11
–Lack of coordination of separate prime
contractors § 2.13
Owner's obligations
–Assurance of ability to pay, providing
§ 2.4
–Information, providing § 2.3
–Insurance, providing § 2.5
–Scope of work, definition § 2.2
Owner's relations with other parties
–Architects § 2.15
–Contractors § 2.14
–Dispute resolution provisions on owner,
effect of § 2.16
–Summary § 2.17
Owner's rights
–Changes, making § 2.6
–Protection from risks which architect,
engineer and contractor should bear
and insure § 2.7
–Suspension or termination of contract
§ 2.8
–Work completed on schedule § 2.9
*ALFRED A. ALTIMONT, INC. VERSUS
CHATELAIN, SAMPERTON & NOLAN*
Defense of qualified privilege in
defamation and commercial tort claims
against architects § 14.19
AMERICAN ARBITRATION
ASSOCIATION (AAA)
CONSTRUCTION INDUSTRY

ARBITRATION RULES
Claims, avoiding and managing §§ 6.8,
6.13
Stoppage of work §§ 18.3, 18.4
AMERICAN INSTITUTE OF
ARCHITECTS (AIA)
Asbestos liability strategies § 19.19
ASCE and NAAG documents, problems
regarding § 5.1
Claims, avoiding and managing
§§ 6.2, 6.5
Construction administration services and
the architect's liability dilemma
§§ 12.4–12.8
Construction management system § 4.2
Design professionals, construction safety
impacts §§ 13.5, 13.6
Progress payments as claim waivers, trust
funds, and partial lien releases § 7.3
Standard trade association contracts
§§ 1.22, 1.23
Stoppage of work §§ 18.3, 18.4
Types of incorporating clauses
§§ 3.2, 3.3
AMERICAN INSTITUTE OF STEEL
CONSTRUCTION (AISC)
ASCE and NAAG documents, problems
regarding § 5.3
AMERICAN SOCIETY OF CIVIL
ENGINEERS (ASCE) AND NATIONAL
ASSOCIATION OF ATTORNEYS
GENERAL (NAAG) DOCUMENTS
Administrative, regulatory, and
registration proceedings involving
design professionals § 11.10
ASCE manual
–ASCE Manual of Professional Practice
for virtually everybody § 5.3
–Overreaction of ASCE § 5.2
Kansas City Hyatt Regency skywalk
collapse § 5.1
NAAG documents
–Agreement between owner and design
professional § 5.5
–Confusion reigns § 5.7
–Construction contract § 5.6
–Overreactions of NAAG § 5.4
Problems regarding §§ 5.2–5.7
ANTITRUST LAWS
Competitive bidding and competitive
negotiation § 1.8
APPEALS
Administrative, regulatory, and
registration proceedings involving

APPEALS (*Continued*)
design professionals §§ 11.3–11.5
Claims, avoiding and managing
§§ 6.10, 6.11
Construction administration services and
the architect's liability dilemma § 12.3
Critical Path Method (CPM) decisions
from 1980 to 1990 §§ 10.13, 10.18,
10.19
Defense of qualified privilege in
defamation and commercial tort claims
against architects § 14.20
Design professionals, construction safety
impacts § 13.3
Manpower shortage and organized labor's
agenda for the 1990's §§ 17.2–17.5
APPORTIONMENT
Recovery for jointly-caused delays
§§ 9.1, 9.4–9.7, 9.9, 9.10, 9.13, 9.14
APPRENTICESHIPS
Manpower shortage and organized labor's
agenda for the 1990's § 17.2
ARBITRATION
See also FEDERAL ARBITRATION ACT
(FAA); UNIFORM ARBITRATION
ACT (UAA)
AIA Document A201 modifications, 1987
edition § 2.16
Construction management system § 4.14
Enforceability, incorporation by reference
§ 3.5
Substantive terms, incorporation of
§§ 3.14, 3.15
ARBITRATORS' FEES
Claims, avoiding and managing § 6.9
ARCHITECTS AND ENGINEERS
See also AMERICAN SOCIETY OF
CIVIL ENGINEERS (ASCE) AND
NATIONAL ASSOCIATION OF
ATTORNEYS GENERAL (NAAG)
DOCUMENTS; CORPS OF
ENGINEERS; LIABILITY OF
ARCHITECT/ENGINEERS FOR
ERRONEOUS SOFTWARE AND
COMPUTER DATA
Administrative, regulatory, and
registration proceedings involving
design professionals § 11.10
AIA Document A201 modification, 1987
edition §§ 2.1, 2.3, 2.6–2.9, 2.12,
2.14, 2.15
Asbestos liability strategies § 19.15
Claims, avoiding and managing §§ 6.2,
6.5, 6.10, 6.13, 6.14, 6.17, 6.21

ARCHITECTS AND ENGINEERS
(*Continued*)
Competitive bidding and competitive
negotiation §§ 1.17, 1.20, 1.21
Construction administration services and
the architect's liability dilemma § 12.5
Construction management system §§ 4.1,
4.17
Critical Path Method (CPM) decisions
from 1980 to 1990 §§ 10.7, 10.15
Design professionals, construction safety
impacts §§ 13.2–13.11
Design professionals, significant cases
§§ 16.1–16.9, 16.11–16.16, 16.23,
16.24, 16.26, 16.28–16.31, 16.33–
16.37, 16.44
Progress payments as claim waivers, trust
funds, and partial lien releases § 7.4
Standard trade association contracts
§§ 1.22–1.24, 1.26
Substantive terms, incorporation of
§ 3.16
ARCHITECT'S LIABILITY DILEMMA
See CONSTRUCTION
ADMINISTRATION SERVICES AND
THE ARCHITECT'S LIABILITY
DILEMMA
ASBESTOS HAZARD EMERGENCY
RESPONSE ACT OF 1986 (AHERA)
Asbestos liability strategies §§ 19.2,
19.26
ASBESTOS LIABILITY EXCLUSION
Polychlorinated biphenyls (PCBS) § 18.4
Stoppage of work § 18.3
ASBESTOS LIABILITY STRATEGIES
Generally § 19.1
Cost recovery
–Miscellaneous theories § 19.9
–Negligence § 19.7
–Product liability § 19.6
–Strict liability § 19.5
–Warranty § 19.8
Cost recovery defenses
–Economic loss versus property damage
§ 19.10
–Product identification § 19.13
–Safe product defense § 19.12
–Statute of limitations § 19.11
Liability and asbestos abatement
–Architects and engineers § 19.15
–Asbestos consultants § 19.16
–Asbestos contractors § 19.17
–Other groups § 19.18
–Owners § 19.14

ASBESTOS LIABILITY STRATEGIES
(*Continued*)
Protection and allocations of liability
–Contracts § 19.19
–Incorporation § 19.25
–Legislation § 19.26
–Liability insurance § 19.24
–Recordkeeping § 19.21
–Supervision § 19.20
–Worker release § 19.23
–Workers' training § 19.22
Regulatory history of asbestos in
buildings
–Criminal enforcement § 19.4
–Federal regulatory history § 19.2
–State regulation § 19.3
ASBESTOS SCHOOL HAZARD
ABATEMENT ACT
Asbestos liability strategies § 19.2
ASSOCIATED GENERAL
CONTRACTORS (AGC)
AIA Document A201 modifications, 1987
edition § 2.8
ASCE and NAAG documents, problems
regarding § 5.7
Claims, avoiding and managing § 6.5
Standard trade association contracts
§§ 1.22, 1.23
Stoppage of work § 18.4
Types of incorporating clauses § 3.2
ATTORNEYS AND ATTORNEYS' FEES
AIA Document A201 modifications, 1987
edition § 2.16
Claims, avoiding and managing
§§ 6.28, 6.30
Construction administration services and
the architect's liability dilemma
§ 12.10
Defense of qualified privilege in
defamation and commercial tort claims
against architects § 14.23
Design professionals, significant cases
§ 16.9
Discovery in construction litigation
§§ 20.8, 20.10, 20.23
Standard trade association contracts
§ 1.24
AWARDS
Claims, avoiding and managing § 6.1
Defense of qualified privilege in
defamation and commercial tort claims
against architects § 14.13
Quantum meruit § 8.7
Recovery for jointly-caused delays § 9.13

BAD FAITH
Competitive bidding and competitive
negotiation § 1.11
Defense of qualified privilege in
defamation and commercial tort claims
against architects §§ 14.4, 14.11,
14.12, 14.15, 14.17, 14.20, 14.23
BALLOU VERSUS BASIC CONSTRUCTION
CO.
Defense of qualified privilege in
defamation and commercial tort claims
against architects § 14.21
BANKRUPTCY
See also U.S. BANKRUPTCY CODE
Claims, avoiding and managing § 6.2
Competitive bidding and competitive
negotiation § 1.9
Progress payments as claim waivers, trust
funds, and partial lien releases § 7.6
Quantum meruit § 8.11
BANKRUPTCY REFORM ACT
AIA Document A201 modifications, 1987
edition § 2.8
BENEFICIARIES
See also THIRD-PARTY BENEFICIARY
STATUS
Design professionals, construction safety
impacts § 13.6
Progress payments as claim waivers, trust
funds, and partial lien releases § 7.6
BIDDING
See also COMPETITIVE BIDDING AND
COMPETITIVE NEGOTIATION;
ESTIMATES
ASCE and NAAG documents, problems
regarding § 5.6
Claims, avoiding and managing §§ 6.4,
6.15, 6.18
Construction management system § 4.10
Quantum meruit §§ 8.3, 8.11
BOARD OF REGISTRATION
PROCEEDINGS
Administrative, regulatory, and
registration proceedings involving
design professionals §§ 11.4, 11.5
BONDS
ASCE and NAAG documents, problems
regarding § 5.6
Claims, avoiding and managing
§§ 6.2, 6.27
Payment bonds
–Competitive bidding and competitive
negotiation § 1.9
–Substantive terms, incorporation of

BONDS (*Continued*)
§ 3.14
Performance bonds
–Claims, avoiding and managing § 6.2
–Competitive bidding and competitive negotiations § 1.9
Substantive terms, incorporation of § 3.15
BREACH OF CONTRACT
Construction administration services and the architect's liability dilemma §§ 12.2, 12.6, 12.8, 12.9
Design professionals, significant cases § 16.7
Progress payment as claim waivers, trust funds, and partial lien releases § 7.6
Quantum meruit § 8.5
Recovery for jointly-caused delays § 9.6
BUILDER'S RISK INSURANCE
AIA Document A201 modifications, 1987 edition § 2.5
ASCE and NAAG documents, problems regarding § 5.6
BUILDING CODES
Design professionals, construction safety impacts § 13.4
BURDEN OF PROOF
Defense of qualified privilege in defamation and commercial tort claims against architects § 14.4
BUREAU OF APPRENTICESHIP TRAINING (BAT)
Manpower shortage and organized labor's agenda for the 1990's § 17.2
BUREAU OF NATIONAL AFFAIRS
Asbestos liability strategies § 19.3

CARDINAL CHANGE CASES
Quantum meruit §§ 8.8, 8.10
CAUSATION
Recovery for jointly-caused delays §§ 9.2, 9.4, 9.7, 9.15
CERTIFIED MECHANICAL CONTRACTORS, INC. VERSUS WIGHT & CO.
Defense of qualified privilege in defamation and commercial tort claims against architects § 14.15
CERTIFIED PUBLIC ACCOUNTANTS (CPAS)
Claims, avoiding and managing §§ 6.28, 6.36

CERTIORARI
See WRIT OF CERTIORARI
"CHAIN OF COMMAND"
AIA Document A201 modifications, 1987 edition § 2.14
CHANGE ORDERS
AIA Document A201 modifications, 1987 edition § 2.6
ASCE and NAAG documents, problems regarding § 5.6
Claims, avoiding and managing §§ 6.5, 6.7, 6.18, 6.22, 6.27
Competitive bidding and competitive negotiation §§ 1.12, 1.18
Construction management system § 4.11
Critical Path Method (CPM) decisions from 1980 to 1990 § 10.16
Defense of qualified privilege in defamation and commercial tort claims against architects § 14.16
Quantum meruit §§ 8.1, 8.3, 8.7, 8.9–8.11
Recovery for jointly-caused delays §§ 9.2, 9.9, 9.13
Stoppage of work § 18.1
CIVIL ACTIONS
Administrative, regulatory, and registration proceedings involving design professionals § 11.6
CIVIL ENGINEERS
See ARCHITECTS AND ENGINEERS
CLAIMS, AVOIDING AND MANAGING
Arbitration alternative
–Generally § 6.8
–Enforceability of agreements to arbitrate § 6.12
–Informality and limited appeals § 6.11
–Multiple parties, special problems involving § 6.13
–Selection of arbitrators § 6.10
–Time and costs § 6.9
Audits § 6.36
Claim development § 6.26
Claim recognition and preparation § 6.27
Communication, lines of § 6.17
Components of a well-prepared claim document § 6.30
Construction industry, avoiding risks and preserving awards § 6.1
Contract framework § 6.4
Contract modification § 6.7
Cost accounting records § 6.24
Damages
–Generally § 6.31

CLAIMS, AVOIDING AND MANAGING
(*Continued*)
–Basic principles § 6.32
Demonstrative evidence, use of § 6.29
Early claim recognition and preparation
§ 6.27
Early involvement of experts and
attorneys § 6.28
Estimating, prudent and responsible
§ 6.15
Express and implied terms, interpreting
and applying § 6.6
Negotiation and settlement, pursuing
§ 6.37
Pricing claims
–Generally § 6.33
–Segregated cost method § 6.35
–Total cost method § 6.34
Project cost reviews and audits § 6.36
Project documentation
–Generally § 6.18
–Correspondence § 6.19
–Jobsite logs or daily reports § 6.21
–Meeting notes § 6.20
–Photographs and videotapes § 6.23
–Standard forms and status logs § 6.22
Proper management and documentation
§ 6.14
Reputable and reliable participants in the
project § 6.2
Rights, responsibilities, and risks § 6.3
Scheduling § 6.25
Standard contract forms and key contract
provisions § 6.5
Standard operating procedures § 6.16
CLAIM WAIVERS
See PROGRESS PAYMENTS AS CLAIM
WAIVERS, TRUST FUNDS, AND
PARTIAL LIEN RELEASES
CLEAN AIR ACT
Asbestos liability strategies §§ 19.2,
19.4, 19.14
CLIENT INFORMATION, ORGANIZING
Basic case established from client data
§ 20.8
Gathering documents
–Generally § 20.9
–Identification and removal of privileged
or exempt documents § 20.11
–Indexing § 20.10
Witness interviews § 20.12
COMMERCIAL IMPRACTICABILITY
Stoppage of work § 18.2
COMMERCIAL TORT CLAIMS AGAINST

ARCHITECTS
See DEFENSE OF QUALIFIED
PRIVILEGE IN DEFAMATION AND
COMMERCIAL TORT CLAIMS
AGAINST ARCHITECTS
"COMMON ENTERPRISE" THEORY
Design professionals, construction safety
impacts § 13.6
COMMUNICATION
Claims, avoiding and managing §§ 6.17,
6.22, 6.26
Construction management system
§§ 4.13, 4.14
Defense of qualified privilege in
defamation and commercial tort claims
against architects §§ 14.5–14.7
COMPETENCE RISK AVOIDANCE
Competitive bidding and competitive
negotiation §§ 1.10, 1.11
COMPETITIVE BIDDING AND
COMPETITIVE NEGOTIATION
Competitive bidding, policy and
frustration
–Generally § 1.8
–Competence risk avoidance in public
sector § 1.10
–Computation errors § 1.14
–Contractor's risk: cost estimating risk
and subcontractor quotes § 1.13
–Cost estimating risks and excessive
change orders § 1.12
–Extra work compensation in public
contracts § 1.17
–Owner's risk: performance risk and
bonds § 1.9
–Private contracts §§ 1.15, 1.18
–Private owners § 1.11
–Public contracts § 1.16
Competitive negotiation
–Generally § 1.19
–Contractor cost estimating risks § 1.21
–Owner's risk § 1.20
COMPLETION OF WORK
AIA Document A201 modifications, 1987
edition § 2.9
COMPREHENSIVE ENVIRONMENTAL
RECOVERY, COMPENSATION AND
LIABILITY ACT (CERCLA)
Asbestos liability strategies §§ 19.4,
19.9, 19.14
COMPUTATION ERRORS
Competitive bidding and competitive
negotiation § 1.14
COMPUTER ASSISTED DRAFTING AND

DESIGN (CADD)
Liability of architect/engineers for
erroneous software and computer data,
generally this heading
COMPUTERS, PERSONAL
See also LIABILITY OF ARCHITECT/
ENGINEERS FOR ERRONEOUS
SOFTWARE AND COMPUTER DATA
Claims, avoiding and managing
§§ 6.20, 6.28
Critical Path Method (CPM) decisions
from 1980 to 1990 §§ 10.2, 10.15
Discovery in construction litigation
§ 20.10
CONCURRENT CAUSE RULE
See JOINTLY-CAUSED DELAYS,
RECOVERY
CONDUIT CLAUSES
Enforceability, incorporation by reference
§§ 3.5, 3.6, 3.9
Incorporation by reference § 3.1
Progress payments as claim waivers, trust
funds, and partial lien releases § 7.4
Substantive terms, incorporation of
§§ 3.10, 3.12–3.14, 3.17
Types of incorporating clauses
§§ 3.2, 3.3
CONFLICTS
Enforceability, incorporation by reference
§ 3.7
CONSOLIDATION
Claims, avoiding and managing § 6.13
CONSTRUCTION ADMINISTRATION
SERVICES AND THE ARCHITECT'S
LIABILITY DILEMMA
Generally § 12.1
Background § 12.2
Limiting liability by contract § 12.9
Recommendations § 12.10
Supervision
–Generally § 12.3
–AIA standard form contract § 12.5
–Early case law § 12.4
–Modern statutes § 12.7
–*Mounds View* case § 12.6
–Recent cases § 12.8
CONSTRUCTION OBSERVATION
SERVICES
Construction administration services and
the architect's liability dilemma § 12.7
"CONSTRUCTION CHANGE
DIRECTIVE"
AIA Document A201 modifications, 1987
edition § 2.6

"CONSTRUCTION CHANGE
DIRECTIVE" (*Continued*)
Quantum meruit § 8.7
Recovery for jointly-caused delays § 9.13
CONSTRUCTION INDUSTRY
ARBITRATION RULES
See AMERICAN ARBITRATION
ASSOCIATION (AAA)
CONSTRUCTION INDUSTRY
ARBITRATION RULES
CONSTRUCTION MANAGEMENT
SYSTEM
Construction Management Association of
America (CMAA) documents,
Construction Manager (CM) as agent
§ 4.2
Concept of construction management,
generally § 4.1
Leadership role of Construction
Manager (CM)
–Construction phase § 4.14
–Design phase § 4.13
–Liability, exposure to § 4.15
–Performance standards of care § 4.16
–Professional liability insurance coverage
§ 4.17
Summary of the CMAA system
–CM and design professional cooperation
§ 4.6
–CM as owner's agent § 4.5
–CM determinations during construction
phase § 4.12
–Compliance with project budget § 4.9
–Construction management plan § 4.4
–Design criteria § 4.8
–Design documentation § 4.10
–Design professional's basic construction
phase services § 4.11
–Project planning and selection of a
design professional § 4.3
–Reliance on CM cost estimates § 4.7
CONSTRUCTION MANAGERS (CMs)
AIA Document A201 modifications, 1987
edition § 2.1
Critical Path Method (CPM) decisions
from 1980 to 1990 § 10.19
CONSULTANTS
Asbestos liability strategies § 19.16
CONSUMER PRODUCT SAFETY
COMMISSION
Asbestos liability strategies § 19.2
CONTRACT CLAIMS
Critical Path Method (CPM) decisions
from 1980 to 1990 §§ 10.1–10.19

CONTRACT DOCUMENTS
AIA Document A201 modifications, 1987 edition §§ 2.2, 2.7, 2.9, 2.12, 2.15
Asbestos liability strategies § 19.19
ASCE and NAAG documents, problems regarding §§ 5.3, 5.6, 5.7
Claims, avoiding and managing §§ 6.5, 6.14
Construction administration services and the architect's liability dilemma § 12.8
Construction management system § 4.14
Enforceability, incorporation by reference § 3.5
Incorporation by reference § 3.1
Types of incorporating clauses § 3.2
CONTRACTOR ADVANTAGES
Price considerations in private contracts §§ 1.4, 1.5
CONTRACTOR RISKS
Competitive bidding and competitive negotiation § 1.13
Price considerations in private contracts § 1.3
CONTRACTORS
See also PRIME CONTRACTORS; SUBCONTRACTORS
AIA Document A201 modifications, 1987 edition § 2.14
Asbestos liability strategies § 19.17
ASCE and NAAG documents, problems regarding §§ 5.1, 5.3, 5.6, 5.7
Claims, avoiding and managing §§ 6.1, 6.2, 6.5, 6.6, 6.10, 6.13, 6.17, 6.21, 6.22, 6.25
Construction administration services and the architect's liability dilemma §§ 12.4, 12.8
Construction management system § 4.1
Critical Path Method (CPM) decisions from 1980 to 1990 §§ 10.3, 10.5–10.8, 10.11, 10.14–10.19
Defense of qualified privilege in defamation and commercial tort claims against architects §§ 14.1, 14.5, 14.6, 14.10–14.21
Design professionals, construction safety impacts §§ 13.3, 13.5–13.11
Design professionals, significant cases §§ 16.1–16.6, 16.9, 16.11, 16.16–16.24, 16.31, 16.33–16.35
Incorporation by reference, generally this heading
Manpower shortage and organized labor's agenda for the 1990's §§ 17.2–17.5

CONTRACTORS (*Continued*)
Progress payments as claim waivers, trust funds, and partial lien releases §§ 7.1–7.9
Quantum meruit §§ 8.1–8.4, 8.7–8.11
Recovery for jointly-caused delays §§ 9.2, 9.8, 9.13
Stoppage of work §§ 18.1–18.5
CONTRACTORS' FEES
AIA Document A201 modifications, 1987 edition § 2.3
Competitive bidding and competitive negotiation §§ 1.19, 1.20
Price considerations in private contracts §§ 1.5, 1.6
CONTRACTUAL LIABILITY
See DESIGN PROFESSIONALS, SIGNIFICANT CASES
CONTRIBUTION AND INDEMNITY
See DESIGN PROFESSIONALS, SIGNIFICANT CASES
CONWAY CORP. VERSUS CONSTRUCTION ENGINEERS, INC.
Defense of qualified privilege in defamation and commercial tort claims against architects § 14.12
COPELAND ANTI-KICKBACK ACT
Manpower shortage and organized labor's agenda for the 1990's § 17.3
CORPS OF ENGINEERS
Critical Path Method (CPM) decisions from 1980 to 1990 § 10.11
CORRESPONDENCE
Claims, avoiding and managing §§ 6.19, 6.20
COST-ACCOUNTING RECORDS
Claims, avoiding and managing § 6.23
COST ESTIMATING RISKS
Competitive bidding and competitive negotiation §§ 1.12, 1.13, 1.21
COST OVERRUNS
Claims, avoiding and managing § 6.29
Price considerations in private contracts §§ 1.3, 1.5, 1.6, 1.21
COSTS
See also ACTUAL COST; ASBESTOS LIABILITY STRATEGIES; HIDDEN COSTS; RECOVERY; SEGREGATED COST METHOD; TOTAL COST METHOD
Claims, avoiding and managing §§ 6.9, 6.16, 6.27, 6.34–6.36
Construction management system §§ 4.7, 4.13, 4.14

COSTS (*Continued*)

Design professionals, significant cases §§ 16.5, 16.27

Progress payments as claim waivers, trust funds, and partial lien releases § 7.4

Quantum meruit §§ 8.2, 8.5, 8.6, 8.9, 8.11

Recovery for jointly-caused delays, generally this heading

CRITICAL PATH METHOD (CPM)

AIA Document A201 modifications, 1987 edition § 2.9

Claims, avoiding and managing § 6.25

Recovery for jointly-caused delays §§ 9.2, 9.4, 9.8

CRITICAL PATH METHOD (CPM) DECISIONS FROM 1980 TO 1990

Generally § 10.1

Acceleration claim analysis § 10.6

CPM, defined § 10.2

Delay claim analysis

–Generally § 10.4

–Parameters § 10.5

Landmark decisions from 1980 to 1990

–Generally § 10.8

–*Fortec Constructors versus United States* § 10.9

–*Gulf Contracting, Inc* § 10.10

–*Weaver-Bailey Contractors, Inc. versus United States* § 10.11

–*Williams Enterprises versus Strait Manufacturing & Welding, Inc.* § 10.12

Loss of productivity analysis § 10.7

Major cases and issues

–Generally § 10.13

–*Ealahan Electric Co.* § 10.17

–*Haney versus United States* § 10.15

–*Santa Fe* decisions, The § 10.16

–*Titan Pacific Construction Corp. versus United States* § 10.18

–*Utley-James, Inc.* § 10.14

State recognition of CPM principles § 10.19

Use of CPM for delay analysis and contract claims § 10.3

DAILY REPORTS

See JOBSITE LOGS AND DAILY REPORTS

DAMAGES

See also CLAIMS, AVOIDING AND MANAGING; DESIGN PROFESSIONALS, SIGNIFICANT CASES; LIQUIDATED DAMAGES; MITIGATING DAMAGES; NO DAMAGES FOR DELAY CLAUSES; PROPERTY DAMAGES

AIA Document A201 modifications, 1987 edition §§ 2.3, 2.7, 2.10

ASCE and NAAG documents, problems regarding § 5.7

Competitive bidding and competitive negotiation §§ 1.9, 1.11

Construction administration services and the architect's liability dilemma §§ 12.8–12.10

Critical Path Method (CPM) decisions from 1980 to 1990 §§ 10.1–10.3, 10.5–10.9, 10.12–10.16

Defense of qualified privilege in defamation and commercial tort claims against architects §§ 14.2, 14.15

Quantum meruit § 8.9

Stoppage of work § 18.3

Substantive terms, incorporation of §§ 3.10, 3.12, 3.13, 3.16

DAVIS-BACON ACT

Manpower shortage and organized labor's agenda for the 1990's § 17.3

DEATHS

Design professionals, construction safety impacts § 13.6

DEFAMATION

See DEFENSE OF QUALIFIED PRIVILEGE IN DEFAMATION AND COMMERCIAL TORT CLAIMS AGAINST ARCHITECTS

DEFAULTS

Claims, avoiding and managing §§ 6.2, 6.5

Defense of qualified privilege in defamation and commercial tort claims against architects § 14.19

Recovery for jointly-caused delays § 9.12

Stoppage of work §§ 18.2, 18.5

DEFECTS

See also DESIGN PROFESSIONALS, SIGNIFICANT CASES

AIA Document A201 modifications, 1987 edition §§ 2.7, 2.12

DEFENSE OF QUALIFIED PRIVILEGE IN DEFAMATION AND COMMERCIAL TORT CLAIMS AGAINST

ARCHITECTS
Generally § 14.1
Case summaries
–Generally § 14.8
–*Alfred A. Altimont, Inc. versus Chatelain, Samperton & Nolan* § 14.19
–*Ballou versus Basic Construction Co.* § 14.21
–*Certified Mechanical Contractors, Inc. versus Wight & Co.* § 14.15
–*Conway Corp. versus Construction Engineers, Inc.* § 14.12
–*Dehnert versus Arrow Sprinklers, Inc.* § 14.16
–*George A. Fuller Co. versus Chicago College of Osteopathic Medicine* § 14.17
–*Joba Construction Co. versus Burns & Roe, Inc.* § 14.11
–*Kecko Piping Co. versus Town of Monroe* § 14.13
–*Riblet Tramway Co. versus Ericksen Associates, Inc.* § 14.9
–*Santucci Construction Co. versus Baxter & Woodman, Inc.* § 14.20
–*Somers Construction Co. versus Board of Education* § 14.10
–*V.M. Solis Underground Utility & Paving Co. versus City of Laredo* § 14.18
–*Vojak versus Jensen* § 14.14
–*Waldinger Corp. versus CRS Group Engineers, Inc.* § 14.22
Communications
–Generally § 14.5
–Owners § 14.6
–Persons other than owners § 14.7
Defamation § 14.2
Guidelines to protect architects § 14.23
Privilege defenses § 14.4
Tortious interference § 14.3
DEFENSIVE DISCOVERY
Generally § 20.24
Depositions
–Designating witnesses § 20.32
–Duty to supplement § 20.34
–Memory of witnesses § 20.31
–Objections § 20.30
–Preparing witness § 20.29
–Requests for admissions § 20.33
Interrogatories
–Preparation of responses § 20.26
–When and how to object § 20.25
Requests for production of documents
–Generally § 20.27

DEFENSIVE DISCOVERY (*Continued*)
–Responding to requests § 20.28
DEHNERT VERSUS ARROW SPRINKLERS, INC.
Defense of qualified privilege in defamation and commercial tort claims against architects § 14.16
DELAYS
See also JOINTLY-CAUSED DELAYS, RECOVERY; NO DAMAGES FOR DELAY CLAUSES
AIA Document A201 modifications, 1987 edition § 2.10
Claims, avoiding and managing §§ 6.5, 6.6, 6.8, 6.28
Construction management system § 4.15
Critical Path Method (CPM) decisions from 1980 to 1990 §§ 10.1–10.5
Defense of qualified privilege in defamation and commercial tort claims against architects § 14.19
Enforceability, incorporation by reference § 3.5
Price considerations in private contracts § 1.7
Quantum meruit § 8.9
Stoppage of work §§ 18.2, 18.5
Substantive terms, incorporation of § 3.16
DEMONSTRATIVE EVIDENCE
Claims, avoiding and managing §§ 6.9, 6.28–6.30
DEPARTMENT OF HEALTH, EDUCATION AND WELFARE
Asbestos liability strategies § 19.2
Manpower shortage and organized labor's agenda for the 1990's § 17.2
DEPARTMENT OF LABOR
Administrative, regulatory, and registration proceedings involving design professionals §§ 11.1–11.6, 11.11
Manpower shortage and organized labor's agenda for the 1990's §§ 17.2, 17.3
DEPOSITIONS
See also DEFENSIVE DISCOVERY
Discovery in construction litigation § 20.17
DESIGN-BUILD CONTRACTS
Generally § 1.25
Joint venture design-build team § 1.26
Sole contractor § 1.27
DESIGNER LIABILITY FOR DEFECTIVE SOFTWARE

DESIGNER LIABILITY FOR
DEFECTIVE SOFTWARE (*Continued*)
Computer Assisted Drafting and Design
(CADD) use guidelines § 15.1
Sale of goods versus sale of services:
rights and responsibilities of software
designer to software user and third
parties § 15.10
Scope of problem § 15.9
Software manufacturer's exposure to
professional malpractice liability
§ 15.15
Substantive or mechanical errors § 15.16
UCC problems facing software dealers
–Generally § 15.11
–Express warranties § 15.12
–Implied warranties § 15.13
–Limitation on remedy provisions
§ 15.14
DESIGN PROFESSIONALS
See also ADMINISTRATIVE,
REGULATORY, AND
REGISTRATION PROCEEDINGS
INVOLVING DESIGN
PROFESSIONALS
ASCE and NAAG documents, problems
regarding §§ 5.3, 5.5, 5.7
Claims, avoiding and managing
§§ 6.1, 6.2
Construction management system §§ 4.2–
4.16
DESIGN PROFESSIONALS,
CONSTRUCTION SAFETY IMPACTS
Generally § 13.1
Construction safety guidelines § 13.11
Current document language § 13.5
Early supervision cases § 13.3
Indemnification, defense by § 13.10
Labor laws § 13.7
Master builder concept § 13.2
Occupational Safety and Health Act
(OSHA) impacts § 13.8
Pending safety legislation § 13.9
Workers' compensation laws, relationship
of § 13.6
Work stoppage cases § 13.4
DESIGN PROFESSIONALS,
SIGNIFICANT CASES
Contractual liability
–Architect's contract and poor
workmanship § 16.1
–Contract disclaimers § 16.3
–Engineering firm liable for failure to
detect fraud § 16.4

DESIGN PROFESSIONALS,
SIGNIFICANT CASES (*Continued*)
–Excess cost of construction does not
defeat architect's fee claim § 16.5
–Exculpatory clause does not absolve
architect § 16.2
Contribution and indemnity
–Apportioned fault verdict upheld
§ 16.15
–Architect allowed indemnity for
attorneys' fees § 16.9
–Architect not entitled to contribution or
indemnity § 16.7
–Contribution action maintained by
defendant § 16.11
–Contribution or indemnity from designer
§ 16.6
–Design engineer could not obtain
contribution from EPA § 16.13
–Engineer not entitled to contribution or
implied indemnity § 16.12
–Equitable indemnity not available from
engineer § 16.8
–Indemnification of joint tortfeasor
§ 16.10
–Indemnity or contribution from design
drawing company § 16.14
Damages
–Consequential damages from engineer
§ 16.28
–Cost to repair § 16.27
Economic loss
–Claim for negligent review of shop
drawing § 16.19
–Negligent misrepresentation case
requires functional equivalent of privity
§ 16.16
–Tort recovery for economic loss not
allowed even to supplier of services
§ 16.18
–Tort recovery for economic loss not
allowed regardless of relationship
between parties § 16.17
Environmental law
–Waste disposal problems § 16.20
Expert witness litigation
–Architect's own expert establishes
architect's negligence § 16.26
–Expert opinion necessary to prove
negligence § 16.22
–Expert witness immune from suit
§ 16.21
–Non-architect as expert witness against
architect § 16.23

DESIGN PROFESSIONALS,
SIGNIFICANT CASES (*Continued*)
–Statute requires filing of expert's
affidavit with complaint against
architects § 16.24
–Surveyor liable as a matter of law
§ 16.25
Jobsite safety
–Architect not liable to injured worker
§ 16.36
–No duty to notify workers § 16.35
–No duty to supervise § 16.37
Patent and latent defects
–Owner's allegation of latent defect
§ 16.30
–Subsequent owner could not recover
§ 16.31
–Question of fact § 16.29
Privity
–Condominium owner third-party
beneficiary § 16.32
Public official immunity
–Suit against state employee engineer
barred § 16.33
Racketeering
–Engineering firm supplying reports and
studies § 16.34
Statutes of limitations
–Architect/engineer firm estopped from
asserting statute of limitations § 16.42
–Damages claim did not change contract
action into tort action § 16.43
–Economic loss action governed by tort
statute of limitations § 16.44
–Suit by governmental agencies not
barred by statute of limitations
§ 16.45
Statutes of repose
–Ohio's statute of repose held
constitutional § 16.40
–Oklahoma's statute of repose held
constitutional § 16.41
–Wisconsin's statute of repose held
unconstitutional § 16.38
–Utah's statute of repose held
unconstitutional § 16.39
DISCOVERY IN CONSTRUCTION
LITIGATION
See also AFFIRMATIVE DISCOVERY,
AVAILABLE METHODS; CLIENT
INFORMATION, ORGANIZING;
DEFENSIVE DISCOVERY
Claims, avoiding and managing § 6.9
Defending against discovery § 20.2

DISCOVERY IN CONSTRUCTION
LITIGATION (*Continued*)
Expert discovery
–Discovery of non-testifying experts
§ 20.36
–Discovery of testifying experts § 20.37
–Experts, defined § 20.35
–Impeachment of trial expert § 20.38
Noncompliance or objections to discovery
–Attorney liability § 20.23
–Duty to preserve documents § 20.22
–Motion practice § 20.20
–Sanctions § 20.21
Purposes of discovery § 20.1
Sources of information, other
–Client sources § 20.3
–Experts § 20.6
–Former employees or representatives of
opponent § 20.5
–Published materials § 20.7
–Third parties § 20.4
DISPUTES AND DISPUTE
RESOLUTIONS
See also CLAIMS, AVOIDING AND
MANAGING
Administrative, regulatory, and
registration proceedings involving
design professionals §§ 11.8, 11.9
AIA Document A201 modifications, 1987
edition §§ 2.7, 2.16
Construction administration services and
the architect's liability dilemma § 12.5
Incorporation by reference § 3.1
Substantive terms, incorporation of
§§ 3.13, 3.14
DISRUPTIONS
Claims, avoiding and managing § 6.6
DOCUMENTS
See also AMERICAN SOCIETY OF
CIVIL ENGINEERS (ASCE) AND
NATIONAL ASSOCIATION OF
ATTORNEYS GENERAL (NAAG)
DOCUMENTS; CONTRACT
DOCUMENTS
Discovery in construction litigation
§§ 20.9–20.11, 20.13–20.15, 20.27
DRAWINGS
See also PLANS AND
SPECIFICATIONS; SHOP DRAWINGS
AIA Document A201 modifications, 1987
edition § 2.7
ASCE and NAAG documents, problems
regarding § 5.6
Competitive bidding and competitive

DRAWINGS (*Continued*)

negotiation § 1.19

Construction management system
§§ 4.11, 4.14

Design professionals, significant cases
§§ 16.2, 16.14, 16.23

Enforceability, incorporation by reference
§ 3.5

Price considerations in private contracts
§ 1.7

Recovery for jointly-caused delays § 9.13

Substantive terms, incorporation of
§ 3.14

EALAHAN ELECTRIC CO.
Critical Path Method (CPM) decisions
from 1980 to 1990 § 10.17

ECONOMIC LOSSES
See also DESIGN PROFESSIONALS,
SIGNIFICANT CASES

Asbestos liability strategies § 19.10

Defense of qualified privilege in
defamation and commercial tort claims
against architects § 14.1

Substantive terms, incorporation of
§ 3.10

EDUCATIONAL FACILITIES
AIA Document A201 modifications, 1987
edition § 2.1

ELECTRIC POWER
ASCE and NAAG documents, problems
regarding § 5.6

Claims, avoiding and managing § 6.2

Critical Path Method (CPM) decisions
from 1980 to 1990 § 10.2

EMPLOYEE RETIREMENT INCOME
SECURITY ACT (ERISA)
Manpower shortage and organized labor's
agenda for the 1990's § 17.2

ENFORCEABILITY
Interpretation
–Generally § 3.4
–Implied incorporation § 3.6
–Scope of incorporation must be clear
§ 3.5
–Subcontract consistency § 3.7
–Surrounding circumstances § 3.8
Third-party beneficiary status § 3.9

ENGINEERS
See ARCHITECTS AND ENGINEERS;
CORPS OF ENGINEERS; LIABILITY
OF ARCHITECT/ENGINEERS FOR

ERRONEOUS SOFTWARE AND
COMPUTER DATA
ENGINEERS' JOINT CONTRACT
DOCUMENTS COMMITTEE (EJCDC)
ASCE and NAAG documents, problems
regarding § 5.3

Claims, avoiding and managing § 6.5

Design professionals, construction safety
impacts §§ 13.5, 13.6

ENVIRONMENTAL LAW
See DESIGN PROFESSIONALS,
SIGNIFICANT CASES

ENVIRONMENTAL PROTECTION
AGENCY (EPA)
Asbestos liability strategies §§ 19.2,
19.4, 19.14, 19.21

ASCE and NAAG documents, problems
regarding § 5.6

Design professionals, significant cases
§ 16.13

Stoppage of work § 18.3

EQUIPMENT
See LABOR AND MATERIALS

ESTIMATES
Claims, avoiding and managing
§§ 6.15, 6.18

Construction management system § 4.13

Critical Path Method (CPM) decisions
from 1980 to 1990 § 10.5

Design professionals, significant cases
§ 16.5

ESTOPPEL
Administrative, regulatory, and
registration proceedings involving
design professionals §§ 11.7–11.9

Design professionals, significant cases
§ 16.42

EVIDENCE
See also DEMONSTRATIVE EVIDENCE

Administrative, regulatory, and
registration proceedings involving
design professionals § 11.9

AIA Document A201 modifications, 1987
edition § 2.4

Claims, avoiding and managing §§ 6.2,
6.11, 6.12, 6.23, 6.27, 6.31

Construction administration services and
the architect's liability dilemma § 12.8

Critical Path Method (CPM) decisions
from 1980 to 1990 § 10.12

Substantive terms, incorporation of
§ 3.16

EXCULPATORY CLAUSE
Design professionals, significant cases

EXCULPATORY CLAUSE (*Continued*)
§ 16.2
EXPERT DISCOVERY
See DISCOVERY IN CONSTRUCTION
LITIGATION
EXPERT WITNESS LITIGATION
See DESIGN PROFESSIONALS,
SIGNIFICANT CASES
EXPRESS WARRANTY
Liability of architect/engineers for
erroneous software and computer data
§ 15.12
EXTRA WORK
AIA Document A201 modifications, 1987
edition § 2.4
Claims, avoiding and managing §§ 6.6,
6.35
Competitive bidding and competitive
negotiation §§ 1.17, 1.18
Progress payments as claim waivers, trust
funds, and partial lien releases § 7.4
Quantum meruit §§ 8.4, 8.11

FAIR MARKET VALUE
Price considerations in private contracts
§ 1.7
FEDERAL ARBITRATION ACT (FAA)
Claims, avoiding and managing § 6.12
Substantive terms, incorporation of
§ 3.14
FEDERAL BUREAU OF INVESTIGATION
(FBI)
Asbestos liability strategies § 19.4
FEDERAL RULES OF CIVIL
PROCEDURE
Discovery in construction litigation
§§ 20.11, 20.20–20.28, 20.30, 20.32,
20.33, 20.35–20.38
FEES
See ADMINISTRATIVE FEES;
ARBITRATORS' FEES; ATTORNEYS
AND ATTORNEYS' FEES;
CONTRACTORS' FEES
FINANCING
Claims, avoiding and managing § 6.2
FIRE
ASCE and NAAG documents, problems
regarding § 5.6
FITZGERALD ACT
Manpower shortage and organized labor's
agenda for the 1990's § 17.2
FIXED PRICE CONTRACTS
See also PRIVATE CONTRACTS, PRICE
CONSIDERATIONS

FIXED PRICE CONTACTS (*Continued*)
Standard trade association contracts
§ 1.23
FLOW DOWN CLAUSES
See CONDUIT CLAUSES
*FORTEC CONSTRUCTORS VERSUS
UNITED STATES*
Critical Path Method (CPM) decisions
from 1980 to 1990 § 10.9
FRAUD
Asbestos liability strategies § 19.9
Design professionals, significant cases
§§ 16.4, 16.34

GENERAL CONTRACTORS
Progress payments as claim waivers, trust
funds, and partial lien releases §§ 7.1–
7.3, 7.6, 7.7
*GEORGE A. FULLER CO. VERSUS
CHICAGO COLLEGE OF OSTEOPATHIC
MEDICINE*
Defense of qualified privilege in
defamation and commercial tort claims
against architects § 14.17
GOOD FAITH
Competitive bidding and competitive
negotiation § 1.10
Defense of qualified privilege in
defamation and commercial tort claims
against architects § 14.14
GOVERNMENT PROPERTY
Substantive terms, incorporation of
§ 3.15
GUARANTEED MAXIMUM
CONTRACTS
Competitive bidding and competitive
negotiation § 1.19
Price considerations in private contracts
§ 1.6
GULF CONTRACTING INC.
Critical Path Method (CPM) decisions
from 1980 to 1990 § 10.10

HANEY VERSUS UNITED STATES
Critical Path Method (CPM) decisions
from 1980 to 1990 § 10.15
HIDDEN COSTS
Competitive bidding and competitive
negotiation § 1.20
HIGH-RISE BUILDINGS
AIA Document A201 modifications, 1987
edition § 2.1

HIGHWAY PROJECT
AIA Document A201 modifications, 1987
edition § 2.1
HOSPITALS AND CLINICS
AIA Document A201 modifications, 1987
edition § 2.1
HOUSING PROJECTS
AIA Document A201 modifications, 1987
edition § 2.1

IMMUNITY
Public official § 16.33
Statutory
–Substantive terms, incorporation of
§ 3.13
IMPEACHMENT OF TRIAL EXPERT
Discovery in construction litigation
§ 20.38
IMPLIED WARRANTY
Liability of architect/engineers for
erroneous software and computer data
§§ 15.8, 15.13
Substantive terms, incorporation of
§ 3.17
INCORPORATION BY REFERENCE
See also ENFORCEABILITY;
SUBSTANTIVE TERMS,
INCORPORATION OF
Generally § 3.1
Incorporating clauses, types of
–Conduit clauses § 3.2
–Incorporation by reference clause § 3.3
INDEMNIFICATIONS
See also CONTRIBUTION AND
INDEMNITY
Construction administration services and
the architect's liability dilemma
§ 12.10
Design professionals, construction safety
impacts § 13.10
Enforceability, incorporation by reference
§§ 3.4–3.6, 3.10, 3.11
Liability of architect/engineers for
erroneous software and computer data
§ 15.6
Substantive terms, incorporation of
§§ 3.12, 3.13
INFLATION
Price considerations in private contracts
§ 1.6
INJURIES
See PERSONAL INJURIES
INSPECTIONS
AIA Document A201 modifications, 1987

INSPECTIONS (*Continued*)
edition § 2.11
Construction administration services and
the architect's liability dilemma § 12.6
INSURANCE
See also BUILDER'S RISK
INSURANCE; PROPERTY
INSURANCE
AIA Document A201 modifications, 1987
edition §§ 2.5, 2.14
Asbestos liability strategies § 19.24
ASCE and NAAG documents, problems
regarding §§ 5.5, 5.7
Claims, avoiding and managing §§ 6.5,
6.18, 6.27
Construction administration services and
the architect's liability dilemma
§§ 12.9, 12.10
Construction management system § 4.17
Design professionals, construction safety
impacts § 13.6
Enforceability, incorporation by reference
§ 3.8
Stoppage of work § 18.3
INTERROGATORIES
See also DEFENSIVE DISCOVERY
Discovery in construction litigation
§ 20.16
INTERSTATE COMMERCE
Claims, avoiding and managing § 6.12
ISSUE PRECLUSION
Administrative, regulatory, and
registration proceedings involving
design professionals §§ 11.7, 11.8

*JOBA CONSTRUCTION CO. VERSUS
BURNS & ROE, INC.*
Defense of qualified privilege in
defamation and commercial tort claims
against architects § 14.11
JOBSITE LOGS AND DAILY REPORTS
Claims, avoiding and managing § 6.21
JOBSITE SAFETY
See DESIGN PROFESSIONALS,
SIGNIFICANT CASES
JOINTLY-CAUSED DELAYS, RECOVERY
Generally § 9.1
Causation and delay to job, proof by both
parties § 9.2
Concurrent cause rule
–Generally § 9.3
–Apportionment still possible under
liberal rule § 9.4
–Breach versus price adjustment § 9.6

JOINTLY-CAUSED DELAYS,
    RECOVERY (*Continued*)
  –Concurrent cause rule used to analyze
    government claims of delay § 9.9
  –Hopelessly intertwined causes § 9.8
  –No apportionment possible under
    conservative version of concurrent
    cause rule § 9.10
  –Other criteria not useful in rule analysis
    § 9.5
  –Suspension of work and government
    delay of work clauses § 9.7
  Consequences of choosing particular rule
    § 9.15
  Presumed sharing rule
  –Generally § 9.11
  –Application of presumed sharing rule to
    costs not time-related § 9.12
  –Application of presumed sharing rule to
    delay § 9.13
  –Criteria used in apportioning under
    presumed sharing rule § 9.14
JOINT TORTFEASORS
  Design professionals, significant cases
    § 16.10
JOINT VENTURE DESIGN-BUILD TEAM
  Design-build contracts § 1.26
JOINT VENTURES
  AIA Document A201 modifications, 1987
    edition § 2.14

*KECKO PIPING CO. VERSUS TOWN OF
MONROE*
  Defense of qualified privilege in
    defamation and commercial tort claims
    against architects § 14.13

LABOR AND MATERIALS
  See also DEPARTMENT OF LABOR;
    ORGANIZED LABOR; UNION AND
    NONUNION LABOR
  AIA Document A201 modifications, 1987
    edition § 2.8
  ASCE and NAAG documents, problems
    regarding § 5.6
  Claims, avoiding and managing
    §§ 6.2, 6.21
  Competitive bidding and competitive
    negotiation § 1.21
  Construction administration services and
    the architect's liability dilemma
    §§ 12.3, 12.8
  Construction management system § 4.7

LABOR AND MATERIALS (*Continued*)
  Critical Path Method (CPM) decisions
    from 1980 to 1990 §§ 10.1, 10.4, 10.5
  Progress payments as claim waivers, trust
    funds, and partial lien releases
    §§ 7.2, 7.6
  Quantum meruit §§ 8.1, 8.6, 8.10, 8.11
  Recovery for jointly-caused delays § 9.13
LABOR LAWS
  Design professionals, construction safety
    impacts § 13.7
LAWSUITS
  Administrative, regulatory, and
    registration proceedings involving
    design professionals § 11.6
  Design professionals, construction safety
    impacts §§ 13.4, 13.6
  Design professionals, significant cases
    §§ 16.7, 16.24, 16.33
  Enforceability, incorporation by reference
    § 3.9
  Progress payments as claim waivers, trust
    funds, and partial lien releases
    §§ 7.3, 7.4
  Quantum meruit § 8.2
  Recovery for jointly-caused delays § 9.8
  Substantive terms, incorporation of
    §§ 3.13, 3.15
LEGISLATION
  Asbestos liability strategies § 19.26
  Design professionals, construction safety
    impacts § 13.9
LIABILITY
  See also ASBESTOS LIABILITY
    STRATEGIES; CONSTRUCTION
    ADMINISTRATION SERVICES AND
    THE ARCHITECT'S LIABILITY
    DILEMMA; CONTRACTUAL
    LIABILITY; INSURANCE;
    PRODUCT LIABILITY; STRICT
    LIABILITY; WORKERS'
    COMPENSATION
  Administrative, regulatory, and
    registration proceedings involving
    design professionals § 11.10
  AIA Document A201 modifications, 1987
    edition §§ 2.5, 2.7, 2.14
  ASCE and NAAG documents, problems
    regarding §§ 5.4, 5.6, 5.7
  Claims, avoiding and managing §§ 6.14,
    6.30, 6.31
  Competitive bidding and competitive
    negotiation § 1.11

LIABILITY (*Continued*)

Construction management system §§ 4.15, 4.17

Critical Path Method (CPM) decisions from 1980 to 1990 § 10.15

Design professionals, construction safety impacts §§ 13.3–13.11

Design professionals, significant cases § 16.15

Enforceability, incorporation by reference § 3.8

Price considerations in private contracts § 1.6

Progress payments as claim waivers, trust funds, and partial lien releases § 7.6

Quantum meruit § 8.9

Recovery for jointly-caused delays § 9.13

Stoppage of work §§ 18.1–18.5

Substantive terms, incorporation of §§ 3.12, 3.13

LIABILITY OF ARCHITECT/ ENGINEERS FOR ERRONEOUS SOFTWARE AND COMPUTER DATA

See also DESIGNER LIABILITY FOR DEFECTIVE SOFTWARE

Generally § 15.1

Traditional areas of architect/engineer liability

–Implied warranty § 15.8

–Indemnification § 15.6

–Legal background and development of the concept of malpractice § 15.2

–Liability to persons with whom the architect/engineer is in privity of contract § 15.3

–Negligence § 15.4

–Third-party beneficiary § 15.5

–Tortious interference with contractual relations § 15.7

LIENS

See also MECHANICS' LIENS; PROGRESS PAYMENTS AS CLAIM WAIVERS, TRUST FUNDS, AND PARTIAL LIEN RELEASES

Claims, avoiding and managing § 6.2

Substantive terms, incorporation of § 3.15

LIQUIDATED DAMAGES

Claims, avoiding and managing §§ 6.5, 6.10, 6.32

Critical Path Method (CPM) decisions from 1980 to 1990 § 10.16

Quantum meruit § 8.9

LIQUIDATED DAMAGES (*Continued*)

Recovery for jointly-caused delays §§ 9.9, 9.10, 9.13

LITIGATION

See also DISCOVERY IN CONSTRUCTION LITIGATION; EXPERT WITNESS LITIGATION

Administrative, regulatory, and registration proceedings involving design professionals § 11.9

Claims, avoiding and managing §§ 6.10– 6.12, 6.26, 6.27

LOSSES

See ECONOMIC LOSSES

LOSS OF PRODUCTIVITY ANALYSIS

Critical Path Method (CPM) decisions from 1980 to 1990 § 10.7

MALICE

See ACTUAL MALICE

MALPRACTICE

Design professionals, significant cases § 16.24

Liability of architect/engineers for erroneous software and computer data §§ 15.2, 15.15

MASTER BUILDER CONCEPT

Design professionals, construction safety impacts § 13.2

MATERIALS

See LABOR AND MATERIALS; SUPPLIERS

MC CARTHY CASE, THE

Stoppage of work §§ 18.3–18.5

MECHANIC'S LIENS

AIA Document A201 modifications, 1987 edition § 2.16

Competitive bidding and competitive negotiation § 1.9

Progress payments as claim waivers, trust funds, and partial lien releases § 7.6

MEETING NOTES

Claims, avoiding and managing § 6.20

MILLER ACT

Competitive bidding and competitive negotiation § 1.9

Substantive terms, incorporation of § 3.15

MISCONDUCT

See also WILLFUL MISCONDUCT

Administrative, regulatory, and registration proceedings involving

MISCONDUCT (*Continued*)
  design professionals § 11.4
  ASCE and NAAG documents, problems regarding § 5.1
MITIGATING DAMAGES
  Claims, avoiding and managing § 6.28
MOTION PRACTICE
  Discovery in construction litigation § 20.20
MOUNDSVIEW CASE
  Construction administration services and the architect's liability dilemma § 12.6

NATIONAL ASSOCIATION OF ATTORNEYS GENERAL DOCUMENTS
  See AMERICAN SOCIETY OF CIVIL ENGINEERS (ASCE) AND NATIONAL ASSOCIATION OF ATTORNEYS GENERAL (NAAG) DOCUMENTS
NATIONAL CONSTRUCTION INDUSTRY ARBITRATION COMMITTEE (NCIAC)
  Stoppage of work § 18.4
NATIONAL EMISSION STANDARDS FOR HAZARDOUS AIR POLLUTANTS (NESHAP)
  Asbestos liability strategies § 19.4
NATIONAL LABOR RELATIONS BOARD (NLRB)
  §§ 17.1–17.5
NATIONAL SOCIETY OF PROFESSIONAL ENGINEERS (NSPE)
  See ARCHITECTS AND ENGINEERS
NEGLIGENCE
  Administrative, regulatory, and registration proceedings involving design professionals §§ 11.3–11.8, 11.10
  AIA Document A201 modifications, 1987 edition § 2.8
  Asbestos liability strategies § 19.7
  ASCE and NAAG documents, problems regarding § 5.1
  Claims, avoiding and managing § 6.32
  Construction administration services and the architect's liability dilemma §§ 12.2, 12.4, 12.5, 12.8, 12.9
  Defense of qualified privilege in defamation and commercial tort claims against architects §§ 14.2, 14.16–14.22
  Design professionals, construction safety impacts § 13.6

NEGLIGENCE (*Continued*)
  Design professionals, significant cases §§ 16.9, 16.10, 16.16, 16.19, 16.22, 16.26
  Liability of architect/engineers for erroneous software and computer data § 15.4
  Substantive terms, incorporation of §§ 3.12, 3.13
NEGOTIATION
  See also COMPETITIVE BIDDING AND COMPETITIVE NEGOTIATION
  Incorporation by reference § 3.1
NO DAMAGES FOR DELAY CLAUSES
  AIA Document A201 modifications, 1987 edition § 2.10
  ASCE and NAAG documents, problems regarding § 5.6
  Claims, avoiding and managing § 6.11
  Quantum meruit §§ 8.8, 8.9
  Substantive terms, incorporation of § 3.16
NONCOMPLIANCE OR OBJECTIONS TO DISCOVERY
  See DISCOVERY IN CONSTRUCTION LITIGATION
NOTICE REQUIREMENTS
  See also WRITTEN NOTICES
  Enforceability, incorporation by reference § 3.5

OCCUPANCY
  AIA Document A201 modifications, 1987 edition § 2.14
OCCUPATIONAL SAFETY AND HEALTH ACT (OSHA)
  Administrative, regulatory, and registration proceedings involving design professionals § 11.3
  Asbestos liability strategies § 19.2
  Design professionals, construction safety impacts § 13.8
  Stoppage of work § 18.3
OCCUPATIONAL SAFETY AND HEALTH REVIEW COMMISSION (OSHRC)
  Design professionals, construction safety impacts § 13.8
OHIO'S STATUTE OF REPOSE
  Design professionals, significant cases § 16.40
OKLAHOMA'S STATUTE OF REPOSE
  Design professionals, significant cases § 16.41

ORGANIZED LABOR
 See MANPOWER SHORTAGE AND
  ORGANIZED LABOR'S AGENDA
  FOR THE 1990S
ORGANIZING TECHNIQUES
 Bottom-up § 17.2
 Top-down § 17.2
OWNERS
 See also AIA DOCUMENT A201
  MODIFICATIONS, 1987 EDITION;
  PRIVATE OWNERS; PUBLIC
  OWNERS; "SPEC" OWNERS
 Asbestos liability strategies § 19.14
 ASCE and NAAG documents, problems
  regarding §§ 5.2–5.7
 Claims, avoiding and managing §§ 6.1,
  6.2, 6.4, 6.6, 6.10, 6.13–6.15, 6.17,
  6.18, 6.22, 6.25
 Construction administration services and
  the architect's liability dilemma
  §§ 12.4, 12.6, 12.7, 12.9, 12.10
 Construction management system §§ 4.2–
  4.4, 4.7, 4.12, 4.13, 4.14, 4.17
 Critical Path Method (CPM) decisions
  from 1980 to 1990 §§ 10.3, 10.5,
  10.6, 10.14, 10.18
 Defense of qualified privilege in
  defamation and commercial tort claims
  against architects §§ 14.1, 14.5–14.7,
  14.18–14.23
 Design professionals, construction safety
  impacts § 13.5
 Design professionals, significant cases
  §§ 16.1, 16.29–16.34
 Enforceability, incorporation by reference
  §§ 3.5, 3.6, 3.9
 Incorporation by reference § 3.1
 Progress payments as claim waivers, trust
  funds, and partial lien releases
  §§ 7.1–7.7
 Quantum meruit §§ 8.1, 8.5–8.7, 8.11
 Recovery for jointly-caused delays § 9.13
 Stoppage of work §§ 18.1–18.5
 Substantive terms, incorporation of
  §§ 3.11, 3.13, 3.14, 3.17
 Types of incorporating clauses § 3.2
OWNER'S ADVANTAGES
 Price considerations in private contracts
  § 1.3
OWNER'S RISKS
 Competitive bidding and competitive
  negotiation §§ 1.9, 1.20
 Price considerations in private contracts
  §§ 1.4, 1.5

PARTIAL LIEN RELEASES
 See PROGRESS PAYMENTS AS CLAIM
  WAIVERS, TRUST FUNDS, AND
  PARTIAL LIEN RELEASES
PARTNERSHIPS
 AIA Document A201 modifications, 1987
  edition § 2.14
PATENT AND LATENT DEFECTS
 See DESIGN PROFESSIONALS,
  SIGNIFICANT CASES
PAYMENT BONDS
 See BONDS
PAYMENTS
 See also PROGRESS PAYMENTS AS
  CLAIM WAIVERS, TRUST FUNDS,
  AND PARTIAL LIEN RELEASES
 Claims, avoiding and managing §§ 6.5,
  6.34–6.36
 Construction administration services and
  the architect's liability dilemma § 12.5
 Progress payments as claim waivers, trust
  funds, and partial lien releases
  §§ 7.1, 7.7
 Quantum meruit, generally this heading
PERFORMANCE BONDS
 See B
PERFORMANCE OF WORK
 ASCE and NAAG documents, problems
  regarding § 5.6
 Claims, avoiding and managing § 6.2
 Construction administration services and
  the architect's liability dilemma § 12.9
 Critical Path Method (CPM) decisions
  from 1980 to 1990 §§ 10.1, 10.4,
  10.9, 10.10, 10.12, 10.14
 Design professionals, construction safety
  impacts § 13.3
 Recovery for jointly-caused delays § 9.12
PERFORMANCE RISK
 Competitive bidding and competitive
  negotiation § 1.9
 Substantive terms, incorporation of
  § 3.11
PERMITS
 AIA Documents A201 modifications,
  1987 edition § 2.3
PERSONAL INJURIES
 Administrative, regulatory, and
  registration proceedings involving
  design professionals § 11.6
 Construction administration services and
  the architect's liability dilemma § 12.2
 Design professionals, construction safety
  impacts § 13.1

PERSONAL INJURIES (*Continued*)

Design professionals, significant cases
§ 16.36

Recovery for jointly-caused delays § 9.12

Stoppage of work § 18.3

Substantive terms, incorporation of
§§ 3.10, 3.13

PETROLEUM PIPELINES

AIA Document A201 modifications, 1987
edition § 2.1

PHOTOGRAPHS AND VIDEOTAPES

Claims, avoiding and managing
§§ 6.23, 6.29

PLANS AND SPECIFICATIONS

ASCE and NAAG documents, problems
regarding §§ 5.3, 5.6

Claims, avoiding and managing §§ 6.6,
6.15, 6.18, 6.22, 6.27, 6.30

Construction administration services and
the architect's liability dilemma
§§ 12.3, 12.6, 12.8

Construction management system
§§ 4.7, 4.14

Defense of qualified privilege in
defamation and commercial tort claims
against architects § 14.22

Design professionals, construction safety
impacts §§ 13.3, 13.4, 13.6–13.11

Design professionals, significant cases
§§ 16.2, 16.14, 16.23

Enforceability, incorporation by reference
§ 3.5

Recovery for jointly-caused delays § 9.12

Substantive terms, incorporation of
§§ 3.14, 3.16, 3.17

PLUMBING

Claims, avoiding and managing § 6.2

Recovery for jointly-caused delays § 9.13

POLYCHLORINATED BIPHENYLS
(PCBS)

See ASBESTOS LIABILITY
EXCLUSION

PREHIRE AGREEMENTS

Manpower shortage and organized labor's
agenda for the 1990's § 17.3

PRELIMINARY EDITION (PE)

ASCE and NAAG documents, problems
regarding §§ 5.1–5.4

PRESUMED SHARING RULE

See JOINTLY-CAUSED DELAYS,
RECOVERY

PRICE ADJUSTMENTS

Enforceability, incorporation by reference
§ 3.7

PRICE ADJUSTMENTS (*Continued*)

Recovery for jointly-caused delays § 9.6

PRICING

See CLAIMS, AVOIDING AND
MANAGING; UNIT PRICING

PRIMA FACIE CASES

Defense of qualified privilege in
defamation and commercial tort claims
against architects § 14.19

PRIME CONTRACTORS

AIA Document A201 modifications, 1987
edition §§ 2.1, 2.13

Claims, avoiding and managing §§ 6.2,
6.6, 6.17, 6.25

Competitive bidding and competitive
negotiation § 1.9

Construction management system § 4.14

Critical Path Method (CPM) decisions
from 1980 to 1990 § 10.12

Enforceability, incorporation by reference
§§ 3.4–3.9

Quantum meruit §§ 8.1, 8.2, 8.5–8.8

Substantive terms, incorporation of
§§ 3.11, 3.12, 3.14, 3.16, 3.17

PRIVATE CONTRACTS

Competitive bidding and competitive
negotiation §§ 1.15, 1.18

PRIVATE CONTRACTS, PRICE
CONSIDERATIONS

Generally § 1.2

Abandonment § 1.7

Cost contracts: contractor advantages,
owner risks § 1.5

Fixed price contracts
–contractor advantages, owner risks § 1.4
–owner advantages, contractor risks § 1.3

Guaranteed maximum contracts § 1.6

PRIVATE OWNERS

Competitive bidding and competitive
negotiation §§ 1.8, 1.9, 1.11, 1.14

PRIVILEGE DEFENSES

Defense of qualified privilege in
defamation and commercial tort claims
against architects § 14.4

PRIVITY OF CONTRACT

See also DESIGN PROFESSIONALS,
SIGNIFICANT CASES

Enforceability, incorporation by reference
§ 3.9

Liability of architect/engineers for
erroneous software and computer data
§ 15.3

PRODUCT IDENTIFICATION

Asbestos liability strategies § 19.13

PRODUCT LIABILITY
Asbestos liability strategies § 19.6
PROGRESS PAYMENTS AS CLAIM
WAIVERS, TRUST FUNDS, AND
PARTIAL LIEN RELEASES
Generally § 7.1
Claims, prompt identification § 7.3
Form; conditional release/unconditional
release of lien § 7.9
Form; contractor's application for
payment § 7.8
Ground rules § 7.2
Release of lien rights § 7.5
Restrictive indorsements § 7.7
Trust funds § 7.6
Waiver of claims for extra cost or time
extension § 7.4
PROJECT DOCUMENTATION
See CLAIMS, AVOIDING AND
MANAGING
PROJECTS, PUBLIC AND PRIVATE
AIA Document A201 modifications, 1987
edition § 2.1
PROPERTY
See also GOVERNMENT PROPERTY
ASCE and NAAG documents, problems
regarding §§ 5.2, 5.3
Claims, avoiding and managing § 6.2
Stoppage of work § 18.4
PROPERTY DAMAGES
Asbestos liability strategies § 19.10
PROPERTY INSURANCE
AIA Document A201 modifications, 1987
edition § 2.5
PUBLIC CONTRACTS
Competitive bidding and competitive
negotiation §§ 1.16, 1.17
PUBLIC OWNERS
Competitive bidding and competitive
negotiation §§ 1.9, 1.14
PUBLIC SECTOR
Competitive bidding and competitive
negotiation § 1.10
PUBLISHED MATERIALS
Discovery in construction litigation
§ 20.7
PURCHASE ORDERS
Claims, avoiding and managing § 6.18

QUALIFIED PRIVILEGE
See DEFENSE OF QUALIFIED
PRIVILEGE IN DEFAMATION AND
COMMERCIAL TORT CLAIMS
AGAINST ARCHITECTS

QUANTUM MERUIT
Generally § 8.1
Payment for work despite contract § 8.7
Recovery despite clause limiting or
controlling recovery
–Generally § 8.8
–Cardinal change cases § 8.10
–No damages for delay cases § 8.9
Recovery despite inequitable contract
provisions that purport to cover the
changed work § 8.11
Source of payment when contract is silent
about some aspect of work
–Extra work § 8.3
–Owner control of methods and materials
§ 8.6
–Owner interference § 8.5
–Work done under unanticipated
conditions § 8.4
Source of payment when there is no
contract § 8.2
QUOTES
See SUBCONTRACTOR QUOTES

RACKETEERING INFLUENCED AND
CORRUPT ORGANIZATIONS ACT
(RICO)
Asbestos liability strategies § 19.9
Design professionals, significant cases
§ 16.34
RECORDKEEPING
See also COST-ACCOUNTING
RECORDS
Administrative, regulatory, and
registration proceedings involving
design professionals § 11.9
Asbestos liability strategies § 19.21
Claims, avoiding and managing §§ 6.18,
6.22, 6.31, 6.34
Discovery in construction litigation
§§ 20.13–20.15
Price considerations in private contracts
§ 1.4
RECOVERY
See also ASBESTOS LIABILITY
STRATEGIES; COSTS; JOINTLY-
CAUSED DELAYS, RECOVERY
AIA Document A201 modifications, 1987
edition §§ 2.3, 2.10
Claims, avoiding and managing §§ 6.24,
6.26, 6.30, 6.31, 6.36
Competitive bidding and competitive
negotiation § 1.15

RECOVERY (*Continued*)

Construction administration services and the architect's liability dilemma § 12.9

Critical Path Method (CPM) decisions from 1980 to 1990 §§ 10.8, 10.9, 10.12

Design professionals, significant cases §§ 16.6, 16.14, 16.17, 16.18, 16.31, 16.43–16.45

Progress payments as claim waivers, trust funds, and partial lien releases § 7.4

Quantum meruit §§ 8.1, 8.5–8.11

REDRESS

Enforceability, incorporation by reference § 3.6

REQUESTS

Discovery in construction litigation §§ 20.18, 20.27, 20.28, 20.33

RESCISSION

Competitive bidding and competitive negotiation § 1.15

Progress payments as claim waivers, trust funds, and partial lien releases § 7.3

RESIDENT PROJECT REPRESENTATIVES

ASCE and NAAG documents, problems regarding § 5.3

RESOURCE CONSERVATION AND RECOVERY ACT (RCRA)

Asbestos liability strategies § 19.14

RESTRICTIVE INDORSEMENT FORMS

Progress payments as claim waivers, trust funds, and partial lien releases §§ 7.1, 7.7

RIBLET TRAMWAY CO. VERSUS ERICKSEN ASSOCIATES, INC.

Defense of qualified privilege in defamation and commercial tort claims against architects § 14.9

RISKS

See also PERFORMANCE RISK

ASCE and NAAG documents, problems regarding § 5.6

Claims, avoiding and managing §§ 6.1–6.3

Construction management system § 4.15

Substantive terms, incorporation of §§ 3.10, 3.17

ROADS

ASCE and NAAG documents, problems regarding § 5.6

RURAL AREAS

AIA Document A201 modifications, 1987 edition § 2.1

SAFETY PROGRAMS

See also ASBESTOS LIABILITY STRATEGIES; DESIGN PROFESSIONALS, CONSTRUCTION SAFETY IMPACTS; DESIGN PROFESSIONALS, SIGNIFICANT CASES

AIA Document A201 modifications, 1987 edition §§ 2.2, 2.8

"SALTING"

Manpower shortage and organized labor's agenda for the 1990's § 17.4

SANCTIONS

Discovery in construction litigation § 20.21

SANTA FE DECISIONS, THE

Critical Path Method (CPM) decisions from 1980 to 1990 § 10.16

SANTUCCI CONSTRUCTION CO. VERSUS BAXTER & WOODMAN, INC.

Defense of qualified privilege in defamation and commercial tort claims against architects § 14.20

SCHEDULING

See also CRITICAL PATH METHOD (CPM)

AIA Document A201 modifications, 1987 edition § 2.9

ASCE and NAAG documents, problems regarding § 5.6

Claims, avoiding and managing §§ 6.10, 6.16, 6.18, 6.21, 6.23, 6.25, 6.28

Construction management system §§ 4.3, 4.4, 4.12–4.16

Critical Path Method (CPM) decisions from 1980 to 1990 §§ 10.1, 10.2, 10.9–10.11, 10.14–10.18

Defense of qualified privilege in defamation and commercial tort claims against architects § 14.19

SCOPE OF THE WORK

AIA Document A201 modifications, 1987 edition §§ 2.2, 2.3

Competitive bidding and competitive negotiation § 1.13

Construction administration services and the architect's liability dilemma § 12.9

Price considerations in private contracts § 1.6

Quantum meruit § 8.2

SEGREGATED COST METHOD

Claims, avoiding and managing § 6.35

SEQUENCING

Construction management system § 4.13

SETTLEMENTS
  Claims, avoiding and managing §§ 6.2, 6.31, 6.36
SEWER AND WATER PROJECTS
  AIA Document A201 modifications, 1987 edition § 2.1
  ASCE and NAAG documents, problems regarding § 5.6
  Defense of qualified privilege in defamation and commercial tort claims against architects § 14.22
  Design professionals, significant cases § 16.13
SHOP DRAWINGS
  ASCE and NAAG documents, problems regarding §§ 5.1, 5.3, 5.6
  Claims, avoiding and managing §§ 6.17, 6.22
  Critical Path Method (CPM) decisions from 1980 to 1990 § 10.12
  Design professionals, significant cases § 16.23
SOFTWARE
  See LIABILITY OF ARCHITECT/ ENGINEERS FOR ERRONEOUS SOFTWARE AND COMPUTER DATA
SOIL TESTS
  AIA Document A201 modifications, 1987 edition § 2.3
SOLE CONTRACTORS
  Design-build contracts §§ 1.25, 1.27
SOLID WASTE INCINERATORS
  AIA Document A201 modifications, 1987 edition § 2.1
SOMERS CONSTRUCTION CO. VERSUS BOARD OF EDUCATION
  Defense of qualified privilege in defamation and commercial tort claims against architects § 14.10
SPEARIN DOCTRINE
  Claims, avoiding and managing § 6.6
SPECIFICATIONS
  See PLANS AND SPECIFICATIONS
"SPEC" OWNERS
  AIA Document A201 modifications, 1987 edition § 2.4
STANDARD FORM OF AGREEMENT
  AIA Document A201 modifications, 1987 edition § 2.2
STANDARD OPERATING PROCEDURES
  Claims, avoiding and managing § 6.16
STANDARD TRADE ASSOCIATION CONTRACTS
  Standard contracts

STANDARD TRADE ASSOCIATION CONTRACTS (*Continued*)
  –Generally § 1.22
  –AIA documents § 1.23
  –Standard contract cautions § 1.24
STATE APPRENTICESHIP COUNCIL (SAC)
  Manpower shortage and organized labor's agenda for the 1990's § 17.2
STATE RECOGNITION OF CPM PRINCIPLES
  Critical Path Method (CPM) decisions from 1980 to 1990 § 10.19
STATE REGULATIONS
  Asbestos liability strategies § 19.3
STATUTE OF LIMITATIONS
  See also DESIGN PROFESSIONALS, SIGNIFICANT CASES
  Asbestos liability strategies § 19.11
STATUTE OF REPOSE
  See DESIGN PROFESSIONALS, SIGNIFICANT CASES
STOPPAGE OF WORK
  Generally § 18.1
  AIA Document A201 modifications, 1987 edition § 2.8
  Construction administration services and the architect's liability dilemma §§ 12.4, 12.5
  Design professionals, construction safety impacts § 13.4
  Impossibility and commercial impracticability § 18.2
  McCarthy case § 18.3
  New AIA clause § 18.4
  Observations § 18.5
  Recovery for jointly-caused delays § 9.7
STRICT LIABILITY
  Asbestos liability strategies § 19.5
STRUCTURALS WORKS ACT
  Design professionals, construction safety impacts § 13.7
STRUCTURES FAILURE CONFERENCE OF 1983
  ASCE and NAAG documents, problems regarding § 5.2
SUBCONTRACTOR QUOTES
  Competitive bidding and competitive negotiation § 1.13
SUBCONTRACTORS
  ASCE and NAAG documents, problems regarding § 5.6
  Claims, avoiding and managing §§ 6.1, 6.2, 6.5, 6.15, 6.18, 6.21, 6.22, 6.25

SUBCONTRACTORS (*Continued*)

Competitive bidding and competitive negotiation §§ 1.9, 1.13

Construction administration services and the architect's liability dilemma § 12.8

Critical Path Method (CPM) decisions from 1980 to 1990 §§ 10.8, 10.12, 10.15

Defense of qualified privilege in defamation and commercial tort claims against architects §§ 14.6, 14.14, 14.21

Design professionals, construction safety impacts § 13.8

Progress payments as claim waivers, trust funds, and partial lien releases §§ 7.1, 7.5–7.7

Quantum meruit §§ 8.1, 8.3, 8.5–8.10

Substantive terms, incorporation of § 3.17

SUBSTANTIVE TERMS, INCORPORATION OF

Arbitration clauses, public policy supports arbitration

–Generally § 3.14

–Incorporated arbitration clauses and the Miller Act § 3.15

Incorporation of implied warranty of the adequacy and suitability of plans and specifications § 3.17

Indemnification clauses

–Generally § 3.10

–Negligence, indemnification for § 3.12

–Scope § 3.11

–Workers' compensation and indemnity § 3.13

No damages for delay and other remedy clauses § 3.16

SUBSURFACE CONDITIONS

AIA Document A201 modifications, 1987 edition §§ 2.3, 2.11

Construction management system §§ 4.11, 4.14

SUPERVISION

See also CONSTRUCTION ADMINISTRATION SERVICES AND THE ARCHITECT'S LIABILITY DILEMMA

Asbestos liability strategies § 19.20

Design professionals, construction safety impacts § 13.3

SUPPLIERS

Claims, avoiding and managing § 6.2

Competitive bidding and competitive

SUPPLIERS (*Continued*)

negotiation §§ 1.9, 1.21

Design professionals, significant cases §§ 16.18, 16.21

Progress payments as claim waivers, trust funds, and partial lien releases §§ 7.2, 7.6, 7.7

Recovery for jointly-caused delays § 9.4

SURETIES

ASCE and NAAG documents, problems regarding § 5.6

Claims, avoiding and managing § 6.2

Competitive bidding and competitive negotiation § 1.9

SURVEYS

AIA Document A201 modifications, 1987 edition §§ 2.3, 2.12

Design professionals, significant cases § 16.25

TESTIMONIES

Discovery in construction litigation §§ 20.35–20.38

THIRD PARTIES

Claims, avoiding and managing § 6.3

Design professionals, significant cases § 16.11

Discovery in construction litigation § 20.4

Liability of architect/engineers for erroneous software and computer data §§ 15.5, 15.10

Progress payments as claim waivers, trust funds, and partial lien releases § 7.6

THIRD-PARTY BENEFICIARY STATUS

Defense of qualified privilege in defamation and commercial tort claims against architects § 14.1

Design professionals, significant cases § 16.32

Enforceability, incorporation by reference § 3.9

Liability of architect/engineers for erroneous software and computer data § 15.5

TIME EXTENSIONS

AIA Document A201 modifications, 1987 edition § 2.10

Claims, avoiding and managing § 6.5

Critical Path Method (CPM) decisions from 1980 to 1990 §§ 10.6, 10.9, 10.16, 10.17

Progress payments as claim waivers, trust funds, and partial lien releases § 7.4

"TIME IS OF THE ESSENCE" CLAUSE
AIA Document A201 modifications, 1987
edition § 2.9
TIME LIMITATIONS
AIA Document A201 modifications, 1987
edition § 2.9
Claims, avoiding and managing § 6.2
Construction management system § 4.13
Progress payments as claim waivers, trust
funds, and partial lien releases § 7.3
Recovery for jointly-caused delays § 9.12
TITAN PACIFIC CONSTRUCTION CORP.
VERSUS UNITED STATES
Critical Path Method (CPM) decisions
from 1980 to 1990 § 10.18
TORTIOUS INTERFERENCE
See also JOINT TORTFEASORS
Defense of qualified privilege in
defamation and commercial tort claims
against architects § 14.3
Liability of architect/engineers for
erroneous software and computer data
§ 15.7
TOTAL COST METHOD
Claims, avoiding and managing § 6.34
TRAINING
See WORKERS' TRAINING
TRUSTEES
Progress payments as claim waivers, trust
funds, and partial lien releases § 7.6
TRUST FUNDS
See PROGRESS PAYMENTS AS CLAIM
WAIVERS, TRUST FUNDS, AND
PARTIAL LIEN RELEASES

UNFAIR LABOR PRACTICE (ULP)
CHARGES
Manpower shortage and organized labor's
agenda for the 1990's § 17.5
UNIFORM ARBITRATION ACT (UAA)
Substantive terms, incorporation of
§ 3.14
UNIFORM COMMERCIAL CODE (UCC)
See also DESIGNER LIABILITY FOR
DEFECTIVE SOFTWARE
Asbestos liability strategies § 19.8
Claims, avoiding and managing § 6.5
Liability of architect/engineers for
erroneous software and computer data
§§ 15.11–15.14
Progress payments as claim waivers, trust
funds, and partial lien releases § 7.7
Stoppage of work § 18.2

UNION AND NONUNION LABOR
AIA Document A201 modifications, 1987
edition § 2.13
Manpower shortage and organized labor's
agenda for the 1990's §§ 17.1–17.5
UNIT PRICING
Competitive bidding and competitive
negotiation § 1.21
Quantum meruit § 8.7
UPSTREAM PARTIES
Enforceability, incorporation by reference
§§ 3.5–3.9, 3.12
Substantive terms, incorporation of
§ 3.15
URBAN AREAS
AIA Document A201 modifications, 1987
edition § 2.1
UTAH'S STATUTE OF REPOSE
Design professionals, significant cases
§ 16.39
U.S. BANKRUPTCY CODE
Progress payments as claim waivers, trust
funds, and partial lien releases § 7.6
U.S. SUPREME COURT
Asbestos liability strategies § 19.9
Progress payments as claim waivers, trust
funds, and partial lien releases § 7.4
Recovery for jointly-caused delays § 9.12
UTLEY-JAMES, INC.
Critical Path Method (CPM) decisions
from 1980 to 1990 § 10.14

VENDOR FILES
Claims, avoiding and managing § 6.18
VERDICTS, APPORTIONED FAULT
Design professionals, significant cases
§ 16.15
VETERANS ADMINISTRATION (VA)
Critical Path Method (CPM) decisions
from 1980 to 1990 § 10.16
VIDEOTAPES
See PHOTOGRAPHS AND
VIDEOTAPES
V.M. SOLIS UNDERGROUND UTILITY &
PAVING CO. VERSUS CITY OF LAREDO
Defense of qualified privilege in
defamation and commercial tort claims
against architects § 14.18
VOJAK VERSUS JENSEN
Defense of qualified privilege in
defamation and commercial tort claims
against architects § 14.14

WAGE APPEALS BOARD (WAB)
Manpower shortage and organized labor's agenda for the 1990's § 17.2
WAIVERS
Claims, avoiding and managing § 6.7
Competitive bidding and competitive negotiation § 1.18
Substantive terms, incorporation of § 3.13
WALDINGER CORP. VERSUS CRS GROUP ENGINEERS, INC.
Defense of qualified privilege in defamation and commercial tort claims against architects § 14.22
WARRANTIES
See also EXPRESS WARRANTY; IMPLIED WARRANTY
AIA Document A201 modifications, 1987 edition § 2.7
Asbestos liability strategies § 19.8
WATER PROJECTS
See SEWER AND WATER PROJECTS
WATER TABLES
ASCE and NAAG documents, problems regarding § 5.6
WEATHER CONDITIONS
See ACTS OF GOD
WEAVER-BAILEY CONTRACTORS, INC. VERSUS UNITED STATES
Critical Path Method (CPM) decisions from 1980 to 1990 § 10.11
WILDERNESS AREAS
AIA Document A201 modifications, 1987 edition § 2.1
WILLFUL MISCONDUCT
Substantive terms, incorporation of § 3.12
WILLIAMS ENTERPRISES VERSUS STRAIT MANUFACTURING & WELDING, INC.
Critical Path Method (CPM) decisions from 1980 to 1990 § 10.12
WISCONSIN'S STATUTE OF REPOSE
Design professionals, significant cases § 16.38
WITNESSES
See also DESIGN PROFESSIONALS, SIGNIFICANT CASES
Discovery in construction litigation §§ 20.29–20.34

WORK
See COMPLETION OF WORK; DEFECTS; PERFORMANCE OF WORK; SCOPE OF THE WORK; STOPPAGE OF WORK
WORKER RELEASE
Asbestos liability strategies § 19.23
WORKERS' COMPENSATION
Design professionals, construction safety impacts § 13.6
Substantive terms, incorporation of § 3.13
WORKERS' TRAINING
Asbestos liability strategies § 19.22
WORK FORCE SHORTAGE AND ORGANIZED LABOR'S AGENDA FOR THE 1990S
Generally § 17.1
Agenda items
–Continuance of apprenticeship battle § 17.2
–Employment of sophisticated top-down organizing techniques § 17.3
–Engaging aggressive bottom-up organizing § 17.4
–Filing of Unfair Labor Practice (ULP) charges § 17.5
WRIT OF CERTIORARI
Manpower shortage and organized labor's agenda for the 1990's § 17.2
WRITTEN AGREEMENTS
Claims, avoiding and managing § 6.7
Construction administration services and the architect's liability dilemma § 12.7
Design professionals, construction safety impacts § 13.5
Design professionals, significant cases § 16.10
Quantum meruit § 8.7
WRITTEN NOTICES
AIA Document A201 modifications, 1987 edition § 2.8
Claims, avoiding and managing § 6.7
Competitive bidding and competitive negotiation § 1.16

ZONING REGULATIONS
ASCE and NAAG documents, problems regarding § 5.6